Richmond

Sheila Dignen

Teacher's GUIDE

A1+

CB078476

Keep it REAL!

Relevant Engaging Achievable Learning

Keep it REAL!

Everything you need to 'Keep it real!' in the class and at home.

Student COMPONENTS

Student's Book

Workbook
and
e-Workbook

Teacher COMPONENTS

Teacher's Guide
and
Student's Book
combined

Audio
Video and animations
***Keep moving!* digital game**
Extended practice

Tests
Worksheets
Scripts
Workbook answer key

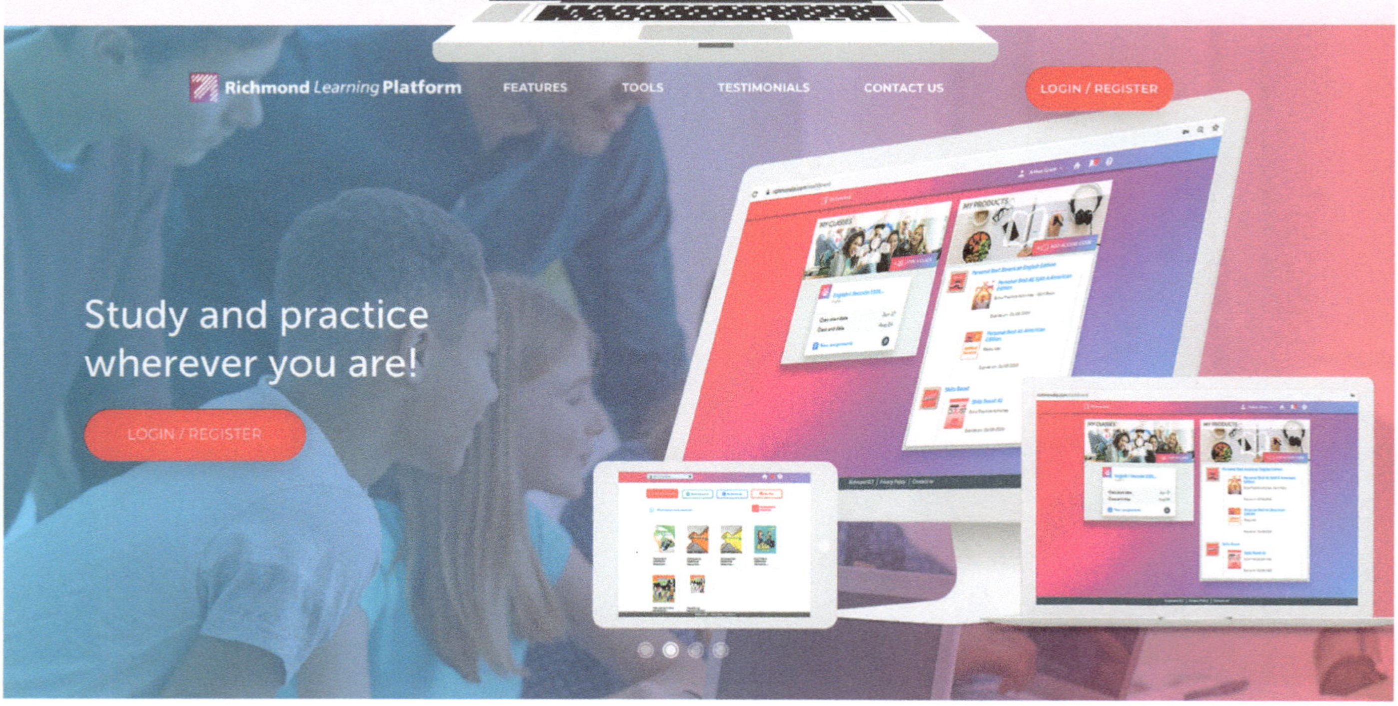

STUDENT'S BOOK CONTENTS

Welcome to *KEEP IT REAL!*

Keep it real! is the ideal 6-level secondary course for today's mixed ability classes, with its flexible blend of dynamic video and digital content, easy-to-use classroom materials, and focus on developing communicative competence and 21st century skills.

Keep it real! throughly develops students' grammar, vocabulary and pronunciation and provides manageable skills development opportunities, including a focus on culture. Optional sections contain project-based work, literature lessons based on extracts from the **Richmond Readers**, and exams lessons that practise common exam tasks.

Keep it real! has a full range of print and digital components including:

- **Student's Book**
- **Workbook** and **e-Workbook**
- **Teacher's Guide** with Student's Book interleaved pages
- **Teacher's resources** including worksheets and tests
- **Teacher's audio, video** and **animated material** as MP3 and MP4 download
- **Teacher's iBook** for interactive whiteboards
- **Richmond Learning Platform** with extended practice activities, assignable and trackable tests and complete teacher's resources

KEY FEATURES

Each *Keep it real!* unit has a number of key features which make the course engaging and unique:

Vocabulary opener pages with vlogs

A focus on vocabulary at the start of each unit with an optional vlog where real vloggers are used in authentic contexts.

Accessible grammar with animated presentations

Simple, effective grammar lessons with animated grammar presentations.

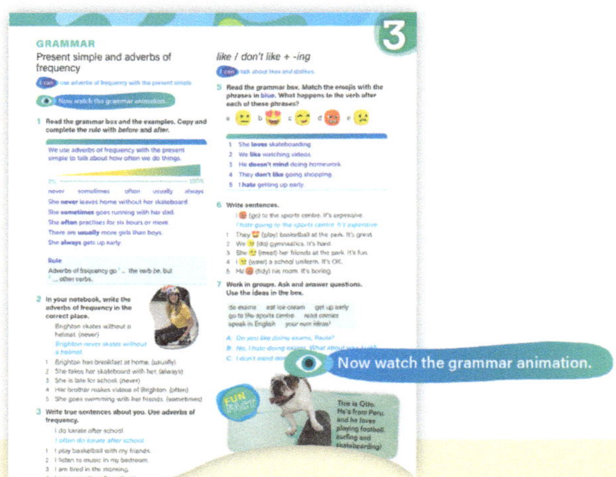

Fun facts

Regular 'fun fact' feature offers fun, but interesting information to arouse curiosity.

Fast finisher

An optional Fast finisher extension activity at the end of each lesson to keep students busy.

FAST FINISHER
Imagine you're enjoying your dream weekend. What are you doing? What do you usually do?
On Saturday, I usually go shopping. But today I'm playing the guitar in a rock band!

FAST FINISHER
Think of your own cool presents for the website on page 74. Write a short description for each present.

Keep talking! speaking lessons with *Keep moving!* game

Each unit includes a functional speaking lesson based on real-world themes and a dynamic board game called *Keep moving!*.

Real Culture! with video

Each unit includes a reading lesson on cultural topics from English-speaking countries and an optional culture video which extends the theme.

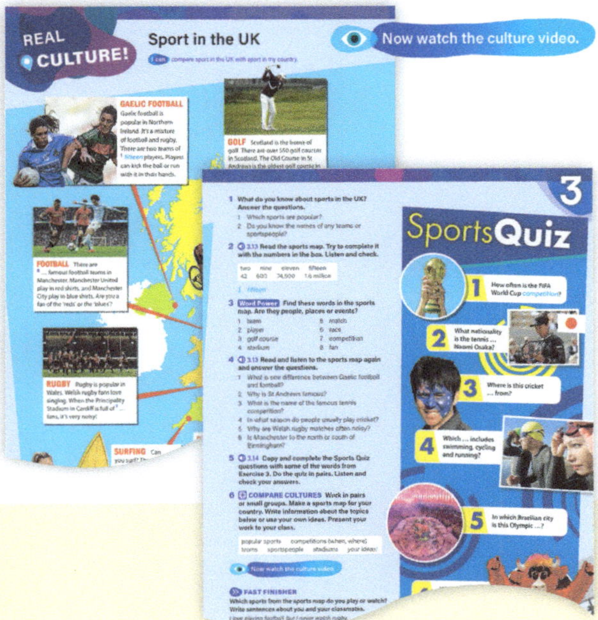

Word Power

Regular word-building exercises through the Word Power feature.

3 Word Power Skateboarding is a new Olympic sport. Work in pairs. Think of other Olympic sports. Which pair can make the longest list?

21st century skills

Four 21st century skills exercises per unit: *Think critically*, *Get creative*, *Find out*, and *Compare cultures* .

4 THINK CRITICALLY Is a school on a ship a good idea? Why/Why not? Discuss as a class and have a class vote.

I think it's a good idea because …

I think it's a bad idea because …

7 GET CREATIVE Work in pairs. Think about a craze that was popular when you were younger. Write a description and present it to the class.

6 FIND OUT In what decade was the first …?
a FIFA World Cup
b phone with a camera
c photograph

5 COMPARE CULTURES What are the main tourist attractions in your town or city? What can tourists see or do there?

Projects, Literature and Exams

Extra sections at the back of the Student's Book for extended learning.

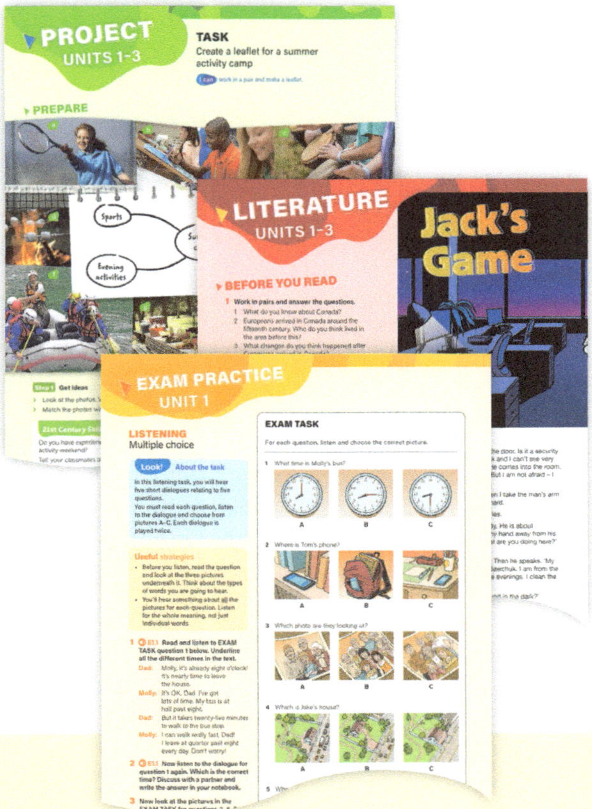

UNIT OVERVIEW

Student's Book

There is a 5-page Starter unit at the beginning of the Student's Book. It reviews basic grammar and vocabulary areas from earlier levels. There is also a short reading and speaking section towards the end of the Starter unit, providing students with a useful introduction to skills work.

The Starter unit is optional. It will depend on your timetable and which areas you think your students would benefit from revising before beginning work on the main units. It can also serve as a useful introduction to the course methodology and features.

The units are 10 pages with 6 main sections:

1 **Vocabulary** (includes a vlog)
2 **Grammar** and **Reading** (includes a grammar animation)
3 **Vocabulary**, **Listening** and **Grammar** (includes a grammar animation)
4 **Reading**, **Listening** and **Speaking** (includes a digital speaking game)
5 **Culture** (includes a culture video)
6 **Writing**

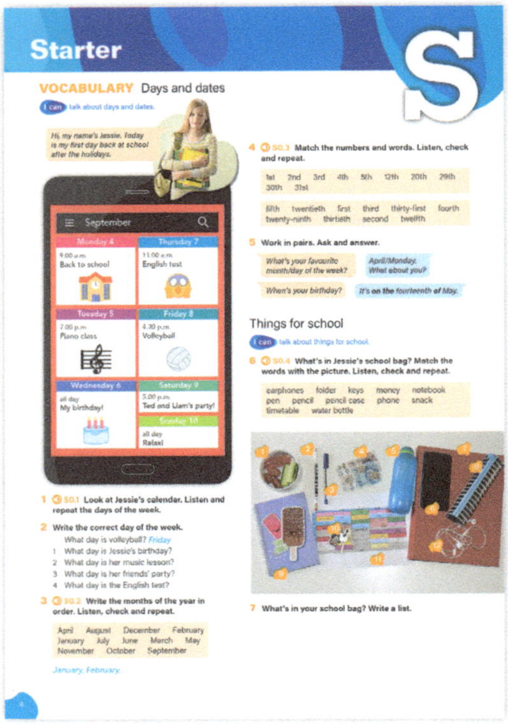

VOCABULARY

There are two vocabulary lessons per unit. The first vocabulary lesson appears on the unit opener page and usually presents the items with colourful visuals, especially at the lower levels. These pages also feature a video in the form of an optional vlog, for use in digital classrooms.

Lesson aims clearly stated in 'I can' statement.

Substantial vocabulary sets with around 10-15 items taught per vocabulary lesson.

Engaging visuals, a text or a quiz to present the vocabulary.

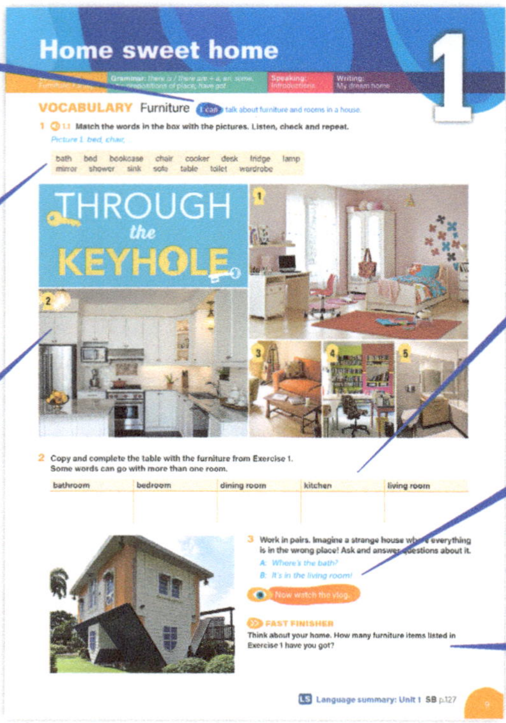

Typically 3 to 5 practice exercises with a pairwork or personalized activity to finish.

Fun, optional vlog on the unit theme including some of the new vocabulary from the lesson.

Fast finisher caters for mixed ability and consolidates what students have learned.

READING and GRAMMAR

There are two grammar lessons per unit. The Reading and grammar spread features the first grammar lesson of the unit and the grammar is presented via a reading text. This lesson also features an optional grammar animation.

Lesson aims clearly stated in 'I can' statement.

Graded reading texts contextualise grammar and practise relevant reading skill.

Texts focus on relevant and engaging topics for today's teenagers.

Word Power word-building task.

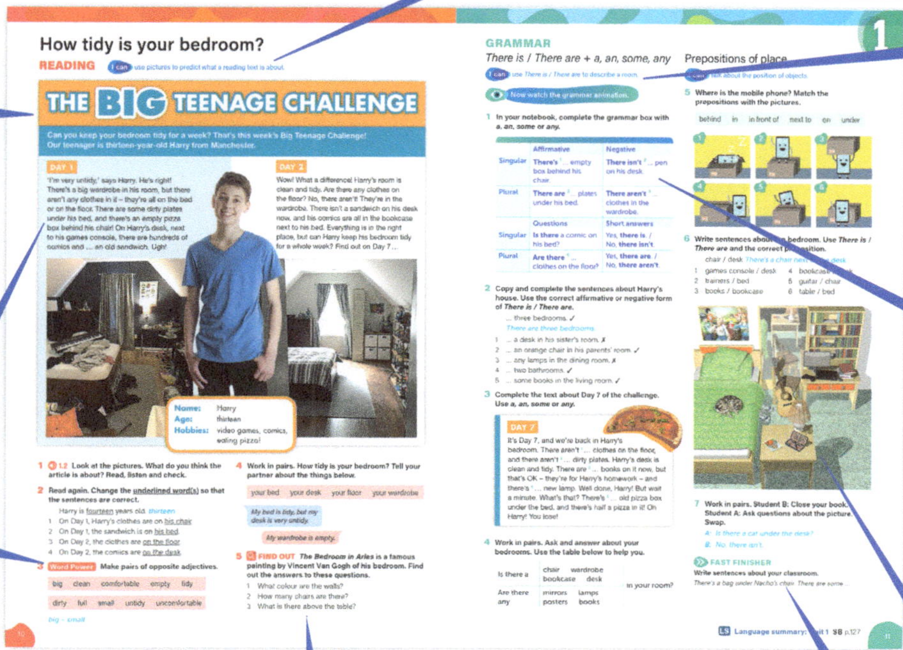

Animated grammar presentations of meaning and form.

Grammar presented inductively and form and use highlighted in tables and rules.

Controlled and freer practice exercises on form and meaning.

4 exercises per unit focus on 21st century skills: *Find out*, *Get creative*, *Think critically* and *Compare cultures*.

Fast finisher caters for mixed ability and consolidates what students have learned.

VOCABULARY, LISTENING and GRAMMAR

The second vocabulary lesson is combined with a listening activity. This spread also features the second grammar lesson of the unit. There is an optional grammar animation.

Lesson aims clearly stated in 'I can' statement.

Vocabulary is presented via a listening with the opportunity to practise a relevant listening skill.

Pronunciation feature allows students to listen and repeat.

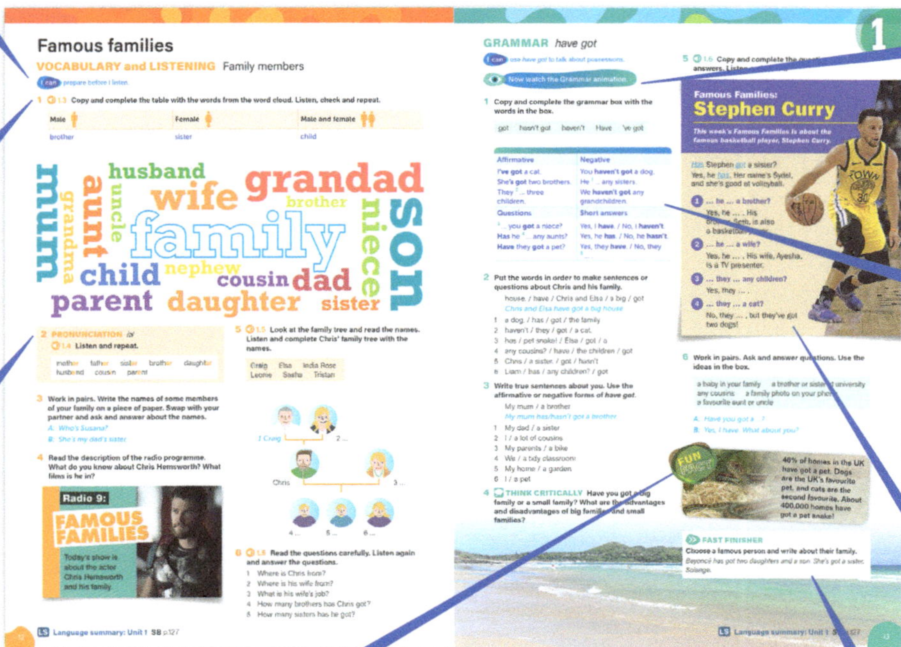

Animated grammar presentations of meaning and form.

Grammar presented inductively and form and use highlighted in tables and rules.

Controlled and freer practice exercises on form and meaning.

Fun facts provide fun but interesting information related to the topic of the lesson.

Fast finisher caters for mixed ability and consolidates what students have learned.

UNIT OVERVIEW

Keep talking!

READING, LISTENING and SPEAKING

The *Keep talking!* lesson starts with a focus on reading and listening before moving on to the functional area of speaking. This spread also features a digital game called *Keep moving!* which encourages spoken interaction. The lesson ends with a structured 'Prepare, Speak, Reflect' output task.

Lesson aims clearly stated in 'I can' statement.

Reading and listening tasks provide context for speaking section. Focus on real world information via blogs, leaflets, signs, adverts and maps.

Exercises for relevant reading and listening skills.

Recorded dialogues model spoken language.

Useful language box highlights key expressions with listen and repeat facility.

Supported 3-stage *Speaking plan* for end-of-lesson speaking task.

Optional digital board game *Keep moving!* for class use. A fun, dynamic way to revise language from the unit.

Fast finisher caters for mixed ability and consolidates what has been learned.

Real culture!

The *Real Culture!* spread contains a text and exercises on a relevant cultural theme. It also practises reading skills. It features an optional video on a related cultural theme.

Lesson aims clearly stated in 'I can' statement.

Reading text on a related cultural theme. Focus on English speaking culture around the world.

Fast finisher caters for mixed ability and consolidates what students have learned.

Word Power word-building task.

4 exercises per unit focus on 21st century skills: *Find out*, *Get creative*, *Think critically* and *Compare cultures*.

Fun optional culture video recycles grammar and vocabulary from the unit.

WRITING

There is a one-page writing lesson at the end of each unit that focuses on a particular text type and the language associated with it. The lesson ends with a structured 'Prepare, Write, Reflect' output task There is a complete Writing summary section at the back of the Workbook with additional model texts and *Tips for writing*.

Lesson aims clearly stated in 'I can' statement.

Model texts such as emails, blog posts, descriptions and letters.

Exercises to focus on the model text and support the writing process.

References to additional sections at the end of the Students Book and the Workbook.

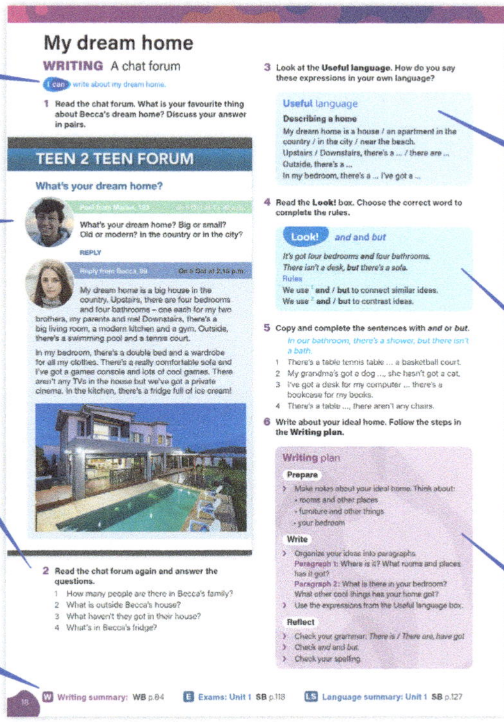

Useful language box highlights key expressions needed for the writing task.

Look! box highlights additional areas of language or text structure needed for the writing task.

Supported 3-stage *Writing plan* for the end-of-lesson writing task.

LANGUAGE SUMMARIES

There is a Language summary page at the end of the Student's Book for each unit. It provides a useful 'at a glance' visual summary of the grammar, vocabulary and functional language taught in the course. This can be used in class or at home as a quick reference whenever needed.

Complete grammar tables for each grammar point from the unit.

Full summary of grammatical forms with clear highlighting.

Comprehensive grammar rules with explanations of meaning.

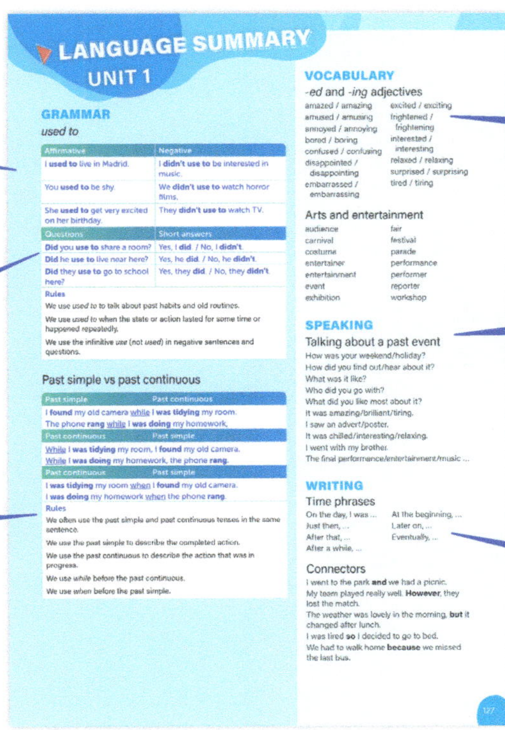

A list of the vocabulary taught in each unit.

A list of the key expressions from the *Keep talking!* speaking lesson.

A list of the key expressions and input from the writing lesson including the language from the *Look!* boxes.

ON-SCREEN LEARNING

Keep it real! offers dynamic on-screen learning for digital classrooms with optional vlogs (video blogs) and culture videos, as well as animated content in the form of an optional alternative grammar presentation. There is also an innovative digital board game called *Keep moving!* at the end of the speaking lesson which can be enjoyed as a whole class activity.

VLOGS

Authentic, real life vloggers in engaging, contemporary contexts.

Informal but graded spoken English and variety of accents including British and American English.

For further teaching notes for each vlog see Teacher's Guide pages 286-294 and for vlog scripts see pages 304-305.

Watch with the teacher in class or for revision at home.

Use as consolidation and revision of vocabulary from the lesson or to set the scene for the unit.

Available with or without subtitles. Useful for mixed ability and supported learning.

CULTURE VIDEOS

Engaging, mini-documentaries on cultural themes from across the English speaking world such as the UK, the USA, Canada, Australia and New Zealand.

Documentaries provide an opportunity for recycling vocabulary and grammar from the unit.

For further teaching notes for each culture video see Teacher's Guide pages 295-303 and for culture video scripts see pages 306-307.

Available with or without subtitles. Useful for mixed ability and supported learning.

Informal but graded English with a variety of accents including British and American English.

Watch with the teacher in class or for revision at home.

GRAMMAR ANIMATIONS

Ready-made optional grammar presentations for each grammar lesson.

A range of characters in fun, bite-sized scenarios and short stories.

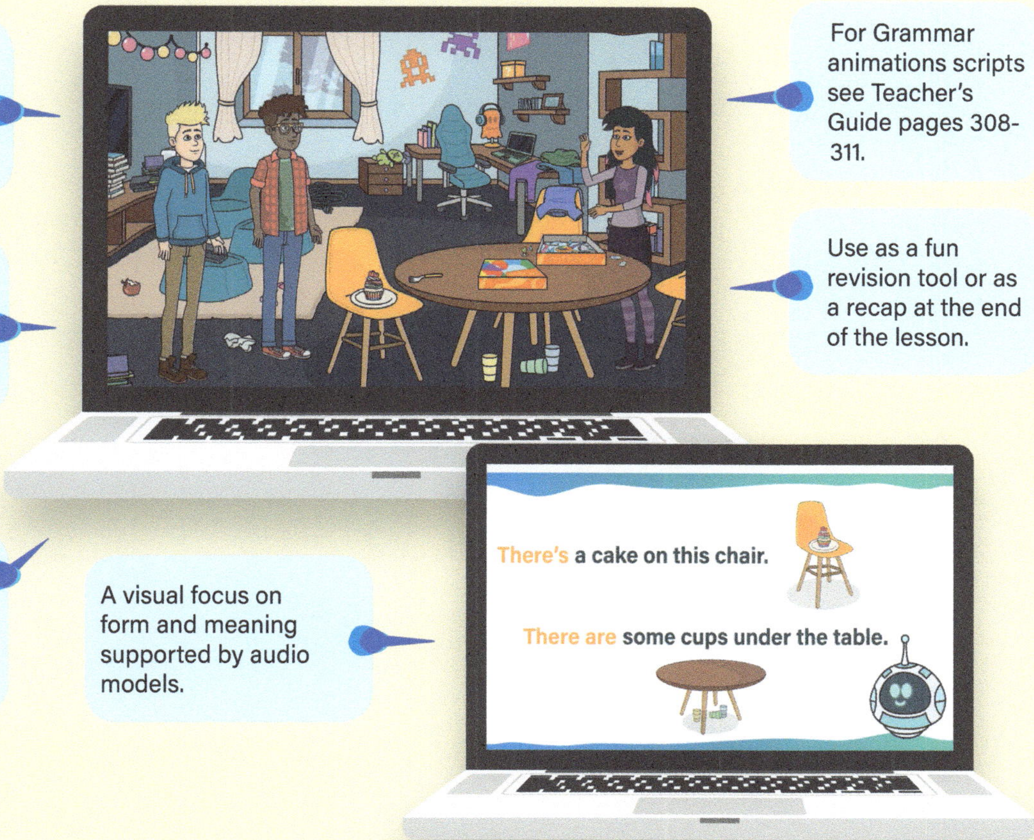

For Grammar animations scripts see Teacher's Guide pages 308-311.

Use as a fun revision tool or as a recap at the end of the lesson.

Available with or without subtitles. Useful for mixed ability and supported learning.

A visual focus on form and meaning supported by audio models.

Keep moving! DIGITAL BOARD GAME

Uniquely developed digital board game at the end of each *Keep talking!* lesson to revise unit content.

Use animated characters to progress along the board.

Win badges and collect treasure.

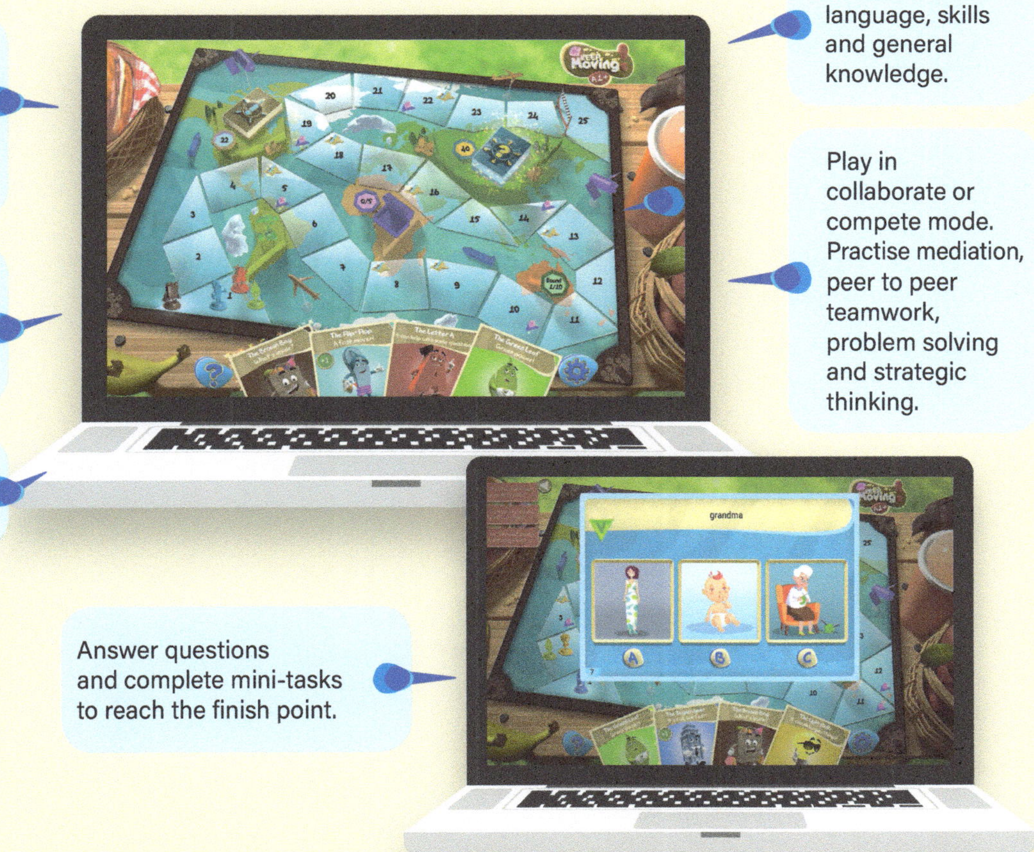

The game tests language, skills and general knowledge.

Play in collaborate or compete mode. Practise mediation, peer to peer teamwork, problem solving and strategic thinking.

Answer questions and complete mini-tasks to reach the finish point.

CONSOLIDATION AND EXTENSION

There are optional lessons at the end of the Student's Book for consolidation and extension. These include termly Reviews, Projects and Literature sections as well as a short Exams practice section for each unit.

REVIEWS

There are 3 termly Reviews that revise grammar and vocabulary via the 4 skills. Each spread starts with a reading, followed by a listening, speaking and writing activity. The aim of these spreads is to consolidate the grammar and vocabulary from the previous 3 units through simple, guided skills activities.

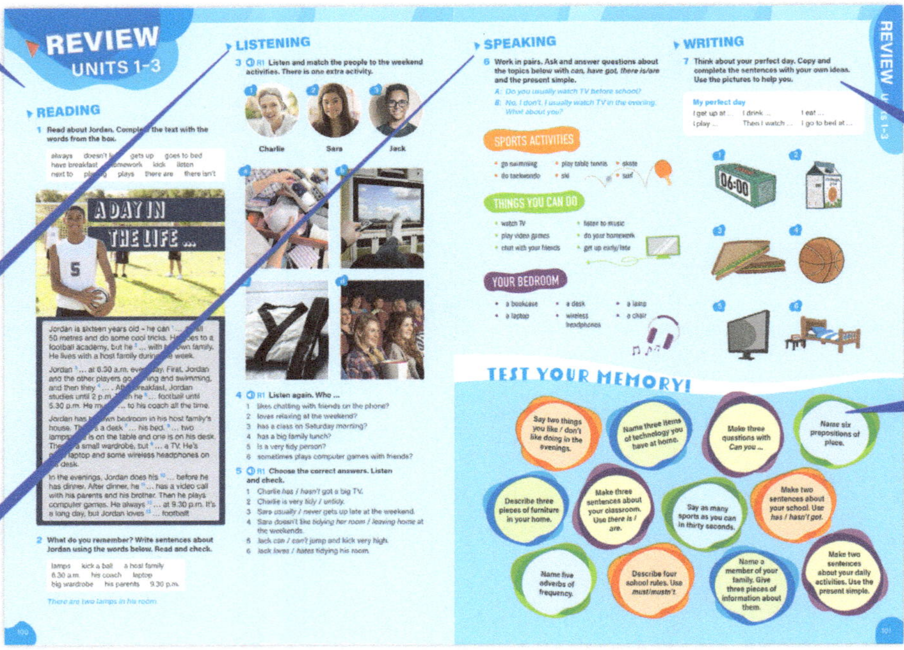

PROJECTS

There are 3 termly Projects that consolidate grammar and vocabulary in a fun, collaborative task. There are 3 clear stages 'Prepare, Do, Reflect' which support students as they create projects in pairs or small groups. A model of the project 'output' is provided for reference throughout the lesson.

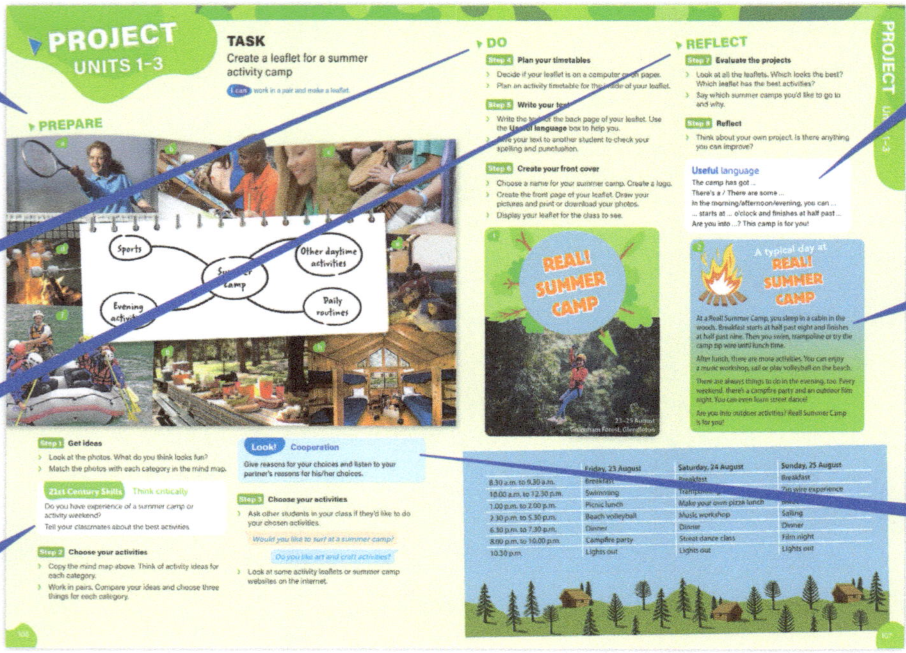

LITERATURE

There are 3 termly Literature lessons that each feature an extract from the **Richmond Readers** series. These provide an opportunity for extensive reading practice in a fun and supported way. There are 3 clear stages 'Before you read, Read, Reflect' which support students with their reading.

Before you read stage prepares students to read the text and think about the context.

Main points of the story are summarized in the *Outline* box.

Read stage helps students to focus on the main points of the story extract.

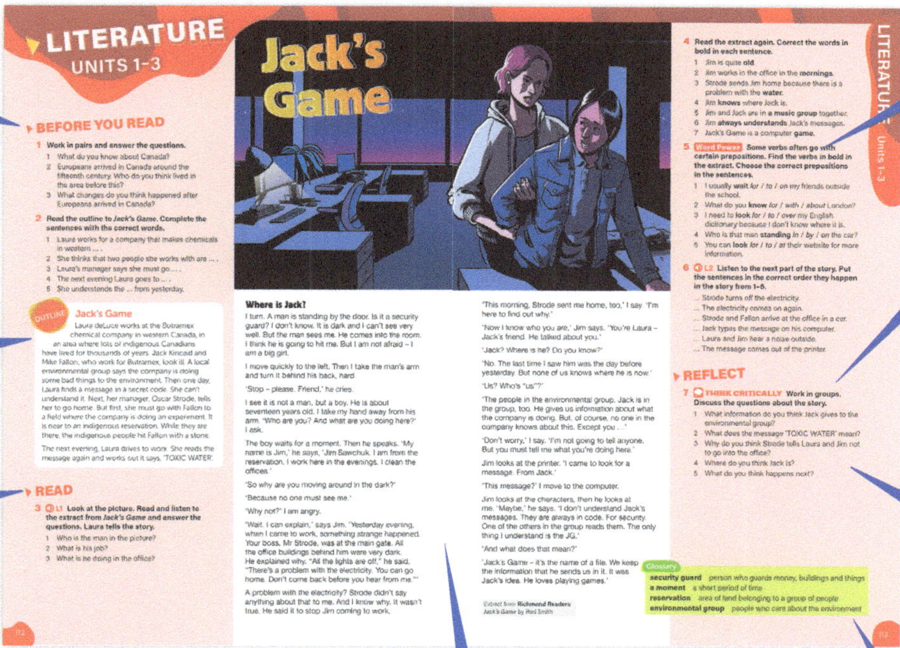

Word Power word-building task.

21st century skills included as part of the literature lesson.

Reflect stage to think about the story in a more general or personalized way.

Extract from the **Richmond Readers** series at the appropriate level with visuals to support details of the story.

Key words from the text are highlighted in the *Glossary*.

EXAMS

There are 9 Exams practice lessons that provide further practice of the grammar and vocabulary from the unit, using common exam question types. These are taken from a wide range of exam boards appropriate for the level and age group. Each section builds towards completing an exam style task.

Each lesson focuses on a skill such as reading, listening, speaking and writing, and a common exam question type such as multiple choice, gapfilling, writing a message and discussing a topic, etc.

Look! boxes provide general information on the scope of the exam task and what students can expect.

Useful strategies box gives guidance and tips on how to approach the exam task.

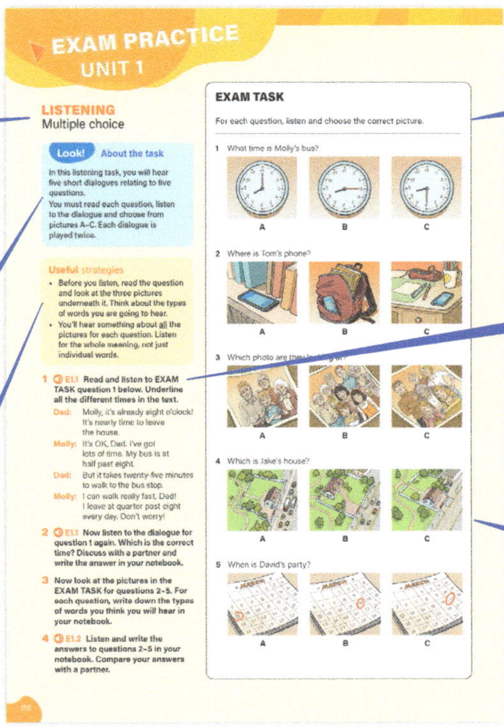

Graded *Exam task* which brings together the themes of the unit.

Exercises build towards and support the *Exam task* at the end of the lesson.

Exam practice lesson finishes with an opportunity to complete a simple *Exam task* based on the skills and strategies taught.

EXTENDED PRACTICE AND ASSESSMENT

Workbook

The Workbook provides thorough practice of the Student's Book material, for students to do in class or at home, with graded activities for mixed ability via the 'star' system. There is a Progress check every 3 units and a writing summary at the back of the book. The Workbook audio is available as an MP3 download on the **Richmond Learning Platform**.

Practice of vocabulary and grammar from the Student's Book. Graded with stars to show 3 levels of difficulty.

Regular 'listen and check' activities. Available as MP3 downloads on the **Richmond Learning Platform.**

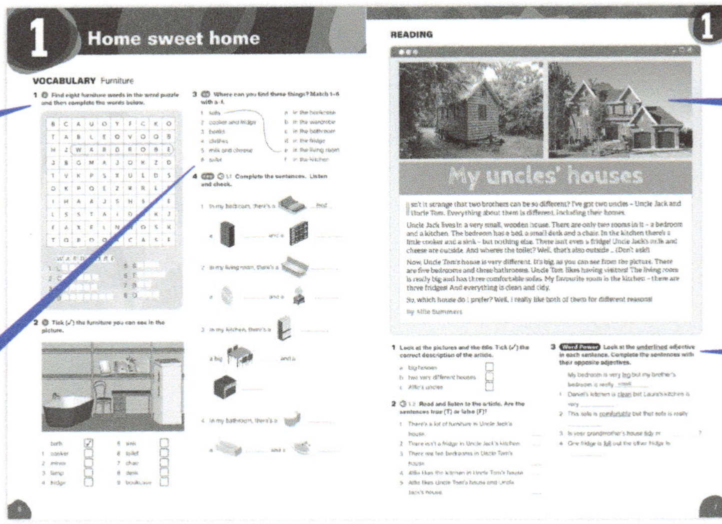

Practice of the 4 skills from the Student's Book: reading, listening, speaking and writing.

Word Power word-building task.

3 termly Progress checks test vocabulary and grammar from the previous 3 units.

A range of exercises test knowledge of vocabulary and grammar across different units.

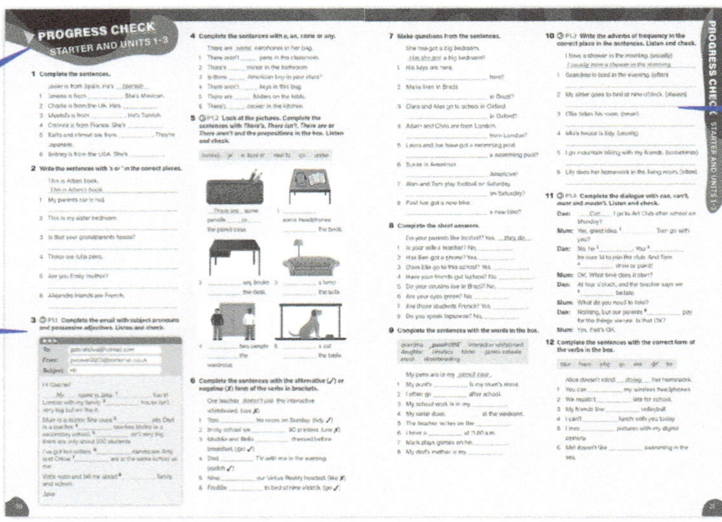

Regular 'listen and check' activities. Available as MP3 downloads on the **Richmond Learning Platform.**

Use as end-of-term revision in class or at home.

Comprehensive Writing summary section at the back of the Workbook.

Model texts for each of the Student's Book writing lessons.

Text features and key language clearly highlighted.

Useful *Tips for writing* in short summary section.

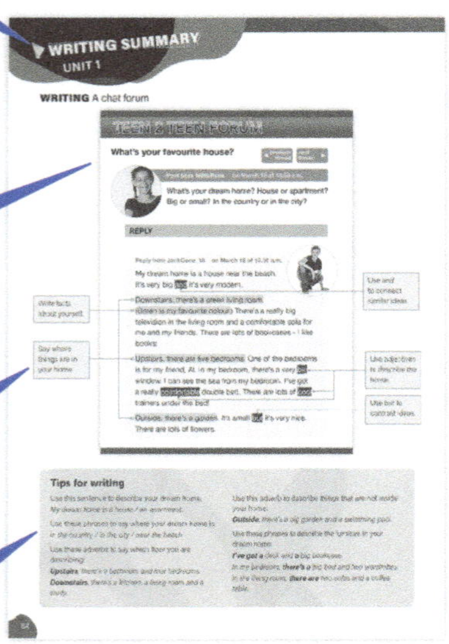

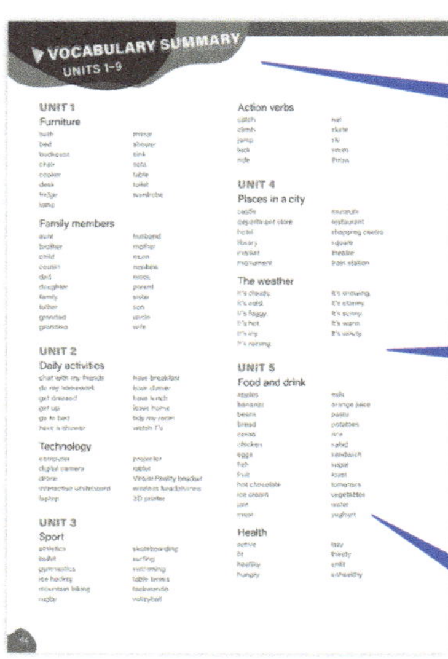

Convenient Vocabulary summary section at the back of the Workbook.

Unit-by-unit reference for items taught in the 2 vocabulary lessons in the Student's Book.

Listed alphabetically for easy use.

Richmond Learning Platform

EXTRA PRACTICE WORKSHEETS

There are 72 print-and-go worksheets that provide students with extra practice of grammar and vocabulary in a variety of different ways, including via the 4 skills. The grammar and vocabulary worksheets are offered at 2 levels of difficulty. All the worksheets can be found on the **Richmond Learning Platform** and can be printed off for use in class or set as homework. Audio for the listening worksheets is available as an MP3 download on the **Richmond Learning Platform**.

- 2 vocabulary and 2 grammar worksheets for every unit.
- The language worksheets are graded for two levels of difficulty via consolidation and extension versions.
- 4 skills worksheets for every unit: reading, listening, speaking and writing.
- The skills worksheets revise grammar and vocabulary via a skills activity at one level of difficulty and end with a short 21st century skills task.

TESTS

There is a comprehensive test package offered on the **Richmond Learning Platform**. Tests are offered at 2 levels of difficulty and are presented in both PDF and digital format.

- Tests for grammar, vocabulary, reading, listening, speaking and writing. The 4 skills are tested separately.
- Consolidation and extension versions of each test (not speaking).
- Tests are auto-marked (except for speaking and writing tasks which require teacher grading).
- Unit-by-unit tests, end-of-term tests, and end-of-year tests.

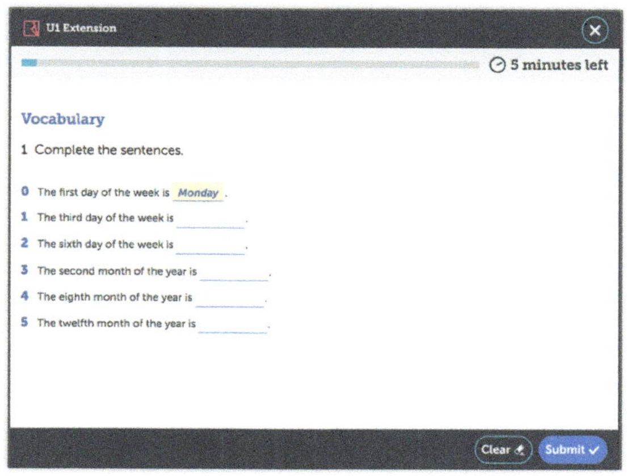

EXTRA PRACTICE ACTIVITIES

Extra practice activities for self study on the **Richmond Learning Platform** in digital format.

- Reading and listening activities use Student's Book texts and audio with new comprehension tasks.
- Speaking and writing activities test Useful language from the Student's Book. Listen, repeat and record facility for speaking and pronunciation.
- Vlogs and culture videos from the Student's Book further exploited using new tasks.

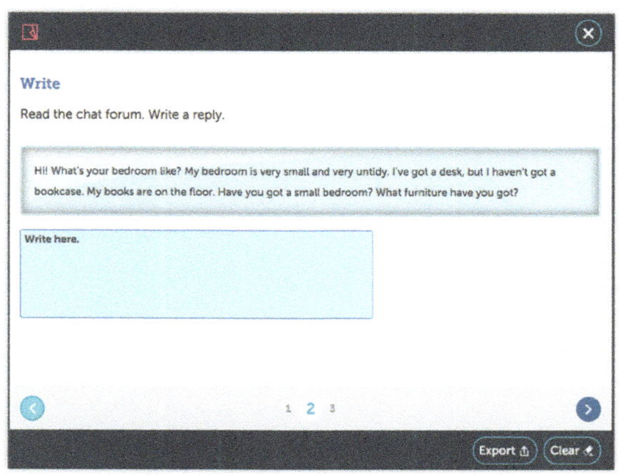

Teacher's Guide

The *Keep it real!* Teacher's Guide is a complete planning and teaching resource with Student's Book pages and teaching notes combined. Student's Book audio scripts, Workbook answer keys and additional teaching notes for the Student's Book vlogs and culture videos are available at the back of the Teacher's Guide.

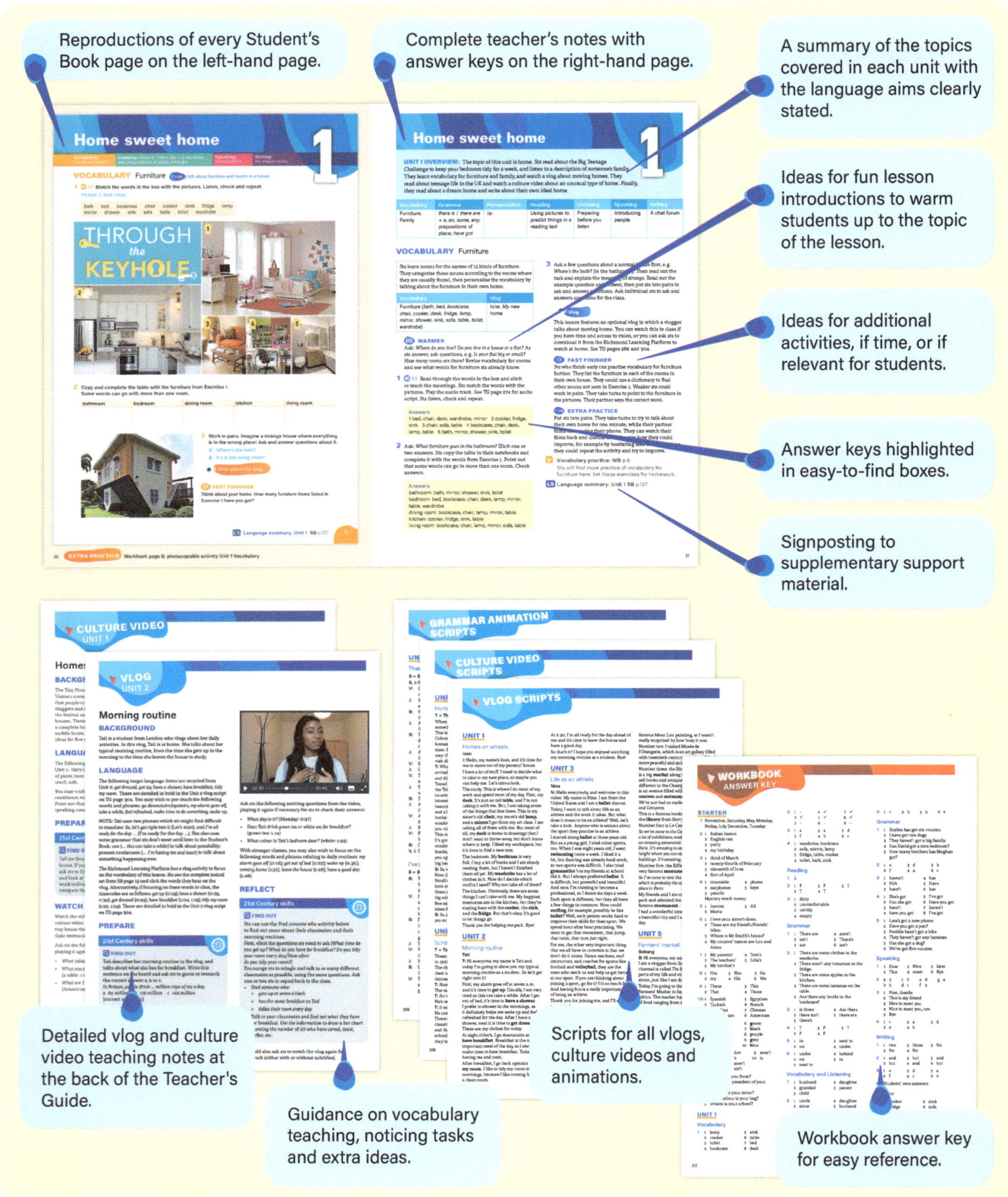

iBook for teachers

The *Keep it real!* iBook is a fully interactive version of the course for use in class. It combines all the teaching and learning elements of the course for use with a Smart Board or projector, in a convenient one-stop resource.

Student's Book pages with pop up answer keys and audio / video scripts.

Includes embedded audio, culture videos and vlogs at a click.

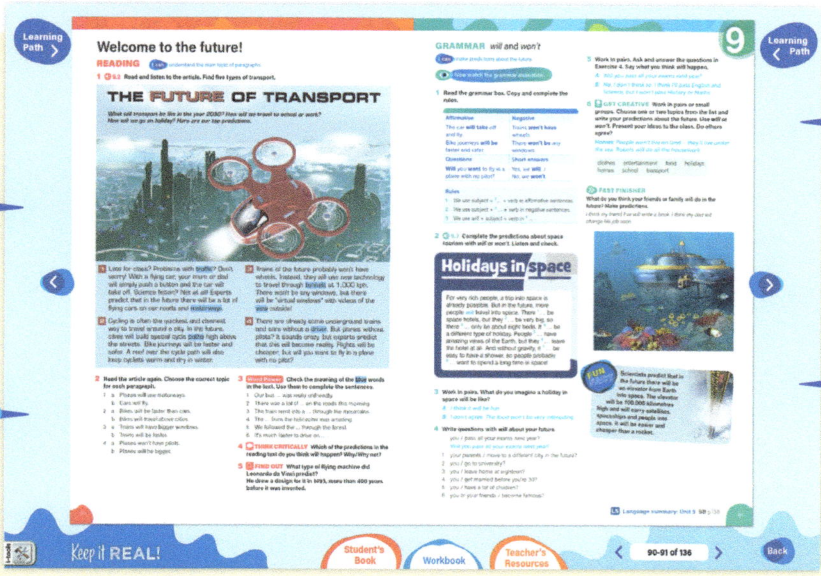

Includes Student's Book, Workbook and Teacher's Guide all in one place.

Easily accessible grammar animations and *Keep moving!* revision game.

Richmond *Learning* Platform

There is a wealth of interactive resources on the **Richmond Learning Platform**. These can be used as self study or assigned by the teacher and assessed and tracked through the mark book. The **Richmond Learning Platform** also includes downloadable PDFs and other key components.

Extra practice activities for skills, pronunciation and video resources that can be assigned, tracked and marked.

Print-and-go worksheets and tests for use in class.

Workbook audio MP3 and answer key.

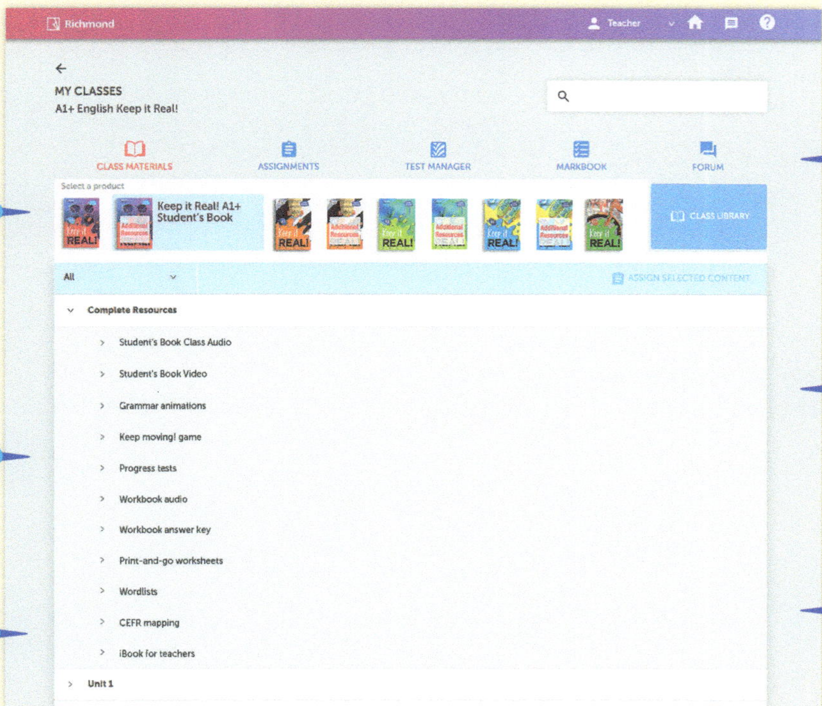

Digital tests that can be assigned, tracked and marked.

Complete downloadable audio, video, animations, and scripts.

Downloadable wordlists and CEFR mapping documents.

Starter

VOCABULARY Days and dates

I can talk about days and dates.

Hi, my name's Jessie. Today is my first day back at school after the holidays.

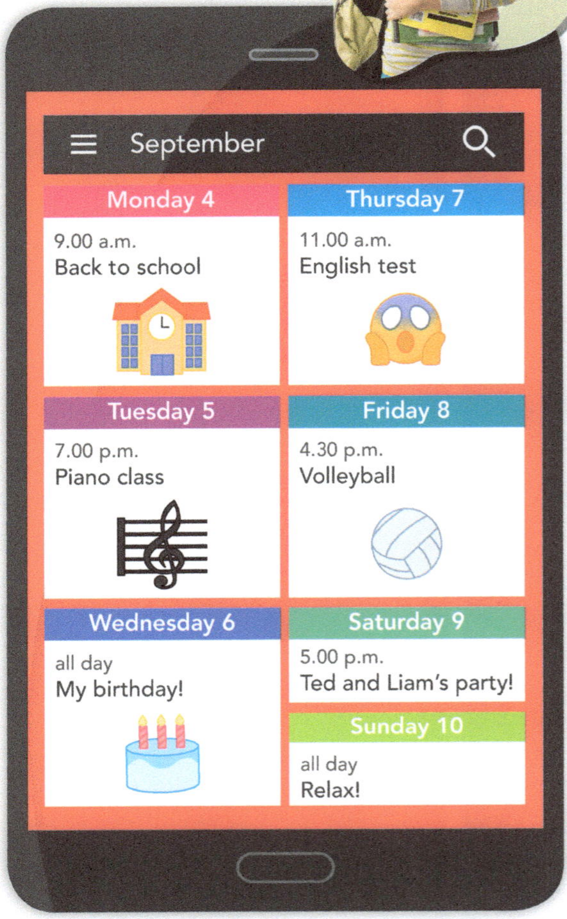

1 S0.1 **Look at Jessie's calendar. Listen and repeat the days of the week.**

2 **Write the correct day of the week.**

What day is volleyball? *Friday*
1 What day is Jessie's birthday?
2 What day is her music lesson?
3 What day is her friends' party?
4 What day is the English test?

3 S0.2 **Write the months of the year in order. Listen, check and repeat.**

April August December February January July June March May November October September

January, February, ...

4 S0.3 **Match the numbers and words. Listen, check and repeat.**

1st 2nd 3rd 4th 5th 12th 20th 29th 30th 31st

fifth twentieth first third thirty-first fourth twenty-ninth thirtieth second twelfth

5 **Work in pairs. Ask and answer.**

What's your favourite month/day of the week?
April/Monday. What about you?
When's your birthday?
*It's **on the** fourteenth **of** May.*

Things for school

I can talk about things for school.

6 S0.4 **What's in Jessie's school bag? Match the words with the picture. Listen, check and repeat.**

earphones folder keys money notebook pen pencil pencil case phone snack timetable water bottle

7 **What's in your school bag? Write a list.**

EXTRA PRACTICE Workbook page 4

Starter

STARTER UNIT OVERVIEW: The aim of this unit is to review language that students already know, to remind them of some familiar vocabulary and grammar before they start the main units of the book. They learn days and dates, and things for school, then revise countries and nationalities and colours. They study the possessive *'s*, subject pronouns, possessive adjectives and demonstrative pronouns. They also revise the present forms of *be* and question words. They read a message board about going back to school and practise transferring information to a table. They also learn how to tell the time.

Vocabulary	Grammar	Pronunciation	Reading	Speaking
Days and dates; Things for school; Countries and nationalities; Colours	Possessive *'s*; subject pronouns and possessive adjectives; demonstrative pronouns; *be*: affirmative, negative and questions; question words	Question words	Transferring information to a table	Telling the time

VOCABULARY Days and dates

Sts revise days and dates and vocabulary to talk about things at school. They study possessive *'s*, subject pronouns, possessive adjectives and demonstrative pronouns.

Vocabulary

Days and dates (*January, February,* etc., *first, second,* etc.); Things for school (*earphones, folder, keys, money, notebook, pen, pencil, pencil case, phone, snack, timetable, water bottle*)

WARMER

Play a game to revise numbers. Ask sts to stand up. Say the number *one* and elicit the next number (two) from a student at the front of the class. Continue around the class, with students saying a number in turn. If they make a mistake or cannot think of the next number, they sit down. You could repeat the game with students counting in twos or threes.

1 S0.1 Read out Jessie's introduction, then ask sts to read the calendar. Play the audio once for students to listen to the days of the week. Play the audio again for sts to listen and repeat.

2 Read out the example question and answer, and point out that the answer is in the calendar. Sts then write the answers to the remaining questions. Check answers.

Answers
1 Wednesday
2 Tuesday
3 Saturday
4 Thursday

3 S0.2 Sts could work in pairs to write the months in order. Play the audio once for sts to listen, check and repeat.

Answers
January, February, March, April, May, June, July, August, September, October, November, December

4 S0.3 Write the first two numbers on the board. Point to each one and ask: *Which words does it match?* Elicit the answers. Sts then match the remaining numbers and words. Play the audio for sts to listen, check and repeat.

Answers
1st first, 2nd second, 3rd third, 4th fourth, 5th fifth, 12th twelfth, 20th twentieth, 29th twenty-ninth, 30th thirtieth, 31st thirty-first

5 Read out the questions and point out the use of *on* to talk about birthdays, e.g. *my birthday is on the tenth of June*. Put sts into pairs to ask and answer questions.

Things for school

6 S0.4 Sts match the words with the items in the picture. Play the audio for students to listen, check and repeat.

Answers
1 snack 2 pencil 3 pen 4 money
5 water bottle 6 phone 7 folder
8 pencil case 9 notebook 10 keys
11 timetable 12 earphones

7 Sts write a list of what is in their school bag. Ask some sts to tell the class what is in their school bag, holding up each thing in turn and saying the words.

V Vocabulary practice: WB p.4
Sts will find more practice of vocabulary for days and dates, and things for school here. Set these exercises for homework.

GRAMMAR Possessive 's

I can talk about possession.

1 Copy and complete the rule. Write *singular* or *plural*.

Singular	Plural
Jessie**'s** birthday is on Wednesday.	Her friends**'** party is on Saturday.

Rules

We use **'s** after a [1] ... noun or name.
We use **'** after a [2] ... noun.

2 Copy and complete the sentences. Use 's or '.

This is the boys' bathroom.
1 That is Mark ... bag.
2 Emma ... birthday is in September.
3 My parents ... names are Sue and Pete.
4 Are these your best friend ... keys?
5 This is Maria ... notebook.
6 Two of my friends ... birthdays are on the same day!

Subject pronouns and possessive adjectives

I can use subject pronouns and possessive adjectives.

3 Copy and complete the grammar box with the words in the box.

he her it ~~my~~ our their your

Subject pronoun	Possessive adjective
I	*my*
you	[1]
[2]	his
she	[3]
[4]	its
we	[5]
they	[6]

4 Change the words in blue to a subject pronoun.

Maria is thirteen years old.
She is thirteen years old.
1 **Daniel** is in Year 7.
2 **The water bottle** is on my desk.
3 **Lucas and I** are in the same class.
4 **The earphones** are in my bag.
5 Are **you and your sister** at the same school?

5 Copy and complete the sentences with a possessive adjective.

She's American, but *her* mum is from Mexico.
1 I'm from Brazil. ... name is Mauro.
2 **A:** When's ... birthday, Anna?
B: ... birthday is on 26th November.
3 That's our neighbour's cat. ... name is Tiger and it's really friendly.
4 **A:** What's the name of the new boy in our class?
B: ... name is Tomasz. He's from Poland.
5 Haruto and Sakura are from Japan. ... home is in Tokyo.
6 I'm in a class with Josie and Leo. We all like ... new teacher.

Demonstrative pronouns

I can use demonstrative pronouns.

6 S0.5 Read the grammar box. Listen and repeat the dialogue.

	 Here	 There
Singular	this	that
Plural	these	those

Student: Excuse me, what's this in English?
Teacher: It's a ruler.
Student: And what are those?
Teacher: They're earphones.
Student: Thanks.
Teacher: You're welcome!

7 Work in pairs. Ask and answer about other things in the classroom.

What's this? *What are these?*
What's that? *What are those?*

FAST FINISHER

Write about your friends' and family's birthdays.

George's birthday is on 22nd October. My mum's birthday is on ...

 EXTRA PRACTICE Workbook pages 4 and 5

GRAMMAR Possessive *'s*

1 Read the grammar box about the possessive *'s* with sts. Make sure they understand the meaning of *singular* and *plural*. Sts could work in pairs to complete the rules. Check answers.

Answers
1 singular 2 plural

Ask questions to check concept.

Concept check questions: Write on the board: *the student's book*. Ask: *One student?* (yes). *One book?* (yes). Write: *the student's books*. Ask: *One book?* (no – more than one). *One student?* (yes). Write: *the students' books*. Ask: *One book?* (no – more than one). *One student?* (no – more than one).

2 Read the example with the class and elicit that it refers to more than one boy. Sts then copy and complete the sentences. Allow sts to compare their answers in pairs, then check answers with the class.

Answers
1 That is Mark**'s** bag.
2 Emma**'s** birthday is in September.
3 My parent**s'** names are Sue and Pete.
4 Are these your best friend**'s** keys?
5 This is Maria**'s** notebook.
6 Two of my friend**s'** birthdays are on the same day!

Subject pronouns and possessive adjectives

3 Demonstrate the grammar by picking up a book and saying: *I am a teacher. It's my book*. Then say to a student: *You are a student. It's* ... Elicit the response *your book*. Sts could work in pairs to copy the grammar box into their notebooks and complete it. Check answers with the class. Point out that English has only one form of *you* for both singular and plural, e.g. *You are my friend. You are all my friends.*

Answers
1 your 3 her 5 our
2 he 4 it 6 their

Ask questions to check concept.

Concept check questions: Use classroom objects such as books or pens to elicit simple sentences to demonstrate the grammar, e.g. *She's Lisa. It's ... pen*. (her). *He's Matteo. It's ... bag*. (his). *Dan and Paul are students. These are ... books*. (their). *Is this his bag?* (no – it's *my* bag).

4 Read out the example answer, then read through the remaining sentences and check that sts understand *water bottle* and *earphones*. Ask sts to rewrite the sentences using subject pronouns. Allow sts to compare their answers in pairs, then check answers with the class.

Answers
1 He 2 It 3 We 4 They 5 you

5 Read out the example answer, then ask sts to copy the sentences and complete them with the correct possessive adjectives. Allow sts to compare their answers in pairs, then check answers with the class.

Answers
1 My 3 Its 5 Their
2 your, My 4 His 6 our

Demonstrative pronouns

6 S0.5 Read through the grammar box with the class. Demonstrate the idea of *here* and *there* in the classroom, by pointing to things close to you and saying: *This is my book. These are my pens*, then pointing to things further away in the classroom and saying: *That is Ana's bag. Those are Ana's pens*. Play the audio for sts to listen to the dialogue. Play it again, pausing for sts to repeat.

Ask questions to check concept.

Concept check questions: Say: *That is my pen – here or there?* (there). *This is my book – here or there?* (here). Point to the far side of the classroom and say: *my books*. Elicit the sentence *Those are my books*. Point to some pens close to you and say: *This is my pens – correct?* (no – these are my pens).

7 Demonstrate the task by picking some things up and asking: *What's this? What are these?* Then point to some objects further away from you and ask: *What's that? What are those?* Elicit some example answers. Sts then work in pairs to ask and answer questions. Monitor and help as necessary.

FAST FINISHER
Sts who finish early can practise the grammar further. Sts write sentences about their friends' and family's birthdays. Weaker sts could write a sentence about their own birthday, then compare with a partner.

G **Grammar practice: WB** pp.4 and 5
Sts will find more practice for possessive *'s*, subject pronouns, possessive adjectives and demonstrative pronouns here. Set these exercises for homework.

VOCABULARY Countries and nationalities

I can talk about countries and nationalities.

1 S0.6 **Match the countries with the flags in the World Quiz. Listen, check and repeat.**

Argentina Brazil China Egypt France Ireland Japan Mexico Spain Turkey the UK the USA

1 Where is this animal from?

a It's from China.

b It's from Japan.

2 Who is Daisy Ridley?

a She's a British actress.

b She's an American singer.

3 What is the capital of Brazil?

a It's Rio de Janeiro.

b It's Brasilia.

4 How old are the pyramids in Egypt?

a They're 4,500 years old.

b They're 450 years old.

5 Where are tacos from?

a They're from Mexico.

b They're from Turkey.

6 What nationality is the footballer Marcos Asensio?

a He's Argentinian.

b He's Spanish.

2 S0.7 **Match the countries in Exercise 1 with the nationalities below. Listen, check and repeat.**

Argentina – Argentinian

-an / -ian	-ese	-ish	Other
American Mexican Egyptian Brazilian Argentinian	Chinese Japanese	Turkish British Spanish Irish	French

3 S0.8 **Work in pairs. Do the quiz. Listen and check.**

Colours

4 S0.9 **Listen and repeat the colours.**

black red white green yellow blue orange pink purple brown grey

5 **Work in pairs. Describe a flag. Can your partner guess it?**

A: It's red and white.

B: Is it Turkey?

A: Yes, it is. / No, it isn't.

EXTRA PRACTICE Workbook page 5

VOCABULARY Countries and nationalities

Sts study vocabulary for countries and nationalities. They read and answer quiz questions, revise colours and work in pairs to describe national flags.

Vocabulary

Countries and nationalities (*Argentina/Argentinian, Brazil/Brazilian, China/Chinese, Egypt/Egyptian, France/ French, Ireland/Irish, Japan/Japanese, Mexico/Mexican, Spain/Spanish, Turkey/Turkish, the UK/British, the USA/ American*); Colours (*black, blue, brown, green, grey, orange, pink, purple, red, white, yellow*)

WARMER

Write the word *country* on the board. Elicit the meaning, then ask: *What's your country?* Elicit the answer, then put sts into pairs and ask them to write five more country names in English. Bring their ideas together on the board and check they understand. Point to one or two of the countries on the board and say: *I'm from (Brazil). I'm (Brazilian).* Try to elicit more nationality words in this way.

1 S0.6 Sts could work in pairs to match the countries with the flags. Play the audio once for sts to listen and check their answers, then play it again, pausing for them to repeat. Ask which sts guessed all the flags correctly.

Answers

1	Egypt	7	Brazil
2	Mexico	8	Spain
3	the USA	9	Ireland
4	Japan	10	Argentina
5	France	11	the UK
6	Turkey	12	China

2 S0.7 Sts could work in pairs to match the countries with the nationalities. Play the audio once for sts to listen and check their answers, then play it again, pausing for them to repeat.

Answers

Brazil – Brazilian	Mexico – Mexican
China – Chinese	Spain – Spanish
Egypt – Egyptian	Turkey – Turkish
France – French	the UK – British
Ireland – Irish	the USA – American
Japan – Japanese	

3 S0.8 Read through the quiz with the class and check that sts understand *actress*, *singer*, *pyramid*, *animal* and *capital*. Sts then do the quiz in pairs. Play the audio for sts to listen and check their answers. Ask who got all the answers right.

Answers

1	a	3	b	5	a
2	a	4	a	6	b

Colours

4 S0.9 Play the audio once for sts to listen to the words. Play the audio again, pausing for sts to repeat. For extra practice, point to some things in the classroom, e.g. sts' clothes or bags and ask: *What colour is this?* Elicit answers.

EXTRA PRACTICE

Ask sts to close their books. Arrange them in small teams and give them a minute to write down the colours they remember from Exercise 4. Elicit all eleven colours and ask teams to spell each one. Write them on the board so teams can check their spelling. They win a point for each correctly spelled colour. When you have all eleven colours on the board, call them out at random, e.g. *blue*. The first team to find something blue on their desk or in their bag, and hold it up in the air, wins another point.

5 Demonstrate the task by describing one or two flags and asking sts to guess them. Sts then work in pairs and take turns to describe and guess the flags. Monitor while they are working, and help if necessary.

V **Vocabulary practice: WB** p.5

Sts will find more practice of countries, nationalities and colours here. Set these exercises for homework.

GRAMMAR

be: affirmative, negative and questions

I can use the verb *be*.

1 **Read and match the long forms with the short forms in the grammar box.**

'm = am

is ~~am~~ are not (x2) is not are (x2) am not

Affirmative	Negative
I**'m** from the UK.	I**'m not** from Ireland.
You**'re** Spanish.	You **aren't** from Colombia.
He/She/It**'s** Brazilian.	He/She/It **isn't** Egyptian.
We/They**'re** German.	We/They **aren't** American.

2 **Choose the correct answers.**

1 My new pencil case *am* / *is* / *are* blue. *is*
2 We *'m* / *'s* / *'re* from Spain.
3 Her keys *am not* / *isn't* / *aren't* in her bag.
4 She *'m not* / *isn't* / *aren't* fourteen.
5 You *'m not* / *isn't* / *aren't* in this class.

3 **Copy and complete the sentences so that they are true for you.**

1 I ... from Spain.
2 My teacher ... American.
3 My parents ... from Mexico.
4 I ... twelve.
5 My friends and I ... interested in sport.
6 My school ... big.

4 **Read the grammar box. Copy and complete the questions and short answers.**

Questions	Short answers
Am I in this class?	Yes, I [1] ... . / No, I**'m not**.
Are you Sarah?	Yes, you [2] .... / No, you aren't.
[3] ... he/she/it in this class?	Yes, he/she/it **is**. / No, he/she/it **isn't**.
Are we/they from London?	Yes, we/they **are**. / No, we/they [4] ... .

5 **Copy and complete the questions. Ask and answer in pairs.**

1 ... you from Italy?
2 ... Lionel Messi from Argentina?
3 ... New York the capital of the USA?
4 ... your parents from Spain?
5 ... kangaroos from Australia?

Question words

I can ask *Wh-* questions with the verb *be*.

6 **Read the example sentences. Complete the dialogue with a question word.**

Where are tacos from?
What is the capital of Brazil?
Who is Daisy Ridley?
How old are the pyramids?

A: [1] ... 's your name?
B: My name is James.
A: [2] ... are you from?
B: I'm from Ireland.
A: [3] ... are you?
B: I'm fourteen years old.
A: [4] ... 's your teacher?
B: My teacher is Mrs Kelly.

7 **PRONUNCIATION Question words**

S0.10 **Listen and repeat the questions from the dialogue in Exercise 6.**

/w/	/h/
What's your name?	How old are you?
Where are you from?	Who is your teacher?

8 **Work in pairs. Ask and answer the questions in Exercise 6. Give true answers for you.**

9 **Work in pairs. Write more quiz questions like those on page 6. Ask and answer with another pair.**

What's the capital of ...?
What colour is the ... flag?
Where is ... from?
Where is ...?
Who is the President of ...?
How old is ...?

FAST FINISHER

Make a list of more countries and nationalities.

Germany – German, ...

 EXTRA PRACTICE Workbook page 5

GRAMMAR *be*: affirmative, negative and questions

1 Read the grammar box with sts about *be*. Draw attention to the different forms, and explain that *be* is an irregular verb, so sts have to learn all the different forms. Point out that it has long forms, but usually when we speak and write we use the short forms. Point out that we use *be* to talk about where someone is from and their nationality, but also their age *(he's fifteen)*, their birthday *(my birthday is on …)* and to talk about things *(this is my bag)*.

Ask sts to match the long forms with the short forms in the grammar box. Check answers.

Answers

'm not – am not	isn't – is not
're – are	're – are
aren't – are not	aren't – are not
's – is	

Ask questions to check concept.

Concept check questions: *I'm a teacher – long form or short form?* (short). *What's the long form?* (I am a teacher). *She are fourteen – correct?* (no – *she is/she's* fourteen). *My book is in my bag – correct?* (yes). *Can you make it negative?* (my book *isn't* in my bag).

2 Sts read the sentences and choose the correct answers. Allow sts to compare their answers in pairs, then check answers with the class.

Answers
2 're 3 aren't 4 isn't 5 aren't

3 Read out the first gapped sentence and elicit a personal answer to complete it. Sts then write the sentences in their notebooks. Check answers by asking individual sts to read out some of their sentences.

4 Read the grammar box with sts. To demonstrate the word order in questions, write a simple affirmative sentence on the board, e.g. *Hugo is from Spain*. Demonstrate with arrows how the word order changes to make a question: *Is Hugo from Spain?* Point out that we use short forms in negative answers, but we always use long forms in affirmative answers. Sts to copy the questions and short answers, and complete them. Check answers.

Answers
1 am 2 are 3 Is 4 aren't

Ask questions to check concept.

Concept check questions: *He's from the USA – can you make that a question?* (Is he from the USA?). *Yes, he's – correct?* (no – *Yes, he is*). *Is they from Brazil – correct?* (no – *Are they from Brazil*). *Yes, they ……* (are), *No, they ……* (aren't).

5 Sts work individually to copy the questions into their notebooks and complete them. Allow them to compare their questions in pairs, then check them with the class. Then put sts into pairs to ask and answer the questions. Go through the answers with the class and check the ones that have a correct answer.

Answers
1 Are 2 Is 3 Is 4 Are 5 Are
2 Is Lionel Messi from Argentina? Yes, he is.
3 Is New York the capital of the USA? No, it isn't.
5 Are kangaroos from Australia? Yes, they are.

Question words

6 Read the example sentences with the class. Point out the word order of Question word + *be* + subject: *What* + *is* + *the capital of Brazil*? Elicit how to say the question words in the sts' own language. Ask sts to complete the dialogue with the correct words. Sts compare answers in pairs then check with the class.

Answers
1 What 2 Where 3 How old 4 Who

Ask questions to check concept.

Concept check questions: *Which question word asks about someone's age?* (How old …). *Which one asks about a place?* (Where). *Which one asks about a person?* (Who). *Which one asks about a thing?* (What).

7 **PRONUNCIATION** S0.10

Model pronunciation of the /w/ and /h/ sounds in isolation. Play the audio once for sts to listen to the questions, then play it again for them to repeat the words.

8 Demonstrate the task by asking one or two sts the questions in Exercise 6 and eliciting true answers. Sts then work in pairs to ask and answer the questions.

9 Read through the question stems with the class and elicit one or two questions with each one. Put sts into pairs to write their quiz questions. Put pairs together into groups of four to ask and answer their questions.

FAST FINISHER
Fast finishers can make a list of more countries and nationalities. They could use a dictionary to help them. Weaker sts could work in pairs.

G **Grammar practice: WB** p.5
Sts will find more practice for the affirmative, negative and question forms of *be* and question words here. Set these exercises for homework.

READING

I can transfer information to a table.

1 S0.11 **Read and listen to the message board. Copy and complete the information for Sam and Jessie.**

Name:	
Age:	
City:	
School:	
School subject 😊:	
School subject ☹:	

Home · Board · Contact

Today's message board

Back to school

Is it your first day back at school this week? Write and tell us about you and your school.

Hi, my name's Sam. I'm thirteen years old, and I'm from Bristol in the UK. I'm at Brandon Park School. It's a big secondary school. My best friends are Jessie, Ted and Liam. We're always together – at break time, lunch and after school! My favourite subjects are Science and English. I'm not very good at Maths – it's difficult!

Hi, I'm Jessie. I'm twelve years old, but I'm nearly thirteen – my birthday's on Wednesday! I'm so excited! I'm also from Bristol, and I'm at the same school as Sam. I like French because I'm quite good at languages, and our teacher's really nice. I like sport, too, and I'm in the school volleyball team. I don't like History.

reply

2 Read the message board again and write true (T) or false (F). Correct the false sentences.

Sam is twelve.
F. Sam is thirteen.

1 Brandon Park is a small school.
2 Sam thinks that Maths is easy.
3 Jessie's birthday is at the weekend.
4 Jessie's French teacher is nice.
5 Jessie is in the school football team.

SPEAKING Telling the time

I can ask for and tell the time.

3 S0.12 **Listen and read. Match the clocks with the times in blue. There is one extra clock.**

Sam: What's the time, Jessie?
Jessie: It's ten o'clock.
Sam: What time is our next lesson?
Jessie: It's at quarter past ten.
Sam: And what time is lunch?
Jessie: It's at half past twelve.
Sam: Oh no, two and a half hours! I'm really hungry!

4 S0.13 **Listen and repeat the Useful language.**

Useful language

Telling the time

What's the time?
It's (ten o'clock / half past ten).
What time is (our next lesson / lunch)?
It's at (quarter past ten / quarter to ten).

5 S0.14 **Listen and choose the correct time.**

6 Work in pairs. Ask about the time now. Ask and answer about two of the things below. Swap roles.

- our English lesson
- our Maths lesson
- our sports class
- break

FAST FINISHER

Write about you and your school for the message board in Exercise 1.

READING

WARMER

Ask: *What days are you at school?* Elicit answers and take the opportunity to revise the days of the week. Ask: *Is school fun?* Elicit a few answers. Teach the word *subject* and ask: *What are your favourite subjects?* Elicit a few answers, and revise or teach the school subjects: *Science, Maths, English, French, History, Geography, Sport*.

1 S0.11 Look at the message board with the class and read out the title *Back to school*. Teach the meaning (at school after the summer holidays). Ask: *When are students back to school in your country?* Read through the table with the class and make sure sts understand how they should complete it. Ask sts to copy the table into their notebooks, then play the audio for them to read and listen to the message board. They then complete the information for Sam and Jessie. Check answers.

Answers

Name:	Sam	Jessie
Age:	13	12
City:	Bristol	Bristol
School:	Brandon Park School	Brandon Park School
School subject (☺):	Science, English	French, Sport
School subject (☹):	Maths	History

2 Sts read the message board again and decide if the sentences are true or false. Ask them to correct the false sentences. Check answers, eliciting the part of the text which confirms each answer.

Answers

1 F Brandon Park School is a big school.
2 F Sam thinks that Maths is difficult.
3 F Jessie's birthday is on Wednesday.
4 T
5 F Jessie is in the school volleyball team.

EXTRA PRACTICE

Ask sts to copy the table in Exercise 1 and complete it with information about themselves. Tell sts to imagine this is their first day at school and they don't know each other. Arrange sts in small groups and ask them to use the information that they wrote in their table to tell the rest of the group about themselves. At the end, ask sts from different groups to tell the class about the group members.

SPEAKING Telling the time

3 S0.12 Focus on the images of the clocks and teach the words *time* and *tell the time*. Explain the task to sts and point out the times in blue. Then play the audio for sts to listen and read. Sts then match the times with the clocks. Check answers with the class and elicit how to say the time on the remaining clock *(quarter to ten)*.

Answers

a half past twelve
c ten o'clock
d quarter past ten

EXTRA PRACTICE

If your sts need more practice of telling the time, draw three or four more clocks on the board, like the ones in Exercise 3. Put sts into teams and ask them to decide how to say the times. Check answers with the class, and see which teams got all the answers right.

4 S0.13 Play the audio once for sts to listen to the Useful language. Read through all the phrases with the class and check that sts understand everything. You could elicit how to say the phrases in the sts' own language. Play the audio again for sts to repeat.

5 S0.14 Play the first time and elicit which clock it matches (c). See TB pages 274–285 for audio script. Play the rest of the audio for sts to listen and note down the correct times. Allow sts to compare their answers in pairs, then play the audio again if necessary for them to check and complete their answers. Check answers with the class.

Answers

1 6.30 – c
2 1.15 – d
3 3.00 – a
4 9.45 – f
5 11.45 – b
6 8.30 – e

6 Elicit the questions that sts will need to ask, using *What time is …?* Sts then work in pairs to ask and answer questions, then swap roles and repeat the activity. Monitor and help while sts are working, then ask the questions to one or two individual sts and elicit answers.

FAST FINISHER

Fast finishers can write about themselves and their school for a message board, using the texts in Exercise 1 as a model. For weaker sts, write some sentence beginnings on the board for them to complete about themselves:

My name's …
I'm from …
I'm … years old.
I like …
I don't like …

Home sweet home

1

Vocabulary: Furniture; Family | **Grammar:** *there is / there are* + *a, an, some, any*; prepositions of place; *have got* | **Speaking:** Introductions | **Writing:** My dream home

VOCABULARY Furniture

I can talk about furniture and rooms in a house.

1 1.1 **Match the words in the box with the pictures. Listen, check and repeat.**

Picture 1: bed, chair, ...

bath bed bookcase chair cooker desk fridge lamp
mirror shower sink sofa table toilet wardrobe

THROUGH *the* KEYHOLE

2 Copy and complete the table with the furniture from Exercise 1. Some words can go with more than one room.

bathroom	bedroom	dining room	kitchen	living room

3 Work in pairs. Imagine a strange house where everything is in the wrong place! Ask and answer questions about it.

A: Where's the bath?

B: It's in the living room!

Now watch the vlog.

FAST FINISHER

Think about your home. How many furniture items listed in Exercise 1 have you got?

LS **Language summary: Unit 1** SB p.127

 EXTRA PRACTICE Workbook page 6

Home sweet home

1

UNIT 1 OVERVIEW: The topic of this unit is home. Sts read about the Big Teenage Challenge to keep your bedroom tidy for a week, and listen to a description of someone's family. They read some penfriend profiles and learn how to introduce people. They read about teenage life in the UK and finally, they read about a dream home and write about their own ideal home. They also watch a vlog about moving homes and a culture video about an unusual type of home.

Vocabulary	Grammar	Pronunciation	Reading	Listening	Speaking	Writing
Furniture; Family	*there is / there are* + *a, an, some, any*; prepositions of place; *have got*	/ə/	Using pictures to predict things in a reading text	Preparing before you listen	Introducing people	A chat forum

VOCABULARY Furniture

Sts learn nouns for the names of 15 kinds of furniture. They categorise these nouns according to the rooms where they are usually found, then personalise the vocabulary by talking about the furniture in their own home.

Vocabulary

Furniture (*bath, bed, bookcase, chair, cooker, desk, fridge, lamp, mirror, shower, sink, sofa, table, toilet, wardrobe*)

Vlog

Ioan: *My new home*

WARMER

Ask: *Where do you live? Do you live in a house or a flat?* As sts answer, ask questions, e.g. *Is your flat big or small? How many rooms are there?* Revise vocabulary for rooms and see what words for furniture sts already know.

1 1.1 Read through the words in the box and elicit or teach the meanings. Sts match the words with the pictures. Play the audio track. See TG page 274 for audio script. Sts listen, check and repeat.

Answers
1 bed, chair, desk, wardrobe, mirror 2 cooker, fridge, sink 3 chair, sofa, table 4 bookcase, chair, desk, lamp, table 5 bath, mirror, shower, sink, toilet

2 Ask: *What furniture goes in the bathroom?* Elicit one or two answers. Sts copy the table in their notebooks and complete it with the words from Exercise 1. Point out that some words can go in more than one room. Check answers.

Answers
bathroom: bath, mirror, shower, sink, toilet
bedroom: bed, bookcase, chair, desk, lamp, mirror, table, wardrobe
dining room: bookcase, chair, lamp, mirror, table
kitchen: cooker, fridge, sink, table
living room: bookcase, chair, lamp, mirror, sofa, table

3 Ask a few questions about a normal house first, e.g. *Where's the bath?* (in the bathroom). Then read out the task and explain the meaning of *strange*. Read out the example question and answer, then put sts into pairs to ask and answer questions. Ask individual sts to ask and answers questions for the class.

Vlog

This lesson features an optional vlog in which a vlogger talks about moving home. You can watch this in class if you have time and access to video, or you can ask sts to download it from the Richmond Learning Platform to watch at home. See TG pages 286 and 304.

FAST FINISHER

Sts who finish early can practise vocabulary for furniture further. They list the furniture in each of the rooms in their own house. They could use a dictionary to find other nouns not seen in Exercise 1. Weaker sts could work in pairs. They take turns to point to the furniture in the pictures. Their partner says the correct word.

EXTRA PRACTICE

Put sts into pairs. They take turns to try to talk about their own home for one minute, while their partner films them using their phone. They can watch their films back and discuss in their pairs how they could improve, for example by hesitating less. If there is time, they could repeat the activity and try to improve.

V **Vocabulary practice: WB** p.6
Sts will find more practice of vocabulary for furniture here. Set these exercises for homework.

LS **Language summary: Unit 1 SB** p.127

How tidy is your bedroom?

READING I can use pictures to predict what a reading text is about.

THE BIG TEENAGE CHALLENGE

Can you keep your bedroom tidy for a week? That's this week's Big Teenage Challenge! Our teenager is thirteen-year-old Harry from Manchester.

DAY 1

'I'm very untidy,' says Harry. He's right! There's a big wardrobe in his room, but there aren't any clothes in it – they're all on the bed or on the floor. There are some dirty plates under his bed, and there's an empty pizza box behind his chair! On Harry's desk, next to his games console, there are hundreds of comics and … an old sandwich. Ugh!

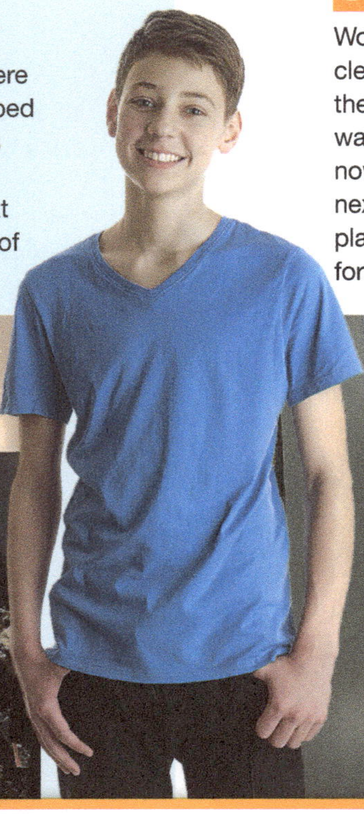

DAY 2

Wow! What a difference! Harry's room is clean and tidy. Are there any clothes on the floor? No, there aren't! They're in the wardrobe. There isn't a sandwich on his desk now, and his comics are all in the bookcase next to his bed. Everything is in the right place, but can Harry keep his bedroom tidy for a whole week? Find out on Day 7 …

Name: Harry
Age: thirteen
Hobbies: video games, comics, eating pizza!

1 1.2 **Look at the pictures. What do you think the article is about? Read, listen and check.**

2 Read again. Change the underlined word(s) so that the sentences are correct.

Harry is fourteen years old. *thirteen*
1 On Day 1, Harry's clothes are on his chair.
2 On Day 1, the sandwich is on his bed.
3 On Day 2, the clothes are on the floor.
4 On Day 2, the comics are on the desk.

3 Word Power Make pairs of opposite adjectives.

~~big~~ clean comfortable empty tidy

dirty full ~~small~~ untidy uncomfortable

big – small

4 Work in pairs. How tidy is your bedroom? Tell your partner about the things below.

your bed your desk your floor your wardrobe

My bed is tidy, but my desk is very untidy.

My wardrobe is empty.

5 FIND OUT *The Bedroom in Arles* is a famous painting by Vincent Van Gogh of his bedroom. Find out the answers to these questions.

1 What colour are the walls?
2 How many chairs are there?
3 What is there above the table?

 EXTRA PRACTICE Workbook page 7

How tidy is your bedroom?

READING

Sts read about Harry, a teenager from Manchester, who takes part in a challenge to keep his bedroom tidy for a week. They focus on using pictures to predict things in a reading text. They learn to use *there is / there are* with *a*, *an*, *some* and *any* to talk about what is in a place, and how to use prepositions of place to say where things are.

Reading text

An article about Harry, a boy from Manchester, who takes part in a challenge to keep his bedroom tidy for a week

Reading skill

Using pictures to predict things in a reading text

WARMER

Ask: *What's in your bedroom? Is there a bed/table/desk*, etc.? Elicit answers from individual sts and use the questions to recycle some of the furniture vocabulary from page 9. Write on the board the words *tidy* and *untidy* and teach the meanings. Ask: *Is your bedroom tidy or untidy?* Elicit a few answers from individual sts, then ask for a show of hands to see how many sts have tidy and untidy bedrooms.

1 1.2 **Using pictures to predict things in a reading text** Ask sts to look at the pictures and elicit what they show (a teenage boy, a tidy bedroom and an untidy bedroom). Ask: *What do you think the article is about?* Explain to sts that predicting what a reading text is about before they read it will help them understand it better, and they can use the pictures to help them predict. Put sts into pairs to look at the pictures again and discuss what they think the article is about. Elicit some of their ideas, but don't confirm them. Check that sts understand *floor*. Play the audio for sts to read, listen and check. Elicit what the article is about and ask who predicted correctly.

2 Ask sts to copy the sentences into their notebooks. They read the text again and change the underlined words in the sentences to make them correct. Check answers with the class.

Answers

1 on the bed or on the floor
2 on his desk
3 in the wardrobe
4 in the bookcase

3 **Word Power** Elicit or remind sts that we use adjectives to describe things. Point out the example answers and demonstrate the opposite meanings of *big* and *small* by using classroom objects, e.g. books. Sts could work in pairs for this task, and could use a dictionary to help them. Tell them they can find some of the adjectives in the article, and can use these to help them understand the meanings. Check answers with the class, and check that sts understand all the adjectives.

Answers

clean, dirty
comfortable, uncomfortable
empty, full
tidy, untidy

4 Read out the question, then read out the example answers. Say some sentences about your own bedroom, as further examples, e.g. *My bedroom is tidy. My bed is tidy and my clothes are in the wardrobe.* Allow sts time to prepare their ideas individually. Weaker sts might like to write some sentences, but encourage stronger sts to just think of ideas and make notes, but not write full sentences. They then work in pairs to tell their partner about their bedroom. Ask some sts to tell the class about their partner's bedroom.

21st Century skills

5 **FIND OUT**

Set this exercise for homework if you prefer. Sts can find this information out by looking online or in other media, or by asking other people. The answers to the questions are: 1 the walls are blue, 2 there are two chairs, 3 there is a mirror above the table.

You could also ask sts to find out some information about Vincent Van Gogh.

EXTRA PRACTICE

Play a game to revise adjectives from Exercise 3. Arrange sts in small teams. Write these nouns on the board: *bag*, *bed*, *bookcase*, *chair*, *classroom*, *clothes*, *desk*, *mirror*, *sandwich*, *table*. Teams have two minutes to match an adjective from Exercise 3 to each noun. They can use each adjective once. Point out that not all the adjectives match all the nouns. For example, *big sandwich* is correct but *uncomfortable sandwich* is incorrect. Award a point for a correct match.

Possible answers

an empty bag, a comfortable bed, an untidy bookcase, clean clothes, an uncomfortable chair, a full classroom, a tidy desk, a dirty mirror, a big sandwich, a small table

R **Reading practice: WB** p.7

You will find more practice for reading here. Set these exercises for homework.

GRAMMAR

There is / There are + a, an, some, any

I can use *There is / There are* to describe a room.

Now watch the grammar animation.

1 In your notebook, complete the grammar box with *a, an, some* or *any*.

	Affirmative	Negative
Singular	**There's** [1] ... empty box behind his chair.	**There isn't** [2] ... pen on his desk.
Plural	**There are** [3] ... plates under his bed.	**There aren't** [4] ... clothes in the wardrobe.
	Questions	**Short answers**
Singular	**Is there** a comic on his bed?	Yes, **there is**. / No, **there isn't**.
Plural	**Are there** [5] ... clothes on the floor?	Yes, **there are**. / No, **there aren't**.

2 Copy and complete the sentences about Harry's house. Use the correct affirmative or negative form of *There is / There are*.

... three bedrooms. ✓

There are three bedrooms.

1 ... a desk in his sister's room. ✗
2 ... an orange chair in his parents' room. ✓
3 ... any lamps in the dining room. ✗
4 ... two bathrooms. ✓
5 ... some books in the living room. ✓

3 Complete the text about Day 7 of the challenge. Use *a, an, some* or *any*.

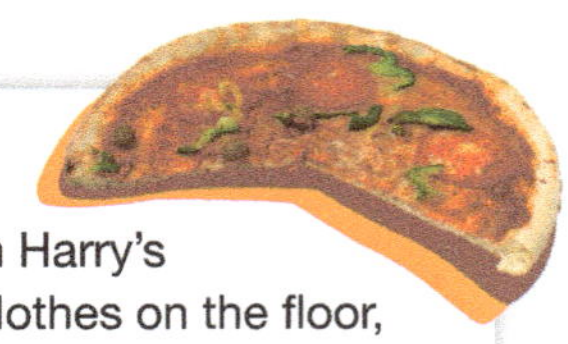

DAY 7

It's Day 7, and we're back in Harry's bedroom. There aren't [1] ... clothes on the floor, and there aren't [2] ... dirty plates. Harry's desk is clean and tidy. There are [3] ... books on it now, but that's OK – they're for Harry's homework – and there's [4] ... new lamp. Well done, Harry! But wait a minute. What's that? There's [5] ... old pizza box under the bed, and there's half a pizza in it! Oh Harry! You lose!

4 Work in pairs. Ask and answer about your bedrooms. Use the table below to help you.

Is there a	chair wardrobe bookcase desk	in your room?
Are there any	mirrors lamps posters books	

Prepositions of place

I can talk about the position of objects.

5 Where is the mobile phone? Match the prepositions with the pictures.

behind in in front of next to on under

6 Write sentences about the bedroom. Use *There is / There are* and the correct preposition.

chair / desk *There's a chair next to the desk.*

1 games console / desk
2 trainers / bed
3 books / bookcase
4 bookcase / desk
5 guitar / chair
6 table / bed

7 Work in pairs. Student B: Close your book. Student A: Ask questions about the picture. Swap.

A: Is there a cat under the desk?

B: No, there isn't.

FAST FINISHER

Write sentences about your classroom.

There's a bag under Nacho's chair. There are some ...

LS Language summary: Unit 1 SB p.127

EXTRA PRACTICE Workbook page 8

GRAMMAR *There is / There are + a, an, some, any*

Grammar animation

This lesson features an optional animated presentation of the grammar in context called There's a cake on this chair! including the form and use of *there is / there are*; *a*, *an*, *some* and *any* and prepositions of place. You can watch this in class if you have time and access to a computer or tablet, or you can ask sts to download it from the Richmond Learning Platform to watch at home. See TG page 308 for animation script.

1 Read the grammar box about *there is / there are* with *a*, *an*, *some* and *any* with sts. Point out that the examples in the grammar box are from the article on page 10. They could look back at the article to find the missing words to complete the grammar box.

Answers
1 an 2 a 3 some 4 any 5 any

Write a singular example on the board, e.g. *There's a book on the floor*. Change *book* to *books* and elicit the other changes that are necessary: *There are some books on the floor*. Then change *there are* to *there aren't* and elicit the necessary changes: *There aren't any books on the floor*. Repeat this with one or two more simple sentences.

Ask questions to check concept.

Concept check questions: *There's a lamp in the living room – one or more than one?* (one). *There are some chairs in the dining room – one or more than one?* (more than one). *There aren't some comics – correct?* (no – *there are some* comics / *there aren't any* comics). *Are there some chairs – correct?* (no – *Are there any* chairs?).

2 Read the example with sts and check that they understand the use of the tick and cross icons. Ask sts to copy the sentences in their notebooks and complete them. Check answers with the class.

Answers
1 There isn't
2 There is
3 There aren't
4 There are
5 There are

3 Read out the first gapped sentence and elicit the answer as an example. Students then read the rest of the text and write the correct missing words. Check answers.

Answers
1 any 2 any 3 some 4 a 5 an

4 Focus attention on the table and ask one or two questions to individual sts. Refer them back to the short answers in the grammar box to help them answer. Put sts into pairs and ask them to take turns to ask and answer questions. When sts have finished, ask some sts to tell the class about their partner's bedroom.

Prepositions of place

5 Explain that the words in the box are prepositions, and we use them to say where something is. You could demonstrate the concept using a book or pen, putting it *on* a desk, *under* a desk, *next to* a book, etc. Sts could work in pairs to match the prepositions with the pictures. Check the answers with the class.

Answers
1 in
2 on
3 under
4 next to
5 behind
6 in front of

Ask questions to check concept.

Concept check questions: Use a classroom object such as a book or pen to ask questions to check that sts understand the prepositions. Hold the object in different positions and give sts a choice of prepositions, e.g. *Is it on the desk or under the desk? Is it next to the chair or behind the chair?* As sts become more confident, hold it in different positions and ask: *Where is it?*

6 Focus on the picture of the bedroom and read the example with sts, then ask sts to write the sentences in their notebooks. Check answers.

Answers
1 There is a games console on the desk.
2 There are some trainers under the bed.
3 There are some books in the bookcase.
4 There is a bookcase behind the desk.
5 There is a guitar in front of the chair.
6 There is a table next to the bed.

7 Allow sts time to look at the picture again and prepare some questions individually. They then work in pairs and take turns to close their books and try to answer the questions from memory. Monitor and help as necessary.

FAST FINISHER
Sts who finish early can practise the grammar further. Sts write sentences about objects in the classroom. Weaker sts could write one or two more sentences about the picture in Exercise 6, using the ideas in Exercise 5 to help them.

G Grammar practice: WB p.8
Sts will find more practice for *there is / there are + a, an, some, any* and prepositions of place here. Set these exercises for homework.

LS Language summary: Unit 1 SB p.127

Famous families

VOCABULARY and LISTENING Family members

I can prepare before I listen.

1 1.3 **Copy and complete the table with the words from the word cloud. Listen, check and repeat.**

Male	Female	Male and female
brother	sister	child

mum grandma aunt uncle husband wife grandad brother family niece son child nephew cousin dad parent daughter sister

2 PRONUNCIATION /ə/

1.4 **Listen and repeat.**

mother father sister brother daughter
husband cousin parent

3 **Work in pairs. Write the names of some members of your family on a piece of paper. Swap with your partner and ask and answer about the names.**

A: Who's Susana?

B: She's my dad's sister.

4 **Read the description of the radio programme. What do you know about Chris Hemsworth? What films is he in?**

5 1.5 **Look at the family tree and read the names. Listen and complete Chris' family tree with the names.**

~~Craig~~ Elsa India Rose
Leonie Sasha Tristan

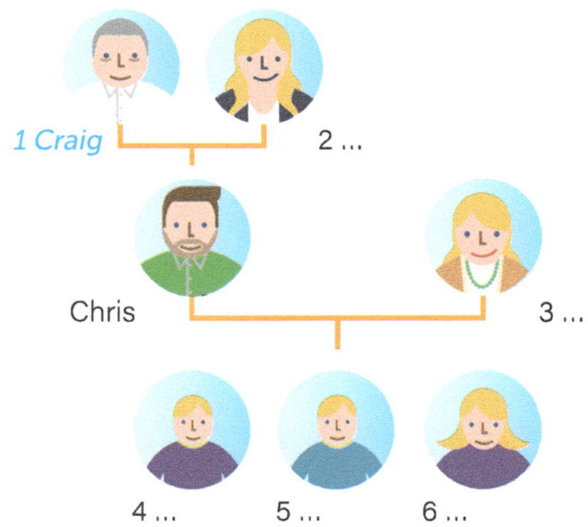

6 1.5 **Read the questions carefully. Listen again and answer the questions.**

1 Where is Chris from?
2 Where is his wife from?
3 What is his wife's job?
4 How many brothers has Chris got?
5 How many sisters has he got?

LS Language summary: Unit 1 SB p.127

Famous families

VOCABULARY and LISTENING
Family members

Sts listen to a radio show about famous families and focus on preparing before they listen. They learn to use *have got* to talk about possessions.

Vocabulary

Family members *(aunt, brother, child, cousin, dad, daughter, grandad, grandma, husband, mum, nephew, niece, parent, sister, son, uncle, wife)*

Listening text

A radio show about famous families

Listening skill

Preparing before you listen

WARMER

With books closed, put sts into groups. Ask them to write three sentences about things there are in their living room, and three sentences about things there are in their kitchen, as quickly as they can. Tell them to put up their hands when they have finished. When a group has finished, check their sentences for accuracy. If the sentences are correct, they are the winners. If there are mistakes, ask them to correct them. Elicit a few examples of correct sentences and take the opportunity to revise furniture words and the use of *there is* / *there are*. Ask: *Who lives in your house?* Elicit a few answers and see what family words sts already know.

1 1.3 Ask sts to look at the family word tree. Read through the words and elicit or teach the meanings. Ask sts to copy the table and complete it with the correct words. Play the audio track for sts to listen and check the answers. See TG page 274 for audio script. Make sure sts understand all the words. Play the audio track again for sts to repeat the words. Point out that *child* has an irregular plural (*children*).

Answers
Male: brother, dad, grandad, nephew, son, uncle
Female: sister, mum, grandma, wife, niece, daughter, aunt
Male and female: cousin, child (children), parent

2 **PRONUNCIATION** 1.4

Model and drill pronunciation of the /ə/ sound in isolation. Point out that in British English, we don't usually pronounce the sound /r/ at the end of a word, but instead use the sound /ə/. Play the audio for sts to repeat. If sts have difficulty producing the /ə/ sound, point out that it is a very short sound and also quite a 'lazy' sound, which you produce simply by opening your mouth a little bit.

3 To demonstrate, write a few names of your family members on the board. Encourage sts to ask you questions, and answer them. Read out the example question and answer and point out the possessive *'s* in *my dad's sister*. Sts then work in pairs to write the names of some family members, then swap and ask and answer questions. Ask some sts to tell the class about someone in their partner's family.

4 **Preparing before you listen** Explain to sts that they are going to hear a radio programme about a famous family. Ask: *Do you find listening difficult?* Elicit a few answers, and tell sts that if they prepare before they listen and think about what they will hear, it will help them understand better. Ask sts to read the description of the radio programme and answer the questions. They could work in pairs for this. Discuss their ideas as a class. Ask: *What words do you think you might hear?* Elicit a few ideas, e.g. *actor*, *acting*, *mum*, *dad*, *son*, *daughter*, *wife*, *brother*, *sister*.

5 1.5 Allow sts time to study the family tree, then read through the names in the box and model pronunciation. Ask sts to copy the family tree into their notebooks, then play the audio once for sts to listen and complete the family tree with the names. See TG pages 274 for audio script. Allow sts to compare their answers in pairs, then play the audio again for them to check and complete the family tree. Check answers, then ask: *Is it a good idea to prepare before you listen? Do you think it helps you understand?*

Answers
2 Leonie
3 Elsa
5 Tristan / Sasha
6 India Rose

6 1.5 Read through the questions with the class and check that sts understand them all. Play the audio again for sts to answer the questions. Check answers with the class.

Answers
1 Chris is from Australia.
2 Chris's wife is from Spain.
3 She is an actress.
4 Chris has got two brothers.
5 Chris hasn't got any sisters.

V L **Vocabulary and Listening practice: WB** p.9
Sts will find more practice for listening, and practice of vocabulary for family here. Set these exercises for homework.

LS **Language summary: Unit 1 SB** p.127

GRAMMAR *have got*

I can use *have got* to talk about possessions.

Now watch the Grammar animation.

1 **Copy and complete the grammar box with the words in the box.**

got hasn't got haven't Have 've got

Affirmative	Negative
I**'ve got** a cat. She**'s got** two brothers. They [2] ... three children.	You **haven't got** a dog. He [1] ... any sisters. We **haven't got** any grandchildren.
Questions	**Short answers**
[3] ... you **got** a niece? **Has** he [4] ... any aunts? **Have** they **got** a pet?	Yes, I **have**. / No, I **haven't**. Yes, he **has**. / No, he **hasn't**. Yes, they **have**. / No, they [5] ... .

2 **Put the words in order to make sentences or questions about Chris and his family.**

house. / have / Chris and Elsa / a big / got
Chris and Elsa have got a big house.

1 a dog. / has / got / the family
2 haven't / they / got / a cat.
3 has / pet snake! / Elsa / got / a
4 any cousins? / have / the children / got
5 Chris / a sister. / got / hasn't
6 Liam / has / any children? / got

3 **Write true sentences about you. Use the affirmative or negative forms of *have got*.**

My mum / a brother
My mum has/hasn't got a brother.

1 My dad / a sister
2 I / a lot of cousins
3 My parents / a bike
4 We / a tidy classroom
5 My home / a garden
6 I / a pet

4 **THINK CRITICALLY** **Have you got a big family or a small family? What are the advantages and disadvantages of big families and small families?**

5 1.6 **Copy and complete the questions and answers. Listen and check.**

Famous Families:
Stephen Curry

This week's Famous Families is about the famous basketball player, Stephen Curry.

Has Stephen got a sister?
Yes, he has. Her name's Sydel, and she's good at volleyball.

1 **... he ... a brother?**
Yes, he ... . His brother, Seth, is also a basketball player.

2 **... he ... a wife?**
Yes, he ... . His wife, Ayesha, is a TV presenter.

3 **... they ... any children?**
Yes, they ... .

4 **... they ... a cat?**
No, they ... , but they've got two dogs!

6 **Work in pairs. Ask and answer questions. Use the ideas in the box.**

a baby in your family a brother or sister at university any cousins a family photo on your phone a favourite aunt or uncle

A: Have you got a ...?
B: Yes, I have. What about you?

FUN FACT

46% of homes in the UK have got a pet. Dogs are the UK's favourite pet, and cats are the second favourite. About 400,000 homes have got a pet snake!

FAST FINISHER
Choose a famous person and write about their family.
Beyoncé has got two daughters and a son. She's got a sister, Solange.

LS Language summary: Unit 1 SB p.127

 EXTRA PRACTICE Workbook page 10

GRAMMAR *have got*

Grammar animation

This lesson features an optional animated presentation of the grammar in context called *I've got funny hair!* including the form and use of *have got*. You can watch this in class if you have time and access to a computer or tablet, or you can ask sts to download it from the Richmond Learning Platform to watch at home. See TG page 308 for animation script.

1 Read the grammar box with sts about *have got*. Draw attention to the different forms, *have got* and *has got*. Point out that we use *have got* for *I*, *we*, *you* and *they*, and we use *has got* for *he*, *she*, *you* and *it*. Explain that we use *have got* to talk about possessions (things that are ours) and also about family members, e.g. *I've got a bike, I've got a sister.* Sts complete the grammar box. Check answers, then ask questions to check concept.

Answers
1 hasn't got
2 have got
3 Have
4 got
5 haven't

Concept check questions: *I've got a big bedroom – is it my bedroom?* (yes). *Jack's got a bike – is it his bike?* (yes). *My cousin have got a cat – correct?* (no – *My cousin has* got a cat). *You have got a brother? – correct?* (no – *Have you got* a brother?). *I've got a sister – can you make that negative?* (I haven't got a sister). *My sister has got a bike – can you make that negative?* (My sister hasn't got a bike).

2 Remind sts of the audio they listened to about Chris. Elicit what they can remember about his family. Ask sts to write the sentences in their notebooks. Check answers.

Answers
1 The family has got a dog.
2 They haven't got a cat.
3 Elsa has got a pet snake!
4 Have the children got any cousins?
5 Chris hasn't got a sister.
6 Has Liam got any children?

3 Read the example answer with the class and ask one or two sts to say the sentence that is true for their family. Sts write their sentences individually. Monitor and help as necessary. Check answers by asking individual sts to read some of their sentences to the class.

21st Century skills

4 **THINK CRITICALLY**
Read out the questions and make sure sts understand *advantages* and *disadvantages*. Put sts into pairs or small groups and encourage them to talk about their own families and brainstorm advantages and disadvantages of big and small families. Help with vocabulary as necessary and encourage them to focus on listing ideas and not to worry too much about writing completely accurate sentences. They might include things such as:

advantages of a big family: you're never lonely, getting help with homework, lots of fun; disadvantages: not much money, parents are very busy, disagreements.

advantages of a small family: close to parents, lots of help and attention from parents, own bedroom; disadvantages: can be lonely, boring in the holidays.

5 1.6 Focus on the photo and ask sts if they recognise Stephen Curry. Explain if necessary that he is an American basketball player, who plays for the Golden State Warriors. Sts copy and complete the questions and answers. Play the audio for sts to listen and check their answers.

Answers

1 Has, got, has	3 Have, got, have
2 Has, got, has	4 Have, got, haven't

6 Read through the ideas in the box and check that sts understand them all. Ask one or two questions to individual sts to demonstrate the task. Read out the example question and answer and point out the phrase *What about you?* to ask your partner the same question. Sts work in pairs to ask and answer questions. Monitor and help, then ask some sts to tell the class something about their partner.

FUN FACT Encourage sts to read this fun fact for pleasure. They might also be interested to know that the most popular kinds of snake for pets are corn snakes and ball pythons, which are both non-poisonous. They eat small mice.

FAST FINISHER
Sts write sentences about a famous person's family. Tell them the famous person can be a music star, a sports star, a film star, etc. Weaker sts could write one or two sentences about their own family.

G Grammar practice: WB p.10
Sts will find more practice for *have got* here. Set these exercises for homework.

LS Language summary: Unit 1 SB p.127

KEEP TALKING!

Nice to meet you!

READING and LISTENING

I can understand a personal profile.

1 Look at the Student Penfriends website. What is a penfriend? Have you got one?

2 Read the website and complete the profiles with emojis a–i.

1 i

Student Penfriends

Home | Log in | Find a penfriend | Schools | Parents

Sara Gonzalez

Profile

Hi. I'm Sara! I'm Spanish **1** and I'm from Valencia. I'm thirteen years old and my birthday is on 2 May.

My mum's Spanish, but my dad's from England. I've got a brother, Santi – he's fifteen.

I'm into music **2** and video games **3**. My favourite type of music is rock and my favourite video game is Minecraft.

Send an email

Send a voice message

Ali Yazgan

Profile

Hello, my name's Ali. I'm from Ankara in Turkey **4**. I'm twelve years old. My birthday **5** is on 23 November.

I've got two sisters. They're twins! Their names are Melek and Zeynep, and they're nine years old.

I love sport, especially basketball **6**. My favourite team are the Houston Rockets. I've got lots of posters of them in my bedroom!

Send an email

Send a voice message

Julia Santos

Profile

Hello! My name's Julia and I'm from Curitiba in Brazil **7**. I'm fourteen years old. My birthday is on 7 July.

I haven't got any brothers or sisters, but I've got a dog and two cats **8**, and I've got a lot of friends!

I'm not into sport, but I'm crazy about films **9**. My favourite actress is Emma Watson. She's amazing!

Send an email

Send a voice message

3 Read the profiles again. Copy and complete the table.

	Sara	Ali	Julia
Age	13	3 ...	14
Country	1 ...	Turkey	Brazil
Brothers	1	0	6 ...
Sisters	0	4 ...	7 ...
Interests	2 ...	5 ...	8 ...

4 Imagine that you want a penfriend. Who do you choose? Why?

5 1.7 Listen to the voice messages from two students, Carla and Felix. Choose a penfriend for each of them: Sara, Ali or Julia.

6 Work in pairs. Talk about your interests.

I'm into ...

I'm crazy about ...

I like ...

My favourite ... is ...

KEEP TALKING!

Nice to meet you!

READING and LISTENING

Sts read a website with profiles of possible penfriends and complete them by adding suitable emojis. They listen to some voice messages and match the students to suitable penfriends. They then learn how to introduce people. They read and hear a model dialogue and personalise the useful language by following the steps in the Speaking plan.

WARMER

Ask: *What do you say when you meet someone for the first time?* Elicit a few ideas, e.g. *Hello. Nice to meet you.* Ask: *What questions do you ask someone when you meet them for the first time?* Elicit a few ideas, e.g. *What's your name? How old are you? Have you got any brothers or sisters? Are you into music? Who's your favourite singer?* Prompt students with question beginnings if necessary, to give them ideas, e.g. *Are you into …? Who's your favourite …? What's your favourite (film/video game)?* As you elicit each question, ask it to one or two sts and elicit their answers. Tell sts they are going to practise meeting new people in English.

1 Look at the Student Penfriends website with the class. Ask them what a penfriend is and if they have got one.

2 Focus on the emojis and ask sts if they use emojis when they message their friends. Ask them to read the profiles and choose the correct emojis to complete them. Check answers.

Answers

1	i	6	a
2	f	7	b
3	c	8	g
4	h	9	d
5	e		

3 Ask sts to copy the table into their notebooks, then read the profiles again and complete the table. Check answers.

Answers

1	Spain	5	basketball
2	music and video games	6	0
3	12	7	0
4	2	8	films

4 Ask sts to read the profiles again and decide who they would choose. Remind them they must have reasons for their choice. Allow sts time to think about their answers, then put them into pairs to say who they chose and why. Ask some sts to tell the class.

5 1.7 Tell sts they will hear two voice messages. Tell them they should listen carefully to hear what the people like, then decide who is the best penfriend for each one. Play the audio once for sts to listen and choose the best penfriend for each one. See TG pages 274 for audio script. Check answers with the class, encouraging sts to give reasons for their answers.

Answers

1 Julia (they are both into films)
2 Ali (they're both into basketball)

6 Read out the sentence beginnings and elicit some possible endings, e.g. *I like video games, I'm crazy about music, My favourite sport is tennis.* Sts work in pairs and talk about their interests. Monitor and help while they are working. For feedback, teach the word *both* then ask some sts to tell the class about an interest that they share, e.g. *We're both into music. We both like football.*

EXTRA PRACTICE

Elicit the types of information that Carla and Felix included in their voice messages in Exercise 5 and write these on the board: *name, nationality/country, hometown, age, brothers and sisters, pets, interests*. If necessary, play the audio again to refresh sts' memories. Tell sts that they are going to make voice messages for the Student Penfriends website. Ask them to make some notes about themselves for their voice message, using the words on the board. Give sts time to practise with their notes, then put them in pairs to record each other's mesage using their phones. They can listen to their messages afterwards and decide if there are any ways they could improve.

SPEAKING Introductions

I can introduce people.

1 1.8 **Listen and read. What sport is Tess into?**

Felix: Hi, Tess. How are things?
Tess: Good, thanks. How are you?
Felix: Not bad. This is my penfriend, Ali. He's here for a week.
Tess: Hello, Ali. Nice to meet you.
Ali: Nice to meet you, too. Are you into basketball?
Tess: My favourite sport is volleyball, but basketball's cool, too.
Ali: Great, let's have a game!
Later ...
Felix: Thanks for the game, Tess.
Tess: You're welcome. See you later.
Ali: See you, Tess.
Felix: Bye.

2 1.9 **Listen and repeat the Useful language.**

Useful language

Greetings
Hi. / Hello.
How are things? / How are you?
Good / Fine, thanks.
Not bad.

Introductions
This is my friend/ cousin, Tess.
Nice to meet you.
Nice to meet you, too.

Saying goodbye
Bye. / See you. / See you later.

3 1.10 **Copy and complete the dialogue. Listen and check.**

Megan: Hi, Ben. *How* are you?
Ben: [1] ... bad, thanks. How are you?
Megan: I'm good. [2] ... is my cousin, Lydia.
Ben: Hi, Lydia. Nice to [3] ... you.
Lydia: Nice to meet you, [4] ... .
Megan: See you [5] ... , Ben.
Ben: Yes, see [6] ... .

4 **Work in groups of three. Have a dialogue where you introduce someone. Follow the steps in the Speaking plan.**

Speaking plan

Prepare
- Choose your roles and decide who you are.
  Student A: You have a visitor for the weekend (cousin, penfriend, etc.)
  Student B: You are Student A's friend.
  Student C: You are Student A's visitor (cousin, penfriend, etc.)
- Decide where you are.
- Make notes for your dialogue.

Speak
- Practise your dialogue.
- Use phrases from the Useful language box.
- Act out your dialogue without notes.

Reflect
- How can you improve next time?
- Swap roles and act out a new dialogue.

Now play *Keep moving!*

FAST FINISHER
Write a personal profile for the Student Penfriends website on page 14.

LS Language summary: Unit 1 SB p.127

EXTRA PRACTICE Workbook page 11

SPEAKING Introductions

1 1.8 Ask sts questions about things they like, e.g. *Are you into music? Who's your favourite singer? Do you like sport? What's your favourite sport?* Encourage them to use full sentences when they answer, and encourage them to use the phrases from page 14 (*I like ..., I'm into ..., My favourite ... is ...*). With stronger classes, you could play the dialogue with books closed and ask: *Who is Ali? What's he into? What sport is Tess into?* With weaker classes, you could play the dialogue for sts to listen and read. See SB page 15 for audio script. Check the answer.

Answers
Tess is into volleyball.

2 1.9 Tell sts there are different ways they can greet people in English. Ask them if they remember or can see any in the dialogue in Exercise 1. Read through the Useful language box with the class and check sts understand all the phrases. Ask questions to check concept.

Concept check questions: Say: *Hi!* Then ask: *What do you say to me now?* (Hi, Hello). Say: *How are you? What do you say now?* (Good, thanks, Fine, thanks, Not bad). *How are you? / How are things? – same meaning?* (yes). *Good, thanks, Fine, thanks, Not bad – same meaning?* (yes). *See you – am I saying hello or goodbye?* (goodbye). *This is my friend, Jack – what do you say?* (nice to meet you).

3 1.10 Ask sts to copy the dialogue in their notebooks and complete it using the Useful language from Exercise 2. Check answers.

Answers

1 Not	2 This	3 meet
4 too	5 later	6 you

4 Sts follow the steps in the Speaking Plan to practise introducing people.

Speaking plan

Prepare

Sts work in groups of three. They decide on which role each of them will play, and decide where they are. They make notes using the Useful language in Exercise 2 to help them. Point out that they should also ask the person they meet some questions about what they like and what they are into.

Speak

Sts decide who will speak first and then practise their dialogue in their groups. They can practise with and then without notes. Monitor and help as necessary. If your sts use smartphones in class, they could record their conversations.

Reflect

Discuss as a class how sts could improve next time. Encourage them to be honest and open about the things they did well and the things they can do better. If you noticed any typical errors, correct them with the class. Sts swap roles and follow the steps again with a different visitor and place. If they record their conversations, ask them to use this to help them think of how they could improve next time. Ask some sts to perform their conversations for the class if they feel confident.

Keep moving!

This lesson features an optional language revision and consolidation game for use in digital classrooms. Players control different characters, each with their own personalities and special abilities.

FAST FINISHER

Sts write their own personal profile for the Student Penfriends website on page 14. Encourage them to use the profiles on page 14 as a model and talk about where they are from, their family and their interests. Weaker sts could write one or two full sentences about things they like and are into.

S **Speaking practice: WB** p.11
Sts will find more practice for introducing people here. Set these exercises for homework.

LS **Language summary: Unit 1 SB** p.127

REAL CULTURE!

My home

I can compare homes in the UK with homes in my country.

TEENAGE LIFE in the UK

What is life like for teenagers in the UK? We talk to Josh, 13 and Poppy, 14.

Josh, 13

WHERE ARE YOU FROM?

I'm from Brixton, in south London.

WHAT'S YOUR HOUSE LIKE?

It's got four bedrooms, a big kitchen and a living room. In the living room, there's a sofa, two chairs and a TV, and there's a red carpet on the floor. Most homes in Britain have got carpets. There's a big garden at the back of the house and a small garden at the front. It's an old house, but it's really comfortable.

WHAT IS THERE FOR YOUNG PEOPLE IN YOUR AREA?

There's a cinema and a sports centre and there are some great parks. There are always things to do!

WHAT ARE THE NEGATIVE THINGS?

There's a lot of traffic and it's sometimes noisy.

Poppy, 14

WHERE ARE YOU FROM?

I'm from a small, quiet village in Wales.

WHAT'S YOUR HOUSE LIKE?

My house is called 'Rose Cottage'. A lot of houses in the UK have got names. It's a beautiful house and there are only two bedrooms. I haven't got my own room – I'm in a room with my sister. It's OK, but I'm very tidy and my sister isn't! We've got a nice garden and there's a trampoline for my sister and me.

WHAT IS THERE FOR YOUNG PEOPLE IN YOUR AREA?

The people are friendly, but there isn't a lot for teenagers. Every summer, there's a village festival.

WHAT ARE THE NEGATIVE THINGS?

It's sometimes boring at the weekend. My friends are in other villages and the buses aren't very good.

REAL CULTURE! My home

Sts learn about a variety of different typical homes in the UK. They practise categorizing adjectives and compare homes in the UK with homes in their country. Sts then make a video about their own home.

This lesson features an optional culture video about an unusual type of home: see SB page 17.

WARMER

Ask: *Where do you live? Do you like your town or city? Do you like your area? Why?* Elicit what sts like about the place where they live. Prompt them with more questions if necessary, e.g. *What is there in your area? A cinema? A sports centre? A park? Is it a good area for young people? Why?* Encourage sts to give their opinions about the place where they live, and give reasons to support their opinions.

BACKGROUND

Brixton is an area of South London. The people who live there come from a range of different ethnic and cultural backgrounds and the area is known for its lively street markets selling foods and other things from all over the world.

Wales is one of the four countries that make up the United Kingdom. The other countries are England, Scotland and Northern Ireland. The four countries are all ruled by the government in London, but Wales, Scotland and Northern Ireland also have their own parliaments which make decisions relating just to their own country. Wales has some industrial towns and cities, but it is also known for its beautiful countryside and mountains.

A lot of people in the UK now live in flats in cities, and more people now rent their home, but home ownership is more popular in the UK than in many other countries, and most people in the UK would still like to own their own home, preferably a house, with its own garden.

1 Read out the five kinds of home and explain the meanings. Put sts into pairs to look at the pictures and decide which home is their favourite and why. Ask pairs in turn to tell the class their ideas and reasons. You could have a class vote to decide on the class's favourite.

2 1.11 Focus on the text about Josh and Poppy and explain that they each live in one of these homes. Tell sts they are going to read and listen to the text, and they should ignore any words they don't understand for now. Play the audio for sts to read and listen and match the people to the homes. See SB page 16–17 for audio script. Check the answers.

Answers

Josh 3 Poppy 2

3 Focus on the table and explain the meaning of *positive* and *negative*. Ask sts if they can remember any positive or negative things about the two homes. Ask sts to copy the table into their notebooks. They can then read the text again in their own time, or you could play the audio again for them to read and listen. They then complete the table with the correct information. Allow sts to compare their answers in pairs, then check answers with the class.

Answers

	Positive things	Negative things
Josh's home	Lots of bedrooms, big garden at the back, it's really comfortable, there's a cinema and sports centre, lots to do, there are some great parks	Lots of traffic, sometimes noisy
Poppy's home	There's a nice garden with a trampoline, people are friendly, in summer there is a village festival	It's a small house, has to share a room with sister, her sister isn't very tidy, there isn't a lot for teenagers, friends aren't nearby, it's sometimes boring, the buses aren't good.

EXTRA PRACTICE

Ask sts to think of a house or flat that they know (not their own) and like, e.g. the home of a relative. Give them time to work individually and make notes about the following: who lives there, where it is, how many rooms there are, which room is their favourite room and why. Arrange sts in pairs and ask them to describe the house/flat to their partner. Their partner should think of one or two general questions to ask at the end, e.g. *Is there a garden? Has it got a garage?*

1 **Look at the pictures of typical homes in the UK. Which home is your favourite? Why?**

1 A block of flats

2 A small cottage in the country

3 A semi-detached house in a city

4 A modern detached house

5 A terraced house

2 1.11 **Read and listen to the text on page 16. Match Josh and Poppy with two of the houses from Exercise 1.**

3 **Read the text again. Copy and complete the table about each home and area. Compare your answers with a partner.**

	Positive things	Negative things
Josh		
Poppy		

4 **Word Power** **Look at the adjectives in blue in the text. Which can describe people? Which can describe things? Find more adjectives in the text.**

People: young   *Things: comfortable*   *Both: quiet*

5 **COMPARE CULTURES** **Work in pairs. Ask and answer the questions.**

1 How are homes in the UK similar to homes in your country?
2 How are they different?

6 **Work in pairs. Think about the area where you live and make notes.**

1 Are there any …?
parks   shops   sports centres   cinemas
2 Is there a problem with …?
traffic   noise   graffiti   pollution
3 Have you got …?
your own bedroom   a garden   a balcony   friends in your road
4 Is your road …?
quiet   noisy   friendly   unfriendly

7 **GET CREATIVE** **Work in small groups. Make a video about your home. Follow steps 1–3.**

1 Use the questions from the text on page 16 and your notes from Exercise 6.
2 Take it in turns to interview each other. Film the interviews.
3 Share your video with your class.

Now watch the culture video.

FAST FINISHER

Choose Josh or Poppy. Write three or four sentences comparing their life with your life.

Poppy's got a sister. I've got two brothers.

REAL CULTURE!

4 **Word Power** Focus on one or two of the adjectives in blue in the text, e.g. *young*, *noisy*. Say some sentences about people and things using the adjectives, to elicit what each one can describe, e.g. *a young person?* (yes) *a young cinema?* (no) *a noisy person?* (yes) *a noisy cinema?* (yes). Sts look at the remaining adjectives in blue and decide what they describe. They could work in pairs for this, and they can use their dictionaries if necessary. Check answers, and check that sts understand all the adjectives. Ask sts to find more adjectives in the text. Discuss the meanings of these adjectives with the class, and discuss whether they describe people, things or both.

Answers
People: young
Things: comfortable
Both: noisy, quiet, tidy, boring, friendly
Other adjectives: big (things), red (things), small (both), old (both), great (both), nice (both), good (both), beautiful (both)

21st Century skills

5 **COMPARE CULTURES**
Put sts into pairs or small groups. Encourage each group to brainstorm information about how homes in their own country are similar and different to homes in the UK. Ask some of the more confident groups to present their ideas to the rest of the class.

6 Read through the questions with the class and make sure sts understand all the vocabulary. Put them into pairs to think about their area and make notes on the topics on the page. Monitor and help while they are working. Ask some pairs to tell the class their ideas. Ask other sts if they agree or disagree, and why.

21st Century skills

7 **GET CREATIVE**
Put sts into pairs or small groups and explain that they are going to make a video by interviewing each other. Read through the three steps with the class and make sure sts understand everything. Allow sts time to prepare their own answers to the questions in the text on page 16 first. Weaker sts might like to write their answers, but stronger sts should be able to answer without writing their ideas first. Demonstrate the task by asking a confident student the questions. Sts then work in their groups and make their video by taking turns to film each other using their phones. Monitor and help as necessary while they are working. If you are able to show the videos to the class on a big screen, you can do this. Alternatively, put groups together for them to share their videos with each other.

Culture video

You can watch this in class if you have time and access to video, or you can ask sts to download it from the Richmond Learning Platform to watch at home. See *Homes on wheels* on TG pages 295 and 306.

FAST FINISHER
Sts write sentences comparing Josh or Poppy's life with their own life. Weaker sts could work in pairs and write two or three sentences about either Josh or Poppy.

My dream home

WRITING A chat forum

I can write about my dream home.

1 **Read the chat forum. What is your favourite thing about Becca's dream home? Discuss your answer in pairs.**

TEEN 2 TEEN FORUM

What's your dream home?

Post from Marius_123 on 5 Oct at 11.30 a.m.

What's your dream home? Big or small? Old or modern? In the country or in the city?

REPLY

Reply from Becca_99 On 5 Oct at 2.15 p.m.

My dream home is a big house in the country. Upstairs, there are four bedrooms and four bathrooms – one each for my two brothers, my parents and me! Downstairs, there's a big living room, a modern kitchen and a gym. Outside, there's a swimming pool and a tennis court.

In my bedroom, there's a double bed and a wardrobe for all my clothes. There's a really comfortable sofa and I've got a games console and lots of cool games. There aren't any TVs in the house but we've got a private cinema. In the kitchen, there's a fridge full of ice cream!

2 **Read the chat forum again and answer the questions.**

1 How many people are there in Becca's family?
2 What is outside Becca's house?
3 What haven't they got in their house?
4 What's in Becca's fridge?

3 **Look at the Useful language. How do you say these expressions in your own language?**

Useful language

Describing a home

My dream home is a house / an apartment in the country / in the city / near the beach.
Upstairs / Downstairs, there's a ... / there are ...
Outside, there's a ...
In my bedroom, there's a ... I've got a ...

4 **Read the Look! box. Choose the correct word to complete the rules.**

Look! ***and* and *but***

It's got four bedrooms ***and*** *four bathrooms.*
There isn't a desk, ***but*** *there's a sofa.*

Rules

We use [1] **and** / **but** to connect similar ideas.
We use [2] **and** / **but** to contrast ideas.

5 **Copy and complete the sentences with *and* or *but*.**

In our bathroom, there's a shower, but there isn't a bath.

1 There's a table tennis table ... a basketball court.
2 My grandma's got a dog ..., she hasn't got a cat.
3 I've got a desk for my computer ... there's a bookcase for my books.
4 There's a table ..., there aren't any chairs.

6 **Write about your ideal home. Follow the steps in the Writing plan.**

Writing plan

Prepare

› Make notes about your ideal home. Think about:
  - rooms and other places
  - furniture and other things
  - your bedroom

Write

› Organize your ideas into paragraphs.
  Paragraph 1: Where is it? What rooms and places has it got?
  Paragraph 2: What is there in your bedroom? What other cool things has your home got?
› Use the expressions from the Useful language box.

Reflect

› Check your grammar: *There is / There are, have got*
› Check *and* and *but*.
› Check your spelling.

W Writing summary: WB p.84 E Exams: Unit 1 SB p.118 LS Language summary: Unit 1 SB p.127

EXTRA PRACTICE Workbook page 12; photocopiable activities for Unit 1: vocabulary, grammar and skills

My dream home

WRITING A chat forum

Sts read a chat forum post about a dream home. They learn useful language for describing a home and study the use of *and* and *but*. They then follow the steps in the Writing plan to write a chat forum post about their own dream home.

Writing

A chat forum

Useful language

Describing a home (*My dream home is …, Upstairs / Downstairs, there's a … / there are …, Outside, there's a …, In my bedroom, there's a …, I've got a …*)

Look!

and and *but*

WARMER

Say: *Imagine your dream home – Is it big or small? How many rooms are there? What is there outside? What is there inside? What is there in your bedroom?* Elicit ideas from individual sts and encourage everyone to contribute their ideas.

1 Focus on the chat forum and teach the word *chat forum*. Ask sts to read the forum and decide on their favourite thing about Becca's dream home. Put them into pairs to discuss their answers.

2 Sts read the chat forum again and answer the questions. Check answers.

Answers
1 There are five people in Becca's family.
2 a swimming pool and a tennis court
3 They haven't got any TVs.
4 ice cream

3 Read the Useful language box with sts about language for describing a home. Ask them how they say these expressions in their first language. Remind sts of the difference between *there is* and *there are*. Elicit or give some examples of each, e.g. *There's a swimming pool. There are some trees.* Remind sts also of the negative forms, *there isn't a …, there aren't any …* .

4 Read the Look! box with sts about *and* and *but*. Sts choose the correct words to complete the rules. Refer sts back to the chat forum post in Exercise 1 to find more examples of each word.

Answers
1 and 2 but

5 Ask sts to copy the sentences in their notebooks and complete them with the correct words. Check answers.

Answers
1 and 2 but 3 and 4 but

6 Ask sts to write a chat forum post about their ideal home following the steps in the Writing plan.

Writing plan

Prepare

Sts work as individuals and make notes about their ideal home. Monitor and help with vocabulary if necessary. Remind them to write about the inside and outside of their home.

Write

Read through the paragraph plan with the class, then refer back to Becca's forum post and show how it follows the paragraph plan. Sts then write their forum post using Becca's post in Exercise 1 as a model. Refer them back to the Useful language box and encourage them to use these phrases. Refer them back to the Look! box and encourage them to use *and* and *but* to connect ideas. They can also use prepositions of place from page 11 and the adjectives from page 17.

Reflect

Ask sts to check their grammar, spelling and punctuation and make any necessary changes. Reassure them that it is normal to make changes to a first draft of written work. Sts then work in pairs. They swap their forum posts with a partner and give feedback on the use of *there is / there are* and *have got*, and also the use of *and* and *but*. Remind sts that they should always be positive and encouraging when they give feedback to a partner.

W **Writing practice: WB** p.12
Sts will find more practice for writing here. Set these exercises for homework.

W **Writing summary: WB** p.84

E **Exams: Unit 1 SB** p.118

LS **Language summary: Unit 1 SB** p.127

School days 2

Vocabulary: Daily activities; Technology | **Grammar:** Present simple; *Wh-* questions | **Speaking:** Asking for and giving information | **Writing:** An email message

VOCABULARY Daily activities

I can use vocabulary for daily activities.

1 2.1 **Match the activities with the pictures. Listen, check and repeat.**

chat with my friends   do my homework   get dressed   get up   go to bed   have a shower
have breakfast   have dinner   have lunch   leave home   tidy my room   watch TV

1

2

3

4

5

6

7

8

9

10

11

12

2 2.2 **Listen to the sounds and write the daily activities in your notebook.**

1 have a shower

3 Complete the blog post with the correct activities.

My day
by Charlie

I *get up* at 7.00 in the morning. I [1] … – usually cereal with milk – and then I [2] … in my school uniform. I [3] … at quarter to eight and I walk to the bus stop. On the bus, I [4] …, Lucas and Emma.

After school, I go home. I [5] … (it's always untidy!), and then I open my schoolbag and I [6] … . We [7] … at about half past six. After dinner, I [8] … with my family in the living room. I'm always tired at 10 p.m. so I [9] …!

4 When do you do the activities in Exercise 1? Write sentences.

I get up at half past seven.
I do my homework after dinner.
I have a shower before breakfast.

5 Work in pairs. Compare your sentences.

A: I get up at half past seven. What about you?
B: I get up at ten past seven.

Now watch the vlog.

FAST FINISHER

Imagine your perfect day. Write sentences.

I get up at ten o'clock. Then I have breakfast. I have hot chocolate and croissants …

LS Language summary: Unit 2 SB p.128

School days

2

UNIT 2 OVERVIEW: The topic of this unit is school life and free time. Sts read about an unusual school on a ship, and listen to a podcast about another unusual school. They read some adverts for school clubs and learn how to ask for and give information. They read about schools in the UK and finally, they read an email from the future about daily life and write an email about their own typical school day. They also watch a vlog about morning routines and a culture video about school life in 1927.

Vocabulary	Grammar	Pronunciation	Reading	Listening	Speaking	Writing
Daily activities; Technology	Present simple: affirmative and negative; present simple: questions; *Wh-* questions	/s/, /z/ and /ɪz/	Scanning a text for specific information	Understanding yes/no questions in a podcast	Asking for and giving information	An email

VOCABULARY Daily activities

Sts learn 12 phrases for daily activities. They complete a blog post with the phrases, then personalise the vocabulary by talking about their own daily activities.

Vocabulary

Daily activities (*chat with my friends, do my homework, get dressed, get up, go to bed, have a shower, have breakfast, have dinner, have lunch, leave home, tidy my room, watch TV*)

Vlog

Tati: *Morning routine*

WARMER

Ask questions about the students' school, e.g. *What time does school start in the morning? What are your favourite subjects?* Elicit answers from different sts.

1 2.1 Read through the phrases in the box and elicit or teach the meanings. Sts match the phrases with the pictures. Play the audio track. See TG page 275 for audio script. Sts listen, check and repeat.

Answers

1 get up
2 leave home
3 chat with my friends
4 have lunch
5 have a shower
6 tidy my room
7 watch TV
8 have dinner
9 go to bed
10 get dressed
11 have breakfast
12 do my homework

2 2.2 Play the sounds for sts to write the activities. Check answers.

Answers

1 have a shower
2 have breakfast
3 get dressed
4 get up
5 leave home
6 chat with my friends
7 go to bed
8 tidy my room

3 Sts read the blog post and complete it with the correct activities. Sts check answers in pairs.

Answers

1 have breakfast
2 get dressed
3 leave home
4 chat with my friends
5 tidy my room
6 do my homework
7 have dinner
8 watch TV
9 go to bed

4 If necessary, revise how to tell the time in English. Read out the example answers, then ask sts to write sentences about what time they do the activities.

5 Put sts into pairs to compare sentences. Point out the question *What about you?* to ask your partner for their answer. Ask some pairs to tell the class which things they do at the same time and which things at different times.

Vlog

This lesson features an optional vlog in which a vlogger talks about her morning routine. You can watch this in class if you have time and access to video, or you can ask sts to download it from the Richmond Learning Platform to watch at home. See TG pages 287 and 304.

FAST FINISHER

Sts who finish early can practise vocabulary for daily activities further. They write sentences about their perfect day. Weaker sts could work in pairs.

EXTRA PRACTICE

Put sts into pairs. They take turns to talk about a typical school day or their perfect day. They should try to talk for one minute, while their partner films them using their phone.

V Vocabulary practice: WB p.14

Sts will find more practice of vocabulary for daily activities here. Set these exercises for homework.

LS Language summary: Unit 2 SB p.128

A school with a difference

READING

I can scan a text for specific information.

The School on a Ship!

A+ World Academy is the world's only school on a ship! Sixty students from all over the world live and study on the ship as it sails around the world. Fifteen-year-old Sophie tells us about it.

Sophie gets up at seven o'clock every day and has a shower. The girls sleep in one room and the boys sleep in another room. 'I have breakfast at 7.30, then we tidy the bedrooms and clean the ship,' Sophie says.

Sophie studies Maths, Science, History, English and Spanish. Students have four to six hours of lessons a day and for two hours they help to sail the ship. 'It's hard work,' Sophie says, 'but it teaches us about teamwork and responsibility.'

After school, Sophie does her homework and chats with her friends. She doesn't watch TV and they don't have Wi-Fi on the ship, but there are exercise classes, clubs and film nights. At ten o'clock, she goes to bed – tired but happy after another day at sea!

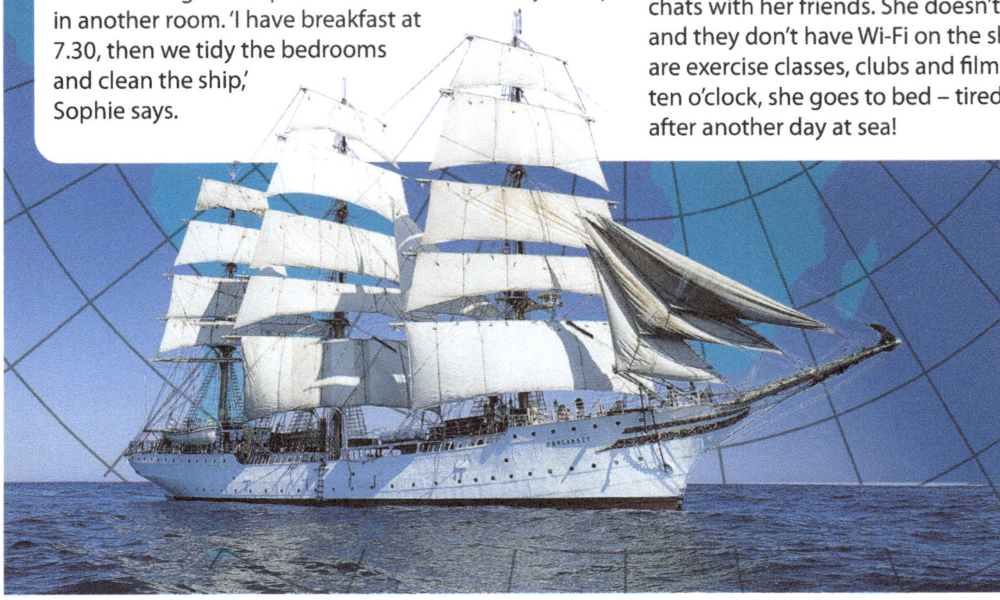

1 **Scan the article and complete the information about Sophie. Don't read every word – just look for the information you need.**

SOPHIE ROBERTS	
Age:	[1] ... years old
Gets up:	At [2] ... a.m.
Has breakfast:	At [3] ... a.m.
Hours of lessons per day:	[4] ...
Goes to bed:	At [5] ... p.m.

2 2.3 **Read and listen. Are the sentences true (T) or false (F)? Correct the false sentences.**

There are 50 students on the ship.

F. There are 60 students on the ship.

1 Sophie has a shower after breakfast.
2 The teachers tidy the bedrooms.
3 They help to sail the ship for six hours.
4 The work on the ship isn't easy.
5 After school, there are clubs and exercise classes.

3 Word Power **Work in pairs. Find five school subjects in the article. Make a list of more subjects.**

4 THINK CRITICALLY **Is a school on a ship a good idea? Why/Why not? Discuss as a class and have a class vote.**

I think it's a good idea because ...

I think it's a bad idea because ...

5 FIND OUT **Find six countries that the A+ World Academy ship visits.**

A school with a difference

READING

Sts read about the A+ World Academy, a school on a ship that sails around the world, and focus on scanning the text for specific information. They learn the affirmative and negative forms of the present simple to talk about routines, and practise pronunciation of the third person *-s* ending. They use the present simple to talk about their own daily routine.

Reading text

An article about the A+ World Academy, a school on a ship

Reading skill

Scanning a text for specific information

WARMER

Focus on the pictures with the article. Ask: *What can you see?* Elicit or teach the words *ship* and *sail*, and elicit or explain that it is a school on a ship. Ask: *What time do you think the students get up? What do they do in the evening?* Elicit a few ideas. Ask: *Do you think a school on a ship is fun? Why/Why not?* Elicit a range of ideas. Remind sts that it is a good idea to look at the pictures and think about what they are going to read before they read a text.

BACKGROUND

The A+ World Academy is an international boarding school for teenagers. The students sail to different countries and experience different ways of life and different cultures while studying for exams. Students usually stay on the ship for a whole school year. As well as studying, students help to sail the ship and prepare meals on board. More details can be found at https://www.aplusworldacademy.org/.

1 Scanning a text for specific information Read out the task and explain to sts that when they scan a text, they don't have to read every single word. Ask them to imagine they are looking for their name in a list of names, and point out that this is scanning. Focus on the table and elicit the words that sts can scan for to find each answer, e.g. *years old, gets up, breakfast, lessons, bed*. Sts then scan the text to find the information. You could do this as a race, to encourage sts to scan rather than reading the whole text. Check answers with the class.

Answers

1 15 2 7 3 7.30 4 4 to 6 5 10

2 2.3 Ask sts to copy the sentences into their notebooks. They read and listen to the article, then decide if the sentences are true or false and correct the false sentences. Check answers with the class.

Answers

1 F She has a shower before breakfast.
2 F The students tidy the bedrooms.
3 F They help to sail the ship for two hours.
4 T
5 T

3 Word Power Sts work in pairs to find five school subjects in the article and then make a list of more. Challenge them to write as many more subjects as they can. They can use a dictionary to help if necessary. Check answers with the class, and check that sts understand all the school subjects. If sts have written some school subjects that are new to other sts, ask them to come and write the words on the board and teach the meaning to their classmates.

21st Century skills

4 THINK CRITICALLY

Read out the question, then write on the board the two headings: *Good idea* and *Bad idea*. As a class, brainstorm some reasons why a school on a ship is a good idea, and why it is a bad idea, e.g.

Good idea: students can travel and see the world, they learn the skill of sailing, they learn teamwork, life is more interesting.

Bad idea: they are away from their families, there's no Wi-Fi so no internet, there might be bad weather, it's not fun if you are sick.

With each idea, encourage sts to express their own opinions and give reasons. Have a class vote to see what sts think of the idea overall.

EXTRA PRACTICE

You could have a class discussion on the following question: *What other activities outside school can you learn a lot from?* Elicit a few ideas, e.g. you can learn teamwork from sports, creativity from doing drama or music, responsibility from looking after a pet, etc. Encourage sts to talk about the activities they do outside school and what they learn from them.

21st Century skills

5 FIND OUT

Set this exercise for homework if you prefer. Sts can find this information out by looking online or in other media. The ship goes to: the Netherlands, Norway, Ireland, Spain, Italy, Morocco, Senegal, Brazil, Barbados, Jamaica, the USA and Portugal.

R **Reading practice: WB** p.15

You will find more practice for reading here. Set these exercises for homework.

GRAMMAR

Present simple: affirmative and negative

I can use the present simple to talk about routines.

Now watch the grammar animation.

1 **Study the grammar box. How does the verb change in the affirmative after *he, she* and *it*? How do we form the negative?**

Affirmative

I/You **have** breakfast at 7.30.
He/She/It **gets up** at 7.00.
We/You/They **clean** the ship after breakfast.

Negative

I/You **don't study** French.
He/She/It **doesn't watch** TV on the ship.
We/You/They **don't have** Wi-Fi on the ship.

2 **Copy and complete the sentences with the correct form of the verb.**

*Sophie **gets up** early. (get up)*

1 The boys and girls … in different rooms. (sleep)
2 Sophie … breakfast at 7.30. (have)
3 After breakfast, she … her room. (tidy)
4 Students … their homework in the evening. (do)
5 The ship … to a lot of countries. (go)
6 Sophie: 'I … film nights!' (love)

3 **PRONUNCIATION** /s/, /z/ and /ɪz/

2.4 **Listen and repeat.**

/s/	/z/	/ɪz/
sleeps	goes	watches

4 2.5 **Copy the table in Exercise 3. Listen to six more verbs and write them in the correct column.**

5 **Correct the sentences so that they are true for you.**

I live on a ship.
I don't live on a ship. I live in a house.

1 I get up at 11.00.
2 I have pizza for breakfast.
3 My school day starts at 12.00.
4 My teacher comes from China.
5 We have two hours of lessons a day.
6 My friends study Russian and Japanese.

6 **Complete the text with the correct form of the verbs in brackets.**

Students at A+ World Academy travel all over the world. When the ship [1] … (arrive) in a new country, the students [2] … (not stay) on board. They [3] … (visit) local schools and they [4] … (learn) about the culture of that country. Sophie's favourite country is Mexico because she [5] … (love) the food! When the ship is at sea, Sophie [6] … (not see) or speak to her family, but she always [7] … (phone) them when the ship is in port.

7 **Write three true and three false sentences using the ideas in the box.**

I My mum My dad My brother My sister	do (my) homework have breakfast study English/Maths play football/basketball chat with (my) friends	at school before/after dinner in the morning/afternoon/evening at lunchtime

8 **Work in pairs. Read your sentences from Exercise 7. Can your partner guess the false information?**

A: My mum studies English in the morning.
B: I think it's false.
A: You're wrong! It's true.

FUN FACT

Space Camp in the USA is a summer school for teenagers. Students build rockets, learn about space and live like astronauts!

FAST FINISHER

Think of a good friend and compare your daily routines.

I watch TV in the evening. Susana doesn't watch TV.

LS **Language summary: Unit 2** **SB** p.128

EXTRA PRACTICE **Workbook page 16**

GRAMMAR Present simple: affirmative and negative

Grammar animation

This lesson features an optional animated presentation of the grammar in context called *He cleans the robots!* including the use of the present simple. You can watch this in class if you have time and access to a computer or tablet, or you can ask sts to download it from the Richmond Learning Platform to watch at home. See TG page 308 for animation script.

1 Read the grammar box about the present simple. Point out that the examples in the grammar box are from the article on page 20. Elicit the answers to the questions.

Answers
In the affirmative after *he*, *she* and *it*, the verb adds *-s*.
We form the negative with *don't* and *doesn't*.

Write an affirmative example on the board, e.g. *I get up at 7.30*. Change *I* to *Ana* and elicit the other changes that are necessary: *Ana gets up at 7.30*. Then write X next to the sentence and elicit the negative form: *Ana doesn't get up at 7.30*. Change *Ana* to *we* and elicit the correct negative form: *We don't get up at 7.30*. Repeat this with one or two more simple sentences. Teach the third person forms *has* and *goes*.

Ask questions to check concept.

Concept check questions: *I have breakfast at eight o'clock – Is this my routine? Is it every day?* (yes). *I don't live on a ship. I live in a flat – Where is my home – a ship or a flat?* (a flat). *I study Maths – can you make this negative?* (I *don't study* Maths). *Sam go to bed at 10 p.m. – correct?* (no – Sam *goes* to bed …). *Sam don't get up at 7 o'clock – correct?* (no – Sam *doesn't get up* …).

2 Read the example with sts, then ask them to copy the sentences in their notebooks and complete them. Check answers with the class.

Answers

1 sleep	2 has	3 tidies
4 do	5 goes	6 love

3 **PRONUNCIATION** 2.4
Play the audio once for sts to listen and notice the three different sounds. Then play the audio again for sts to repeat. Point out that the /ɪz/ sound adds an extra syllable to the verb, whereas the other two sounds don't.

4 2.5 Ask sts to copy the table from Exercise 3 into their notebooks. Play the audio once for sts to listen and add the verbs to the table. Allow sts to compare their answers in pairs, then play the audio again for them to listen and check their answer. Check answers.

Answers
/s/ talks, chats
/z/ loves, has
/ɪz/ teaches, finishes

5 Read out the example sentence, then ask sts to correct the sentences so they are true for them, and write them in their notebooks. Check answers.

6 Pre-teach the words *on board* and *on dry land*. Then ask sts to read the text and write the correct verb forms in their notebooks. Check answers.

Answers

1 arrives	2 don't stay	3 visit
4 learn	5 loves	6 doesn't see
7 phones		

7 Elicit one or two sentences using the ideas in the box, then ask sts to write three true and three false sentences about themselves. Monitor and help as necessary.

8 Read out the example answers, and teach the meaning of *You're wrong* and also *You're right*. Sts then work in pairs and take turns to read their sentences to each other and guess if they are true or false. Ask one or two sts to read some of their sentences to the class.

FUN FACT
Encourage sts to read this fun fact for pleasure. They might also be interested to know that young people travel from over 100 different countries to take part in the space camp each summer.

FAST FINISHER
Sts who finish early can practise the grammar further. Sts write sentences about their own routines and a good friend's routines. Weaker sts could write two or three sentences about their own routines.

G **Grammar practice: WB** p.16
Sts will find more practice for the present simple (affirmative and negative) here. Set these exercises for homework.

LS **Language summary: Unit 2 SB** p.128

Do you play video games?

VOCABULARY and LISTENING Technology

I can understand yes/no questions in a podcast.

1 2.6 **Match the items of technology with the pictures. Listen, check and repeat.**

computer digital camera drone interactive whiteboard laptop projector tablet Virtual Reality headset wireless headphones 3D printer

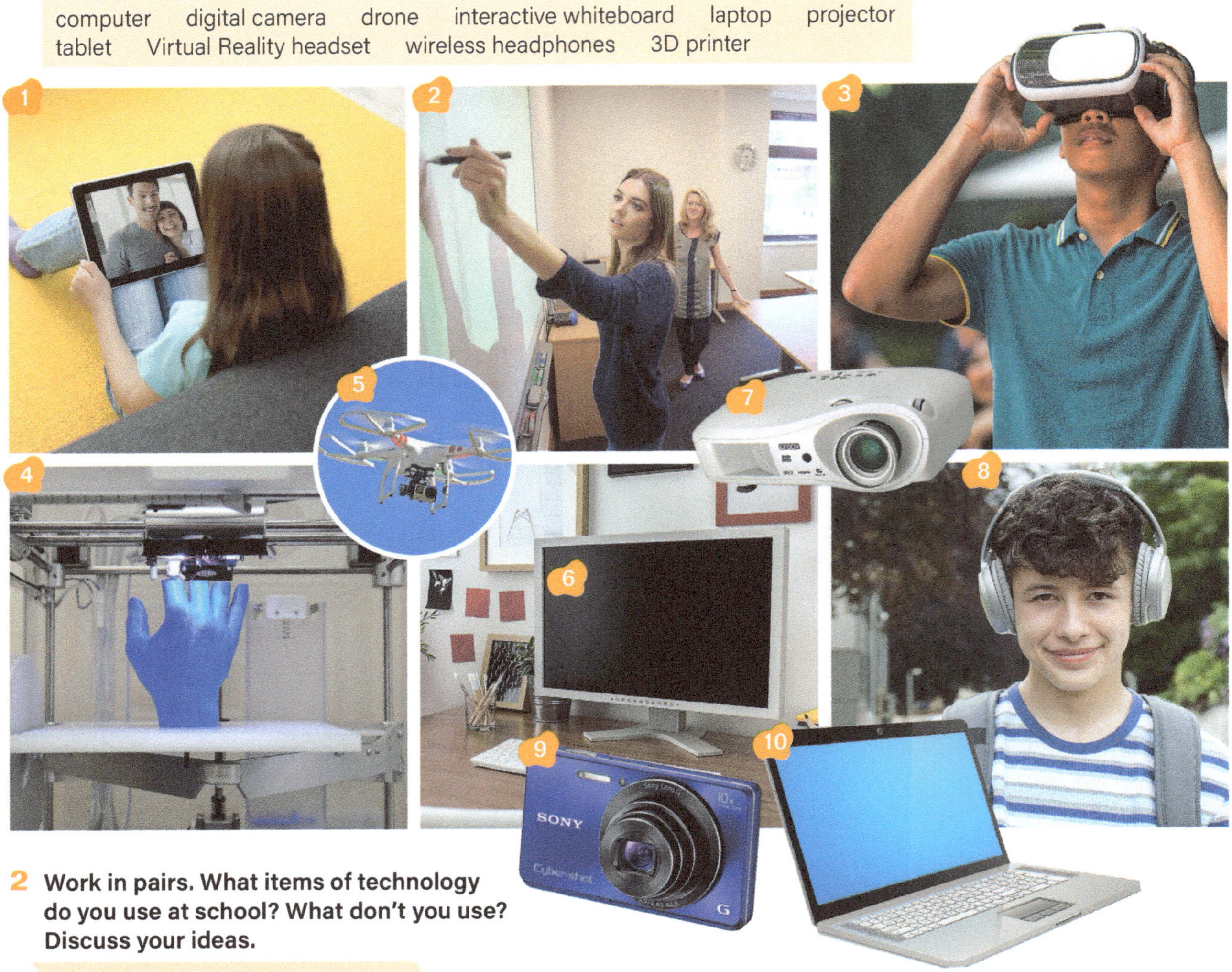

2 **Work in pairs. What items of technology do you use at school? What don't you use? Discuss your ideas.**

Our English teacher uses a projector.

We don't use Virtual Reality headsets.

3 2.7 **Read about the podcast. How do you think the school in the podcast is different from other schools? Listen and check.**

TODAY'S PODCAST

Most teenagers use computers, laptops or tablets at school, or they use them at home to do their homework. But at this school, things are different …

Listen Download

4 2.7 **Read the questions. Listen again and answer *Yes* or *No*.**

1 Does Alfie's teacher use an interactive whiteboard?
2 Do the students study with books?
3 Does Alfie do sport at school?
4 Does he watch TV at home?
5 Does he like his school? Why/Why not?

5 **Think and write sentences. What technology do you have at home? What do you use it for? Use the ideas in the box and your own ideas.**

I do my homework on my mum's laptop.

chat with my friends do my homework listen to music play games read books take photos watch videos

(digital) camera computer games console (wireless) headphones laptop phone tablet

LS Language summary: Unit 2 SB p.128

 EXTRA PRACTICE Workbook page 17

Do you play video games?

VOCABULARY and LISTENING
Technology

Sts listen to a podcast about a 'no technology' school in London and practise understanding *yes/no* questions in a podcast. They learn vocabulary for technology and learn present simple questions and *Wh-* questions.

Vocabulary

Technology (*computer, digital camera, drone, interactive whiteboard, laptop, projector, tablet, Virtual Reality headset, wireless headphones, 3D printer*)

Listening text

A podcast about a 'no technology' school in London

Listening skill

Understanding *yes/no* questions in a podcast

WARMER

Ask: *Who has a phone? How often do you look at it? Once a day? Ten times a day? Fifty times a day?* Elicit a range of answers. Ask: *What do you use your phone for?* Elicit a few ideas, e.g. to chat to friends, to buy things, to look for information. Teach the meaning of technology. Ask: *What other kinds of technology are there?* Elicit a few ideas, e.g. computer, TV. Ask: *Can you live with no technology? Why/Why not?* Elicit a few ideas.

1 2.6 Read through the words in the box and elicit or teach the meanings. Ask sts to match the words with the pictures. Play the audio track for sts to listen and check the answers. See TG page 275 for audio script. Make sure sts understand all the words. Play the audio track again for sts to repeat the words.

Answers

1 tablet
2 interactive whiteboard
3 Virtual Reality headset
4 3D printer
5 drone
6 computer
7 projector
8 wireless headphones
9 digital camera
10 laptop

2 Read out the example answers. If necessary, focus on the present simple affirmative and negative forms and revise the grammar rules. Put sts into pairs to look at the pictures again and decide which they use and don't use at school. Elicit answers from the class.

3 2.7 Ask sts to read the information about the podcast, then ask sts how they think this school is different. Elicit a range of ideas, but don't confirm them. Play the audio for sts to listen and check the answer. See TG page 275 for audio script. Check the answer with the class.

Answer

The school doesn't use any technology.

4 2.7 **Understanding *yes/no* questions in a podcast** Allow sts time to read through the questions. Point out that the answer to all the questions is *yes* or *no*. Read out the first question, then play the first part of the audio, as far as *Does she use a computer or an interactive whiteboard? No, she doesn't.* Stop the audio and elicit the answer to the first question (no). Point out to sts that to hear the answers to these kinds of questions, they should listen for affirmative or negative verbs. Play the rest of the audio for sts to listen and answer the questions. Check answers with the class, playing the audio again and pausing it for sts to hear the answers.

Answer

1 No
2 Yes
3 Yes
4 No
5 Yes

5 Read through the activities in the box with the class and make sure sts understand them all. Read out the example sentence and elicit one or two more examples. Point out the use of the preposition *on* (on my laptop/computer/tablet). Sts then write their sentences individually. Ask one or two sts to read some of their sentences to the class.

EXTRA PRACTICE

Arrange sts in small groups and ask them to look at the technology words in Exercise 1 and Exercise 5. Tell them to imagine that they are on a deserted island and they can have three pieces of technology. Groups have to decide which three things they want and why. For example, a digital camera to take photos of wildlife. Monitor while sts work, then nominate one person from each group to tell the rest of the class which three things they want to have.

V L **Vocabulary and Listening practice: WB** p.17
Sts will find more practice for listening, and practice of vocabulary for technology here. Set these exercises for homework.

LS **Language summary: Unit 2 SB** p.128

GRAMMAR

Present simple: questions

I can ask yes/no questions with the present simple.

Now watch the grammar animation.

1 **Copy and complete the grammar box.**

Questions and short answers	
Do you **like** your school?	Yes, I **do**. / No, I [1] ... .
[2] ... Sophie **live** on a boat?	Yes, she **does**. / No, she [3] ... .
[4] ... students **use** books?	Yes, they **do**. / No, they **don't**.

2 **Complete the questions with *Do* or *Does* and write short answers.**

Does your dad play games on his phone?
No, he doesn't.

1 ... your parents listen to music in the car?
2 ... your phone take good photos?
3 ... you read a lot of books?
4 ... you and your friends use VR headsets?
5 ... your Science teacher use a whiteboard?

3 **Do the questionnaire in pairs. Check your score.**

DOES TECHNOLOGY CONTROL YOUR LIFE?

1 ... (you use) use a phone or watch TV in bed at night?
A Yes, I do. **B** No, I don't.

2 ... (you do) your homework in front of the TV?
A Yes, I do. **B** No, I don't.

3 ... (you look) at your phone at dinner time?
A Yes, I do. **B** No, I don't.

4 ... (you wear) headphones in the street?
A Yes, I do. **B** No, I don't.

5 ... (you play) a lot of video games?
A Yes, I do. **B** No, I don't.

Mostly As: You think technology is great, but it's important to do other things. Do exercise, read books and chat with your family and friends!

Mostly Bs: Does technology control your life? No, it doesn't. That's good! You know that it's important to do other things.

Wh- questions

I can ask *Wh-* questions with the present simple.

4 **Study the grammar table. What other question words can you think of?**

Question word	do/does	subject	verb
Where	**do**	you	**go** to school?
What	**does**	he	**do** at home?
When	**do**	they	**watch** TV?

5 **Tanmay is a schoolboy with an interesting hobby. Put the words in order to make questions. Match the questions and answers.**

1 he / does / do / What *What does he do? d*
2 to school / go / does / Where / he
3 does / When / he / his videos / make
4 like / What subjects / he / does
5 relax / he / does / How

a He likes Maths, Science and Computer Studies!
b He plays table tennis and he rides his bike.
c He doesn't go to school. His parents teach him at home.
d He makes videos about computer programming. He's got 300,000 fans!
e He makes them in the evening and at the weekend.

6 **Write questions for your partner. Ask and answer.**

WEEKEND SURVEY

1 How / relax at the weekend?
2 What time / get up?
3 What / eat for breakfast?
4 What TV programmes / watch?
5 Where / go shopping?
6 When / go to bed?

A: How do you relax at the weekend?
B: I listen to music and do sport.

FAST FINISHER
Write questions for an interview with a celebrity. Imagine the answers.

LS Language summary: Unit 2 SB p.128

EXTRA PRACTICE Workbook page 18

GRAMMAR Present simple: questions

Grammar animation

This lesson features an optional animated presentation of the grammar in context called *What does it do?* including the use of questions in the present simple and the use of *Wh-* questions. You can watch this in class if you have time and access to a computer or tablet, or you can ask sts to download it from the Richmond Learning Platform to watch at home. See TG page 308 for animation script.

1 Read the grammar box with sts about present simple questions. Elicit the correct words to complete it. Draw attention to the word order, with *do* or *does* before the subject: *Do you like ...?* NOT ~~*You like ...?*~~ Point out also that we use *does* for the *he*, *she* and *it* forms, and *do* for all the other forms. Point out that we don't repeat the main verb in short answers: *Yes, I do.* NOT ~~*Yes, I do like*~~ or ~~*Yes, I like*~~.

Write a simple affirmative sentence on the board, e.g. *Sophie likes Maths*. Elicit the changes we need to make to form a question: ***Does*** *Sophie* ***like*** *Maths?* Repeat this with one or two more sentences. Elicit the short answers to the questions on the board.

Answers
1 don't 2 Does 3 doesn't 4 Do

Ask questions to check concept.

Concept check questions: *What words do we add to make present simple questions?* (do, does). *You live in a flat? – correct?* (no – *Do you live* in a flat?). *Yes, I am – correct?* (no – Yes, *I do*). *Do he watch TV? – correct?* (no – *Does he watch* TV?) *Yes, he watches. – correct?* (no – *Yes, he does.*). *Does she likes music? – correct?* (no – *Does she like* music?). *No, she doesn't. – correct?* (yes).

2 Ask sts to write the questions and short answers in their notebooks. Point out that that they should write short answers that are true for them. Check answers.

Answers
1 Do, Yes, they do. / No, they don't.
2 Does, Yes, it does. / No, it doesn't.
3 Do, Yes, I do. / No, I don't.
4 Do, Yes, we do. / No, we don't.
5 Does, Yes, he/she does. / No, he/she doesn't.

3 Read out the title of the questionnaire and explain the meaning if necessary. Focus on each question in turn and elicit the correct question form. Check that sts understand all the questions. They then work in pairs to ask and answer the questions and check their scores. Get feedback on whose life is controlled by technology.

Answers
1 Do you use
2 Do you do
3 Do you look
4 Do you wear
5 Do you play

Wh- questions

4 Read the grammar box with sts about *Wh- questions*. Check that sts understand the questions in the table. Point out that *where* asks about places and *when* asks about a time. Elicit other question words that sts know, e.g. *Why? Who? How many?* Point out the word order in the questions.

Ask questions to check concept.

Concept check questions: *What word asks about a place?* (where). *What word asks about a time?* (when). *What word asks about a thing?* (what). *Where you live? – correct?* (no – *Where do you* live?). *When he does have breakfast – correct?* (no – *When does he have* breakfast?).

5 Read out the example question, and point out that it matches answer *d*. Sts then write the questions in their notebooks and match them with the answers. Check answers. Ask: *Do you think this is an interesting hobby? What hobbies do you have?* Elicit a few answers.

Answers
2 Where does he go to school? c
3 When does he make his videos? e
4 What subjects does he like? a
5 How does he relax? b

6 Check that sts understand the meaning of *relax*. Ask sts to write the questions first. Check these, and check that sts understand them all. Allow sts time to prepare their answers to the questions individually, then put them into pairs to ask and answer them. Tell them to listen carefully to their partner's answers, so they can tell the class. Ask some sts to tell the class something about their partner, e.g. *Ali gets up at 7.30.*

Answers
1 How do you relax at the weekend?
2 What time do you get up?
3 What do you eat for breakfast?
4 What TV programmes do you watch?
5 Where do you go shopping?
6 When do you go to bed?

FAST FINISHER
Sts write questions to ask a celebrity, then imagine the answers. Tell them the celebrity can be a music star, a sports star, a film star, etc. Weaker sts could work in pairs and write one or two more questions to ask each other, then ask and answer them.

G **Grammar practice: WB** p.18
Sts will find more practice for present simple questions and *Wh-* questions here. Set these exercises for homework.

LS **Language summary: Unit 2 SB** p.128

KEEP TALKING!

Join the club!

READING and LISTENING

I can ask for information about school clubs.

Parkside School

Sign in

Home | Our School | School Clubs | News | Contact

Do you want to have fun and meet new friends? Then join one of our clubs.

SAILING CLUB

Have fun and learn to sail!
Tuesday, 4.00–6.00
Bluewater Lake (bus from school)

DANCE CLUB

Salsa, jazz, street dance and more!
Thursday, 3.30–4.30
In the gym

Music Club

Do you play an instrument?
Come to our music club!

Monday lunchtime (12.30–1.30)
School Hall

COMPUTER CLUB

Do you want to learn to code?
Join the Computer Club!

Contact Mr Green for more information.

Art Club

Do you love art?
Learn to draw, paint and more …
When: Thursday, 12.30–1.30
Where: In the Art Room

BASKETBALL CLUB

Are you the next Anthony Davis or Maya Moore? We want you in our club!

We play every Friday from 3.45–4.45, in the gym.

1 **Work in pairs. What clubs are there at your school? Which clubs do you go to? What clubs would you like to have?**

2 **Look at the school website and answer the questions.**

1 What day does the Art Club meet?
2 Which clubs meet at lunchtime?
3 What time does the Dance Club start and finish?
4 Who do you speak to about the Computer Club?
5 How do students go to the Sailing Club?
6 Where does the Basketball Club meet?

3 2.8 **Megan wants to join one of the clubs. Listen to Megan and her sister, Flora. What days is Megan free?**

4 2.8 **Listen again and complete the sentences in your notebook. Compare your answers in pairs. Look at the school website and find a club for Megan.**

Megan isn't interested in [1] … or [2] …
She's busy after school on [3] … and [4] …
She doesn't want to go to a club at [5] ….
The club for Megan is the [6] …

KEEP TALKING! Join the club!

READING and LISTENING

Sts read a school website with information about school clubs. They answer questions about the website, then listen to a conversation between two sisters about joining one of the clubs and choose a suitable club for them. They then learn how to ask for and give information. They read and hear a model dialogue and personalise the useful language by following the steps in the Speaking plan.

WARMER

Write these gapped words on the board: *d _ nce, f _ _ tb _ ll, a _ t, d _ _ ma, m _ s _ c, t _ nn _ s.*
Tell sts they are all fun activities that young people enjoy. Put them into pairs and ask them to complete the words as quickly as they can. When the first pair finishes, invite them to come to the front of the class and complete the words on the board. Check their answers, and check that sts understand all the words. Ask: *Which of these activities do you enjoy?* Elicit a range of answers.

Answers
dance, football, art, drama, music, tennis

1 Look at the school website with the class. Ask: *Does your school have a website? What information is on it?* Teach the meaning of *club* if necessary, then put sts into pairs to answer the questions. Discuss answers.

2 Read out the questions and check that sts understand them all. If necessary, briefly revise the days of the week. Ask sts to look at the website and answer the questions. Check answers, eliciting the part of the website which confirms each answer.

Answers

1 Thursday	4 Mr Green
2 Music Club, Art Club	5 by bus from school
3 3.30, 4.30	6 in the gym

3 2.8 Tell sts they will hear Megan and her sister, Flora, talking about the clubs. Point to the picture of the two girls and explain that they are looking at the school website on their computer. Read out the question, then play the audio for sts to listen and answer the question. See TG page 275 for audio script. Check the answer.

Answer
She's free on Monday, Wednesday and Thursday.

4 2.8 Allow sts time to read through the gapped sentences and copy them into their notebooks. Make sure they understand them all. Explain to sts that they must listen carefully to hear the details they need to complete gaps 1–6. They will then look at the information and choose the club for Megan. Play the audio again for sts to listen and complete the sentences. Allow sts to compare their answers in pairs, then check with the class, playing the audio again if necessary and pausing for sts to hear the answers. Sts then work in their pairs to choose a club for Megan. Discuss the answer with the class and the reasons why this is the club for Megan.

Answers

1 computers	4 Friday
2 art	5 lunch time
3 Tuesday	6 Dance Club

EXTRA PRACTICE

Explain that the purpose of the adverts on the Parkside School webpage is to encourage people to join the clubs. Elicit or point out that they do this with big headings, bright colours, nice photos, questions (e.g. Do you play an instrument?). Ask: *What information do the adverts include?* (name of the club, time, location, contact details).

In pairs or small groups, sts then think of a new club for their school and design a poster. Display the posters for everyone to see and ask sts to choose one or two clubs to join.

NOTE: If you have the facilities in your classroom, you could get sts to produce a webpage instead of a poster.

SPEAKING

Asking for and giving information

I can ask for and give information about school clubs.

Mr Green:	Hello, Liam. Can I help you?
Liam:	Yes, I'm interested in the Computer Club.
Mr Green:	OK. What would you like to know?
Liam:	What day is it on?
Mr Green:	It's on Wednesday.
Liam:	Cool. And what time does it start?
Mr Green:	It starts at quarter to four and it finishes at five o'clock.
Liam:	Where do they meet?
Mr Green:	Let me see. They meet in Room C3.
Liam:	Great. I'd like to join, please.
Mr Green:	No problem. Have fun!

1 2.9 **Listen and read. Copy and complete the information.**

Student	**Liam Baker**
Club	1 …
Day	2 …
Time	3 … to 4 …
Where	5 …

2 2.10 **Listen and repeat the Useful language.**

Useful language

Asking for and giving information

Can I help you?
I'm interested in …
What would you like to know?
What day is it on?
What time does it start/finish?
Where do they meet?

3 2.11 **Put the dialogue in order. Listen and check.**

1 c

a What time does it start?
b Cool. I'd like to join, please.
c Hello. Can I help you?
d They meet on Monday.
e Yes, I'm interested in the Drama Club. When do they meet?
f It finishes at 4.30.
g Of course. Have fun!
h It starts at 3.30.
i And what time does it finish?

4 **Work in pairs. Ask for information about a school club. Follow the steps in the Speaking plan.**

Speaking plan

Prepare

- Decide on your roles.
- Choose a club from the school website on page 24 or use your own ideas.
- Make notes for your dialogue.

Speak

- Practise your dialogue.
- Use phrases from the Useful language box.
- Act out your dialogue without notes.

Reflect

- How can you improve next time?
- Swap roles and choose a new club.

Now play *Keep moving!*

FAST FINISHER

Imagine your ideal school club and write an advertisement for it, like the ones on page 24.

LS Language summary: Unit 2 SB p.128

SPEAKING Asking for and giving information

1 2.9 Explain to sts that they will hear a dialogue between Liam and Mr Green. Ask them to copy the information into their notebooks. With stronger classes, you could play the dialogue with books closed and ask: *Which club does Liam ask about? What information does he want?* They can then complete the information. With weaker classes, you could play the dialogue for sts to listen and read, then complete the information. See SB page 25 for audio script. Check the answers.

Answers

1	Computer Club	4	5.00
2	Wednesday	5	Room C3
3	3.45		

2 2.10 Read through the Useful language box with the class and check sts understand all the phrases. Elicit which phrases Mr Green says, and which ones Liam says.

Ask questions to check concept.

Concept check questions: Ask: *Which questions does Liam use to ask for information?* (I'm interested in … What day is it on? What time does it start/finish? Where do they meet?). *Which phrase does Mr Green use to start the conversation?* (How can I help you?). *Which phrase does he use to ask Liam what information he wants?* (What would you like to know?).

3 2.11 Ask sts to read the sentences in the dialogue, then write the dialogue in the correct order in their notebooks. Play the audio for sts to listen and check their answers. Sts could then practise the dialogue in pairs.

Answers

1	c	2	e	3	d
4	a	5	h	6	i
7	f	8	b	9	g

4 Sts follow the steps in the Speaking plan to practise asking for and giving information.

Speaking plan

Prepare

Sts work in pairs. They decide on a club to ask about, either from the website on page 24 or using their own ideas. You could brainstorm some more ideas for clubs with the class first. They then make notes using the Useful language in Exercise 2 to help them.

Speak

Sts decide who will speak first and then practise their dialogue in their pairs. They can practise with and then without notes. Monitor and help as necessary. If your sts use smartphones in class, they could record their conversations.

Reflect

Discuss as a class how sts could improve next time. Encourage them to be honest about things they did well and things they can do better. If you noticed any typical errors, correct them with the class. Sts swap roles and follow the steps again with a different club. If they record their conversations, ask them to listen to their recording and use it to help them think of how they could improve next time. Ask some sts to perform their conversations for the class if they feel confident.

Keep moving!

This lesson features an optional language revision and consolidation game for use in digital classrooms. Players control different characters, each with their own personalities and special abilities.

FAST FINISHER

Sts think of their own idea for their ideal school club and write an advertisement for it, like the ones on page 24. Weaker sts could write one or two questions asking for information about different clubs on page 24. They could then ask and answer their questions with a partner.

S **Speaking practice: WB** p.19

Sts will find more practice for asking for and giving information here. Set these exercises for homework.

LS **Language summary: Unit 2 SB** p.128

REAL CULTURE!

UK education

I can compare schools in my country with schools in the UK.

SCHOOLS IN THE UK

Everything you need to know about schools in the UK ... and some surprises!

SCHOOL UNIFORM

Most schools have a school uniform. It's often a shirt with trousers or a skirt. 63% of students wear a tie.

SCHOOL LUNCHES

Students have lunch at school or bring sandwiches from home. A typical school lunch is pasta with tomato sauce and vegetables, as well as fruit.

SCHOOL DAY

Students have five and a half hours of lessons a day. School usually starts at about 8.30 and finishes at about 3.00, with an hour for lunch.

JOURNEY TO SCHOOL

How do secondary school students go to school? 38% go on foot, 29% go by bus and 23% go by car. Only 3% go by bike.

HOMEWORK

How many hours of homework do students have a week in the UK compared to other countries?

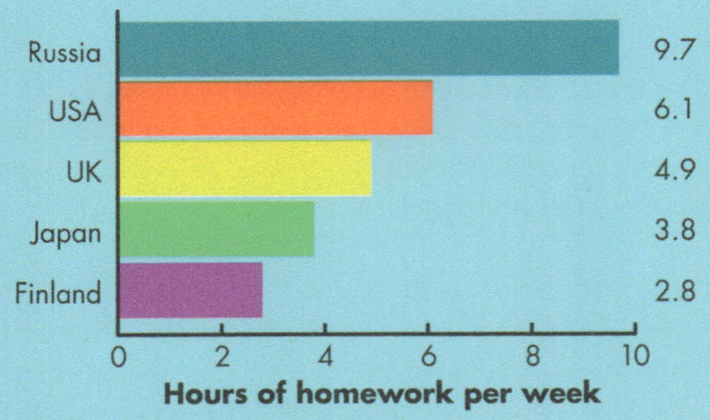

LANGUAGES

What languages do students learn at secondary school?

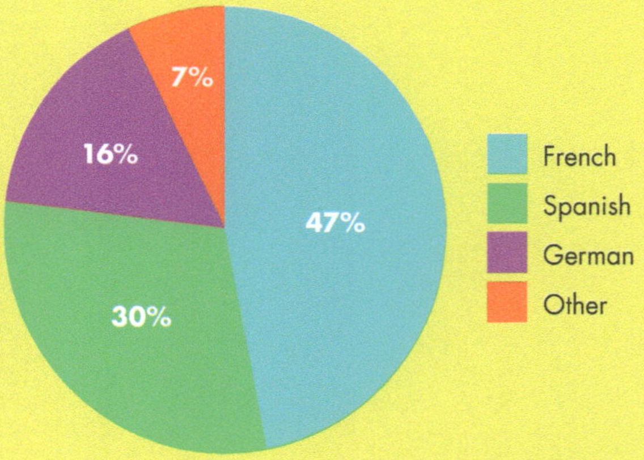

Foreign languages in UK schools

SCHOOL PETS

At some schools in the UK, dogs help in the classroom. The dogs don't teach, but they help students to relax and that helps students to read.

REAL CULTURE! Schools in the UK

Sts read an infographic text and learn about some different aspects of school life in the UK. They compare this to school life in their own country. Sts then make, and present, a digital presentation about schools and school life.

This lesson features an optional culture video about school life in 1927: see SB page 27.

WARMER

Put sts into groups. Ask them to imagine someone from another country is coming to their school. Ask them to think of three important things about their school to tell the person. Elicit a few ideas first, e.g. *It's a very big school. The teachers are friendly. We have Maths every day.* Monitor and help while sts are working, then ask groups in turn to read their sentences to the class.

BACKGROUND

Schools in the UK are divided into Primary Schools (5–11 years) and Secondary Schools (11–18 years). There are also some schools, called Sixth form colleges, for students between the ages of 16 and 18. Some students choose to leave school at 16, but they must continue some kind of training, either as an apprentice or at a specialist college such as an art college.

Around 7% of children in the UK go to private schools. These are usually stricter than state schools, and often focus more on academic subjects. They are also often boarding schools, where students stay during term time and only return home during the school holidays.

In the UK, parents can also choose to educate their children at home, and a small number of students are home-educated in this way.

1 Put sts into pairs to discuss the question. Tell them they can look at the infographic to give them ideas. Ask pairs in turn to tell the class their ideas, and share the Background information with them.

2 2.12 Tell sts they are going to read and listen to the infographic, and they should ignore any words they don't understand for now. Read through the gapped sentences with the class and check that sts understand them all. Ask sts to copy the sentences into their notebooks. Play the audio for sts to read, listen and complete the sentences. See SB page 26–27 for audio script. Check the answers.

Answers
1 8.30 2 4.9 3 23 4 30

3 Ask sts to read through the questions. Check they understand them all. Sts could read the text again in their own time, or you could play the audio again for them to read and listen. They then answer the questions. Encourage stronger sts to write full sentences for their answers. Weaker sts can write short answers. Allow sts to compare their answers in pairs, then check answers with the class.

Answers
1 It's a shirt with trousers or a skirt, and usually a tie.
2 They have lunch at school.
3 Most students walk to school.
4 An American student has more homework.
5 They help students to relax, and that helps them to read.
6 The most popular language is French.

4 2.13 Explain to sts that they will hear five young people talking about different topics to do with school. Play the first speaker and point out the example answer. Play the rest of the audio for sts to listen and write down the topics. See TG page 275 for audio script. Allow sts to compare their answers in pairs, then play the audio again if necessary for them to check and complete their answers. Check answers with the class.

Answers
2 uniform
3 languages
4 journey to school
5 school lunches

EXTRA PRACTICE

Arrange sts in pairs and ask them to draw a plan of their school and label all of the different places. You could elicit some ideas before they begin. For example, classroom, teachers' room, headteacher's office, toilets/bathroom, art room, library, computer room, music room, playground, classroom, corridor). Sts can use their dictionaries to look up new words or check spellings. At the end, rearrange sts into groups of four to compare their plans and check they have included everything. Remind sts to make a note of new vocabulary in their notebooks.

1 **Work in pairs. What do you know about schools in the UK?**

2 2.12 **Read and listen to the infographic. Complete the sentences.**

1 Schools start at ... a.m.
2 UK students have ... hours of homework.
3 ... per cent of students go to school by car.
4 ... per cent of students study Spanish.

3 **Read the infographic again. Answer the questions in your notebook.**

1 What is a typical school uniform?
2 Do students have lunch at home or at school?
3 How do most students go to school?
4 Who has more homework: a British student or an American student?
5 How do dogs help in some classrooms?
6 What is the most popular foreign language in UK schools?

4 2.13 **Look at the seven topics in the infographic (*School uniform, School lunches*, etc.) Listen. What topic does each speaker talk about?**

1 Homework

5 **COMPARE CULTURES** **How is your school similar or different to typical schools in the UK? Make a list.**

Similar: We wear a uniform.
Different: We don't learn German.

6 **Work in pairs. What is a boarding school? What famous boarding schools in books or films do you know? Complete the text below with the words in the box.**

do	does	doesn't	gets
goes	has	start	study

7 **Word Power** **Read the text in Exercise 6 again. Find four places for the definitions in the text.**

1 You have lunch here.
2 There are a lot of books here. You can read or study.
3 You do Science classes here.
4 You do exercise here.

8 **GET CREATIVE** **Create a digital presentation about your school or schools in your country. Include text, pictures and charts to make it attractive. Present your work to the class.**

Lessons start at ... and finish at ...
Students wear / don't wear a uniform.
Most students go to school by ...

Now watch the culture video.

FAST FINISHER

Imagine a funny school. Write sentences.

School starts at 10.00 p.m. We play football in the Science lab ...

Life at a BOARDING SCHOOL

In the UK, a small number of students go to boarding schools – they eat, sleep and [1]... there. What's life like at a boarding school?

Fourteen-year-old Tom [2]... up at 7.00 and [3]... breakfast in the canteen. Lessons [4]... at 8.45 and finish at 4.30, with an hour for lunch. His favourite subject is Chemistry – he loves the Science lab!

In the evening, he [5]... to Drama Club or he plays sport in the gym. Dinner is at 6.00. Then from 7.00 to 9.00, students [6]... their homework in their rooms or in the library.

[7]... he see his family at the weekend? No, he [8]... . He only sees them in the holidays.

REAL CULTURE!

21st Century skills

5 **COMPARE CULTURES**

Put sts into pairs or small groups. Encourage each group to brainstorm information about how schools in their own country are similar and different to schools in the UK and make a list. Ask some of the more confident groups to present their ideas to the rest of the class.

6 Read out the questions with the class, then put sts into pairs to discuss what they know about boarding schools. Elicit their ideas, and elicit the names of any boarding schools they know in books or films. They then work in their pairs to read the text and complete it with the correct words. Check answers. Ask: *What do you learn from the text about boarding schools?* Elicit what sts have learned from the text about boarding schools.

Answers

1 study
2 gets
3 has
4 start
5 goes
6 do
7 Does
8 doesn't

7 **Word Power** Ask sts to read the definitions and find the words in the text to match them. They could work in pairs for this. Check answers and model pronunciation of the words. Ask sts which of the places their school has.

Answers

1 canteen
2 library
3 Science lab
4 gym

21st Century skills

8 **GET CREATIVE**

Put sts into pairs or small groups and explain that they are going to create a digital presentation to present to the class. Read through the task with the class and discuss as a class what kinds of pictures and charts they could include to make their presentations attractive, e.g. pictures of the different activities in their school, charts about how most sts travel to school, etc.

Tell sts they should divide the work between them, so each person contributes to the presentation. Sts then work in their pairs or groups to prepare their presentations. Monitor and help while they are working.

Allow sts time to practise presenting their work in their pairs or groups. They could film each other to help them see things they can improve. Then start with a confident pair or group and ask them in turn to present their work to the class. Alternatively, put pairs or groups together for them to share their work with each other.

Culture video

You can watch this in class if you have time and access to video, or you can ask sts to download it from the Richmond Learning Platform to watch at home. See School in 1927 on TG pages 296 and 306.

FAST FINISHER

Sts imagine a funny school and write sentences describing it. Weaker sts could work in pairs and write sentences about a typical day at their school.

My school day

WRITING An email

I can write an email about my school day.

1 **Look at the message. Who is it from? What's unusual about it?**

MESSAGE FROM THE FUTURE

From: Alex Cole
Date: 14 October 2056

Hi there!

I'm Alex. I'm fourteen years old and I go to school in Sky City.

I want to tell you about my day. I get up at 9.30 and have breakfast. I go to school by drone. I meet my friends and we chat about our pet robots.

School starts at 11.00. My favourite day is Wednesday. We have Computer Science in the morning, and Space Studies in the afternoon.

After school, I play virtual reality sport or I go to a club. I go to Robotics Club on Monday and Time Travel Club on Thursday. In the evening, I do my homework. I go to bed at 10.30.

That's my day! Write soon and tell me about your day.

Bye for now,

Alex

2 **Read the message and find three differences between Alex's day and your day. Tell your partner.**

I don't get up at 9.30 on a school day. I get up at 7.00.

3 **Look at the Useful language. How do you say these expressions in your language?**

Useful language

Starting and finishing an email

Hi there / Hi ... / Dear ...	Bye for now
I want to tell you about ...	Best wishes
Write soon	

4 **Study the Look! box. Find an example of each preposition in Alex's email.**

Look! Prepositions of time

We use prepositions of time to help us talk about when something happens.

at *9.30,* ***at*** *11.00*
in *the morning,* ***in*** *the afternoon,* ***in*** *the evening*
on *Friday,* ***on*** *Saturday*
BUT: ***at*** *night,* ***at*** *the weekend*

5 **Complete the sentences with the correct preposition.**

1 Alex has lunch ... one o'clock.
2 ... Tuesday, he has History and Art.
3 Alex tidies his room ... the weekend.
4 He doesn't listen to music ... the evening.
5 Alex's pet robot sleeps in Alex's bedroom ... night.

6 **Write an email to Alex about your school day. Follow the steps in the Writing plan.**

Writing plan

Prepare

› Make notes about your school day.
  • What time do you get up / start school?
  • How do you go to school?
  • What is your favourite school day / lesson? Why?
› What do you do after school?

Write

› Organize your ideas into three paragraphs:
  • Before school • During school • After school
› Use the expressions from the Useful language box.

Reflect

› Check your grammar: Present simple
› Check prepositions of time.
› Check your spelling.

W Writing summary: WB p.85 E Exams: Unit 2 SB p.119 LS Language summary: Unit 2 SB p.128

EXTRA PRACTICE Workbook page 00; photocopiable activities for Unit 2: vocabulary, grammar and skills

My school day

WRITING An email

Sts read a message from the future, describing a typical school day in the future. They learn useful language for starting and finishing an email and study prepositions of time. They then follow the steps in the Writing plan to write an email to a friend about their school day.

Writing
An email

Useful language
Starting and finishing an email (*Hi there / Hi ..., Dear ..., I want to tell you about ..., Write soon. Bye for now / Best wishes*)

Look!
Prepositions of time

WARMER

Say two sentences about a typical school day, one true and one false, e.g. *I get up at 7.30. I go to school by ship*. Invite students in turn to say a sentence about their school day, either true or false. Their classmates listen and decide if the sentence is true or false.

1 Ask sts to look at the message without reading it. Ask: *Who is it from? What is unusual about it?* Elicit the answers.

Answers
It is from Alex.
It is unusual because it is from the future. The date is 2056.

2 Sts read the message and find three differences between Alex's day and theirs. Elicit a range of answers from individual sts.

Example answers
I don't go to school by drone. I go by bus.
We don't chat about our pet robots. We chat about computer games.
School doesn't start at 11.00. It starts at 8.30.

3 Read the Useful language box with sts about language for starting and finishing an email. Sts look at the email again to see which expressions it uses. Ask sts how they say these expressions in their first language.

4 Read the Look! box with sts about prepositions of time. Ask sts to find an example of each preposition in Alex's email. Point out that we use *at* for times of day. Point out that we use *in* with *morning, afternoon* and *evening*, and we use *the: In **the** morning/afternoon/evening*, but *at ~~the~~ night*. Explain that we use *on* with days of the week, but *at* with *the weekend*.

Answers
at 9.30, at 11.00, in the morning, in the afternoon, on Monday, on Thursday, in the evening, at 10.30

Ask questions to check concept.

Concept check questions: *Which prepositions do we use with times of day?* (at). *Do we use the same preposition with morning, afternoon, evening, night?* (no – *in* the morning/afternoon/evening; *at* night). *I have Maths Friday – correct?* (no – *on* Friday). *I see my friends on weekend – correct?* (no – *at the* weekend).

5 Ask sts to copy the sentences in their notebooks and complete them with the correct prepositions. Check answers with the class.

Answers
1 at 2 On 3 at 4 in 5 at

6 Ask sts to write an email to Alex about their school day using the Writing plan.

Writing plan

Prepare
Sts work as individuals or in pairs and make notes about their school day, including things they do before school. Monitor while they are working, and help with vocabulary if necessary.

Write
Read through the paragraph plan with the class, then refer back to Alex's email and show how it follows the plan. Sts then write their email using their notes, and Alex's email in Exercise 1 as a model. They should write three paragraphs. Refer them back to the Useful language box and encourage them to use these phrases to start and finish their email. Refer them back to the Look! box and encourage them to use prepositions of time correctly.

Reflect
Ask sts to check their grammar, spelling and punctuation and make any necessary changes. Reassure them that it is normal to make changes to a first draft of written work. Sts then work in pairs. They swap their emails with a partner and give feedback on the use of the present simple and prepositions of time. Remind sts that they should always be positive and encouraging.

W **Writing practice: WB** p.20
Sts will find more practice for writing here. Set these exercises for homework.

W **Writing summary: WB** p.85

E **Exams: Unit 2 SB** p.119

LS **Language summary: Unit 2 SB** p.128

School days

Vocabulary: Daily activities; Technology | **Grammar:** Present simple; *Wh-* questions | **Speaking:** Asking for and giving information | **Writing:** An email message

2

VOCABULARY Daily activities

I can use vocabulary for daily activities.

1 2.1 **Match the activities with the pictures. Listen, check and repeat.**

chat with my friends   do my homework   get dressed   get up   go to bed   have a shower
have breakfast   have dinner   have lunch   leave home   tidy my room   watch TV

2 2.2 **Listen to the sounds and write the daily activities in your notebook.**

1 have a shower

3 Complete the blog post with the correct activities.

My day
by Charlie

I *get up* at 7.00 in the morning. I [1] … – usually cereal with milk – and then I [2] … in my school uniform. I [3] … at quarter to eight and I walk to the bus stop. On the bus, I [4] …, Lucas and Emma.

After school, I go home. I [5] … (it's always untidy!), and then I open my schoolbag and I [6] … . We [7] … at about half past six. After dinner, I [8] … with my family in the living room. I'm always tired at 10 p.m. so I [9] …!

4 When do you do the activities in Exercise 1? Write sentences.

I get up at half past seven.
I do my homework after dinner.
I have a shower before breakfast.

5 Work in pairs. Compare your sentences.

A: I get up at half past seven. What about you?
B: I get up at ten past seven.

Now watch the vlog.

FAST FINISHER

Imagine your perfect day. Write sentences.

I get up at ten o'clock. Then I have breakfast. I have hot chocolate and croissants …

LS Language summary: Unit 2 SB p.128

EXTRA PRACTICE Workbook page 22

Crazy about sport

3

UNIT 3 OVERVIEW: The topic of this unit is sport. Sts read about a young skateboarding superstar, and listen to a radio advertisement for an urban sports week. They read some public signs and notices and learn how to make suggestions. They read about sport in the UK and do a sports quiz and finally, they read a blog post about someone's typical weekend and write a blog post about their own typical weekend. They also watch a vlog about someone's life as an athlete and a culture video about an unusual kind of football.

Vocabulary	Grammar	Pronunciation	Reading	Listening	Speaking	Writing
Sport; Action verbs	Adverbs of frequency; *like / don't like + -ing; can/can't* and *must/mustn't*	/ə/, /æ/ and /ɑː/	Working out the meaning of new words	Listening for specific information in an advertisement	Making suggestions	A blog post

VOCABULARY Sport

Sts learn nouns for the names of 12 different sports. They categorise these nouns according to the verb they are typically used with (*play, go, do*), then personalise the vocabulary by asking and answering questions about different sports.

Vocabulary

Sport (*athletics, ballet, gymnastics, ice hockey, mountain biking, rugby, skateboarding, surfing, swimming, table tennis, taekwondo, volleyball*)

Look!

play, *go* and *do*

Vlog

Nina: *Life as an athlete*

WARMER

Mime playing tennis and ask: *What sport is this?* Elicit the answer, then invite sts in turn to mime a sport. If sts don't know the word in English, you can teach the words as they mime.

1 3.1 Read through the words in the box and elicit or teach the meanings. Sts match the words to the pictures. Play audio track. See TG page 275 for audio script. Sts listen, check and repeat.

Answers

1 rugby
2 taekwondo
3 volleyball
4 skateboarding
5 ice hockey
6 table tennis
7 swimming
8 ballet
9 gymnastics
10 mountain biking
11 athletics
12 surfing

2 Read the Look! box with sts about *play*, *go* and *do*. Ask: *What other sports are ball sports?* Elicit one or two answers, e.g. volleyball. Ask sts to copy the table in their notebooks and complete it with the rest of the sports words from Exercise 1. Check answers with the class.

Answers

play: ice hockey, rugby, table tennis, volleyball
go: mountain biking, skateboarding, surfing, swimming
do: athletics, taekwondo, gymnastics, ballet

3 Put sts into pairs to add more sports to the table. Draw the table on the board and elicit sports words to add to each column.

Possible answers

play: tennis, football
go: running, cycling
do: judo, karate

4 Demonstrate the task with a confident student. Sts then work in pairs to ask and answer questions about the sports in Exercise 1.

Vlog

This lesson features an optional vlog in which vlogger Nina talks about life as an athlete. You can watch this in class if you have time and access to video, or you can ask sts to download it from the Richmond Learning Platform to watch at home. See TG pages 288 and 304.

FAST FINISHER

Sts who finish early write sentences about people in their class or their family members. Weaker sts could work in pairs.

EXTRA PRACTICE

Put sts into pairs. They take turns to talk about the sports they do and like for one minute, while their partner films them using their phone. They can watch their films back and discuss in their pairs how they could improve.

V Vocabulary practice: WB p.22

Sts will find more practice for vocabulary for sport here. Set these exercises for homework.

LS Language summary: Unit 3 SB p.129

A school with a difference

READING I can scan a text for specific information.

The School on a Ship!

A+ World Academy is the world's only school on a ship! Sixty students from all over the world live and study on the ship as it sails around the world. Fifteen-year-old Sophie tells us about it.

Sophie gets up at seven o'clock every day and has a shower. The girls sleep in one room and the boys sleep in another room. 'I have breakfast at 7.30, then we tidy the bedrooms and clean the ship,' Sophie says.

Sophie studies Maths, Science, History, English and Spanish. Students have four to six hours of lessons a day and for two hours they help to sail the ship. 'It's hard work,' Sophie says, 'but it teaches us about teamwork and responsibility.'

After school, Sophie does her homework and chats with her friends. She doesn't watch TV and they don't have Wi-Fi on the ship, but there are exercise classes, clubs and film nights. At ten o'clock, she goes to bed – tired but happy after another day at sea!

1 **Scan the article and complete the information about Sophie. Don't read every word – just look for the information you need.**

SOPHIE ROBERTS	
Age:	[1] ... years old
Gets up:	At [2] ... a.m.
Has breakfast:	At [3] ... a.m.
Hours of lessons per day:	[4] ...
Goes to bed:	At [5] ... p.m.

2 2.3 **Read and listen. Are the sentences true (T) or false (F)? Correct the false sentences.**

There are 50 students on the ship.
F. There are 60 students on the ship.

1 Sophie has a shower after breakfast.
2 The teachers tidy the bedrooms.
3 They help to sail the ship for six hours.
4 The work on the ship isn't easy.
5 After school, there are clubs and exercise classes.

3 Word Power **Work in pairs. Find five school subjects in the article. Make a list of more subjects.**

4 THINK CRITICALLY **Is a school on a ship a good idea? Why/Why not? Discuss as a class and have a class vote.**

I think it's a good idea because ...

I think it's a bad idea because ...

5 FIND OUT **Find six countries that the A+ World Academy ship visits.**

20

Secrets of success

READING

Sts read about Brighton Zeuner, an American teenager who is a skateboarding star. They focus on working out the meaning of new words from their context. They learn to use the present simple with adverbs of frequency to talk about their daily routines and *like / don't like + -ing* to talk about their likes and dislikes.

Reading text

A web page about Brighton Zeuner, an American teenager who is a skateboarding star

Reading skill

Working out the meaning of new words

WARMER

Ask: *Do you go skateboarding? Is it easy or difficult?* If there are sts in the class who go skateboarding, encourage them to talk about their experiences. Ask them more questions, e.g. *Where do you go skateboarding? When?* Teach the word *trick* and ask: *Can you do tricks?* If no sts in the class go skateboarding, ask: *Do you think it's a fun / difficult sport? Why?*

1 3.2 Focus on the text and elicit or point out that it is a web page. Ask sts to look at the picture and explain that it shows Brighton, an American teenager. Read out the question, then play the audio for sts to read and listen to the web page. Elicit the answer to the question. Teach the meaning of *winner* and *gold medal*, but don't teach the meaning of *champion*.

Answers

She is a world champion skateboarder; she is the youngest winner of an X Games gold medal at the age of 13.

2 3.2 Ask sts to copy the sentences into their notebooks. They read the text again and complete the sentences with the correct words. Check answers with the class.

Answers

1	school	2	afternoon	3	skatepark
4	boys	5	Olympic Games		

3 **Word Power** Put sts into pairs and set a time limit of two or three minutes for sts to write as many Olympic sports as they can. When time is up, ask sts how many sports they have on their list. Invite the pair with the largest number to write their words on the board. Check sts understand all the words, and, if they are all correct, declare the pair the winner.

4 **Working out the meaning of new words** Focus attention on the blue words and read out the task. Explain to sts that when they read, there will often be words that they don't understand, but they can learn to guess the meaning of a word by thinking about similar words in their language and looking at the sentence around the word. Read out the sentence with the word *champion* in. Ask: *Is there a similar word in your language? What do you think the word means?* Elicit answers, and point out that the sentence also says she is a *winner* and has a *gold medal*, so this can help us work out the meaning. Put sts into pairs to look at the remaining blue words. Check answers with the class, eliciting similar words in the sts' own language and eliciting what in each sentence helped them understand the meaning.

Answers

champion: someone who has beaten all competitors in a competition
success: achieving results hoped for or wanted
helmet: a strong, hard hat that protects the head
tricks: clever moves or interesting routines
ambition: desire and determination to achieve success

21st Century skills

5 **THINK CRITICALLY**

Put sts into pairs or small groups and ask them to think of five secrets for success, either at school or in a sport. You could elicit one or two from the class first, e.g. Do your homework, Get lots of sleep, Eat healthy food. Monitor and help while sts are working. Elicit ideas from the class and write them on the board. Discuss all the ideas with the class and see if the class can agree on the top 5 overall.

EXTRA PRACTICE

Write on the board: *Talent* and *Hard work*. Ask: *Which is more important for success?* Have a brief class discussion. Encourage as many sts as possible to join in and express their opinions. Ask more questions if necessary to help sts think of ideas, e.g. *How many hours a day do professional sports people practise? Can you be a professional sports person just with talent, but no practice? Can anyone become a professional if they practise enough?*

21st Century skills

6 **FIND OUT**

Set this exercise for homework if you prefer. Sts can find this information out by looking online or in other media, or by asking other people. The answers to the questions are: Summer : Tokyo 2020 or 2024 Paris; Winter : Beijing 2022

You could also ask sts to find out what new Olympic sports there will be at the next Olympic Games.

R **Reading practice: WB** p.23

You will find more practice for reading here. Set these exercises for homework.

GRAMMAR

Present simple: affirmative and negative

I can use the present simple to talk about routines.

Now watch the grammar animation.

1 **Study the grammar box. How does the verb change in the affirmative after *he, she* and *it*? How do we form the negative?**

Affirmative

I/You **have** breakfast at 7.30.
He/She/It **gets up** at 7.00.
We/You/They **clean** the ship after breakfast.

Negative

I/You **don't study** French.
He/She/It **doesn't watch** TV on the ship.
We/You/They **don't have** Wi-Fi on the ship.

2 **Copy and complete the sentences with the correct form of the verb.**

*Sophie **gets up** early. (get up)*

1 The boys and girls ... in different rooms. (sleep)
2 Sophie ... breakfast at 7.30. (have)
3 After breakfast, she ... her room. (tidy)
4 Students ... their homework in the evening. (do)
5 The ship ... to a lot of countries. (go)
6 Sophie: 'I ... film nights!' (love)

3 **PRONUNCIATION** /s/, /z/ and /ɪz/

2.4 **Listen and repeat.**

/s/	/z/	/ɪz/
sleeps	goes	watches

4 2.5 **Copy the table in Exercise 3. Listen to six more verbs and write them in the correct column.**

5 **Correct the sentences so that they are true for you.**

I live on a ship.
I don't live on a ship. I live in a house.

1 I get up at 11.00.
2 I have pizza for breakfast.
3 My school day starts at 12.00.
4 My teacher comes from China.
5 We have two hours of lessons a day.
6 My friends study Russian and Japanese.

6 **Complete the text with the correct form of the verbs in brackets.**

Students at A+ World Academy travel all over the world. When the ship [1] ... (arrive) in a new country, the students [2] ... (not stay) on board. They [3] ... (visit) local schools and they [4] ... (learn) about the culture of that country. Sophie's favourite country is Mexico because she [5] ... (love) the food! When the ship is at sea, Sophie [6] ... (not see) or speak to her family, but she always [7] ... (phone) them when the ship is in port.

7 **Write three true and three false sentences using the ideas in the box.**

I My mum My dad My brother My sister	do (my) homework have breakfast study English/Maths play football/basketball chat with (my) friends	at school before/after dinner in the morning/afternoon/evening at lunchtime

8 **Work in pairs. Read your sentences from Exercise 7. Can your partner guess the false information?**

A: My mum studies English in the morning.
B: I think it's false.
A: You're wrong! It's true.

FUN FACT

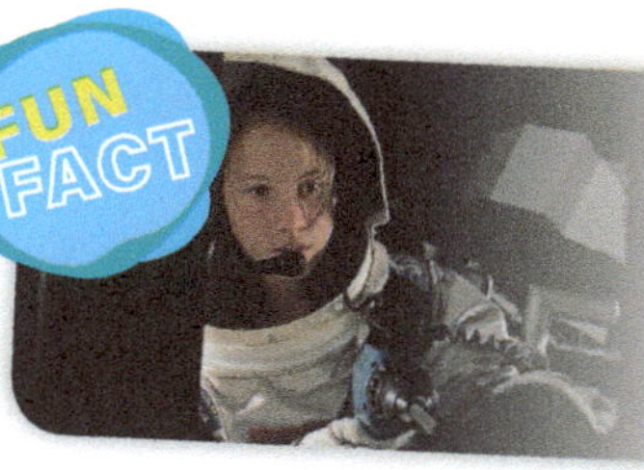

Space Camp in the USA is a summer school for teenagers. Students build rockets, learn about space and live like astronauts!

FAST FINISHER

Think of a good friend and compare your daily routines.

I watch TV in the evening. Susana doesn't watch TV.

LS **Language summary: Unit 2** **SB** p.128

EXTRA PRACTICE **Workbook page 24**

GRAMMAR Present simple and adverbs of frequency

Grammar animation

This lesson features an optional animated presentation of the grammar in context called *I love eating popcorn!* including the form and use of the present simple with adverbs of frequency and the use of *like / don't like + -ing*. You can watch this in class if you have time and access to a computer and tablet, or you can ask sts to download it from the Richmond Learning Platform to watch at home. See TG page 308–309 for animation script.

1 Read the grammar box and examples. Point out the meanings from *never* (0%) to *always* (100%). Ask sts to copy the rule into their notebooks, then look at the examples and complete the rule with the correct words. Check answers.

Answers
1 after
2 before

Write a present simple sentence on the board, with an adverb of frequency, e.g. *I sometimes play tennis at school.* Elicit the same sentence with different adverbs of frequency. Repeat this with a sentence with *be*, e.g. *Gymnastics is always fun.*

Ask questions to check concept.

Concept check questions: *What do adverbs of frequency tell us?* (how often we do something). *Tom sometimes goes swimming, Ana often goes swimming – who goes swimming more?* (Ana). *Lucia practises on Monday, Wednesday and Saturday – does she always practise?* (no – she *sometimes* practises). *Sam wins usually – correct?* (no – Sam *usually* wins). *Jack is always happy – correct?* (yes).

2 Ask sts to copy the sentences in their notebooks and add the adverbs of frequency. Check answers.

Answers
1 Brighton **usually** has breakfast at home.
2 She **always** takes her skateboard with her.
3 She is **never** late for school.
4 Her brother **often** makes videos of Brighton.
5 She **sometimes** goes swimming with her friends.

3 Read out the first sentence and ask two or three sts to repeat it with an adverb of frequency, so it is true for them. Sts then write true sentences about themselves.

4 Put sts into pairs to compare their answers. Monitor and help as necessary. Ask some sts to tell the class something that their partner *often* or *usually* does.

like / don't like + -ing

5 Sts match the sentences with the emojis. Check answers, then ask: *What happens to the verb after each of these phrases?* Elicit that it adds *-ing* on the end.

Answers
1 b 2 c 3 a 4 e 5 d

Ask questions to check concept.

Concept check questions: *I like swimming and my brother loves swimming – who likes it more?* (my brother). *Paul doesn't mind doing taekwondo and Max doesn't like it – who likes it more?* (Paul). *I love do ballet – correct?* (no – I *love doing* ballet).

6 Focus on the example sentence and point out how the emoji becomes *I hate …* in the sentence. Ask sts to write the sentences in their notebooks. Check answers.

Answers
1 They love playing basketball at the park. It's great.
2 We don't like doing gymnastics. It's hard.
3 She likes meeting her friends at the park. It's fun.
4 I don't mind wearing a school uniform. It's OK.
5 He hates tidying his room. It's boring.

7 Read out the task and the example answers. Put sts into groups to ask and answer questions. Ask some sts to tell the class something their classmates love.

FUN FACT Encourage sts to read this fun fact for pleasure. Ask: *Do you sometimes watch animals like this online?* Elicit other sporty dogs or cats that sts sometimes watch online. You could suggest that they search online for Benny the ice-skating dog, to see pictures of a dog who loves playing on the ice and has his own ice skates.

FAST FINISHER
Fast finishers can write sentences about things that members of their family do or don't do, and things they like and dislike. Weaker sts could write one or two sentences about Brighton, looking back at the web page on page 30 to help them.

G Grammar practice: WB p.24
Sts will find more practice for Present simple and adverbs of frequency and *like / don't like + -ing* here. Set these exercises for homework.

LS Language summary: Unit 3 SB p.129

Do you play video games?

VOCABULARY and LISTENING Technology

I can understand yes/no questions in a podcast.

1 2.6 **Match the items of technology with the pictures. Listen, check and repeat.**

computer   digital camera   drone   interactive whiteboard   laptop   projector
tablet   Virtual Reality headset   wireless headphones   3D printer

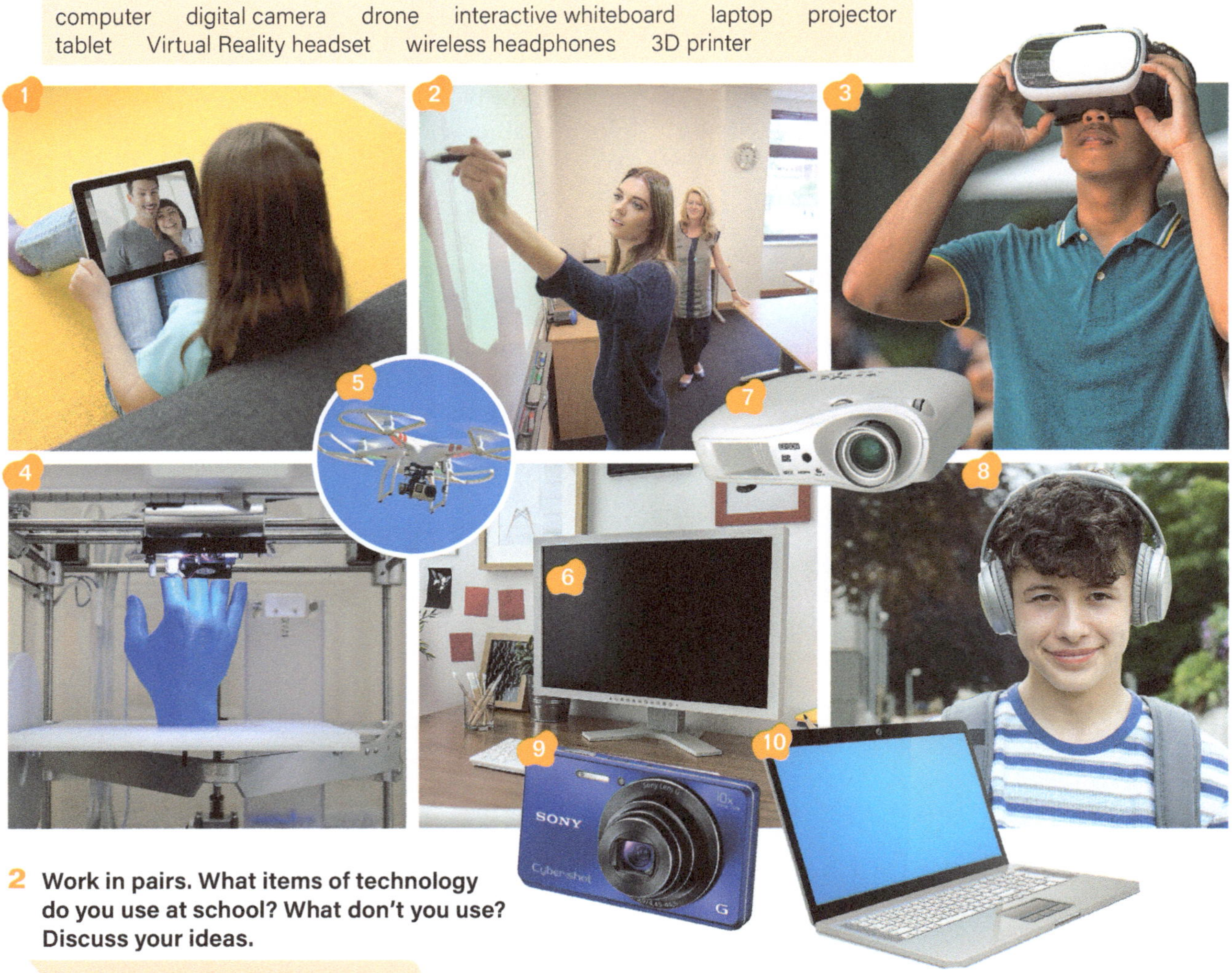

2 **Work in pairs. What items of technology do you use at school? What don't you use? Discuss your ideas.**

Our English teacher uses a projector.

We don't use Virtual Reality headsets.

3 2.7 **Read about the podcast. How do you think the school in the podcast is different from other schools? Listen and check.**

TODAY'S PODCAST

Most teenagers use computers, laptops or tablets at school, or they use them at home to do their homework. But at this school, things are different …

Listen   Download

4 2.7 **Read the questions. Listen again and answer *Yes* or *No*.**

1 Does Alfie's teacher use an interactive whiteboard?
2 Do the students study with books?
3 Does Alfie do sport at school?
4 Does he watch TV at home?
5 Does he like his school? Why/Why not?

5 **Think and write sentences. What technology do you have at home? What do you use it for? Use the ideas in the box and your own ideas.**

I do my homework on my mum's laptop.

chat with my friends   do my homework
listen to music   play games   read books
take photos   watch videos

(digital) camera   computer   games console
(wireless) headphones   laptop   phone   tablet

LS Language summary: Unit 2 SB p.128

EXTRA PRACTICE Workbook page 24

Can you run, jump and climb?

VOCABULARY and LISTENING
Action verbs

Sts listen to a radio advert for an Urban Sports Week and focus on listening for specific information. They learn action verbs, and learn how to use *can/can't* to talk about ability and permission, and *must/mustn't* to talk about obligation

Vocabulary
Action verbs (*catch, climb, jump, kick, ride, run, skate, ski, swim, throw*)

Listening text
A radio advert for an Urban Sports Week

Listening skill
Listening for specific information in an advertisement

WARMER
Tell sts they are going to test each other on the language they learned in the last lesson. On the board, draw a picture representing a sport, e.g. a bicycle and draw an emoji showing how you feel about it. Elicit the correct sentence, e.g. *I love mountain biking*. Ask sts to draw three similar 'picture sentences'. Sts swap their sentences in pairs and try to guess their partner's sentences. Ask who guessed all three sentences correctly.

1 Focus on the poster and explain the meaning of *urban* (in a city, not the countryside). Read the names of the sports and elicit or explain the meaning of *3-on-3 basketball* (basketball with only 3 people in each team) and *5-a-side football* (football with 5 people in each team). Read out the question and the example answers. Check that sts understand all the adjectives in the example answers. Sts could work in pairs to say which sports they would and wouldn't like to try, or you could ask individual sts and elicit a range of answers.

2 3.3 Read through the verbs in the box and elicit or teach the meanings. Play the audio once for sts to listen to the verbs. Play the audio again for sts to repeat the words. Sts then look at the pictures and say which verbs they can see. Check answers.

Answers
BMX biking: ride, jump
Free running: run, jump
Climbing: climb
3-on-3 basketball: throw, catch
5-a-side football: kick, run
Inline skating: skate

3 Focus on the example answer and point out that we *ride a bike* and *ride a horse*. Focus on the next two nouns and elicit the correct verb (climb). Sts then copy all the phrases into their notebooks and complete them with the correct verbs. Allow sts to compare their answers in pairs, then check with the class.

Answers
1 climb
2 swim
3 run
4–6 throw, catch, kick

4 3.4 Read out the question, then play the audio for sts to listen and identify the sports that the advert mentions. TG page 276 for audio script. Tell sts not to worry at this stage if they don't understand everything in the audio. Check answers with the class.

Answers
Free running, BMX biking, 3-on-3 basketball,

5 3.4 **Listening for specific information in an advertisement** Ask sts to copy the table into their notebooks. Read through the table with the class and elicit the kind of information that is missing in each gap, e.g. a day, a time, a place. Elicit a few possible answers sts might hear, e.g. *on Saturday, at two o'clock, in the park*. Ask: *Do you think you need to listen very carefully to hear this information?* (yes). Elicit that when you are listening for general meaning, as in Exercise 4, you don't need to listen to every single word, but when you are listening for specific information, you need to listen very carefully to hear the answers. Play the audio again for sts to listen and complete the information in their notebooks. See TG page 276 for audio script. Check answers with the class, playing the audio again if necessary and pausing for sts to hear the answers.

Answers
1 11 o'clock
2 park
3 Thursday
4 10 o'clock
5 skate park
6 Saturday
7 9.30
8 sports centre

6 3.5 Ask sts to write the gapped sentences in their notebooks. Model pronunciation of the words in the box, then play the audio again for sts to listen and complete the sentences with the correct words. Check answers, and check that sts understand the meaning of all the sentences.

Answers
1 Can 2 must 3 can, can't 4 mustn't

V L **Vocabulary and Listening practice: WB** p.25
Sts will find more practice for listening, and practice of vocabulary for action verbs here. Set these exercises for homework.

LS **Language summary: Unit 3 SB** p.130

GRAMMAR

Present simple: questions

I can ask yes/no questions with the present simple.

Now watch the grammar animation.

1 **Copy and complete the grammar box.**

Questions and short answers

Do you **like** your school?	Yes, I **do**. / No, I [1] ... .
[2] ... Sophie **live** on a boat?	Yes, she **does**. / No, she [3] ... .
[4] ... students **use** books?	Yes, they **do**. / No, they **don't**.

2 **Complete the questions with *Do* or *Does* and write short answers.**

Does your dad play games on his phone?
No, he doesn't.

1 ... your parents listen to music in the car?
2 ... your phone take good photos?
3 ... you read a lot of books?
4 ... you and your friends use VR headsets?
5 ... your Science teacher use a whiteboard?

3 **Do the questionnaire in pairs. Check your score.**

DOES TECHNOLOGY CONTROL YOUR LIFE?

1 ... (you use) use a phone or watch TV in bed at night?
A Yes, I do. B No, I don't.

2 ... (you do) your homework in front of the TV?
A Yes, I do. B No, I don't.

3 ... (you look) at your phone at dinner time?
A Yes, I do. B No, I don't.

4 ... (you wear) headphones in the street?
A Yes, I do. B No, I don't.

5 ... (you play) a lot of video games?
A Yes, I do. B No, I don't.

Mostly As: You think technology is great, but it's important to do other things. Do exercise, read books and chat with your family and friends!

Mostly Bs: Does technology control your life? No, it doesn't. That's good! You know that it's important to do other things.

Wh- questions

I can ask *Wh-* questions with the present simple.

4 **Study the grammar table. What other question words can you think of?**

Question word	do/does	subject	verb
Where	**do**	you	**go** to school?
What	**does**	he	**do** at home?
When	**do**	they	**watch** TV?

5 **Tanmay is a schoolboy with an interesting hobby. Put the words in order to make questions. Match the questions and answers.**

1 he / does / do / What *What does he do? d*
2 to school / go / does / Where / he
3 does / When / he / his videos / make
4 like / What subjects / he / does
5 relax / he / does / How

a He likes Maths, Science and Computer Studies!
b He plays table tennis and he rides his bike.
c He doesn't go to school. His parents teach him at home.
d He makes videos about computer programming. He's got 300,000 fans!
e He makes them in the evening and at the weekend.

6 **Write questions for your partner. Ask and answer.**

WEEKEND SURVEY

1 How / relax at the weekend?
2 What time / get up?
3 What / eat for breakfast?
4 What TV programmes / watch?
5 Where / go shopping?
6 When / go to bed?

A: How do you relax at the weekend?
B: I listen to music and do sport.

FAST FINISHER
Write questions for an interview with a celebrity. Imagine the answers.

LS Language summary: Unit 2 SB p.128

EXTRA PRACTICE Workbook page 26

GRAMMAR *can* and *can't*

Grammar animation

This lesson features an optional animated presentation of the grammar in context called *You mustn't give up!* including the form and use of *can / can't* and *must / mustn't*. You can watch this in class if you have time and access to a computer or tablet, or you can ask sts to download it from the Richmond Learning Platform to watch at home. See TG page 309 for animation script.

1 Read the grammar box with sts about *can* and *can't*. Ask sts to look at the example sentences carefully and answer the questions. Check the answers, then draw attention to the word order in questions: *Can she swim?* NOT ~~*She can swim?*~~ Check answers.

Answers
1 No, it doesn't. 2 a verb without *to*

Ask questions to check concept.

Concept check questions: *Joey can swim, Laura can't swim – who is safe in the water?* (Joey). *You can play football in the park – is it OK to play football in the park?* (yes). *You can't skate here – are you allowed to skate here?* (no). *Sam can't to ride a bike – correct?* (no – Sam can't ride a bike). *You can ski – how do you make that into a question?* (Can you ski?).

2 Point out the example answer and the tick prompt. Ask sts to write the sentences in their notebooks. Check answers.

Answers

1 can't	2 can	3 can't
4 can	5 A: Can, B: can't	

3 **PRONUNCIATION** 3.6

Model and drill pronunciation of the three sounds in isolation. Point out that in English, vowels are often pronounced as /ə/ when they are not stressed, but they are pronounced in their full form when they are stressed. Play the audio for sts to repeat.

4 3.7 Play the audio once for sts to listen to the questions and answers. Play the audio again for them to listen and repeat.

5 Read out the example question and answer, then ask the question to one or two sts and elicit their answers. Then put sts into pairs to ask and answer questions. Monitor and help while sts are working, and remind them to think about how they pronounce *can* and *can't*. Check answers by inviting one or two sts to ask one of their classmates a question.

must and *mustn't*

6 3.8 Read through the grammar box with the class. Point out that *must* is similar to *can* in that it doesn't change in the 3rd person singular and we use it with a verb without *to*. Explain that we use *must* and *mustn't* to talk about rules. Ask sts to read the club rules and complete them with *must* or *mustn't*. Play the audio for them to listen and check. Check answers with the class.

Answers

2 mustn't	3 must	4 must
5 mustn't	6 must	

Ask questions to check concept.

Concept check questions: *You must wear a white T shirt – is that a rule?* (yes). *Can I wear a blue T shirt?* (no). *You mustn't play on your phone in class – is that a rule?* (yes). *Is it OK to play with your phone?* (no – *you mustn't*).

21st Century skills

7 **GET CREATIVE**

Read out the task, then put sts into pairs to invent a club and write the rules. Encourage them to use their imagination, and tell them they can invent crazy rules if they want. You could elicit a few rules with the class first, e.g. *You must bring your own ball. You mustn't chat during games.* Monitor and help while sts are working, then ask some pairs to read their rules to the class.

EXTRA PRACTICE

Sts could make a poster advertising their club. You could use these as a display on the classroom walls. Alternatively, remind them of the radio advert they listened to for the Urban Sports Week. Ask them to write a radio advert for their new club. They could record it on their phones and share with their classmates in groups.

FAST FINISHER

Sts write sentences about what they and their family can and can't do. Weaker sts could work in pairs. They each say three sentences about things they can and can't do, e.g. *I can swim*. They then write three sentences about what their partner can and can't do, e.g. *Maria can swim*.

G **Grammar practice: WB** p.26
Sts will find more practice for *can* and *can't*, and *must* and *mustn't* here. Set these exercises for homework.

LS **Language summary: Unit 3 SB** p.129

KEEP TALKING!

Join the club!

READING and LISTENING

I can ask for information about school clubs.

Sign in

Parkside School

Home | Our School | School Clubs | News | Contact

Do you want to have fun and meet new friends? Then join one of our clubs.

SAILING CLUB

Have fun and learn to sail!
Tuesday, 4.00–6.00
Bluewater Lake (bus from school)

DANCE CLUB

Salsa, jazz, street dance and more!
Thursday, 3.30–4.30
In the gym

Music Club

Do you play an instrument? Come to our music club!

Monday lunchtime (12.30–1.30)
School Hall

COMPUTER CLUB

Do you want to learn to code? Join the Computer Club!

Contact Mr Green for more information.

Art Club

Do you love art?
Learn to draw, paint and more …
When: Thursday, 12.30–1.30
Where: In the Art Room

BASKETBALL CLUB

Are you the next Anthony Davis or Maya Moore? We want you in our club!

We play every Friday from 3.45–4.45, in the gym.

1 Work in pairs. What clubs are there at your school? Which clubs do you go to? What clubs would you like to have?

2 Look at the school website and answer the questions.

1 What day does the Art Club meet?
2 Which clubs meet at lunchtime?
3 What time does the Dance Club start and finish?
4 Who do you speak to about the Computer Club?
5 How do students go to the Sailing Club?
6 Where does the Basketball Club meet?

3 2.8 Megan wants to join one of the clubs. Listen to Megan and her sister, Flora. What days is Megan free?

4 2.8 Listen again and complete the sentences in your notebook. Compare your answers in pairs. Look at the school website and find a club for Megan.

Megan isn't interested in [1] … or [2] …
She's busy after school on [3] … and [4] …
She doesn't want to go to a club at [5] ….
The club for Megan is the [6] …

KEEP TALKING! What shall we do?

READING and LISTENING

Sts read some notices with rules and match them with the places they might see them. They listen to some conversations and identify where each conversation takes place. They then learn how to make suggestions. They read and hear a model dialogue and personalise the useful language by following the steps in the Speaking plan.

WARMER

Ask: *Do you ever feel bored at the weekend or in the school holidays? What do you do when you're bored?* Elicit a few ideas and suggest some ideas if necessary to prompt sts, e.g. *Do you go to the cinema? Do you go shopping? Do you watch a film at home?* Encourage sts to talk about things they do with their friends when they are bored. Tell sts they are going to practise making suggestions and deciding what to do.

1 Look at the notices with the class. Explain that they all have rules about things you must and mustn't do in different places. Ask: *Where do you see signs with rules?* Elicit a few ideas, e.g. at the swimming pool, at the cinema. Read through the places in the box with the class and check they understand them all. Then ask sts to look at the notices and decide where you can find each one. Check answers.

Answers

a	sports centre	e	beach
b	skatepark	f	cinema
c	café	g	park
d	swimming pool	h	climbing wall

2 Read out the first sentence and elicit which sign it matches (b). Ask: *Does it match sign g?* (no – that says no bikes). Sts read the remaining sentences and match each one to a notice. Point out that one sentence matches two notices. Allow sts to compare their answers in pairs then check with the class, eliciting the part of each sign which confirms the answer.

Answers

1 b 2 d 3 c 4 f 5 e, g 6 a

3 Read out the example answers and remind sts about the adverbs of frequency they studied on page 31. You could elicit the adverbs and write them on the board to help sts. Point out the use of *Me, too* to agree with your partner. Ask: *Can you remember what you say if you are surprised by your partner's sentence?* (Really?). Sts then work in pairs to say how often they go to each place. Ask some sts to tell the class which places they often go to.

4 3.9 Tell sts they will hear three dialogues in some of the places in Exercise 1. Tell them they should listen for clues to guess where the people are. Play the audio for sts to listen and identify the places. See TG page 276 for audio script. Check answers with the class, encouraging sts to give reasons for their answers.

Answers

1 cinema 2 beach 3 sports centre

5 3.9 Read out the questions and point out that to answer these questions they must listen very carefully for the specific information. Play the audio again for sts to listen and answer the questions. Check answers with the class, playing the audio again if necessary and pausing for sts to hear the answers.

Answers

1 £14 (£7 each)
2 an ice cream
3 The girl's sister is too young to use the gym.

EXTRA PRACTICE

Arrange sts in pairs or small groups and focus on the list of places in the box in Exercise 1. Ask sts to write one more piece of advice or information for each place. Monitor while sts work, then elicit ideas from around the classroom.

Example answers

beach: No dogs
café: Opening times 10 a.m. to 4 p.m.
cinema: No hot food
climbing wall: No phones
park: No camping, No barbecues
skatepark: No skating or cycling without a helmet
sports centre: No food or drink
swimming pool: No shoes

SPEAKING
Asking for and giving information

I can ask for and give information about school clubs.

Mr Green:	Hello, Liam. Can I help you?
Liam:	Yes, I'm interested in the Computer Club.
Mr Green:	OK. What would you like to know?
Liam:	What day is it on?
Mr Green:	It's on Wednesday.
Liam:	Cool. And what time does it start?
Mr Green:	It starts at quarter to four and it finishes at five o'clock.
Liam:	Where do they meet?
Mr Green:	Let me see. They meet in Room C3.
Liam:	Great. I'd like to join, please.
Mr Green:	No problem. Have fun!

1 2.9 **Listen and read. Copy and complete the information.**

Student	Liam Baker
Club	1 …
Day	2 …
Time	3 … to 4 …
Where	5 …

2 2.10 **Listen and repeat the Useful language.**

Useful language

Asking for and giving information

Can I help you?
I'm interested in …
What would you like to know?
What day is it on?
What time does it start/finish?
Where do they meet?

3 2.11 **Put the dialogue in order. Listen and check.**

1 c

a What time does it start?
b Cool. I'd like to join, please.
c Hello. Can I help you?
d They meet on Monday.
e Yes, I'm interested in the Drama Club. When do they meet?
f It finishes at 4.30.
g Of course. Have fun!
h It starts at 3.30.
i And what time does it finish?

4 Work in pairs. Ask for information about a school club. Follow the steps in the Speaking plan.

Speaking plan

Prepare
- Decide on your roles.
- Choose a club from the school website on page 24 or use your own ideas.
- Make notes for your dialogue.

Speak
- Practise your dialogue.
- Use phrases from the Useful language box.
- Act out your dialogue without notes.

Reflect
- How can you improve next time?
- Swap roles and choose a new club.

Now play *Keep moving!*

FAST FINISHER

Imagine your ideal school club and write an advertisement for it, like the ones on page 24.

LS Language summary: Unit 2 SB p.128

EXTRA PRACTICE Workbook page 27

SPEAKING Making suggestions

1 3.10 Focus on the picture and explain that it shows Jack and Alice. Ask: *How does Alice feel? Is she happy?* Elicit that she is bored. Read out the question, then play the audio of the dialogue. With stronger classes, you could play the dialogue with books closed and ask: *What do they decide to do?* With weaker classes, you could play the dialogue for sts to listen and read. See SB page 35 for audio script. Check the answer.

Answer
They decide to go mountain biking and take a picnic.

2 3.11 Ask sts if they can remember any of the phrases Alice and Jack used to make suggestions. Read through the Useful language box with the class and check sts understand all the phrases. Play the audio for sts to listen and repeat.

3 3.12 Ask sts to copy the dialogue in their notebooks and complete it using the Useful language from Exercise 2. Play the audio for sts to listen and check their answers. Check answers with the class.

Answers

1 Let's	2 shall	3 don't
4 sound	5 playing	6 fun

4 Sts follow the steps in the Speaking plan to practise making suggestions.

Speaking plan

Prepare
Sts work in pairs. They choose an activity and decide on a place to meet, then make notes for their dialogue using the Useful language in Exercise 2 to help them. You could brainstorm some ideas for a dialogue with the class first and make notes on the board as a model.

Speak
Sts practise their dialogue in their pairs. They can practise with and then without notes. Monitor and help as necessary. If your sts use smartphones in class, they could record their conversations.

Reflect
Discuss as a class how sts could improve next time. Encourage them to be honest and open about the things they did well and the things they can do better. If you noticed any typical errors, correct them with the class. Sts swap roles and follow the steps again with a different activity and a different place. If they record their conversations, ask them to use this to help them think of how they could improve next time. Ask some sts to perform their dialogues for the class if they feel confident.

Keep moving!

This lesson features an optional language revision and consolidation game for use in digital classrooms. Players control different characters, each with their own personalities and special abilities.

FAST FINISHER
Sts write suggestions for things to do with their family or friends on their birthday. Weaker sts could find the suggestions that Alice and Jack use in the dialogue in Exercise 1 and rewrite them, changing the details.

S Speaking practice: WB p.27
Sts will find more practice for making suggestions here. Set these exercises for homework.

LS Language summary: Unit 3 SB p.129

REAL CULTURE!

UK education

I can compare schools in my country with schools in the UK.

SCHOOLS IN THE UK

Everything you need to know about schools in the UK ... and some surprises!

SCHOOL UNIFORM

Most schools have a school uniform. It's often a shirt with trousers or a skirt. 63% of students wear a tie.

SCHOOL LUNCHES

Students have lunch at school or bring sandwiches from home. A typical school lunch is pasta with tomato sauce and vegetables, as well as fruit.

SCHOOL DAY

Students have five and a half hours of lessons a day. School usually starts at about 8.30 and finishes at about 3.00, with an hour for lunch.

JOURNEY TO SCHOOL

How do secondary school students go to school? 38% go on foot, 29% go by bus and 23% go by car. Only 3% go by bike.

HOMEWORK

How many hours of homework do students have a week in the UK compared to other countries?

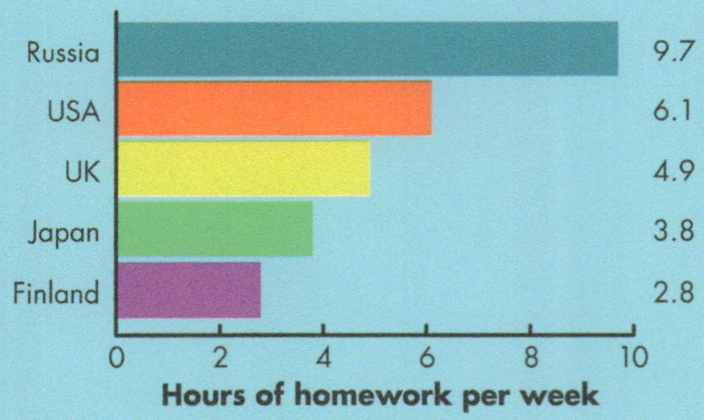

LANGUAGES

What languages do students learn at secondary school?

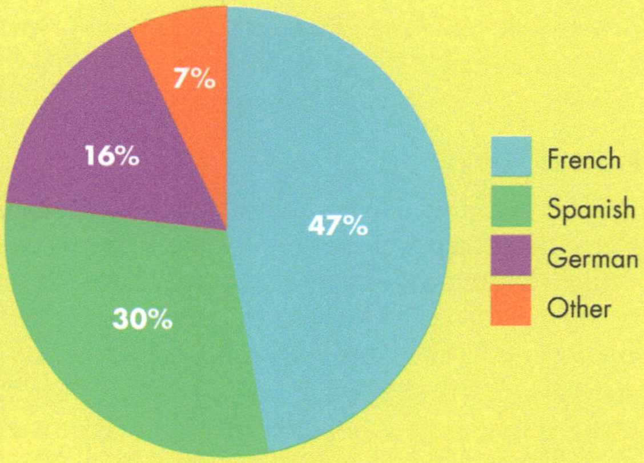

Foreign languages in UK schools

SCHOOL PETS

At some schools in the UK, dogs help in the classroom. The dogs don't teach, but they help students to relax and that helps students to read.

26

REAL CULTURE! Sport in the UK

Sts read a sports map and learn about a variety of different sports that are popular in the UK. They compare sports in the UK with sport in their own country. Sts then work in groups to make a sports map about their country.

This lesson features an optional culture video about an unusual kind of football: see SB page 37.

WARMER

Ask: *Which sports are popular in your country?* Elicit a few ideas and ask more questions if necessary to help sts, e.g. *What sports can you watch on TV? What sports can people do at school? Who are the big sports stars in your country? What big sporting events take place each year?* Elicit a range of answers, then ask: *What's your favourite sport? Why?*

BACKGROUND

Gaelic football is popular in Northern Ireland and also the Republic of Ireland. It is an amateur sport, and players are not allowed to receive any money for playing.

Cricket is popular especially in England. Traditional cricket games can go on for many hours, but recently, shorter versions of the game have been introduced which only last for two or three hours.

Surfing is popular in Devon and Cornwall, in the south west of England, where there are large waves suitable for the sport.

Golf originated in Scotland and remains extremely popular there. Many of the golf courses are close to the coast and set in stunning countryside, which makes them popular with players from all over the world.

1 Read out the questions and put sts into groups to brainstorm ideas about sports, teams and sportspeople in the UK. Ask groups in turn to report back to the class.

2 3.13 Focus on the sports map and explain to sts that they are going to learn about some popular sports in the UK. Explain that they should read the information on the sports map and try to complete it with the correct numbers. Tell them to guess the numbers if they aren't sure. Allow sts to compare their answers in pairs, then play the audio for sts to listen and check. See TG page 276 for audio script. Ask sts which facts they find the most surprising and why.

Answers

2 600
3 nine
4 1.6 million
5 42
6 eleven
7 74,500
8 two

3 **Word Power** Read out the question, then ask sts to find the words in the sports map and decide which category they belong to. Allow sts to compare their answers in pairs, then check with the class. Ask questions to check that sts understand the meaning of all the words, e.g. *What do you call people who play football together?* (a team). *What do you call someone who plays tennis?* (a tennis player). *Where do you play golf?* (on a golf course), etc.

Answers

1 people
2 person/people
3 place
4 place
5 event
6 event
7 event
8 person/people

4 3.13 Sts read and listen to the sports map again and answer the questions. Allow sts to check their answers in pairs. Check answers with the class, eliciting the part of the text which confirms each answer.

Answers

1 In Gaelic football, players can kick the ball or run with it in their hands; there are fifteen players per team
2 The Old Course is the oldest golf course in the world.
3 Wimbledon
4 summer
5 singing; there are lots of fans in the stadium
6 north

1 **Work in pairs. What do you know about schools in the UK?**

2 2.12 **Read and listen to the infographic. Complete the sentences.**

1 Schools start at … a.m.
2 UK students have … hours of homework.
3 … per cent of students go to school by car.
4 … per cent of students study Spanish.

3 **Read the infographic again. Answer the questions in your notebook.**

1 What is a typical school uniform?
2 Do students have lunch at home or at school?
3 How do most students go to school?
4 Who has more homework: a British student or an American student?
5 How do dogs help in some classrooms?
6 What is the most popular foreign language in UK schools?

4 2.13 **Look at the seven topics in the infographic (*School uniform, School lunches*, etc.) Listen. What topic does each speaker talk about?**

1 Homework

5 **COMPARE CULTURES** **How is your school similar or different to typical schools in the UK? Make a list.**

Similar: We wear a uniform.
Different: We don't learn German.

6 **Work in pairs. What is a boarding school? What famous boarding schools in books or films do you know? Complete the text below with the words in the box.**

do	does	doesn't	gets
goes	has	start	study

7 **Word Power** **Read the text in Exercise 6 again. Find four places for the definitions in the text.**

1 You have lunch here.
2 There are a lot of books here. You can read or study.
3 You do Science classes here.
4 You do exercise here.

8 **GET CREATIVE** **Create a digital presentation about your school or schools in your country. Include text, pictures and charts to make it attractive. Present your work to the class.**

Lessons start at … and finish at …
Students wear / don't wear a uniform.
Most students go to school by …

Now watch the culture video.

FAST FINISHER

Imagine a funny school. Write sentences.

School starts at 10.00 p.m. We play football in the Science lab …

Life at a BOARDING SCHOOL

In the UK, a small number of students go to boarding schools – they eat, sleep and [1] … there. What's life like at a boarding school?

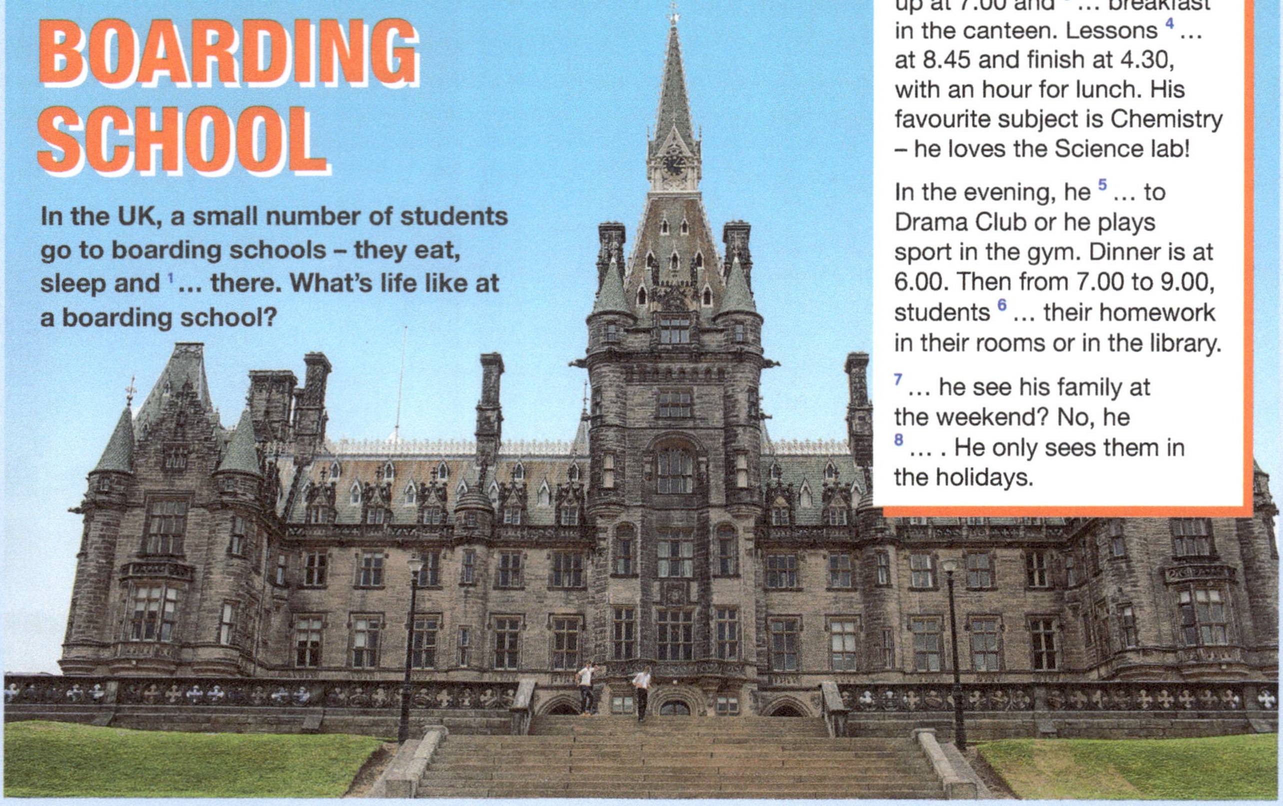

Fourteen-year-old Tom [2] … up at 7.00 and [3] … breakfast in the canteen. Lessons [4] … at 8.45 and finish at 4.30, with an hour for lunch. His favourite subject is Chemistry – he loves the Science lab!

In the evening, he [5] … to Drama Club or he plays sport in the gym. Dinner is at 6.00. Then from 7.00 to 9.00, students [6] … their homework in their rooms or in the library.

[7] … he see his family at the weekend? No, he [8] … . He only sees them in the holidays.

REAL CULTURE!

5 3.14 Focus sts' attention on the sports quiz. Explain that they are now going to test their knowledge of sport. Ask sts to copy the quiz questions into their notebooks and complete them with some of the words from Exercise 3. Check these answers, then put sts into pairs to read the questions and answer them. Play the audio for sts to listen and check their answers. See TG page 276 for audio script. Ask how many questions sts answered correctly, and see which pair got the most answers right.

Answers
1 every four years
2 player; Japanese
3 fan; Australia
3 race; triathlon
4 stadium; Rio de Janeiro
5 team; Chicago Bulls

21st Century skills

6 **COMPARE CULTURES**

Put sts into pairs or small groups. Encourage each group to brainstorm information about sports and sports events in their country first. Bring this information together into a class discussion and make notes on useful information and vocabulary on the board. Sts then work in pairs or groups to produce their map. Ask some of the more confident sts to present their maps to the rest of the class.

Culture video

You can watch this in class if you have time and access to video, or you can ask sts to download it from the Richmond Learning Platform to watch at home. See *Soccer in Soweto* on TG pages 297 and 306.

FAST FINISHER

Sts write sentences about sports from the sports map that they or their classmates play or watch. Weaker sts could work in pairs and look at the sports map again, then write two or three sentences about some of the sports and events.

EXTRA PRACTICE

Put sts into small teams and explain that they are going to do a quiz. They will need a piece of paper to write their answers on and a team name. Ask them to write the name of their team at the top of the piece of paper. Explain that all of the questions are about the sports in the text on page 36 and allow one minute for teams to quickly ready the text, then tell them to close their books. Read out the questions and allow time for teams to record their answers. Read out the correct answers (these are given in brackets).

1 What do people like to eat when they watch tennis? (strawberries)
2 How many people are in a Gaelic football team? (15)
3 What colour shirts do Manchester United and Manchester City wear? (red and blue)
4 Which country is the home of golf? (Scotland)
5 Why do cricket players stop their game in the middle of the day? (to eat)
6 Where is rugby popular? (Wales)
7 How long in kilometres is the London Marathon? (42 km)
8 What water sport is popular in Newquay? (surfing)

My school day

WRITING An email

I can write an email about my school day.

1 **Look at the message. Who is it from? What's unusual about it?**

MESSAGE FROM THE FUTURE

From: Alex Cole
Date: 14 October 2056

Hi there!

I'm Alex. I'm fourteen years old and I go to school in Sky City.

I want to tell you about my day. I get up at 9.30 and have breakfast. I go to school by drone. I meet my friends and we chat about our pet robots.

School starts at 11.00. My favourite day is Wednesday. We have Computer Science in the morning, and Space Studies in the afternoon.

After school, I play virtual reality sport or I go to a club. I go to Robotics Club on Monday and Time Travel Club on Thursday. In the evening, I do my homework. I go to bed at 10.30.

That's my day! Write soon and tell me about your day.

Bye for now,

Alex

2 **Read the message and find three differences between Alex's day and your day. Tell your partner.**

I don't get up at 9.30 on a school day. I get up at 7.00.

3 **Look at the Useful language. How do you say these expressions in your language?**

Useful language

Starting and finishing an email

Hi there / Hi ... / Dear ...	Bye for now
I want to tell you about ...	Best wishes
Write soon	

4 **Study the Look! box. Find an example of each preposition in Alex's email.**

Look! Prepositions of time

We use prepositions of time to help us talk about when something happens.

***at** 9.30, **at** 11.00*
***in** the morning, **in** the afternoon, **in** the evening*
***on** Friday, **on** Saturday*
BUT: ***at** night, **at** the weekend*

5 **Complete the sentences with the correct preposition.**

1 Alex has lunch ... one o'clock.
2 ... Tuesday, he has History and Art.
3 Alex tidies his room ... the weekend.
4 He doesn't listen to music ... the evening.
5 Alex's pet robot sleeps in Alex's bedroom ... night.

6 **Write an email to Alex about your school day. Follow the steps in the Writing plan.**

Writing plan

Prepare

› Make notes about your school day.
 • What time do you get up / start school?
 • How do you go to school?
 • What is your favourite school day / lesson? Why?
› What do you do after school?

Write

› Organize your ideas into three paragraphs:
 • Before school • During school • After school
› Use the expressions from the Useful language box.

Reflect

› Check your grammar: Present simple
› Check prepositions of time.
› Check your spelling.

W Writing summary: WB p.85   E Exams: Unit 2 SB p.119   LS Language summary: Unit 2 SB p.128

EXTRA PRACTICE Workbook page 28; photocopiable activities for Unit 3: vocabulary, grammar and skills

A typical weekend

WRITING A blog post

Sts read a blog post about a typical weekend. They learn expressions of frequency and study the use of punctuation in English. They then follow the steps in the Writing plan to write a blog post about their typical weekend.

Writing

A blog post

Useful language

Expressions of frequency (*Every Saturday/Sunday/weekend, I ...; Once a month, Twice a week, I ...;I always/usually/often/sometimes/never ...*)

Look!

Punctuation

WARMER

Say: *What do you usually do at the weekend? Do you play sports? Do you meet your friends?* Elicit ideas and encourage sts to use some of the adverbs of frequency they learned on page 31, e.g. *I sometimes go shopping. I usually play tennis.*

1 Focus on the blog post and teach the meaning of *typical*. Look at the mind map and explain that it shows Molly's notes before she wrote her blog post. Ask sts to read the blog post, then copy the mind map into their notebooks and complete it with the correct information, then do Molly's mind map for Sunday. Check answers.

Answers

1 park, cinema, café 2 friends

Sunday

What: Sunday lunch, homework, writes a blog

Who with: Molly's grandparents

Where: Molly's house

2 Put sts into pairs to ask and answer the questions. Ask some sts to tell the class what their partner usually does.

3 Read the Useful language box with sts. Ask how they say these expressions in their first language. Refer sts back to the blog post and ask them to find some of the expressions. Elicit or point out that expressions of frequency such as *every Saturday, once a month*, etc. go at the beginning of a sentence or after the verb, but adverbs of frequency go before the main verb or after the verb *be*. Write one or two simple sentences on the board to demonstrate, e.g. *I play tennis every Saturday. Every Saturday, I play tennis. I always play tennis. Tennis is always fun.*

4 Read the Look! box with sts about punctuation. Sts find an example of each type of punctuation in the blog post. Elicit these from the class and make sure sts can all see the punctuation marks in context. Point out that we use a comma after expressions of frequency when they are at the beginning of a sentences, e.g. *Once a month, my grandparents come ... .*

5 Ask sts to copy the sentences in their notebooks and complete them with the correct punctuation. Invite individual sts to come and write the sentences on the board.

Answers

1 Where do you do gymnastics?
2 That's amazing!
3 I sometimes play tennis with my mum, dad and brother.
4 Where does your best friend live?

6 Ask sts to write a blog post about their typical weekend following the steps in the Writing plan.

Writing plan

Prepare

Sts work as individuals and make a mind map about their weekend. Monitor while they are working, and help with vocabulary if necessary.

Write

Sts write their blog post using Molly's post in Exercise 1 as a model. They should write two short paragraphs: one about what they usually do on Saturday and one about what they usually do on Sunday. Refer them back to the Useful language box and encourage them to use expressions of frequency in their forum post. Refer them back to the Look! box and encourage them to check their punctuation. Encourage them also to use some of the sports vocabulary from page 29 and *like / don't like*.

Reflect

Ask sts to check their grammar, spelling and punctuation and make any necessary changes. Then, in pairs, sts could swap their blog posts with a partner and give feedback on the use of expressions of frequency and punctuation. Remind sts that they should always be positive and encouraging when they give feedback to a partner.

W **Writing practice: WB** p.28. There is more practice for writing in the Workbook. Set these exercises for homework.

W **Writing summary: WB** p.86

R **Review: Units 1–3 SB** pp.100–101

P **Project: Units 1–3 SB** pp.106–107

L **Literature: SB** pp.112–113

E **Exams: Unit 3 SB** p.120

LS **Language summary:** SB p.129

Out and about

4

Vocabulary: Places in a city; The weather | **Grammar:** Present continuous; Present continuous and present simple | **Speaking:** Asking for and giving directions | **Writing:** A text message

VOCABULARY Places in a city

I can describe my town or city.

1 4.1 **Complete the website with eight of the words in the box. Listen and check.**

castle department store hotel library market monument museum restaurant shopping centre square theatre train station

What's On | Inside Tips | Things to do | Maps

Things to do in Dublin

Are you planning a visit to Dublin?

Click on the pictures for more information.

Explore a [1] …

Stay in a [2] …

Watch a play at the [3] …

Walk round a [4] …

Eat in a [5] …

Spend a day at a [6] …

Go shopping at a [7] …

Visit a famous [8] …

2 4.2 **Listen to eight dialogues. Where are the people? Choose words from Exercise 1.**

3 **In pairs, think of more places in a town or city.**

café, stadium, …

4 **Discuss your town or city. What is there to do?**

There are some cafés and restaurants in the main square.

There isn't a shopping centre, but there's a department store.

Now watch the vlog.

FAST FINISHER

Imagine you are the mayor of your town or city. Write three things you want to do.

I want to build an IMAX cinema with a big screen and comfortable sofas.

LS **Language summary: Unit 4** SB p.130

EXTRA PRACTICE Workbook page 32

Out and about

4

UNIT 4 OVERVIEW: This unit focuses on the topic of travel and tourism. Sts read about a jetpack tour of Paris, and listen to a conversation about the weather in different parts of the world. They read a tourist map and learn how to ask for and give directions. They read about the seasons in New York and finally, they read a text message by someone who is visiting a place, then imagine they are visiting a different city and write their own text message from there. They also watch a vlog about someone's recent trip to Paris and a culture video about visiting tourist attractions in the UK.

Vocabulary	Grammar	Pronunciation	Reading	Listening	Speaking	Writing
Places in a city; The weather	Present continuous; Present continuous and present simple	/ŋ/	Using existing knowledge to help understand a text	Listening for time expressions	Asking for and giving directions	A text message

VOCABULARY Places in a city

Sts learn nouns for the names of 12 places in a city. They listen to dialogues and guess where the people are, then personalise the vocabulary by talking about things there are to do in their own city.

Vocabulary

Places in a city (*castle, department store, hotel, library, market, monument, museum, restaurant, shopping centre, square, theatre, train station*)

Vlog

Natalie: *My top five things in Paris*

WARMER

Ask: *Do you live in a city, a town or a village?* Encourage sts to use full sentences when they answer. As they answer, ask additional questions, e.g. *Is your city big or small? What things can you do there?* Use these questions and sts' answers to revise *can* and *can't* and assess what vocabulary for places in a city sts already know.

1 4.1 Read through the words in the box and elicit or teach the meanings. Sts match eight of the words to the pictures. Play the audio for sts to listen and check.

Answers

1	museum	5	restaurant
2	hotel	6	castle
3	theatre	7	shopping centre
4	market	8	monument

2 4.2 Explain to sts that they will hear eight short dialogues in different places in a city, and they need to say where the people are. Play the audio. See TG pages 276–277 for audio script. Allow sts to compare their answers in pairs, then check answers.

Answers

1	a restaurant	5	a theatre
2	a train station	6	a department store
3	a library	7	a hotel
4	a market	8	a monument

3 Put sts into pairs to think of more places in a city. Elicit sts' ideas and write them on the board. Check that sts understand them all.

Possible answers

swimming pool, sports centre, park, cinema, university, bus station, airport

4 Read out the example answers and briefly revise the use of *there is / there are* if necessary. Elicit one or two more examples of things that there are and aren't in the sts' own city. Then put sts into pairs to discuss. Ask some sts to tell the class some of the things they discussed.

Vlog

This lesson features a vlog in which vlogger Natalie talks about her recent trip to Paris. You can watch this in class if you have time and access to video, or you can ask sts to download it from the Richmond Learning Platform to watch at home. See TG pages 289 and 304.

FAST FINISHER

Sts imagine they are mayor of their town or city and write three things they want to do. Weaker sts could work in pairs.

EXTRA PRACTICE

In pairs, sts imagine they are a city guide, talking about their city and explaining all the things visitors can do. Elicit some examples first, e.g. *There's a big shopping mall. You can go shopping there. You can eat in lots of restaurants.* Sts take turns to talk while their partner films them using their phone. They can watch their films back and discuss in their pairs how they could improve.

V **Vocabulary practice: WB** p.32

Sts will find more practice for vocabulary for places in a city here. Set these exercises for homework.

LS **Language summary: Unit 4 SB** p.130

A city tour

READING

I can use existing knowledge to help me understand a text.

HOME ABOUT ME LATEST POSTS

Leo's Blog

Paris by jetpack!

I'm in France on a school trip. Today we're in the French capital, Paris. But we aren't walking or taking a bus tour. Instead, we're exploring the city by jetpack!

12.15 p.m. We're putting on our seatbelts and getting ready for our flight. '5-4-3-2-1 ... lift off!'

12.17 p.m. This is amazing – I'm flying over Paris! Below us, people are walking in the streets and sitting outside restaurants. There's an old man reading a newspaper in the park.

12.20 p.m. We're now flying over the Louvre, the world's biggest art museum. The views are incredible. Look, there's the Arc de Triomphe! Some tourists are taking photos and a girl is buying an ice cream.

12.25 p.m. We're travelling really fast now, and in front of us is the Eiffel Tower. There's a lift that goes to the top, but a few people are climbing the 1,665 stairs!

12.30 p.m. Our tour is over. And it's time to tell you the truth. We aren't really flying jetpacks – we're at *Flyview®*, a virtual reality attraction in the centre of Paris, and we're wearing virtual reality headsets. It's a great way to see the city.

1 **Work in pairs. Before you read, discuss the questions about the blog.**

1 What do you know about Paris? What country is it in? What are some of its famous monuments?
2 Look at the jetpack in the picture. What can you do with a jetpack?

2 4.3 **Read and listen to the blog. What is special about Leo's tour of Paris?**

3 **Read the blog again and answer the questions.**

1 Why is Leo in Paris?
2 How long is the jetpack tour?
3 Leo sees lots of people on the ground.
  a What is the old man reading?
  b What is the girl buying?
  c What are people climbing?
4 What is Leo's opinion of the tour?

4 **Word Power** **Copy and complete the nationalities. Put the missing letters in the correct order to spell another European capital city. What country is it in?**

1 Fre◯ch
2 P◯lish
3 ◯razilian
4 Ita◯ian
5 Russ◯an
6 ◯panish

5 **THINK CRITICALLY** **In your opinion, what is the best way to explore a city and why? By bus, on foot or another way?**

6 **FIND OUT** **How tall is the Eiffel Tower? How many people visit it a year?**

EXTRA PRACTICE Workbook page 33

A city tour

READING

Sts read a blog by Leo about a jetpack tour of Paris and focus on using existing knowledge to help them understand a text. They learn to use affirmative and negative forms of the present continuous and practise the /ŋ/ sound. They then practise using the present continuous to talk about things that are happening now by saying what they and their family are doing now.

Reading text
A blog by Leo, a teenage boy, about a jetpack tour of Paris

Reading skill
Using existing knowledge to help me understand a text

Pronunciation
the /ŋ/ sound

WARMER

Ask: *How can people travel around your city?* Elicit a range of answers and revise words for forms of transport if necessary, e.g. *by bus, by metro, on foot, by bike.* Ask: *How do you usually travel around your city? Which forms of transport do you enjoy? Which don't you like? Why?* Elicit answers from individual sts and encourage them to give reasons for their answers.

1 **Using existing knowledge to help understand a text** Ask sts to look at the pictures. Elicit or explain that the city in the picture is Paris, and the other picture shows a person wearing a *jetpack*. Point out the jetpack, but don't explain what it is for. Explain to sts that before they read a text, it is a good idea to think about what they already know about the topic of the text. Read out the title of the blog, then read out the two questions. Put sts into pairs to discuss the questions. Get feedback on their discussions, and bring sts' knowledge together collectively into a class discussion.

Possible answers
1 France; Eiffel Tower, Arc de Triomphe, The Louvre, etc.
2 (especially in science fiction) You can fly.

2 4.3 Read out the question, then play the audio for sts to read and listen to the blog. Check the answer to the question, then ask: *Do you think it helps to think about what you know before you read? Why?*

Answers
It is a virtual reality tour at a virtual reality attraction in the centre of Paris called *Flyview®*.

3 Ask sts to read through the questions. Check they understand everything. Sts read the blog again and answer the questions. Check answers.

Answers
1 He's on a school trip.
2 15 minutes.
3 a A newspaper
  b An ice cream
  c The Eiffel Tower
4 It is a great way to see the city.

4 **Word Power** Ask sts to copy the nationalities into their notebooks and complete them with the correct letters, then use the letters to make another European city. You could do this activity as a race, to make it more motivating. Check answers with the class.

Answers
1 French
2 Polish
3 Brazilian
4 Italian
5 Russian
6 Spanish
Lisbon–Portugal

21st Century skills

5 **THINK CRITICALLY**
Read out the questions, then put sts into pairs or small groups to discuss them. You could teach or revise a few phrases for giving opinions first, e.g. *I think ..., For me, ..., In my opinion, ...* Ask sts to note down opinions they agree about and their reasons. Ask groups in turn to tell the class their opinions and reasons.

EXTRA PRACTICE

You could ask sts to imagine a jetpack tour of their city. Discuss as a class what they would see and what things would be fun to fly over.

21st Century skills

6 **FIND OUT**
Set this exercise for homework if you prefer. Sts can find this information out by looking online or in other media, or by asking other people. The answers to the questions are: 324m; about 6.9 million people.

You could also ask sts to find out about another of the places in Leo's blog, e.g. the Louvre or the Arc de Triomphe.

R **Reading practice: WB** p.33
You will find more practice for reading here. Set these exercises for homework.

GRAMMAR Present continuous: affirmative and negative

I can use the present continuous to talk about things that are happening now.

Now watch the grammar animation.

1 Read the grammar box. Write the *-ing* form of the verbs in the box.

have leave read sit swim watch

Affirmative

I'**m flying** over Paris.
He/She/It'**s buying** an ice cream.
You/We/They'**re putting** on our seatbelts.

Negative

I'**m not taking** a bus tour.
He/She/It **isn't taking** a photo.
We/You/They **aren't walking**.

2 PRONUNCIATION /ŋ/

4.4 Listen and repeat.

reading walking taking climbing putting

3 4.5 Listen and repeat.

1 I'm not walking, I'm flying!
2 We're having a fantastic time!

4 4.6 Leo can see these people from his 'jetpack'. Write sentences and match them with the pictures. Listen and check.

1 She's walking to work. Picture c.

1 She / walk to work
2 They / play a game
3 He / run
4 She / go to a party
5 She / ride a bike
6 We / have fun on the river
7 He / play the trumpet
8 I / read a book

5 Write an affirmative and negative sentence about each picture in Exercise 4.

Picture a: read a comic / a book
He isn't reading a comic. He's reading a book.

1 Picture b: play the guitar / the trumpet
2 Picture c: look at her phone / her watch
3 Picture d: walk / run
4 Picture e: play tennis / table tennis
5 Picture f: carry a cake / balloons
6 Picture g: travel by jetpack / by canoe
7 Picture h: wear a hat / a helmet

6 Imagine you and your family are at the places on page 39. Write sentences about what you're doing.

My sister is watching a concert at the theatre.
My dad is having a pizza in a restaurant.

7 Work in pairs. Say what you and your family are doing, but don't say the place. Can your partner guess?

A: My sister is watching a concert.
B: Is she at the theatre?

FUN FACT

The *Mona Lisa* is the most famous painting in the Louvre Museum. But look carefully! She hasn't got any eyebrows. And is she smiling or is she sad? Art experts can't agree. What do you think?

FAST FINISHER

Choose a town or city and imagine you're spending a day there. Write sentences about what you're doing at different times.

10.00 I'm visiting the Picasso Museum in Málaga.

LS Language summary: Unit 4 SB p.130

EXTRA PRACTICE Workbook page 34

GRAMMAR Present continuous: affirmative and negative

Grammar animation

This lesson features an optional animated presentation of the grammar in context called *Drew is playing the guitar!* including the use of the present continuous. You can watch this in class if you have time and access to a computer or tablet, or you can ask sts to download it from the Richmond Learning Platform to watch at home. See TG page 309 for animation script.

1 Read the grammar box about the present continuous with sts. Point out that there are two parts to the present continuous form: the correct part of the verb *be* and the verb with an *-ing* ending. Ask sts to check the spelling rules on page 130, then write the *-ing* forms of the verbs. Check answers by writing the *-ing* forms on the board.

Answers
having, leaving, reading, sitting, swimming, watching

To check the form, write a simple gapped sentence on the board, e.g. I … *(walk) around Paris*. With the class, elicit the correct present continuous form: *I am walking around Paris*. Change the subject of the sentence to *he/she* and then to *we* and elicit the necessary changes to the verb form. Then write X next to the sentence and elicit the negative forms. Each time, focus on which parts change and which parts stay the same.

Ask questions to check concept.

Concept check questions: We're studying English – does that mean we study English often, or does it mean we're doing it right now? (right now). My dad sitting at home – correct? (no – My dad *is sitting* at home).

2 **PRONUNCIATION** 4.4
Model and drill pronunciation of the /ŋ/ sound in isolation. Point out that this sound is used in the *-ing* form of verbs in the present continuous, and point out that it is also used in the names of some of the sports they learned in the last unit, e.g. *skateboarding*. Play the audio for sts to repeat.

3 4.5
Play the audio once for sts to listen and read the sentences, and notice the pronunciation. Play the audio again for them to repeat.

4 4.6 Read the example with the class and show how it matches picture c. Ask sts to write the remaining sentences in their notebooks and match them with the pictures. Sts compare their answers in pairs, then play the audio for them to listen and check. See TG page 277 for audio script. Check answers.

Answers
2 They're playing a game. – e
3 He's running. – d
4 She's going to a party. – f
5 She's riding a bike. – h
6 We're having fun on the river. – g
7 He's playing the trumpet. – b
8 I'm reading a book. – a

5 Read out the example sentences and point out how they refer to picture *a*. Ask sts to write the affirmative and negative sentences in their notebooks. Check answers.

Answers
1 He isn't playing the guitar. He's playing the trumpet.
2 She isn't looking at her phone. She's looking at her watch.
3 He isn't walking. He's running.
4 They aren't playing tennis. They're playing table tennis.
5 She isn't carrying a cake. She's carrying balloons.
6 They aren't travelling by jetpack. They're travelling by canoe.
7 She isn't wearing a hat. She's wearing a helmet.

6 Focus on one or two more places of the places on page 39 and ask: *Who is at (the shopping centre / a famous monument)?* Elicit sentences about these places. Sts then write sentences about themselves and members of their own family.

7 Demonstrate the task by reading out the example, then saying a sentence using a different place, e.g. *My brother is having lunch*. Elicit the answer (Is he in a restaurant?). Sts work in pairs and take turns to say what they and their family are doing. Their partner guesses the places. At the end, ask who guessed all their partner's places correctly.

FUN FACT Encourage sts to read this fun fact for pleasure. They might also be interested to know that experts disagree about the Mona Lisa's eyebrows. Some think that she hasn't got any because they weren't fashionable at that time, so women removed them. Others think that she did originally have eyebrows, but they have gradually faded over time.

FAST FINISHER
Sts imagine they are spending a day in another city and write sentences about what they are doing. Weaker sts can work in pairs.

G Grammar practice: WB p.34
Sts will find more practice for the present continuous here. Set these exercises for homework.

LS Language summary Unit 4 SB p.130

Is it snowing over there?

VOCABULARY and LISTENING The weather

I can listen for time expressions.

1 4.7 **Match the phrases in the box with the pictures. Listen, check and repeat.**

It's cloudy.	It's cold.	It's foggy.	It's hot.
It's icy.	It's raining.	It's snowing.	It's stormy.
It's sunny.	It's warm.	It's windy.	

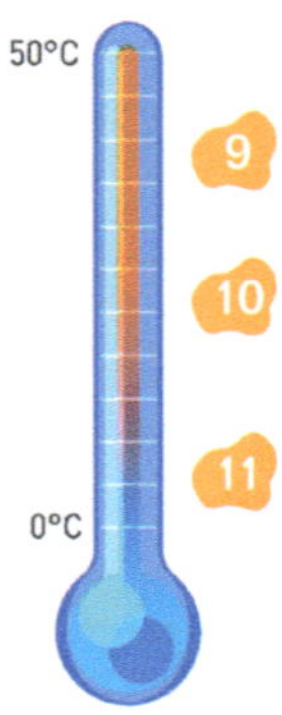

2 Work in pairs. What's the weather like today where you are?

It's cold and cloudy this morning.

LS Language summary: Unit 4 SB p.130

3 Read the Look! box. In pairs, ask and answer the questions.

> **Look!** *rain and snow*
>
> *Rain* and *snow* are verbs. We use *It's raining* and *It's snowing* to talk about the weather now.
> We use *It rains* or *It snows* to talk about the weather in general: *It often snows in winter.*

1 Does it rain a lot in your town? In which months does it rain the most?
2 Does it sometimes snow in your country in winter? In which regions does it snow a lot?

4 4.8 **Liv is calling her Australian cousin, Josh. Listen and answer the questions.**

1 Why is Liv calling Josh?
2 What time is it in Glasgow?
3 What time is it in Perth?
4 Where is Josh?
5 What is Liv doing at the moment?

Liv (Glasgow, UK)

Josh (Perth, Australia)

5 4.8 **Listen again. Are the sentences true (T) or false (F)? Correct the false sentences.**

It's windy in Perth.
F. It's hot and sunny.

1 It's snowing in Glasgow.
2 Josh is surfing and playing volleyball.
3 At Christmas, Josh usually has a picnic or a barbecue on the beach.
4 Josh's mum and dad are good at surfing.
5 Liv's dad is cleaning the kitchen.

6 4.8 **Listen again and complete the sentences with time expressions.**

1 Is it snowing ...?
2 It ... snows in Perth!
3 What are you doing ..., Josh?
4 Do you ... go to the beach on Christmas Day?
5 What are you doing ..., Liv?

EXTRA PRACTICE Workbook page 35

Is it snowing over there?

VOCABULARY and LISTENING
The weather

Sts listen to a phone conversation between cousins in different parts of the world, and focus on listening for time expressions. They learn vocabulary for weather and learn the question forms of the present continuous, then focus on the difference between the present simple and present continuous.

Vocabulary
The weather (*it's cloudy, it's cold, It's foggy, It's hot, It's icy, It's raining, It's snowing, It's stormy, It's sunny, It's warm, It's windy*)

Listening text
A phone conversation between people in different parts of the world

Listening skill
Listening for time expressions

Look!
rain and *snow*

WARMER
With books closed, put sts into teams. Tell them you are going to say the name of a person and a place and they must race to make a correct sentence about what the person is doing there. Do an example first, e.g. *My brother / the theatre – He's watching a play*. Call out names or words for family members and some of the places on page 39. Sts race to say a correct sentence about what the person is doing. Use the game as a way of checking how able sts are to use the present continuous correctly.

1 4.7 Read through the phrases in the box and elicit or teach the meanings. Sts match the phrases with the pictures. Play the audio. See TG page 277 for audio script. Sts listen and check their answers. Play the audio again for sts to repeat the words.

Answers
1 It's sunny.
2 It's cloudy.
3 It's windy.
4 It's raining.
5 It's snowing.
6 It's foggy.
7 It's icy.
8 It's stormy.
9 It's hot.
10 It's warm.
11 It's cold.

2 Sts work in pairs to say what the weather is like where they are today. Elicit the answer.

3 Read through the Look! box with the class. Then put sts into pairs to ask and answer the questions. Encourage them to answer using full sentences. Elicit answers from the class.

4 4.8 Explain to sts that they are going to hear a phone dialogue between two cousins who live in different parts of the world. Focus attention on the pictures and model pronunciation of the people's names and the city names. Allow sts time to read through the questions, then play the audio for sts to listen and answer the questions. See TG pages 277 for audio script. Check answers with the class.

Answers
1 Liv is calling because it's Christmas.
2 It's 8 a.m.
3 It's 4 p.m.
4 He's at the beach.
5 Helping her dad in the kitchen.

5 4.8 Allow sts time to read through the sentences, then play the audio again for them to listen and decide if the sentences are true or false, and correct the false sentences. Allow sts to compare their answers in pairs, then check answers with the class, playing the audio again and pausing to confirm the answers.

Answers
1 T
2 F (Josh is surfing and swimming)
3 T
4 F (They aren't very good at surfing)
5 F (Liv's dad is cooking lunch)

6 4.8 **Listening for time expressions** Ask sts to read through the gapped sentences and copy them into their notebooks. Ask: *What kind of information is missing?* Elicit that the missing words are all time expressions. Remind sts that for this kind of task they need to listen very carefully to hear the specific information they need. Play the audio again for sts to listen and complete the time expressions. Check answers with the class, and check that sts understand all the time expressions.

Answers
1 Is it snowing **at the moment**?
2 It **never** snows in Perth!
3 What are you doing **today**, Josh?
4 Do you **always** go to the beach on Christmas Day?
5 What are you doing **right now**, Liv?

V L **Vocabulary and Listening practice:** WB p.35
Sts will find more practice for listening, and practice of vocabulary for the weather here. Set these exercises for homework.

LS **Language summary: Unit 4 SB** p.130

GRAMMAR

Present continuous: questions

I can ask questions using the present continuous.

Now watch the grammar animation.

1 **Copy and complete the grammar box with *are, aren't, is, isn't* and *am*.**

Questions	Short answers
Are you **having** a nice day?	Yes, I [1] ... . / No, I'**m not**.
[2] ... your dad **cooking**?	Yes, he **is**. /No, he **isn't**.
Is it **snowing**?	Yes, it **is**. / No, it [3] ... .
[4] ... they **surfing**?	Yes, they **are**. /No, they [5] ... .

2 **In your notebook, complete the questions and short answers.**

Is it *snowing* in Glasgow? (snow)
Yes, *it is*.

1 .... it ... in Perth? (rain)
No, ...

2 ... Josh's parents ...? (surf)
Yes, ...

3 **Josh:** ... you ... lunch at the moment? (have)
Liv: No, I ... .

4 ... Liv's dad ... lunch? (cook)
Yes, ...

3 **Write questions and answers about what is happening now at school.**

you / write in your notebook?
Are you writing in your notebook? Yes, I am.

1 you / wear trainers?
2 it / rain?
3 What / your teacher / wear?
4 Who / you and your friends / talk to?
5 Who / you / sit next to?

4 **Work in pairs. Choose an activity from the box below and mime it. Can your partner guess the activity?**

climb a mountain   cook dinner   do yoga
do your homework   get dressed   go to bed
have lunch   listen to music   play a video game
play ice hockey   ride a horse   swim
take a photo   tidy your room   use a computer

A: Are you swimming?
B: No, I'm not.
A: Are you riding a horse?
B: Yes, I am!

Present continuous and present simple

I can use the present continuous and present simple.

5 **Read the grammar box. Complete the rules with *present simple* or *present continuous*.**

Present continuous	Present simple
We'**re having** a picnic on the beach today.	We usually **have** a picnic on the beach.
It'**s snowing** now.	It never **snows** in Perth.
What **are** you **doing** at the moment?	What **do** you usually **do** at the weekend?

Rules

We use the [1] ... for things that we are doing now.
We use the [2] ... for things that we do regularly.

6 **Choose the correct answers.**

1 My dad *is having* / *has* a shower at the moment.
2 I *am often going* / *often go* to the beach.
3 Oh no, *it's raining!* / *it rains!* Quick, let's go home.
4 It *isn't usually snowing* / *doesn't usually snow* in summer.
5 They *are playing* / *play* tennis in the park right now.

7 **Complete the blog. Use the present simple or present continuous.**

A WEEKEND AWAY!

The Ross Family are spending the weekend at a holiday park. There's lots to do.

Lottie usually *plays* (play) volleyball on Saturday, but at the moment she [1] ... (learn) to climb. It's difficult, but she [2] ... (have) fun!

Dylan usually [3] ... (get up) late and then he sometimes [4] ... (meet) his friends. Today he [5] ... (paddleboard). The water's warm, so he [6] ... (not wear) a wetsuit.

At the weekend, Mr and Mrs Ross usually [7] ... (go) shopping. Right now, they [8] ... (relax) outside.

FAST FINISHER

Imagine you're enjoying your dream weekend. What are you doing? What do you usually do?

On Saturday, I usually go shopping. But today I'm playing the guitar in a rock band!

LS Language summary: Unit 4 SB p.130

GRAMMAR Present continuous: questions

Grammar animation

This lesson features an optional animated presentation of the grammar in context called *Is it snowing now?* including the form and use of questions in the present continuous, and present continuous and present simple. You can watch these in class if you have time and access to a computer or tablet, or you can ask sts to download them from the Richmond Learning Platform to watch at home. See TG page 309 for animation script.

1 Read the grammar box with sts about questions in the present continuous. Draw attention to the word order in questions, with the subject coming before the verb, e.g. *Is it raining?* NOT ~~*It is raining?*~~ Point out that we don't usually repeat the main verb in short answers, e.g. Yes, *it is*. NOT ~~*Yes, it is raining*~~. Sts complete the grammar box. Check answers, then ask questions to check concept.

Concept check questions: *Are you watching TV? – am I asking about your usual habits, or something that is happening now?* (something that is happening now). *What you are doing? – correct?* (no – *What are you doing?*) *It snowing now? – correct?* (no – *Is it snowing now?*)

Answers
1 am 2 Is 3 isn't 4 Are 5 aren't

2 Remind sts of the dialogue they listened to between Liv and Josh, and explain that these questions and answers come from that dialogue. Ask sts to write the questions and answers. Check answers.

Answers
1 **Is** it **raining** in Perth? No, **it isn't**.
2 **Are** Josh' parents **surfing**? Yes, **they are**.
3 Josh: **Are** you **having** lunch at the moment? Liv: No, **I'm not**.
4 **Is** Liv's dad **cooking** lunch? Yes, **he is**.

3 Read the example with the class, then ask sts to write the questions and answers in their notebooks. Allow sts to check in pairs, then check with the class.

Answers
1 Are you wearing trainers?
2 Is it raining?
3 What is your teacher wearing?
4 Who are you and your friends talking to?
5 Who are you sitting next to?

4 Demonstrate the activity by miming *swimming* and *riding a horse*, then reading out the example question and answer. Put sts into pairs to take turns to mime and guess the activity. Monitor while sts are working. End by correcting any mistakes you noticed while sts were working.

Present continuous and present simple

5 Read the grammar box with sts about the present continuous and present simple. Point out that the different tenses are used with different time expressions. Elicit which time expressions are used with each (present continuous: *today, at the moment, now;* present simple: *usually, never*). Then ask sts to copy the rules into their notebooks and complete them with the correct tense names. Check answers.

Answers
1 present continuous
2 present simple

Concept check questions: *What do you do on Saturdays? – present continuous or present simple?* (present simple). *What are you doing now? – present continuous or present simple?* (present continuous). *Which tense do we use for things that are happening right now?* (present continuous). *Which tense do we use for things we often or usually do?* (present simple).

6 Ask sts to read the sentences and choose the correct verb forms. Tell them they can use the time expressions to help them choose the correct verb form. Check answers with the class.

Answers
1 is having
2 often go
3 it's raining!
4 doesn't usually snow
5 are playing

7 Check sts understand *paddleboard*. Ask sts to read the blog and complete it with the correct verb forms. Check answers.

Answers
1 's/is learning
2 's/is having
3 gets up
4 meets
5 's/is paddleboarding
6 isn't wearing
7 go
8 're/are relaxing

FAST FINISHER

Sts imagine their dream weekend and write sentences about things they usually do and things they are doing this weekend. Weaker sts could work in pairs. They refer back to the blog in Exercise 7. They imagine they are Lottie or Dylan and write two sentences about things they usually do, and two sentences about things they are doing this weekend.

G **Grammar practice: WB** p.36
Sts will find more practice for present continuous questions and the present continuous and present simple here. Set these exercises for homework.

LS **Language summary: Unit 4 SB** p.130

KEEP TALKING!

Is it far?

READING and LISTENING A tourist map

I can understand information on a tourist map.

1 Look at the map of Oxford. Where can you go to ...

change some money? *the bank*

1 have a picnic?
2 learn about animals and plants?
3 travel to another city?
4 buy a book?
5 ask about places to visit in Oxford?

2 Read the Look! box. Use the words in bold to complete sentences 1–4 about the map.

> **Look!** **Prepositions**
>
> We use prepositions to talk about where something is.
> *The art museum is **opposite** the hotel.*
> *The hotel is **next to** the bus station.*
> *The bank is **near** the department store.*
> *The market is **between** the bank and the library.*

1 The Natural History Museum is ... the park.
2 The market is ... the hotel.
3 The shopping centre is ... the department store.
4 The university library is ... the market and a café.

3 4.9 **Listen to a tour guide in Oxford. Where does the tour start? Which places does it visit?**

4 4.9 **Listen again and choose the correct answer.**

1 The theatre is more than ... years old.
 a 250 b 350
2 The seats in the theatre are ... .
 a comfortable b uncomfortable
3 The bookshop sells ... .
 a all types of books b only children's books
4 Inside the bookshop, there is a ... .
 a cake shop b café
5 The tour guide's favourite things at the museum are ... .
 a the insects b the dinosaurs

5 COMPARE CULTURES What are the main tourist attractions in your town or city? What can tourists see or do there?

KEEP TALKING! Is it far?

READING and LISTENING
A tourist map

Sts study a tourist map of Oxford and listen to a tour guide taking tourists around the city, then talk about tourist attractions in their own town or city. They then learn how to ask for and give directions. They read and hear a model dialogue and personalise the useful language by following the steps in the Speaking plan.

WARMER
Ask: *What do you enjoy doing when you visit a city? Shopping? Visiting museums? Eating in restaurants?* Elicit a few ideas, then ask: *How do you find your way to places in a new city? Do you use a map? Your phone? What do you do if you get lost?* Elicit a range of answers, and introduce the idea of asking for directions. Tell sts they are going to practise asking for and giving directions in English.

1 Focus on the tourist map with the class. Put sts into pairs to look at the map and answer the questions. Check answers and check that sts understand all the places on the map.

Answers
1 the park
2 the Natural History Museum
3 the bus station
4 the bookshop
5 the Tourist Information Office

2 Read the Look! box with sts about prepositions. Use the map to teach the meaning of each preposition. Sts then look at the map and complete the sentences with the correct prepositions. Check answers. To check that sts have understood the meanings, take a classroom object, e.g. a bag or a book. Place it in different positions and say two statements about each position, one true and one false. Sts can race to choose the correct sentence. For example, place it between two sts and say: *The bag is opposite Tomas and Andrea. The bag is between Tomas and Andrea*. Sts choose the correct sentences. Alternatively, you could ask individual sts to stand up and to go and stand in particular positions, e.g. *Go and stand next to Ana. Go and stand between George and Hana*.

Answers
1 next to
2 near
3 opposite/across from
4 between

3 4.9 Explain to sts that they are going to hear a tour guide taking a group of tourists around the city. Read out the questions, then play the audio. See TG pages 277 for audio script. Sts listen and note down the answers. Check answers.

Answers
It starts at the Tourist Information office. It visits the theatre, the bookshop and the Natural History Museum.

4 4.9 Allow sts time to read the sentences and possible answers. Elicit how to say the two numbers in sentence 1. Play the audio again for sts to listen and choose the correct answers. Check answers, playing the audio again and pausing if necessary to confirm the answers.

Answers
1 b 2 b 3 a 4 b 5 b

21st Century skills

5 **COMPARE CULTURES**
Put sts into pairs or small groups and ask them to brainstorm a list of tourist attractions in their town or city and discuss what tourists can do there. You could brainstorm some categories for them to think about as a class first, e.g. museums, theatres, cinemas, natural places to visit, historical places, places where there are sports events, theme parks, places where there are music events, etc. Ask pairs or groups in turn to tell the class their ideas. As a class, discuss all the tourist attractions and try to agree on the top five.

EXTRA PRACTICE
Sts work individually and draw a map showing their house / flat and the area around it. They make a note of any places (buildings, parks, etc.) that they visit, why they go there and who they go with. Arrange sts in pairs or small groups to take turns describing the area where they live. Sts could take turns to film each other using their phones and watch the films back, then discuss how they could improve their descriptions.

SPEAKING Asking for and giving directions

I can ask for and give directions.

1 4.10 **Listen and read. A visitor to Oxford is at the bus station. Where does she want to go?**

Visitor: Excuse me. I'm looking for the Rose Café.
Sam: Hmm, let me think. Oh yes, it's on High Street.
Visitor: Is it far?
Sam: No, it's a ten-minute walk. Go straight on, then turn right.
Visitor: Straight on, then right?
Sam: Yes. Then go past the shopping centre and the bank and turn left. The café is on the left near the university library.
Visitor: Great! Thanks very much.
Sam: You're welcome. Bye!

2 4.11 **Listen and repeat the Useful language.**

Useful language

Asking for directions	Giving directions
Excuse me, I'm looking for ...	It's a five-minute walk.
Is it far?	**Go straight on.**
	Turn right/left.
	Go past the bank.
	It's on the left/right.

3 **Match the directions in bold from the Useful language box with the pictures.**

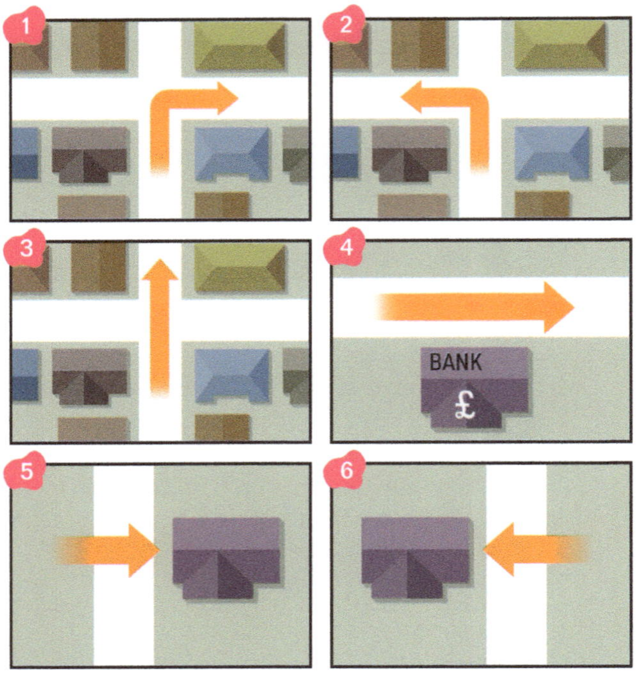

4 4.12 **Listen to three more dialogues at the bus station. Look at the map on page 44. Follow the directions and find the places.**

5 **Work in pairs. Ask and answer about places near your school, and how you get there. Follow the steps in the Speaking plan.**

Speaking plan

Prepare
- Choose a place near your school.
- Write directions to get there from your school.
- Make notes for your dialogue.

Speak
- Practise your dialogue.
- Use phrases from the Useful language box.
- Act out your dialogue without notes.
- Be polite! Use *Excuse me* and *Thank you*.

Reflect
- How can you improve next time?
- Swap roles and ask for directions to a different place.

Now play *Keep moving!*

FAST FINISHER

Draw a map of part of your town or city. Describe where the buildings are.

The sports centre is opposite the park. There's a small museum in the park.

LS Language summary: Unit 4 SB p.130

 EXTRA PRACTICE Workbook page 37

SPEAKING Asking for and giving directions

1 4.10 Focus on the picture and ask: *What do you think the people are saying?* Elicit a few ideas for what each person is saying. Read out the situation and the question, then play the dialogue. With stronger classes, you could play the dialogue with books closed, then elicit the answers to the questions. With weaker classes, you could play the dialogue for sts to listen and read. See SB page 45 for audio script. Check the answer.

Answers
She wants to go to the Rose Café.

2 4.11 Ask sts if they can remember the phrases the visitor uses to ask for directions and the phrases Sam uses to give directions. Read through the Useful language box with the class and check sts understand all the phrases. Play the audio once for sts to listen to the phrases, then play it again for them to repeat.

Ask questions to check concept.

Concept check questions: *I want to find the Science Museum – What can I say?* (Excuse me, I'm looking for the Science Museum). I want to know if it will take me 10 minutes or 30 minutes – What can I ask? (Is it far?). *I want to tell you that you stay on this road – What can I say?* (Go straight on). *I want to say that if you walk, you will be there in 10 minutes – What can I say?* (It's a ten-minute walk). *I want to say it's on this side* (indicate your right hand) – *What can I say?* (It's on the right). *I want to say go this way* (indicate turning left) – *What can I say?* (Turn left).

3 Ask sts to match the directions in bold with the pictures. Check answers.

Answers

Go straight on. – 3	Go past the bank. – 4
Turn right. – 1	It's on the left. – 6
Turn left. – 2	It's on the right. – 5

4 4.12 Read out the task, then refer sts back to the map on page 44. Play the audio. See TG pages 277 for audio script. Sts listen and follow the directions to find the places. They could work in pairs for this, and use their finger to trace the route that each person follows. Check answers, playing the audio again if necessary and pausing to show the route each person takes.

Answers
1 (art) museum
2 park
3 market

5 Sts follow the steps in the Speaking plan to practise asking for and giving directions.

Speaking plan

Prepare

Sts work in pairs and decide on a place near their school. You could brainstorm a few ideas as a class for places sts could choose. Sts then write directions on how to get to the place, and plan their dialogue, using the Useful language in Exercise 2 to help them.

Speak

Sts practise their dialogue in their pairs. They can practise with and then without notes. Monitor and help as necessary. If your sts use smartphones in class, they could record their conversations.

Reflect

Discuss as a class how sts could improve next time. Encourage them to be honest and open about the things they did well and the things they can do better. If you noticed any typical errors, correct them with the class. Sts swap roles and follow the steps again with a different place. If they record their conversations, ask them to use this to help them think of how they could improve next time. Ask some sts to perform their dialogues for the class if they feel confident.

Keep moving!

This lesson features an optional language revision and consolidation game for use in digital classrooms. Players control different characters, each with their own personalities and special abilities.

FAST FINISHER

Sts draw a map of part of their town or city, then write sentences about where the buildings are. Encourage them to use the prepositions on page 44. Weaker sts could work in pairs. They look at the map of Oxford again and write sentences about where some of the buildings are.

S **Speaking practice: WB** p.37
Sts will find more practice for asking for and giving directions here.
Set these exercises for homework.

LS **Language summary: Unit 4 SB** p.130

REAL CULTURE!

New York, New York

I can compare the seasons in my country with another country.

Home | Posts | About | Search

THE SEASONS IN NEW YORK

I'm Alisha and I'm from New York. I love the different seasons here! Here's my guide:

1 FALL*

Weather: The days are warm. It doesn't often rain.

What to do: The trees change color and it's a beautiful time to explore Central Park. On 31 October, two million people walk around the streets in crazy costumes to celebrate Halloween!

Food and drink: Fall is the season of apples. Why not try an apple donut?

2 WINTER

Weather: Winters in New York are cold, and it usually snows.

What to do: You can go ice skating at the Rockefeller Center in front of the famous Christmas tree. Or visit a museum! At the Museum of Modern Art, you can see paintings by Picasso and Warhol.

Food and drink: Are you feeling cold? Then have a hot chocolate – yum!

3 SPRING

Weather: It's usually warm, but be prepared – it can rain!

What to do: Spring is the start of the baseball season. You can watch a game at the Yankee Stadium. Or, if you prefer music, you can go and see a musical in Broadway, New York's theater district.

Food and drink: Start your day with a typical American breakfast of pancakes and fruit!

4 SUMMER

Weather: The days are long, hot and sunny. Leave your coat at home!

What to do: Summer is an exciting time in the city. There are lots of free concerts and outdoor movies in the parks. You can also visit the beach at Coney Island or take a ride on the funfair.

Food and drink: Try one of New York's famous bagels – they're delicious!

* fall (American English) = autumn

REAL CULTURE! New York, New York

Sts read and learn about the different seasons in New York and do a quiz about the differences between British and American English. Sts then work in groups to write a guide to the seasons in their town or city.

This lesson features an optional culture video about a student visiting tourist attractions in Brighton, UK: see SB page 47.

WARMER

Ask: *What's the weather like today?* Elicit the answer, then ask: *What's the weather like here in the summer?* Elicit a range of answers and take the opportunity to revise the weather vocabulary from page 42. Ask: *What are the summer months here?* Elicit answers, then ask: *What comes next?* How does the weather change? Elicit the names of the four seasons, the months for each one, and the weather for each one. Teach the word *season* and ask: *What's your favourite season? Why?*

BACKGROUND

New York City is the largest city in the United States. It is known for many famous landmarks, including the Statue of Liberty, the Empire State Building, Central Park, Times Square, Wall Street, the beach at Coney Island and the Broadway theatre district. It has featured in many Hollywood films, so many parts of the city look familiar to people, even if they have never been there.

1 Ask sts to look at the pictures and read out the questions. Elicit what sts know about New York and what places they recognise from the pictures. Encourage as many sts as possible to join in and share any information they have. If any sts have been to New York, encourage them to share their experiences with the class. If no sts have been to New York, discuss with the class why they recognise some of the places, e.g. if they have appeared in films or TV series.

2 4.13 Read out the question, then play the audio for sts to listen. Put sts into pairs to discuss which season sounds the most fun and why, then discuss their ideas as a class.

3 Ask sts to read the guide again and answer the questions. Allow sts to compare their answers in pairs, then check answers with the class.

Answers

1 The trees change color (colour *British English*).
2 Two million people walk around the streets in crazy costumes.
3 It is cold and it usually snows.
4 the Museum of Modern Art
5 spring
6 You can see a musical.
7 hot and sunny
8 the beach at Coney Island

4 **Word Power** Read through the Look! box with the class. Elicit any other words sts know that are different in British and American English. Then put sts into pairs to do the quiz. Explain that the quiz is meant to be fun, so they shouldn't worry if they don't know all the answers, but should try to guess. Check answers with the class, and see who got the most answers right.

Answers

1 movie theater
2 soccer
3 mall
4 sneakers
5 vacation
6 cookie
7 apartment
8 elevator

EXTRA PRACTICE

Arrange sts in pairs to test each other on American and English words. One student says an American word, the other says the English word without looking at the book. The first student can give clues. For example, *You wear them on your feet*. When they have finished, they swap roles.

Alternatively, prepare a list of British words from Units 1–4 and their American equivalents. Draw a large circle on the board and write these British words inside: *bath, cooker, film, garden, mum, sink, sofa, taxi, toilet, wardrobe*. Draw another circle and write these American words inside: *back yard, bath tub, cab, closet, couch, mom, movie, restroom, stove, washbasin*.

Arrange sts in pairs and have a race to see who can match all the words correctly. Tell sts they can use their dictionaries to check their ideas.

Answers (US words in brackets)

bath (bath tub); cooker (stove); film (movie); garden (back yard); mum (mom); sink (washbasin); sofa (couch); taxi (cab); toilet (restroom); wardrobe (closet)

1 Look at the pictures. What do you know about New York? What places can you see?

2 4.13 Read and listen to Alisha's guide to the seasons. Which season sounds most fun to you? Why?

3 Read the guide again and answer the questions.

1. Why is autumn (or fall) a beautiful time in New York?
2. How do people celebrate Halloween?
3. What is the weather like in winter?
4. Where can you go if you're interested in art?
5. In which season do you probably need an umbrella?
6. What can you do in Broadway?
7. What is the weather like in summer?
8. Where can you go if you want to see the sea?

4 **Word Power** Read the **Look!** box. Work in pairs and do the quiz.

Look! British and American English

Some words in British English are different (or spelled differently) in American English, for example:

British English	American English
autumn	*fall*
colour	*color*

5 4.14 Listen to the interviews with three people in New York. Which American English words do you hear?

6 4.14 Listen again. Copy and complete the table in your notebook.

	Favourite season?	Why?
Speaker 1		
Speaker 2		
Speaker 3		

7 **GET CREATIVE** Write a guide to the seasons in your town or city. Follow the steps:

1. Work in groups of four and choose a season each.
2. Discuss each season: What is the weather like? What can you do? What typical food and drink is there?
3. Use the ideas to write about your season. Add photos and display your guide in the classroom.

Now watch the culture video.

FAST FINISHER

Write down the four seasons. Make a list of words that each season makes you think of.

Summer: sun, camping, ice cream, August, holidays, ...

THE BIG QUIZ: British and American English

How much do you know about British and American English? Do our quiz to find out. Choose from the answers in the box.

apartment   cookie   elevator   mall   movie theater   sneakers   soccer   vacation

1 In the UK, people go to a cinema to watch a film. Where do people in the USA go?

2 What do people in the USA call the sport: football?

3 In the UK, you go shopping at a shopping centre. In the USA, you go to a … .

4 If an American likes your trainers, they say 'I like your … .'

5 In the UK, people go on holiday, but in the USA, people take a … .

6 A British speaker calls this a biscuit. An American speaker calls it a … .

7 In British English, this is called a block of flats. In American English, it's called an … block.

8 In the UK, you take a lift to travel to the top of a tall building. In the USA, you take an … .

REAL CULTURE!

5 4.14 Read out the question, then play the audio. See TG pages 278 for audio script. Sts listen and note down the American English words they hear. Check answers with the class, playing the audio again and pausing if necessary to confirm the answers. Check that sts understand all the words and elicit the British English words for the same meanings (*football*, *autumn*, *ice hockey*, *trainers*, *holiday*).

Answers
soccer, fall, hockey, sneakers, vacation

6 4.14 Ask sts to copy the table into their notebooks and complete any information they can remember from the first listening. Play the audio again for them to listen and complete the table. Check answers, playing the audio again if necessary and pausing to confirm the answers.

Answers

	Favourite season?	Why?
Speaker 1	winter	He plays hockey in the winter and he loves it.
Speaker 2	fall	The weather is perfect for running outside and there is the New York Marathon.
Speaker 3	spring	The weather is usually good so you can picnic in the park and sit outside at restaurants.

21st Century skills

7 **GET CREATIVE**

Read out the task, then put sts into groups of four. Read through the three steps with the class and make sure sts understand everything. Tell them that although they should each write about one season, they can help each other with ideas and with the writing if necessary. Sts then work in their groups and make their guide to the seasons in their town or city. Monitor and help as necessary while they are working. If they have online access in class, they can download and print out photos to add, otherwise they can bring these to the next lesson and add them to their guide. Collect in the guides and make a display on the classroom wall. Allow sts time to look at all the guides and discuss as a class which they like best and why.

Culture video

You can watch this in class if you have time and access to video, or you can ask sts to download it from the Richmond Learning Platform to watch at home. See *Holidays at home* on TG pages 298 and 306.

FAST FINISHER

Sts write words they associate with the four seasons. Weaker sts could work in pairs and decide on their favourite season. They then write a list of words and activities they associate with that season.

A message to a friend

WRITING A text message

I can write a message about what I'm doing now.

1 **Work in pairs. Describe the photo. Use the words in the box.**

aquarium	fish	shark	swimming

2 **Read the messages. Where is Emma? What is she doing?**

Hey there, how are things? What are you doing today? Tom 11.00

Hi Tom! I'm spending the weekend in Brighton 😊. I'm staying with my friend, Sara. At the moment, we're exploring the aquarium – it's very interesting. We're watching the sharks. They're all swimming round in circles. I think it's their lunchtime! 😨 Emma 11.05

Sounds cool! Have fun and speak later! 11.08

Hi again! How's your afternoon going? 15.50

Great, thanks! We're at the beach now 🏖. It's a bit cloudy, but it's quite hot. We're with some of Sara's friends, and we're having a picnic and playing volleyball. Brighton's a cool place, and I'm having a really good time. See you at school on Monday! x 15.58

3 **Read the Useful language box. How do you say these expressions in your language?**

Useful language

Writing a message

I'm spending the weekend in ...
I'm staying with my ...
At the moment / Now, we're ...-*ing* ...
I'm having a really good time!
See you at/on ...! / See you soon!

4 **Read the Look! box. Find an example of each adverb of degree in Emma's texts.**

Look! Adverbs of degree

We use:
It's *quite* hot. ☀
It's *very* hot. ☀☀
It's *really* hot. ☀☀☀

5 **In your notebooks, rewrite the sentences with *quite* (*), *very* (**) or *really* (***).**

The park is beautiful. 🌷🌷🌷
The park is really beautiful

1 The people are friendly. 😊😊
2 It's cold at the moment. ❄
3 The shops are expensive. 💵💵💵
4 The museum is interesting. 👍
5 It's cloudy today. ☁☁

6 **Imagine you are spending the weekend in a different city. Reply to Tom's messages in Exercise 2. Follow the steps in the Writing plan.**

Writing plan

Prepare

› Make notes about your day.
First message (in the morning)
Which city are you visiting? Where are you staying? What are you doing there?
Second message (in the afternoon)
What are you doing now? What is the weather like? Are you having a good time?

Write

› Write your messages.
› Use the expressions from the Useful language box.

Reflect

› Check your grammar: present continuous.
› Check adverbs of degree. › Check your spelling.

W Writing summary: WB p.87   E Exams: Unit 4 SB p.121   LS Language summary: Unit 4 SB p.130

EXTRA PRACTICE Workbook page 38; photocopiable activities for Unit 4 vocabulary, grammar and skills

A message to a friend

WRITING A text message

Sts read a text message from a friend about what they are doing now. They study adverbs of degree and learn useful language for writing a message. They then follow the steps in the Writing plan to imagine they are spending a weekend in a different city and write a text message about what they are doing.

Writing
A text message

Useful language
Writing a message *(I'm spending the weekend in ..., I'm staying with my ..., At the moment / Now, we're ... -ing ..., I'm having a really good time! See you at/on ...! / See you soon!*

Look!
Adverbs of degree

WARMER

Say: *What city would you like to visit for a weekend?* Elicit a few ideas, and suggest a few cities if necessary to help sts, e.g. *New York, London, Paris.* Ask: *Do your friends sometimes send you messages if they are doing something exciting? Do they send photos?* Elicit a range of ideas.

1 Focus on the messages and the picture. Read through the words in the box with the class and elicit or teach the meanings. Put sts into pairs to describe the picture. Elicit a description from the class.

2 Sts read the messages and answer the questions. Check answers.

Answers
She's spending the weekend in Brighton. She's watching the sharks at the aquarium; She's at the beach, having a picnic and playing volleyball.

3 Read the Useful language box with sts about language for writing a message. Ask them how they say these expressions in their first language. Elicit which tense the verbs are in (present continuous) and remind sts that we use the present continuous for things we are doing now, so we often use it in text messages or to describe photos.

4 Read the Look! box with sts about adverbs of degree. Sts find examples of the adverbs in the text messages.

Ask questions to check concept.

Concept check questions: *It's 45 degrees today – is it quite hot or really hot?* (really hot). *It's 10 degrees today – is it very cold or quite cold?* (quite cold).

Answers
quite: it's quite hot
very: it's very interesting
really: I'm having a really good time

5 Ask sts to write the sentences in their notebooks, using *quite*, *very* or *really*. Check answers with the class.

Answers
1 The people are very friendly.
2 It's quite cold at the moment.
3 The shops are really expensive.
4 The museum is quite interesting.
5 It's very cloudy today.

6 Ask sts to imagine they are spending the weekend in a different city and write a text message to reply to Tom's questions in Exercise 2, following the steps in the Writing plan.

Writing plan

Prepare
Sts work as individuals and make notes about their day in another city. Monitor while they are working, and help with vocabulary if necessary.

Write
Sts write their messages using Emma's replies in Exercise 1 as a model. They should write two short messages: the things they are doing in the morning, the things they are doing in the afternoon. Refer them back to the Useful language box and encourage them to use these expressions in their messages. Refer them back to the Look! box and encourage them to use adverbs of degree. Encourage them also to use some of the weather vocabulary from page 42, and remind them to use verbs in the present continuous.

Reflect
Ask sts to check their grammar, spelling and punctuation and make any necessary changes. Sts could then swap their messages with a partner and give feedback on the use of the Useful language, adverbs of degree and the present continuous. Remind sts that they should always be positive and encouraging when they give feedback to a partner.

W **Writing practice: WB** p.38
Sts will find more practice for writing here. Set these exercises for homework.

W **Writing summary: WB** p.87

E **Exams: Unit 4 SB** p.121

LS **Language summary: Unit 4 SB** p.130

Fantastic food!

5

Vocabulary: Food and drink; Adjectives: health | **Grammar:** Countable and uncountable nouns + *some* and *any*; Quantifiers: *much, many, a lot of* | **Speaking:** Ordering food | **Writing:** A recipe

VOCABULARY Food and drink

I can talk about food and drink.

1 5.1 **Look at the food diary. Match the words in the box with the pictures. Listen, check and repeat.**

Breakfast: cereal, milk, ... 2nd Breakfast: ...

beans cereal chicken eggs fish fruit hot chocolate jam milk orange juice pasta potatoes rice salad sandwich toast vegetables yoghurt

2 **Work in pairs. How many more food words can you think of? Make a list and compare with the rest of the class.**

3 5.2 **Listen to a gymnast talking about her food diary. In your notebook, write what she has for breakfast, lunch and dinner.**

Breakfast:
Lunch:
Dinner:

4 **Interview your partner and write their food diary. Is it similar to the athletes' diaries?**

A: What do you have for breakfast?
B: I usually have toast and coffee.

Ruth's Food Diary

Breakfast: toast, coffee
Lunch:
Dinner:

Now watch the vlog.

FAST FINISHER

What's your idea of a perfect breakfast, lunch or dinner?

LS Language summary: Unit 5 SB p.131

 EXTRA PRACTICE Workbook page 40

Fantastic food! 5

UNIT 5 OVERVIEW: The focus for this unit is food. Sts read about two young people who make and sell food and drink, and listen to someone talking about their healthy and unhealthy food and exercise habits. They read a restaurant menu and learn how to order food and drink. They read about festivals in different parts of the world and finally, they read a recipe for spaghetti Bolognese and write a recipe for a dish they know. They also watch a vlog about a visit to a local farmer's market and a culture video about celebrating *Diwali* in New York.

Vocabulary	Grammar	Pronunciation	Reading	Listening	Speaking	Writing
Food and drink; Adjectives: health	Countable and uncountable nouns + *some* and *any*; Quantifiers: *much, many, a lot of*	/h/	Understanding an author's opinion	Making notes when I'm listening	Ordering food and drink in a restaurant or café	A recipe

VOCABULARY Food and drink

Sts learn words for food and drink. They listen to people talking about the food they eat, then personalise the vocabulary by talking about their own food diary. This lesson also features an optional vlog in which people talk about a visit to a local farmers' market.

Vocabulary

Food and drink (*beans, cereal, chicken, eggs, fish, fruit, hot chocolate, jam, milk, orange juice, pasta, potatoes, rice, salad, sandwich, toast, vegetables, yoghurt*)

Vlog

Bokang: *Farmer's market*

WARMER

Write on the board: *breakfast, lunch, dinner*. Elicit or teach the meanings. Ask: *What do you usually eat for breakfast/lunch/dinner?* Elicit a few ideas, then ask: *What kinds of food do you like? What kinds don't you like?* Teach the word *snack*, and ask: *What's your favourite snack?*

1 5.1 Read through the words in the box and elicit or teach the meanings. Sts look at the food diary and match the words to the pictures. Play the audio for sts to listen, check and repeat.

Answers
Breakfast: cereal, milk, yoghurt, orange juice
2nd breakfast: eggs, beans, toast, jam
Lunch: fish, pasta, salad, fruit
Snack: sandwich, hot chocolate
Dinner: chicken, rice, potatoes, vegetables

2 Put sts into pairs to think of more food words they know. Bring their ideas together on the board and ask: *Which of these foods do you love / hate?*

3 5.2 Explain to sts that they will hear a gymnast talking about her food diary. Ask: *What do you think she has for breakfast/lunch/dinner?* Elicit a few ideas. Play the audio for sts to listen and note down her meals. See TG page 278 for audio script. Allow sts to compare their answers in pairs, then check answers.

Answers
Breakfast: cereal and fruit
Lunch: chicken, vegetables, glass of orange juice
Dinner: fish, pasta, salad

4 Focus on the food diary and read out the example question. Sts work in pairs to ask questions and complete their partner's food diary. Ask some sts to tell the class what their partner eats, and discuss how it is similar or different to the athletes' diaries.

Vlog

This lesson features a vlog in which vlogger Bokang talks about her trip to a local farmers' market. You can watch this in class if you have time and access to video, or you can ask sts to download it from the Richmond Learning Platform to watch at home. See TG pages 290 and 304.

FAST FINISHER

Sts who finish early can write their perfect breakfast, lunch or dinner. Weaker sts could work in pairs. They cover the words in Exercise 1, then look at the pictures again and try to remember the words.

EXTRA PRACTICE

Put sts into pairs. They take turns to imagine they are a famous sports star and talk about the food they eat each day, while their partner films them using their phone. They can watch their films back and discuss in their pairs how they could improve.

V **Vocabulary practice: WB** p.40
Sts will find more practice of vocabulary for food and drink here. Set these exercises for homework.

LS **Language summary: Unit 5 SB** p.131

Recipe for success

READING

I can understand an author's opinion.

1 Word Power **Before you read, match the blue words in the article with the pictures. Think of three more things from a kitchen cupboard and three more things from a fridge.**

butter f

2 5.3 **Read and listen to the article. What do the two young people in the pictures have in common?**

A sweet idea

It's the summer holidays and you want to earn some money. What can you do? You look in the kitchen. There's some butter in the fridge and some flour and sugar in the cupboard. There aren't any eggs, so you can't make a cake, but there's some chocolate. You decide to make some cookies. You can sell them to your neighbours. Perhaps you can make some lemonade, too. Are there any lemons? Yes, there are. Perfect!

A few hours later, you start selling your cookies and lemonade. Your neighbours love them. The next day, you make some more. People tell their friends and soon you are earning hundreds of euros a day. Impossible? Not at all! Meet teenagers **Mikaila Ulmer** and **Cory Nieves**.

Cory makes delicious cookies with natural ingredients and sells them online. In the future, he plans to use the money from his business to pay for his university studies.

Mikaila makes 'healthy' lemonade. She doesn't use sugar – instead she uses honey. She's now got a successful business and she sells her lemonade in shops across the USA.

So if you want to start your own business, remember: *You're never too young!*

3 Read the article again. What is the author's opinion? Choose a, b, c or d.

a It's impossible for teenagers to earn a lot of money.
b Mikaila and Cory are too young to start a business.
c Young people can be successful in business.
d It's a good idea for students to have a job when they're at university.

4 THINK CRITICALLY **Do you think it's a good idea for young people to have a job? Why/Why not?**

5 FIND OUT **It's true – there is a National Cookie Day in the USA! When is it?**

 EXTRA PRACTICE Workbook page 41

Recipe for success

READING

Sts read an article about two young people who have started their own food businesses and focus on understanding an author's opinion. They match food words to pictures and learn to use countable and uncountable nouns correctly with *some* and *any*. They then practise using countable and uncountable nouns to talk about food.

Reading text

An article about two young people who have started their own businesses, making and selling cookies and healthy lemonade

Reading skill

Understanding an author's opinion

WARMER

Ask: *Do you like cooking?* Teach the meaning of *cook* if necessary. Ask: *What kinds of food can you make? Who eats your food?* Elicit a few answers and help with vocabulary where necessary. Teach the word *cookie* and ask: *Can you make cookies? Who eats them? Are they nice?*

1 **Word Power** Focus on the blue words in the text and elicit or teach the meanings. Sts then match the words with the pictures. Alternatively, sts could work in pairs and use a dictionary to find the meaning of the words and match them with the pictures. Check answers, and model pronunciation of the words. Then put sts into pairs to think of three more things from a kitchen cupboard and a fridge. Bring their ideas together on the board and teach the meaning of all the words.

Answers

a	lemonade	e	sugar
b	lemons	f	butter
c	honey	g	chocolate
d	cookies	h	flour

(Possible answers: Kitchen cupboard: pasta, rice, jam; Fridge: milk, yoghurt, orange juice)

2 5.3 Read out the question and encourage sts to guess the answer. Elicit a few ideas. Teach the words *delicious*, *healthy* and *business*, then play the audio for sts to read and listen to the article. Check the answer.

Answer

They are both teenagers who own their own businesses.

3 **Understanding an author's opinion** Ask: *Does the author think that what Mikaila and Cory are doing is good or bad? How do you know?* Elicit a few ideas, e.g. the author says that Mikaila's lemonade is healthy and Cory's cookies are delicious. Ask: *Does the author think it is easy or difficult to start your own business?* Elicit that the author suggests it is easy because all the things you need are in the fridge and the cupboard, you can sell to your neighbours, etc. Ask sts to read the final sentence of the article again, then ask them to read the four possible opinions and choose the best one. Check the answer with the class, discussing why the other answers are not correct.

Answer

c

21st Century skills

4 **THINK CRITICALLY**

Read out the question, then write on the board: *Yes, because …* and *No, because …* . Put sts into pairs or small groups. Ask them to discuss the question and think of two reasons for *yes*, and two reasons for *no*. You could revise a few phrases for giving opinions first, e.g. *I think …, For me, …, In my opinion, …* and you could teach some phrases for agreeing and disagreeing, e.g. *I agree, Yes, you're right. No, I don't agree because …* . Ask pairs or groups in turn to tell the class their opinions and reasons.

EXTRA PRACTICE

You could ask sts in pairs or groups to plan their own business. Ask them to think about what they can make and who they can sell it to. Ask pairs or groups to present their ideas to the class. The class could vote for their favourite.

21st Century skills

5 **FIND OUT**

Set this exercise for homework if you prefer. Sts can find this information out by looking online or in other media, or by asking other people. The answer to the question is: 4 December.

EXTRA PRACTICE

Focus on Exercise 5. Ask sts to work individually and make up a new national day for their favourite food. Tell them to decide on the name of the national day, the date, and what people do on this day. Then arrange sts in small groups to tell each other about their new favourite food day. If you have time, sts could make posters to advertise their food day and display them around the classroom. Sts could walk around and choose their top three food days.

R **Reading practice: WB** p.41

You will find more practice for reading here. Set these exercises for homework.

GRAMMAR Countable and uncountable nouns + *some* and *any*

I can identify countable and uncountable nouns and use *some* and *any*.

Now watch the grammar animation.

1 Read the grammar box. Complete the rules with *countable, uncountable, some, any, a* and *an*.

	Affirmative	Negative and questions
Countable singular	There's **a** lemon.	There isn't **an** orange. Is there **a** banana?
Countable plural	There are **some** cookies.	There aren't **any** eggs. Are there **any** lemons?
Uncountable	There's **some** butter.	There isn't **any** flour. Is there **any** sugar?

Rules

1 [1] ... nouns only have a singular form. [2] ... nouns have a singular and a plural form.
2 With singular countable nouns, we use [3] ... or [4] ... .
3 With uncountable nouns and plural countable nouns, we use [5] ... in affirmative sentences and [6] ... in negative sentences and questions.

2 Copy and complete the table with the words in the box. For countable nouns, write the singular and plural form.

~~apple~~ banana ~~bread~~ egg fruit
ice cream meat milk pasta potato
sugar tomato vegetable water

Countable nouns	Uncountable nouns
an apple (plural: apples)	*bread*

3 Choose the correct answer.

1 There's *a / some* pasta in the cupboard.
2 I don't want *some / any* meat, thanks. I'm a vegetarian.
3 Do you want a drink? We've got *some / any* orange juice.
4 I always have *a / an* apple at break time.
5 There are *some / any* eggs in the fridge.
6 Let's make a salad. Have you got *some / any* tomatoes?
7 I usually have *a / an* banana for lunch.
8 There's *some / any* pasta in the bowl.

4 Complete the dialogue with *a, an, some* or *any*.

Leo: It's Milly's birthday today. Let's make her [1] ... birthday cake.
Theo: Great idea. Are there [2] ... eggs in the fridge?
Leo: Yes, there are. And there's [3] ... butter and [4] ... milk, too.
Theo: Is there [5] ... flour in the cupboard?
Leo: Yes, there is. Oh, but there isn't [6] ... sugar. We can't make a cake without sugar. What can we do?
Theo: I know – we can make [7] ... pancakes!
Leo: Good idea. Milly loves pancakes. What can we put on them? Have we got [8] ... chocolate sauce?
Theo: No, we haven't, but there are [9] ... bananas and there's [10] ... honey.
Leo: Pancakes with bananas and honey. Mmm, delicious!

5 Copy the picture of a shopping basket and draw five items of food or drink in it. In pairs, ask questions to find out about your partner's basket.

A: Are there any apples in your basket?
B: Yes, there are.
A: Is there any meat?
B: No, there isn't.

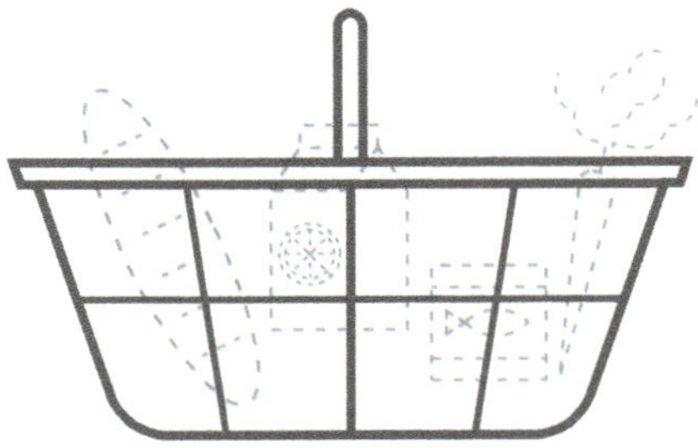

FUN FACT

Every year, there is a Pancake Day in the UK on a Tuesday in February or March. People cook and eat pancakes, and there are also pancake races. People run and throw pancakes in the air!

FAST FINISHER

What's in your fridge at home? Can you remember?

There's some milk. There aren't any eggs.

LS Language summary: Unit 5 SB p.131

EXTRA PRACTICE Workbook page 42

GRAMMAR Countable and uncountable nouns + *some* and *any*

Grammar animation

This lesson features an optional animated presentation of the grammar in context called *Is there any cheese?* including the form and use of *some* and *any* with countable and uncountable nouns. You can watch this in class if you have time and access to a computer or tablet, or you can ask sts to download it from the Richmond Learning Platform to watch at home. See TB pages 309 for animation script.

1 Read the grammar box about countable and uncountable nouns with sts. Sts could look back at the article on page 50 to find more examples of countable and uncountable nouns and notice how they are used with *some*, *any*, *a*, and *an*. Put sts into pairs to complete the rules. Check answers.

Answers

1 Uncountable	4 an
2 Countable	5 some
3 a	6 any

Ask questions to check concept.

Concept check questions: *I'd like a banana – countable or uncountable?* (countable). *Can I say two bananas / three bananas?* (yes – countable / plural). *I'd like some cereal – countable or uncountable?* (uncountable). *Can I say two cereals / three cereals?* (no – uncountable). *A apple or an apple?* (an apple). *In the fridge there is some butter or any butter?* (some butter). *There isn't some milk – correct?* (no – There *isn't any* milk).

2 Put sts into pairs. Ask them to copy the table into their notebooks and complete it with the nouns. Tell them to think about whether they can count each thing, and suggest that they use a learner's dictionary to help them too. Point out that learners' dictionaries say whether nouns are countable [C] or uncountable [U]. Check answers with the class, and for each word elicit a simple sentence, e.g. *There isn't any bread, There is some fruit.*

Answers

Countable nouns: a banana (plural: bananas); an egg (plural: eggs); an ice cream (plural: ice creams); a potato (plural: potatoes); a tomato (plural: tomatoes); a vegetable (plural: vegetables)
Uncountable nouns: fruit, meat, milk, pasta, sugar, water

3 Sts choose the correct words to complete the sentences. Sts compare their answers in pairs. Check answers.

Answers

1 some	4 an	7 a
2 any	5 some	8 some
3 some	6 any	

4 Ask sts to read the dialogue quickly, ignoring the gaps. Ask: *What do Leo and Theo want to make?* Elicit the words *cake* and *pancakes* and teach the meaning. Sts then read the dialogue again and complete it with the correct words. Allow sts to compare their answers in pairs, then check answers with the class.

Answers

1 a	6 any
2 any	7 some
3 some	8 any
4 some	9 some
5 any	10 some

5 Ask sts individually to copy the picture of a shopping basket and add five items of food or drink. Tell them not to show anyone their basket. Demonstrate the activity by asking individual sts some questions, e.g. *Is there any meat in your basket? Is there a banana?* Sts then work in pairs and take turns to guess what is in their partner's basket. You could do this activity as a game, telling sts they should try to guess what is in their partner's basket as quickly as possible. Monitor while they are working and note down mistakes in the use of countable and uncountable nouns and *some* and *any*. Correct the mistakes in a feedback session at the end.

FUN FACT Encourage sts to read this fun fact for pleasure. Ask if there are similar food days in their country, and ask what people do on these days. They might be interested to know that in the USA, 9 February is National Pizza Day, when people celebrate by making and eating pizzas.

FAST FINISHER

Sts who finish early can think about their fridge at home and write sentences about what things there are and aren't in it. Weaker sts can work in pairs. They write sentences about their baskets from Exercise 5, saying what things there are and aren't in it.

G Grammar practice: WB p.42

Sts will find more practice for countable and uncountable nouns with *some* and *any* here. Set these exercises for homework.

LS Language summary: Unit 5 SB p.131

How much exercise do you do?

VOCABULARY and LISTENING Adjectives: health

I can make notes when I'm listening.

1 **Match the adjectives in the box with the pictures a–e below. Some pictures have more than one adjective.**

active	fit	healthy	hungry
lazy	thirsty	unfit	unhealthy

2 5.4 **Make pairs of adjectives from the words in Exercise 1. Listen, check and repeat. Which pairs aren't opposites?**

active – lazy

3 **Complete the sentences with an adjective from Exercise 1.**

Olympic athletes need to be very *fit*.

1 I'm ... . Can I have some water, please?
2 Sam eats a lot of ... food like burgers.
3 What time is dinner? I'm really ... .
4 Igor, it's 11.30. Get out of bed, and don't be ...!
5 Saskia has a very ... diet. She eats fish and vegetables every day.
6 It's important to be ... . I hate staying at home all day.

4 5.5 **Read the questionnaire. Listen to an interview with Jamie and make notes for his answers. Only write important words or information.**

Notes

Question 1: a lot – 5 or more

Question 2: ...

5 5.5 **Work in pairs and compare your notes. Listen again and check.**

6 **What are Jamie's healthy habits? What are his unhealthy habits? Make a list.**

7 **Work in pairs. Do the questionnaire.**

How HEALTHY are you?

1 How much fruit and how many vegetables do you eat in a day?

2 How much exercise do you do in a day?

3 How many hours do you sleep at night?

4 How much time do you spend watching TV, playing video games or using your phone?

5 How much water do you drink in a day?

6 It's two hours before dinner and you're hungry. What do you do?

a

b

c

d

e

LS Language summary: Unit 5 SB p.131

How much exercise do you do?

VOCABULARY and LISTENING

Adjectives: health

Sts listen to an interview with Jamie, a teenage boy, about his food and exercise habits, and focus on making notes when they are listening. They learn adjectives to talk about health and learn the quantifiers *much*, *many* and *a lot of*. They then ask and answer personal questions using *how much* and *how many*.

Vocabulary

Adjectives: health (*active, fit, healthy, hungry, lazy, thirsty, unfit, unhealthy*)

Listening text

An interview about healthy and unhealthy food and exercise habits

Listening skill

Making notes when listening

Pronunciation

/h/

WARMER

With books closed, mime one or two forms of exercise, e.g. running, playing football. Ask: *What am I doing?* Elicit the answers, then teach the word *exercise*. Ask: *What kinds of exercise do you do?* Elicit answers, revise the words for sports that sts learned in Unit 3.

1 Read through the adjectives in the box and elicit or teach the meanings. Sts then match the words with the pictures. Explain that some pictures can match more than one adjective. Check answers.

Answers

a thirsty, healthy
b lazy, unfit
c healthy, hungry
d hungry, unhealthy
e unfit, unhealthy, fit, active, healthy

2 5.4 Read out the example and point out that the two adjectives have opposite meanings. Sts put the remaining adjectives into pairs of opposites. Play the audio for sts to listen, check and repeat the words.

Answers

active – lazy
fit – unfit
healthy – unhealthy
hungry/thirsty are not opposites.

3 Sts read the sentences and complete them with the correct adjectives. Allow sts to compare their answers in pairs, then check with the class.

Answers

1 thirsty
2 unhealthy
3 hungry
4 lazy
5 healthy
6 active

4 5.5 **Making notes when listening** Explain to sts that they are going to hear an interview in which Jamie answers a questionnaire about health. Explain that they must make notes when they listen. Focus on the example answers, and point out that the answer for question 1 only includes important words, because there is not time to write a lot while you listen. Read through the questionnaire with the class and elicit the kinds of answers sts might need to write, e.g. questions 2 and 3 will be a number of hours. Play the audio for sts to listen and make notes. See TG page 278 for audio script.

5 5.5 Put sts into pairs to compare their answers, then play the audio again for them to listen and check their answers. Check answers with the class, playing the audio again and pausing to confirm the answers. Ask sts what they found difficult about making notes when they listened, and discuss what things they could do to help next time.

Answers

Question 2: not much; sometimes plays football after school
Question 3: about 9 hours; goes to bed at 10 p.m. and gets up at 7 a.m.
Question 4: about 3 hours a day; doesn't watch much TV but uses phone a lot and plays a lot of games
Question 5: a litre and a half a day; glass of orange juice at breakfast
Question 6: has toast with jam or honey

6 Put sts into pairs to make a list of Jamie's healthy and unhealthy habits. Discuss the answers with the class and elicit some more examples of healthy and unhealthy habits.

Answers

Healthy: eats a lot of fruit; plays football after school; gets nine hours of sleep; doesn't watch much TV; drinks a lot of water; drinks fruit juice
Unhealthy: doesn't eat many vegetables; not very active; uses phone a lot; eats toast with jam

7 Sts work in pairs to do the questionnaire. Ask: *Who has healthy habits? What habits do you need to change?* Encourage sts to join in and talk about themselves, but don't force sts to talk about their own habits if they are uncomfortable with this.

V L **Vocabulary and Listening practice: WB** p.43
Sts will find more practice for listening, and practice of vocabulary for health here. Set these exercises for homework.

LS **Language summary: Unit 5 SB** p.131

GRAMMAR
Quantifiers: *much, many, a lot of*

I can talk about quantity.

Now watch the grammar animation.

1 **Read the grammar box. Choose the correct answer in the rules.**

	Countable	Uncountable
+	I play **a lot of** games.	I eat **a lot of** fruit.
–	I **don't** eat **many** vegetables.	I **don't** do **much** exercise.
?	**How many** hours do you sleep at night?	**How much** water do you drink?
	A lot. / Not many.	**A lot. / Not much.**

Rules

1 We use *How much* and *not much* with *countable / uncountable* nouns.

2 We use *How many* and *not many* with *countable / uncountable* nouns.

3 We use *a lot of* in affirmative sentences with *only countable / all* nouns.

2 **Complete the sentences with the words below.**

a lot of   many   much

1 There are *a lot of* bananas.

2 There's ... snow.

3 There aren't ... fans.

4 Hurry up! We haven't got ... time.

3 **PRONUNCIATION** /h/

5.6 **Listen and repeat. Focus on the /h/ sound.**

How much? How many? healthy hungry happy his her

4 5.7 **Listen and repeat.**

1 Harry's happy. He's having a hot dog!
2 How much honey have you got at home?
3 Here – have a hot chocolate!

5 5.8 **Complete the Fun Food Quiz with *How much* or *How many*. Match the questions with the answers. Listen and check.**

FUN FOOD QUIZ

1 ... sugar is there in a can of cola?

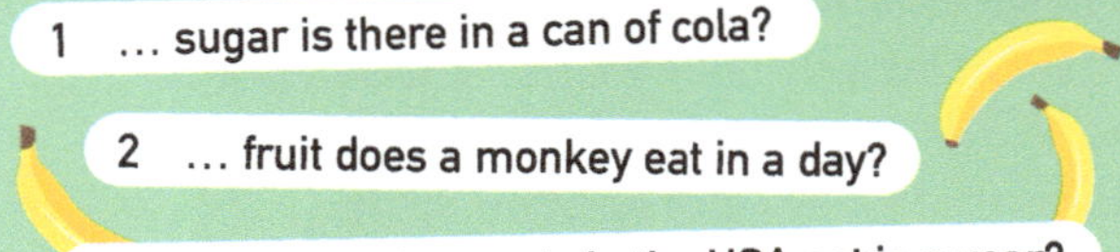

2 ... fruit does a monkey eat in a day?

3 ... burgers do people in the USA eat in a year?

4 ... honey does a bee make in its life?

5 ... eggs does a chicken produce in a week?

ANSWERS

a A lot – nearly fifty billion!

b Not much – only 1/12 (one twelfth) of a teaspoon.

c A lot – about fifty different types.

d Not many – about five.

e A lot – about nine teaspoons.

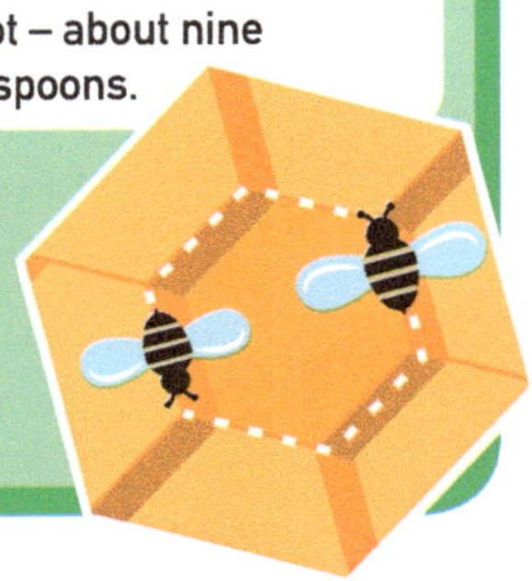

6 **Work in pairs. Ask and answer the questions.**

A: How many sports do you play?
B: Not many. I only play tennis and basketball. What about you?
A: A lot! I play six different sports.

1 How much chocolate do you eat in a week?
2 How many languages can you speak?
3 How many people are there in your family?
4 How much homework do you get in a week?
5 How many films do you watch in a month?

FAST FINISHER

Imagine an interview with your favourite sports person. Use *how much* and *how many*.

Interviewer: *How much coffee do you drink?*
Paul Pogba: *Not much. I prefer tea.*

LS Language summary: Unit 5 SB p.131

EXTRA PRACTICE Workbook page 44

GRAMMAR

Quantifiers: *much, many, a lot of*

Grammar animation

This lesson features an optional animated presentation of the grammar in context called *How many questions are there?* including the form and use of the quantifiers *much*, *many* and *a lot of*. You can watch this in class if you have time and access to a computer or tablet, or you can ask sts to download it from the Richmond Learning Platform to watch at home. See TG page 309 for animation script.

1 Read the grammar box with sts about quantifiers. Point out that the example sentences are all things that Jamie said in his interview. Draw attention to the headings *Countable* and *Uncountable* and point out that it is important to know whether nouns are countable or uncountable because we use different quantifiers with the two kinds of nouns, e.g. *I don't eat many vegetables*, NOT ~~*I don't eat much vegetables*~~. Point out that we use *a lot of* in affirmative sentences, e.g. *I play a lot of games*, NOT ~~*I play many games*~~. Sts complete the rules. Check answers, then ask questions to check concept.

Answers
1 uncountable 2 countable 3 all

Concept check questions: *Do we use 'a lot of' with countable or uncountable nouns, or both?* (both). *Many – countable or uncountable nouns?* (countable). *Much – countable or uncountable nouns?* (uncountable). *How do I ask questions about quantity?* (*how much* and *how many*). *How much fruit do you eat? – correct?* (yes). *What are the answers?* (*a lot* or *not much*).

2 Sts look at the pictures and complete the sentences with the correct words. Check answers, referring back to the grammar box to explain them if necessary.

Answers
2 a lot of 3 many 4 much

3 **PRONUNCIATION** 5.6

Model and drill pronunciation of the /h/ sound in isolation. Point out that this sound is often used at the beginning of a word. Play the audio once for sts to listen, then play it again for them to repeat the words.

4 5.7

Put sts into pairs and ask them to practise saying the sentences. Play the audio for them to listen and compare, then play the audio again. Ask individual sts to repeat, or get the whole class to repeat together. You could ask sts in pairs to write their own sentence using words with the /h/ sound. They could swap sentences with another pair and practise saying the sentence they are given.

5 5.8 Ask sts to complete the quiz with the correct words. Check these answers, then put sts into pairs to match the questions with the answers. Play the audio for them to listen and check. See who guessed all the answers correctly. Ask: *Which facts do you find surprising? Why?*

Answers
1 How much; e
2 How much; c
3 How many; a
4 How much; b
5 How many; d

6 Read through the questions with the class and check that sts understand them all. Put sts into pairs to ask and answer the questions. Point out they should use quantifiers in their answers. Ask some sts to tell the class something about their partner, using quantifiers, e.g. *Ana doesn't each much chocolate*.

FAST FINISHER

Sts imagine they are interviewing their favourite sports person and write questions with *how much / how many*, then write the answers. You could ask sts in pairs to perform some of their interviews for the class. Weaker sts could work in pairs. They think of one more question to ask their partner, using *how much / how many*. They then work with a different partner to ask and answer their questions, using quantifiers.

EXTRA PRACTICE

Play a game of noughts and crosses / tic tac toe. Draw a 3 x 3 grid on the board and fill the nine squares randomly with quantifiers from the lesson: *a lot of*, *much*, *many*, *a lot of*, *how much*, *how many*, *many*, *much a lot of*. Some quantifiers will be repeated. Arrange sts into two teams: O and X. Teams take turns to choose a square and make a sentence with the quantifier. If the sentence is correct, put an O or an X in the square. To win the game, teams have to make a line of three Os or three Xs. Play once or twice as a class, then put sts into pairs to play against each other.

G **Grammar practice: WB** p.44
Sts will find more practice for quantifiers here. Set these exercises for homework.

LS **Language summary: Unit 5 SB** p.131

KEEP TALKING!

What can I get you?

READING and LISTENING

I can understand a menu.

1 **Work in pairs. Do you have a favourite restaurant or café? What do you usually order there?**

2 **Read the menu for The Natural Kitchen and answer the questions.**

1 Which salads have got fruit in them?
2 What type of meat is in the meatballs?
3 What meals can vegetarians eat?
4 You've only got £1.00. What can you buy?
5 You don't like fruit juice. What can you order?

3 **Work in pairs and discuss the questions.**

1 Do you think The Natural Kitchen is a healthy or unhealthy place to eat? Why?
2 What is your favourite thing on the menu?

4 5.9 **Listen to two friends at The Natural Kitchen. What do they decide to order?**

5 5.9 **Listen again. Which ingredients do they mention?**

KEEP TALKING!

What can I get you?

READING and LISTENING

Sts study a café menu and discuss what things on the menu they like. They listen to two friends who are deciding what to order. They then learn how to order food and drink in a restaurant or café. They read and hear a model dialogue and personalise the Useful language by following the steps in the Speaking plan.

WARMER

Play a game to revise food vocabulary. Say: *In my shopping basket, I have ….* Elicit an answer from a student sitting near the front of the class, e.g. *some apples*. Ask the next student to repeat this and add another item, e.g. *In my shopping basket, I have some apples and some cereal*. Continue around the class, with each student repeating all the previous items and adding one more. Continue until the list becomes too long to remember!

1 Put sts into pairs to discuss the question. Ask some sts to tell the class about their favourite café or restaurant and what they order there.

2 Read through the menu with the class. Teach the meaning of words that are new to sts. Check they understand *vegetarian*, then ask them to read the questions and answer them. They could work in pairs for this. Check answer with the class.

Answers
1 Taste of Thailand
2 chicken
3 Plant Power; Korean Curry
4 bread; chocolate cookie
5 mineral water

3 Sts discuss the questions in pairs. Discuss the answers with the class, encouraging sts to give reasons for their answers.

4 5.9 Explain to sts that they will hear two friends who are in the café, looking at the menu. Read out the question, and remind sts that when they listen and make notes they should write only the important words. Play the audio for sts to listen and note down what the people order. See TG page 278 for audio script. Allow sts to compare their answers in pairs, then play the audio again for them to listen and check their answers. Check answers with the class, playing the audio again and pausing if necessary to confirm the answers.

Answers
1 Plant Power, bottle of mineral water
2 Super Salmon; bread

5 5.9 Read out the question and teach the meaning of *ingredients*. Ask: *Can you remember any ingredients they mention?* Play the audio again for sts to listen and note down the ingredients the people mention. Check answers, playing the audio again and pausing if necessary to confirm the answers.

Answers
mango, seafood, vegetables, nuts, chicken, meatballs, salmon, fish

EXTRA PRACTICE

Write these gapped sentences on the board:

1 *It's … seafood in it.*
2 *I … Mexican food.*
3 *I don't … chicken.*
4 *I'm … about the Mexican Meatballs.*
5 *Why … have the Super Salmon?*
6 *Yes, … idea.*
7 *… we order?*

Put sts into pairs to try to remember the missing words. Play the audio again for them to check, and check that sts understand all the sentences.

Answers
1 got
2 love
3 really like
4 not sure
5 don't you
6 good
7 Shall

EXTRA PRACTICE

Sts could work in pairs. They imagine they are in the Natural Kitchen and they are deciding what to order. Ask them to prepare and practise a conversation. You could write some useful phrases from the audio on the board to help them. Monitor and help while they are working, then invite one or two confident pairs to perform their conversations for the class.

SPEAKING Ordering food and drink

I can order food and drink in a restaurant or café.

1 **Read the dialogue and look at the menu on page 54. How much does Alina's order cost?**

2 5.10 **Listen and read. Check your answer.**

Server: Can I help?
Alina: Hi, I'd like the Plant Power salad, please.
Server: Anything to drink?
Alina: Can I have an orange juice?
Server: OK. Anything else? Any dessert?
Alina: Yes please, I'll have a chocolate cookie.
Server: Is that to eat in or take away?
Alina: To take away.
Server: OK, that's £ ..., please.
Alina: Here you are.
Server: Thank you. Your food is just coming.

3 5.11 **Listen and repeat the Useful language.**

Useful language
Ordering food

Server	Customer
Can I help? / What can I get you?	I'd like ..., please.
Anything to drink? / Anything else?	Can I have ...?
Is that to eat in or take away?	I'll have ...
That's ... pounds, please.	To take away. / To eat in.
Your food is just coming.	Here you are.

4 5.12 **Read the Look! Box. Put the dialogue in order. Listen and check.**

Look! *water* vs *a water*

Food and drink words like *juice, water* and *salad* are usually uncountable. But when you order food, you can say: *a salad, a water* or *an orange juice.*

a **Server:** Hello, what can I get you?
b **Boy:** Here you are.
c **Server:** OK, that's £7.75, please.
d **Boy:** To eat in.
e **Server:** One Korean Curry. Anything else?
f **Boy:** I'd like the Korean Curry, please.
g **Server:** Sure. Is that to eat in or take away?
h **Boy:** Yes, can I have a fruit salad?
i **Server:** Thank you.

5 **GET CREATIVE** **Work in pairs. Invent your own restaurant or café and create a menu. Choose a name for your restaurant and illustrate the menu with pictures.**

6 **Work in pairs. Choose what you want to eat and drink, and order it. Follow the steps in the Speaking plan.**

Speaking plan

Prepare
- Decide on your roles.
- Use your menu from Exercise 5 or the menu on page 54.
- Make notes for your dialogue.

Speak
- Practise your dialogue.
- Use phrases from the Useful language box.
- Be polite: use *please* and *thank you.*
- Act out your dialogue without notes.

Reflect
- How can you improve next time?
- Swap roles and act out a new dialogue.

Now play *Keep moving!*

FAST FINISHER
Write a review of your favourite restaurant.
My favourite restaurant is Café Rio. It's a Brazilian restaurant. My favourite thing on the menu is ... .

LS Language summary: Unit 5 SB p.131

SPEAKING Ordering food and drink

1 Focus on the picture and explain that it shows two friends at the Natural Kitchen. Use the picture to teach the words *server* and *customer*. Read out the question, then ask sts to read the dialogue and work out how much Alina's order costs. You could do this as a race, to make it more challenging. Don't check the answer yet.

Answer
£8

2 5.10 Play the audio for sts to listen and check the answer to Exercise 1. See TG page 278 for audio script. Check the answer with the class.

3 5.11 Ask sts if they can remember some of the phrases the server and customers use. Read through the Useful language box with the class and check sts understand all the phrases. Play the audio once for sts to listen to the phrases, then play it again for them to repeat.

Ask questions to check concept.

Concept check questions: *What does the server say to ask me what I want?* (Can I help? / What can I get you?). *How do I order Super Salmon?* (I'd like Super Salmon, please. / Can I have ...? / I'll have ...). *If I want to take the food home with me, what do I say?* (to take away). *My meal is £6. What does the server say?* (That's six pounds, please). *When I give the server the money, what do I say?* (Here you are).

4 5.12 Read the Look! box with the class. Give one or two examples to illustrate the different uses of *salad*, e.g. *I love salad!* (uncountable) *I'd like a salad, please*. (countable). Elicit similar examples using *water* and *orange juice*. Ask sts to read the dialogue and put it in the correct order. Allow sts to compare their answers in pairs, then play the audio for them to listen and check. See TG pages 278–279 for audio script. If your sts would benefit from some controlled practice before the personalised practice, they could practise this dialogue in pairs.

Answers
a, f, e, h, g, d, c, b, i

21st Century skills

5 **GET CREATIVE**

Read out the task, then put sts into pairs to invent their own restaurant or café. Encourage them to look back through the unit for ideas of food and drinks they can include on their menu. You could also brainstorm some ideas with the class first. Teach any vocabulary that sts might need, e.g. *pizza*, *burger*, *ice cream*. Ask some pairs to present their restaurant or café and menu to the class.

6 Sts follow the steps in the Speaking plan to practise ordering food and drink in a restaurant or café.

Speaking plan

Prepare

Sts work in their pairs and decide who is the customer and the server. They use their own menu or the menu on page 54 to make notes for their dialogue. Remind sts to use the Useful language in Exercise 3 to help them.

Speak

Sts practise their dialogue in their pairs. They can practise with and then without notes. Monitor and help as necessary. If your sts use smartphones in class, they could record their conversations.

Reflect

Discuss as a class how sts could improve next time. Encourage them to be honest and open about the things they did well and the things they can do better. If you noticed any typical errors, correct them with the class. If sts record their conversations, ask them to use this to help them think of how they could improve next time. Sts could swap menus and practise again. Ask some sts to perform their dialogues for the class if they feel confident.

Keep moving!

This lesson features an optional language revision and consolidation game for use in digital classrooms. Players control different characters, each with their own personalities and special abilities.

FAST FINISHER

Sts write a review of their favourite restaurant, saying why they like it and what food they like there. Weaker sts could work in pairs. They could talk about restaurants they know and say which ones they like and what food they enjoy eating there.

S **Speaking practice: WB** p.45
Sts will find more practice for ordering food and drink in a restaurant or café here. Set these exercises for homework.

LS **Language summary: Unit 5 SB** p.131

REAL CULTURE!

International festivals

I can compare festivals and celebrations in other countries with my country.

Favourite Festivals

What's your favourite festival or celebration? Write and tell us.

1 Ethan,
Washington DC, USA

My favourite celebration is Independence Day on the fourth of July. What happens? We decorate the house, and we invite family and friends to a barbecue. Dad makes a lot of food – burgers, sweetcorn, fried chicken and salads. For dessert, my grandma always makes a fruit pie in the colours of the American flag – red, white and blue! In the evening, we watch the fireworks over the city. It's beautiful!

2 Yanlin,
London, UK

I'm from London, but my parents are Chinese. I love Chinese New Year! It happens in January or February. We clean our homes and we put up red decorations for good luck. On the evening before New Year, we have a family dinner. We eat fish and chicken with vegetables and rice. At midnight, there are fireworks – it's very noisy! The next day, there's a parade in the street, with lion dances and traditional Chinese music.

3 Meera,
Mumbai, India

My favourite festival is Diwali, or 'the festival of lights'. It takes place in October or early November, and it lasts for five days. We clean the house and decorate it with lights, and we wear new clothes. We have a big family meal with vegetarian curries, rice, samosas (Indian snacks with potatoes and vegetables) and special cakes. In the evening, there's music, dancing and fireworks.

REAL CULTURE!

International festivals

Sts learn about three different festivals in different countries, focusing on how people celebrate and what kinds of food they eat. They study verb-noun collocations then discuss celebrations and festivals in their own country.

This lesson features an optional culture video about how people celebrate Diwali in New York: see SB page 57.

WARMER

Ask: *What special days do people celebrate in your country?* Elicit a few ideas, e.g. Christmas, Easter. Ask: *Do you have a special meal? Who with? In a restaurant or at home? What special food do you eat?* Elicit a range of answers and teach any food vocabulary that sts need. Teach the words *festival* and *celebrations* Ask: *What festivals and celebrations do you know about in other countries or cultures? When are they? What do people do to celebrate?* Elicit what sts know about other festivals.

BACKGROUND

American Independence Day celebrates the date when the United States became an independent country. Until 1776, America was ruled by Britain.

Diwali is celebrated by Hindus, Jains, Sikhs and Buddhists. It symbolises the victory of light (good) over dark (evil).

Chinese New Year is celebrated by Chinese communities all over the world. The Chinese calendar is not the same as the standard Western calendar, so the date of Chinese New Year varies slightly each year.

1 Read out the names of the three festivals and elicit what sts know about them. Ask more questions if necessary to help them, e.g. *Which countries do people celebrate them in? When do they celebrate them? When are they?* Put sts into pairs to look at the pictures and try to match them to the celebrations. Elicit a few ideas, but don't confirm them.

2 5.13 Play the audio for sts to read and listen to the article to check their answers to exercise 1. Check answers with the class, and ask: *What else did you learn about each festival?* Elicit what sts can remember about the festivals.

Answers
1 c, d 2 e, f 3 a, b

3 Ask sts to read the article again and decide which celebration each sentence describes. Point out that some sentences describe more than one celebration. Allow sts to compare their answers in pairs, then check answers with the class, eliciting the part of the article which confirms each answer.

Answers
1 American Independence Day, Chinese New Year, Diwali
2 Diwali
3 Chinese New Year
4 Chinese New Year, Diwali
5 American Independence Day, Chinese New Year, Diwali
6 American Independence Day
7 Chinese New Year, Diwali
8 Chinese New Year, Diwali

4 **Word Power** Read out the task and explain to sts that some verbs and nouns go together to make phrases, and it is useful to learn these phrases. Ask sts to look at the article on page 56 again and match the verbs and nouns. Check answers, and check that sts understand all the phrases. Then focus on each phrase in turn and elicit other nouns that go with each verb.

Answers
2 d 3 c 4 b 5 e 6 a

Other nouns (example answers):
1 clean: your bedroom, a car, windows
2 wear: jeans, a coat, new shoes
3 decorate: your bedroom, the school, the classroom
4 invite: friends, your classmates, your cousins
5 make: a salad, pizzas, cookies, a cake
6 watch: TV, a film, a band

EXTRA PRACTICE

Before sts move on to the listening task, put them into pairs and ask them to find as many words for food and drink as they can in the article on page 56. Write all the words on the board and check that sts understand them all. Ask: *Which of these foods do you like? Which don't you like?*

Answers
barbecue, burgers, sweetcorn, fried chicken, salad, dessert, fruit pie, fish, chicken, vegetables, rice, curries, samosas, potatoes

1 What do you know about celebrations 1–3? Match them with pictures a–f.

1 American Independence Day
2 Chinese New Year
3 Diwali

2 5.13 Read and listen to the magazine article and check your answers.

3 Read the article again. Say which celebration or celebrations the sentences describe.

People clean their homes.
Diwali and Chinese New Year.

1 People decorate their houses.
2 People don't usually eat meat.
3 Red is a lucky colour.
4 People eat rice.
5 People watch fireworks.
6 It takes place in the middle of the year.
7 The festival is on more than one day.
8 People dance.

4 Word Power Match the verbs with the nouns to make phrases. Can you think of other nouns that go with these verbs?

1 c clean the house — clean your room, clean the car

1	clean	a	fireworks
2	wear	b	family and friends to a barbecue
3	decorate	c	the house
4	invite	d	new clothes
5	make	e	a fruit pie
6	watch	f	the house with lights

5 5.14 Listen to three dialogues. Match each conversation with a festival.

6 5.14 Listen again and answer true (T) or false (F).

1 In dialogue 1, the boy's father is decorating the house.
2 The weather isn't very good.
3 In dialogue 2, the girl is talking to her aunt and uncle.
4 Her grandmother is wearing a new dress.
5 In dialogue 3, the boy and girl are watching fireworks.
6 The girl's friend is a dancer.

7 5.15 Complete the text below about American Independence Day with the numbers in the box. Listen and check.

4 43 65 1776 16,000 7 billion

8 COMPARE CULTURES Think about a festival or celebration in your country. Work in pairs and ask and answer the questions. Can you guess your partner's festival or celebration?

1 Do people decorate their houses?
2 Do people wear special clothes?
3 Do people invite friends to their homes?
4 What food do people make or eat?
5 Do people watch fireworks?
6 What special things do people do?

Now watch the culture video.

FAST FINISHER

Imagine you are making the food for a celebration at your house. Write a shopping list.

INDEPENDENCE DAY
in numbers

Every year on [1] … July, millions of Americans celebrate Independence Day.

It's a celebration of America's independence from Great Britain in [2] … .

[3] … % of Americans have a barbecue or picnic. Altogether, people spend more than [4] … dollars on food.

Offices and schools close for the day, and friends and families get together.

Americans love fireworks on Independence Day! There are more than [5] … firework displays in the country, and [6] … % of people go to one.

REAL CULTURE!

5 5.14 Explain to sts that they will hear three dialogues with people who are celebrating one of the festivals on page 56. See TG page 279 for audio script. Play the audio. Sts listen and match each dialogue with a festival. Check answers with the class.

Answers
1 American Independence Day
2 Diwali
3 Chinese New Year

6 5.14 Allow sts time to read through the sentences. Play the audio again for them to listen and decide if the sentences are true or false. Check answers.

Answers
1 F 2 F 3 F 4 T 5 T 6 T

7 5.15 Read through the numbers in the box with the class and elicit how to say them. Allow sts time to read through the information about Independence Day. Puts sts into pairs to complete the information with the correct numbers. Play the audio for them to listen and check their answers. Check answers.

Answers

1 4	3 43	5 16,000
2 1776	4 7 billion	6 65

21st Century skills

8 **COMPARE CULTURES**

As a class, brainstorm some ideas for festivals and celebrations in the students' own country. Ask sts individually to think of one of the festivals you have brainstormed, or an idea of their own. Ask them to read the questions and think about the answers for their festival. When sts have finished, explain that they will now ask and answer the questions in pairs and try to guess their partner's festival. Put sts into pairs to ask and answer the questions. Ask some sts to tell the class which festival their partner chose, and whether they guessed it easily.

Culture video

You can watch this in class if you have time and access to video, or you can ask sts to download it from the Richmond Learning Platform to watch at home. See Diwali in New York on TG pages 299 and 306–307.

EXTRA PRACTICE

Arrange sts in small groups and ask each group to research a different festival that people in English-speaking countries celebrate. For example: Bonfire Night (England), Hogmanay (Scotland), Halloween (the USA), Thanksgiving (the USA and Canada), St Patrick's Day (Ireland), Christmas / Easter / Eid (various countries). They should prepare a short presentation using the questions in Exercise 8 to help them. Allow time for sts to practise their presentation in their group. They could use phones to film each other and then discuss what they need to improve. Then, ask sts to present their work to the class.

FAST FINISHER

Sts think of the food they need to make for a festival and write a shopping list. You could ask some sts to read their shopping list to the class, and see if other sts can guess the festival. Weaker sts could work in pairs. They could choose a festival they both like and write two or three sentences about the food they eat for this festival.

Enjoy!

WRITING A recipe

I can write a simple recipe.

1 Ask and answer in pairs. Do you like cooking? Do you sometimes cook for your family? What is your favourite recipe?

2 Read the recipe for Spaghetti Bolognese. How long does it take to make the Bolognese sauce?

SPAGHETTI BOLOGNESE

This is a popular pasta dish. It's delicious and very easy to make. I often make it for my friends!

DIFFICULTY	TIME	SERVES
4/10	70 mins	4

INGREDIENTS

- 400 g beef
- Olive oil
- Onion
- Garlic
- 800 g tomato sauce
- 400 g spaghetti
- Salt and pepper
- Cheese

INSTRUCTIONS

1. First, fry the beef in some oil for about ten minutes until it is brown.
2. Then, cut the onion and garlic into small pieces and add them to the meat. Cook for another five minutes.
3. Next, add the tomato sauce and mix everything together.
4. Cook for about 45 minutes. Add some salt and pepper.
5. Finally, cook the spaghetti in water for about ten minutes.
6. Put the spaghetti on the plate and add the sauce. Serve with some cheese. Enjoy!

3 Look at the **Useful language**. Notice how we give instructions using the imperative. How do you say these instructions in your language?

Useful language

Instructions

Fry *some onions.*
Add *some cheese.*
Cut *up some fruit.*
Cook *in an oven.*
Serve *in a bowl.*

4 Study the **Look!** box. We use sequence words to show the order of instructions. What punctuation do we use after a sequence word?

Look! Sequence words

We use sequencing words to help us order events in our writing.

First, *cook the beef.*
Then, *cut the garlic.*
Next, *add the tomato sauce.*
Finally, *cook the spaghetti.*

5 Put the instructions for making fries in order. Include sequence words and write the instructions in your notebook.

a cut the potatoes into long, thin pieces
b serve the potatoes with ketchup. Enjoy!
c wash the potatoes *1*
d fry the potatoes

6 Write a recipe for a dish that you know. Follow the steps in the **Writing plan**.

Writing plan

Prepare

› Choose a simple dish.
› Research the ingredients and instructions.

Write

› Write the recipe. Add a short introduction and a picture.
› Use the expressions from the Useful language box.
› Use sequence words to show the order.

Reflect

› Check your grammar: *some*, *any*, *a*, *an*, imperatives.
› Check sequence words.
› Check your spelling.

W Writing summary: WB p.88   E Exams: Unit 5 SB p.122   LS Language summary: Unit 5 SB p.131

Enjoy!

WRITING A recipe

Sts read a recipe for Spaghetti Bolognese. They study sequence words and learn useful language for writing instructions. They then follow the steps in the Writing plan to write a recipe for a dish that they know.

Writing
A recipe
Useful language
Instructions *Fry ..., Cut ..., Cook ..., Add ..., Serve ...*
Look!
Sequence words

WARMER

Remind sts about the two teenagers they read about earlier in the unit, Cory and Mikaila. Ask: *Can you remember the ingredients that Cory uses for his cookies?* Elicit the ingredients he uses (flour, butter, sugar, chocolate). Ask: *What do you think he does with the ingredients? Does he put the flour with the chocolate first? Does he mix the butter with the sugar?* Elicit a few ideas, then teach the word *recipe*. Explain to sts that they are going to read a recipe and then write their own recipe. Teach the word *dish*.

1 Put sts into pairs to discuss the questions. Elicit who in the class likes cooking and what their favourite recipes are.

2 Focus on the picture and ask: *Do you recognise this dish? Do you like it? What ingredients does it have? Do you know how to make it?* Elicit a range of answers. Then read out the question and explain the meaning of *sauce*. Ask sts to read the recipe and answer the question. Check the answer.

> **Answer**
> 60 minutes in total

3 Read the Useful language box with sts about instructions. Check they understand all the verbs and ask them how they say these instructions in their first language. Point out that when we give instructions in English, we use the imperative form of the verb (the same as the base form) and we don't use the pronoun *you*, e.g. *Fry the onions*, NOT ~~*You fry the onions*~~. Elicit or teach the negative form: *Don't ...*, e.g. *Don't cook it for very long.*

4 Read the Look! box with sts about sequence words. Check they understand them all, and explain that when we give instructions, sequence words are important to make it clear what order we should do things in. Ask sts to find examples of the sequence words in the recipe and elicit that we use a comma after them.

> **Answer**
> A comma

5 Ask sts to write the instructions in the correct order, using sequence words. Allow sts to compare their answers in pairs, then check answers with the class.

> **Answers**
> c, a, d, b
> First, wash the potatoes. Then, cut the potatoes into long, thin pieces. Next, fry the potatoes. Finally, serve the potatoes with ketchup. Enjoy!

6 Explain to sts that they will now write a recipe for a dish that they know, following the steps in the Writing plan.

Writing plan

Prepare

Sts work as individuals to choose a simple dish and research the ingredients and instructions. You could brainstorm a few ideas for dishes with the class. If you are short of time, you could choose one or two dishes as a class and elicit or teach the ingredients for them. Make notes on the board for sts to use to write their recipe.

Write

Sts then write their recipes using the recipe in Exercise 2 as a model. Refer them back to the Useful language box for instructions and remind them to use sequence words.

Reflect

Ask sts to check their grammar, spelling and punctuation and make any necessary changes. Sts could then swap their recipes with a partner and give feedback on the use of the Useful language, sequence words and quantifiers.

W **Writing practice: WB** p.46
Sts will find more practice for writing here. Set these exercises for homework.

W **Writing summary: WB** p.88

E **Exams: Unit 5 SB** p.122

LS **Language summary: Unit 5 SB** p.131

Wonderful world

6

Vocabulary: The natural world; Wild animals | **Grammar:** Comparative adjectives; (*not*) *as ... as ...*; Superlative adjectives | **Speaking:** Buying a ticket | **Writing:** A fact sheet

VOCABULARY The natural world

I can talk about the natural world.

1 6.1 **Match the words in the box with the picture. Listen, check and repeat.**

beach desert forest island lake mountain
rainforest river sea sky volcano waterfall

2 6.2 **Work in pairs. Do the Geography quiz. Listen and check your answers.**

1 K2 is a very high *mountain / forest* between China and Pakistan.
2 The Amazon is *a river / an island* in South America. It's home to piranhas and caimans.
3 Half of the Earth's animal species live in *rainforests / deserts*.
4 Vesuvius is *a volcano / a beach* in Italy near the old city of Pompeii.
5 Angel Falls is *a waterfall / a lake* in Venezuela. It's 979 metres high.
6 Bali is a beautiful *island / sea* in Indonesia. It's very popular with tourists.

3 **Work in pairs. Write three true or false sentences about other places in the world. Read your sentences to another pair.**

A: Kilimanjaro is a mountain. True or false?
B: We think it's true.
A: You're right.

Now watch the vlog.

FAST FINISHER

Write sentences about the geography of your country.

There are mountains, rivers and forests in La Rioja.

LS **Language summary: Unit 6** **SB** p.132

Wonderful world 6

UNIT 6 OVERVIEW: The topic for this unit is the natural world. Sts read an article about a distant planet, Trappist-1e and listen to two people doing a quiz about wild animals. They read online adverts for activities and learn how to buy a ticket. They read about the natural wonders of the USA and finally, they read a fact sheet about orangutans and write a fact sheet about another animal. They also watch a vlog about travelling in East Java and a culture video about taking part in an extreme cycle race.

Vocabulary	Grammar	Pronunciation	Reading	Listening	Speaking	Writing
The natural world; Wild animals	Comparative adjectives; (*not*) *as ... as*; Superlative adjectives	/ɜː/	Understanding the main idea of a text	Using existing knowledge to help before listening	Buying a ticket	A fact sheet

VOCABULARY The natural world

Sts learn words for the natural world. They identify these from picture clues, then listen and check their answers. They do a geography quiz, then personalise the vocabulary by writing some true and false sentences about places around the world.

Vocabulary

The natural world (*beach, desert, forest, island, lake, mountain, rainforest, river, sea, sky, volcano, waterfall)*

Vlog

Steve: *Exploring the island of East Java*

WARMER

Tell sts you are going to describe some places and they must say the words. Say: *This is a lot of water. When you go on holiday, it's nice to swim in it. Boats go on it, to go to another country.* Elicit the word (*sea*). Repeat this with *mountain* (*This is a very high place. You can go up to the top, and then you can see all around*). Write the words on the board as sts guess them, then teach the expression *natural world*. Ask: *Do you know any more words for things in the natural world?*

1 6.1 Read through the words in the box and elicit or teach the meanings. Sts look at the picture and match the words with the places in the picture. Play the audio for sts to listen, check and repeat.

Answers

1 sky	5 forest	9 waterfall
2 volcano	6 rainforest	10 island
3 mountain	7 lake	11 sea
4 desert	8 river	12 beach

2 6.2 Put sts into pairs to do the Geography quiz. You could pre-teach *piranhas* (= a kind of fierce fish), *caiman* (= a kind of crocodile) and *species*. Play the audio for sts to check their answers. Check answers.

Answers

1 mountain	3 rainforests	5 a waterfall
2 a river	4 a volcano	6 island

3 Explain the task to sts and read out the example answers. Sts then work in pairs and write three true or false sentences. Put pairs together into groups of four to read their sentences to each other and guess if they are true or false. When they have finished, ask who guessed all the sentences correctly.

Vlog

This lesson contains an optional vlog in which travel vlogger Steve talks about his visit to the island of East Java. You can watch this in class if you have time and access to video, or you can ask sts to download it from the Richmond Learning Platform to watch at home. See TG pages 291 and 305.

FAST FINISHER

Sts who finish early can write sentences about the geography of their country. Weaker sts could work in pairs. They each write three of the words from Exercise 1 with the letters in a jumbled order. They then swap with their partner and try to guess their partner's words.

EXTRA PRACTICE

Put sts into pairs. They take turns to talk about the geography of their own country, saying what interesting places there are to visit. Their partner films them using their phone. Ask them to try to speak for one minute. They can watch their films back and discuss in their pairs how they could improve. If there is time, they could repeat the activity and try to improve.

V **Vocabulary practice: WB** p.48

Sts will find more practice of vocabulary for the natural world here. Set these exercises for homework.

LS **Language summary: Unit 6 SB** p.132

Your new planet!

READING

I can understand the main idea of a text.

Welcome to your new planet!

'Ladies and gentlemen, we are arriving at our destination. Please return to your seats.' While the pilot makes his final announcements, I look through the window of the spaceship. On the planet below, I can see oceans, rivers and icy lakes. The mountains are higher than on Earth, and the oceans are more beautiful. The spaceship lands on a large island in the middle of a lake. 'Welcome to Trappist-1e,' says the pilot. We step out on to the planet. It isn't as warm as Earth, but the air is cleaner. It's the start of a better life for me and my family …

The story is science fiction, but Trappist-1e is a real planet. It's about 40 light years from the Sun, and scientists are very excited about it. Why? Because it's very similar to Earth, and it's possible that there is water – and life – on the planet. Scientists are using special telescopes to take a closer look and to find out more. So is Trappist-1e a possible destination for humans? Not at the moment. It's further than 300 trillion* kilometres from Earth – a journey of 800,000 years! But in the future, with faster and more powerful spaceships, who knows?

(*1 trillion = 1 million million)

1 6.3 **Read and listen to the article. Which is correct, a, b or c?**

a It's about a real planet. A spaceship is planning to go there.
b It's a science fiction story. The planet isn't real.
c It's about a real planet – possibly with water and life.

2 Read the article again and answer the questions.

1 What can the person in the spaceship see on Trappist-1e?
2 Why is he/she travelling there?
3 Is he/she travelling alone? How do you know?
4 Why are scientists excited about Trappist-1e?
5 What are scientists using to explore the planet?
6 Is it possible for people to fly there? Why/Why not?

3 Word Power Match the numbers with the words.

100 1,000 100,000 1,000,000
1,000,000,000 1,000,000,000,000

a billion a hundred a hundred thousand
a million a thousand a trillion

4 Choose three of the numbers in Exercise 3 and write sentences with them.

The population of my country is about 50 million.

The Earth is billions of years old.

5 THINK CRITICALLY Imagine you are going to another planet. There is food and water, and you can also take three more things. What do you take? Make a list and discuss your ideas in groups.

6 FIND OUT What is the name of the large volcano on Mars? How tall is it? Is it active?

60

 EXTRA PRACTICE Workbook page 49

Your new planet!

READING

Sts read an article about a distant planet, Trappist-1e. The article contains part of a science fiction story about the planet, and some factual information about the planet. While they are reading, they focus on understanding the main idea of a text. They learn to use comparative adjectives and (*not*) *as* … *as* to compare things. They then practise using comparative adjectives and (*not*) *as* … *as* by comparing people and things that they know.

Reading text

An article about the planet Trappist-1e

Reading skill

Understanding the main idea of a text

WARMER

Write the word *planet* on the board and elicit or teach the meaning. Ask: *What planets are close to the Earth? How many can you name?* Elicit the names of any that sts know, e.g. *Mars, Jupiter, Saturn, Mercury, Venus, Uranus, Neptune*. Ask: *Do you know the names of any planets that are a long way away? Do you like reading stories or watching films about space travel? Which ones have you read or seen?* Elicit a few ideas.

1 6.3 **Understanding the main idea of a text**
Read out the question and the three possible answers. Point out to sts that to choose the correct answer, they don't need to understand every detail in the text, but they need to understand the main idea. Explain that when they read a new text for the first time, it is a good idea to read it to understand the main idea, and not worry if they don't understand all the details. Play the audio for sts to read and listen to the article. Check the answer, and elicit why the other two answers are not correct.

Answer
c

2 Ask sts to read the article again and answer the questions. Check answers with the class, eliciting the part of the text which confirms each answer.

Answers
1 oceans, rivers, icy lakes, mountains
2 to start a new life with his/her family
3 No, the person is travelling with his / her family (and others). The pilot says, 'Ladies and gentlemen' and the person mentions his / her family.
4 it's very similar to Earth; it's possible that water and life are on the planet
5 special telescopes
6 not at the moment; it would take 800,000 years to get there.

3 **Word Power** Sts could work in pairs to match the numbers with the words. Check answers with the class, and elicit how to say all the numbers. For extra practice, you could invite two or three sts to come and write a different big number on the board. Other sts can work out how to say it.

Answers
100 – a hundred
1,000 – a thousand
100,000 – a hundred thousand
1,000,000 – a million
1,000,000,000 – a billion
1,000,000,000,000 – a trillion

4 Sts could work individually or in pairs to write their sentences. Ask some sts to read their sentences to the class.

EXTRA PRACTICE

Arrange sts in pairs. Write three headings on the board: *People*, *The natural world*, *Parts of a space ship*. Ask sts to copy them, then read the text *Welcome to your new planet!* again and find words for each category. Tell them to look up any new words to check the meaning. Put sts in pairs to compare their ideas at the end.

Possible answers
People: ladies, gentlemen, pilot, scientists, humans
The natural world: planet, oceans, rivers, lakes, Earth, island, the Sun
Parts of a spaceship: seat, window

21st Century skills

5 **THINK CRITICALLY**
Read out the task and elicit a few examples of things sts might decide to take, e.g. a telescope, a tablet for playing games, etc. Ask sts individually to think about three things they would like to take, then put them into groups. Tell them they should each explain their choices, then discuss which are the best ideas and why. Ask them to see if they can agree on three things they would all like to take. Ask groups in turn to tell the class what they decided on and why.

21st Century skills

6 **FIND OUT**
Set this exercise for homework if you prefer. Sts can find this information out by looking online or in other media, or by asking other people. The answer to the question is Olympus Mons.

You could also ask sts to find out if there are any other planets that could possibly support life.

R **Reading practice: WB** p.49
You will find more practice for reading here. Set these exercises for homework.

GRAMMAR Comparative adjectives

I can use comparative adjectives to compare things.

Now watch the grammar animation.

1 **Copy and complete the grammar box with words from the article on page 60.**

	Adjective	Comparative adjective
Short adjectives	high close easy big	high**er** [1] … eas**ier** bi**gger**
Long adjectives	beautiful exciting	[2] … **more** exciting
Irregular adjectives	good bad far	[3] … **worse** **further**

2 **Write sentences with a comparative adjective and *than*. Use your notebook.**

Everest is *higher than* Kilimanjaro. (high)

1. The Sahara Desert is … the Atacama desert. (hot)
2. Some volcanoes are … others. (dangerous)
3. The Indian Ocean is … the Pacific Ocean. (warm)
4. The Amazon rainforest is … France, Spain and Germany together. (large)
5. Camping on a beach is … camping in the desert. (easy)
6. Food on Earth is … food in space! (good)

3 6.4 **Complete the text. Use the comparative form of the adjectives in the box. Listen and check.**

active clean happy healthy ~~long~~ old sunny

THE SECRETS OF
A LONGER LIFE

Okinawa is a beautiful island in Japan, with mountains, forests and beaches. The people there enjoy a <u>*longer*</u> life than people in other parts of the world. A lot of them are [1] … than 100! What's their secret?

- The weather in Okinawa is [2] … than in other parts of Japan.
- People eat [3] …food, with lots of vegetables.
- People are [4] … in their free time. For example, they walk, work in their gardens or do *tai chi*.
- The air is [5] … than in a big modern city.
- People are [6] … because they spend a lot of time with family and friends.

4 **Read the Look! box. Complete each second sentence so that it means the same as the first sentence. Use the adjective in brackets.**

Look! ***(not) as … as***

Trappist-1e is as big as Earth. (= it's the same size)
Earth isn't as big as the Sun. (= the Sun is bigger than Earth)

a Spain is warmer than the UK. (warm)
b The UK isn't *as warm as Spain*.

1 a An ocean is bigger than a lake. (big)
b A lake isn't … .

2 a Cities are noisier than villages. (noisy)
b Villages aren't … .

3 a My grandfather is the same age as my grandmother. (old)
b My grandfather is … .

4 a The traffic in Los Angeles is worse than the traffic in London. (bad)
b The traffic in London is not … .

5 a The Burj Khalifa tower in Dubai is the same height as some mountains. (high)
b The Burj Khalifa tower is … .

5 **In pairs, discuss your opinions about these things.**

A: I think that basketball is more exciting than football.
B: I don't agree. I think that football is more exciting.

1. basketball or football? (exciting)
2. Mexican food or Chinese food? (good)
3. money or friends? (important)
4. classical music or jazz? (bad)
5. Science or History? (interesting)
6. a day at the beach or a day at the shops? (relaxing)

FUN FACT

On an island in the Philippines, there's a big lake. In the lake, there's a smaller island called Volcano Island. On this island, there's another smaller lake, and in this lake there's a tiny island called Vulcan Point. So … Vulcan Point is an island in a lake on an island in a lake on an island. Confused?!

FAST FINISHER

Write sentences comparing people and things at home. Use these adjectives:

comfortable modern noisy old tall tidy

My mum is older than my dad. My bed is more comfortable than my sister's bed.

LS Language summary: Unit 6 **SB** p.132

 EXTRA PRACTICE Workbook page 50

GRAMMAR Comparative adjectives

Grammar animation

This lesson features an optional animated presentation of the grammar in context called *Which place is more interesting?* including the form and use of comparative adjectives and (*not*) *as ... as*. You can watch this in class if you have time and access to a computer and tablet, or you can ask sts to download it from the Richmond Learning Platform to watch at home. See TG page 309–310 for animation script.

1 Read the grammar box about comparative adjectives with sts. Put sts into pairs to complete the box with more comparative adjectives from the article on page 60. Check answers. Point out that short adjectives ending in *-y* change to *-ier*, e.g. *easy*, *easier* and some adjectives which end in a consonant double the consonant, e.g. *big*, *bigger*. Point out that we use *than* after comparative adjectives, e.g. *She is taller than me*.

Answers
1 closer 2 more beautiful 3 better

Ask questions to check concept.

Concept check questions: *Why do we use comparative adjectives?* (to compare two things). *How do we make short comparative adjectives?* (we add *-er*). *What about long comparative adjectives?* (with *more*). *What word comes after the comparative adjective?* (than). *Tom is fourteen years old and Jack is fifteen – make a sentence comparing them* (Jack is older than Tom). *Maths is quite interesting, but Science is really interesting – make a sentence comparing them* (Science is more interesting than Maths). *This film is more good than the other one – correct?* (no – *better than*).

2 Ask sts to write sentences with comparative adjectives in their notebooks. Allow sts to compare their answers in pairs, then check answers with the class. Write the correct comparative adjectives on the board for sts to check their spellings.

Answers
1 hotter than
2 more dangerous than
3 warmer than
4 larger than
5 easier than
6 better than

3 6.4 Ask sts to read the text first for general meaning, ignoring the gaps. Ask: *What is different about Okinawa?* (people there live a long time). Ask sts to read the text again and complete it with the correct comparative adjectives. Allow sts to compare their answers in pairs, then play the audio for sts to listen and check. Point out that *healthy* can behave either as a short or a long adjective, so both forms are possible.

Answers
1 older
2 sunnier
3 healthier / more healthy
4 more active
5 cleaner
6 happier

4 Read through the *Look!* box with the class. Point out that we say *as big as*, NOT ~~*as big than*~~. Ask one or two concept questions to check understanding: *Ana is as tall as Amy – are they the same size?* (yes). *Paul isn't as tall as Mark – are they the same size?* (no). *Who is taller?* (Mark). Read out the example answer, then ask sts to write the sentences in their notebooks. Allow sts to compare their answers in pairs, then check answers with the class.

Answers
1 A lake isn't as big as an ocean.
2 Villages aren't as noisy as cities.
3 My grandfather is as old as my grandmother.
4 The traffic in London is not as bad as the traffic in Los Angeles.
5 The Burj Khalifa tower in Dubai is as high as some mountains.

5 Ask sts individually to look at the prompts and decide on their opinions. Point out that they can use a comparative adjective or *as ... as* to express their opinion. Sts then work in pairs to discuss their opinions. Monitor while they are working, and note down any typical mistakes to correct in a feedback session at the end. Ask some pairs to tell the class which things they agreed about, and which they disagreed about.

FUN FACT Encourage sts to read this fun fact for pleasure. Ask if they know any similar fun facts about the natural world. They might be interested to know that Lake Hillier in Western Australia is unusual because the water is pink. Scientists believe the pink colour comes from microorganisms that live in the water.

FAST FINISHER
Sts who finish early can practise the grammar further. They write sentences comparing people and things at home. Weaker sts write some sentences based on their opinions in Exercise 5.

G Grammar practice: WB p.50
Sts will find more practice of comparative adjectives here. Set these exercises for homework.

LS Language summary: Unit 6 SB p.132

The wonderful world of animals

VOCABULARY and LISTENING Wild animals

I can use my existing knowledge to help me before I listen.

1 6.5 **Match the animals with the photos. Listen, check and repeat.**

bat bear beetle elephant frog leopard lion monkey
mosquito parrot penguin shark snake spider tortoise whale

1. What is the strongest animal in the world?
2. What is the oldest animal alive today?
3. What is the hungriest animal – the animal that eats the most food?
4. What is the most dangerous animal to humans?
5. What animal can jump the furthest?

2 **Work in pairs. Copy and complete the table with the words from Exercise 1. Can you add more animals to the table?**

Birds	
Fish	
Insects and other invertebrates	
Mammals	*bear*
Reptiles and amphibians	

3 **Complete the animal quiz in pairs. Use the animal words in Exercise 1.**

4 6.6 **Listen to two friends doing the quiz and check your answers.**

5 6.6 **Listen again and complete the sentences with the numbers. Try to guess the answers first.**

15 200 1,000 4,000 800,000

1 The strongest animal can carry an object that is ... times heavier than it is.
2 The oldest animal alive today is about ... years old.
3 The hungriest animal eats ... kg of food a day.
4 The most dangerous animal kills ... people a year.
5 The furthest that an animal can jump is ... metres.

6 **Work in pairs. Choose an animal and describe it to your partner. Can he/she guess your animal?**

A: It's a mammal. It lives in forests. It can climb.
B: Is it a monkey?

LS Language summary: Unit 6 SB p.132

The wonderful world of animals

VOCABULARY and LISTENING
Wild animals

Sts learn vocabulary for wild animals and complete an animal quiz. They then listen to two people doing the quiz to check their answers, and practise using their existing knowledge to help before they listen. They learn superlative adjectives and practise pronouncing the /ɜː/ sound. They then give their opinions on the best, funniest, etc. things they know.

Vocabulary

Wild animals (*bat, bear, beetle, elephant, frog, leopard, lion, monkey, mosquito, parrot, penguin, shark, snake, spider, tortoise, whale*)

Listening text

Two friends doing a quiz about wild animals

Listening skill

Using existing knowledge to help before listening

Pronunciation

/ɜː/

WARMER

With books closed, ask: *What's your favourite animal? Why?* Elicit a few ideas, then ask sts to look at the pictures on page 62. Ask: *Which of these animals do you like? Why? Which don't you like? Why?* If sts don't know the words in English, they can point to the pictures, or say the letters. Encourage them to join in and express their opinions about animals that they like and dislike.

1 6.5 Read through the words in the box and elicit or teach the meanings. Sts then match the words with the pictures. Play the audio once for sts to listen, check and repeat.

Answers

a	elephant	g	monkey	m	tortoise
b	bear	h	penguin	n	snake
c	frog	i	mosquito	o	spider
d	lion	j	shark	p	leopard
e	beetle	k	whale		
f	parrot	l	bat		

2 Read through the table with the class and check that sts understand all the headings. Ask them to copy the table into their notebooks. Read out the example and elicit one or two more examples. Sts then work in pairs to complete the table and add more animals. Check answers by drawing the table on the board and inviting sts in turn to come and add animals to it. If sts add animals that their classmates don't know, encourage them to try to explain what they are in English, before they give the word in their own language.

Answers

Birds: parrot, penguin
Fish: shark
Insects and other invertebrates: beetle, mosquito, spider
Mammals: elephant, bear, lion, monkey, bat, leopard, whale
Reptiles and amphibians: frog, snake, tortoise

3 Focus on the Amazing Animals quiz. Read out the questions and check that sts understand everything. Sts work in pairs to complete the quiz with the animals in Exercise 1. Don't check answers yet.

4 6.6 Play the audio for sts to listen and check their answers. See TG page 279 for audio script. Check answers with the class, and see which pair got the most answers right. Ask: *Which amazing animal facts do you find the most surprising? Why? Do you know any more amazing facts about animals?*

Answers

1	beetle	3	whale	5	leopard
2	tortoise	4	mosquito		

5 6.6 **Using existing knowledge to help before listening** Focus on the task and explain to sts that they are going to listen to the friends doing the animal quiz again and complete the sentences with the correct numbers. Elicit how to say the numbers in the box, then explain that thinking and using your existing knowledge before you listen can make it easier to hear the correct answers when you do the listening task. Put sts into pairs to read the sentences and try to guess the answers. Elicit one or two possible answers, but don't confirm them. Play the audio for sts to listen and complete the sentences. Check answers with the class and ask: *Do you think it helps to think and use your knowledge before you listen?*

Answers

1	1,000	3	4,000	5	15
2	200	4	800,000		

6 Explain the task and read out the example answer. Demonstrate further if necessary by describing another of the animals in Exercise 1, e.g. *It's a fish. It's very big. It's dangerous* (shark). Put sts into pairs to take turns to describe and guess animals. For feedback, ask: *Which animals are difficult to describe? Which are difficult to guess? Why?*

V L **Vocabulary and Listening practice: WB** p.51
Sts will find more practice for listening, and practice of vocabulary for wild animals here. Set these exercises for homework.

LS **Language summary: Unit 6 SB** p.132

GRAMMAR Superlative adjectives

I can use superlative adjectives to compare things.

Now watch the grammar animation.

1 **Read the grammar box. Write the superlative form of these adjectives.**

colourful heavy lazy loud
slow strange thin wet

Adjective	Comparative	Superlative
Short adjectives		
strong	stronger	**the** strong**est**
large	larger	**the** large**st**
hungry	hungrier	**the** hungr**iest**
hot	hotter	**the** hot**test**
Long adjectives		
dangerous	more dangerous	**the most** dangerous
Irregular adjectives		
good	better	**the best**
bad	worse	**the worst**
far	further	**the furthest**

2 **PRONUNCIATION** /ɜː/

6.7 **Listen and repeat.**

person Earth furthest bird worst journey

3 6.8 **Listen and repeat the sentences. Focus on the /ɜː/ sound.**

1 This is the worst journey in the world!
2 Perfect! It's my birthday on Thursday.

4 **Complete the sentences with the superlative form of the adjectives in the box.**

big dangerous far fast ~~heavy~~ lazy slow

The heaviest reptile is the crocodile. Some crocodiles can weigh 1,000 kg.

1 The koala bear is ... animal. It sleeps for twenty hours a day.
2 The ... snake is the black mamba. It can kill a person in 30 minutes.
3 ... spider is a type of tarantula. It's bigger than a person's hand!
4 The ... bird in water is the Gentoo penguin. It can swim at 36 kilometres per hour.
5 The ... reptile is the Galapagos tortoise. It walks at 0.3 kilometres per hour.
6 Neptune is ... planet from the Sun.

5 **Look at the information. Write sentences about the animals. Use comparative and superlative adjectives.**

Polar bears are heavier than lions.

Great white sharks are the heaviest.

	Great white shark	African lion	Polar bear
Heavy?	1100 kg	190 kg	680 kg
Fast?	60 kph	80 kph	40 kph
Long?	6 m	2.5 m	3 m
Dangerous?	30 attacks per year	100 attacks per year	1–3 attacks per year
Rare?	8,000 in wild	20,000 in wild	26,000 in wild

6 **Work in pairs. One student closes his/her book, and the other student asks questions. Use comparative and superlative adjectives. Swap.**

A: Which are heavier – polar bears or African lions?

B: I think African lions are heavier.

A: Wrong! Polar bears are heavier.

7 **Work in pairs. Discuss the topics below. Give your opinions.**

A: Who's the best singer, in your opinion?

B: In my opinion, Adele is the best singer. What do you think?

the best singer **the most boring game**
the most exciting film **the funniest animal**
the worst food

FAST FINISHER

Write sentences about people in your class. Use these adjectives.

old short tall young friendly

Jorge is the oldest.

LS Language summary: Unit 6 SB p.132

GRAMMAR Superlative adjectives

Grammar animation

This lesson features an optional animated presentation of the grammar in context called *The most intelligent animal!* including the form and use of superlative adjectives. You can watch this in class if you have time and access to a computer or tablet, or you can ask sts to download it from the Richmond Learning Platform to watch at home. See TG page 310 for animation script.

1 Read the grammar box with sts about superlative adjectives. Elicit or explain that we use superlative adjectives to compare more than two things. Point out that the spelling rules and rules on irregular adjectives are the same for comparative and superlative adjectives. Point out that we use *the* before superlative adjectives, e.g. *What is the fastest animal?* NOT ~~*What is fastest animal?*~~ Read through the adjectives in the box with the class and check that sts understand them all. Ask sts to write the superlative form of the adjectives in the box. Allow sts to compare their answers in pairs, then check with the class, writing the superlative adjectives on the board for sts to check their spellings.

Answers

colourful – the most colourful
heavy – the heaviest
lazy – the laziest
loud – the loudest
slow – the slowest
strange – the strangest
thin – the thinnest
wet – the wettest

Ask questions to check concept.

Concept check questions: *How do we make short superlative adjectives?* (we add *-est*). *What about long superlative adjectives?* (with *most*). *What word comes before the superlative adjective?* (the). *A beetle – not very big, a frog – not very big, an elephant – very big; Make a sentence with a superlative adjective* (An elephant is the biggest). *A tortoise – not dangerous; a parrot – not dangerous, a shark – very dangerous – Make a sentence with a superlative adjective* (A shark is the most dangerous).

2 PRONUNCIATION 6.7

Model and drill pronunciation of the /ɜː/ sound in isolation. Play the audio once for sts to listen, then play it again for them to repeat the words.

3 6.8

Play the audio once for sts to listen to the sentences. Play the audio again and ask individual sts to repeat, or get the whole class to repeat together. Sts can then practise saying the sentences in pairs. You could ask sts in pairs to write their own sentence using words with the /ɜː/ sound. They could swap sentences with another pair and practise saying the sentence they are given.

4 Read through the animals in the sentences and check that sts understand them all. You may need to explain *crocodile*, *koala bear*, and *tarantula*. Ask sts to complete the sentences with the correct superlative adjectives. Allow sts to compare their answers in pairs, then check with the class. Write the superlative adjectives on the board, for sts to check their spellings.

Answers

1 the laziest
2 the most dangerous
3 The biggest
4 fastest
5 slowest
6 furthest

5 Read out the example answer and point out how it relates to the information in the chart. Ask sts to write the sentences individually. Check answers with the class. Ask: *Which facts do you find the most surprising?*

Answers

African lions are the fastest.
Great white sharks are the longest.
African lions are the most dangerous.
Great white sharks are the rarest.
Polar bears are the slowest.

6 Focus on the chart again. Point out that we can use superlative adjectives for the heaviest, fastest, etc. but we can also use the information to compare pairs of animals, using comparative adjectives. Give one or two examples, e.g. *Polar bears are heavier than African lions*. Read out the example question and elicit a question using a superlative, e.g. *Which are the heaviest – great white sharks, African lions or polar bears?* With weaker classes, allow sts time to prepare four or five questions before they work in pairs. Stronger classes can go straight into the pairwork. They take turns to close their books and try to answer their partner's questions from memory. Ask who answered all their partner's questions correctly.

7 Read out the topics and check sts understand them all. Sts work in pairs to discuss the topics. Ask some sts which topics they agree on.

FAST FINISHER

Sts who finish early can practise the grammar further. They write sentences about their classmates using comparative and superlative adjectives. Weaker sts could work in pairs. They write four sentences about the animals in Exercise 5, using comparative and superlative adjectives.

G Grammar practice: WB p.52

Sts will find more practice of superlative adjectives here. Set these exercises for homework.

LS Language summary: Unit 6 SB p.132

KEEP TALKING!

How much is it?

READING and LISTENING

I can understand information on a web page.

1 **Look at the web page. What activity would you like to try?**

WALTON FOREST ACTIVITIES

Home | Activities | Contact us

COME TO WALTON FOREST FOR A FUN DAY OUT!

Come to Walton Forest for a fun day out! Go for a walk or a bike ride, or enjoy a picnic with your family or friends. If you love nature, the forest is home to lots of mammals, birds and insects. Or for a different kind of adventure, why not try one of our special activities?

Discounts for children and teenagers!

TREETOP CHALLENGE

- Climb, swing, jump and fly through the forest!
- Three hours of fun and adventure – this is our most popular activity!
- Age: 12+
- Minimum height: 1.2 metres

COST: £15

FOREST SURVIVAL

- Spend a day in the forest.
- Learn how to build a fire, and then cook lunch! (We give you the ingredients.)
- Look for insects with our expert!
- Great for all the family!

COST: £10

KAYAK ADVENTURE

- If you love the water, then try our Kayak Adventure!
- After a quick lesson, go on a two-hour trip down the river with one of our guides.
- Bring a snack!
- Age: 15+. All levels welcome.

COST: £20

Opening times: Open every day, 10.00–18.00

Transport: **By train to:** Walton Station **By bus to:** Greenwood Bus Station

2 **Read the leaflet. Are the sentences true (T) or false (F)?**

1 Walton Forest is only open at the weekend.
2 You can cycle in the forest.
3 If you're younger than 15, you can't go kayaking.
4 You must be taller than 1.2 metres to do the Treetop Challenge.
5 You must take your own food to Forest Survival.
6 Forest Survival is more popular than Treetop Challenge.
7 If you haven't got much time, Kayak Adventure is the shortest activity.
8 Treetop Challenge is the most expensive activity.

3 6.9 **Lisa phones Anneka to invite her to Walton Forest. Choose the correct answers.**

1 They decide to go on *Saturday* / *Sunday*.
2 They decide to go by *bus* / *train*.
3 They decide to meet at *9.15* / *9.30*.

4 6.9 **Listen again and complete the sentences.**

1 Sunday is ... for me than Saturday.
2 The bus is ... than the train.
3 The train is ... than the bus.
4 The bus station is ... to the forest than the train station.
5 The forest isn't as ... in the morning.

5 COMPARE CULTURES **Can you do activities in the forest in your country? Where? What activities can you do?**

KEEP TALKING!

How much is it?

READING and LISTENING

Sts study a web page about adventure days out in a forest and discuss what fun activities they can do in forests in their own country. They listen to two friends who are buying tickets for a Treetop Challenge and learn how to buy tickets. They read and hear a model dialogue and personalise the useful language by following the steps in the Speaking plan.

WARMER

Play a game to revise the vocabulary for the natural world. With books closed, write the words from page 59 on the board, with some gapped letters, e.g. *b _ _ c h*, *f _ r _ _ t*, etc. Sts work in pairs and race to complete the words. Complete the words on the board and ask who wrote them all correctly. Ask: *Which places do you enjoy visiting? Why?*

1 Put sts into pairs to discuss the question. Ask some sts to tell the class which activity they would like to try and why.

2 Sts read the web page and decide if the sentences are true or false. Check answers with the class, eliciting the part of the text which confirms each answer. Read through the web page with the class and explain any vocabulary that sts don't understand or cannot guess.

Answers

1 F	4 T	7 T
2 T	5 F	8 F
3 T	6 F	

3 6.9 Explain to sts that they will hear two friends talking about Walton Forest. Read out the situation, then allow sts time to read through the sentences and possible answers. Play the audio for sts to listen and choose the correct answers. See TG pages 279–280 for audio script. Allow sts to compare their answers in pairs, then check answers with the class, playing the audio again and pausing if necessary to confirm the answers.

Answers

1 Sunday 2 bus 3 9.15

4 6.9 Allow sts time to read through the gapped sentences. Elicit the kinds of words that might be missing, and elicit that they are all adjectives or comparative adjectives. Play the audio again for sts to listen and complete the sentences. Check answers, playing the audio again and pausing if necessary to confirm the answers.

Answers

1 better	4 nearer
2 cheaper	5 busy
3 faster	

EXTRA PRACTICE

Write these gapped sentences on the board:

1 ... you like to go to Walton Forest?
2 Are you ... on Saturday?
3 OK, ... go on Sunday then.
4 What time ... meet?
5 ... we get the 9.30 train?
6 Great. ... you then.

Put sts into pairs to try to remember the missing words. Play the audio again for them to check, and check that sts understand all the sentences. Elicit that the sentences are all used for making arrangements to do something together.

Answers

1 Would	5 shall we
2 free	5 Shall
3 let's	6 see

21st Century skills

5 **COMPARE CULTURES**

As a class, brainstorm a few places where sts can visit forests in their country. Sts then work in pairs and discuss what activities they can do there. Discuss their ideas as a class.

EXTRA PRACTICE

Arrange sts in small teams for a reading race. Explain that you will read a definition and sts have to find the word somewhere on the web page. Read the definitions below (all or as many as you want). Award a point to the first team to find and call out the answer.

Definitions

A meal you eat outside – on the beach or in the countryside (picnic)
An animal that flies (bird)
Go up a tree (climb)
An animal such as a dog, a cat or a human (mammal)
Someone who shows you around a new place (guide)
Someone who knows a lot about something (expert)
A place that has a lot of trees (forest)
You can travel on water in one of these (kayak)
Money that you take off the usual price of something (discount)
A small animal with 6 legs and three body parts, such as a bee (insect)

SPEAKING Buying a ticket

I can buy a ticket.

1 6.10 **Lisa and Anneka are at Walton Forest. Listen and read. Are the tickets cheaper for young people?**

Assistant: Good morning. Can I help you?
Lisa: Hello. We'd like to do the Treetop Challenge. Is there a discount for young people?
Assistant: Yes, it's £12 if you're under 16.
Lisa: Oh good, we're 13. We'd like two tickets please.
Assistant: OK, that's £24 in total.
Lisa: Here you are.
Assistant: Thank you. Here are your tickets.
Lisa: Great.
Assistant And here's your change. Have fun!
Lisa: Thanks.

2 6.11 **Listen and repeat the Useful language.**

Useful language

Buying a ticket

Can I help you?
I'd like a ticket / two tickets, please.
Is there a discount for children / young people / students?
That's ... in total.
Here you are.
Here are your tickets.
Here's your change.

3 6.12 **Copy and complete the dialogue. Listen and check.**

Assistant: Hello, can I [1] ... you?
Boy: Yes, we'd like to visit the museum. Is there a [2] ... for students?
Assistant: Yes, it's half price if you have a student card.
Boy: Great! We'd like four [3] ..., please.
Assistant: OK, that's £16 in total.
Boy: Here you [4] ... .
Assistant: Here are your tickets and your [5] ... .
Boy: Thanks.
Assistant: Enjoy your visit!

4 Work in pairs. Buy tickets for an activity or place in the box, or use your own idea. Follow the steps in the Speaking plan.

an activity at Walton Forest on page 64
a concert a film a museum a theme park

Speaking plan

Prepare

- Decide on your roles.
- Decide on: ticket prices and discounts
- Make notes for your dialogue.

Speak

- Practise your dialogue.
- Use phrases from the Useful language box.
- Act out your dialogue without notes.

Reflect

- How can you improve next time?
- Swap roles, and choose another place to buy a ticket.

Now play *Keep moving!*

FAST FINISHER

Invent your own activity for a fun day out. Write a short advert for it like the web page for Walton Forest.

LS Language summary: Unit 6 SB p.132

SPEAKING Buying a ticket

1 6.10 Focus on the picture and explain that it shows two friends at Walton Forest. Read out the question, then play the audio of the dialogue. With stronger classes, you could play the dialogue with books closed and ask: *Are tickets cheaper for young people?* With weaker classes, you could play the dialogue for sts to listen and read. See SB page 65 for audio script.

Answer
Yes, they are cheaper (£12 for under 16s)

2 6.11 Ask sts if they can remember some of the phrases Lisa and the assistant used. Read through the Useful language box with the class and check sts understand all the phrases. Play the audio once for sts to listen to the phrases, then play it again for them to listen and repeat.

3 6.12 Ask sts to copy the dialogue into their notebooks and complete it with the correct words. Allow sts to compare their answers in pairs, then play the audio for them to listen and check. If your sts would benefit from some controlled practice before the personalised practice, they could practise this dialogue in pairs.

Answers

1 help	4 are
2 discount	5 change
3 tickets	

4 Sts follow the steps in the Speaking plan to practise buying a ticket for an activity or a place.

Speaking plan

Prepare

Sts work in their pairs and decide who is the assistant and the customer. They decide on the ticket prices and discounts. Weaker sts can write their dialogue out in full, but encourage stronger sts to just make notes, to make their dialogue more spontaneous and natural. Remind sts to use the Useful language in Exercise 2 to help them.

Speak

Sts practise their dialogue in their pairs. They can practise with and then without notes. Monitor and help as necessary. If your sts use smartphones in class, they could record their conversations.

Reflect

Discuss as a class how sts could improve next time. Encourage them to be honest and open about the things they did well and the things they can do better. If you noticed any typical errors, correct them with the class. Sts swap roles and follow the steps again. If they recorded their conversations, ask them to use this to help them timprove next time.

Keep moving!

This lesson features an optional language revision and consolidation game for use in digital classrooms. Players control different characters, each with their own personalities and special abilities.

FAST FINISHER

Sts invent their own activity for a fun day out, and write an advert for it. You could ask some sts to read their advert to the class. Ask sts which activity they would like to try. Weaker sts could work in pairs. They look at the dialogue in Exercise 3 again and write prompts to help them remember it, writing no more than two words for each line. They then close their books and try to practise the dialogue from memory.

S **Speaking practice: WB** p.53

Sts will find more practice of buying a ticket here. Set these exercises for homework.

L **Language summary: Unit 6** p.132

REAL CULTURE!

Amazing America

I can compare natural places in the USA with natural places in my country.

NATURAL WONDERS of the USA

What do you imagine when you think of the USA? Big cities? Burgers? American football? It's much more than that. Here are six natural wonders.

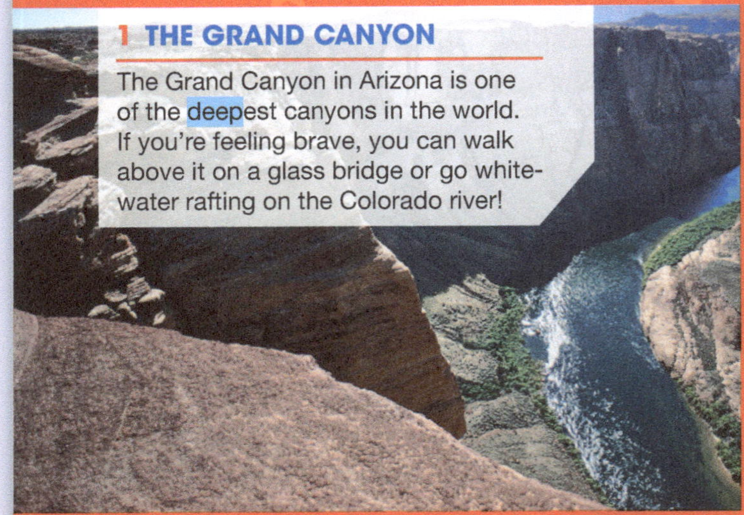

1 THE GRAND CANYON

The Grand Canyon in Arizona is one of the deepest canyons in the world. If you're feeling brave, you can walk above it on a glass bridge or go white-water rafting on the Colorado river!

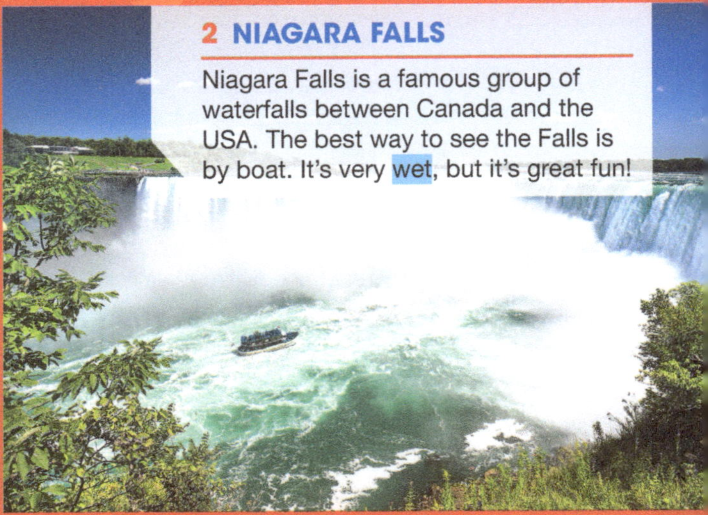

2 NIAGARA FALLS

Niagara Falls is a famous group of waterfalls between Canada and the USA. The best way to see the Falls is by boat. It's very wet, but it's great fun!

3 MAMMOTH CAVE

Mammoth Cave in Kentucky is the longest cave in the world. It's full of amazing stalagmites and stalactites. It's also home to lots of bats!

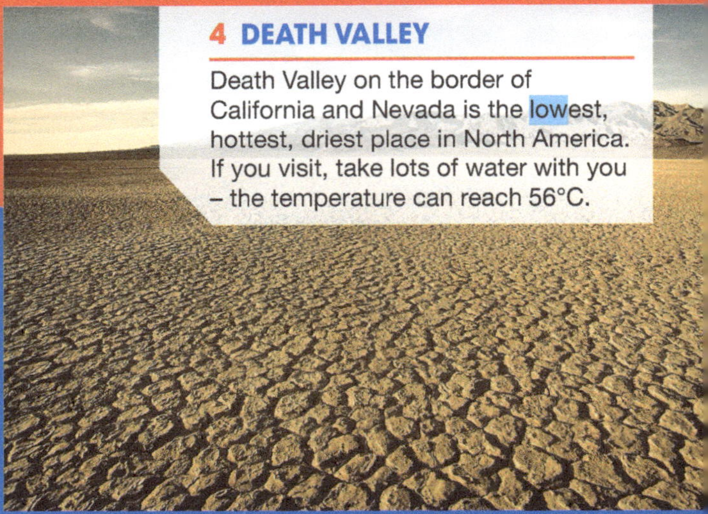

4 DEATH VALLEY

Death Valley on the border of California and Nevada is the lowest, hottest, driest place in North America. If you visit, take lots of water with you – the temperature can reach 56°C.

5 THE EVERGLADES

The Everglades is a beautiful area of rivers and lakes in Florida. It's popular for walking and kayaking. But watch out – there are more than 200,000 alligators and crocodiles!

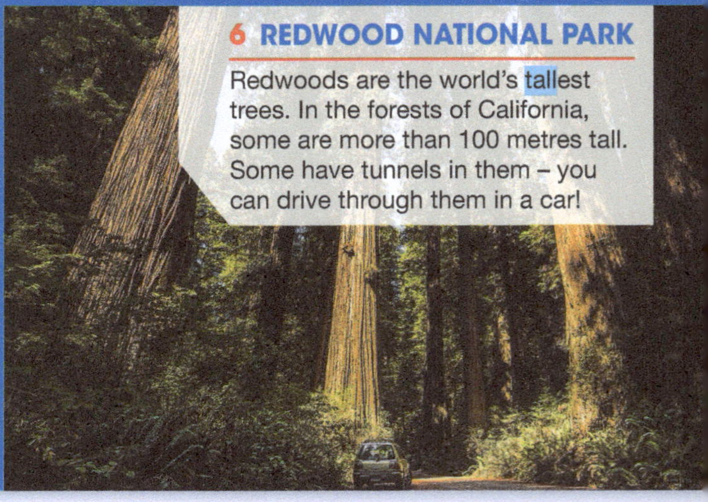

6 REDWOOD NATIONAL PARK

Redwoods are the world's tallest trees. In the forests of California, some are more than 100 metres tall. Some have tunnels in them – you can drive through them in a car!

REAL CULTURE! Amazing America

Sts learn about some exciting natural places in the USA, including the Grand Canyon and Niagara Falls, and compare these places to natural places in their own country. This lesson features an optional culture video about a man taking part in an extreme cycle race. See SB page 67.

WARMER

Ask: *What natural places do tourists visit in your country? Do you sometimes go to these places?* Elicit a few ideas. If sts have visited some of the places, encourage them to describe the places for the class and talk about what they did there. Ask: *What do you know about the USA? What natural places can you visit there?* Elicit a few ideas, and ask more questions if necessary to prompt sts, e.g. *What about waterfalls? What about deserts?* Encourage sts to share their knowledge about places in the USA.

BACKGROUND

The Grand Canyon is over 400 km long and up to 29 km wide. Some parts are over 1,800 metres deep.

Niagara Falls is on the border between the USA and Canada. It is made up of 3 separate waterfalls, and is over 50 metres deep.

Mammoth Cave is the longest cave system in the world. It has over 600 km of underground passages.

Death Valley is part of the Mojave Desert, and is one of the hottest places in the world. It is surrounded by mountains, so most of the rain falls on the mountains before it reaches Death Valley.

The Everglades is an area of tropical wetlands. Because it is wet, it is impossible to walk around the area, so people visit in boats or kayaks.

Redwood National Park is an area of national park along the coast of northern California. As well as being a tourist site, it has also been used as the location for many films, including the Star Wars films.

1 Sts can work in pairs to look at the photos and identify the things they can see. Check answers. Use the picture of the Grand Canyon to teach the meaning of *canyon*, and use the picture of Mammoth Cave to teach the meaning of *stalagmites* (= pointed pieces of rock sticking up from the floor of a cave) and *stalactites* (= pointed pieces of rock hanging down from the roof of a cave). Also teach the words *kayaking* and *tunnel*.

Answers

a forest: 5,6
a desert: 4
a river: 1,2,5
a waterfall: 2
mountains: 1

2 Focus on the map and point out the letters a–f. Use the map to teach the meaning of *border*. Ask sts to read the guide and match the places with a–f on the map. Check answers with the class.

Answers

1 c
2 e
3 d
4 b
5 f
6 a

3 Ask sts to read the guide again and answer the questions. Allow sts to compare their answers in pairs, then check answers with the class, eliciting the part of the guide which confirms each answer.

Answers

1 It's the hottest place in North America; it can reach 56°C.
2 bats
3 It's very wet.
4 redwoods
5 Mammoth Cave and The Everglades
6 You can walk above it on a glass bridge or go white water rafting.

4 **Word Power** Read out the task and elicit or explain the meaning of *opposite*. Ask sts to look at the guide again and match the adjectives in blue with their opposites. Check answers, and check that sts understand all the adjectives. Model pronunciation of words that sts might find difficult, e.g. *beautiful*.

Answers

1 wet
2 beautiful
3 low
4 tall, long
5 deep

1 **Look at the photos on page 66. In which photo(s) can you see ...?**

a forest   a desert   a river
a waterfall   mountains

2 **Read the guide and match places 1–6 to a–f on the map.**

1 c

3 **Read the guide again and answer the questions.**

1 How hot is it in Death Valley?
2 What animals can you find in Mammoth Cave?
3 Why is it a good idea to wear a coat at Niagara Falls?
4 What are the tallest trees in the world called?
5 In which two places in the guide can you see animals?
6 What can you do at the Grand Canyon if you like adventure?

4 **Word Power** **Match the blue adjectives in the guide with their opposites 1–5.**

1 dry
2 ugly
3 high
4 short
5 shallow

5 **6.13 Listen. Where are the people? Choose from the places in the text.**

1 Mammoth Cave

6 **GET CREATIVE** **Work in pairs or small groups. Think of one or two natural wonders in your country. Research information, and prepare a short presentation to give to your class. Use the questions below to help you.**

- What is it? (a mountain / a forest / river, etc.)
- Where is it?
- What is special about it?
- What can you do there?

Our presentation is about El Teide. It's a volcano on Tenerife in the Canary Islands.

It's the highest volcano in Spain and one of the biggest in the world.

Now watch the culture video.

FAST FINISHER

Which natural wonder in the world would you like to visit, and why? Describe the place and explain your reasons.

I'd like to visit ...

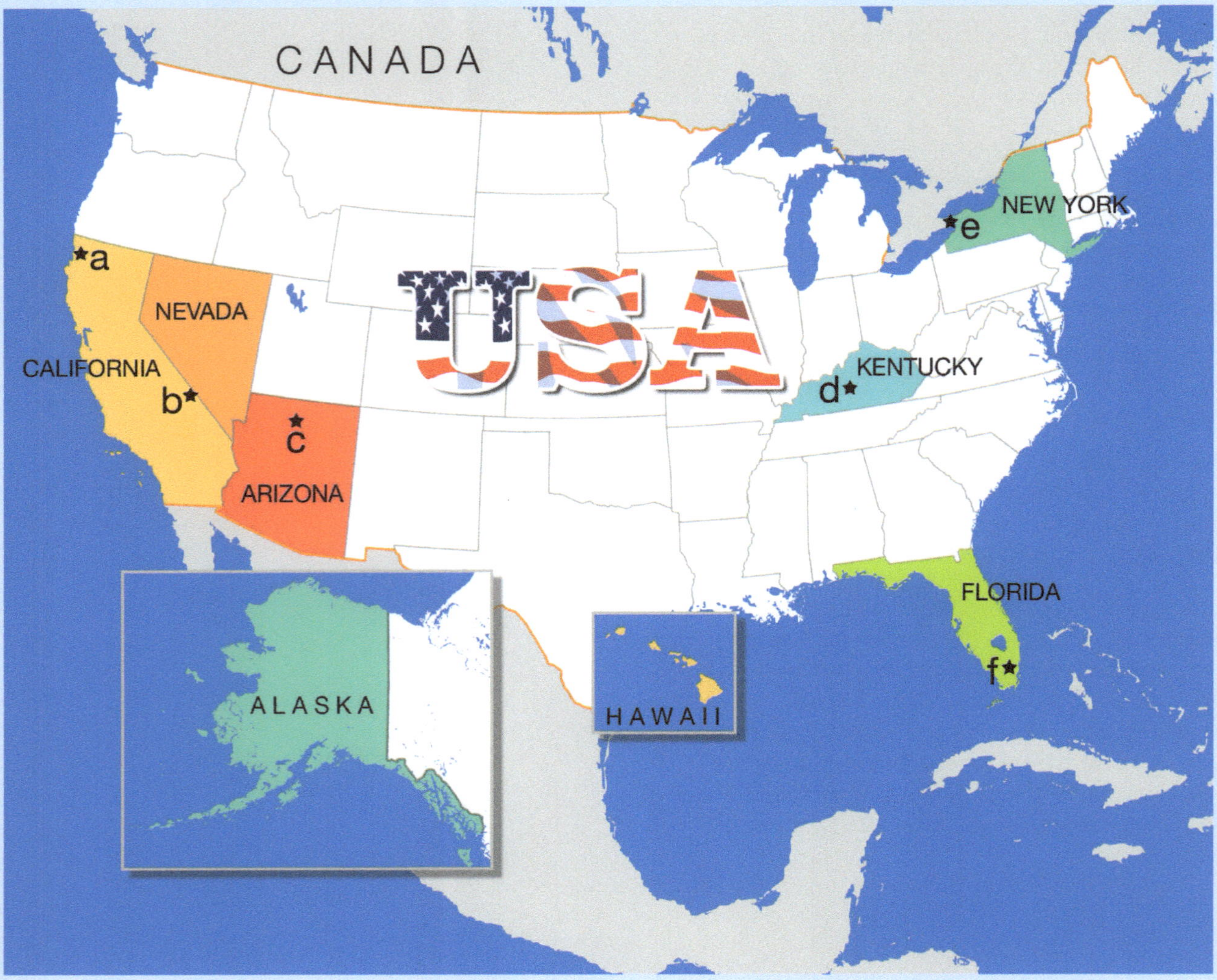

REAL CULTURE!

5 6.13 Explain to sts that they will hear six short monologues or dialogues, and they must guess where the people are in each one. Play the first person and point out the example answer. Play the rest of the audio. See TG page 280 for audio script. Sts listen and decide where the people are in each one. Check answers with the class and ask sts what clues helped them choose the place each time.

Answers
2 Redwood National Park
3 Death Valley
4 The Grand Canyon
5 The Everglades
6 Niagara Falls

EXTRA PRACTICE

Put sts into pairs and ask them to prepare their own dialogue in one of the places in the guide. Tell them to include some clues, but not to say where they are. Monitor and help while they are working. Ask pairs in turn to perform their dialogue for the class. Other sts can listen and guess where they are.

21st Century skills

6 **GET CREATIVE**

Read out the task, then put sts into pairs or groups to choose a natural wonder in their country and prepare a presentation on it. Read out the questions and example sentences to give them ideas for what information they should find and include. Sts can do the research in class if they have access to the internet, or they can do it for homework and prepare their presentation in the next lesson. When sts are preparing their presentations, encourage as many of them as possible to take part in the presentation. Ask pairs or groups in turn to give their presentations to the class. Then discuss as a class which places sts would like to visit and why.

Culture video

You can watch this in class if you have time and access to video, or you can ask sts to download it from the Richmond Learning Platform to watch at home. See *Marvellous mountain biking* on TG pages 300 and 307.

EXTRA PRACTICE

Put sts in pairs or small groups. Explain that there are seven natural wonders of the world. Write them on the board: the *Grand Canyon*, *Parícutin*, the *Northern Lights*, *Victoria Falls*, the *Harbour of Rio de Janeiro*, the *Great Barrier Reef*, *Mount Everest*.

Ask sts to find out what they are and where they are. If they have internet access in class, they can search online. If not, write the places and type of natural wonder on the board and ask sts to match them.

Answers
the Grand Canyon – a canyon / USA
Parícutin – a volcano / Mexico
the Northern (or Southern) Lights – a feature of the night sky / many places in the Northern/Southern polar areas
Victoria Falls – waterfall / Zimbabwe and Zambia
the Harbour of Rio De Janeiro – a big harbour / Brazil
the Great Barrier Reef – an area of ocean / near Australia
Mount Everest – a mountain / Tibet

FAST FINISHER

Sts think of a natural wonder in the world that they would like to visit, then write a description and explain why they would like to go there. You could ask some sts to read their descriptions to the class and ask who else would like to visit this place and why. Weaker sts could work in pairs. They could imagine they are at one of the places on page 66 and write a text message to a friend saying where they are and describing the place.

Awesome animals

WRITING A fact sheet

I can write a description of an animal.

1 **Work in pairs. Look at the photo and discuss the questions.**

1 What are these animals called?
2 Where do they live?
3 What do they eat?
4 Do you know any more facts about them?

2 **Read the fact sheet and check your answers.**

1 ...

Orangutans live in the forests in Sumatra and Borneo, two islands in Indonesia. They are some of the most intelligent animals on Earth. They are also very rare.

2 ...

They can grow to about 1.4 m long, and they can weigh 100 kg. They have red fur and long strong arms. They can live for 40 years or longer.

3 ...

Orangutans love fruit. They often eat leaves and insects, too. Mothers teach their babies what food to eat and where to find it.

4 ...

During the day, orangutans spend a lot of time in trees. They also sleep in trees at night because they are safer there from leopards and other animals.

FUN FACTS!

* The name *orangutan* means 'person of the forest'.
* Orangutans use leaves as umbrellas when it rains!

3 **Read the fact sheet again and match the headings to the paragraphs.**

a Food
b Size and appearance
c Lifestyle
d Habitat

4 **Look at the Useful language. How do you say these expressions in your language?**

Useful language

Animal facts

... are one of the most dangerous animals on Earth.
They live in the forests/mountains/ocean in ...
They can grow to ... m long. / They can weigh ... kg.
They can live for ... They usually eat ...
During the day, they ... At night, they ...

5 **Study the Look! box. Complete the rules with *too* and *also*.**

Look! ***too* and *also***

We use *too* and *also* to introduce a similar idea.
Lions usually hunt at night. Leopards also hunt at night.
Lions usually hunt at night. Leopards hunt at night, too.

Rules
1 ... usually goes at the end of a sentence.
2 ... goes before most verbs, but after the verb *be*.

6 **Rewrite the sentences with *too* or *also*.**

Rhinos live in Africa. They live in Asia. (too)
Rhinos live in Africa. They live in Asia, too.

1 Sharks eat fish. Some sharks eat seals. (too)
2 During the day, elephants look for food. They swim and play. (also)
3 Snakes live in forests. They live in deserts. (too)
4 Polar bears are beautiful. They are dangerous. (also)

7 **Write a fact sheet about an animal. Follow the steps in the Writing plan.**

Writing plan

Prepare
› Choose a wild animal and research some facts about it. Use the headings below:
  - Habitat
  - Lifestyle
  - Food
  - Size and appearance
  - Fun Facts

Write
› Use the headings to organize your ideas into paragraphs.
› Use the expressions from the Useful language box.

Reflect
› Check your grammar: comparatives and superlative adjectives.
› Check *too* and *also*.
› Check your spelling.

W **Writing summary:** **WB** p.89
R **Review: Units 4–6** **SB** pp.102–103
P **Project: Units 4–6** **SB** pp.108–109
L **Literature: Units 4–6** **SB** pp.114–115
E **Exams: Unit 6** **SB** p.123
LS **Language summary: Unit 6** **SB** p.132

Awesome animals

WRITING A fact sheet

Sts read a fact sheet about orangutans. They study *too* and *also* and learn useful language for writing animal facts. They then follow the steps in the Writing plan to write a fact sheet about another animal.

Writing

A text fact sheet

Useful language

Animal facts (*... are one of the most dangerous animals on Earth, They live in the forests/mountains/ocean in ..., They can grow to ... m long, They can weigh ... kg, They can live for ..., They usually eat ..., During the day, they ..., At night, they ...*)

Look!

too and *also*

WARMER

Ask: *What animals have you learned about in this unit?* Put sts into pairs and give them two minutes to write as many of the animal words they have learned as they can. Bring their ideas together on the board, and ask: *What have you learned about these animals?*

1 Put sts into pairs to look at the photo and discuss the questions. Elicit one or two possible answers, but don't confirm them yet.

2 Ask sts to read the fact sheet to check their answers to Exercise 1. Check the answers with the class.

Answers
1 orangutans
2 in the forests in Sumatra and Borneo
3 fruit, leaves and insects
4 They are very intelligent and very rare; they can weigh 100 kg and can live for 40 years; they spend a lot of time in trees.

3 Sts read the fact sheet again and match the headings with the paragraphs. Check answers.

Answers
1 Habitat
2 Size and appearance
3 Food
4 Lifestyle

4 Read the Useful language box with sts about animal facts. Check they understand all the expressions and ask them how they say these expressions in their first language. Point out that we often use *can* when describing animals, e.g. *They can grow to ...* . Point out also the use of *usually* in the expression *They usually eat ...* . Point out that we can also use other adverbs of frequency in some of the other expressions, e.g. *During the day, they often ..., At night, they always ...* .

5 Read the Look! box with sts about *too* and *also*. Check they understand the meaning of the words and the difference in their use. Ask sts to complete the rules, and check the answers.

Answers
1 too 2 also

6 Ask sts to rewrite the sentences using *too* or *also*. Point out that they only need to rewrite the second sentence in each pair. Allow sts to compare their answers in pairs, then check answers with the class.

Answers
1 Some sharks eat seals, too.
2 They also swim and play.
3 They live in deserts, too.
4 They are also dangerous.

7 Explain to sts that they will now write a fact sheet about another animal, following the steps in the Writing plan.

Writing plan

Prepare

Sts choose an animal and research some facts. Weaker sts could work in pairs for this. You could brainstorm a few ideas for animals they could choose.

Write

Sts then write their fact sheets using the fact sheet in Exercise 2 as a model. Refer them back to the Useful language box for expressions to talk about animal facts, and remind them to use *too* and *also*.

Reflect

Ask sts to check their grammar, spelling and punctuation and make any necessary changes. Sts could then swap their fact sheets with each other in pairs and give feedback on the use of the Useful language, comparative and superlative adjectives and *too* and *also*.

W **Writing practice: WB** p.54. There is more practice for writing in the Workbook. Set these exercises for homework.
W **Writing summary: WB** p.89
R **Review: Units 4–6 SB** pp.102–103
P **Project Units 4–6 SB** pp.108–109
L **Literature: SB** pp.114–115
E **Exams: Unit 6 SB** p.123
LS **Language summary: SB** p.132

Then and now

7

Vocabulary: Clothes; Regular verbs | **Grammar:** *be*: past simple; Past simple: regular verbs; Object pronouns | **Speaking:** Shopping for clothes | **Writing:** A review of a year

VOCABULARY Clothes

I can talk about clothes.

1 7.1 **Match the words in the box with the pictures. Listen, check and repeat.**

boots coat dress hat jacket jeans jumper shirt
shoes shorts skirt socks T-shirt tie trainers trousers

2 Work in pairs. Ask and answer the questions in the questionnaire.

WHAT'S YOUR STYLE?

1. What clothes do you usually wear in summer?
2. What clothes do you usually wear in winter?
3. What clothes do you wear to a party?
4. What clothes do you never wear?
5. What do you usually wear to school?

Look! Plural nouns

Trousers, *jeans* and *shorts* are always plural.
She's wearing red trousers. NOT ~~a red trousers~~
I need some new jeans. NOT ~~a new jeans~~

3 Read the Look! box. Work in pairs. Student A: choose a person from a unit in this book, and describe them. Student B: try to find the person.

A: Unit 1. This person is wearing a blue T-shirt and black jeans.

B: Is it the boy on page 10?

Now watch the vlog.

FAST FINISHER

Imagine it's your birthday. What clothes would you like as a birthday present?

I'd like some new jeans, a red jacket, …

LS **Language summary: Unit 7 SB** p.133

EXTRA PRACTICE Workbook page 58

Then and now 7

UNIT 7 OVERVIEW: The topic for this unit is life and fashions in the past. Sts read about a TV show in which families experience life in different decades, and listen to a radio show about past crazes. They read a shopping website and learn about shopping for clothes. They read about the history of film in the USA and finally, they read a review of a year and write their own review of a year. They also watch a vlog about someone's fashion sense and a culture video about a family who take part in a TV programme.

Vocabulary	Grammar	Pronunciation	Reading	Listening	Speaking	Writing
Clothes; Regular verbs	*be*: past simple; *There was / There were*; Past simple affirmative: regular verbs; Object pronouns	*-ed* endings	Understanding what pronouns refer to in a text	Understanding the main idea when I listen	Shopping for clothes	A review of a year

VOCABULARY Clothes

Sts learn words for clothes. They identify these from picture clues, then listen and check their answers. They answer questions in a clothes questionnaire, then personalise the vocabulary by describing what people in the pictures in this unit are wearing.

Vocabulary

Clothes (*boots, coat, dress, hat, jacket, jeans, jumper, shirt, shoes, shorts, skirt, socks, T-shirt, tie, trainers, trousers*)

Vlog

Ben: *I know nothing about fashion.*

WARMER

Point to some of the clothes you are wearing and ask: *What's this?* Elicit the word. Elicit or teach the word *clothes* and write it on the board. Put sts into pairs and give them two minutes to write as many words for clothes as they can. Bring all the words together on the board and briefly revise colour words.

1 7.1 Read through the words in the box and elicit or teach the meanings. Sts then match the words to the pictures. Play the audio for sts to listen, check and repeat.

Answers

1 jeans	9 shorts
2 coat	10 skirt
3 boots	11 T-shirt
4 shirt	12 jumper
5 shoes	13 tie
6 hat	14 trousers
7 dress	15 jacket
8 trainers	16 socks

2 Put sts into pairs to do the questionnaire. When sts have finished, ask some sts to tell the class what their partner usually wears and never wears.

3 Read through the Look! box with the class. Explain that these words are always plural and can never be singular. Point out that some other clothes words are often plural, e.g. *shoes*, *boots*, *socks*, but these can also be singular, e.g. *I can only find one sock*. Demonstrate the task by describing one of the people in the pictures in Unit 7. Get sts to look through Unit 7 and guess who you are describing. Read out the example answer and elicit or point out that we use the present continuous to say what someone is wearing now. Then put sts into pairs to continue the activity.

Vlog

This lesson features an optional vlog in which vlogger Ben talks about clothes. You can watch this in class if you have time and access to video, or you can ask sts to download it from the Richmond Learning Platform to watch at home. See TG pages 292 and 305.

FAST FINISHER

Sts who finish early can practise clothes vocabulary further. They write sentences about what clothes they would like for their birthday. Weaker sts could write some sentences about what they are wearing today.

EXTRA PRACTICE

Put sts into pairs. They take turns to talk about the clothes they are wearing today and the clothes they like. Their partner films them using their phone. Ask them to try to speak for one minute. They can watch their films back and discuss in their pairs how they could improve.

V **Vocabulary practice: WB** p.58

Sts will find more practice of clothes vocabulary here. Set these exercises for homework.

LS **Language summary: Unit 7 SB** p.133

Which decade was best?

READING

I can understand what pronouns refer to in a text.

1 7.2 **Read and listen to the article. Match the pictures with the decades.**

BACK IN TIME

Back in Time for Dinner is a British living history TV show. Every week, a family experiences life in a different decade, from the 1900s to the present day. The family members live in a house from that time and wear typical clothes. [1]They also eat typical food. We talk to two fans of the programme.

In your opinion, what was the worst decade to live in?

Susie: The 1900s. Girls' dresses were long and heavy, and the colours were boring. The hairstyles were horrible, too.

Ted: I agree. There were shirts and ties for boys, and [2]they were really uncomfortable. Also, the food wasn't very exciting – there weren't any fridges or easy meals like pizza or pasta! Cooking was hard work.

Susie: Yes, [3]it was – for the women in the house, Ted!

What was your favourite decade in the show?

Susie: [4]It was probably the 1960s. There were shorter skirts and more colourful dresses. The food was more interesting, too. There was cereal for breakfast, and there were supermarkets and Chinese restaurants.

Ted: My favourite decade was the 1970s. The clothes were more comfortable. Jeans and T-shirts were in fashion, and there were games consoles and cool cars!

2 Read the article again. Complete the sentences with the words in the box. There are two extra words.

best better colourful comfortable easy heavy uncomfortable worse worst

1 Clothes in the 1900s were ... and ... .
2 Food in the 1900s wasn't ... to make.
3 For Susie, the 1960s were ... than the 1900s.
4 For Ted, the ... decade was the 1970s.
5 In the 1960s and 1970s, clothes were more ... and more ... .

3 Find four blue pronouns in the text. Match them with the nouns that each refers to.

1 they = a the family members b typical clothes
2 they = a boys b shirts and ties
3 it = a pasta b cooking
4 it = a your favourite decade b the show

4 Word Power Find a word in the article which means 'ten years'. Add it to the following units of time and put them in order, from the shortest to the longest.

second, minute, ...

century day hour minute month second week year

5 THINK CRITICALLY Imagine you can go back in time. What year, decade or century do you want to go back to? Why?

I want to go back to the 1980s because I love the music and fashion.

I want to go back to 3000 BC because I'm interested in Ancient Egypt.

6 FIND OUT In what decade was the first ...?

a FIFA World Cup
b phone with a camera
c photograph

Which decade was best?

READING

Sts read an article about a TV show that takes families back in time to experience life in different decades, and practise the skill of understanding what pronouns refer to in a text. They learn the past simple form of *be*, and *there was* / *there were* to talk about the past. They then read about life in the 1950s, and practise understanding and using the past simple form of *be* and *there was* / *there were* in context.

Reading text
An article about a TV show

Reading skill
Understanding what pronouns refer to in a text

WARMER

Ask: *What year is it now?* Elicit the answer, then say: *Imagine it's 1975 and you're at school – what do you think is different?* Elicit a few answers, and ask more questions to prompt sts, e.g. *What about your clothes? What about your hair? What about computers and phones? What about music? What about food?* Elicit a few ideas.

1 7.2 Focus on the pictures and teach the word *decade*. Elicit or model how to say different decades, e.g. *the nineteen fifties, the nineteen sixties*, etc. Ask: *Which decade do you think each picture shows?* Elicit a few ideas, but don't confirm them. Play the audio for sts to read and listen to the article and match the pictures with the decades. Check the answers with the class.

Answers
1 the 1900s 2 the 1960s 3 the 1970s

2 Ask sts to read the article again and complete the sentences with the correct words. Check answers with the class, eliciting the part of the text which confirms each answer.

Answers
1 heavy, uncomfortable
2 easy
3 better
4 best
5 colourful, comfortable

3 Understanding what pronouns refer to in a text
Read out the task and elicit or explain that pronouns are words like *he*, *she*, *it*, *they*, etc., which can replace nouns. Explain that writers often use pronouns to avoid repeating nouns, so understanding what pronouns refer to in a text can help you to understand the meaning better. Ask sts to find the first pronoun in the text. Read out the two possible answers and elicit the correct one. Ask a student to read out the sentence from the text, replacing the pronoun with the correct noun (the family members). Ask: *Does it make sense?* Elicit that the sentence makes sense, so it is the correct answer. Sts then complete the task. Check answers.

Answers
1 a 2 b 3 b 4 a

4 Word Power Elicit the word that means 'ten years'. Sts then put all the units of time in order. Check answers, and check that sts understand all the words.

Answers
second, minute, hour, day, week, month, year, decade, century

5 **21st Century skills**

THINK CRITICALLY
Read out the task and elicit a few examples of times that sts might choose. Ask sts to think about their ideas individually. Point out they should think of reasons why they have chosen this time. Put sts into groups to compare their ideas, then ask some sts to tell the class their ideas.

6 **21st Century skills**

FIND OUT
Set this exercise for homework if you prefer. Sts can find this information out by looking online or in other media, or by asking other people. You could ask sts to choose one of the three things and find out a few facts about it. When you check the answers, elicit what sts found out about each of the things.

Answers
a 1930s b 2000 c 1820s

R **Reading practice: WB** p.59
You will find more practice for reading here. Set these exercises for homework.

GRAMMAR *be:* past simple

I can use *was* and *were* to talk about the past.

Now watch the grammar animation.

1 **Copy and complete the grammar box with *was, were, wasn't* or *weren't*.**

Affirmative
I **was** at home yesterday.
He/She/It [1] ... a fan of the show.
You/We/They **were** babies in 2012.

Negative
I **wasn't** happy.
He/She/It **wasn't** at school.
You/We/They [2] ... comfortable.

Questions	Short answers
Were you at home?	Yes, I **was**. / No, I [3] ....
Was the food nice?	Yes, it **was**. / No, it **wasn't**.
[4] ... the cars cool?	Yes, they **were**. / No, they **weren't**.

2 **Complete the text. Use *was, were, wasn't* or *weren't*.**

In the 1960s, the mini skirt [1] ✓ <u>*was*</u> in fashion. Trousers for women [2] ✓ ... also popular. Clothes [3] ✗ ... as expensive as in earlier decades. Fashion [4] ✓ ... for everybody!
In the 1970s, platform shoes and boots [5] ✓ ... cool. It [6] ✗ ... easy to walk in them! They [7] ✗ ... very comfortable and they [8] ✗ ... good for your feet!

3 **Read the Look! box. How do you say the expressions in your language?**

Look! **Past time expressions**

We use:
yesterday *last night/week/month/year*
in 2016/the 1960s (in the nineteen sixties)

4 **Copy and complete the dialogues. Use *Where* and short answers.**

A: Where / Mia yesterday? / at school?
B: ✗ / at home
A: Where was Mia yesterday? Was she at school?
B: No, she wasn't. She was at home.

1 **A:** Where / Oliver last Tuesday? / at the library?
B: ✓
2 **A:** Where / Sam and Eli last Friday? / at a café?
B: ✗ / at the sports centre
3 **A:** Where / Isabella yesterday? / at drama club?
B: ✗ / at basketball practice

There was / There were

5 **Read the grammar box. Copy and complete the rules with *there was* and *there were*.**

	Affirmative	Negative
Singular	**There was** a phone.	**There wasn't** a TV.
Plural	**There were** cool cars.	**There weren't** any fridges.
	Questions	**Short answers**
Singular	**Was** there cereal for breakfast?	Yes, there **was**. No, there **wasn't**.
Plural	**Were** there any games consoles?	Yes, there **were**. No, there **weren't**.

Rules
We use [1] ... ... with singular nouns.
We use [2] ... ... with plural nouns.

6 7.3 **Complete the text about life in the USA in the 1950s. Use affirmative and negative forms of *there was* and *there were*. Listen and check.**

THE 1950S

<u>*There was*</u> often a phone in people's homes, but [1] ... any mobile phones.
Fridges were very popular in the 1950s. [2] ... often a fridge in the kitchen, but [3] ... always a washing machine because they were expensive.
For children, [4] ... books and toys, but [5] ... any computers or games consoles.
Clothes for adults were a bit boring. [6] ... dresses and skirts for women and suits for men.
But for teenagers, [7] ... colourful skirts, jeans and leather jackets. And [8] ... rock 'n' roll music!

FUN FACT
In the fifteenth century, long shoes like this were popular with men. Some were 60 cm long. It was difficult to walk in them and it was impossible to run!

FAST FINISHER
Write sentences about your favourite music, film, toy or hobby when you were younger.
When I was younger, my favourite toy was a Star Wars *lightsaber.*

LS Language summary: Unit 7 SB p.133

GRAMMAR *be:* past simple

Grammar animation

This lesson features an optional animated presentation of the grammar in context called *There weren't any laptops!* including the form and use of the past simple of *be* and *there was / there were*. You can watch this in class if you have time and access to a computer and tablet, or you can ask sts to download it from the Richmond Learning Platform to watch at home. See TG page 310 for animation script.

1 Read the grammar box about the past simple of *be* with sts. Put sts into pairs to complete the box with the correct forms. Check answers. Point out that the full negative forms are *was not* and *were not*, but we usually use the contracted forms *wasn't* and *weren't*. Point out the word order in questions: *Was he happy?* NOT ~~*He was happy?*~~

Answers
1 was 2 weren't 3 wasn't 4 Were

Ask questions to check concept.

Concept check questions: *I'm happy – is this now or yesterday?* (now). *She was happy – now or yesterday?* (yesterday). *The 1970s are fun or were fun?* (were fun). *Ted was bored or were bored?* (was bored). *Can you make that negative?* (Ted *wasn't* bored). *Can you make it a question?* (*Was* Ted bored?).

2 Focus on the picture of the shoes and ask: *When were these shoes fashionable?* Elicit the answer (1970s). Point out the example and point out that the affirmative form is used because there is a tick. Point out the cross with some answers. Sts read the text again and complete it with the correct words. Allow sts to compare their answers in pairs, then check answers with the class.

Answers
2 were 3 weren't 4 was 5 were 6 wasn't 7 weren't 8 weren't

3 Read through the Look! box with the class. Elicit how sts say the expressions in their language.

4 Read out the example answers and point out the use of *where* and the short answers. Sts then copy the dialogues into their notebooks and complete them with the correct words. To check answers, invite pairs of sts to read out the completed dialogues.

Answers
1 A: **Where was** Oliver last Tuesday? **Was he** at the library?
B: **Yes, he was.**
2 A: **Where were** Sam and Eli last Friday? **Were they** at a café?
B: **No, they weren't. They were** at the sports centre
3 A: **Where was** Isabella yesterday? **Was she** at drama club?
B: **No, she wasn't. She was** at basketball practice.

There was / There were

5 Read the grammar box about *There was / There were* with sts. Put sts into pairs to copy the rules into their notebooks and complete them. Check answers.

Answers
1 there was 2 there were

Ask questions to check concept.

Concept check questions: *There was a phone in the house – now or in the past?* (in the past). *There wasn't many cars – correct?* (no – *there weren't* many cars). *There was a TV – can you make this a question?* (*Was there* a TV?).

6 7.3 Focus on the picture and ask: *What do you know about the 1950s? What kind of music was popular?* (rock 'n' roll music). Play the audio. Sts read the text again and complete it with the correct words. Check answers.

Answers
1 there weren't
2 There was
3 there wasn't
4 there were
5 there weren't
6 There were
7 there were
8 there was

FUN FACT Encourage sts to read this fun fact for pleasure. They may also be interested to know that high heels first became popular in Europe in the 1700s, but were only worn by men. It was a hundred years later that women started to wear them.

FAST FINISHER

Sts who finish early can write sentences about their favourite music, film, toy or hobby when they were younger. Weaker sts can look back at the text on page 70, and write sentences about different decades in the past.

G Grammar practice: WB p.60

Sts will find more practice of the past simple of *be* and *there was / there were* here. Set these exercises for homework.

LS Language summary: Unit 7 SB p.133

We loved it!

VOCABULARY and LISTENING Regular verbs

I can understand the main idea when I listen.

1 **Read the dictionary definition of the word *craze*. What are some recent crazes in your country?**

craze *noun*
Something that is suddenly very popular, usually for a short time.
Minecraft *was a craze when I was younger.*

2 **Read and match the paragraphs with the photos. Were you, or are you, crazy about any of these things? There is one extra photo – do you know what it is?**

a
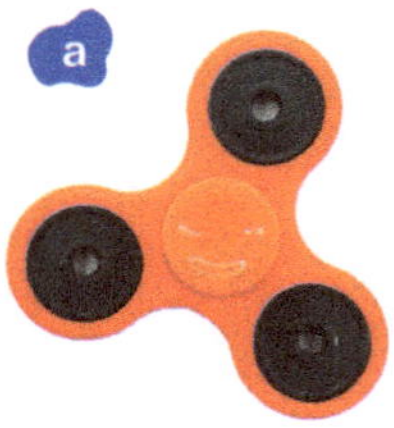
b

c

d

Home | Trending | Crazes | Quizzes

Four Crazy Crazes

Posted 20th April

1 Rubik's Cube

In the 1980s, everybody **wanted** a Rubik's Cube. Children, teenagers and adults **loved** them! It is still the best-selling toy of all time.

2 Pokémon cards

In 1999, Pokémon cards **arrived** from Japan. Millions of children around the world **collected** the cards and **played** games with them.

3 Mini scooters

In the 2000s, children everywhere **used** these small scooters to go school. Parents **borrowed** the scooters for short journeys, and some people even **travelled** to work by scooter!

4 Fidget Spinners

Fidget spinners were a more recent craze. Kids **enjoyed** playing with them in class, but they weren't popular with a lot of teachers, and some schools **tried** to ban them.

e

3 7.4 **Copy the table in your notebook. Complete it with the blue verbs in the text. Listen, check and repeat.**

Infinitive	Past simple
want	*wanted*

4 7.5 **Listen to a radio show about crazes. Try to understand the main idea. Answer these questions.**

1 What does Amy talk about – a game, a dance or a sport?
2 True or false? Amy hated the craze.
3 What does Zac talk about – a game, a dance or a sport?
4 True or false? The craze was only popular with famous people.

5 7.5 **Listen again and answer the questions.**

1 Where were the monsters in *Pokémon Go*? Name two places.
2 Why does Amy think the game was popular? Name one reason.
3 Who danced the Floss? Name two groups of people.
4 Why does Zac think the dance was popular? Name one reason.

LS Language summary: Unit 7 SB p.133

We loved it!

VOCABULARY and LISTENING
Regular verbs

Sts read about four gadgets that have been crazes. They listen to a radio show about crazes and focus on understanding the main idea when they listen. They study the past simple affirmative form of regular verbs and learn some common regular verbs, then practise pronouncing *-ed* endings on past simple verbs. They learn object pronouns and practise these in context.

Vocabulary
Regular verbs (*arrived, borrowed, collected, enjoyed, loved, played, travelled, tried, used, wanted*)

Listening text
A radio show about crazes

Listening skill
Understanding the main idea when listening

Pronunciation
-ed endings

WARMER
With books closed, teach the word *gadget* and ask: *Are there any toys or gadgets that are very popular at the moment?* Elicit a few ideas and ask more questions to prompt sts if necessary, e.g. *What about computer games? What about popular movies or TV shows?* Ask: *Can you remember any things that were very popular when you were younger?* Elicit a few ideas.

1 Read through the dictionary definition with the class, then elicit some recent *crazes* in the sts' country. If they want to mention ideas from the warmer, encourage them to repeat their ideas using the word *craze*, e.g. *There was a craze for ... .*

2 Focus on the pictures and ask sts if they recognise any of the things. Sts read the text and match the paragraphs with the pictures. Check answers with the class, and elicit or explain that the remaining picture (d) shows a Tamagotchi, a kind of virtual pet that was popular in the 1990s. Find out who in the class was crazy about each thing.

Answers
1 c
2 b
3 e
4 a

3 7.4 Focus on the verbs in blue in the text. Ask: *Do they refer to the past or the present?* (the past). Explain that the verbs are in the past simple form, and they are all regular verbs. Elicit the regular ending (*-ed*). Ask sts to copy the table into their notebooks and complete it. Play the audio for sts to listen, check and repeat. Check answers with the class.

Answers
Infinitive: love, arrive, collect, play, use, borrow, travel, enjoy, try
Past simple: loved, arrived, collected, played, used, borrowed, travelled, enjoyed, tried

4 7.5 **Understanding the main idea when listening** Read out the task and allow sts time to read through the questions. Ask: *To do this task, do you need to understand every word when you listen, or just the main idea?* (just the main idea). Explain to sts that when they listen for the first time, it is a good idea to focus on understanding the main idea, and not worry about understanding all the details. Play the audio for sts to listen and answer the questions. See TG page 280 for audio script. Check answers with the class.

Answers
1 a game
2 F – She loved it.
3 a dance
4 F – Everybody wanted to do it.

5 7.5 Allow sts time to read through the questions. Check they understand *monsters*. Play the audio again for sts to listen and answer the questions. Point out that it is easier to understand the details if they have understood the main idea first. Allow sts to compare their answers in pairs, then check answers with the class.

Answers
1 parks, restaurants, museums, cinemas, in front of famous buildings
2 It started in summer, so it was hot and people wanted to be outside. It was easy to play, new and exciting.
3 school students, teachers, famous people, footballers
4 People wanted to learn it to be able to do it faster than their friends because it was difficult.

V L **Vocabulary and Listening practice: WB** p.61
Sts will find more practice for listening, and practice of vocabulary for regular verbs here. Set these exercises for homework.

LS **Language summary: Unit 7 SB** p.133

GRAMMAR

Past simple affirmative: regular verbs

I can use the past simple to talk about the past.

Now watch the grammar animation.

1 Look at the grammar box and answer the questions.

1 How do we form the past simple affirmative of regular verbs?

2 Is the past simple form different for different subjects in a sentence?

I **loved** *Pokémon Go*!
Everybody **wanted** a Rubik's Cube.
Some schools **tried** to ban fidget spinners.
People **travelled** to work by scooter.

2 7.6 Complete the text. Use the past simple form of the verbs in brackets. Listen and check.

The Story of the Floss

A few years ago, a fifteen-year-old schoolboy, Russell Horning, *invented* (invent) a funny new dance called 'the Floss'. He [1] … (upload) a video of the dance to YouTube. The singer Katy Perry [2] … (watch) the video and she liked it. She [3] … (invite) Russell to dance with her on a TV show. Russell [4] … (travel) to New York to be on the show. He [5] … (dance) the Floss on national TV! Children and adults [6] … (try) to copy him. Later, Epic Games [7] … (use) the dance in their video game, *Fortnite*. Suddenly the Floss was a global craze!

3 PRONUNCIATION *-ed* endings

7.7 Listen and repeat.

/t/	/d/	/ɪd/
watched	loved	wanted
danced	travelled	invited

4 7.8 Add these verbs to the table in Exercise 3. Listen, check and repeat.

collected finished liked
started arrived tried

5 Read the Look! box. How do you say *ago* in your language?

Look! *ago*

We use *ago* to talk about something that happened at some point in the past up to now.
Russell Horning invented the Floss a few years ago.
I played 'Fortnite' two days ago.

6 Write sentences that are true for you. Use the expressions in the box or your own ideas.

an hour ago a week ago a month ago
a year ago (two/three) minutes/days ago

1 I / watch a film at the cinema …
2 This English lesson / start …
3 I / visit (my cousins/grandparents/a museum) …

7 GET CREATIVE Work in pairs. Think about a craze that was popular when you were younger. Write a description and present it to the class.

Object pronouns

I can use object pronouns.

8 Read the sentences and complete the grammar box.

Fidget spinners weren't popular. Schools tried to ban **them**.
Katy Perry watched the video and she liked **it**.
Russell danced on TV. Children tried to copy **him**.

Singular		Plural	
Subject pronoun	Object Pronoun	Subject pronoun	Object Pronoun
I	me	we	us
you	you	you	you
he she it	[1] … her [2] …	they	[3] …

9 Complete the sentences with an object pronoun.

1 Katy Perry is great. I really like …!
2 I've got a new guitar. I practise … every day.
3 It's Dan's birthday. I've got a present for … .
4 Excuse … . Is this the train to London?
5 Daisy and I are at the shops. Dad is with …, too.

FAST FINISHER

Imagine all your friends are famous people. Write sentences about last week. Use these verbs.

cook dance listen phone play visit watch

Last Monday, I cooked pizza for LeBron James. On Tuesday, …

LS Language summary: Unit 7 SB p.133

GRAMMAR Past simple affirmative: regular verbs

Grammar animation

This lesson features an optional animated presentation of the grammar in context called Ben *needed some new clothes!* including the form and use of the past simple affirmative of regular verbs, and object pronouns. You can watch this in class if you have time and access to a computer or tablet, or you can ask sts to download it from the Richmond Learning Platform to watch at home. See TG page 310 for animation script.

1 Read the examples of past simple forms in the grammar box with sts. Elicit that we add *-ed* to verbs, but point out the spelling changes in *try* – *tried* and *travel* – *travelled*. Elicit that the form stays the same for all subjects in a sentence, e.g. *I wanted a fidget spinner, my brother wanted a fidget spinner, we wanted a fidget spinner*.

Answers
1 We add *-ed* 2 No, it stays the same.

Ask questions to check concept.

Concept check questions: *I want a Rubik's cube – now or in the past?* (now). *I wanted a Mini scooter – now or in the past?* (in the past).

2 7.6 Focus on the picture and ask: *What is this? Do you know this dance?* Elicit answers, and explain that the English name is the Floss. Ask sts to read the text and complete it with the correct past simple forms. Allow sts to compare their answers in pairs, then play the audio for them to listen and check.

Answers
1 uploaded
2 watched
3 invited
4 travelled
5 danced
6 tried
7 used

3 **PRONUNCIATION** 7.7

Model and drill pronunciation of the three endings in isolation. Play the audio once for sts to listen, then play it again for them to repeat the words.

4 7.8

Put sts into pairs to copy the table and complete it with the verbs. Play the audio for sts to listen, check and repeat.

5 Read through the Look! box with the class. Elicit how sts express the word in their own language, and point out that we say *a few days ago*, NOT ~~*ago a few days*~~.

6 Read out the prompts and an example sentence for the first prompt. Sts then write their sentences individually. Ask some sts to read their sentences to the class.

21st Century skills

7 **GET CREATIVE**

Read out the task, then put sts into pairs to choose a craze that was popular in their country and write a description of it. Monitor and help while sts are working, then ask pairs in turn to read their descriptions to the class, without saying the name of the craze. Other sts can listen and guess the craze.

Object pronouns

8 Read the grammar box with sts about object pronouns and elicit the missing pronouns. If necessary, use a simple pair of sentences to demonstrate the idea of subject and object pronouns, e.g. *I like him. / He likes me.* Point out that the pronoun before the verb is the subject pronoun, and the one after the verb is the object pronoun. Point out that *you* and *it* are the same as subject and object pronouns, but all the others are different.

Answers
1 him 2 it 3 them

Ask questions to check concept.

Concept check questions: *Mini scooters – they are fun – subject or object pronoun?* (subject). *Mini scooters – I love them – subject or object pronoun?* (object). *This scooter is for you – subject or object pronoun?* (object).

9 Sts read the sentences and complete them with the correct object pronouns. Check answers.

Answers
1 her 2 it 3 him 4 me 5 us

FAST FINISHER

Sts who finish early can write sentences about last week, imagining their friends are all famous people. Weaker sts could write two true sentences about things they did last week.

G **Grammar practice: WB** p.62
Sts will find more practice of the past simple affirmative form of regular verbs and object pronouns here. Set these exercises for homework.

LS **Language summary: Unit 7 SB** p.133

KEEP TALKING!

Have you got this in black?

READING and LISTENING

I can understand a shopping website.

1 Work in pairs. Do you or your family shop online? What type of things do you buy?

2 Look at the website for an online shop. What type of things can you buy on the website?

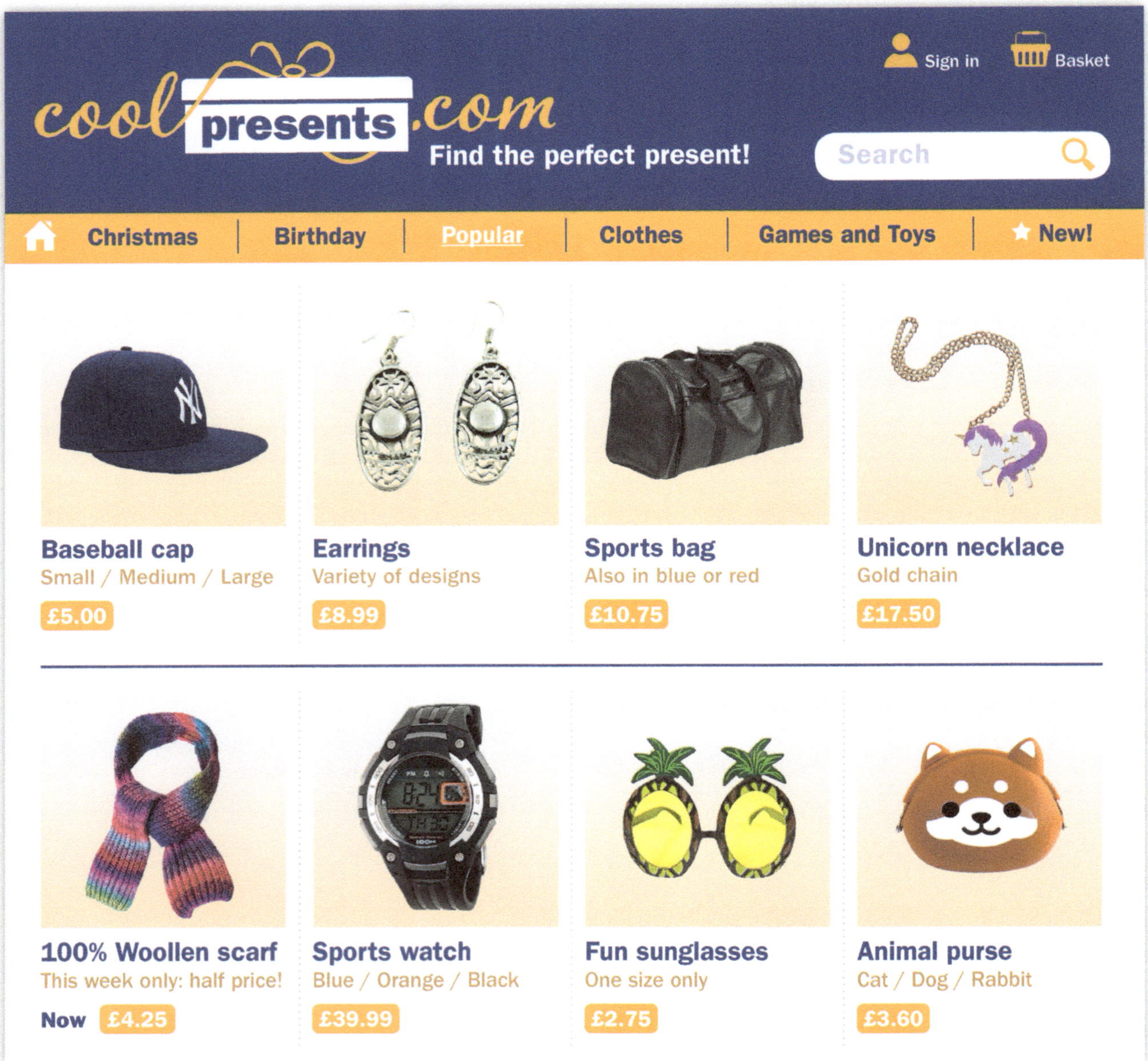

3 Scan the website quickly and find the answers to these questions.

1 What is the cheapest thing on the website?
2 What is the most expensive thing?
3 How many sizes are there of the baseball cap?
4 How much was the scarf last week?
5 You want to buy a Rubik's Cube. What page do you click on?
6 Your dad is 45 next week. What page do you click on?

4 7.9 Listen. Eva is shopping on coolpresents.com. Who is she buying a present for? What does she decide to buy?

5 7.9 Listen again and answer the questions.

1 Why doesn't she buy the sports bag?
2 Why doesn't she buy the watch?
3 When is Eva's brother's birthday?

6 Work in pairs. What is your favourite thing on the coolpresents.com website? Why?

KEEP TALKING!

Have you got this in black?

READING and LISTENING

Sts study a website for an online shop and listen to a dialogue about online shopping. They then discuss their favourite thing on the website. They listen to someone who is shopping for clothes and learn how to shop for clothes and say prices. They read and hear a model dialogue and personalise the useful language by following the steps in the Speaking plan.

WARMER

Play a game to revise the clothes vocabulary from page 69. Ask sts individually to look back at the pictures on page 69, then draw four things to test their classmates. Put sts into groups. They take turns to show their pictures to each other and guess the words. The first person to say each word correctly gets a point (they cannot get points when they are showing their own pictures). Ask who in each group got the most points.

1 Put sts into pairs to discuss the questions. Ask some sts to tell the class what things they buy online.

2 Sts look at the website and notice the types of things you can buy on it. Read through the things with the class and check that sts understand all the words.

Answer
You can buy presents.

3 Sts read the website again and answer the questions. You could do this as a race to motivate sts. Check answers with the class.

Answers

1	Fun sunglasses	4	£8.50
2	Sports watch	5	Games and Toys
3	3: small, medium, large	6	Birthday

4 7.9 Read out the situation and explain to sts that they will hear Eva talking to a friend. Read out the questions, and remind sts that for this task they are listening for the main meaning, not for details. Play the audio for sts to listen and answer the questions. See TG pages 280–281 for audio script. Allow sts to compare their answers in pairs, then check answers with the class, playing the audio again and pausing if necessary to confirm the answers.

Answers
1 Her brother; cap and sunglasses

5 7.9 Allow sts time to read through the questions, then play the audio again for sts to listen and answer the questions. Check answers, playing the audio again and pausing if necessary to confirm the answers.

Answers
1 Her brother has already got a new sports bag.
2 It's too expensive.
3 It was yesterday.

EXTRA PRACTICE

Write these gapped sentences on the board:

1 I'm ... a present for my brother.
2 I don't know ... to get him.
3 What ... this bag?
4 This cap's really ... .
5 ... idea!
6 I'm a bit ... with the present.

Put sts into pairs to try to remember the missing words. Play the audio again for them to check, and check that sts understand all the sentences. Elicit that the sentences are all used for talking about presents.

Answers

1	looking for	4	cool
2	what	5	Great
3	about	6	late

6 Put sts into pairs to discuss which are their favourite things on the website and why. Discuss their ideas as a class. Ask: *What other good ideas for presents can you find online?*

EXTRA PRACTICE

Ask: *When do you give or receive presents?* Elicit some ideas from the class, e.g. birthdays, Christmas, because you pass an exam. Arrange sts in small groups and ask them to think of the best and worst presents they received, and tell their group members what the present was, who it was from, and what it was for. At the end, groups decide what was the best and worst present and tell the rest of the class.

SPEAKING Shopping for clothes

I can ask about things in a shop.

1 7.10 **Frank is looking for some new shorts. Listen and read. What colour and size does he buy?**

Assistant: Hello. Can I help you?
Frank: Have you got these shorts in white?
Assistant: I'm afraid not, but we've got them in black.
Frank: OK, can I try them on, please?
Assistant: Of course. What size do you need?
Frank: Medium.
Assistant: Here's a medium in black. The changing rooms are over there.
Later ...
Assistant: Any good?
Frank: They're perfect, thanks. How much are they?
Assistant: £15.99.
Frank: Great! I'll take them.
Assistant: OK. You can pay over there.
Frank: Thanks very much.

2 7.11 **Listen and repeat the Useful language.**

Useful language

Shopping for clothes

Assistant	Customer
Can I help you?	Have you got this shirt / these shorts in (red/ green)?
What size do you need?	Small/Medium/Large
The changing rooms are over there.	Can I try it/them on, please?
Any good?	How much is it / are they?
You can pay over there.	I'll take it/them.

3 7.12 **Copy and complete the dialogue. Listen and check.**

Assistant: Hello. Can I [1] ... you?
Girl: Have you got this sweatshirt in red?
Assistant: Yes, we have.
Girl: Can I [2] ... it on, please?
Assistant: Of course. What [3] ... do you need?
Girl: Small.
Assistant: Here's a small in red. The changing rooms are [4] ... there.
Later ...
Assistant: Any good?
Girl: Yes, thanks. I'll [5] ... it.
Assistant: OK. You can [6] ... over there.

4 7.13 **Read the Look! box. Listen and repeat the prices on the website on page 74.**

Look! Saying prices

We use:

£5	*Five pounds*
£8.99	*Eight pounds ninety-nine or Eight ninety-nine*
75p	*75 p* or *75 pence*

5 7.14 **Listen and write the prices.**

1 £24.99

6 **Work in pairs and prepare a new dialogue. Follow the steps in the Speaking plan.**

Shopping list

Trousers: blue – medium
Jacket: red – small
T-shirt: orange – extra small
Jeans: white – large

Speaking plan

Prepare

- Decide on your roles.
- Choose an item of clothing from the shopping list or use your own ideas.

Speak

- Practise your dialogue.
- Use phrases from the Useful language box.
- Act out the dialogue without notes.

Reflect

- How can you improve next time?
- Choose a new item of clothing and swap roles.

Now play *Keep moving!*

FAST FINISHER

Think of your own cool presents for the website on page 74. Write a short description for each present.

LS Language summary: Unit 7 SB p.133

 EXTRA PRACTICE Workbook page 63

SPEAKING Shopping for clothes

1 7.10 Focus on the picture and explain that it shows Frank looking for some new shorts. Read out the question and elicit some words for sizes (small, medium, large), then play the audio of the dialogue. With stronger classes, you could play the dialogue with books closed and ask: *What colour and size does he buy?* With weaker classes, you could play the dialogue for sts to listen and read. See SB page 75 for audio script.

Answers
He buys medium in black.

2 7.11 Ask sts if they can remember some of the phrases Frank and the assistant used. Read through the Useful language box with the class and check sts understand all the phrases. Play the audio once for sts to listen to the phrases, then play it again for them to repeat.

3 7.12 Ask sts to copy the dialogue into their notebooks and complete it with the correct words. Allow sts to compare their answers in pairs, then play the audio for them to listen and check. If your sts would benefit from some controlled practice before the personalised practice, they could practise this dialogue in pairs.

Answers

1	help	4	over
2	try	5	take
3	size	6	pay

4 7.13 Read through the Look! box with the class. Model pronunciation of the prices. Refer sts back to the prices on page 74. Play the audio once for them to listen, then play it again for them to listen and repeat. For extra practice, you could write some more prices on the board. As you write each one, sts race to say it correctly.

5 7.14 Play the first price as an example, then play the rest of the prices, pausing if necessary to allow sts time to write. Check answers by playing the audio again and writing the prices on the board.

Answers

2	£12.35	4	65p	6	80p
3	£17.70	5	£3.49		

6 Sts follow the steps in the Speaking plan to practise buying clothes.

Speaking plan

Prepare

Sts work in their pairs and decide who will be the customer and who will be the assistant. The customer chooses what they are going to buy. Remind them to think about the colour and size. The assistant can look back at the Useful language in Exercise 2 and think about what they need to say.

Speak

Sts practise their dialogue in their pairs. They can practise with and then without notes. Monitor and help as necessary. If your sts use smartphones in class, they could record their conversations.

Reflect

Discuss as a class how sts could improve next time. If you noticed any typical errors, correct them with the class. Sts swap roles and follow the steps again. If they record their conversations, ask them to use this to help them think of how they could improve next time. Ask some sts to perform their dialogues for the class if they feel confident.

Keep moving!

This lesson features an optional language revision and consolidation game for use in digital classrooms. Players control different characters, each with their own personalities and special abilities.

FAST FINISHER

Sts think of their own cool presents for a website and write a short description of each one. Remind them to add a price, too. You could ask some sts to read their descriptions to the class. Ask who would buy each present, and who for. Weaker sts could work in pairs. They look at the website on page 74 again, choose two presents and change some of the details then write a description of each one.

S Speaking practice: WB p.63
Sts will find more practice for shopping for clothes here. Set these exercises for homework.

LS Language summary: Unit 7 SB p.133

REAL CULTURE!

The history of film in the USA

I can compare the American film industry to the film industry in my country.

a

b

c

THE HISTORY OF AMERICAN CINEMA

1 Cinema started in the USA in the 1890s. Thomas Edison, an inventor, showed some films to an audience in New York. They were less than a minute long and there was no sound, but people loved them!

2 In 1911, a film studio opened in a village in California. What was the name of the village? Hollywood! Today, Hollywood is full of big hotels, restaurants and theatres, and is part of the city of Los Angeles.

3 In 1925, a Hollywood studio used special effects to make the first dinosaur movie, *The Lost World*. When a Tyrannosaurus Rex walked on screen, audiences were amazed and frightened!

4 In 1927, an actor talked for the first time in a film. *The Jazz Singer* was a big success. Soon there weren't any silent films. They were all 'talkies'.

5 Walt Disney was an American film-maker. In 1928, he created the cartoon character Mickey Mouse. People loved Mickey and that was the start of Disney films.

6 The first colour films arrived in the 1930s. *The Wizard of Oz* was an early colour film. Some people still think it is one of the best films in cinema history.

7 In the 1970s and 1980s, popular films included *Jaws* and *Star Wars*. Film studios used computers to create special effects. These were more and more amazing during the 1990s and into the twenty-first century.

d

e

f

g

REAL CULTURE! The history of film in the USA

Sts learn about the history of film making in the USA, including early silent films, the first 'talking' films, the first cartoons and the first special effects. They then discuss the film industry in their own country.

This lesson also features an optional culture video about a family who take part in a TV programme: see SB page 77.

WARMER

Explain to sts that they are going to learn about the film industry in the USA. Put them into groups. Ask them to try and think of a film title beginning with every letter of the alphabet. Tell them the titles can be in English or in their own language. Give them two or three minutes, then elicit a film title beginning with each letter of the alphabet in turn. See if, as a class, they can come up with a film for every letter!

BACKGROUND

Students might enjoy some of this movie trivia.

- Hollywood is the biggest film industry in the world, followed by China, Japan, India and the UK.
- So far, five Hollywood films have earned over $2 billion: *Avengers: Endgame*, *Avatar*, *Titanic*, *Star Wars: The Force Awakens* and *Avengers: Infinity War*.
- The famous Hollywood sign was first installed in 1923. The sign originally said Hollywoodland, and was an advertisement for a housing development. In 1949, it was agreed that the 'land' should be removed and a new sign put up saying simply Hollywood.
- The name Hollywood has been adapted into names for other film industries around the world. The Indian film industry is known as Bollywood (Bombay + Hollywood) and the Nigerian film industry is known as Nollywood (Nigeria + Hollywood)

1 Put sts into pairs to discuss the questions. Discuss as a class who likes going to the cinema and why, and elicit some of the favourite films that sts have, encouraging them to give reasons for their choices. You could use the discussion to introduce some extra film vocabulary by asking questions like: *Who is your favourite character? What's your favourite scene in the film? Does it have a happy ending?*

2 7.15 Focus on the pictures and ask sts if they recognise any of the films or characters. Read out the task, then play the audio. Sts read and listen to the article and match the paragraphs with the pictures. Check answers.

Answers

1 f	4 g	7 a
2 b	5 c	
3 e	6 d	

3 Ask sts to read the article again and choose the correct answers. Allow sts to compare their answers in pairs, then check answers with the class, eliciting the part of the article which confirms each answer.

Answers

1 b	3 b	5 b
2 a	4 a	6 c

4 **Word Power** Read out the task and point out the paragraph numbers in brackets after each sentence. Explain that sts will find the correct word in this paragraph. Sts copy the sentences into their notebooks and complete them with the correct words. Check answers, and check that sts understand all the words. Model pronunciation of words that sts might find difficult, e.g. *frightened*.

Answers

2 audience	5 cartoon
3 sound	6 special effects
4 frightened	

EXTRA PRACTICE

NOTE: You will need to find out the name of the films used here before doing this activity. Explain that many Hollywood films have one English title and one title in the language of the country where people will watch them. Write the titles of some popular films on the board. For example, *Home Alone*, *Toy Story*, *Harry Potter and the Philosopher's Stone*, *Jungle Book*, *The Lion King*, *Cats*, *Star Wars*, *Pirates of the Caribbean*, *Men in Black*, *Ice Age*. Ask sts to work in pairs or small groups and try to guess the title in their own language.

1 **Work in pairs. Do you like going to the cinema? Have you got a favourite film?**

2 7.15 **Read and listen to the article about the history of cinema. Match the paragraphs with the pictures.**

3 **Read the article again and choose the correct option.**

1 The first films were ...
 a long
 b short
 c loud

2 100 years ago, Hollywood was ...
 a a small village
 b a film studio in California
 c part of Los Angeles

3 *The Lost World* was the first movie ...
 a about dinosaurs
 b with special effects
 c for an American audience

4 The *Jazz Singer* was the first film that ...
 a wasn't silent
 b was popular
 c used actors

5 The *Wizard of Oz* was ...
 a the best film of all time
 b in colour
 c the first film of the 1930s

6 In the 1970s and 80s, films ...
 a were more amazing than in the 1990s
 b weren't very popular
 c started to use computers to create special effects

4 **Word Power** **Copy and complete the sentences with words from the text.**

1 Our English teacher *showed* us a video about London. (Paragraph 1)
2 The film was very popular – there was a large ... in the cinema. (Paragraph 1)
3 I always turn off the ... on my phone when I'm at the cinema. (Paragraph 1)
4 I can't watch horror films. I get really ... . (Paragraph 3)
5 My favourite ... is *The Simpsons*. (Paragraph 5)
6 I love this film because of its amazing ... . (Paragraph 7)

5 7.16 **Do the quiz in pairs. Listen and check your answers.**

Quiz: Are you a film expert?

How much do you know about the most famous films of our times? Try our quiz to find out!

1 She played Hermione Granger in the *Harry Potter* films. Who is she?
 a Emma Stone
 b Emma Watson
 c Kristen Stewart

2 He directed the first two *Jurassic Park* films. Who is he?
 a Steven Spielberg
 b Peter Jackson
 c George Lucas

3 How old was Macauley Culkin when he acted in the film *Home Alone*?
 a Seven years old
 b Nine years old
 c Twelve years old

4 In the *Toy Story* films, Woody and Buzz Lightyear lived with a boy called ...
 a Andy
 b Kenny
 c Bobby

5 In the movie *E.T.*, the alien wanted to phone ...
 a a doctor
 b the police
 c home

6 At the end of *Titanic*, Rose dropped something into the sea. What was it?
 a some earrings
 b a letter
 c a necklace

6 **COMPARE CULTURES** **Discuss the questions.**

1 Is there a big film industry in your country?
2 What are some famous films, or some recent films, from your country?
3 Who are your country's most famous actors and directors?
4 Do you prefer films from your country or films from other countries? Why?

Now watch the culture video.

FAST FINISHER

Write about a recent film that you watched.

Two weeks ago, I watched Coco. It's about a twelve-year-old boy. He wants to be a musician, but ...

REAL CULTURE!

5 7.16 Puts sts into pairs to do the quiz. Play the audio for them to check their answers, and find out who got all the answers right. Ask: *Have you seen any of these films? Do you like them?*

Answers

1	b	3	b	5	c
2	a	4	a	6	c

EXTRA PRACTICE

Put sts into pairs and ask them to prepare one more quiz question about films. Tell them to give three possible answers, as in the quiz. When they are ready, ask pairs in turn to read their question and possible answers to the class. Other sts can race to give the correct answers.

21st Century skills

6 **COMPARE CULTURES**

Put sts into pairs or small groups to discuss the questions. Have a brief class discussion on the film industry in the sts' own country, and films they like.

Culture video

You can watch this in class if you have time and access to video, or you can ask sts to download it from the Richmond Learning Platform to watch at home. See *TV time travellers* on TG pages 301 and 307.

EXTRA PRACTICE

Put sts in pairs and ask them to look at pages 76 and 77 and find as many film-related words as possible. Elicit the following words: *acted*, *actor*, *audience*, *cartoon*, *character*, *cinema*, *colour film*, *directed*, *director*, *film*, *film industry*, *Hollywood*, *horror film*, *movie*, *silent film*, *special effects*, *studio*, *talkie*. Check that sts understand them and ask them if they know any more film words. Elicit these so that everyone can add them to their list.

FAST FINISHER

Sts write a paragraph about a recent film they watched. You could ask some sts to read their paragraphs to the class, leaving out the name of the film. Other sts can listen and guess the film. Weaker sts could write two or three sentences about their favourite film, saying what it is, who is in it and why they like it.

A great year!

WRITING A review of a year

I can write a review about past events.

Zoe's Blog

Latest posts Archives

A great year

Posted 12 April

For me, 2018 was a fantastic year. There were some great films, for example, *Incredibles 2* and *Black Panther*. I loved *Incredibles 2*. It was really exciting and also very funny.

There were some great singers and groups in 2018, for example Shawn Mendes and Bruno Mars. My friends and I also loved listening to Taylor Swift.

What video games were popular? My brother and his friends played *Fortnite*, but I was too young. I liked *Just Dance 2018*. My friends and I learned some great new dances!

Were there any big events in 2018? Yes, there were, for example the FIFA World Cup. We watched the final on TV. France were the winners and Kylian Mbappé scored an amazing goal – he was only nineteen!

I loved 2018. It was one of my favourite years ever!

1 **Read Zoe's review of the year 2018. Copy and complete the mind map.**

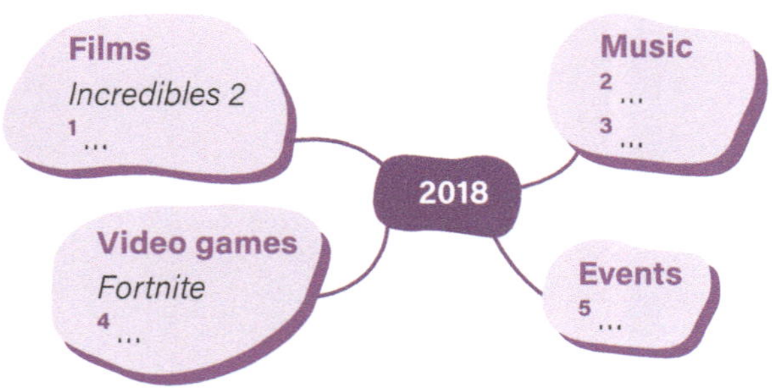

2 **Look at the Useful language. How do you say these expressions in your language?**

Useful language

Writing about past events

For me, ... was a fantastic / an interesting year.
There were some great films.
There was some great music.
We listened to ... / We watched ...
We loved/liked ...
It was exciting/funny/cool/great.

3 **Study the Look! box. Find another sentence with *for example* in the review.**

Look! Giving examples

We add examples in an essay to make it more interesting.
There were some great films, for example Incredibles 2 *and* Black Panther.

4 **In your notebooks, rewrite sentences 1–4 with examples. Use your own ideas.**

1 At the weekend, I wear comfortable clothes, ...
2 I eat a lot of healthy food, ...
3 I love all types of sport, ...
4 There were some great video games when I was younger, ...

5 **Work in pairs. Think of one or two recent years. What films, games, music and events can you remember in each year?**

6 **Write a review of a year. Follow the steps in the Writing plan.**

Writing plan

Prepare

› Choose a year that you remember well.
› Make a mind map like the one in Exercise 1.

Write

› Use a different paragraph for each category of your mind map.
› Use the expressions from the Useful language box.
› Give examples.

Reflect

› Check your grammar: *be*: past simple, past simple regular verbs.
› Check examples. Check your spelling.

W Writing summary: WB p.90 E Exams: Unit 7 SB p.124 LS Language summary: Unit 7 SB p.133

EXTRA PRACTICE Workbook page 64; photocopiable activities for Unit 7: vocabulary, grammar and skills

A great year!

WRITING A review of a year

Sts read a review of the year 2018. They study a mind map and learn useful language for writing about past events. They look at how examples make a text more interesting. They then follow the steps in the Writing plan to write a review of a year, using a mind map to plan their ideas before they write.

Writing
A review of a year

Useful language
Writing about past events (*For me, ... was a fantastic / an interesting year, There were some great films, There was some great music, We listened to ... / We watched ..., We loved/liked ..., It was exciting/funny/cool/great.*)

Look!
Giving examples

WARMER

Ask: *What can you remember about last year? What things happened in your country? What music was popular? What films were there? Were there any big sports events?* Elicit a range of ideas and make notes on the board under headings such as *Music, Films, Sport, Events*, etc. Point to the notes and ask: *Was it a good year?* Explain to sts that you can write about all the ideas on the board to make a review of a year. Tell sts they are going to read a review of a year, then write their own.

1 Focus on the mind map and point out that this is what they have done together on the board. Ask sts to copy the mind map into their notebooks, then read Zoe's review and complete the mind map. Check answers with the class.

Answers
1 *Black Panther*
2 Shawn Mendes
3 Bruno Mars
4 *Just Dance 2018*
5 FIFA World Cup

2 Read the Useful language box with sts about writing about past events. Check they understand all the expressions and ask them how they say these expressions in their first language. Point out that *For me, ...* is a way of expressing your own opinion. You could elicit one or two more expressions for expressing your opinion, e.g. *I think ..., In my opinion ...* .

3 Read the Look! box with sts about *for example*. Check they understand the meaning and point out the use of a comma before the expression.

4 Ask sts to rewrite the sentences adding their own examples. Allow sts to compare their answers in pairs, then ask some sts to read some of their sentences to the class.

5 Put sts into pairs to think of one or two recent years and make notes on the films, games, music and events they can remember. Alternatively, sts could use the notes on the board from the warmer activity, or you could brainstorm ideas about another year with the class.

6 Explain to sts that they will now write a review of a year, following the steps in the Writing plan.

Writing plan

Prepare
Sts work as individuals and prepare a mind map of the year they have chosen. Weaker sts could work in pairs for this.

Write
Focus on the review in Exercise 1 and elicit or point out that each category (films, music, video games, events) has its own paragraph. Point out to sts that they should do this in their own review. Sts then write their review, using the review in Exercise 1 as a model. Refer them back to the Useful language box for expressions to write about the past, and remind them to include examples.

Reflect
Ask sts to check their grammar, spelling and punctuation and make any necessary changes. Sts could then swap their reviews with each other in pairs and give feedback on the use of the Useful language, the past simple of *be* and past simple regular verbs. Alternatively, they could share their reviews with each other in small groups and discuss which years were the most amazing and why.

W **Writing practice: WB** p.64
Sts will find more practice of writing here. Set these exercises for homework.

W **Writing summary: WB** p.90

E **Exams: Unit 7 SB** p.124

Life stories 8

Vocabulary: Life events; Physical appearance | **Grammar:** Past simple: affirmative and negative; Past simple: questions | **Speaking:** Talking about past events | **Writing:** A personal description

VOCABULARY Life events

I can talk about life events.

1 8.1 **Match the life events in the box with the pictures. Listen, check and repeat.**

be born   buy a house   die   get a job   get married   go to university   grow up
have a baby   learn to drive   leave school   make friends   start school

2 Copy and complete the table. Use the verbs from Exercise 1 and the past tense forms in the box. Are the verbs regular or irregular?

Verb	Past tense	Regular or Irregular?
be	was/were	Irregular
buy	bought	Irregular

~~bought~~   got   made   left   died   ~~was/were~~
grew up   started   learned   had   went

3 8.2 **Do the quiz in pairs. Listen and check.**

1993   84   a clown   eighteen
Hawaii   Spain   thirteen

4 Work in pairs. In which order do people usually do the life events from Exercise 1?

1 be born

Now watch the vlog.

FAST FINISHER

Write sentences about famous people.

Novak Djokovic grew up in Belgrade.

QUIZ: FAMOUS LIVES

1 The footballer Lionel Messi left Argentina to play for Barcelona when he was …

2 The actor Daniel Radcliffe bought his first house when he was …

3 The singer Ariana Grande was born in …

4 The singer Bruno Mars went to school in …

5 The actress Penélope Cruz grew up in …

6 Before he was famous, the actor Hugh Jackman got a job as …!

7 Kimani Maruge from Kenya started primary school when he was … – the oldest person ever!

LS Language summary: Unit 8 SB p.134

EXTRA PRACTICE Workbook page 66

Life stories

8

UNIT 8 OVERVIEW: This unit focuses on life stories. Sts read about the singer Camila Cabello, and listen to a podcast about make-up and special effects in films. They read some adverts for events and learn how to talk about their weekend. They read about the life and achievements of Nelson Mandela and finally, they write a description of someone in their family. They also watch a vlog about someone's family history and a culture video about a popular British actor and his life story.

Vocabulary	Grammar	Pronunciation	Reading	Listening	Speaking	Writing
Life events; Physical appearance	Past simple: affirmative and negative; Past simple: questions	Intonation in questions	Answering multiple choice questions	Listening for key words in a podcast	Talking about past events	A description of a person

VOCABULARY Life events

Sts learn words for life events. They do a quiz about the lives of some famous people, then personalise the vocabulary by talking about the order in which people usually do different life events.

Vocabulary

Life events (*be born, buy a house, die, get a job, get married, go to university, grow up, have a baby, learn to drive, leave school, make friends, start school*)

Vlog

Rebecca: *My grandpa and his life story*

WARMER

Ask: *What do you want to do when you're 18? What about when you're 30?* Elicit a few ideas and teach English words and phrases for things that sts want to talk about, e.g. *get a job, go travelling, get married*.

1 8.1 Read through the phrases in the box and elicit or teach the meanings. Sts match the phrases to the pictures. Play the audio for sts to listen, check and repeat.

Answers

1 leave school
2 learn to drive
3 start school
4 get a job
5 get married
6 be born
7 buy a house
8 have a baby
9 die
10 make friends
11 grow up
12 go to university

2 Sts copy the table into their notebooks and complete it with the correct verb forms. Remind them that regular verbs add *-ed* in the past simple. Check answers.

Answers

Regular verbs: die/died, start/started, learn/learned or learnt
Irregular verbs: get/got, make/made, leave/left, grow up/grew up, have/had, go/went

3 8.2 Sts work in pairs to do the quiz. Play the audio for them to listen and check.

Answers

1 thirteen
2 eighteen
3 1993
4 Hawaii
5 Spain
6 a clown
7 84

4 Put sts into pairs and ask them to write the order in which people usually do the things in Exercise 1. Explain that there is no single right answer. Discuss the answers.

Possible answers

be born, start school, make friends, grow up, leave school, go to university, get a job, learn to drive, buy a house, get married, have a baby, die

Vlog

This lesson features a vlog in which vlogger Rebecca talks about her family history. You can watch this in class if you have time and access to video, or you can ask sts to download it from the Richmond Learning Platform to watch at home. See TG pages 293 and 305.

FAST FINISHER

Sts who finish early can write sentences about famous people. Weaker sts could work in pairs. They cover the vocabulary in Exercise 1, then take turns to point at a picture and try to remember the correct phrase.

EXTRA PRACTICE

Put sts into pairs. They take turns to talk about life events that they want to do, and when they want to do them, e.g. *I want to leave school when I'm eighteen and ....* Their partner can film them using their phone. They can watch their films back and discuss in their pairs how they could improve.

V **Vocabulary practice: WB** p.66

Sts will find more practice of life events vocabulary here. Set these exercises for homework.

LS **Language summary: Unit 8 SB** p.134

My heart is in Havana

READING

I can answer multiple choice questions.

1 **Look at the picture. Who is the singer? What do you know about her?**

2 8.3 **Read and listen to the article. Match the headings with the paragraphs A–C. There is one extra heading.**

1 A new life in a new country
2 Early life in Cuba
3 The journey to Cuba
4 You can do it!

JOURNEY TO SUCCESS: Camila Cabello

A

Camila Cabello was born in Cuba and grew up in a small fishing village near the capital, Havana. Her mother, Sinuhe, dreamed of a better future for Camila, so when Camila was nearly seven, they left Cuba. They travelled to Mexico, and then by bus to the USA. Camila's Mexican dad, Alejandro, planned to join them later.

B

After a long journey, Camila and her mum arrived in Florida and started their new life. They only had a small backpack and $200. Sinuhe got a job in a shoe shop, and Camila went to school. Things were difficult at first. Camila didn't speak English, and she missed her dad.

C

Camila worked hard at school and learned English, and finally Alejandro joined the family. Camila loved singing, but she was shy and didn't like singing in front of other people. When she was fifteen, she decided to enter *The X Factor* on TV. When she saw the audience, she was really nervous, but it didn't stop her. She learned from her family that if you really want something and you work hard, you can do the impossible. Camila didn't win the competition, but it was the start of her next journey … in music.

3 8.3 **Read the article again. Choose the correct answers. Listen and check.**

1 Sinuhe travelled to the USA because …
  a she grew up there.
  b she wanted a better life for her daughter.
  c her husband, Alejandro, was there.
2 Life in America was difficult for Camila because …
  a she worked in a shoe shop.
  b they didn't speak English at her school.
  c she was sad that her dad wasn't there.
3 Camila liked singing …
  a with her family.
  b to a lot of people.
  c alone.
4 On *The X Factor*, Camila …
  a was a little frightened.
  b was the winner.
  c sang with her mother.

4 Word Power **Look at the words in the box. Which word is not connected with music? Write sentences with the other words.**

My favourite group is … Their best album is …

album	audience	competition	concert
group	singer	song	village

5 THINK CRITICALLY **Imagine your family goes to live in another country. What things do you miss about home and why?**

6 FIND OUT **Find the flags for Cuba, Mexico and the USA. What colour(s) do the flags have in common?**

 EXTRA PRACTICE Workbook page 67

My heart is in Havana

READING

Sts read an article about the singer Camila Cabello, and practise answering multiple choice questions. They learn affirmative and negative forms of regular and irregular past simple verbs. They then read about the Egyptian footballer Mo Salah, and practise using the past simple by talking about things they did and didn't do in the recent past.

Reading text

An article about Camila Cabello

Reading skill

Answering multiple choice questions

WARMER

Ask: *Who is your favourite singer?* Elicit a few answers, then put sts into pairs to try to agree on three singers they both like and say why they like them. Elicit some ideas from the class.

1 Ask sts to look at the picture. Elicit that it shows Camila Caballo, and elicit what sts know about her. Some sts may know quite a lot about the singer and her songs, so encourage them to share what they know with the class.

2 8.3 Use the map to elicit or show sts where Cuba is. Ask sts to read the four headings, then play the audio for sts to read and listen to the article and match the headings with the paragraphs. Check the answers with the class.

Answers

A 2 B 1 C 4

3 8.3 **Answering multiple choice questions**
Read out the task and point out the multiple choice questions. Explain to sts that when they answer multiple choice questions they need to read the relevant parts of the text very carefully. Point out that ideas from all the options may be mentioned in the text, but only one answer matches the meaning in the text exactly. Play the audio. Ask sts to read the article again and choose the correct answers. Check answers with the class, eliciting the part of the text which confirms each answer.

Answers

1 b 2 c 3 c 4 a

EXTRA PRACTICE

Ask sts to close their books. Write these gapped sentences on the board:

1 Camila was born in … .
2 She grew up in a … .
3 Camila and her … travelled from Mexico to … by bus.
4 They only had $… .
5 Camila's mum worked in a … .
6 Camila entered a singing … when she was … .

Put sts in pairs to complete the information about Camila Cabello, without looking at the text. Go through the answers to find out who remembers the most about her story.

Answers

1 Cuba
2 small fishing village
3 mum, the USA
4 200
5 shoe shop
6 competition, 15

4 **Word Power** Sts could work in pairs to look at the words and decide which one is not connected with music. Elicit the answer (*village*), then read through the other words in the box with the class and elicit or explain the meanings. Sts then work individually or in pairs to write a sentence with each of the words. Ask some sts to read their sentences to the class.

Answer

village

21st Century skills

5 **THINK CRITICALLY**

Read out the task and elicit a few examples of things that sts might miss about home. Ask sts to think about their ideas individually. Point out they should think of reasons for each thing they choose. Put sts into groups to compare their ideas, then ask some sts to tell the class what things they all miss about home.

21st Century skills

6 **FIND OUT**

Set this exercise for homework if you prefer. Sts can find this information out by looking online or in other media, or by asking other people. When you check the answers, see if sts can describe each of the flags.

Answer

blue, white, red

R **Reading practice:** **WB** p.67

You will find more practice for reading here. Set these exercises for homework.

GRAMMAR
Past simple: affirmative and negative

I can talk about the past.

Now watch the grammar animation.

1 Read the grammar box and answer the questions.

1 Which of the verbs in the table are regular? How do you know?
2 Which of the verbs are irregular?
3 How do we form the past simple negative? Is it different for regular and irregular verbs?

Affirmative	Negative
Camila **worked** hard at school.	It **didn't stop** her.
They only **had** a small backpack and $200.	Camila **didn't win** the competition.
Alejandro **joined** the family.	
She **saw** the audience.	

2 Match these irregular verbs with their past simple forms.

verbs	past simple
give know meet see sing speak win write	sang won gave spoke knew wrote met saw

3 Complete the text about the next part of Camila Cabello's life. Use the past simple affirmative.

During *The X Factor*, Camila *joined* (join) a girl group, *Fifth Harmony*. They [1] … (make) two albums, and they [2] … (give) concerts in a lot of different countries.

Then Camila [3] … (meet) the singer, Shawn Mendes, and they [4] … (sing) a song together. A year later, Camila [5] … (leave) *Fifth Harmony*. She [6] … (want) to be a solo singer. Camila [7] … (write) some new songs. One of them was about her home city in Cuba. *Havana* was Number 1 all over the world!

4 Write true negative and affirmative sentences.

Camila / grow up in Costa Rica / Cuba
Camila didn't grow up in Costa Rica. She grew up in Cuba.

1 Camila / speak English in Cuba / Spanish
2 Camila and her mum / go to Canada / the USA
3 Sinuhe / get a job in a bookshop / shoe shop
4 Camila / sing with Ed Sheeran / Shawn Mendes
5 Camila / write a song about Barcelona / Havana

5 Complete the text. Use the correct form of the verbs in the box.

THE MO SALAH STORY

~~be born~~ join love not like

Mo Salah *was born* in a small village in Egypt. As a child, he [1] … school, but he [2] … football. When he was fourteen, he [3] … a club in Cairo, the Egyptian capital.

leave make not get

The club was four hours from his village by bus. Every day, Mo [4] … school early to go to training. After training, he [5] … the same four-hour journey back to his village. He [6] … home until very late.

get have not stay

Mo [7] … with the club. In 2012, he moved to Europe. He played for some big clubs there, and he also played for the Egypt national team. He joined Liverpool's team in 2017. In 2013, Mo [8] … married to Magi. They [9] … their first child in 2014.

6 Write true affirmative or negative sentences about you.

I (grow up) in another country.
I didn't grow up in another country.

1 I (have) toast for breakfast this morning.
2 I (go) to the beach last month.
3 I (make) a drink for my parents last night.
4 I (meet) my friends last weekend.
5 I (win) a competition last year.

7 Work in pairs. How many things from Exercise 6 do you have in common?

A: I had toast for breakfast this morning.
B: Me, too! / Really? I didn't. I had cereal.

FUN FACT

When Mo Salah got married, he invited his whole village to the wedding!

FAST FINISHER

Write sentences about your life. Use the verbs from Exercise 2 and from page 79.

I grew up in Granada. I spoke my first words when I was one.

LS Language summary: Unit 8 SB p.134

 EXTRA PRACTICE Workbook page 68

GRAMMAR Past simple: affirmative and negative

Grammar animation

This lesson features an optional animated presentation of the grammar in context called *He became famous!* including the form and use of past simple affirmative and negative verbs. You can watch this in class if you have time and access to a computer or tablet, or you can ask sts to download it from the Richmond Learning Platform to watch at home. See TG page 310–311 for animation script.

1 Read the grammar box. Put sts into pairs to answer the questions. Check answers with the class. Point out that irregular verbs do not follow any patterns, so sts need to learn them all individually.

Answers
1 work, join, stop – we add *-ed* if it is regular
2 have, see, win
3 *didn't* + infinitive; no, it isn't different for irregular verbs.

Ask questions to check concept.

Concept check questions: *How do we form the past simple with regular verbs?* (we add *-ed*). *Do we add -ed for irregular verbs?* (no). *Are there rules for irregular verbs?* (no – they are all different). *How do we form the negative of regular past simple verbs?* (*didn't* + base form). *Is it the same for irregular verbs?* (yes).

2 Students match the irregular verbs with their past simple forms. Check answers, and model pronunciation.

Answers
give/gave, know/knew, meet/met, see/saw, sing/sang, speak/spoke, win/won, write/wrote

3 Ask sts to read the text about Camila Cabello's life and write the correct past simple forms to complete it. Check answers.

Answers

1 made	4 sang	7 wrote
2 gave	5 left	
3 met	6 wanted	

4 Read out the example answer and point out that the information is true, based on the article on page 80. Sts then write the sentences in their notebooks. Allow sts to compare their answers in pairs, then check with the class.

Answers
1 Camila didn't speak English in Cuba. She spoke Spanish.
2 Camila and her mum didn't go to Canada. They went to the USA.
3 Sinuhe didn't get a job in a bookshop. She got a job in a shoe shop.
4 Camila didn't sing with Ed Sheeran. She sang with Shawn Mendes.
5 Camila didn't write a song about Barcelona. She a song wrote about Havana.

5 Focus on the picture of Mo Salah and ask: *Who is this? What do you know about him?* Ask sts to read the text and write the correct verb forms in their notebooks. Allow sts to compare their answers in pairs, then check answers with the class.

Answers

1 didn't like	4 left	7 didn't stay
2 loved	5 made	8 got
3 joined	6 didn't get	9 had

6 Read out the example, then ask sts to write true affirmative and negative sentences about themselves. Ask some sts to read their sentences to the class.

7 Read out the example conversation. Point out that we use *Me too!* to agree with an affirmative sentence. Write on the board: *I didn't, either* and explain that we use this to agree with a negative sentence, e.g. *I didn't have toast this morning – I didn't, either*. Put sts into pairs to compare their sentences from Exercise 6 and see how many things they have in common. Ask some pairs to tell the class which things they have in common.

FUN FACT Encourage sts to read this fun fact for pleasure. They might be interested to know that, according to the Guinness World Records, the biggest ever wedding took place in India in 1995. There was a meal for over 150,000 people, who watched the wedding on big screens in the grounds of the bride's family home.

FAST FINISHER
Sts who finish early can write sentences about their life, using verbs from the page. Weaker sts can work in pairs. They cover the past simple forms in Exercise 2, then take turns to say one of the verbs and try to remember the past simple form.

G **Grammar practice: WB** p.68
Sts will find more practice of the affirmative and negative forms of the past simple here. Set these exercises for homework.

LS **Language summary: Unit 8 SB** p.134

How did they do that?

VOCABULARY and LISTENING Physical appearance

I can listen for key words in a podcast.

1 **Look at the photos. What films are these characters from?**

In *The Lord of the Rings*, he played Gollum, a short, thin, bald creature with big ears. But in real life, the actor Andy Serkis has got curly, grey hair and blue eyes. He's often got a beard and a moustache.

The actor Zoe Saldana has got dark brown, wavy hair and brown eyes. In *Avatar*, she played Neytiri, an alien with blue skin, yellow eyes and long, straight hair. As Gamora in *Guardians of the Galaxy*, she had green skin and red hair!

Dave Bautista is tall and well-built, and he sometimes wears glasses. He played the character Drax in *Guardians of the Galaxy*. Drax is also tall and well-built, but he's got grey skin and red tattoos!

2 8.4 **Copy and complete the table with the blue words from the text. Listen, check and repeat.**

Height and build	Hair colour	Hair type	Eyes	Other
short	*grey*	*curly*	*blue*	*beard*

3 **Add these words to the table. Can you add any more words?**

blond light brown slim green

4 **Work in pairs. Think of a famous person and describe him/her. Can your partner guess the person?**

He's a footballer. He's quite short.
He's got dark brown hair and a beard.

5 8.5 **Listen to a podcast, *Film Magic*, about make-up and special effects in films. Which of these words do you hear?**

camera cinema computer digital make-up skin special effects

6 8.5 **Listen again and answer the questions. Use the words in Exercise 5 to help you.**

1 How did they create Neytiri's appearance?
2 How did they create Gamora's appearance?
3 How long did the make-up take?

LS **Language summary: Unit 8** **SB** p.134

How did they do that?

VOCABULARY and LISTENING
Physical appearance

Sts read about some actors who changed their appearance with make-up and special effects to play well-known film characters. They learn vocabulary for describing physical appearance, then listen to a podcast about make-up and special effects in films and focus on listening for key words. They study questions in the past simple and practise intonation in questions. They end by asking and answering questions using the past simple.

Vocabulary

Physical appearance (*bald, beard, blue, brown, curly, dark brown, glasses, grey, long, moustache, red, short, straight, tall, thin, wavy, well-built*)

Listening text

A podcast about make-up and special effects in films

Listening skill

Listening for key words in a podcast

Pronunciation

Intonation in questions

WARMER

With books closed, ask: *What are your favourite films? Why?* Elicit a few answers, encouraging sts to say why they like them. Teach the word *character*, then ask: *Who are the actors in your favourite film? What characters do they play?* Teach the meaning of *special effects*, then ask: *Do you know any films that used good special effects?* Elicit a few ideas.

1 Sts look at the photos and try to identify the films. They could work in pairs for this. Check answers and ask: *Do you know these films? Do you like them?*

Answers
1 Gollum – *The Lord of the Rings*
2 Neytiri – *Avatar*
3 Gamora – *Guardians of the Galaxy*
4 Drax – *Guardians of the Galaxy*

2 8.4 Read through the table with the class and check that sts understand all the headings. Put sts into pairs to copy the table into their notebooks and complete it with the correct words. Play the audio for them to listen and check their answers. Check answers with the class and check that sts understand all the words. Then play the audio again for sts to repeat.

Answers
Height and build: short, thin, tall, well-built
Hair colour: grey, dark brown, red
Hair type: curly, bald, wavy, long, straight
Eyes: blue, brown
Other: beard, moustache, glasses

3 Sts work in their pairs and add the words to the table then they try to think of more words they could add. Check answers and check that sts understand all the words. Elicit other words that sts have added and write them on the board. Explain the meanings to the class if necessary.

Answers
Hair colour: blond, light brown
Height and build: slim
Eyes: green

4 Read out the example description and elicit who the person is (Mo Salah). Point out that we use *be* to describe someone's height and build, e.g. *He's tall / short*. We use *has got* to describe someone's hair, eyes, and other features, e.g. *She's got brown hair / blue eyes / glasses*. Allow sts time to prepare their descriptions individually, then put them into pairs to read out their descriptions and guess the people. Ask which famous people were easy to guess, and which were difficult to guess.

5 8.5 **Listening for key words in a podcast**
Read out the task and allow sts time to read through the words in the box. Model pronunciation of the words. Ask: *How carefully do you think you need to listen if you want to hear these words?* Elicit that you need to listen very carefully, to every word. Play the audio for sts to listen and make a note of the words they hear. See TG page 281 for audio script. Check answers with the class.

Answers
make-up, special effects, skin, camera, computer, digital

6 8.5 Allow sts time to read through the questions. Check they understand *create*. Play the audio again for sts to listen and answer the questions. Remind them to use words from Exercise 5 in their answers. Allow sts to compare their answers in pairs, then check answers.

Answers
1 They used a special camera to film Zoe's face and they used a computer to change the colour of her skin and make her eyes bigger, etc.
2 They used lots of make-up.
3 It took five hours in the first film and four hours in the later films.

V L **Vocabulary and Listening practice: WB** p.69
Sts will find more practice for listening, and practice of vocabulary for physical appearance here. Set these exercises for homework.

LS **Language summary: Unit 8 SB** p.134

GRAMMAR Past simple: questions

I can ask questions about events in the past.

Now watch the grammar animation.

1 **Read the grammar box. Put the words in the correct order to show how we make questions. What type of words can go before *did*?**

main verb | did | ? | subject

Questions	Short answers
Did you **watch** ***Avatar***?	Yes, I **did**. / No, I **didn't**.
Did Zoe **wear** make-up?	Yes, she **did**. / No, she **didn't**.
Did they **use** computers?	Yes, they **did**. / No, they **didn't**.
***Wh-* questions**	
What did they **do**?	
How long did the make-up **take**?	

2 **Put the words in 1–5 in the correct order to make questions. Match the questions with answers a–f.**

you / did / in Barcelona / grow up / ?
Did you grow up in Barcelona? c

1 English / Eva / at university / study / did / ?
2 go / the same school / they / did / to / ?
3 George / a job / last summer / did / get / ?
4 enjoy / you / did / the film / ?
5 last night / TV / did / watch / Lucy / ?

a No, she didn't. She went to bed early.
b Yes, I did. The actors were really good.
c ~~No, I didn't. I grew up in Madrid.~~
d Yes, he did. He got a job in a café.
e No, she didn't. She studied law.
f No, they didn't. They went to different schools.

3 **PRONUNCIATION Intonation in questions**
8.6 **Listen and repeat.**

1 Did you watch a film? ↗
2 What film did you watch? →

4 8.7 **Practise saying these sentences. Listen, check and repeat.**

1 What did you wear yesterday?
2 Did you wear a jacket?
3 How much homework did you have?
4 Did you have a lot of homework?

5 **Read the answers. Complete the questions about Dave Bautista.**

Questions and Answers: DAVE BAUTISTA

Q Where [1]…?
A He grew up in Washington DC.
Q Did [2]…?
A No, he didn't act at school.
Q When [3]…?
A He became an actor in 2010 when he was 41 years old.
Q Wow, that's old! What did [4]… before that?
A Before that he was a wrestler. He was a world champion!
Q When [5]… for the first time?
A He played Drax for the first time in 2014.
Q [6]… *Guardians of the Galaxy* … any awards?
A Yes, it did. It won a lot of awards.

6 **GET CREATIVE In pairs, choose a famous person and write six questions for an interview. Invent the answers. Practise the interview and act it out.**

Interview with …
Where did you go to school?
Did you work hard at school?
When did you become a …?

7 **Work in pairs. Ask and answer questions.**
A: What did you do after school yesterday?
B: I went swimming.

1 What / do after school yesterday?
2 What time / go to bed last night?
3 How / get to school this morning?
4 When / last go to the cinema?
5 Who / go with?
6 What film / see?

FAST FINISHER
Write your partner's answers to Exercise 7.
Enrique went shopping after school yesterday.

LS Language summary: Unit 8 SB p.134

EXTRA PRACTICE Workbook page 70

GRAMMAR Past simple: questions

Grammar animation

This lesson features an optional animated presentation of the grammar in context called *Did they like your photo?* including the form and use of past simple questions. You can watch this in class if you have time and access to a computer or tablet, or you can ask sts to download it from the Richmond Learning Platform to watch at home. See TG page 311 for animation script.

1 Read through the examples in the grammar box with the class. Ask sts to use the examples to help them put the words in the correct order to show how we make questions. Check answers. Point out that we use the base form of the verb, not the past simple form of the verb, in questions: *Did you wear make-up?* NOT ~~*Did you wore make-up?*~~. In short answers, we just use *did* or *didn't*, but not the main verb: *Yes, I did*. NOT ~~*Yes, I did wear*~~.

Answers
did – subject – main verb – ?
question words

Ask questions to check concept.

Concept check questions: *Do you like this film? – present or past?* (present) *Did you like this film? – present or past?* (past) *What are the short answers?* (Yes, I did. / No, I didn't.).

2 Ask sts to write the questions in their notebooks, and match them with the answers. Allow sts to compare their answers in pairs, then check answers.

Answers
1 Did Eva study English at university? – e
2 Did they go to the same school? – f
3 Did George get a job last summer? – d
4 Did you enjoy the film? – b
5 Did Lucy watch TV last night? – a

3 **PRONUNCIATION** 8.6
Play the audio and ask sts to listen and notice the intonation in the two different kinds of questions. Play the audio again for sts to repeat the questions. Encourage them to copy the intonation on the audio.

4 8.7
Put sts into pairs to practise saying the sentences. Play the audio. Ask individual sts to repeat, or get the whole class to repeat together. Sts can then practise saying the questions again in pairs. This time, they could give true answers about themselves.

5 Read out the first answer and elicit the correct question. Sts then read the remaining answers and write the questions in their notebooks. Allow sts to compare their answers in pairs, then check with the class.

Answers
1 Where did he grow up?
2 Did he act at school?
3 When did he become an actor?
4 What did he do before that?
5 When did he play Drax for the first time?
6 Did *Guardians of the Galaxy* win any awards?

21st Century skills

6 **GET CREATIVE**
Read out the task, then put sts into pairs to choose a famous person and write six questions to interview them. Monitor and help while they are working, then ask some sts to read their questions to the class. Correct any mistakes. Sts then work in their pairs to prepare answers and practise their interview. Ask some pairs to act out their interview for the class, without saying the name of the famous person. See if other sts can guess who the interview is with.

7 Weaker sts will probably need to prepare the questions first. Check these, then put them into pairs to ask and answer them. Stronger sts should be able to go straight into the pairwork. Ask some sts to tell the class something they learned about their partner.

Answers
2 What time did you go to bed last night?
3 How did you get to school this morning?
4 When did you last go to the cinema?
5 Who did you go with?
6 What film did you see?

FAST FINISHER
Sts who finish early can practise the grammar further. They write their partner's answers to the questions in Exercise 7. Weaker sts could choose two of the questions in Exercise 7 and write their own answers to them.

G **Grammar reference: WB** p.70
Sts will find more practice of past simple questions here. Set these exercises for homework.

LS **Language summary: Unit 8 SB** p.134

KEEP TALKING!

Did you have a good weekend?

READING and LISTENING

I can find out information about events.

1 **Work in pairs. Look at these words. Which is your favourite type of event?**

barbecue   basketball match   birthday party   concert   dance show

2 **Match the events in Exercise 1 with a–e below.**

3 **Find the answers to these questions.**

1 Where is the birthday party?
2 What time is the concert?
3 How many nights is the dance show on for?
4 How much was the ticket to the basketball match?
5 Who is having a barbecue?
6 What is there to eat at the barbecue?

4 8.8 **Three people are talking about last weekend. Listen. Which event did each person go to? Did he/she have a good time?**

5 8.8 **Listen again and answer the questions for each speaker.**

1 Who did he/she go to the event with?
2 What did he/she do before or after the event?

KEEP TALKING!

Did you have a good weekend?

READING and LISTENING

Sts study some notices about events and invitations to events and practise finding out information from them. They then listen to three people talking about what they did last weekend. They read and hear a model dialogue and personalise the useful language by following the steps in the Speaking plan.

WARMER

Play a game to revise the irregular past simple forms that students learned on pages 79 and 81. Put students into pairs, then write a selection of base forms on the board, e.g. *get, buy, make, leave, have, go, give, know, meet, see, sing, speak, win, write*. Teams take turns to choose a verb and say a correct sentence using the verb in the past simple. If their sentence is correct, award a point and cross the verb off the board. If their sentence is not correct, don't correct it but move to the next team. Continue the game until all the verbs are crossed off. See which team has the most points.

1 Put sts into pairs to discuss the events. Ask some sts to tell the class which events they like and why.

2 Sts match the events with the notices and invitations. Check answers, and elicit which are notices and which are invitations.

Answers
a birthday party
b concert
c barbecue
d basketball match
e dance show

3 Sts read the notices and invitations again and answer the questions. You could do this as a race to motivate sts to find out the information quickly. Check answers with the class.

Answers
1 Josie's house
2 18.00
3 3 nights
4 £15
5 Mark
6 burgers, chicken, vegetarian sausages

4 8.8 Read out the questions, then play the audio. See TB pages 281–282 for audio script. Pause after each speaker to give sts time to write the answers. Allow sts to compare their answers in pairs, then check answers with the class, playing the audio again and pausing if necessary to confirm the answers.

Answers
1 concert, one of the best evenings ever
2 basketball match, yes and no: great day and exciting game, but the team didn't win
3 performed in a dance show, great fun, audience loved it

5 8.8 Allow sts time to read through the questions, then play the audio again for sts to listen and answer the questions. Check answers, playing the audio again and pausing if necessary to confirm the answers.

Answers
1 1 his family
  2 her dad
  3 his dance club
2 1 bought a T-shirt at the stadium shop
  2 had lunch next to the arena
  3 went to a party after

EXTRA PRACTICE

Write these gapped sentences on the board:

1 It was one of the ... evenings ever!
2 The band was ... !
3 It was ... good fun.

Put sts into pairs to try to remember the missing words. Play the audio again for them to check, and check that sts understand all the sentences. Elicit that the sentences are all used for talking about fun things you did last weekend.

Answers
1 best 2 fantastic 3 really

EXTRA PRACTICE

Focus on the events in Exercise 1. Ask sts to think of a similar event that they went to recently and enjoyed. Ask them to make notes about when / where it was, who they were with, how much it cost, what they did.

Arrange sts in pairs. They take turns to use their phones to film their classmates describing their weekend. Allow sts time to watch their films to see if they could improve – for example, by speaking more fluently or including more details. Sts could film themselves again to see if they can improve their descriptions.

SPEAKING Talking about your weekend

I can talk about past events.

1 8.9 **Listen and read. Which events did Oli and Mia go to?**

Mia: Hi Oli. Did you have a good weekend?
Oli: Yes, it was great, thanks. I went to Josie's party.
Mia: Cool. How was it?
Oli: It was really good fun. There was music and dancing, and everyone dressed as a film character.
Mia: Really? Who were you?
Oli: Well, I wore a long white beard, long white hair and glasses.
Mia: Don't tell me – Professor Dumbledore, right?
Oli: That's right! How about you? What did you do?
Mia: I went to a barbecue at Mark's house.
Oli: That sounds like fun! What was the food like?
Mia: It was delicious. We had burgers, chicken and salad.
Oli: Mmm, that sounds good!

2 8.10 **Listen and repeat the Useful language.**

Useful language

Asking about the weekend

Did you have a good weekend?
What did you do?
How was it?
What was the food/music/weather like?
How about you?

Responding

It was great / amazing / really good / OK.
I went to ...
That sounds like fun! / That sounds good!

3 8.11 **Put the words of the dialogue in order. Listen and check.**

Boy: weekend? / you / Did / a nice / have
Girl: thanks. / was / it / really / Yes, / good,
Boy: do? / What / you / did
Girl: the cinema / I / to / went / with Harry. We saw the new *Star Wars* film.
Boy: it / was / like? / What
Girl: It / fantastic. / was The special effects were amazing!
Boy: good! / sounds / That

4 **Work in pairs. Ask and answer about your weekends. Follow the steps in the Speaking plan.**

Speaking plan

Prepare

› Make notes about your weekend. Choose one of the events from page 84, or use your own ideas.
 • Where did you go?
 • What did you do?
 • Did you have a good time?

Speak

› Practise your dialogue.
› Use phrases from the Useful language box.
› Act out your dialogue without notes.

Reflect

› How can you improve next time?
› Swap roles and choose new events to talk about.

Now play *Keep moving!*

FAST FINISHER

Imagine that you had the best weekend ever! Write about what you did.

LS Language summary: Unit 8 SB p.134

SPEAKING Talking about your weekend

1 8.9 Focus on the picture and elicit that it shows two friends chatting. Explain that they are chatting about their weekend. Read out the question, then play the audio of the dialogue. With stronger classes, you could play the dialogue with books closed and ask: *Which events did Oli and Mia go to?* With weaker classes, you could play the dialogue for sts to listen and read. See SB page 85 for audio script.

Answers
Oli went to Josie's party. Mia went to a barbecue at Mark's house.

2 8.10 Ask sts if they can remember some of the phrases Oli and Mia used. Read through the Useful language box with the class and check sts understand all the phrases. Play the audio once for sts to listen to the phrases, then play it again for them to repeat.

3 8.11 Ask sts to put the words in the correct order and write the dialogue in their notebooks. Allow sts to compare their answers in pairs, then play the audio for them to listen and check. If your sts would benefit from some controlled practice before the personalised practice, they could practise this dialogue in pairs, or they could change some of the details and practise.

Answers
Boy: Did you have a nice weekend?
Girl: Yes, it was really good, thanks.
Boy: What did you do?
Girl: I went to the cinema with Harry. We saw the new *Star Wars* film.
Boy: What was it like?
Girl: It was fantastic. The special effects were amazing!
Boy: That sounds good!

4 Sts follow the steps in the Speaking plan to practise talking about their weekend.

Speaking plan

Prepare
Sts work individually to make notes about their weekend. Tell them they don't need to talk about what they really did, but can invent something, using one of the ideas from page 84 or their own ideas.

Speak
Sts practise their dialogue in their pairs. Remind them to use the Useful language in Exercise 2. They can practise with and then without notes. If your sts use smartphones in class, they could record their conversations.

Reflect
Discuss as a class how sts could improve next time. If you noticed any typical errors, correct them with the class. Sts swap roles and choose a new event, then follow the steps again. If they record their conversations, ask them to use this to help them think of how they could improve next time. Ask some sts to perform their dialogues for the class if they feel confident.

Keep moving!

This lesson features an optional language revision and consolidation game for use in digital classrooms. Players control different characters, each with their own personalities and special abilities.

FAST FINISHER
Sts imagine their best weekend ever and write about what they did. Weaker sts could work in pairs. They look at the model dialogue again and write some sentences about what Mia or Oli did at the weekend.

S **Speaking reference: WB** p 81
Sts will find more practice for talking about your weekend here. Set these exercises for homework.

LS **Language summary: Unit 8 SB** p.134

REAL CULTURE!

Great lives

I can compare a historical figure from another country with someone from my country.

NELSON MANDELA 1918–2013

1 When Nelson Mandela was young, white people and black people in South Africa lived very different lives. White people had better jobs and nicer homes. Most black people were poor. They didn't go to the same schools or hospitals as white people, and they couldn't vote in elections. Nelson helped to change that …

2 Nelson Mandela was born on 18 July 1918, and grew up in a small village.

3 He was the first person in his family to go to school. He worked hard, and he went to university to study law.

4 At university, Nelson was the only black person in his class. He couldn't use the swimming pool, gym or restaurant. They were for white students only.

5 Nelson got a job in a lawyer's office. He often met his friends to talk about politics.

6 Nelson started to organize protests. He was unpopular with the white government. In 1962, the police arrested him, and he went to prison.

7 All around the world, people protested against the South African government.

8 In 1989, South Africa had a new president. He wanted to change things. After 27 years in prison, Nelson was finally free!

9 In 1994, there were new elections. Millions of black South Africans voted for the first time. Nelson became South Africa's first black president.

10 Nelson Mandela died in 2013. There are still a lot of problems in South Africa, but Nelson helped to make it a fairer country for everyone.

REAL CULTURE! Great lives

Sts learn about the life and achievements of Nelson Mandela in helping to bring about democratic reform in South Africa. They then talk about a famous person from their own country that they admire.

This lesson also features an optional culture video about popular British actor, Danny Dyer and his family history: see SB page 87.

WARMER

Ask: *Do you know about any famous people from the past?* What did they achieve? Elicit a few ideas, e.g. Albert Einstein, Martin Luther King. Put sts into pairs to think of two famous people from the past that they know about and note down everything they know about them. Ask pairs in turn to tell the class their ideas. Teach the word *biography* and tell sts they are going to read the biography of a famous person.

1 Put sts into pairs to discuss what they know about Nelson Mandela. Discuss as a class what sts know. Encourage sts who know more to share their knowledge with the class.

Answers

South Africa; he was South Africa's first black head of state; he was an anti-apartheid revolutionary; he was a political leader and philanthropist

2 **Word Power** Read through the words in the box with the class and elicit or explain the meanings. Sts then match the words with the pictures. Check answers with the class.

Answers

lawyer: 4,5; protest: 7; arrest: 6; prison: 6; free: 8; election: 9; vote: 9

3 8.12 Read through the events with the class and check that sts understand everything. Play the audio. Sts read and listen to the biography and order the events. Check answers.

Answers

1	d	6	g
2	c	7	j
3	f	8	a
4	b	9	h
5	e	10	i

4 Ask sts to read the biography again and answer the questions. Allow sts to compare their answers in pairs, then check answers with the class, eliciting the part of the biography which confirms each answer.

Answers

1 18 July 1918
2 No, they didn't.
3 He studied law.
4 He got a job in a lawyer's office.
5 He was protesting and was unpopular with the white government.
7 27 years
8 He became president in 1994.

EXTRA PRACTICE

Arrange sts in pairs. Read out true and false statements about Nelson Mandela, e.g. *Nelson Mandela grew up in a city*. (FALSE) *He was the first person in his family to go to university*. (TRUE) *All the students at Nelson's university were black*. (FALSE) *Nelson went to prison in 1962*. (TRUE) *He was in prison for 30 years*. (FALSE) *He won the Nobel Peace Prize*. (TRUE). Sts work in pairs and decide if the sentences are true or false. Go through the answers at the end.

1 What do you know about Nelson Mandela? Where was he from? Why is he famous?

2 **Word Power** Before you read the biography, match these words with the pictures.

lawyer *(n)*	protest *(v)*	arrest *(v)*	prison *(n)*
free *(adj)*	election *(n)*	vote *(v)*	

3 8.12 **Read and listen to the biography. In your notebook, put the events in order.**

1 d

a Nelson left prison.
b He got a job.
c He went to school.
d Nelson was born in South Africa.
e He protested against the government.
f He studied at university.
g He went to prison.
h He became president of South Africa.
i Nelson Mandela died.
j People organized protests in other countries.

4 **Read the biography again and answer the questions.**

1 When was Nelson born?
2 Did his parents go to school?
3 What did Nelson study at university?
4 What did he do after university?
5 Why did the police arrest him?
6 How long did he spend in prison?
7 When did he become president?

5 8.13 **Work in pairs. Do the quiz. Listen and check.**

NELSON MANDELA:

Did you know?

1 Nelson's real name was Rolihlahla. He started using the name Nelson on his first day at …!

a school b university c work

2 For eighteen years, Nelson was in prison on an island. His room was … metres. There was no bed – Nelson slept on the floor.

a 4 x 4 b 3 x 3 c 2 x 2

3 As a young man, Nelson loved sport, especially … . He exercised regularly in his room in prison.

a boxing b table tennis c swimming

4 In 1993, he won … .

a an Olympic gold medal b an Oscar c the Nobel Peace Prize

5 Nelson always made his own …, even when he was president.

a food b bed c clothes

6 **COMPARE CULTURES** **Work in pairs or small groups. Choose a famous person from your country that you admire. Research information about their life and prepare a presentation. Use the ideas below. Find photos to illustrate your presentation.**

- Why is he/she famous?
- When and where was he/she born?
- Where did he/she go to school?
- Did he/she go to university?
- What is/was his/her job?
- What are some interesting facts about him/her?
- Why do you admire him/her?

Now watch the culture video.

REAL CULTURE!

5 8.13 Puts sts into pairs to do the quiz. Play the audio for them to check their answers, and find out who got all the answers right. Ask: *Which fact about Nelson Mandela do you find the most surprising? Why?*

Answers

1 school	4 the Nobel Peace Prize
2 2 x 2	5 bed
3 boxing	

EXTRA PRACTICE

Put sts into pairs. Give them two minutes to find as many irregular past simple verbs in the biography as they can, and write the base forms. Elicit answers.

Answers

was – be	grew up – grow up
had – have	got – get
were – be	met – meet
went – go	became – become

EXTRA PRACTICE

Ask sts to close their books. Put them in groups and make a list of important events in Nelson Mandela's life – without looking at the text. Sts use their list of events to retell Mandela's biography. Give them time to practise and to add details that they remember. Then ask sts to open their books and look at the text on page 86 again to see what they included / left out.

21st Century skills

6 **COMPARE CULTURES**

Put sts into pairs or small groups to think of a famous person from their own country, research information about them and answer the questions. You could brainstorm a few names with the class first, to give sts ideas. Ask pairs or groups to report back to the class when they have finished the research, or in the next lesson. Discuss as a class which person sts admire the most and why.

Culture video

This lesson features an optional culture video about popular British actor, Danny Dyer. You can watch this in class if you have time and access to video, or you can ask sts to download it from the Richmond Learning Platform to watch at home. See *A family history* on TG pages 302 and 307.

EXTRA PRACTICE

Arrange sts in small teams. Say two interesting facts about your life, one true and one false. For example, *I won a singing competition*. *I was in a film last year*. Explain that sts have two minutes to ask as many questions as possible, then teams have to decide which is the true sentence and which is the false, e.g. *Where was the competition? What was the film? How old were you? What did you sing?* Teams that get the answer correct score a point.

My favourite uncle

WRITING A description of a person

I can write about a family member or friend.

1 Work in pairs. Have you got a favourite relative or person? What makes them special?

2 Read Lottie's description of her uncle. Which tenses does she use in each paragraph: present simple, past simple or both?

My Uncle Chris

by Lottie

1 My uncle Chris is tall and quite slim. He's got dark brown hair, a beard and a moustache, and he wears glasses. He's got a friendly face, and he's really funny.

2 Chris is my mum's brother. He was born in Manchester, but my grandparents moved to London when he was a baby, so he grew up there. After he finished school, he got a job in a restaurant and learned to be a chef. He got married to Laura when he was 29. They've got two children, my cousins, Susie and Ted.

3 Uncle Chris' hobbies are music – and cooking, of course! He plays the guitar in a band and sings. For his birthday last year, he had a big party in his garden. It was a sunny day, and Chris cooked an amazing lunch. After that, he and his band played some songs. It was really good fun!

3 Look at the **Useful language.** How do you say these expressions in your language?

Useful language

Describing someone

He's/She's tall/slim/well-built.
He's/She's got blond/dark hair and blue/brown eyes.
He's/She's got a kind/friendly/serious face.
He/She was born in ... / He grew up in ...
After he/she (finished school), he/she ...
After that, ...
His/Her hobbies are ...

4 Read the **Look!** box. Match paragraphs 1–3 of Lottie's description with these topics.

His life story | His hobbies | His appearance

Look! Using paragraphs

When you write an essay, organize your ideas into paragraphs.
Each paragraph contains a sentence about one topic.
When you change topic, start a new paragraph.

5 Put the sentences about Lottie's grandmother in order. In your notebook, copy the sentences into three paragraphs.

a After she finished her studies, she got a job in a hospital and met another doctor.
b Grandma grew up in Scotland and she studied Medicine at university.
c Grandma's hobbies are reading and playing card games.
d My grandmother has got short, wavy hair and blue eyes. *1*
e When we play together, she always wins!
f She's got a kind face and a nice smile.
g Two years later, they got married!

6 Write a description of a special person you know. Follow the steps in the **Writing plan.**

Writing plan

Prepare

› Choose an adult member of your family.
Ask questions about their life, for example:
- When and where were they born?
- Where did they grow up?
- What was their first job?
- What do they do now?
- Are they married?
- How did they meet their husband/wife?
- What are their hobbies?

Write

› Organize your ideas into paragraphs.
› Use the expressions from the Useful language box.

Reflect

› Check your grammar: present tense for description; past simple for events in the past.
› Check your use of paragraphs and spelling.

W Writing summary: WB p.91 E Exams: Unit 8 SB p.125 LS Language summary: Unit 8 SB p.134

 EXTRA PRACTICE Workbook page 72; photocopiable activities for Unit 8: vocabulary, grammar and skills

My favourite uncle

WRITING A description of a person

Sts read a description of a favourite relative. They learn about using paragraphs and learn useful language for describing someone. They then follow the steps in the Writing plan to write a description of a member of their own family, organizing their ideas into paragraphs.

Writing

A description of a person

Useful language

Describing someone (*He's/She's tall/slim/well-built, He's/She's got blond/dark hair and blue/brown eyes, He's/She's got a kind/friendly/serious face, He/She was born in …, He/She grew up in …, After he/she (finished school), he/she …, After that …, His/Her hobbies are …*)

Look!

Using paragraphs

WARMER

Ask: *What do you know about your parents and grandparents? What about uncles and aunts? Where were they born?* Put sts into pairs to talk about members of their family and what they know about them. Ask: *Do your family members enjoy talking about their lives?*

1 Read out the question and point out to sts that they can talk about a family member or another person that they know. Ask some sts to tell the class what makes the person they talked about special.

2 Ask sts to read the description and answer the questions. They could work in pairs for this. Check answers.

Answers
1 present simple
2 both
3 both

3 Read the Useful language box with sts. Check they understand all the expressions and ask them how they say these expressions in their first language. Point out that we say someone *was born*, NOT ~~*is born*~~.

4 Read the Look! box with sts about paragraphs. Explain that we organize a text into paragraphs to give it a logical structure, so each paragraph is about a different topic. Ask sts to match the paragraphs in the description with the topics. Check answers.

Answers
1 His appearance
2 His life story
3 His hobbies

5 Ask sts to read the sentences and put them in order first. Check these answers, then ask sts to copy the sentences into their notebooks, putting them into 3 paragraphs. Check answers.

Answers
1 d
2 f
3 b
4 a
5 g
6 c
7 e

My grandmother has got short, wavy hair and blue eyes. She's got a kind face and a nice smile.

Grandma grew up in Scotland and she studied Medicine at university. After she finished her studies, she got a job in a hospital and met another doctor. Two years later, they got married!

Grandma's hobbies are reading and playing card games. When we play together, she always wins!

6 Explain to sts that they will now write a description of a special person, following the steps in the Writing plan.

Writing plan

Prepare

Read through the questions with the class and check that sts understand them all. For homework, ask them to interview the family member they have chosen and note down their answers.

Write

Sts then organize the information they have into paragraphs, using the description in Exercise 2 as a model. Refer them back to the Useful language box for expressions to use in their descriptions.

Reflect

Ask sts to check their grammar, spelling and punctuation and make any necessary changes. Sts could then swap their descriptions with each other in pairs and give feedback on the use of the Useful language, and the present and past simple. Alternatively, they could share their descriptions with each other in small groups and discuss which people they enjoyed learning about and why.

W **Writing practice: WB** p.72
Sts will find more practice of writing here. Set these exercises for homework.

W **Writing summary: WB** p.84

E **Exams: Unit 8 SB** p.125

LS **Language summary: Unit 8 SB** p.134

Getting around 9

Vocabulary: Transport; Holiday activities | **Grammar:** *will* and *won't*; *be going to* | **Speaking:** Making arrangements | **Writing:** An email about holiday plans

VOCABULARY Transport

I can talk about different types of transport.

WHERE IN THE WORLD?

Can you name the type of transport and the country?

1 9.1 **Do the quiz. Match the transport and the countries in the boxes with the pictures. Listen and check.**

1 a ship in Australia

bike boat coach helicopter on foot lorry motorbike plane scooter ~~ship~~ tram underground

~~Australia~~ Eygpt Canada France India Italy Japan Portugal Switzerland the Netherlands the UK the USA

2 Copy and complete the table with the types of transport from Exercise 1.

air	sea	land
plane	*boat*	*bike*

3 Work in pairs. Ask and answer the questions.

1 How do you usually get to school?
2 What's your favourite way to travel on holiday?
3 When did you learn to ride a bike?
4 In your opinion, what is the best way to travel long distances in your country?
5 What are the advantages and disadvantages of the different types of transport?

Now watch the vlog.

FAST FINISHER

Describe three amazing journeys you'd like to take.

I'd like to fly in a helicopter over the Great Wall of China ...

LS Language summary: Unit 9 SB p.135

 EXTRA PRACTICE Workbook page 74

Getting around

9

UNIT 9 OVERVIEW: The topic for this unit is travel and holidays. Sts read about the future of transport, and listen to a radio show about holiday plans. They read an online chat forum and learn how to make arrangements. They read about some cool tours in London and finally, they read an email about holiday plans and write an email to a friend about their own holiday plans. They also watch a vlog about a someone using different types of transport in Europe and a culture video about a celebrity chef travelling around Bangladesh.

Vocabulary	Grammar	Pronunciation	Reading	Listening	Speaking	Writing
Transport; Holiday activities	*will* and *won't*; *be going to*	Sentence stress	Understanding the main topic of paragraphs	Identifying the type of information to listen for	Making arrangements	An email about holiday plans

VOCABULARY Life events

Sts learn vocabulary for different types of transport. They do a quiz about transport around the world, then personalise the vocabulary by talking about the ways they travel and like to travel.

Vocabulary

Transport (*bike, boat, coach, helicopter, on foot, lorry, motorbike, plane, scooter, ship, tram, underground*)

Vlog

Natalie: *Transport in Europe*

WARMER

Ask: *How do people travel around your town or city?* Elicit a few answers, e.g. *by bus*, *by train*, etc. Ask: *Which are fast ways to travel? Which are slow?* Discuss the best way to travel around the sts' own town or city.

1 9.1 Read through the words in the box and elicit or teach the meanings. Sts then match the words to the pictures. Play the audio for sts to listen and check their answers. See TG page 282 for audio script.

Answers

1 a ship in Australia
2 a scooter in Italy
3 a lorry in India
4 a motorbike in the USA
5 a coach in Switzerland
6 a bike in the Netherlands
7 an underground train in Japan
8 a helicopter in Canada
9 a tram in Portugal
10 a boat in France
11 on foot in the UK
12 a plane in Egypt

2 Put sts into pairs to copy the table into their notebooks and complete it with the correct words. Check answers.

Answers

air: plane, helicopter
sea: boat, ship
land: bike, scooter, lorry, motorbike, coach, underground, tram, on foot

3 Allow sts time to prepare their answers individually, then put them into pairs to ask and answer the questions. Discuss the questions with the class.

Vlog

This lesson also features an optional vlog in which vlogger Natalie talks about visiting cities in Europe, using different types of transport. You can watch this in class if you have time and access to video, or you can ask sts to download it from the Richmond Learning Platform to watch at home. See TG pages 294 and 305.

FAST FINISHER

Sts who finish early can practise the vocabulary further. They write descriptions of three amazing journeys they would like to take. Weaker sts could work in pairs. They take turns to say a form of transport from the box in Exercise 1. Their partner points to the correct picture.

EXTRA PRACTICE

Put sts into new pairs. They choose two questions from Exercise 3 and ask and answer them again, while their partner films them using their phone. Tell them to focus on speaking fluently, without hesitating. They can watch their films back and discuss how fluently they spoke, and how they could improve.

V Vocabulary practice: WB p.74

Sts will find more practice of transport vocabulary here. Set these exercises for homework.

LS Language summary: Unit 9 SB p.135

Welcome to the future!

READING

I can understand the main topic of paragraphs.

1 9.2 **Read and listen to the article. Find five types of transport.**

THE FUTURE OF TRANSPORT

What will transport be like in the year 2050? How will we travel to school or work? How will we go on holiday? Here are our top predictions.

1 Late for class? Problems with traffic? Don't worry! With a flying car, your mum or dad will simply push a button and the car will take off. Science fiction? Not at all! Experts predict that in the future there will be a lot of flying cars on our roads and motorways.

2 Cycling is often the quickest and cleanest way to travel around a city. In the future, cities will build special cycle paths high above the streets. Bike journeys will be faster and safer. A roof over the cycle path will also keep cyclists warm and dry in winter.

3 Trains of the future probably won't have wheels. Instead, they will use new technology to travel through tunnels at 1,000 kph. There won't be any windows, but there will be "virtual windows" with videos of the view outside!

4 There are already some underground trains and cars without a driver. But planes without pilots? It sounds crazy, but experts predict that this will become reality. Flights will be cheaper, but will you want to fly in a plane with no pilot?

2 Read the article again. Choose the correct topic for each paragraph.

1 a Planes will use motorways.
  b Cars will fly.
2 a Bikes will be faster than cars.
  b Bikes will travel above cities.
3 a Trains will have bigger windows.
  b Trains will be faster.
4 a Planes won't have pilots.
  b Planes will be bigger.

3 Word Power Check the meaning of the blue words in the text. Use them to complete the sentences.

1 Our bus ... was really unfriendly.
2 There was a lot of ... on the roads this morning.
3 The train went into a ... through the mountains.
4 The ... from the helicopter was amazing.
5 We followed the ... through the forest.
6 It's much faster to drive on ... .

4 THINK CRITICALLY Which of the predictions in the reading text do you think will happen? Why/Why not?

5 FIND OUT What type of flying machine did Leonardo da Vinci predict?
He drew a design for it in 1493, more than 400 years before it was invented.

Welcome to the future!

READING

Sts read an article about the future of transport, and practise understanding the main topic of paragraphs. They learn *will* and *won't* for future predictions. They then read some predictions about holidays in space, and practise using *will* and *won't* to make their own predictions about the future.

Reading text
An article about the future of transport

Reading skill
Understanding the main topic of paragraphs

WARMER

Ask: *Where do you usually go on holiday? How do you usually travel there?* Elicit a few answers, then ask: *What about in the future? How do you think people will travel in the future?* Elicit a few ideas, and prompt sts with a few ideas if necessary, e.g. *What about cars that can drive themselves? What about small planes for everyone? What about holidays to the Moon?* Discuss a range of different possibilities with the class.

1 9.2 Ask sts to look at the picture. Elicit that it shows a city in the future, with a future form of transport. Read out the task, then play the audio for sts to read and listen to the article and find five types of transport. Check the answers with the class.

Answers
plane, car, bike, train, underground

2 Understanding the main topic of paragraphs
Point out the four paragraphs in the article. Explain that writers organize texts into different paragraphs, and each paragraph focuses on a different topic. Point out that when we read a text, we can use this structure to help us understand the text better. Ask sts to read the article again and choose the best topic for each paragraph. Check answers with the class.

Answers
1 b 2 b 3 b 4 a

3 Word Power Sts could work in pairs to look at the blue words in the text and check their meanings. Encourage them to use the context to guess the meanings, and then check in a dictionary. Sts then read the sentences and complete them with the blue words. Check answers with the class, and check that sts understand all the words.

Answers
1 driver
2 traffic
3 tunnel
4 view
5 paths
6 motorways

21st Century skills

4 THINK CRITICALLY
Read out the questions and point out that sts should think of reasons why they think the predictions in the text will or won't come true. Allow sts to think about their ideas individually, then put them into pairs or small groups to discuss the predictions. Discuss each of the predictions with the class, encouraging as many sts as possible to join in and express their opinions.

EXTRA PRACTICE

Put sts into new pairs. They talk about the predictions they think will/won't happen while their partner records them using their phone. Tell them to focus on speaking fluently and giving clear reasons for their opinions. They can watch or listen to their recordings and discuss how they could improve.

21st Century skills

5 FIND OUT
Set this exercise for homework if you prefer. Sts can find this information out by looking online or in other media, or by asking other people. Encourage them to find pictures of Leonardo da Vinci's designs if possible. When you check the answers, ask what else sts found out about the design, and what they find surprising about it.

Answers
Leonardo da Vinci predicted the invention of the helicopter.

EXTRA PRACTICE

Arrange sts into teams of two, then put two teams together to compete against each other in a game of 'word tennis'. Teams take turns to find and say a travel-related word from the text. If a team repeats a word, or they can't find a word, they lose the game and start again. At the end, elicit a list of travel-related words from the text.

Possible words
bike, car, cycle path, cycling, cyclist, driver, flight, flying, journey, motorway, pilot, plane, road, traffic, train, transport, travel, tunnel, underground train, wheel.

R Reading practice: WB p.75

You will find more practice for reading here. Set these exercises for homework.

GRAMMAR *will* and *won't*

I can make predictions about the future.

Now watch the grammar animation.

1 **Read the grammar box. Copy and complete the rules.**

Affirmative	Negative
The car **will take** off and fly. Bike journeys **will be** faster and safer.	Trains **won't have** wheels. There **won't be** any windows.
Questions	**Short answers**
Will you **want** to fly in a plane with no pilot?	Yes, we **will**. / No, we **won't**.

Rules

1 We use subject + [1] ... + verb in affirmative sentences.
2 We use subject + [2] ... + verb in negative sentences.
3 We use *will* + subject + verb in [3] ... .

2 9.3 **Complete the predictions about space tourism with *will* or *won't*. Listen and check.**

Holidays in space

For very rich people, a trip into space is already possible. But in the future, more people *will* travel into space. There [1] ... be space hotels, but they [2] ... be very big, so there [3] ... only be about eight beds. It [4] ... be a different type of holiday. People [5] ... have amazing views of the Earth, but they [6] ... leave the hotel at all. And without gravity, it [7] ... be easy to have a shower, so people probably [8] ... want to spend a long time in space!

3 **Work in pairs. What do you imagine a holiday in space will be like?**

A: I think it will be fun.

B: I don't agree. The food won't be very interesting.

4 **Write questions with *will* about your future.**

you / pass all your exams next year?
Will you pass all your exams next year?

1 your parents / move to a different city in the future?
2 you / go to university?
3 you / leave home at eighteen?
4 you / get married before you're 30?
5 you / have a lot of children?
6 you or your friends / become famous?

5 **Work in pairs. Ask and answer the questions in Exercise 4. Say what you think will happen.**

A: Will you pass all your exams next year?

B: No, I don't think so. I think I'll pass English and Science, but I won't pass History or Maths.

6 **GET CREATIVE** **Work in pairs or small groups. Choose one or two topics from the list and write your predictions about the future. Use *will* or *won't*. Present your ideas to the class. Do others agree?**

Homes: People won't live on land – they'll live under the sea. Robots will do all the housework.

clothes entertainment food holidays
homes school transport

FAST FINISHER

What do you think your friends or family will do in the future? Make predictions.

I think my friend Eva will write a book. I think my dad will change his job soon.

FUN FACT

Scientists predict that in the future there will be an elevator from Earth into space. The elevator will be 100,000 kilometres high and will carry satellites, spaceships and people into space. It will be easier and cheaper than a rocket.

LS Language summary: Unit 9 SB p.135

EXTRA PRACTICE Workbook page 76

GRAMMAR *will* and *won't*

Grammar animation

This lesson features an optional animated presentation of the grammar in context called *When will it be ready?* including the form and use of *will* and *won't*. You can watch this in class if you have time and access to a computer or tablet, or you can ask sts to download it from the Richmond Learning Platform to watch at home. See TG page 311 for animation script.

1 Read the grammar box about *will* and *won't*. Put sts into pairs to copy the rules into their notebooks and complete them with the correct words. Check answers. Point out that the form of *will* and *won't* is the same for all persons, and they are followed by the base form of the verb, NOT the infinitive with *to*: *We will have flying cars.* NOT ~~*We will to have flying cars*~~.

Answers
1 will 2 won't 3 questions

Ask questions to check concept.

Concept check questions: *People drive to work – past, present or future?* (present). *Cars will fly above cities – past, present or future?* (future). *How do we make the prediction negative?* (Cars *won't fly* above cities). *I will to travel to the Moon one day – correct?* (no – I *will travel* to the Moon). *Will fly cars one day? – correct?* (no – *Will cars fly* one day?).

2 9.3 Sts read the predictions about space tourism and complete them with *will* or *won't*. Allow sts to compare their answers in pairs, then play the audio for them to listen and check. Ask: *Do you agree that people will take trips into space in the future? Why/Why not?* Discuss the question as a class.

Answers

1 will	5 will
2 won't	6 won't
3 will	7 won't
4 will	8 won't

3 Read out the task and the example answers. You could brainstorm a few more ideas for describing holidays in space, e.g. *boring, scary, exciting, amazing*. Put sts into pairs to discuss what they think a holiday in space will be like and why. Ask some pairs to tell the class their ideas. Ask other sts if they agree or disagree, and why.

4 Read out the example question and point out the word order. Ask sts to write the questions. Allow sts to compare their answers in pairs, then check with the class. Make sure sts understand all the questions.

Answers
1 Will your parents move to a different city in the future?
2 Will you go to university?
3 Will you leave home at 18?
4 Will you get married before you're 30?
5 Will you have a lot of children?
6 Will you or your friends become famous?

5 Read out the example question and answer. Point out that we often use *I (don't) think* when talking about the future, because we don't know for certain what will happen. Allow sts time to prepare their answers individually, then put them into pairs to ask and answer the questions. Ask some sts to tell the class something they learned about their partner.

21st Century skills

6 **GET CREATIVE**

Read out the task and the example answer. Put sts into pairs or small groups to discuss the topics and write their predictions. With weaker classes, you could work as a class and brainstorm a few ideas for each topic first, to help sts with ideas. Encourage sts to use their imagination and think about all the things that might be possible in the future. Monitor and help while sts are working. Ask pairs or groups in turn to tell the class their ideas. Discuss as a class which ideas are the most likely, and which are the most exciting.

FUN FACT Encourage sts to read this fun fact for pleasure. Ask if they know any similar fun facts about space travel. They might be interested to know that the idea of an elevator going up into space was first proposed in 1895 by Konstantin Tsiolkovsky, a Russian scientist.

FAST FINISHER

Sts who finish early can practise the grammar further. They write sentences with predictions about what their family or friends will do in the future. Weaker sts can work in pairs. They try to remember some of the predictions from the texts on pages 90 and 91 and write sentences. They can check their ideas in the texts.

G Grammar practice: WB p.76
Sts will find more practice of *will* and *won't*. Set these exercises for homework.

LS Language summary: Unit 9 p.135

What are you going to do?

VOCABULARY and LISTENING Holiday activities

I can identify the type of information I need to listen for.

1 9.4 **Check the meaning of the blue phrases in the questionnaire. Listen and repeat. Do the questionnaire.**

What's your ideal holiday?

1 Where do you like to stay on holiday?
- **a** I like to stay in an apartment next to the beach
- **b** I prefer to stay in a hotel in a city.
- **c** I prefer to stay in a campsite.

2 It's time to pack your bag. What do you take?
- **a** My swimming things and some sun cream.
- **b** My phone (to take pictures) and a guide book.
- **c** A tennis racket and a surfboard.

3 What's your favourite thing to do on holiday?
- **a** relax on a beach or by a pool.
- **b** go sightseeing, for example visit a castle or museum.
- **c** go hiking in the mountains or surfing in the sea.

4 You're visiting a city. Which option sounds best to you?
- **a** I relax in a café and share photos from my phone.
- **b** I take a bus tour and explore the city.
- **c** I rent a bike and ride around the city's parks.

5 What's the first thing you do when you arrive on holiday?
- **a** I unpack my bag and jump in the pool!
- **b** I put on my trainers and explore the area.
- **c** I get on my mountain bike. Time for an adventure!

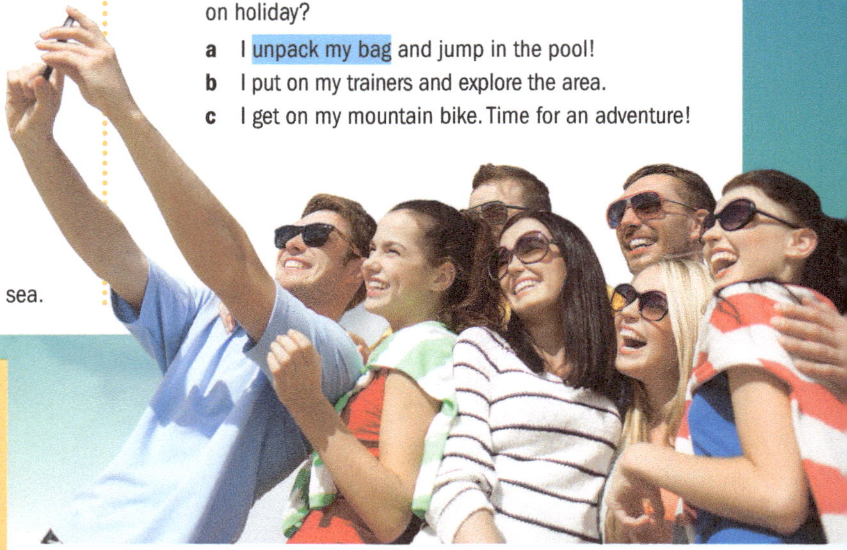

RESULTS

Mostly a: You're a **Beach Boy/Girl**! You just want to lie in the sun and relax!

Mostly b: You're a **City Boy/Girl**! You love visiting cities and learning about new places!

Mostly c: You're an **Action Boy/Girl**! You prefer activity holidays and being busy!

2 Complete the phrases with the words in the box. Use the questionnaire to help you.

a bus tour	a city	a guide book	a museum
hiking	in a hotel	~~in a campsite~~	surfing

1 stay: in an apartment, *in a campsite*, ...
2 go: sightseeing, ..., ...
3 take: pictures, ..., ...
4 visit: a castle, ..., ...

3 Work in pairs. Talk about your last holiday. Where did you go? What did you do?

We went to ...
We stayed in a ...
We went ... -ing

4 You're going to hear three callers to a radio show. Before you listen, read the interviewer's questions and think of possible answers.

SUMMER HOLIDAYS!

1 Where are you going to go in the summer?
2 How are you going to travel?
3 Where are you going to stay?
4 What are you going to do there?

5 9.5 **Now listen to the radio show. Answer Questions 1–4 for the three callers, Conor, Jaz and Luke. Listen again and check.**

LS Language summary: Unit 9 SB p.135

What are you going to do?

VOCABULARY and LISTENING
Holiday activities

Sts do a quiz about their ideal holiday. They learn vocabulary for holiday activities, then listen to a radio show and practise identifying the type of information they need to listen for. They study *be going to* for future plans and practise pronunciation of sentence stress. They end by planning their ideal holiday.

Vocabulary

Holiday activities (*explore the city, go hiking, go sightseeing, pack your bag, relax on a beach, rent a bike, stay in an apartment, take a bus tour, take pictures, unpack your bag, visit a castle*)

Listening text

A radio show about holiday plans

Listening skill

Identifying the type of information you need to listen for

Pronunciation

Sentence stress

WARMER
Write on the board: *I love holidays because ….* . Ask sts to complete the sentence with their own ideas. Tell them not to think too much about it, but just put down the first idea that comes into their mind. Put sts into groups to compare their ideas and make a list of reasons why they love holidays. Ask groups in turn to tell the class their ideas.

1 9.4 Puts sts into pairs to look at the blue phrases and check the meanings. Encourage them to read the phrases in context first and try to work out the meanings, then check in a dictionary. Check the answers, and make sure sts understand all the phrases. Then play the audio for them to listen and repeat. Finally, ask sts to do the questionnaire.

2 Read out the example, then ask sts to complete the phrases with the words in the box. Check answers.

Answers
1 stay: in a hotel
2 go: hiking, surfing
3 take: a bus tour, a guide book
4 visit: a city, a museum

3 Demonstrate the task by talking about a holiday that you had recently, e.g. *We went to Paris. We stayed in a hotel. We went sightseeing and I took lots of pictures.* Allow sts time to prepare their ideas individually, then put them into pairs to talk about their last holiday. Encourage them to ask each other questions, to find out more information. Ask some sts to tell the class what they learned from their partner.

4 **Identifying the type of information you need to listen for** Explain to sts that they are going to hear a radio show in which people call the show to talk about their holiday plans. Ask: *Do you find listening tasks difficult? Why?* Elicit that sometimes it is difficult to hear the correct answer. Point out to sts that it is easier to hear the correct answers if you can identify the type of information you need to listen for before you listen. Ask sts to read the interviewer's questions and think of some possible answers. They could work in pairs for this. Discuss the answers as a class, and discuss what type of information sts must listen for to answer each question.

Answers
1 a place, e.g. a city name
2 a form of transport, e.g. train, plane, car
3 a place to stay, e.g. a hotel, an apartment
4 holiday activities, e.g. go sightseeing, relax on a beach

5 9.5 Write the names of the three callers on the board for sts to refer to (Conor, Jaz, Luke). Play the audio once for sts to listen and note down the answers to the four questions for each speaker. See TG page 282 for audio script. Allow sts to compare their answers in pairs, then play the audio again for sts to listen and check their answers. Check answers with the class.

Answers

1
Conor: I'm going to go to Wales with my family.
Jaz: I'm going to France with my sister and my mum and dad.
Luke: We're going to stay at home in London.

2
Conor: We're going to travel by train.
Jaz: We're going to go by coach and by boat.
Luke: [no answer]

3
Conor: We're going to stay with my cousins, near the beach.
Jaz: We're going to stay in a campsite.
Luke: A Spanish friend is going to stay with us.

4
Conor: I'm going to go surfing.
Jaz: We're going to rent bikes and visit some castles.
Luke: We're going to go sightseeing in London.

V L **Vocabulary and Listening practice: WB** p.77
Sts will find more practice for listening, and practice of vocabulary for holiday activities here. Set these exercises for homework.

LS **Language summary: Unit 9 SB** p.135

GRAMMAR *be going to*: future plans

I can talk about future plans.

Now watch the grammar animation.

1 Copy and complete the grammar box.

Affirmative	
I'm going to stay with my cousins.	
He/She/It**'s going to travel** by train.	
We/You/They [1] ... **going to go** sightseeing.	
Negative	
I'm not going to have a holiday.	
He/She/It [2] ... **going to stay** at home.	
We/You/They **aren't going to go** surfing.	
Questions	**Short answers**
Are you **going to stay** at home?	Yes, I **am**. / No, I [3] ... .
[4] ... she **going to visit** friends?	Yes, she **is**. / No, she **isn't**.
Are they **going to rent** bikes?	Yes, they **are**. / No, they [5] ... .

2 Write sentences with the correct form of *be going to*.

We (stay) in our aunt's apartment.

We're going to stay in our aunt's apartment.

1 I (pack) my bag tomorrow.
2 James (not go) on holiday this year.
3 My sister and I (rent) mountain bikes.
4 I (not take) my phone to the beach.
5 Elena (fly) to Istanbul.

3 Write questions and answers about Jamal, Laura and Henry's holiday plans.

	Jamal	Laura and Henry
Go ...	to Liverpool	to Ireland
Travel ...	by train	by boat
Stay ...	with uncle	in a campsite
Do ...	see a football match	go hiking
Pack ...	scarf, hat	walking boots, raincoats

Is Jamal going to go to London?

No, he isn't. He's going to go to Liverpool.

1 Jamal / stay with his uncle?
2 Laura and Henry / go surfing?
3 Jamal / pack his raincoat?
4 How / Laura and Henry / travel?
5 What / Jamal / do there?
6 Where / Laura and Henry / stay?

4 Complete the interview with *be going to* and the verbs in the box.

go (x3) | not miss | relax | see | take (x2)

Young Photographer of the year

Winner

Thirteen-year-old Ben won a photography competition with this photo of a zebra at his local zoo. His prize is a free family holiday! Our reporter, Tanya, asked him about his plans.

Tanya: Congratulations, Ben! So where [1] ... you ... on holiday?
Ben: We [2] ... to Kenya.
Tanya: Wow! [3] ... you ... on a beach?
Ben: No, we're [4] ... on safari! We [5] ... elephants and lions, and zebras, of course!
Tanya: [6] ... you ... your camera?
Ben: Yes, of course. I [7] ... lots of pictures! I [8] ... an opportunity like this!
Tanya: Thanks, Ben. Have a great time.

5 PRONUNCIATION Sentence stress

9.6 Listen and repeat.

1 **A:** Where are you going to go?
B: I'm going to go to France.
2 **A:** How are you going to travel?
B: We're going to travel by car.

6 9.7 Practise these sentences. Listen, check and repeat.

1 **A:** Where are you going to stay?
B: I'm going to stay in a hotel.
2 **A:** What are you going to do?
B: I'm going to relax by the pool.

7 Plan your ideal holiday. Copy the table from Exercise 3 and make notes. Ask and answer.

A: Where are you going to go?

B: I'm going to go to Croatia.

FAST FINISHER

Imagine you're planning a party for a friend or relative. Write about your plans.

We're going to have a barbecue. I'm going to make a cake. I'm going to buy ...

LS Language summary: Unit 9 SB p.135

GRAMMAR *be going to*: future plans

Grammar animation

This lesson features an optional animated presentation of the grammar in context called *We're going to go on holiday!* including the form and use of *be going to*. You can watch this in class if you have time and access to a computer and tablet, or you can ask sts to download it from the Richmond Learning Platform to watch at home. See TG page 311 for animation script.

1 Read through the examples in the grammar box with the class, then ask sts to copy the grammar box into their notebooks and complete it with the correct words. Check answers. Point out that *going to* remains the same for all persons, and only the form of *be* changes: *I'm going to, she's going to, we're going to*. Point out the word order in questions: *Are you going to go surfing?* NOT ~~*You are going to go surfing?*~~

Answers
1 are 2 isn't 3 'm not 4 Is 5 aren't

Ask questions to check concept.

Concept check questions: *I'm going to travel by train – past, present or future?* (future). *Is it a prediction or a plan?* (a plan). *We don't going to stay in a hotel – correct?* (no – *We aren't going to stay* in a hotel). *You going to go sightseeing? – correct?* (no – *Are you going to go* sightseeing?).

2 Sts write the sentences in their notebooks. Allow sts to compare their answers in pairs, then check answers.

Answers
1 I'm going to pack my bag tomorrow.
2 James isn't going to go on holiday this year.
3 My sister and I are going to rent mountain bikes.
4 I'm not going to take my phone to the beach.
5 Elena is going to fly to Istanbul.

3 Focus on the table and ask sts to read through the people's holiday plans. Read out the example question and answer. Allow sts time to write their questions. Check the questions, but not the answers, with the class. Then put sts into pairs to ask and answer the questions. To make the activity into a game, ask sts to close their books before they ask and answer, and tell them they should answer the questions from memory.

Answers
1 Is Jamal going to stay with his uncle? Yes, he is.
2 Are Laura and Henry going to go surfing? No, they aren't. They are going to go hiking.
3 Is Jamal going to pack his raincoat? No, he isn't. He is going to pack his scarf and hat.
4 How are Laura and Henry going to travel? They are going to travel by boat.
5 What is Jamal going to do there? He is going to see a football match.
6 Where are Laura and Henry going to stay? They are going to stay in a campsite.

4 Ask sts to read the interview and complete it with the correct forms of *be going to* and the verbs. To check answers, invite two sts to read out the interview.

Answers
1 are, going to go
2 are going to go
3 are, going to relax
4 going to go
5 are going to see
6 Are, going to take
7 'm going to take
8 'm not going to miss

5 PRONUNCIATION 9.6
Play the audio and ask sts to listen and notice how the highlighted words are stressed. Play the audio again for sts to repeat the sentences. Encourage them to copy the intonation on the audio.

6 9.7
Put sts into pairs to practise saying the sentences, focusing on using the correct sentence stress. Play the audio once for sts to listen and check their answers. Play the audio again. Ask individual sts to repeat, or get the whole class to repeat together.

7 Ask sts to copy the table from Exercise 3 and complete it with their own ideal holiday plans. Explain to sts that they are now going to ask each other questions about their ideal holiday. Weaker sts will probably need to prepare some questions first. Stronger sts should be able to go straight into the pairwork. Ask some sts to tell the class something about their partner's ideal holiday.

FAST FINISHER
Sts who finish early can practise the grammar further. They imagine they are planning a party for a friend and write about their plans. Weaker sts could write some sentences about their ideal holiday, using their ideas from Exercise 7.

G Grammar practice: WB p.77
Sts will find more practice of *be going to* for future plans here. Set these exercises for homework.

LS Language summary: Unit 9 SB p.135

KEEP TALKING!

What are you doing at the weekend?

READING and LISTENING

I can understand a group chat.

1 **Read the group chat between a group of friends. What is happening on Sunday?**

George *12:15*
Who's going to the Festival in the Park on Sunday? I'm playing some songs with my band. Come and watch us!

Daisy *12:16*
Adam and I are going! We can't wait!

Lola *12:16*
I can't make it, I'm afraid. We're going to Edinburgh on Saturday. 😭😭😭😭😭

George *12:18*
That's a shame. Have a great time!

Jordan *12:19*
What time are you playing? I'm seeing my cousins in the morning, but I'm free later.

George *12:20*
No problem – we aren't playing until 4.00, so come along in the afternoon!

Daisy *12:20*
Adam and I are meeting at the park at 2.00. We're taking a picnic. Why don't you join us, Jordan?

Jordan *12:21*
Thanks, Daisy. I'd love to. See you then.

George *12:22*
See you all on Sunday! 🙂🎵

2 **Read the dialogue again and answer the questions.**

1 Who is going to the festival? Write the names.
2 Who can't go? Why not?
3 What time is George's band playing?
4 What is Jordan doing before the concert?
5 What time does Daisy arrange to meet Jordan?

3 **Read the Look! box. Read the dialogue again and find more examples of the present continuous for future arrangements.**

Look! **Present continuous for future arrangements**

We use the present continuous to talk about arrangements in the near future. We often use time expressions: *tonight, tomorrow, on Saturday, at the weekend.*
Who's going to the Festival in the Park on Sunday?
I'm playing some songs with my band.

4 **Look at George's diary for the weekend. Write sentences about his arrangements. Use the present continuous.**

1 *He's having a haircut at 10.00 on Saturday.*

Saturday

10.00 a.m.	Have a haircut
11.30 a.m.	Practise with the band at Joe's house
3.00 p.m.	Buy some new T-shirts for the band

Sunday

10.30 a.m.	Meet the band at the bus station
10.45 a.m.	Take the bus to Preston Park
4.00 p.m.	Play with the band at the festival!

5 🔊 9.8 **Daisy is phoning Jordan. Listen. Why is she phoning him?**

6 🔊 9.8 **Listen again and answer the questions.**

1 When is George's band playing?
2 Why is Jordan late?
3 Where is he now?
4 What are Daisy and Adam doing later?
5 Who is meeting them at 8.00?
6 What does Daisy suggest?

KEEP TALKING!

What are you doing at the weekend?

READING and LISTENING

Sts read a group chat about an event that is happening at the weekend. They learn the present continuous for future arrangements, then listen to a conversation about arrangements for the weekend. They personalise the useful language by following the steps in the Speaking plan.

WARMER

Ask: *Do you have any plans for the weekend?* You could give an example of your plans, e.g. *I'm going shopping on Saturday, and I'm just relaxing at home on Sunday.* Put sts into pairs to talk about their plans for the weekend.

1 Focus on the group chat and ask: *Do you have group chats like this with your friends?* Ask sts to read the chat quickly and answer the question. Check the answer.

Answer
There is a festival in the park.

2 Sts read the group chat again and answer the questions. Check answers.

Answers
1 George, Adam, Daisy, Jordan
2 Lola. She's going to Edinburgh on that day.
3 at 4.00
4 He's seeing his cousins.
5 at 2.00

3 Read the Look! box with sts about the present continuous for future arrangements. Explain that we use *be going to* for plans, e.g. *I'm going to invite Sam to the festival*, and we use the present continuous for things that are already agreed and arranged, e.g. *We're meeting at 2 p.m.* Ask sts to read the group chat again and find more examples of the present continuous for future arrangements. Check answers.

Answers
Adam and I are going!; We're going to Edinburgh on Saturday; What time are you playing?; I'm seeing my cousins in the morning; we aren't playing until 4.00; Adam and I are meeting at the park at 2.00; We're taking a picnic.

Ask questions to check concept.

Concept check questions: *I'm reading my book at the moment – present or future?* (present). *I'm going to a festival on Saturday – present or future?* (future). *Do I know for certain that I'm going, or is it just a plan?* (I know for certain – it's an arrangement).

4 Focus on George's diary and point out that all the activities are arrangements, because George knows he is definitely doing all the things at the times in his diary. Sts write the sentences. Allow sts to compare their answers in pairs, then check with the class.

Answers
2 He's practising with the band at Joe's house at 11.30 on Saturday.
3 He's buying some new T-shirts for the band at 3.00 on Saturday.
4 He's meeting the band at the bus station at 10.30 on Sunday.
5 He's taking the bus to Preston Park at 10.45 on Sunday.
6 He's playing with the band at the festival at 4.00 on Sunday.

5 9.8 Read out the question, then play the audio. See TG page 282 for audio script. Elicit the answer to the question.

Answer
Jordan is late and he's going to miss George's band.

6 9.8 Play the audio again for sts to listen and answer the questions. Check answers.

Answers
1 George's band is playing in 10 minutes.
2 Jordan/He had some homework.
3 He is on the bus.
4 Daisy and Adam are staying to watch the fireworks.
5 Daisy's mum is meeting them at 8.00.
6 Daisy suggests that her mum take Jordan home, too.

EXTRA PRACTICE

Write these phrases on the board:

Don't worry.	*That sounds cool.*	*Brilliant, thanks.*
Just in time!	*See you!*	

Ask sts in pairs to try to remember who said each phrase and why. Discuss the answers as a class, playing the audio again and pausing for sts to hear the phrases.

Answers
1 Jordan: Don't worry = It isn't a problem.
2 Jordan: That sounds cool = That's a fun idea.
3 Jordan: Brilliant, thanks = that's great, thank you.
4 Daisy: Just in time = you are almost late, but not quite.
5 Daisy: See you = I will see you soon/later.

SPEAKING Making arrangements

I can arrange to meet a friend.

1 9.9 **Listen and read. Where and when do Ethan and Vicky arrange to meet?**

Ethan: What are you doing on Saturday, Vicky?
Vicky: I'm having lunch at my grandma's.
Ethan: Oh really? What about in the evening? Are you doing anything then?
Vicky: No, nothing special. Why's that?
Ethan: I'm going to the cinema with a few people. Would you like to come?
Vicky: That sounds great. Who are you going with?
Ethan: Oh, just some people from my class.
Vicky: Cool. What time are you meeting?
Ethan: We're meeting outside the cinema at half past seven.
Vicky: Great. I'll see you then.
Ethan: Yes, see you on Saturday.

2 9.10 **Listen and repeat the Useful language.**

Useful language

Making arrangements

What are you doing on Saturday / at the weekend?
Are you doing anything in the afternoon/evening?
Would you like to ...?
We're meeting at ... .

Responding

Nothing special.
Sorry, I'm busy.
That sounds great.
Where are you meeting?
I'll see you then.

3 9.11 **Copy and complete the dialogue. Use one or two words for each space. Listen and check.**

Jess: Hi Greg. Are you doing [1]... on Saturday afternoon?
Greg: [2]... special. Why's that?
Jess: I'm going to a football match. [3]... like to come?
Greg: Sure! That [4]... great. What time are you going?
Jess: We're leaving my house at 2.00.
Greg: OK, [5]... you then.

4 **Work in pairs. Arrange to meet a friend. Follow the steps in the Speaking plan.**

Speaking plan

Prepare

- Student A: Choose an activity to go to with Student B. Choose from the box or use your own ideas.

go to a festival	go swimming
go for a picnic	go to a football match

- Student B: Think of three plans for this weekend. Decide when you're doing them. Choose from the box or use your own ideas.

go to the doctor	visit (family)
play (a sport)	paint my bedroom

Speak

- Practise your dialogue.
- Use phrases from the Useful language box.
- Act out your dialogue without notes.

Reflect

- How can you improve next time?
- Swap roles and choose a new activity.

Now play *Keep moving!*

FAST FINISHER

Imagine it's your birthday next weekend. Write sentences to describe your plans.

On Saturday, I'm having lunch in a new restaurant with my family.

LS Language summary: Unit 9 SB p.135

 EXTRA PRACTICE Workbook page 79

SPEAKING Making arrangements

1 9.9 Focus on the picture and elicit that it shows two friends chatting. Explain that they are making arrangements for next weekend. Read out the question, then play the audio of the dialogue. With stronger classes, you could play the dialogue with books closed and ask: *When do Ethan and Vicky arrange to meet?* With weaker classes, you could play the dialogue for sts to listen and read. See SB page 95 for audio script.

Answer
On Saturday at half past seven.

2 9.10 Ask sts if they can remember some of the phrases Ethan and Vicky used. Read through the Useful language box with the class and check sts understand all the phrases. Play the audio once for sts to listen, then again for them to repeat.

EXTRA PRACTICE
Give sts time to read through the phrases in the Useful language box again, then ask them to close their books. Write the following phrases on the board and put sts in pairs to rewrite them correctly. Go through the answers at the end and elicit the correct phrases. (See Useful language box for the correct phrases).

1 *Are you doing nothing tomorrow?*
2 *Nothing especially.*
3 *You would like to go swimming?*
4 *That is sounding great.*
5 *What you do tomorrow?*
6 *Sorry, I busy.*

3 9.11 Ask sts to copy the dialogue into their notebooks and complete it with one or two words in each gap. Allow sts to compare their answers in pairs, then play the audio for them to listen and check. If your sts would benefit from some controlled practice before the personalised practice, they could practise this dialogue in pairs.

Answers
1 anything
2 Nothing
3 Would
4 sounds
5 see

4 Sts follow the steps in the Speaking plan to practise making arrangements.

Speaking plan

Prepare
Put sts into pairs and ask them to decide which of them is Student A and which is Student B. They then work individually and follow the instructions to prepare their ideas. Tell them they can use the ideas in the box or their own ideas.

Speak
Sts practise their dialogue in their pairs. Remind them to look at the Useful language box in Exercise 2 to help them. They can practise with and then without notes. If your sts use smartphones in class, they could record their conversations.

Reflect
Discuss as a class how sts could improve next time. If you noticed any typical errors, correct them with the class. Sts swap roles and choose a new activity, then follow the steps again. If they record their conversations, ask them to use this to help them think of how they could improve next time. Ask some sts to perform their dialogues for the class if they feel confident.

Keep moving!

This lesson features an optional language revision and consolidation game for use in digital classrooms. Players control different characters, each with their own personalities and special abilities.

FAST FINISHER
Sts imagine it is their birthday weekend and write sentences to describe their plans. Weaker sts could work in pairs. They look at the model dialogue again and write some sentences about what Ethan and Vicky are doing at the weekend.

S **Speaking practice: WB** p.79
Sts will find more practice for making arrangements here. Set these exercises for homework.

LS **Language summary: Unit 9 SB:** p.135

REAL CULTURE!

Cool tours in London

I can compare transport in London with transport in my city.

MUSIC **TRAVEL** VIDEOS BOOKS TECHNOLOGY CONTACT

TEEN EXPLORERS

Our two reporters, Hayley and Josh, try some unusual ways to explore London.

HAYLEY

JOSH

1 GHOST BUS TOUR

This is a bus tour with a difference: it's at night, and the bus isn't red – it's black! The bus drives past some of London's famous buildings, and actors tell you scary stories about things that happened there many years ago! The tour is 75 minutes long and costs £15 if you're fifteen or under.

Hayley ★★★
It was fun to go sightseeing in the dark, but the stories weren't very scary!

Josh ★★★★★
Our guide was called Mr Bones. His stories made us all laugh … and scream!

2 STREET ART TOUR BY BIKE

Are you interested in street art? Then you'll love this bike tour! You'll visit some of London's amazing street art, including paintings by the artist Banksy! The tour is two hours long and costs £16 (including bike and helmet). Don't forget your camera!

Hayley ★★★★★
My favourite artist was called ROA. His huge paintings of animals are amazing. I took some great pictures.

Josh ★★★
Most of the tour was on quiet streets, but there were some busy roads with lots of traffic.

3 SPEEDBOAT TOUR

Would you like to be a secret agent for the day? You can with this exciting tour! The speedboat travels along the River Thames and under Tower Bridge at 60 kph, and plays songs from James Bond movies! The price is £29.50 if you're under fifteen, and it lasts 50 minutes.

Hayley ★★★★★
It was a warm sunny day, and this tour was an amazing way to see London!

Josh ★★★★
The tickets were expensive, but it was great fun, especially when the boat went fast!

REAL CULTURE! Cool tours in London

Sts learn about three fun tours that you can do in London. They then think about unusual tours in their town or city, or invent one that they think would be fun.

This lesson also features an optional culture video about a celebrity chef travelling around Bangladesh: see SB page 97.

WARMER

Ask: *What cities have you visited? What did you do when you were there? What did you enjoy most?* Elicit a few ideas. Then ask: *What do you know about London?* If any sts have been to London, encourage them to tell the class about their visit, which parts of London they explored and what they did. If sts have not visited London, encourage them to talk about pictures or films they have seen, or things they have read about London.

1 Read out the question and elicit what sts know about transport in London. Prompt them with more questions if necessary, e.g. *What colour are the buses?* (red). *What is a double decker bus?* (a bus with two levels). *What are taxis like in London? Are they yellow?* (no, black). *Is there a river in London?* (yes). *Do you think you can travel by boat sometimes?*

BACKGROUND

London is known for its red double-decker buses and its iconic black taxi cabs. There is also an extensive network of underground trains, as well as overground trains which travel out to the parts of London further from the centre. Boats travel up and down the River Thames. There are bikes available for people to use, and also cars and vans, which people can use for a short time and pay for using their phone.

2 9.12 Focus on the pictures of the three tours. Check that sts understand the meaning of *ghost*. Use the pictures to teach *street art* and *speedboat*. Read out the task and the four facts sts must find. Play the audio. Sts read and listen to the blog and write the answers. Check answers, then ask: *Which tour would you like to go on? Why?* Elicit a range of answers.

Answers

1 the ghost bus tour
2 the speedboat tour
3 the street art tour
4 the speedboat tour

3 Ask sts to read the blog again and decide if the sentences are true or false, or doesn't say. Allow sts to compare their answers in pairs, then check answers with the class, eliciting the part of the blog which confirms each answer.

Answers

1 F
2 F
3 DS
4 F
5 T
6 F

4 **Word Power** Ask sts to read the blog again and find three of the prepositions in the box. Check answers, and elicit the meanings of all the prepositions. Sts then look at the pictures and complete the sentences with the correct prepositions. Check answers with the class.

Answers

In the blog: The bus drives **past** some of London's famous buildings. The speedboat travels **along** the River Thames and **under** Tower Bridge.

1 along
2 past
3 under
4 between
5 around

EXTRA PRACTICE

Write these numbers on the board: *2, 15, 16, 29.50, 50, 60, 75*. Put sts in pairs to read the text quickly and find out what the numbers refer to.

Answers

2 – the Street Art Tour lasts 2 hours.
15 – the Ghost Bus Tour costs £15 for people 15 or under.
16 – the Street Art Tour costs £16.
29.50 – the Speedboat Tour costs £29.50 if you're under 15.
50 – the Speedboat Tour lasts 50 minutes.
60 – the speedboat travels at 60 kph.
75 – the Ghost Bus Tour is 75 minutes long.

EXTRA PRACTICE

Write the following prepositions on the board: *along, past, under, between, around*. Arrange sts in pairs. They take turns to describe their journey to school today using as many of the prepositions as possible. Ask one or two sts to tell the rest of the class about their journey. Check they use the prepositions correctly.

1 **What do you know about transport in London? How can you travel around the city?**

2 **9.12 Read and listen to the blog about three unusual tours of London. Find:**

1 the cheapest tour
2 the most expensive tour
3 the longest tour
4 the shortest tour

3 **Read the blog again and write True (T), False (F) or Doesn't Say (DS).**

The bus tour visits Buckingham Palace. *DS*
1 Hayley thought the bus tour was frightening.
2 You mustn't take photos of the street art.
3 You can learn how to make your own street art.
4 The weather was bad when Josh and Hayley took the speedboat tour.
5 There was music on the speedboat tour.
6 Josh didn't like it when the boat went fast.

4 **Word Power** **Find three of the prepositions below in the blog. Look at the pictures. Complete the sentences with the correct preposition.**

~~along~~ around between past under

1 The speedboat went *along* the river.
2 It went ... Big Ben.
3 It went ... a bridge.
4 It went ... two other boats.
5 It went ... a police boat.

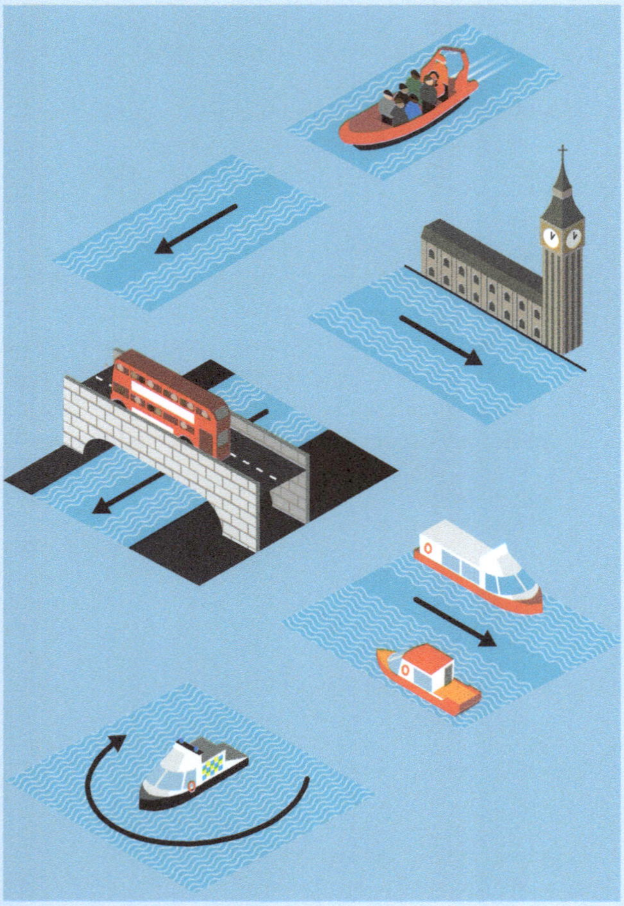

5 **Work in pairs. Discuss what you think the pictures and numbers in *5 Facts about the London Underground* mean.**

Maybe a baby was born on the Underground!

Or maybe babies travel free on the Underground?

6 **9.13 Listen and check. What do the pictures mean? Were you right?**

7 **9.13 Listen again and answer the questions.**

1 How many Underground stations are there today?
2 How many people use the London Underground every day?
3 What is the distance between Leicester Square station and Covent Garden?
4 What is the name of the station where a baby was born?
5 How many musicians play in the London Underground every day?

Now watch the culture video.

8 **COMPARE CULTURES** **Work in pairs or small groups. Think of an unusual tour for your town or city like on page 96, or invent one. Write a description of the tour.**

REAL CULTURE!

5 Put sts into pairs and ask them to look at the pictures. Point out that the pictures refer to five facts about the London Underground, numbered 1–5. Sts work in their pairs and try to guess what facts the pictures refer to. Elicit a few possible ideas for each picture, but don't confirm them at this stage.

6 9.13 Play the audio for sts to listen and check their answers. TG pages 282–283 for audio script. Elicit what each picture refers to, and elicit which ones sts guessed correctly.

Answers
1 1863 – the year the Underground first opened, with seven stations.
2 mice – there are half a million mice in the underground tunnels.
3 20 seconds – the shortest journey, between Leicester Square and Covent Garden.
4 a baby – a baby was born on the Underground.
5 musicians – Ed Sheeran often played in the Underground before he was famous.

7 9.13 Allow sts time to read the questions, then play the audio again for them to listen and answer the questions. Allow sts to compare their answers in pairs, then check with the class, playing the audio again and pausing if necessary for sts to hear the answers.

Answers
1 270
2 five million
3 260 metres
4 Elephant and Castle
5 hundreds of musicians

Culture video

This lesson features an optional culture video about Nadiya, a celebrity chef in the UK, travelling around Bangladesh. You can watch this in class if you have time and access to video, or you can ask sts to download it from the Richmond Learning Platform to watch at home. See *Tasty travels* on TG pages 303 and 307.

21st Century skills

8 **COMPARE CULTURES**

Put sts into pairs or small groups to think of an unusual tour for their town or city. You could brainstorm a few ideas with the class first, to give sts ideas. Ask pairs or groups to tell the class about their tour when they have finished. Discuss as a class which tour sounds the most interesting or fun and why.

EXTRA PRACTICE

When sts have completed Exercise 8, ask them to work in their pairs/groups and produce a blog for their tour. Explain that this is for a travel web page. The blog should include the following details: what you can see on the tour, the length of the tour, how much it costs. Ask each member of the group to imagine they have been on the tour and write a comment about it with a star rating. Refer sts to Hayley and Josh's blog for ideas.

If you have time and you have access to computers in your classroom, sts could add some pictures to their blog and make it into a digital presentation.

My holiday plans

WRITING An email

I can write an email about my holiday plans.

1 **Work in pairs. Ask and answer about your plans for the summer. Tell the class about your partner.**

Lucia is going to go to Mallorca with her family.

2 **Read the email. In your notebook, copy and complete two mind maps about Callum's holidays plans.**

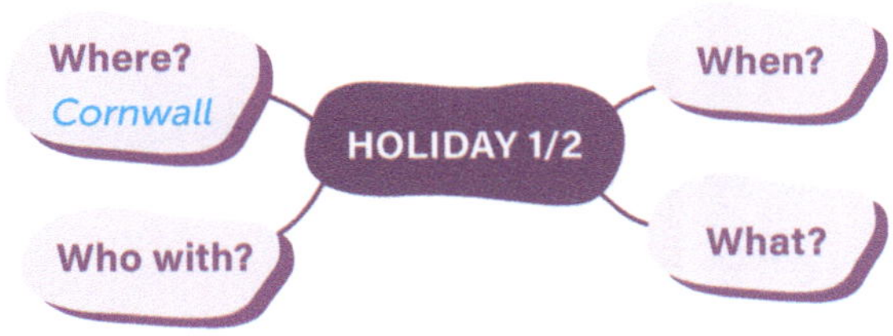

Hi Bruno,

How are you? I'm really excited because it's the last week of school! Just four more days and then it's the holidays. I can't wait!

In July, we're going to go to Cornwall, in south-west England. We're going to stay in a campsite for a week. It's next to a really nice beach, so I'm going to go swimming every day! We're going to rent a sailing boat because Mum and Dad love sailing. I want to learn, too, so Mum's going to give me some lessons.

Then in August, I'm going to spend a week in Spain. I want to improve my Spanish, so I'm going to do a language course in San Sebastian. I'm a bit nervous because I'm not going to be with my friends. I hope I'll meet some nice people there.

Write and tell me about your plans for the summer.

Bye for now!

Callum

3 **Look at the Useful language. How do you say these expressions in your language?**

Useful language

Writing about holiday plans

In July/August, I'm going to go to ...
We're going to stay in a campsite/hotel.
I'm going to spend a week / a few days in ...
I can't wait.
I'm excited/nervous because ...
Write and tell me about your plans.

4 **Study the Look! box. Find more examples of *so* and *because* in Callum's email.**

Look! *so* and *because*

We use *so* to introduce a consequence:
I want to improve my Spanish, so I'm going to do a language course.
We use *because* to introduce a reason:
I'm really excited because it's the last week of school!

5 **Copy and complete these sentences with your own ideas.**

1 I love the summer because ...
2 I don't like flying, so ...
3 We aren't going to stay in a hotel because ...
4 My dad wants to go hiking, so ...
5 We're going to rent bikes because ...

6 **Write an email to a friend about your holiday plans. Follow the steps in the Writing plan.**

Writing plan

Prepare

› Make a mind map about your holiday plans.
  • Where and when are you going to go?
  • Who are you going to go with?
  • What are you going to do on holiday?
  • How are you going to travel?

Write

› Look at *Starting and finishing an email* on page 28.
› Use the expressions from the Useful language box.

Check

› Check your grammar: *going to* for future plans
› Check *because* and *so*.
› Check your spelling.

W **Writing summary:** WB p.92
R **Review: Units 7–9** SB pp.104–105
P **Project: Units 7–9** SB pp.110–111
L **Literature: Units 7–9** SB pp.116–117
E **Exams: Unit 9** SB p.126
LS **Language summary: Unit 9** SB p.135

My holiday plans

WRITING An email

Sts read an email about holiday plans and complete a mind map. They learn how to use *so* and *because* to talk about reasons and consequences. They follow the steps in the Writing plan to write an email about their holiday plans, using a mind map to plan their ideas.

Writing

An email about holiday plans

Useful language

Writing about holiday plans (*In July/August, I'm going to go to ..., We're going to stay in a campsite/hotel, I'm going to spend a week/a few days in ..., I can't wait, I'm excited/ nervous because ..., Write and tell me about your plans.*)

Look!

so and *because*

WARMER

Revise the vocabulary for holiday activities from page 92. Write the verbs from the phrases on the board: *stay*, *pack*, *take*, *relax*, *go*, *visit*, *take*, *explore*, *rent*, *unpack*. Put sts into pairs and give them two minutes to try to remember all the phrases they learned. Check answers.

1 Read out the task and elicit some possible questions that sts can ask, e.g. *Where are you going? Who are you going with? What are you going to do?* Put sts into pairs to ask and answer questions. Ask some sts to tell the class about their partner's plans.

2 Read out the task and explain that Callum is planning two holidays. Ask sts to draw two mind maps in their notebooks, like the one in Exercise 2. They then read the email and complete the mind maps. Check answers.

Answers

1 Where? *Cornwall*, in a campsite; When? July; Who with? Mum and Dad; What? swimming, sailing
2 Where? Spain, San Sebastian; When? August; Who with? alone; What? language course

3 Read the Useful language box with sts about writing about holiday plans. Check they understand all the expressions and ask them how they say these expressions in their first language.

4 Read the Look! box with sts about *so* and *because*. To demonstrate the meanings, you could write a pair of similar sentences on the board, to show the difference between the two words: *I'm excited because it's the last week of school*. (reason) *It's the last week of school, so I'm excited*. (consequence). Sts find more examples of *so* and *because* in Callum's email. Check answers.

Answers

It's next to a really nice beach, **so** I'm going to go swimming every day.
We're going to rent a sailing boat **because** Mum and Dad love sailing.
I want to learn, too, **so** Mum's going to give me some lessons.
I want to improve my Spanish, **so** I'm going to do a language course in San Sebastian.
I'm a bit nervous **because** I'm not going to be with my friends.

Ask questions to check concept.

Concept check questions: *We like Greece because it's hot – reason or consequence?* (reason). *We like Greece, so we go there every year – reason or consequence?* (consequence).

5 Ask sts to copy the sentence beginnings into their notebooks and complete them with their own ideas. Ask some sts to read their sentences to the class.

6 Sts now write an email about their holiday plans, following the steps in the Writing plan.

Writing plan

Prepare

Sts make a mind map about their holiday plans.

Write

Refer sts back to the information on starting and finishing an email on page 28. They then write their emails. Refer them back to the Useful language box for expressions to use in their emails.

Reflect

Ask sts to check their grammar, spelling and punctuation and make any necessary changes. Sts could then swap their emails with each other in pairs and give feedback on the use of the Useful language, *be going to* and *so* and *because*. Discuss which holidays sound the most fun and why.

W **Writing practice: WB** p.80 There is more practice for writing in the Workbook. Set these exercises for homework.

W **Writing summary: WB** p.92

R **Review: Units 7–9 SB** pp.104–105

P **Project: Units 4–6 SB** pp.110–111

L **Literature: SB** pp.116–117

E **Exams: Unit 9 SB SB** p.126

LS **Language summary: SB** p.135

REVIEW
UNITS 1–3

READING

1 **Read about Jordan. Complete the text with the words from the box.**

always	doesn't live	gets up	goes to bed	
have breakfast	homework	kick	listen	
next to	playing	plays	there are	there isn't

Jordan is sixteen years old – he can [1] … a ball 50 metres and do some cool tricks. He goes to a football academy, but he [2] … with his own family. He lives with a host family during the week.

Jordan [3] … at 6.30 a.m. every day. First, Jordan and the other players go running and swimming, and then they [4] … . After breakfast, Jordan studies until 2 p.m. Then he [5] … football until 5.30 p.m. He must [6] … to his coach all the time.

Jordan has his own bedroom in his host family's house. There's a desk [7] … his bed. [8] … two lamps: one is on the table and one is on his desk. There's a small wardrobe, but [9] … a TV. He's got a laptop and some wireless headphones on his desk.

In the evenings, Jordan does his [10] … before he has dinner. After dinner, he [11] … has a video call with his parents and his brother. Then he plays computer games. He always [12] … at 9.30 p.m. It's a long day, but Jordan loves [13] … football!

2 **What do you remember? Write sentences about Jordan using the words below. Read and check.**

lamps	kick a ball	a host family
6.30 a.m.	his coach	laptop
big wardrobe	his parents	9.30 p.m.

There are two lamps in his room.

LISTENING

3 R1 **Listen and match the people to the weekend activities. There is one extra activity.**

1 
Charlie

2 
Sara

3 
Jack

a 

b 

c 

d 

4 R1 **Listen again. Who …**

1 likes chatting with friends on the phone?
2 loves relaxing at the weekend?
3 has a class on Saturday morning?
4 has a big family lunch?
5 is a very tidy person?
6 sometimes plays computer games with friends?

5 R1 **Choose the correct answers. Listen and check.**

1 Charlie *has* / *hasn't* got a big TV.
2 Charlie is very *tidy* / *untidy*.
3 Sara *usually* / *never* gets up late at the weekend.
4 Sara doesn't like *tidying her room* / *leaving home* at the weekends.
5 Jack *can* / *can't* jump and kick very high.
6 Jack *loves* / *hates* tidying his room.

REVIEW UNITS 1–3

LESSON OVERVIEW: This lesson reviews the grammar and vocabulary sts have learned in Units 1–3 of the book. Sts read about the life and daily routine of a young football star and listen to three people talking about what they do at the weekend. They talk about things they typically do at the weekend, and write sentences about things they like and don't like doing at the weekend, and their perfect day. The lesson ends with a fun memory test of language sts have learned in Units 1–3.

WARMER

Say: *At the weekend, I ...* Invite a student at the front of the class to complete the sentence, e.g. *go shopping*. Invite the next student to repeat this and add their own idea, e,g, *At the weekend, Ana goes shopping and I watch TV*. Continue around the class, with each student repeating what their classmates do and adding their own idea. Help out with ideas and vocabulary if necessary. Continue until the list of things to remember becomes too long!

READING

1 Read out the title of the text and focus on the picture. Ask: *What do you think Jordan does each day? What kind of school does he go to? Does he play football every day?* Elicit a few ideas, then ask sts to read the text quickly, ignoring the gaps, to check their ideas. Discuss the answers, and elicit what sts learned about Jordan. Then ask them to read the text again and complete it with the correct words. Check answers.

Answers

1	kick	8	There are
2	doesn't live	9	there isn't
3	gets up	10	homework
4	have breakfast	11	always
5	plays	12	goes to bed
6	listen	13	playing
7	next to		

2 Read through the words in the box with the class and check that sts understand them all. Sts write sentences about Jordan from memory, using the words. Weaker sts could work in pairs for this. Ask some sts to read some of their sentences to the class and ask other sts if they think they are correct. Sts then read the text again to check.

Possible answers

Jordan can kick a ball 50 metres.
Jordan lives with a host family during the week.
He gets up at 6.30 a.m. every day.
He always listens to his coach.
Jordan has got a laptop.
There isn't a big wardrobe in his bedroom. There's a small wardrobe.
He always has a video call with his parents after dinner.
He goes to bed at 9.30 p.m.

LISTENING

3 R1 Focus on the pictures and elicit what they show. Focus on the photos of Charlie, Sara and Jack and explain to sts that they will hear them talking about their weekend activities. Play the audio for sts to listen and match the people to the activities. See TG page 283 for audio script. Check answers.

Answers

Charlie b
Sara a
Jack c

4 R1 Allow sts time to read through the questions, then play the audio again for them to listen and answer the questions. Check answers with the class, playing the audio again and pausing if necessary for sts to hear the answers.

Answers

1	Sara	4	Sara
2	Charlie	5	Sara
3	Jack	6	Charlie

5 R1 Sts read the sentences and choose the correct answers. Play the audio again for them to listen and check. Check answers with the class and check that sts understand all the sentences.

Answers

1	has	4	leaving home
2	untidy	5	can
3	never	6	hates

EXTRA PRACTICE

Say one or two sentences about yourself using phrases from exercises 4 and 5, e.g. *I'm a very tidy person. I always get up late at the weekend.* Ask: *True or False?* Get sts to guess. Ask sts individually to write four sentences, three true and one false, about themselves, using phrases from exercises 4 and 5. They then work in pairs to read their sentences to each other and guess which are false.

SPEAKING

6 **Work in pairs. Ask and answer questions about the topics below with *can, have got, there is/are* and the present simple.**

A: Do you usually watch TV before school?
B: No, I don't. I usually watch TV in the evening. What about you?

SPORTS ACTIVITIES

- go swimming
- do taekwondo
- play table tennis
- ski
- skate
- surf

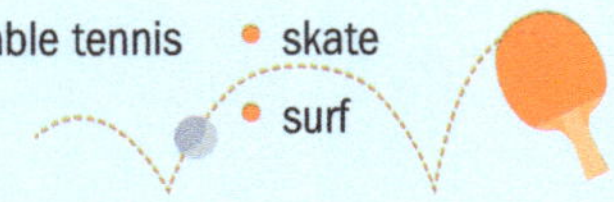

THINGS YOU CAN DO

- watch TV
- play video games
- chat with your friends
- listen to music
- do your homework
- get up early/late

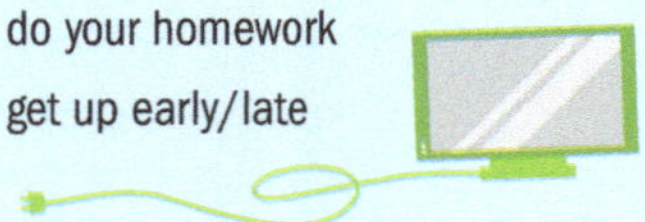

YOUR BEDROOM

- a bookcase
- a laptop
- a desk
- wireless headphones
- a lamp
- a chair

WRITING

7 **Think about your perfect day. Copy and complete the sentences with your own ideas. Use the pictures to help you.**

My perfect day

I get up at ... I drink ... I eat ...
I play ... Then I watch ... I go to bed at ...

1 

2 

3 

4 

5 

6 

TEST YOUR MEMORY!

Say two things you like / don't like doing in the evenings.

Name three items of technology you have at home.

Make three questions with *Can you ...*

Name six prepositions of place.

Describe three pieces of furniture in your home.

Make three sentences about your classroom. Use *there is / are*.

Say as many sports as you can in thirty seconds.

Make two sentences about your school. Use *has / hasn't got*.

Name five adverbs of frequency.

Describe four school rules. Use *must/mustn't*.

Name a member of your family. Give three pieces of information about them.

Make two sentences about your daily activities. Use the present simple.

REVIEW UNITS 1-3

SPEAKING

6 Read out the task and explain to sts that they are going to ask and answer questions in pairs. Ask sts to read through all the topics and check they understand everything. Read out the example question and answer, then elicit one or two more example questions about the different topics. With weaker classes, sts could write five or six questions individually about the different topics. Check these before sts work in pairs. Monitor while sts are working in pairs and note down any typical errors to correct in a feedback session at the end. When sts have finished asking and answering questions, ask some sts to tell the class something they learned about their partner. For extra practice, sts could repeat the activity with a new partner.

Sample answers

Sports activities

Do you go swimming after school? Yes, I go every Friday evening.
Can you play table tennis? No, I can't but I can play volleyball.
Do you skate in winter? Yes, if it's very cold.
Do you do Taekwondo? No, I don't.
Can you ski? No, but I'd like to learn.
Do you surf in the summer? Yes, with my friends.

Things you can do

Can you watch TV late at night? No, I can't.
Can you play video games on your mobile? Yes, of course.
Can you chat with your friends online? Yes, I can.
Can you listen to music at school? No, I can't.
Can you do your homework on the bus? No, it's very busy.
Can you get up late / early on Saturday mornings? Yes, I can. No I can't.

Your bedroom

Is there a bookcase in your bedroom? Yes, a small one.
Can you use a laptop in your bedroom? No, the Wi-Fi is not good.
Have you got a desk in your bed? No, I haven't.
Do wireless headphones work in your bedroom? Yes, they do.
Is there a lamp near your bed? Yes, there is.
Have you got a chair in your bedroom? No, I haven't.

EXTRA PRACTICE

Play a game to practise more vocabulary from Units 1-3. Put sts into teams, and write these words on the board: *mother, brother, cousin, fridge, wardrobe, sofa, mirror, dinner, lunch, laptop, tablet, drone, athletics, volleyball, catch, climb, run, ride, throw.* Teams take turns to choose a word and say it in a sentence. If their sentence is correct, they get a point and the word or phrase is crossed off the board. If their sentence is not correct, don't correct it but move on to the next team. Continue until all the vocabulary has been practised. See which team has the most points.

WRITING

7 Focus on the pictures and elicit what they show. Read out one or two sentence beginnings and elicit some possible endings. Sts then work individually to complete the sentences with their own ideas. Ask some sts to read their sentences to the class.

Sample answers

Your perfect day

I get up at 11 o clock.
I drink 2 glasses of fresh orange juice.
I eat a very big sandwich for lunch.
I play basketball with my friends in the afternoon.
In the evening, I watch my favourite TV series.
I go to bed very late.

TEST YOUR MEMORY

This is a fun way for sts to review the vocabulary and grammar from the unit. They could do the task individually or in pairs, and you could do the activity as a race to provide extra motivation. Alternatively, sts could work in pairs and take turns to choose one of the tasks for their partner. With weaker classes, you could challenge sts to choose 6 tasks to complete from memory, then refer back to the units to help them complete the remaining tasks. Elicit a range of example answers for each task.

REVIEW
UNITS 4–6

READING

1 Read and choose the correct words to complete the text.

Home · Board · Contact

The Great Bear Project

Come and see us at Eastern Europe's [1] *bigger / biggest* bear sanctuary, near the city of Brasov in the [2] *monuments / mountains* of Romania. More than 70 bears live here and the [3] *older / oldest* bear, Betsy, is 40 years old!

At the moment, four volunteers [4] *work / are working* here to help the staff. Right now, it's early in the morning and the volunteers [5] *prepare / are preparing* the bears' food. Bears are very [6] *thirsty / hungry* animals and eat [7] *a lot of / many* food. Every day, each bear [8] *eats / is eating* more than 10 kg of food to stay [9] *hungry / healthy* – that's [10] *much / a lot of* food! There are [11] *some / any* vegetables and fruit for them today. Don't worry, they [12] *don't eat / aren't eating* people!

Right now, some of the bears [13] *climb / are climbing* trees and others are swimming in the [14] *beach / lake*. Some of the bears are [15] *the laziest / lazier* than the others and they're sleeping! It's summer here, so it's warm and [16] *foggy / sunny*.

We think this is one of [17] *better / the best* wildlife attractions in the world! Why not come and see for yourself?

2 Complete the sentences. Use the correct form of the word in brackets. Read and check.

1 The bear sanctuary ... in Romania. (be)
2 Today, four volunteers ... . (help)
3 There ... some vegetables for the bears today. (be)
4 Some of the bears are ... than the others. (active)
5 There ... some bears in the lake. (be)
6 Bears are ... than smaller animals like foxes, but they don't eat people. (dangerous)
7 It's one of the ... wildlife attractions in the world! (good)

LISTENING

3 R2 Read the words in the box. Who do you think mentions these things: Hannah, Pierre or Alba? Listen and check your answers.

a beach · a hotel · a lake · a theatre · fish · ice hockey · sandwiches · street food · volleyball

a

b

c

4 R2 Listen again and answer the questions.

1 What are Hannah's friends cooking on the barbecue?
2 What is Hannah's favourite food?
3 What is the weather like in Quebec City at the moment?
4 Where are Pierre and his friends playing ice hockey?
5 What ingredients are in Alba's favourite street food?

5 R2 Listen again. Complete the sentences with the correct comparative or superlative form of the adjectives in the box.

cold · early · fit · good · near · sunny

1 In Hannah's opinon, Perth is ... city in Australia.
2 Perth is ... to Indonesia than another Australian city.
3 Pierre is ... in winter than he is in summer.
4 The Ice Hotel in Quebec is ... hotel in North America.
5 It's an hour ... in Mexico City than it is in Quebec.
6 In Alba's opinion, ... street food is a chicken torta.

REVIEW UNITS 4-6

LESSON OVERVIEW: This lesson reviews the grammar and vocabulary sts have learned in Units 4–6 of the book. Sts read about a bear sanctuary in Romania and listen to a radio phone-in programme in which people from around the world talk about what's happening and what the weather is like where they are. They talk about what is happening in a pictures, and write an entry about a town or city for an online tour guide. The lesson ends with a fun memory test of language sts have learned in Units 4–6.

WARMER

Mime playing tennis or football and ask: *What am I doing?* Elicit the answer, using the present continuous. Repeat this using one or two more actions, e.g. reading a book and eating a burger. Then invite sts to mime an action for their classmates to guess. Monitor how well sts use the present continuous and revise the form and use of the tense if necessary.

READING

1 Read out the title of the text and focus on the picture. Check that sts understand *bear*. Ask: *What do you think the Great Bear Project is? Where do you think it is?* Elicit a few ideas, then ask sts to read the text quickly to check their ideas. Discuss the answers, and elicit what sts learned about the bears. Explain the meaning of *sanctuary*. Then ask them to read the text again and choose the correct answers to complete it. Check answers and revise any language points that sts have struggled with.

Answers

1 biggest
2 mountains
3 oldest
4 are working
5 are preparing
6 hungry
7 a lot of
8 eats
9 healthy
10 a lot of
11 some
12 don't eat
13 are climbing
14 lake
15 lazier
16 sunny
17 the best

2 Sts complete the sentences with the correct form of the words in brackets. Weaker sts could work in pairs for this. Check answers.

Answers

1 is
2 are helping
3 aren't
4 more active
5 are
6 more dangerous
7 best

LISTENING

3 R2 Focus on the pictures and explain to sts that they will hear people talking about what they are doing and what is happening in different parts of the world. Read through the words in the box with the class and check that sts understand them all. Then put sts into pairs to discuss who they think mentions each thing. Elicit a few ideas, but don't confirm them.
Play the audio for sts to listen and check their answers. See TG page 283 for audio script. Check answers with the class.

Answers

Hannah: a beach, fish, volleyball
Pierre: a hotel, a lake, ice hockey
Alba: a theatre, sandwiches, street food

4 R2 Allow sts time to read through the questions, then play the audio again for them to listen and answer the questions. Encourage them to write full sentences for their answers. Check answers with the class, playing the audio again and pausing if necessary for sts to hear the answers.

Answers

1 They're cooking fish, chicken and vegetables.
2 Hannah's favourite food is fish.
3 It's cold and icy, but it isn't snowing.
4 They're playing on a frozen lake.
5 The ingredients are bread, meat, chicken, cheese, salad and tomato sauce.

5 R2 Sts complete the sentences with the correct comparative or superlative form of the adjectives. Play the audio again for them to listen and check. Check answers with the class, writing the correct forms on the board for sts to check their spellings. Check that sts understand all the sentences. Revise the form and use of comparatives and superlatives if necessary.

Answers

1 the sunniest
2 nearer
3 fitter
4 the coldest
5 earlier
6 The best

EXTRA PRACTICE

Ask sts to look at the pictures in exercise 3 again and choose one to talk about. Tell sts to imagine they are in that place and talk about what they are doing and what they like about the city. Allow sts time to prepare their ideas individually. Encourage them to read exercises 1-3 again to help with ideas and vocabulary. You could also play the audio again for them to listen and make notes. Sts then work in pairs and take turns to speak. Encourage them to try to speak for 30 seconds.

SPEAKING

6 Work in pairs. Look at the picture and write as many sentences as you can. Use *much, many, a lot of* and the present continuous. Use positives and negatives.

Two people are playing volleyball.

There aren't many clouds.

WRITING

7 Choose a town/city in your country or around the world. Write an entry for an online tour guide. Use the ideas below to help you.

Milan is in the north of Italy. The weather is warm and sunny in the summer, but it often rains. In winter, it's cold and cloudy. It's a big city, with a population of ...

Think about ...

- where it is.
- the weather at different times of the year.
- the best time of year to visit.
- the most interesting things to see and do there.
- food you can eat in the local restaurants.
- the best nature reserves to visit near the town/city.
- animals you can see near the city.

TEST YOUR MEMORY!

- Name four adjectives to describe your health.
- Give the comparative and superlative forms of these adjectives: *bad, big, good, hot, hungry, lazy*
- Make two questions. One with *How much ...?* and one with *How many ...?*
- Say as many animals as you can in thirty seconds.
- Name three countable and three uncountable food nouns.
- Make two sentences starting with *The best ...*
- Describe three places in your town/city.
- Make a sentence with *I'm not as ... as ...*
- Describe the weather today. Use two or more weather words.
- Say one thing you do every day and one thing you're doing now.
- Make two sentences starting with *The worst ...*
- Name three natural world features for *water* and three for *land*.

SPEAKING

6 Focus on the picture and elicit what it shows. Elicit any vocabulary that sts might need, e.g. *mountains, volleyball, barbecue, dog, salad, orange juice, frog*. Read out the task and the example sentences. Ask: *Are some people playing football?* Elicit a negative sentence as the answer: *People aren't playing football*. Elicit some more examples of quantifiers, e.g. *some, any, not much, not many, a lot of*. You could write these on the board for sts to refer to. Sts then work in pairs to write sentences. Monitor while sts are working in pairs and note down any typical errors to correct in a feedback session at the end. Ask pairs in turn to read some of their sentences to the class.

Sample answer
There's a lot of orange juice on the table.
One person is cooking / barbecuing chicken.
There's a lot of meat on the barbecue.
A dog is looking at the chicken on the barbecue.
A frog is sitting on some tomatoes.
There are a lot of tomatoes.
A boy and a girl are looking at each other.
There's a lot of salad on the table.
There are a lot of mountains in the background.
There aren't many trees.
There isn't much rice.

EXTRA PRACTICE

Ask sts to close their books. Say some sentences about the picture in exercise 6, some true and some false, e.g. *A woman is cooking food.* (true) *Two boys are playing volleyball.* (false – a boy and a girl are playing). Put sts into pairs. Ask them to look at the picture again and write four true or false sentences about it. Monitor and help while they are working. Ask sts to close their books again, then put pairs together into groups of four to read their sentences to each other, guess if they are true or false and correct the false sentences.

WRITING

7 Focus on the picture and elicit or explain that it shows Milan, in Italy. Read out the task, then read through the ideas with the class and make sure sts understand everything. Read out the example answer, then elicit a few towns or cities that sts could write about. With weaker classes, you could choose a city and brainstorm ideas as a class before sts do the writing task. Sts could work individually or in pairs to write their own entry for an online tour guide. Ask some sts to read their tour guides to the class.

Sample answer
Milan is in the north of Italy. The weather is warm and sunny in the summer but it often rains. In winter it's cold and cloudy and often foggy. It's a big city with a population of over 3 million people. The best time of year to go is spring or early autumn. There are a lot of museums and galleries in Milan and it's got two famous football clubs - Inter Milan and AC Milan. You can get tickets and watch a live match. You can also visit some historic buildings. There is a famous cathedral and castle. The food in Milan is fantastic and there are many great restaurants. You can visit the lakes near Milan such as Lake Como. There aren't many wild animals to see in Italy but if you go to the mountains, you may see marmots, ibex goats or possibly a lynx at night.

TEST YOUR MEMORY

This is a fun way for sts to review the vocabulary and grammar from the unit. They could do the task individually or in pairs, and you could do the activity as a race to provide extra motivation. Alternatively, sts could work in pairs and take turns to choose one of the tasks for their partner. With weaker classes, you could challenge sts to choose 6 tasks to complete from memory, then refer back to the units to help them complete the remaining tasks. Elicit a range of example answers for each task.

REVIEW
UNITS 7–9

READING

1 Read and complete the text. Use the correct form of the verbs in brackets. Which answer doesn't use the past simple?

by Nora Lucas
Posted at 9.30p.m.

Hi everyone. I'm back!

Last week, I [1] … (be) on holiday with my parents and my younger brother. Where did we [2] … (go)? We went to San Sebastián in the north of Spain. We [3] … (travel) by boat from the south of England. We [4] … (not stay) in a hotel – we stayed in an apartment near the beach.

We relaxed on the beach and we went sightseeing. One day, we [5] … (go) by bus to the Cristóbal Balenciaga museum in Getaria. Cristóbal was a clothes designer and he was born in Getaria on 21 January 1895 . He [6] … (die) on 23 March 1972. His mother [7] … (make) clothes for a rich family, and Cristóbal [8] … (start) working with her when he was twelve. He [9] … (open) his first shop in San Sebastián in 1919 and his first design studio, in Paris, in 1937.

He designed a lot of clothes and there were more than 1,200 outfits in the museum. I [10] … (take) a lot of pictures of the coats, jackets, skirts, dresses, trousers and shoes. As you can see, my favourite clothes at the museum [11] … (be) the colourful long dresses and beautiful jackets!

No more trips now until next summer. We're [12] … (go) to visit my cousins in Scotland!

2 In your notebooks, correct the sentences.

1 Nora was on holiday with her grandparents.
2 Nora travelled to Spain by plane.
3 They stayed in a hotel.
4 They didn't go sightseeing.
5 Nora didn't take any pictures of the clothes.
6 Nora is going to visit her cousins next week.

3 Find two words for each of these topics in Nora's blog:

1 transport
2 holiday activities
3 life events
4 clothes

LISTENING

4 R3 Listen and match Daz, Ines and Nick to their clothes. There is one set that you don't need.

1 Daz 2 Ines 3 Nick

a

b

c

d

5 R3 Listen again. Complete the sentences with verbs in the box. Use a past or future form.

arrive	buy	get	go	not be	wear

1 Daz's trousers … this morning.
2 Daz is … his new trainers to his friend's party.
3 Ines' sister is … her a white T-shirt for her birthday.
4 Ines … her red baseball cap in New York City.
5 Nick … sightseeing in Paris.
6 The weather in Paris … cold.

6 R3 Listen again. Are the sentences true (T) or false (F)? Correct the false sentences.

1 Daz has got a new green T-shirt with writing on it.
2 Daz's new trousers are blue.
3 Ines' baseball cap isn't from London.
4 Ines hates the skater style.
5 Nick is going to go sightseeing in Paris.
6 It isn't going to be cold in Paris.

REVIEW UNITS 7–9

LESSON OVERVIEW: This lesson reviews the grammar and vocabulary sts have learned in Units 7–9 of the book. Sts read a blog post about a recent trip to Spain and listen to about the life and daily routine of a young football star and listen to three people talking about the kinds of clothes they like to wear. They talk about a holiday they had in the past, and write six sentences about a famous person. The lesson ends with a fun memory test of language sts have learned in Units 7–9.

WARMER

Ask: *Where do you usually go on holiday? Where would you like to go? Why?* Elicit a few answers, then ask: *What do you enjoy doing on holiday?* Elicit a few answers and review some of the vocabulary for holiday activities that sts have learned. Then ask: *What do you usually wear on holiday?* Elicit a few answers, and review some of the clothes vocabulary that sts have learned. Ask: *Where did you go on holiday last year? What did you do?* Elicit a few answers and review the form and use of the past simple if necessary.

READING

1 Focus on the text and explain that it is a blog post by someone about their holiday. Ask sts to look at the pictures, then ask: *Where do you think Nora went? What do you think she did on holiday?* Elicit a few ideas, then ask sts to read the text quickly, ignoring the gaps, to check their ideas. Discuss the answers, and elicit what sts learned about Nora's holiday. Then ask them to read the text again and complete it with the correct past simple verb forms. Check answers, and elicit which verbs are regular and which are irregular.

Answers

1 was	7 made
2 go	8 started
3 travelled	9 opened
4 didn't stay	10 took
5 went	11 were
6 died	12 going

2 Sts write the sentences in their notebooks and correct them. Weaker sts could work in pairs for this. Check answers.

Answers

1 Nora's was on holiday with her parents.
2 Nora travelled to Spain by boat.
3 They stayed in an apartment.
4 They went sightseeing.
5 Nora took a lot of pictures of the clothes.
6 Nora is going to visit her cousins next summer.

3 Sts find the words in the blog. Check answers, and check that sts understand the words. You could brainstorm more words for each category with the class.

Answers

1 boat, bus
2 relax on the beach, go sightseeing
3 be born, die
4 coat, jacket, skirt, dress, trousers, shoes

LISTENING

4 R3 Focus on the pictures and elicit what they show. Explain to sts that they will hear Daz, Ines and Nick talking about their favourite clothes. Play the audio for sts to listen and match the people to the clothes. See TG page 283 for audio script. Check answers.

Answers

1 Daz c 2 Ines b 3 Nick d

5 R3 Allow sts time to read through the sentences, then play the audio again for them to listen and complete them with the correct form of the verbs in the box. Check answers with the class, playing the audio again and pausing if necessary for sts to hear the answers.

Answers

1 arrived	4 got / bought
2 going to wear	5 is going to go
3 going to buy	6 won't be

6 R3 Sts read the sentences and decide if they are true or false. Allow sts to compare their answers in pairs, then play the audio again for them to listen and check. Check answers with the class, playing the audio again and pausing if necessary to confirm the answers.

Answers

1 F He's got a new red T-shirt with writing on it.
2 T
3 T
4 F She loves the skater style.
5 T
6 T

EXTRA PRACTICE

Play a game to practise irregular past simple verbs. Put sts into teams and write some verbs on the board, e.g. *buy, get, give, go, see, know, make, meet, sing, speak, take, wear, win, write*. Point to individual verbs in turn. Teams race to say a correct sentence using the verb in the past simple. Continue until all the verbs have been practised. See which team has the most points.

SPEAKING

7 **Work in pairs. Ask and answer questions about your holiday. Use the prompts in the box or your own ideas.**

Where / go? When / go? Who / go with?
How / travel? Where / stay? What / do?
What / see? How long / stay there?

8 **Look at the photos below. In pairs, describe the people in the past and now.**

Her jumper was pink. Her dress is black.

His hair was curly. Now, his hair is straight.

a

b

c

d

WRITING

9 **Write six sentences to describe a famous person: a fashion designer, a musician, an actor, a sportsperson, a YouTuber. Use the ideas below or use your own.**

Luka Sabbat is an American YouTuber. He's tall and thin …

Think about …

- his/her appearance.
- his/her style.
- his/her clothes.
- his/her life story.
- what his/her life story is.
- why you like him/her.
- something cool that he/she did.
- what he/she will do next.

TEST YOUR MEMORY!

Describe a famous person. Use adjectives of appearance.

Say five things you're going to do on your next holiday.

Give the past simple of these verbs: *be, go, have, make, play, see, travel, watch*

Say as many items of clothing as you can in 30 seconds.

Make three questions starting with *Did you …*

Say where you were yesterday at 9.00 a.m., 5.00 p.m. and 10.00 p.m.

Give two predictions about your life in the future. Use *will/won't*.

Make two sentences about last week: one positive, one negative.

Name six different types of transport.

Make sentences with the past simple. Use these verbs: *be born, grow up, start school, learn to drive*

Name five object pronouns.

Make sentences with time expressions. Use the past simple: *yesterday, last month, ago, in 2012*

REVIEW UNITS 7-9

SPEAKING

7 Read out the task and explain to sts that they are going to ask and answer questions in pairs about their last holiday. Focus on the prompts in the box and elicit one or two questions, then ask individual sts the questions and elicit their answers. With weaker classes, sts could write the questions first. Check these before sts work in pairs. Monitor while sts are working in pairs and note down any typical errors to correct in a feedback session at the end. When sts have finished asking and answering questions, ask some sts to tell the class something about their partner's holiday.

Sample answer
Where did you go on your holiday? We went to India.
When did you go? We went last summer/in August.
Who did you go with? I went with my parents and my sister.
How did you travel there? We went by car.
Where did you stay? We stayed in a lovely hotel.
What did you do there? We spent a lot of time at the beach.
What did you see? We saw lots of interesting places and lots of fish.
How did you stay there? We stayed for 2 weeks.

8 Focus on the pictures and ask sts if they recognise the people. Focus on the first pair and elicit some sentences describing the person in the past and the present. Point out that we need to use the past simple to talk about the person in the past and the present simple to describe them in the present. Put sts into pairs to continue describing the people. Elicit some descriptions from the class.

Sample answer
Photo A and B is the actress from Harry Potter Emma Watson.
Photo C and D is the actor and film maker Ben Affleck.

Emma Watson
Her hair was long. Now it's shorter.
Her hair was blonde. Now it's brown.

Ben Affleck
His hair was blond. Now it's darker.
He didn't have a beard and a moustache. Now he does.

WRITING

9 Focus on the picture and elicit who it shows. Ask: *Do you watch him on YouTube? Do you like his videos? Why/ Why not?* Read out the task and elicit some other famous people that sts could write about. Choose someone as a class and brainstorm a sentence for each of the ideas in the list. Sts then work individually to write their sentences. Ask some sts to read their sentences to the class. You could ask them to read their sentences without saying the name of the person, and the class could guess who the person is.

Sample answer
Luka Sabbat is an American YouTuber. He's tall and thin and he's got great hair and a thin moustache. He looks cool and he's wearing a T-shirt and jeans. He's a young, model, actor and social media personality on YouTube. He lived in Paris as a young child and went to Arts school in New York. He joined Instagram when he was 14. He is also a good skier. In the future I think he will be a famous actor and win an Oscar!

EXTRA PRACTICE

Ask sts individually to write six sentences describing themselves, using the ideas in exercise 9. Ask them to write their sentences on a piece of paper. Collect all the descriptions then read them out to the class in turn. See if the class can guess which of their classmates wrote each description.

TEST YOUR MEMORY

This is a fun way for sts to review the vocabulary and grammar from the unit. They could do the task individually or in pairs, and you could do the activity as a race to provide extra motivation. Alternatively, sts could work in pairs and take turns to choose one of the tasks for their partner. With weaker classes, you could challenge sts to choose 6 tasks to complete from memory, then refer back to the units to help them complete the remaining tasks. Elicit a range of example answers for each task.

PROJECT UNITS 1-3

TASK

Create a leaflet for a summer activity camp

I can work in a pair and make a leaflet.

PREPARE

Step 1 **Get ideas**

› Look at the photos. What do you think looks fun?
› Match the photos with each category in the mind map.

21st Century Skills Think critically

Do you have experience of a summer camp or activity weekend?

Tell your classmates about the best activities.

Step 2 **Choose your activities**

› Copy the mind map above. Think of activity ideas for each category.
› Work in pairs. Compare your ideas and choose three things for each category.

Look! **Cooperation**

Give reasons for your choices and listen to your partner's reasons for his/her choices.

Step 3 **Choose your activities**

› Ask other students in your class if they'd like to do your chosen activities.

Would you like to surf at a summer camp?

Do you like art and craft activities?

› Look at some activity leaflets or summer camp websites on the internet.

PROJECT UNITS 1-3

LESSON OVERVIEW: In this project, sts work in pairs to create a leaflet for a summer activity camp. They work through different stages of planning and writing to create their leaflet, then evaluate their work and reflect on what they could improve. They also focus on the skill of cooperating and working together.

Task	Skill
Create a leaflet for a summer activity camp	Cooperation

WARMER

Ask: *What do you know about summer camps? Do you sometimes go to summer camps? What activities can you do there? Do you think they are fun? Why?* Elicit a range of answers and encourage sts to share with the class their experiences of summer camps or what they know about them. Explain to sts that they are going to create a leaflet for a summer camp.

PREPARE

Step 1 Get ideas

Focus on the pictures and elicit the activities that they show. Ask sts to look at the pictures and discuss in pairs which activities look fun and why. You could ask them to choose the top three fun activities. Elicit a few answers, then focus on the mind map. Elicit or explain that mind maps are a good way of brainstorming ideas and noting them down. Ask sts to match the pictures with the categories in the mind map. Check answers.

Answers
sports: a, e
other daytime activities: b, c
evening activities: d, e
daily routines: g, h

21st Century skills

THINK CRITICALLY

Read out the information in the *21st Century Skills* box on thinking critically. Explain that using your own experience can be a good way of helping you to make decisions.

Step 2 Choose your activities

Explain to sts that they are now going to choose activities for their summer camp. Ask sts to copy the mind map into their notebooks, then work individually to think of ideas for each category. Explain to sts that they are now going to compare their ideas and choose the best ones for their own summer camp. Read through the *Look!* box with the class and point out to sts that it is important to listen to other people when you are working with them, and respect their ideas and opinions. Sts then work in pairs to compare their ideas and choose their activities. Ask some pairs to tell the class what they chose and why.

Step 3 Choose your activities

Explain that when you have to plan something, it can be useful to ask other people for their opinions, or look online for ideas. Put pairs of sts together into groups of four to ask each other if they would like to do the activities at their summer camps. Encourage sts to give reasons for their answers, and try to give helpful feedback to their classmates. Sts can then look at some activity leaflets or summer camp websites online for ideas. Ask some pairs to tell the class which feedback they found useful and what ideas they found online.

DO

Step 4 **Plan your timetables**

- Decide if your leaflet is on a computer or on paper.
- Plan an activity timetable for the inside of your leaflet.

Step 5 **Write your text**

- Write the text for the back page of your leaflet. Use the **Useful language** box to help you.
- Give your text to another student to check your spelling and punctuation.

Step 6 **Create your front cover**

- Choose a name for your summer camp. Create a logo.
- Create the front page of your leaflet. Draw your pictures and print or download your photos.
- Display your leaflet for the class to see.

REFLECT

Step 7 **Evaluate the projects**

- Look at all the leaflets. Which looks the best? Which leaflet has the best activities?
- Say which summer camps you'd like to go to and why.

Step 8 **Reflect**

- Think about your own project. Is there anything you can improve?

Useful language

The camp has got ...
There's a / There are some ...
In the morning/afternoon/evening, you can ...
... starts at ... o'clock and finishes at half past ...
Are you into ...? This camp is for you!

2

A typical day at **REAL! SUMMER CAMP**

At a Real! Summer Camp, you sleep in a cabin in the woods. Breakfast starts at half past eight and finishes at half past nine. Then you swim, trampoline or try the camp zip wire until lunch time.

After lunch, there are more activities. You can enjoy a music workshop, sail or play volleyball on the beach.

There are always things to do in the evening, too. Every weekend, there's a campfire party and an outdoor film night. You can even learn street dance!

Are you into outdoor activities? Real! Summer Camp is for you!

	Friday, 23 August	Saturday, 24 August	Sunday, 25 August
8.30 a.m. to 9.30 a.m.	Breakfast	Breakfast	Breakfast
10.00 a.m. to 12.30 p.m.	Swimming	Trampolining	Zip wire experience
1.00 p.m. to 2.00 p.m.	Picnic lunch	Make your own pizza lunch	Barbecue lunch
2.30 p.m. to 5.30 p.m.	Beach volleyball	Music workshop	Sailing
6.30 p.m. to 7.30 p.m.	Dinner	Dinner	Dinner
8.00 p.m. to 10.00 p.m.	Campfire party	Street dance class	Film night
10.30 p.m.	Lights out	Lights out	Lights out

DO

Step 4 Plan your timetables

Decide as a class whether sts will produce their leaflets on paper or on a computer, depending on what is possible in your class situation. Focus on the activity timetable at the bottom of page 107 and read through it with the class. Then ask sts in their pairs to plan a timetable for their summer camp and write it on the inside of their leaflet. Monitor and help while they are working.

Step 5 Write your text

Focus on the text 'A typical day at Real! Summer Camp'. Ask sts to read the text, and elicit that it describes what happens on a typical day at the camp. Read through the Useful language with the class, then ask sts to read the text about Real! Summer Camp and make a note of any other useful words and phrases that they could use, e.g. *After lunch, there are more activities. You can enjoy ..., There are always things to do. ...You can even ...* . Sts work in their pairs and write their own text about their summer camp, on the back page of their leaflet. Monitor and help while they are working. Ask pairs to swap texts and check each other's spelling and punctuation. Ask some pairs to read their text to the class.

Step 6 Create your front cover

Focus on the front cover of the Real! Summer Camp leaflet. Elicit that it has an exciting picture and details of when the camp takes place. Sts then work in their pairs to think of a name for their camp and create their own front cover for their leaflet. They could download a photo from the internet or draw a picture. When they have finished, put all the leaflets around the class for sts to see.

REFLECT

Step 7 Evaluate the projects

Explain to sts that they are now going to evaluate the leaflets. Remind them that they should always be respectful when they are commenting on each other's work, and they should focus on saying positive things and making helpful suggestions. Allow sts to walk around the class and look at all the leaflets. Ask them to note down which ones they think look the best, and which have the best activities. Discuss their ideas and reasons as a class, and discuss which summer camps they would most like to go to and why.

Step 8 Reflect

Sts work in their pairs to think about their own project again and think about what they could improve. Point out to sts that when they have done a big piece of work like this one, they should always think about what they did well, and what things they could do better next time. Ask some sts to tell the class what they think they did well, and how they could improve.

EXTRA PRACTICE

As an extension activity, sts could imagine that they are at one of the summer camps in the leaflets. Tell them they are going to record a short video diary for their family. Discuss as a class what topics they can talk about in their video diary. Make notes on the board, e.g. *the weather, daytime activities, evening activities, the food, the bedrooms, the activity leaders, new friends*. Sts can work in pairs to prepare their ideas, then use their phones to record each other's video diaries. Encourage them to speak for a minute if they can, and try to make their diary sound exciting. Monitor and help while they are working. Sts can show their video diaries to each other in groups.

PROJECT
UNITS 4-6

TASK
Create a poster advertising a new shop for your town

I can work in a pair and make a poster.

PREPARE

Step 1 **Get ideas**

- Look at the photos. Which of the shops in the mind map sell these products?
- Work in pairs. Talk about which of these shops your town already has.

Step 2 **Choose a shop for your town**

- With your partner, choose one of the shops from the mind map for your advert.
- Think about how your shop can be different.
- Copy the mind map above and write notes in each section. Decide on your products and prices.
- Think of a name for your shop.

21st Century Skills Find out

Compare prices of the same item in different online shops. What do you notice?

Step 3 **Do your research**

- Ask other students in your class what they think about your shop's products.

Would you like to buy a skateboard in a sports shop?

Do you like cookies?

- Look at the prices of similar products online or in shops in your town.

Look! **Mediation**

If you don't understand your partner's ideas, ask him/her to explain in a different way.

PROJECT
UNITS 4–6

LESSON OVERVIEW: In this project, sts work in pairs to create a poster advertising a new shop for their town. They work through different stages of planning and writing to create their poster, then evaluate their work and reflect on what they could improve. They also focus on the skill of mediation when working together.

Task	Skill
Create a poster advertising a new shop for your town	Mediation

WARMER
Ask: *What kinds of shops are there in your town?* Elicit a few ideas, e.g. *sports shop*, *shoe shop*, then put sts into pairs and give them two minutes to think of as many different kinds of shops in their town as they can. Elicit their ideas, then ask: *What new shops would you like to see in your town?* Elicit a few ideas. Explain to sts that they are going to create a poster advertising a new shop in their town.

PREPARE

Step 1 Get ideas
Focus on the pictures and elicit the things that they show. Then focus on the mind map. Ask sts to match the pictures with the shops in the mind map. Check answers. Sts then work in pairs and talk about which of the shops their town already has. Discuss their ideas as a class.

Answers
Sports shop: a, g
sandwich shop: b, d
cake shop: c, e
tech store: f, h

Step 2 Choose a shop for your town
Explain to sts that they are now going to choose a new shop for their town. Ask them to copy the mind map into their notebooks and complete it with information about their new shop. Tell them to think of a good name for their shop.

21st Century skills

FIND OUT
Read out the information in the *21st Century Skills* box on finding out. Explain that it is important to find out some facts before you make decisions about prices and products. Sts can look online to find information, then complete their mind map with their own ideas.

Step 3 Do your research
Explain to sts that they are now going to do some research. Explain that when you are planning something new, it is important to ask other people for their opinions, or look online for ideas. Read out the information on mediation in the *Look!* box and encourage sts to try hard to understand each other's ideas, so they benefit from feedback. Put pairs of sts together into groups of four to ask each other what they think about their shop's products and prices. Encourage sts to give reasons for their answers, and try to give helpful feedback to their classmates.

DO

Step 4 **Plan your poster**

- Decide if your advert is on a computer or on paper.
- Make a sketch of your advert. Plan where each section can go on your poster.
- Decide which photos or drawings you want.

Step 5 **Write the text for your poster**

- Write the text for each section of your advert. Use the **Useful language** box to help you.
- Give your text to another student to check your spelling and punctuation.

Step 6 **Create your poster**

- Draw your pictures and print or download your photos and text.
- Make your poster.
- Display your poster for your class to see.

REFLECT

Step 7 **Evaluate the projects**

- Look at all the posters. Which looks the best? Which has the best information?
- Say which shops you'd like to go to and what you'd like to buy there.

Step 8 **Reflect**

- Think about your own project. Is there anything you can improve?

Useful language

We make/sell ...
It's next to / near ...
It's between the ... and the ...
There's a discount for ... / There are some ...
There aren't any ...
Our shop is bigger / better / closer than ...

Santi and Sofia's Sandwich Shop

Open every day, 10.00 a.m. – 5.00 p.m.

Where to find us

Santi and Sofia's Sandwich Shop is opposite the theatre, between the hotel and the library.

We're only a five-minute walk from the market square!

Our sandwiches

White or brown bread:

Chicken and salad	£2.50
Cheese and tomato	£1.90
Tuna and sweetcorn	£1.90
Egg mayonnaise	£1.90

Bagels:

Cream cheese	£2.30
Cheese and salad	£2.80
Jam or honey	£2.00
Chocolate and banana	£2.30

Wraps:

Duck	£3.00
Barbecue chicken	£2.50

Praise for Santi and Sofia's Sandwich Shop

'I go to this sandwich shop every day. I'm eating a duck wrap right now!'
John Turner

'All the straws and packaging are biodegradable. Fantastic!'
Josh White

'The sandwiches are cheaper and more delicious than in all the other shops!'
Katy Williams

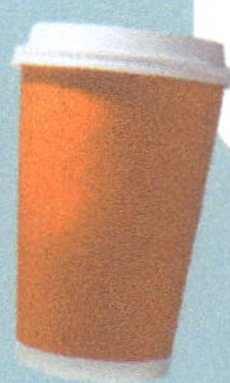

'When it's cold in winter, the hot chocolate is perfect!'
Holly Thomas

PROJECT
UNITS 4-6

DO

Step 4 Plan your poster

Decide as a class whether sts will produce their posters on paper or on a computer, depending on what is possible in your class situation. Focus on the poster for Santi and Sofia's Sandwich Shop and ask sts to read through it. Point out the different sections (*Where to find us*, *Our sandwiches*, *Praise …*). Then ask sts in their pairs to make a sketch of their poster and decide where each section will go, and what pictures or drawings they want. Monitor and help while they are working.

Step 5 Write the text for your poster

Read through the Useful language with the class, then ask sts to read the text about Santi and Sofia's Sandwich Shop again and make a note of any other useful words and phrases that they could use, e.g. *We're only a five-minute walk from …*, *The … is perfect!*, *The … are cheaper and more delicious than …* . Sts work in their pairs and write the text for their own poster. Monitor and help while they are working. Ask pairs to swap texts and check each other's spelling and punctuation. Ask some pairs to read their text to the class.

Step 6 Create your poster

Focus on the pictures on the poster for the sandwich shop. Elicit that they look attractive and exciting. Sts then work in their pairs to create their own poster. They could download photos from the internet or draw pictures. When they have finished, put all the posters around the class for sts to see.

REFLECT

Step 7 Evaluate the projects

Explain to sts that they are now going to evaluate the posters. Remind them that they should always be respectful when they are commenting on each other's work, and they should focus on saying positive things and making helpful suggestions. Allow sts to walk around the class and look at all the posters. Ask them to note down which ones they think look the best, and which ones they would like to go to. Discuss their ideas and reasons as a class, and discuss which shops sts would like to go to, and what they would buy there.

Step 8 Reflect

Sts work in their pairs to think about their own project again and think about what they could improve. Point out to sts that when they have done a big piece of work like this one, they should always think about what they did well, and what things they could do better next time. Ask some sts to tell the class what they think they did well, and how they could improve.

EXTRA PRACTICE

As an extension activity, sts could work in groups of three or four. They choose one of the new shops in the posters they and their classmates have produced and plan a TV advert for it. Explain that one person will film the advert on their phone, and the others will do the acting. Ask them to think about what they should show, e.g. a customer using the shop, customers talking about why they like the shop, etc. Remind sts that in an advert they should try to persuade people that the shop is the best! Monitor and help while sts are working. They can then watch their advert in their groups and discuss how they could improve it. Sts could share their advert with another group.

PROJECT
UNITS 7-9

TASK

Create a past and future timeline of your life

I can work in a pair and make a timeline.

PREPARE

a

b

c

d

Last year	Next year	
Best moments	Plans / Arrangements	Predictions
• *I won a singing competition.*	• *I'm going to visit my brother in the USA.*	• *I'll score ten goals!*
• *I went kayaking.*	• *I'm going to start a new school.*	•
•	•	•
•	•	•

e

f

g

h

Step 1 **Get ideas**

› Look at the photos. What's happening? Which do you think are the most interesting, most exciting and funniest experiences?

Step 2 **Do your research**

› Look at photos to remember what you did last year.
› Ask your family about plans or events next year.

21st Century Skills Get creative

Think of different, original ways to create your timeline. Look at images of timelines on the internet for ideas.

Step 3 **Choose ideas for your timeline**

› Make a list of your best moments last year.
› Make other lists of your predictions and plans for next year.
› Work in pairs. Share your lists. Decide which of your ideas to use in your timeline.

Look! Collaboration

If your partner has difficulty thinking of ideas, make suggestions or ask questions to help him/her.

PROJECT UNITS 7–9

LESSON OVERVIEW: In this project, sts work in pairs to create a past and future timeline of their life. They work through different stages of planning and writing to create their timeline, then evaluate their work and reflect on what they could improve. They also focus on the skill of collaboration and helping each other.

Task	Skill
Create a past and future timeline of your life	Collaboration

WARMER

Ask: *What are the best things in your life so far?* Elicit or suggest a few ideas, e.g. winning a race or competition, doing well in exams, visiting an exciting place. Ask sts individually to write down three exciting things they have done or experienced. Put them into groups to talk about their experiences. Ask some sts to tell the class about their experiences. Explain to sts that they are going to create a timeline of their life, showing exciting experiences in the past and predictions for the future.

PREPARE

Step 1 Get ideas

Focus on the pictures and elicit what they show. Ask sts in pairs to discuss which pictures show the most interesting, most exciting and funniest experiences. You could ask them to choose the top three experiences. Elicit a few ideas.

Step 2 Do your research

Explain to sts that they are now going to work individually to think of ideas for their own timeline. Tell them they can look at old photos to remind themselves of things they did in the past, and they can ask their family about plans and events that are happening next year. They could do this research for homework, if they need to ask their family for information.

21st Century skills

GET CREATIVE

Read out the information in the *21st century skills* box on getting creative. Explain that the internet can be a useful source for creative design ideas and how to make things look good visually. Ask them to research different kinds of timelines online and compare ideas.

Step 3 Choose ideas for your timeline

Sts work individually to make a list of their best moments last year and their predictions and plans for next year. Read the information in the *Look!* box with the class encourage sts to help each other think of ideas. They then discuss their ideas in their pairs and decide which ideas to use in their timeline. Tell them they should include a mixture of ideas from each of their lists. Read through the information in the *21st Century Skills* box on getting creative, and encourage sts to look online for ways of creating a timeline and try to think of an attractive and original way to present their own timeline.

DO

Step 4 **Plan your timeline**

- Decide if your timeline is on a computer or on paper.
- Make a sketch of your timeline. Plan where each past and future experience can go.
- Decide which photos or drawings and text captions you want.

Step 5 **Create your timeline**

- Write your text captions. Use the **Useful language** box to help you.
- Draw your pictures and print or download your photos.
- Put your timeline together.

Step 6 **Present your timeline**

- Decide what you will say about your timeline. Use the **Useful language** box to help you.
- Practise your presentation with your partner.
- Present your timeline to your class.

REFLECT

Step 7 **Evaluate the projects**

- Listen to the other presentations. What did you like about them? Which was the best timeline?
- Say which past experiences and future plans are the most interesting and exciting.

Step 8 **Reflect**

- Think about your own project. Is there anything you can improve?

Useful language

Last year / Six months ago / In February 2018 ...
I watched/visited/loved ...
I saw/met/won/made ...
My ... was born.
I'll pass my exams.
I'm going to fly to ...
My ... is getting married.

DO

Step 4 Plan your timeline

Decide as a class whether sts will produce their timelines on paper or on a computer, depending on what is possible in your class situation. Focus on the timeline at the bottom of page 111 and read through it with the class. Then ask sts in their pairs to make a sketch of their timeline and plan where their experiences can go, then decide which photos or drawings they want to include. Monitor and help while they are working.

Step 5 Create your timeline

Focus on the model timeline again and point out the text captions. Read through the Useful language with the class and point out the different verb forms for the past events and future predictions. Sts work in their pairs and write their own text captions, then download their photos or draw their pictures and put their timeline together. Monitor and help while they are working.

Step 6 Present your timeline

Explain to sts that they are going to present their timeline to the class in their pairs. Explain that they should give more information about each of the events on the timeline, e.g. when it happened, why it was fun, etc. Tell them they should both give the presentation together. Sts work in their pairs to prepare and practise their presentations. Before they give their presentations to the class, read through the instructions in Step 7 with the class. Ask sts to listen carefully to all the presentations and make notes about things they like, and experiences they enjoyed hearing about. Sts then take turns to give their presentations in their pairs.

REFLECT

Step 7 Evaluate the projects

When sts have listened to all the presentations, discuss as a class which ones sts most enjoyed listening to and why.

Step 8 Reflect

Sts work in their pairs to think about their own project again and think about what they could improve. Point out to sts that when they have done a big piece of work like this one, they should always think about what they did well, and what things they could do better next time. Ask them to think not only about their timeline, but also about how well they presented it to the class. Ask some sts to tell the class what they think they did well, and how they could improve.

EXTRA PRACTICE

As an extension activity, ask sts to work individually. Ask them to imagine they are a celebrity and note down two things they did last year, two things they are doing at the moment and two things they are planning in the future. You could brainstorm some ideas as a class first for some exciting events they could add to their timelines, e.g. give a concert in *New York, go to Hollywood to make a movie*. Sts could then work in pairs and take turns to interview each other about their past, present and future. Ask some sts to tell the class about the exciting things their 'celebrity' partner did last year, is doing now and is planning to do next year.

LITERATURE
UNITS 1–3

BEFORE YOU READ

1 Work in pairs and answer the questions.

1 What do you know about Canada?
2 Europeans arrived in Canada around the fifteenth century. Who do you think lived in the area before this?
3 What changes do you think happened after Europeans arrived in Canada?

2 Read the outline to *Jack's Game*. Complete the sentences with the correct words.

1 Laura works for a company that makes chemicals in western … .
2 She thinks that two people she works with are … .
3 Laura's manager says she must go … .
4 The next evening Laura goes to … .
5 She understands the … from yesterday.

OUTLINE

Jack's Game

Laura deLuce works at the Butramex chemical company in western Canada, in an area where lots of indigenous Canadians have lived for thousands of years. Jack Kincaid and Mike Fallon, who work for Butramex, look ill. A local environmental group says the company is doing some bad things to the environment. Then one day, Laura finds a message in a secret code. She can't understand it. Next, her manager, Oscar Strode, tells her to go home. But first, she must go with Fallon to a field where the company is doing an experiment. It is near to an indigenous reservation. While they are there, the indigenous people hit Fallon with a stone.

The next evening, Laura drives to work. She reads the message again and works out it says, 'TOXIC WATER'.

READ

3 L1 Look at the picture. Read and listen to the extract from *Jack's Game* and answer the questions. Laura tells the story.

1 Who is the man in the picture?
2 What is his job?
3 What is he doing in the office?

Where is Jack?

I turn. A man is standing by the door. Is it a security guard? I don't know. It is dark and I can't see very well. But the man sees me. He comes into the room. I think he is going to hit me. But I am not afraid – I am a big girl.

I move quickly to the left. Then I take the man's arm and turn it behind his back, hard.

'Stop – please. Friend,' he cries.

I see it is not a man, but a boy. He is about seventeen years old. I take my hand away from his arm. 'Who are you? And what are you doing here?' I ask.

The boy waits for a moment. Then he speaks. 'My name is Jim,' he says, 'Jim Sawchuk. I am from the reservation. I work here in the evenings. I clean the offices.'

'So why are you moving around in the dark?'

'Because no one must see me.'

'Why not?' I am angry.

'Wait. I can explain,' says Jim. 'Yesterday evening, when I came to work, something strange happened. Your boss, Mr Strode, was at the main gate. All the office buildings behind him were very dark. He explained why. "All the lights are off," he said. "There's a problem with the electricity. You can go home. Don't come back before you hear from me."'

A problem with the electricity? Strode didn't say anything about that to me. And I know why. It wasn't true. He said it to stop Jim coming to work.

LITERATURE
UNITS 1–3

LESSON OVERVIEW: In this lesson, sts read an extract of the novel *Jack's Game*. They read an outline of the novel, then read an extract and listen to the next part of the story. They end by discussing some of the issues that the extract raises, and predicting what happens next in the story.

WARMER

Read out the title of the book and focus on the picture. Explain to sts that they are going to read an extract from a book called *Jack's Game*. Write these words on the board: *chemical company, toxic water, environmental group, information, message, computer file*. Teach the meaning of the words, then put sts into pairs to discuss what the book might be about, using the title, the picture and the words on the board to help them. Elicit a few ideas but don't confirm them.

BACKGROUND INFORMATION

A range of different people lived in Canada before the arrival of the Europeans, including the Inuit, who lived in the far north of Canada. Many of the native Canadians were removed from their lands by the European settlers and moved onto reservations, areas of land that were reserved for the indigenous people. Many still complain of unfair treatment by the Canadian government. The book *Jack's Game* is by the writer Rod Smith.

BEFORE YOU READ

1 Put sts into pairs to discuss the questions. Ask them to note down all their ideas. Ask pairs in turn to share their ideas with the class, and encourage sts to share any information they have about Canada and its history. Share the Background information on this page with the class and teach the meaning of *indigenous*.

2 Ask sts to read the outline to the story, then complete the sentences with the correct words. Allow sts to compare their answers in pairs, then check with the class. Ask which of their ideas from the Warmer were correct.

Answers

1 Canada	4 work	5 message
2 ill	3 home	

READ

3 L1 Read out the questions, then play the audio. Sts read and listen to the extract and answer the questions. Check answers.

Answers

1 The man is Jim Sawchuk.
2 He is the office cleaner.
3 He is looking for a message from Jack.

'This morning, Strode sent me home, too,' I say. 'I'm here to find out why.'

'Now I know who you are,' Jim says. 'You're Laura – Jack's friend. He talked about you.'

'Jack? Where is he? Do you know?'

'No. The last time I saw him was the day before yesterday. But none of us knows where he is now.'

'Us? Who's "us"?'

'The people in the environmental group. Jack is in the group, too. He gives us information about what the company is doing. But, of course, no one in the company knows about this. Except you …'

'Don't worry,' I say. 'I'm not going to tell anyone. But you must tell me what you're doing here.'

Jim looks at the printer. 'I came to look for a message. From Jack.'

'This message?' I move to the computer.

Jim looks at the characters, then he looks at me. 'Maybe,' he says. 'I don't understand Jack's messages. They are always in code. For security. One of the others in the group reads them. The only thing I understand is the JG.'

'And what does that mean?'

'Jack's Game – it's the name of a file. We keep the information that he sends us in it. It was Jack's idea. He loves playing games.'

Extract from **Richmond Readers**: *Jack's Game* by Rod Smith

4 Read the extract again. Correct the words in bold in each sentence.

1. Jim is quite **old**.
2. Jim works in the office in the **mornings**.
3. Strode sends Jim home because there is a problem with the **water**.
4. Jim **knows** where Jack is.
5. Jim and Jack are in **a music group** together.
6. Jim **always understands** Jack's messages.
7. Jack's Game is a computer **game**.

5 Word Power Some verbs often go with certain prepositions. Find the verbs in bold in the extract. Choose the correct prepositions in the sentences.

1. I usually **wait** *for* / *to* / *on* my friends outside the school.
2. What do you **know** *for* / *with* / *about* London?
3. I need to **look** *for* / *to* / *over* my English dictionary because I don't know where it is.
4. Who is that man **standing** *in* / *by* / *on* the car?
5. You can **look** *for* / *to* / *at* their website for more information.

6 L2 Listen to the next part of the story. Put the sentences in the correct order they happen in the story from 1–6.

… Strode turns off the electricity.
… The electricity comes on again.
… Strode and Fallon arrive at the office in a car.
… Jack types the message on his computer.
… Laura and Jim hear a noise outside.
… The message comes out of the printer.

REFLECT

7 THINK CRITICALLY Work in groups. Discuss the questions about the story.

1. What information do you think Jack gives to the environmental group?
2. What does the message 'TOXIC WATER' mean?
3. Why do you think Strode tells Laura and Jim not to go into the office?
4. Where do you think Jack is?
5. What do you think happens next?

Glossary

security guard person who guards money, buildings and things
a moment a short period of time
reservation area of land belonging to a group of people
environmental group people who care about the environment

4 Explain that the words in bold in each sentence are incorrect. Read out the first sentence and elicit the correct information. Sts then read the extract again and write the correct sentences in their notebooks. Check answers, eliciting the part of the extract which confirms each answer.

Answers
1 Jim is quite young.
2 Jim works in the office in the evenings.
3 Strode sends Jim home because there is a problem with the electricity.
4 Jim doesn't know where Jack is.
5 Jim and Jack are in an environmental group together.
6 Jim doesn't understand Jack's messages.
7 Jack's Game is a computer file.

5 **Word Power** Explain to sts that it is important to learn which prepositions go with different verbs. Ask sts to find the verbs in the extract, then choose the correct prepositions to complete the sentences. Check answers.

Answers

1 for	3 for	5 at
2 about	4 by	

EXTRA PRACTICE
To help sts engage more with the story, divide the class into three groups: Jim, Laura and Mr Strode. Explain to the class that they are going to do a class reading of the text. Explain that you will be the narrator, and they will speak for Jim, Laura and Mr Strode. Start by reading aloud the first two paragraphs, then indicate to the 'Jim' group when it is time for them to speak ('Stop – please. Friend.' Encourage them to speak with feeling, all at the same time. Continue with the narration and bring the groups in where appropriate to say the words that the characters say. As you narrate, omit the words such as 'Jim says', so the dialogue flows freely between the different characters. Encourage sts to play their parts with feeling. When you have finished, ask sts if the activity helped them understand the text better.

6 L2 Explain to sts that they will now hear the next part of the story. Read out the task, then allow sts time to read through the sentences. Play the audio. See TB TG page 283 for audio script. Sts listen and put the sentences in order. Check answers, playing the audio again and pausing if necessary to confirm the answers.

Answers
1 Jack types the message on his computer.
2 Strode turns off the electricity.
3 The electricity comes on again.
4 The message comes out of the printer.
5 Laura and Jim hear a noise outside.
6 Strode and Fallon arrive at the office in a car.

REFLECT

21st Century skills

7 **THINK CRITICALLY**
Ask sts to read through the questions. Check they understand everything. Put them into groups to discuss the questions. Explain that there are no correct answers to the questions, so they must think for themselves and express their own ideas and opinions. Elicit some possible answers to each question and discuss as a class what sts think might happen next. Ask: Who wants to read this story now? Explain to sts where they can buy the book if they want to read it.

LITERATURE
UNITS 4-6

BEFORE YOU READ

1 Work in pairs and answer the questions.

1 What type of places do people like going to on their summer holidays?
2 Where can you stay when you go on holiday?

2 Read the outline to the story. Are the sentences true (T) or false (F)? Correct the false sentences.

1 The Dale family live in Sea Bird Cottage.
2 Smuggling means taking things out from people's houses and out of the country without permission.
3 Mrs Dale doesn't take the children to the hospital.

OUTLINE

The Boy from Yesterday

Pattie and Will Dale are two teenagers on holiday with their mother, Mrs Dale. They are staying in an old house called Sea Bird Cottage, in a village by the sea. Many years ago, men in the village used boats to bring things like tobacco and alcohol into the country from other countries without permission. This crime is called smuggling.

Sea Bird Cottage belongs to Mr Webb. He lives nearby in a large house with his grandson, Roger. Mrs Dale learns of a secret from Mrs Burns, a woman who lives in the village. She doesn't tell Pattie and Will.

The next day, Mrs Dale gets a telephone call. Her mother is in hospital. Mrs Dale leaves the children alone in the cottage and drives to the hospital for a few days.

The Boy from Yesterday

The Boy in the garden

At six o'clock, Pattie got out of bed and went across to her bedroom window.

'It's raining again!' she thought. She looked across the garden. 'We need to buy food from the village this morning. We're going to get wet!'

Then she saw someone. A figure moved between the trees.

The boy wore* black trousers, a grey shirt and some heavy shoes. But he had no coat. He moved slowly, very slowly, through the trees. Pattie could not see his face.

'Who is it?' Pattie thought. 'Of course, it's Roger! Mr Webb's grandson.'

She watched him for another minute or two.

Then, suddenly, he wasn't there!

▪■▪

'I think it was Roger,' Pattie said.

It was breakfast time.

'Did he see you?' Will asked.

'No, he didn't look at the cottage,' Pattie said. 'But there was something…'

'What?' Will said.

'His clothes,' Pattie said. 'They were … strange*. They were clothes that people wore a long time ago.'

'Maybe Roger likes old clothes,' Will said.

He finished his breakfast and got up. Suddenly, he heard the noise again. The noise under the cottage.

'What's that?' Pattie said.

'I don't know,' Will said. 'I heard it earlier. I think it's something in the cellar.'

'What cellar?' Pattie said.

LITERATURE
UNITS 4-6

LESSON OVERVIEW: In this lesson, sts read an extract of the novel *The Boy from Yesterday*. They read an outline of the novel, then read an extract and listen to the next part of the story. They end by discussing some of the issues that the extract raises.

WARMER

Read out the title of the book and focus on the picture. Explain to sts that they are going to read an extract from a book called *The Boy from Yesterday*. Write these words on the board: *Pattie and Will, holiday cottage, sea, smugglers in the past, boy in the wood, old-fashioned clothes, noise in the cellar*. Teach the meaning of the words, then put sts into pairs to discuss what the book might be about, using the title, the picture and the words on the board to help them. Elicit a few ideas but don't confirm them.

BACKGROUND INFORMATION

Smuggling was quite common around the coast of Britain in the past. People smuggled tobacco and alcohol into the country, so they didn't have to pay tax on it. Boats arrived at quiet places on the coast in the middle of the night, and the goods were unloaded secretly and carried ashore. Smuggling was a dangerous business, because soldiers guarded the coast and smugglers were often arrested or killed. The book *The Boy from Yesterday* is by the writer John Davage.

BEFORE YOU READ

1 Put sts into pairs to discuss the questions. Elicit answers from the class.

2 Ask sts to read the outline to the story, then decide if the sentences are true or false. Allow sts to compare their answers in pairs, then check with the class. Ask which of their ideas from the Warmer were correct.

Answers

1 F They are on holiday in Seabird Cottage.
2 F Smuggling means bringing things into the country without permission.
3 T

They looked for a cellar door for the next ten minutes. But they did not find one.

Their mother phoned again, an hour later. 'Gran is a little better,' Mrs Dale said to Pattie. 'But I'm going to stay here today. Are you all right?'

'We're OK, don't worry, Mum,' Pattie said.

'You need some food,' Mrs Dale began to say.

'We're going to the village shop later,' Pattie said.

'Is everything all right?' Mrs Dale asked.

'What do you mean?' Pattie said.

'At the cottage,' Mrs Dale said. 'Is everything all right at the cottage?'

Pattie thought about the strange noises, but she said, 'Yes, everything is all right. Give our love to Gran and Grandad.'

Twenty minutes later, she and Will went out. The rain was still very heavy and they walked through big pools of water to get across the garden. There was a stream next to the road, about twenty metres from the cottage. The water in the stream was very high.

'The water's nearly on the road,' Pattie said.

Will stopped and looked round.

'What's the matter?' Pattie asked.

'I saw somebody … yes, look! In the trees!' he said.

Pattie looked. 'I don't see anybody,' she said.

'He's not there now,' Will said.

'He?' she said.

'A boy.' Will looked at Pattie, then said, 'Roger? Maybe he's watching us.'

'But … why?' Pattie said.

'I don't know,' Will said.

Extract from **Richmond Readers**: *The Boy from Yesterday* by John Davage

READ

3 L3 **Read and listen to the extract from *The Boy from Yesterday*. Who did Will see in the trees?**

4 Read the extract again and choose the correct answers.

1 Pattie first sees a boy in the garden *in the morning / at night.*
2 The unusual thing about the boy in the garden is his *face / clothes.*
3 *Pattie / Will* hears the strange noise in the cottage first.
4 Mrs Dale was at the *cottage / hospital* all day.
5 Pattie and Will go outside *after / before* the rain stops.
6 While they are out, Will sees a boy *in the trees / on the road.*

5 Word Power When you learn an adjective, it's a good idea to also learn its opposite. Find these adjectives 1–5 in the text. Match them to their opposites a–e.

1 wet	a low
2 strange	b new
3 old	c light
4 heavy	d normal
5 high	e dry

6 L4 **Listen to the next part of the story. Complete the sentences with the correct words.**

1 By the time the teenagers arrive at the village shop, they are … and … .
2 In the shop, they buy some … and a … of cola.
3 They see old … and pictures of the … in a shop window.
4 Pattie sees a photo of … … house.
5 It says that in the past, smugglers … in the house.

REFLECT

7 THINK CRITICALLY Work in groups. Discuss the questions about the story.

1 Who is the strange boy in the old clothes Will and Pattie see?
2 What is the noise Will and Pattie hear under the cottage?
3 What is the secret that Mrs Burns tells Mrs Dale?
4 Why is the story called *The Boy from Yesterday*?
5 Do you know any other ghost stories? Do you think ghosts are real?

Glossary

cottage a small house in the country
cellar underground room in a house
all right when something is OK
stream a small, narrow river

3 L3 Read out the question, then play the audio. Sts read and listen to the extract and answer the question. Check the answer.

Answer
He saw a boy.

4 Read out the first sentence and elicit the correct answer. Sts then read the extract again and choose the correct words to complete the sentences. Check answers, eliciting the part of the extract which confirms each answer.

Answers
1 in the morning
2 clothes
3 Will
4 hospital
5 before
6 in the trees

5 **Word Power** Explain to sts that learning pairs of opposite adjectives is a good way to learn the meanings and increase your vocabulary. Ask sts to find the adjectives in the extract, then match them with their opposites. Check answers, and check that sts understand all the adjectives.

Answers
1 e 4 c 5 a
2 d 3 b

6 L4 Explain to sts that they will now hear the next part of the story. Read out the task, then allow sts time to read through the gapped sentences. Play the audio. See TG page 284 for audio script. Sts listen and complete the sentences. Check answers, playing the audio again and pausing if necessary to confirm the answers.

Answers
1 wet, cold
2 vegetables, bottle
3 postcards, village
4 Sea Bird
5 lived

REFLECT

21st Century skills

7 **THINK CRITICALLY**
Ask sts to read through the questions. Check they understand everything. Put them into groups to discuss the questions. Explain that there are no correct answers to the questions, so they must think for themselves and express their own ideas and opinions. Elicit some possible answers to each question and discuss as a class what sts think might happen next. Ask: *Who wants to read this story now?* Explain to sts where they can buy the book if they want to read it.

EXTRA PRACTICE
Put sts into groups of three. Explain that they are going to imagine that Pattie and Will see the boy again and manage to speak to him. Ask: *What questions do you think Pattie and Will might ask him?* Elicit a few example questions, e.g. *Who are you? What's your name? Why are you here? What do you know about the smugglers?* Write the questions on the board and elicit a few possible answers that the boy might give. Put sts into groups of three to role play a conversation between Pattie, Will and the boy. Monitor and help while they are working. Encourage them to use their imagination and think about what the boy's story might be. Ask some groups to perform their role play for the class.

LITERATURE
UNITS 7–9

MARIA'S DILEMMA

BEFORE YOU READ

1 What is a dilemma? Choose the correct definition a–c.

a an angry conversation between two people
b when two people have a different opinion about something
c when someone has to make a difficult choice between two different options

2 How do you feel when you have a dilemma? What do you do?

3 Read the outline to *Maria's Dilemma* and correct the sentences.

1 Maria's father is ill and can't pay for her to go on holiday.
2 Maria finds a dead woman next to the river.
3 Maria keeps the watch the woman was wearing.
4 The dead woman got married last Saturday.

OUTLINE

Maria's Dilemma

Maria is a foreign student at a university in England. One morning, she receives a letter from her father. He is unwell and can't work, and has no more money to pay for her studies. She goes for a walk by the river and finds the body of a woman in the water. The woman has an expensive necklace. Maria takes the necklace and runs off. She meets a friend and then calls the police.

The next morning, Maria reads about herself and the dead woman in the newspaper. Her name was Harriet Beecham. She was rich. She was at her sister's wedding when she ran to the river. The police think she was afraid of something. Her husband, Melvin, wants to know what happened.

Maria wants to sell the necklace. Then the police arrive.

READ

4 L5 Read and listen to the extract from *Maria's Dilemma*. What is the dilemma that Maria has?

A VISIT FROM THE POLICE

A tall, dark man and a shorter, dark woman were at the door.

'Maria Adami?' the man asked.

'Yes.'

'We are police detectives,' the woman said. 'I am Maggie and this is Bill. Can we come in?'

'Yes,' Maria said. They came in. Bill saw the newspaper.

'You're famous,' he said.

Maria couldn't speak. Her face was white.

'Sit down, Maria,' Maggie said. 'I must ask you some questions.' They all sat down. 'Now. What time did you find Mrs Beecham?' she asked.

'About seven thirty in the morning,' Maria answered.

'Did you see what clothes she had on?'

Maria knew what to say. 'I saw a shoe – only one shoe. And a green dress. I saw white arms – and a lot of long, dark hair.'

'Did you see a necklace, an emerald necklace?'

'I didn't see anything more. I was afraid. I ran away.'

'Yes, of course.'

'Harriet Beecham's husband wants to know about the necklace,' Bill explained. 'He thinks it is important. It was very expensive. Maybe someone killed Mrs Beecham because they wanted it.'

LITERATURE UNITS 7–9

LESSON OVERVIEW: In this lesson, sts read an extract of the novel *Maria's Dilemma*. They read an outline of the novel, then read an extract and listen to the next part of the story. They end by discussing some of the issues that the extract raises, and predicting what happens next in the story.

WARMER

Read out the title of the book and focus on the picture. Explain to sts that they are going to read an extract from a book called *Maria's Dilemma*. Write these words on the board: *Maria, university, money, walk by the river, dead body, expensive necklace, police*. Teach the meaning of the words, then put sts into pairs to discuss what the book might be about, using the title, the picture and the words on the board to help them. Elicit a few ideas but don't confirm them.

BACKGROUND INFORMATION

A lot of foreign students study at universities in England and the fees are very high. British students pay around £9,000 a year for their studies, but foreign students pay two or three times this amount. The book *Maria's Dilemma* is a crime novel by the writer Julia Newsome.

BEFORE YOU READ

1 Put sts into pairs to discuss the question. Check the answer with the class, and check that sts understand the meaning of *dilemma*.

Answer

c

2 Read out the question and elicit or suggest some possible answers, e.g. talk to a friend, ask for advice online, talk to parents, etc. Put sts into pairs to discuss the question. Discuss their answers as a class.

3 Ask sts to read the outline of the story, then correct the false sentences. Check answers. Ask sts which of their ideas from the Warmer were correct.

Answers

1 Maria's father is ill and can't pay for her studies.
2 Maria finds a dead woman in the river.
3 Maria keeps the necklace the woman was wearing.
4 The dead woman's sister got married last Saturday.

READ

4 L5 Read out the question, then play the audio. Sts read and listen to the extract and answer the question. Check the answer.

Answer

Her dilemma is that she took the dead woman's necklace, and now she doesn't know what to do.

'I – I don't know. I didn't see it.' Maria waited. She felt ill.

'OK, Maria, thank you,' Maggie said. She stood up. 'So we can tell Mr Beecham there was no necklace when you found her.' She looked at Maria for some moments.

Maria looked at Maggie.

'That's right,' she said.

'If you remember anything more, please telephone us.' Bill gave Maria the number.

'Yes, of course,' she said quietly.

'Goodbye, Maria.'

They left. Maria closed the door.

'What am I doing?' she thought, 'I take a necklace from a dead person. I tell a lie to the police. What am I going to do …?

'I'm going to take this very expensive necklace to London. I'm going to find someone to buy it. I'm going to put the money in the bank. I'm going to finish my studies. I'm going to go home to my family and get a very good job. That's what I'm going to do. It isn't going to be easy, but I must do it.'

It was eleven o'clock. Maria had a class. She took her books and went out.

A man got out of a car and walked behind her.

Extract from **Richmond Readers**: *Maria's Dilemma* by Julia Newsome

5 Read the extract again and complete the sentences with the correct words.

1 One of the police officers says Maria is famous after he sees the … .
2 The dead woman was wearing a green … and one … when Maria found her.
3 The police detectives ask Maria about the … .
4 One of the detectives gives Maria a … number.
5 Maria decides to sell the … in London.
6 When she goes to class, a … follows her.

6 Word Power In the story, Maria found the woman wearing a green dress. How many other items of clothes can you think of? Add them to the correct category.

Clothes for men	Clothes for women	Clothes for men or women
	dress	*shoes*

7 L6 Listen to the next part of the story. Discuss the questions with your partner.

1 How does Maria feel first of all?
  a happy
  b scared
  c surprised
2 Where is Maria going?
  a to university
  b home
  c to the police
3 How does the man feel when she talks to him?
  a angry
  b happy
  c surprised
4 Who is the man?
  a a police officer
  b Harriet's husband
  c the husband of Harriet's sister
5 What does he ask Maria?
  a Does she know Harriet?
  b What was Harriet wearing when she found her?
  c Where is Harriet now?
6 Where does the man want to go with Maria?
  a to university
  b to the place she found Harriet
  c to the police station

8 THINK CRITICALLY Work in groups. Discuss the questions about the story.

1 What do you think Barry Lyle wants from Maria?
2 Why do you think the necklace is so important?
3 What do you think Maria should do with the necklace?
4 What do you think happens next?

Glossary

detective a person who catches criminals
emerald bright green colour
run away to escape from a person or a place
some moments a long period of time

5 Read out the first sentence and elicit the missing word. Sts then read the extract again and complete the sentences with the correct words. Check answers, eliciting the part of the extract which confirms each answer.

Answer

1 newspaper	4 phone
2 necklace, shoe	5 necklace
3 necklace	6 man

6 **Word Power** Explain to sts that it is useful to learn vocabulary in sets. Put sts into pairs to copy the table into their notebooks and add as many more items of clothing as they can. Draw the table on the board and elicit words to complete it. Check that sts understand all the words.

Possible answers
Clothes for men: tie
Clothes for women: dress, skirt, tights, blouse, top
Clothes for men or women: trousers, shorts, jacket, shirt, coat, T-shirt, jumper, boots

7 L6 Explain to sts that they will now hear the next part of the story. Read out the task, then allow sts time to read through the questions and possible answers. Play the audio. See TG page 284 for audio script. Sts listen and choose the correct answers. Check answers, playing the audio again and pausing if necessary to confirm the answers.

Answer

1 b	4 c	6 b
2 a	3 c	5 a

REFLECT

21st Century skills

8 **THINK CRITICALLY**
Ask sts to read through the questions. Check they understand everything. Put them into groups to discuss the questions. Explain that there are no correct answers to the questions, so they must think for themselves and express their own ideas and opinions. Elicit some possible answers to each question and discuss as a class what sts think might happen next. Ask: *Who wants to read this story now?* Explain to sts where they can buy the book if they want to read it.

EXTRA PRACTICE
Ask: *Is Maria a criminal? Should she go to prison for what she did?* Elicit a few answers from individual sts, then divide the class in half. Ask sts in one half of the class to work in pairs and prepare reasons why Maria is a criminal and should go to prison. Ask sts in the other half of the class to work in pairs and prepare reasons why she is not a criminal and should not go to prison. Monitor and help while sts are working. Tell sts they are now going to debate the question. Elicit all the reasons why Maria is a criminal and should go to prison. Make notes on the board. Then do the same with all the reasons why she is not a criminal and should not go to prison. Ask: Which reasons do you think are the strongest? Why? Elicit answers from individual sts, and encourage sts to agree and disagree with each other. End with a class vote to decide the final 'verdict'.

EXAM PRACTICE
UNIT 1

LISTENING
Multiple choice

Look! **About the task**

In this listening task, you will hear five short dialogues relating to five questions.
You must read each question, listen to the dialogue and choose from pictures A–C. Each dialogue is played twice.

Useful strategies

- Before you listen, read the question and look at the three pictures underneath it. Think about the types of words you are going to hear.
- You'll hear something about all the pictures for each question. Listen for the whole meaning, not just individual words.

1 E1.1 **Read and listen to EXAM TASK question 1 below. Underline all the different times in the text.**

Dad: Molly, it's already eight o'clock! It's nearly time to leave the house.
Molly: It's OK, Dad. I've got lots of time. My bus is at half past eight.
Dad: But it takes twenty-five minutes to walk to the bus stop.
Molly: I can walk really fast, Dad! I leave at quarter past eight every day. Don't worry!

2 E1.1 **Now listen to the dialogue for question 1 again. Which is the correct time? Discuss with a partner and write the answer in your notebook.**

3 **Now look at the pictures in the EXAM TASK for questions 2–5. For each question, write down the types of words you think you will hear in your notebook.**

4 E1.2 **Listen and write the answers to questions 2–5 in your notebook. Compare your answers with a partner.**

EXAM TASK

For each question, listen and choose the correct picture.

1 What time is Molly's bus?

A

B

C

2 Where is Tom's phone?

A

B

C

3 Which photo are they looking at?

A

B

C

4 Which is Jake's house?

A

B

C

5 When is David's party?

A

B

C

EXAM PRACTICE
UNIT 1

LESSON OVERVIEW: This lesson provides practice of a Listening multiple choice exam task. It also reviews some of the language sts have learned in Unit 1.

Skill	Exam task
Listening	Multiple choice

WARMER
Play a game to revise numbers, times and dates. Put sts into teams. Write a selection of six numbers on the board first, e.g. 7, 11, 14, 23, 30. Teams race to decide how to say the numbers. Once a team is confident, they put up their hands. If they can say all the numbers correctly, they get a point. If not, don't correct them but wait until a team can say all the numbers correctly. Repeat this with six times of day, e.g. 7.00, 8.15, 9.30, 11.45, 12.00, then repeat it with six dates, e.g. 13/03, 12/05, 22/06, 27/08, 30/09.

BACKGROUND INFORMATION
In this exam task, sts hear five short dialogues. For each dialogue, there is a question and three pictures. Sts listen to each dialogue and choose the picture which gives the correct answer to the question. They will have enough time before they listen to look at all the pictures and read the questions. They hear the recording twice.

1 E1.1 Explain to sts that they are going to practise a listening exam task. Read the information in the Look! box with the class. Point out that the answers to the multiple choice questions are pictures rather than words.

Read through the Useful strategies with the class. Point out to sts that it is really important to listen carefully and not choose an answer just because they hear a word related to that answer. Tell them they will hear words related to all the answers, so they need to listen carefully to hear which one is correct.

Play the audio. See TG page 284 for audioscript. Sts read and listen to Exam task question 1 and underline all the different times in the text. Check answers.

Answer
The times are eight o'clock, half past eight, quarter past eight

2 E1.1 Play the audio for sts to listen to the dialogue again. Sts discuss with a partner and note down the correct time. Elicit which is the correct answer and why.

Answer
The correct picture is C, half past eight.
A is wrong because 8 o'clock is the time now.
B is wrong because Molly leaves the house at quarter past eight.
C is right because Molly says 'My bus is at half past eight.'

3 Remind sts of the information in the Useful strategies box to think about some of the words you might hear. Put them into pairs to look at the pictures for Questions 2–5 and write down some words they might hear in their notebooks. Discuss their ideas as a class.

Sample answers
2 phone, bookshelf, bag, desk
3 parents, grandparents, mother, father, aunt, uncle, brother, man, woman
4 garden, house, park, road, cars
5 12 March, 16 March, 17 March, party day, weekend

4 E1.2 Play the audio for sts to listen and complete Questions 2–5. See TG page 284 for audioscript. Play the audio again for them to check and complete their answers. Put sts into pairs to compare their answers and say and write why they chose each answer. To check answers, focus on each question in turn. Ask sts which answer they chose and why, then play the audio for that question, pausing to confirm the correct answer.

Answers
2 B 3 C 4 A 5 C

EXAM PRACTICE UNIT 2

READING
Open cloze

Look! About the task

In this reading task, you will complete a short text with some words missing. You will need to write one word for each gap. Your spelling must be correct.

Useful strategies

- Read through the text once to get an idea of the topic.
- Think about the type of word you need for each gap. Does it fit with the meaning of the whole sentence?
- Read the whole text again. This time, check your spelling and make sure it all makes sense.

1 Read sentences 1–8 below. What type of word is missing in each sentence? Choose the correct answer.

1 ... does she live?
 a a question word
 b a preposition
2 I come from ... in Colombia.
 a a verb
 b a noun
3 There aren't many people ... my class, it's very small.
 a a preposition
 b a pronoun
4 I ... to the cinema every Saturday.
 a a verb
 b a preposition
5 The English test is ... Monday morning.
 a a question word
 b a preposition
6 It's really cold. ... is the temperature today?
 a a noun
 b a question word
7 Lucy isn't Spanish, ...'s English.
 a a pronoun
 b a question word
8 We play ... after school.
 a a noun
 b a preposition

2 Look at gap 1 in the EXAM TASK and answer questions 1–3 below. Use example answer 0 to help you.

1 What type of word do you need here?
2 How do you know? Discuss with a partner.
3 What do you think the correct word is here? Why?

3 Now complete the gaps for 2–5 of the EXAM TASK. Compare your answers with a partner. What type of words did you use?

EXAM TASK

This is a blog about Rosa's life, school and favourite sport. Read the text and complete the sentences by writing one word for each gap in your notebook.

Example 0 *you*

Home · Board · Reply

Thank [0] ... for visiting my blog. It's full of articles about my life, my school and my favourite sport – football!

So, [1] ... am I? Well, my name is Rosa, and I'm fourteen years old. I come from Manchester, [2] ... England, and I go to a secondary school [3] ... to my house. There [4] ... 1,500 students at my school! My P.E. teacher [5] ... really nice, and we've got a lot of clubs to go to. I'm in the football club, of course! It's on Wednesdays after school and it's [6] ... the gym. It's really good fun. [7] ... about your school? Which is your favourite [8] ...? Is it football, too?

I hope you enjoy my blog. If you do, please leave me a comment and tell me about your life.

EXAM PRACTICE
UNIT 2

LESSON OVERVIEW: This lesson provides practice of a Reading open cloze exam task. It also reviews some of the language sts have learned in Unit 2.

Skill	Exam task
Reading	Open cloze

WARMER

Put sts into teams. Tell them you are going to read out some sentences with a missing word, and they must guess the missing word. Read out these sentences in turn, pausing or coughing to indicate the gap. Teams race to say the missing word in each sentence. Repeat each correct sentence once sts have guessed the answers.

1 *Have you ... any brothers or sisters?*
2 *There's ... pen on the table.*
3 *There aren't ... clothes in the wardrobe.*
4 *Where ... you live?*
5 *What time ... Sam get up?*
6 *I go ... bed at nine o'clock.*

Answers

1 got	3 any	5 does
2 a	4 do	6 to

BACKGROUND INFORMATION

In this exam task, sts read a short text. There are eight missing words, and sts must complete the gaps with one word in each. The words are usually grammatical words, e.g. articles, auxiliary verbs, prepositions, pronouns, etc. Students must spell the words correctly in order to get the marks.

1 Explain to sts that they are going to practise a reading exam task. Read the information in the Look! box with the class. Point out that they must only write one word in each gap, and they must spell the word correctly. Explain that the words are usually grammatical words such as articles, auxiliary verbs, prepositions or pronouns.

Read through the Useful strategies with the class. Point out to sts that it is really important to read the text around each gap carefully and think about what type of word is missing, rather than just guessing. Tell them it is also important to read the whole text when they have finished, to make sure it makes sense with the words added.

Put sts into pairs to look at the sentences and decide what type of word is missing in each sentence. Check the answers. You could then ask them in their pairs to think about what word is missing in each sentence. Check answers.

Answers

1 a	3 a	5 b	7 a
2 b	4 a	6 b	8 a

2 Ask sts to read the text quickly, ignoring the gaps. Ask some questions to check comprehension, e.g. *What kind of text is it?* (a blog). *How old is Rosa?* (14). *What sports does she do?* (football). Point out the example and answer. Ask sts to look at the first gap carefully and answer the questions. Check the answers.

Answers

1 You need a question word.
2 You know because there is a question mark (?).
3 The correct answer is 'who'. You know because she tells you her name.

3 Remind sts of the information in the Useful strategies box, and remind them to read the text through when they have finished, to check that it makes sense. Sts then complete the exam task. Allow them to compare their answers in pairs, then check answers with the class.

Answers

1 who	3 next	5 is	7 What
2 in	4 are	6 in	8 sport

EXAM PRACTICE
UNIT 3

SPEAKING
Introductions

Look! About the task

In this speaking task, the examiner will ask you for some simple personal information. They will also ask about your daily life and your interests. Practise asking and answering these types of questions with a partner to help you with the EXAM TASK.

Useful strategies

- Try to relax before you answer each question.
- If you don't understand the question, ask the examiner to repeat it.
- When the examiner says, 'Tell me about ...', try to give a long answer using two or three sentences.

1 E3.1 **Maria and her teacher are practising for the speaking test. Match questions 1–6 with answers a–f. Listen and check.**

1 What's your name?
2 How old are you?
3 Where do you live?
4 What's your favourite subject at school?
5 What do you usually do at the weekend?
6 Tell me something about your bedroom.

a I watch TV.
b Madrid.
c It's small.
d Maria.
e History.
f 13.

2 Read the statements below. Are they true (T) or false (F)? Correct the false sentences.

1 Maria doesn't answer all the questions.
2 Maria gives a lot of information.
3 Maria gives short answers.
4 Maria asks the teacher to repeat a question.

3 E3.2 **Now listen to Maria in her speaking test. Copy and complete the sentences below, in your notebook. Why are Maria's answers better this time? Discuss with a partner.**

1 I'm Maria. ... 13. I ... ... Madrid.
2 Well, I'm ... at Maths, but I ... History.
3 Lots of things! I usually ... TV and ... computer games. I also like ... my bike and I sometimes visit my grandma, too.
4 Well, I share it with my ... . It isn't ... big, but we like it. We've got a ... for our books and ... of pictures on the walls.

4 Now complete the EXAM TASK.

EXAM TASK

Work in pairs. Student A and Student B take turns to ask and answer the questions.

Student A
1 What's your name?
2 How old are you?
3 Where do you live?
4 Who do you live with?
5 What do you usually do in the evening?
6 Tell me something about your home.

Student B
1 What's your name?
2 How old are you?
3 Where do you come from?
4 What clothes do you wear to school?
5 What do you never do at the weekend?
6 Tell me something about your favourite teacher.

EXAM PRACTICE
UNIT 3

LESSON OVERVIEW: This lesson provides practice of a Speaking exam task. It also reviews some of the language sts have learned in Unit 3.

Skill	Exam task
Speaking	Introductions

WARMER

Put sts into teams. Tell them you are going to give some answers to some questions, and they must guess the questions. Read out these answers. Award a point to the first team that gives a correct possible question.

1 *My name's Sam.*
2 *I'm fourteen years old.*
3 *I live in London.*
4 *My favourite sport is tennis.*
5 *I've got one brother and one sister.*
6 *I like to go swimming.*

Sample answers
1 What's your name?
2 How old are you?
3 Where do you live?
4 What's your favourite sport?
5 Have you got any brothers and sisters?
6 What do you like to do (at the weekend)?

BACKGROUND INFORMATION

In this exam task, sts talk to an examiner. They go into the exam in pairs, but for this part of the exam they only talk to the examiner, not their partner. They answer six questions about themselves, their daily life and their interests. They can give short, factual answers to the first few questions, but they should try to give slightly longer answers to the last few questions.

1 E3.1 Explain to sts that they are going to practise a speaking exam task. Read the information in the Look! box with the class. Explain to sts that there is no need to be nervous about this part of the exam because they just need to relax and talk about themselves. Tell them that the examiner will be friendly and encouraging.

Read through the Useful strategies with the class. Elicit some ways of asking the examiner to repeat a question, e.g. *Can you repeat the question, please? Can you say that again, please?* Tell sts they don't have to give longer answers to all the questions, just the ones that begin *Tell me about …* . Sts match the questions with the answers.

Play the audio for sts to listen and check their answers. See TG page 284 for audio script. Check answers with the class.

Answers

1 d	3 b	5 a
2 f	4 e	6 c

2 Sts could work in pairs to read the statements and decide if they are true or false, then correct the false statements. Check answers.

Answers
1 F. Maria answers all the questions.
2 F. Maria doesn't give a lot of information.
3 T
4 T

3 E3.2 Allow sts time to copy Maria's answers, then play the audio for them to listen and complete the answers into their notebooks. See TG page 285 for audio script. Allow sts to compare their answers in pairs and discuss why Maria's answers are better this time. Check answers.

Answers
1 I'm, live in
2 good, love
3 watch, play, riding
4 sister, very, bookcase, walls

4 Ask sts to look at the exam task and read the instructions. Put them into pairs and ask them to decide who is Student A and who is Student B. Read through all the questions with the class and check sts understand them all. Sts then work in pairs to ask and answer the questions. When they have finished, ask which questions they found difficult to answer and why, and ask who managed to give longer answers to the last two questions. If sts need more practice, they could work with a new partner and repeat the task. Point out to them that the more they practise, the more their speaking will improve.

EXAM PRACTICE
UNIT 4

READING
Multiple matching

Look! About the task

In this reading task, you will read a long text with five paragraphs. You will match each paragraph to a list of six titles. There is one title that isn't needed.

Useful strategies

- Read the text through once to help you understand the topic. Underline the important words in each paragraph.
- Now read all the paragraph titles and underline the important words in each title.
- Carefully read through each paragraph. Remember to choose the title because it matches the main idea of each paragraph, not just because it matches a word in the paragraph.

1 **Read the EXAM TASK instructions and look at the pictures. Why do you think people go to Cancun? Discuss with a partner.**

2 **Next, read the text from start to finish. Write down any important words you find in each paragraph, in your notebook.**

3 **Now read paragraph titles a–f and choose the best title for paragraph 1. The title must match the main idea in the paragraph.**

4 **Now work with a partner to match the other titles to Paragraphs 2–5, using the same strategy. Which title was not needed?**

EXAM TASK

Read the text about Cancun. Choose the best title for each paragraph.

Paragraph 1

More than two million tourists travel to the Mexican city of Cancun each year. They go there for its beautiful, white, sandy beaches, and because there is a lot to do. Most visitors come from the USA, but people from all over Mexico, and other parts of the world, also come to stay in this amazing city.

Paragraph 2

Cancun has a tropical climate so the weather is hot all year round. There are just two seasons – a rainy season from May to October and a dry season from November to April. It's a good idea to book your holiday in the dry season if you can. It's a bit cooler then, and of course you won't get wet!

Paragraph 3

There are lots of fantastic activities to choose from in Cancun. You can lie on the beach, swim with dolphins, go surfing or go for a boat trip to a beautiful island. There are also several museums to visit or you can go to the Mayan ruins near the city.

Paragraph 4

The Zona Hotelera, or Hotel Zone in Cancun, is 27 km long. It has accommodation, restaurants, beaches, shops and even an underwater museum of art, called MUSA! There are many different kinds of hotels for families and young people.

Paragraph 5

People with a driver's licence, who are over 25, can rent a car. If that is not possible, you can take a taxi or a bus. Buses in Cancun go between the Hotel Zone and popular tourist attractions from 6.00 a.m. until midnight every day. There are also many ferries to take you to the islands near Cancun.

1 Paragraph 1 ...
2 Paragraph 2 ...
3 Paragraph 3 ...
4 Paragraph 4 ...
5 Paragraph 5 ...

a The best time of year to visit Cancun
b Where to stay in Cancun
c How to travel around Cancun
d Things to do in Cancun
e Interesting buildings in Cancun
f Why Cancun is so popular

EXAM PRACTICE
UNIT 4

LESSON OVERVIEW: This lesson provides practice of a Reading multiple matching exam task. It also reviews some of the language sts have learned in Unit 4.

Skill	Exam task
Reading	Multiple matching

WARMER

Ask: *What do you know about Cancun? Which country is it in? Is it a small town or a big city? What's the weather like there?* Elicit what sts know about Cancun. If they don't know much about the city, ask them to look at the pictures and guess the answers.

BACKGROUND INFORMATION

In this exam task, sts read a longer text, with five paragraphs. They have to choose a title for each paragraph, from a list of six titles. There is one title they don't need to use. In order to do the task, they have to read each paragraph to understand the general meaning, and match this to the correct title. They do not need to understand all the details of the text, so they should not be put off if there are words they don't understand.

1 Explain to sts that they are going to practise a reading multiple matching exam task. Read the information in the Look! box with the class. Point out the paragraph headings in the text, and the list of titles at the bottom of the text. Read through the Useful strategies with the class. Point out to sts that it is important to read the text right through first, to get a general idea of what it is about. Tell them they shouldn't worry if they don't understand every word, but should keep reading to the end, to get an idea of what the whole text is about before they do the matching task. Read out the Exam task instructions, then ask: *Why do you think people go to Cancun?* Ask sts to discuss their ideas with a partner. Elicit a few ideas, but don't confirm them.

2 Ask sts to read the whole text through. They write down any important words in their notebooks. Allow sts to compare their answers in pairs, then check with the class. to see if their ideas from Exercise 1 were correct.

Sample answer
To have a holiday, to relax, to swim, to see wildlife, to visit museums, to go to restaurants, etc.

3 Ask sts to read paragraph titles a–f and choose the best title for paragraph 1. Tell them to note down the words and phrases in the paragraph that match the idea in the title. Check the answer with the class, eliciting which words and phrases in the paragraph match the title.

Answer
f
More than <u>two million tourists travel to the Mexican city of Cancun each year</u>. They go there for its beautiful white sandy beaches, its crystal-clear water, and because there is so much to do there. <u>Most visitors come from the USA but people from all over Mexico, and other parts of the world too</u>, come to stay in this wonderful city.

4 Sts work with a partner to match the other titles to paragraphs 2–5. Check answers with the class, eliciting the words and phrases from each paragraph which match the idea in the correct title. Ask sts which title was not needed.

Answers
2 a (hot all year round, two seasons, good idea to book your holiday in the dry season)
3 d (lots of fantastic activities, lie on the beach, swim with dolphins, go surfing, boat trip, museums, Mayan ruins)
4 b (accommodation, many different kinds of hotels)
5 c (rent a car, take a taxi, go by bus, ferries)

Title e was not needed.

EXAM PRACTICE
UNIT 5

LISTENING
A set of notes

Look! **About the task**

In this listening task, you will hear a short monologue and complete a set of notes. You will fill each gap with a word, number, time, date or price. You will hear the monologue twice.

Useful strategies

- Before listening, read the set of notes from start to finish. What kind of information is missing?
- The first time you listen, try to write down all the answers in one go. Listen again and check your answers.
- Remember to write prices and times in numbers, not words.
- Remember to also check your spelling.

1 E5.1 **Look at the pairs of dates, times, prices and numbers below. Listen, choose and write the correct answers in your notebook.**

1 17 October / 7 October
2 £6.00 / £9.00
3 1.15 / 1.30
4 07386 446 281 / 07376 885 291
5 Jones / James

2 **Now look at the EXAM TASK. Match each question to the type of answer it is.**

Question 1	a price
Question 2	a date
Question 3	an item
Question 4	a time
Question 5	a person

3 E5.2 **Read and listen to the first part of the teacher's talk. Which days of the week do you hear? Discuss with a partner.**

OK, everyone. Listen, please. I want to give you some information about the new school cooking club. Some of you have activities every Thursday and Friday, so this club is on Wednesday.

4 **Why is the new school cooking club on Wednesday? Discuss with a partner.**

5 E5.3 **Now read the EXAM TASK instructions and copy the set of notes into your notebook. Finally, listen and complete the notes with your answers.**

EXAM TASK

You will hear a teacher talking about a school cooking club. Complete the missing information in the leaflet for items 1–5. Remember to write one word, a number, a date or a time.

SCHOOL COOKING CLUB

Day:	*Wednesday*
Start date:	(1) ...
Time:	(2) ... p.m. to ... p.m.
Name of teacher:	(3) Mr ...
Cost per week:	(4) £...
What to take next week:	(5) ...

6 **Which parts of the EXAM task did you find easy and which parts did you find difficult? Discuss your answers with a partner.**

EXAM PRACTICE
UNIT 5

LESSON OVERVIEW: This lesson provides practice of a Listening note completion exam task. It also reviews some of the language sts have learned in Unit 5.

Skill	Exam task
Listening	Note completion

WARMER

Put sts into teams. Tell them you are going to test them on numbers, dates, prices and spellings. Read out the following sentences and ask teams to write down the number or name in each one. Check answers by inviting sts to come to the board to write the correct numbers or words on the board.

1 *My phone number is 07978 462 015.*
2 *These shoes cost £49.80.*
3 *My birthday is on 23 July.*
4 *The train leaves at 10.15.*
5 *My family name is Hardwick – that's H – A – R – D – W – I – C- K.*

See which team got the most answers right and discuss with sts which ones they found difficult and why.

BACKGROUND INFORMATION

In this exam task, sts hear an announcement or message. They have a set of notes which they must complete with the details that they hear. The details can be an individual word, or they can be a number, date or price. They can also be a name, which will be spelled for sts to listen and write.

1 E5.1 Explain to sts that they are going to practise a listening note completion exam task. Read the information in the Look! box with the class. Point out to sts that they will hear the recording twice, so they shouldn't worry if they don't manage to complete all the notes the first time they listen.

Read through the Useful strategies with the class. Remind sts that with all listening tasks, it is helpful to read through all the information before you listen, to try to predict the kind of information you are listening for. Point out to sts that it is better to write times and prices in numbers (e.g. 4.30 rather than *half past four*), as there is less chance they will make a mistake.

Allow sts time to read through the pairs of numbers and words. Elicit which one is a date, a time, a price and a phone number. Play the audio for sts to listen and choose the ones they hear. See TG page 285 for audio script. Check answers, playing the audio again and pausing to confirm the answers.

Answers
1 17 October
2 £9.00
3 1.30
4 07386 446 281
5 Jones

2 Ask sts to read through the exam task. Ask: *Who will you hear speaking?* (a teacher) *What are they giving information about?* (the school cooking club). Sts then focus on the notes and match each question to the kind of information they need to write in the gap. Check answers.

Answers
1 a date
2 a time
3 a person
4 a price
5 an item

3 E5.2 Focus on the example answer in the notes. Point out that in the recording, more than one day, price, time, etc. will be mentioned for each answer, so it is important to listen carefully to hear the correct one. Play the audio. See SB page p122 for audio script. Sts read and listen to the recording and answer the questions. Check the answers.

Answer
The teacher mentions three days (Thursday, Friday, Wednesday).
Wednesday is the correct answer because the teacher says: *this club is on Wednesday.*

4 Ask sts to discuss the question with a partner. Check the answer.

Answer
Some of the students have activities every Thursday and Friday.

5 E5.3 Read the exam task instructions with the class and give them time to copy the set of notes into their notebooks. Play the audio for sts to listen and complete the exam task. See TG page 285 for audio script. Play the audio again for them to check and complete their answers. Put sts into pairs to compare their answers and discuss why they wrote each answer. Check answers, playing the audio again and pausing to confirm the answers.

Answers
1 9 January
2 3.30 / 4.30
3 Gastrell
4 2
5 chicken and vegetables

6 Give sts time to discuss the questions. Ask some pairs to tell the class their answers. Discuss with the whole class.

EXAM PRACTICE
UNIT 6

WRITING
A short message

Look! **About the task**

In this writing task, you will write a short note or message, such as an email. You must answer all the questions or prompts and use the correct number of words written in the EXAM TASK instructions.

Useful strategies

- When writing an email, think about the type of information you need to include: Who are you writing to? Why are you writing to them?
- Make sure you have included all the information you need for the EXAM TASK and have used the correct number of words.
- Remember to check your writing for spelling and punctuation errors.

1 Read the email below and answer questions 1–2.

1 What is Alex's email about? Discuss with a partner.

2 What four pieces of information does Alex ask for in his email? Write them down in your notebook.

From: Alex

To Ana,

How are you? Guess what? My parents and I are visiting your country for a holiday next year! I'm so excited – I can't wait! What's the best time of year to visit and why? Where should we go? What activities can we do there? Which are the best attractions to visit?

Write soon,

Alex

2 Read the Useful Strategies and Alex's email again. Read and compare Sofia and Devrim's responses. Remember to check that they include all the information needed. Which reponse is better? Why? Discuss with a partner.

Hi Alex,

I think it's a great idea you come to Slovakia! Come in autumn because the weather is warm and dry.

You can go at capital city, Bratislava and visit the castle. It's very interesting!

Bye!

Sofia

Hello Alex,

Turkey is great for a holiday. You can, go to beautiful beeches the best time to come is spring or autumn. In summer is too hot and there is too much tourists.

Devrim

3 Read and complete the example email reponse to Alex's email below, using the words and phrases from the box. Is this email response better than Sophia and Devrim's email responses? Why? Discuss with a partner.

football stadium	spring	warm and sunny	match	Madrid

Hi Alex,

Spain is great! You must visit [1] … in [2] … because it's [3] … . You can visit the [4] … and watch a [5] … .

Have fun!

4 Now complete the EXAM TASK. Check it carefully. Answer all the questions and correct any mistakes.

EXAM TASK

You are going to the wildlife park with your English friend Jo, tomorrow. Write a note to Jo using 25 words or more.

Say:

- Where you want to meet
- What time you want to meet
- What animals you want to see

EXAM PRACTICE
UNIT 6

LESSON OVERVIEW: This lesson provides practice of a short message writing exam task. It also reviews some of the language sts have learned in Unit 6.

Skill	Exam task
Writing	A short message

WARMER

Ask: *What kinds of messages can you write to people?* Elicit a few ideas, e.g. emails, notes, text messages. Ask: *Who do you write messages to? Who writes messages to you? What do you write messages about?* Elicit a few answers from individual sts.

BACKGROUND INFORMATION

In this exam task, sts write a short message to a friend. The instructions for the message include three questions or prompts, and sts must answer all of these in their message. They should write a minimum of 25 words. They can write more words than this, but they should aim not to write too many more.

1 Explain to sts that they are going to practise a writing exam task in which they have to write a short message to a friend. Read the information in the Look! box with the class. Point out that in order to get a good mark, they must answer all the questions or prompts in the task, and they must write at least 25 words.

Read through the Useful strategies with the class. Reinforce the point that it is really important to answer all the questions and write at least 25 words. Remind them that with any writing task, they should always check their grammar and spelling carefully when they have finished.

Sts read the email and answer the questions. They could work in pairs for this. Check the answers with the class.

Answers
1 asking for information/advice about visiting Ana's country
2 the best time to come / why; where they should go; what activities they can do / which attractions to visit

2 Ask sts to read the Useful strategies again, then read the two answers. Tell them they should check each answer against the instructions in the Useful language, to decide which one is better and why. Allow sts to compare their answers in pairs, then check with the class. As an extra activity, sts could work in pairs and correct the mistakes in the two answers.

Answers
Sofia's answer is better. Devrim's answer has enough words, but there are spelling and punctuation mistakes and he hasn't answered the question *What activities can we do there?*

3 Sts read the email and complete it with the correct words and phrases. Check answers and point out that although this email is quite short, it is still over 25 words and answers all the questions in the task, so it is a good answer.

Answers
1 Madrid
2 spring
3 warm and sunny
4 football stadium
5 match

4 Ask sts to read the exam task. Ask a few questions to check comprehension: *What do you need to write?* (a note). *Who do you write to?* (your friend Jo). *Where are you going?* (to the wildlife park). *What three things should you include?* (where to meet, what time to meet, what animals you want to see). Sts then complete the exam task. Refer them back to the Useful strategies to help them check their answer. Sts could check each other's messages in pairs. Elicit a model answer and write it on the board.

Sample answer
Hi Jo,
I'm excited about our visit to the wildlife park tomorrow. Let's meet at the bus stop at 9.30 in the morning. I really want to see the monkeys!
See you tomorrow!

EXAM PRACTICE UNIT 7

LISTENING
Multiple choice

Look! About the task

In this listening task, you will hear a conversation and answer five multiple-choice questions about it. Some questions include facts and details, others talk about feelings or opinions. You will hear the conversation twice.

Useful strategies

- Before listening, read all the instructions and questions.
- You will hear some information about all three answers, but only one answer is correct. Listen for the whole meaning.
- The first time you listen, choose an answer. Listen again and check your answer.

1 **Look at the instructions and questions 1–5 in the EXAM TASK. Work with a partner and answer questions 1–4 below.**

1 Who is speaking?
2 What are they talking about?
3 Which questions in this task are about facts?
4 Which questions in this task are about opinions or feelings?

2 E7.1 **Look at EXAM TASK question 1. Now read and listen to the first part of the conversation below. Which is the correct answer: a, b or c? Why? Discuss with a partner.**

Mum: How was your shopping trip, Toby? Was the new shopping centre nice?

Toby: Yes, I liked it Mum. It's really big, and I found some amazing trainers ... and they were cheap, too! But there were a lot of people at the shopping centre. It was very busy!

3 E7.2 **Now complete the rest of the EXAM TASK. Listen to the full conversation and answer questions 2–5.**

EXAM TASK

You will hear Toby talking to his mum about a shopping trip. For each question, choose the correct answer.

1 Toby thinks the shopping centre was ...
  a small.
  b busy.
  c expensive.
2 Toby travelled to the shopping centre ...
  a on foot.
  b by train.
  c by bus.
3 The shopping centre does not have a ...
  a sandwich shop.
  b cinema.
  c restaurant.
4 How much were Toby's new jeans?
  a £20
  b £30
  c £50
5 Toby's mum isn't happy about ...
  a the price of Toby's jeans.
  b the colour of Toby's jeans.
  c the size of Toby's jeans.

4 **Compare your answers with a partner. Which questions were difficult to answer? Why? Discuss your answers.**

EXAM PRACTICE
UNIT 7

LESSON OVERVIEW: This lesson provides practice of a Listening multiple choice exam task. It also reviews some of the language sts have learned in Unit 7.

Skill	Exam task
Listening	Multiple choice

WARMER

Ask: *Do you like shopping or hate it? Why? Where do you usually go shopping for clothes?* Elicit a few ideas, and elicit or teach the word *shopping centre*. Ask: *Is there a big shopping centre in your town? Where is it? How can you get there? Are there cafés and restaurants there? Is there a cinema? Which are your favourite shops there? Are the clothes cheap or expensive?* Elicit a few answers from individual sts.

BACKGROUND INFORMATION

In this exam task, sts hear a longer dialogue. They answer five multiple-choice questions, with three choices for each question. Some questions are about specific information in the recording, and others are about the feelings or opinions of the speakers.

1 Explain to sts that they are going to practise a listening multiple choice exam task. Read the information in the Look! box with the class. Remind sts that they have already practised one multiple choice listening task, where the answers were pictures rather than words. Point out that in this task the answers are written. Remind them that for all listening exam tasks, they hear the recording twice, so they shouldn't worry if they can't answer all the questions the first time they listen.

Read through the Useful strategies with the class. Emphasise the point that the recording will mention all the options in the answers, so they shouldn't choose an answer just because they hear it. They must listen carefully to hear which one is the correct answer.

Ask sts to read the exam task and all the questions. They then work in pairs to answer the questions. Check answers.

Answers

1 A boy (called Toby) and his mum.
2 They're talking about the boy's trip to a new shopping centre.
3 Questions 2,3 and 4 are about facts.
4 Questions 1 and 5 are about opinions and feelings.

2 E7.1 Ask sts to read the first question and possible answers again, then play the audio. See TG page 285 for audio script. Sts read and listen to the first part of the dialogue and choose the correct answer. Elicit which is the correct answer and why.

Answer

The answer is B – busy. This is because Toby says 'But there were a lot of people there. It was very busy!'

3 E7.2 Play the audio for sts to listen and complete the exam task. See TG page 285 for audio script. Play the audio again for them to check and complete their answers.

4 Put sts into pairs to compare their answers and discuss which were difficult and which were easy. Check the answers with the class, playing the audio again and pausing for sts to hear the correct answers.

Answer

1 b 2 c 3 b 4 a 5 b

EXAM PRACTICE UNIT 8

READING
Multiple choice

Look! About the task

In this reading task, you will read a long text and answer five multiple-choice questions. There is roughly one question for each paragraph.

Useful strategies

- Read through the whole text once to get an idea of the topic.
- Look at each question and underline any important words.
- Read and underline any words in the text that match the words you underlined in the questions. This will help you to choose the correct answer for each question.

1 **Read the title of the text and look at the picture. What would you like to know about Leo? Write three questions in your notebook.**

2 **Read the whole text in the EXAM TASK. Can you find the answers to your three questions? Write them in your notebook.**

3 **Next, read question 1 in the EXAM TASK. Find the words 'became interested in dance'. Which sentences in Paragraph 1 give you more information about this? Discuss with a partner.**

4 **Read answers a, b and c under question 1. Which answer matches the information presented in paragraph 1?**

5 **Now complete the rest of the EXAM TASK. Work with a partner and answer questions 2–5. Write your answers in your notebook.**

EXAM TASK

Read the text below. For each question, choose the correct answer.

A young dancer: eighteen-year-old Leo Hunter talks about his life

I was seven years old when I first learned about ballet. A dancer visited our school to teach us for an afternoon. She spoke to the class about her job and showed us a video of her dancing in a beautiful theatre. It looked amazing! That afternoon, I went home and asked my parents for dance lessons.

My parents were very surprised. They're both scientists, and they aren't interested in dance. It's funny how different we are! However, they found me a teacher and I started lessons.

I worked hard and I improved quickly. Then, when I was twelve, I got a place at a top ballet school. I was very happy, as it's a good school. It was a boarding school, so I lived at the school, and went home to my parents for the holidays.

I entered lots of dance competitions when I was at school. I didn't do them for the prizes – I did them to help me to get work as a dancer. They were a great way to meet famous dancers and directors, and to practise in front of people.

I left school last year, and got my first job with a dance company. We have a new show, and we're performing it all over the world. I was in France last week and I'm in Spain next week. I get tired, but I'm enjoying it a lot. I made my dreams come true, and that's a fantastic feeling.

1 Leo became interested in dance after ...
   a a trip to the theatre.
   b a special lesson at school.
   c a chat with his parents.

2 What does Leo say about his parents?
   a They wanted him to study science.
   b They know a lot about dance.
   c They are not the same as him.

3 What do we learn about Leo's boarding school?
   a It was close to Leo's home.
   b It was only for the best young dancers.
   c It wasn't as good as everyone thought.

4 Why did Leo enter dance competitions?
   a They were fun to do.
   b He wanted to win prizes.
   c They were important for his future.

5 Leo says that at the moment he is ...
   a travelling a lot.
   b learning dances for a show.
   c trying to get a new job.

EXAM PRACTICE
UNIT 8

LESSON OVERVIEW: This lesson provides practice of a Reading multiple choice exam task. It also reviews some of the language sts have learned in Unit 8.

Skill	Exam task
Reading	Multiple choice

WARMER

Ask: *Do you like dancing? Do you have dance lessons?* Find out if anyone in the class has dance lessons, and encourage them to tell the class what kinds of dance they do and where they have lessons. If no sts do dance, ask: *What different kinds of dance are there? How can you learn them?* Use the discussion to teach the word *ballet*. Ask: *Do you think it's easy to become a famous dancer? Why/Why not?*

BACKGROUND INFORMATION

In this exam task, sts read a longer text and answer five multiple choice questions. There is usually one question for each paragraph of the text, and the questions come in the same order as the information in the text. There are three options for each question. The questions ask about detailed information in the text. The ideas in the incorrect options are often mentioned in the text, so sts need to read the relevant parts of the text very carefully to choose the correct answers.

1 Explain to sts that they are going to practise a multiple choice reading exam task. Read the information in the Look! box with the class. Point out the five paragraphs in the text and the five questions, and point out that there are three possible answers for each question.

Read through the Useful strategies with the class. Remind sts that with any reading task, it is important to read the whole text before you start, to get a general idea of the topic. Explain that ideas from all the options may be mentioned in the text, but only one answer matches the meaning in the text exactly.

Ask sts to read the title of the text and look at the picture, and write three questions about Leo in their notebooks. They could work in pairs for this. Elicit a few example questions.

Sample answers
When did Leo start dancing?
Where did he learn to dance?
Does he like being a dancer?

2 Ask sts to read the text quickly to see if it answers any of their questions. Get feedback on which questions it answers, and elicit what else sts learned about Leo from the text.

3 Read through the first question with the class and focus on the words 'became interested in dance'. Ask sts to read paragraph 1 and find the words that are about Leo becoming interested in dance. Check the answer with the class.

Answer
<u>I was seven years old when I first learned about ballet</u>. <u>A dancer visited our school to teach us for an afternoon</u>. She spoke to the class about her job and showed us a video of her dancing in a beautiful theatre. <u>It looked amazing</u>! That afternoon I went home and asked my parents for dance lessons.

4 Sts look at the three options for question 1 and choose the one that matches the meaning in the text. Allow them to compare their answers in pairs, then check with the class.

Answer
b

5 Refer sts back to the Useful strategies. Ask them to look at questions 2–5 and underline the important words. With weaker classes, you could check these answers before they complete the task. Sts then read the text carefully and write the correct answers in their notebooks. Check answers, eliciting the part of the text which confirms each answer.

Answer
2 c – They're both scientists, and they aren't interested in dance. It's funny how different we are!
3 b – I got a place at a top ballet school.
4 c – I didn't do them for the prizes – I did them to help me to get work as a dancer. They were a great way to meet famous dancers and directors, and to practise in front of people.
5 a – we're performing it all over the world. I was in France last week and I'm in Spain next week.

EXAM PRACTICE
UNIT 9

SPEAKING
A personal topic

Look! **About the task**

In this speaking task, you will choose a topic to talk about and make notes in the topic form before the exam. The examiner will take your form and will ask you questions about the topic. You must also ask the examiner a question.

Useful strategies

- Choose a topic that you like or one that you enjoy talking about.
- Plan your topic well. Include different tenses, different structures and give some opinions in your answers.
- Remember to always answer the examiner's questions. Don't just read your plan.
- If you didn't understand the question, ask the examiner to repeat it.

1 **Read and match the examiner's questions 1–4 below with items a–d in the example topic form.**

1 How old were you when you started skiing?
2 Why do you like skiing so much?
3 Can you snowboard as well?
4 Are you going skiing again soon?

Topic form

Title of topic: *My favourite sport – skiing*

a Why I love skiing
b When I learned to ski
c My next skiing holiday
d Differences between skiing and other winter sports

2 **Look at the example topic questions below, and imagine that you love skiing. Ask and answer with a partner.**

When did you learn ...?
Why do you like ...?
Who do you ... with?
Which ... do you prefer?
How often do you ...?

3 E9.1 **Listen to Tomas practising talking about skiing with his teacher. Copy and complete the table below, in your notebook with true (T) or false (F).**

The student ...	T	F
1 gives full answers.		
2 answers all the questions.		
3 uses a good range of grammar and vocabulary.		
4 asks for help.		
5 asks the examiner a question about the topic.		

4 E9.2 **Now listen to Tomas completing the speaking test with the examiner. Why are Tomas' answers better this time? Discuss with a partner.**

5 **Now choose your own topic to talk about. Copy the topic form below and complete it with your own ideas.**

Topic form

Title of topic:

1 ... **2** ... **3** ... **4** ...

6 **Now read the instructions below and complete the EXAM TASK. Remember to use question words 1–4 in your responses.**

EXAM TASK

Work in pairs. Student A: ask Student B questions about their topic form. Student B: ask Student A questions about their topic form. Swap forms and repeat the same task. Remember to include the question words below.

1 What ...
2 Why ...
3 Who ...
4 Which ...

EXAM PRACTICE
UNIT 9

LESSON OVERVIEW: This lesson provides practice of a Speaking exam task. It also reviews some of the language sts have learned in Unit 9.

Skill	Exam task
Speaking	A personal topic

WARMER

Ask: *What topics can you talk about in English? What activities do you enjoy? What things are you interested in?* Elicit a few possible ideas, e.g. a favourite sport, a favourite kind of music, a hobby. Put sts into pairs to discuss what things they are interested in, and what topics they can talk about in English. Elicit a few ideas from sts.

BACKGROUND INFORMATION

In this exam task, sts choose a topic to talk about. They make notes on a topic form before the exam, and the examiner asks them questions about their topic. This task is an opportunity for sts to show the range of language they can use. They should aim to talk about the past, present and future to use different tenses. They should also express their opinions and they must ask the examiner a question about the topic.

1 Explain to sts that they are going to practise a speaking exam task. Read the information in the Look! box with the class and tell sts this is an opportunity for them to talk about something they are interested in, and show the range of English they can use.

Read through the Useful strategies with the class. Point out to sts that it is useful to plan their ideas, so they can try to include information about the past, present and future to use different tenses, but they should listen carefully to the examiner's questions and answer these.

Refer sts to the topic form and point out headings a–d. Ask sts to read the questions and match each one with a heading on the topic form. Check answers.

Answers
1 b 2 a 3 d 4 c

2 Ask sts to look at the example topic questions and imagine that they love skiing. Put sts into pairs and ask them to ask and answer the example topic questions.

3 E9.1 Tell sts they're going to listen to Tomas answering the questions with his teacher. Allow sts time to read through the sentences, then play the audio. See TG page 285 for audio script. Sts listen and decide if the sentences are true or false. Check answers.

Answers
1 F 2 T 3 F 4 T 5 F

4 E9.2 Read out the questions, then play the audio. See TG page 285 for audio script. Put sts into pairs to discuss what is different and how Tomas' answers are better. Discuss the answer with the class.

Answer
This time Tomas gives full answers to all the questions, gives extra information, uses a good range of grammar and vocabulary. He also asks for help when he needs it, and asks the examiner a question.

5 Sts work individually to choose a topic. They copy the topic form and complete it with their own ideas. With weaker classes, you could check some of these with the class and encourage sts to look back at the sentences and descriptions in Exercise 3, to make sure they cover a range of topics and tenses.

6 Put sts into pairs then read through the instructions with the class. Sts take turns asking each other questions about their topic forms.When all sts have finished, put them into groups to discuss what they found easy and difficult about the task. Discuss their ideas as a class, and discuss what they could do to improve next time.

LANGUAGE SUMMARY
UNIT 1

GRAMMAR

There is / There are + a, an, some, any

	Singular	Plural
+	**There's a** folder in the cupboard. **There's a** bag on the desk. **There's an** apple in my bag.	**There are some** keys in the kitchen. **There are** two lamps in the living room.
–	**There isn't a** table.	**There aren't any** pencils.
?	**Is there a** wardrobe?	**Are there any** chairs?
Y/N	Yes, **there is**. No, **there isn't**.	Yes, **there are**. No, **there aren't**.

Rules

We use *there is* + *a*/*an* with singular nouns.

We use *there are* + *some* or *any* with plural nouns. We use *some* in affirmative sentences and *any* in negative sentences and questions.

Prepositions of place

*The bookcase is **behind** the chair.*

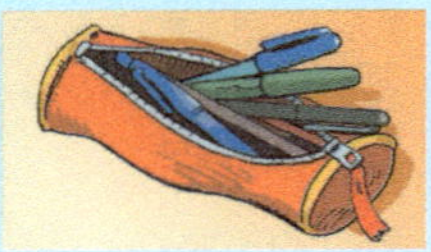
*The pens are **in** the pencil case.*

*The table is **in front of** the sofa.*

*The lamp is **next to** the chair.*

*The keys are **on** the table.*

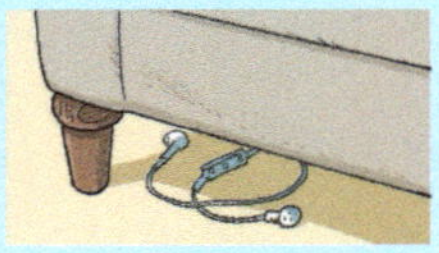
*The earphones are **under** the sofa.*

have got

Affirmative	Negative
I**'ve got** a computer.	I **haven't got** a laptop.
You**'ve got** a new bike.	You **haven't got** a brother.
He/She/It**'s got** green eyes.	He/She/It **hasn't got** any cousins.
We**'ve got** two cats.	We **haven't got** a cat.
They**'ve got** black hair.	They **haven't got** any red pens.
Questions	**Short answers**
Have I **got** your address?	Yes, you **have**. / No, you **haven't**.
Have you **got** a phone?	Yes, I **have**. / No, I **haven't**.
Has he/she/it **got** any pets?	Yes, he/she/it **has**. / No, he/she/it **hasn't**.
Have we **got** any tacos?	Yes, we **have**. / No, we **haven't**.
Have they **got** a dog?	Yes, they **have**. / No, they **haven't**.

Rules

We use *have got* to talk about possessions, and to describe people and their appearance.

VOCABULARY

Furniture

bath
bed
bookcase
chair
cooker
desk
fridge
lamp
mirror
shower
sink
sofa
table
toilet
wardrobe

Family members

aunt
brother
child
cousin
dad
daughter
family
father
grandad
grandma
husband
mother
mum
nephew
niece
parent
sister
son
uncle
wife

SPEAKING

Introductions

Hi. / Hello.
How are things? / How are you?
Good/Fine, thanks.
Not bad.
This is my friend/cousin, ...
Nice to meet you.
Nice to meet you, too.
Bye. / See you. / See you later.

WRITING

Describing a home

My dream home is a house / an apartment in the country / in the city / near the beach.
Upstairs/Downstairs, there is ... / there are ...
Outside, there's a ...
In my bedroom, there's ...
I've got a ...

and and *but*

It's got four bedrooms **and** four bathrooms.
There isn't a desk, **but** there's a sofa.

LANGUAGE SUMMARY
UNIT 2

GRAMMAR

Present simple: affirmative and negative

Affirmative	Negative
I **leave** home at 7.30.	I **don't have** lunch at school.
You **paint** beautiful pictures.	You **don't get up** early.
He/She/It **likes** pizzas.	He/She/It **doesn't like** chocolate.
We **walk** to school.	We **don't play** tennis.
They **study** in the evening.	They **don't like** Maths.

Rules

We use the present simple to talk about routines and facts.

For the third person singular (*he*/*she*/*it*), we add *-s* to the infinitive to form the affirmative.

When a verb ends in *-ch*, *-sh*, *-ss*, *-x* and *-o*, we add *-es*, e.g. *goes*

When a verb ends in consonant + *-y*, we change the *-y* to *-ies*.

The third person singular of *have* is *has*.

We form the negative with *don't* (*do not*) or *doesn't* (*does not*) + the infinitive of the verb.

Present simple: questions

Questions	Short answers
Do I **take** good photos?	Yes, you **do**. / No, you **don't**.
Do you **play** basketball?	Yes, I **do**. / No, I **don't**.
Does he/she/it **like** bagels?	Yes, he/she/it **does**. / No, he/she/it **doesn't**.
Do we **drink** a lot of coffee?	Yes, you **do**. / No, you **don't**.
Do you **watch** TV after school?	Yes, we **do**. / No, we **don't**.
Do they **play** video games?	Yes, they **do**. / No, they **don't**.

Rules

We form questions with *do* + subject + the infinitive of the verb.

For the third person singular (*he*/*she*/*it*) we form questions with *does* + subject + the infinitive of the verb.

Present simple: *Wh-* questions

Question word	*do*/*does*	subject	verb
Where	**do**	you	**live**?
What	**does**	he	**do** at the weekend?
When	**does**	she	**leave** home?
Who	**do**	you	**chat** with online?
How	**do**	they	**go** to school?
Why	**does**	Daniel	**get up** early?
What time	**does**	it	**start**?
Which subjects	**do**	you	**like**?

Rules

We make questions with question words to ask for specific information.

VOCABULARY

Daily activities

chat with my friends
do my homework
get dressed
get up
go to bed
have a shower
have breakfast
have dinner
have lunch
leave home
tidy my room
watch TV

Technology

computer
digital camera
drone
interactive whiteboard
laptop
projector
tablet
Virtual Reality headset
wireless headphones
3D printer

SPEAKING

Asking for and giving information

Can I help you?
I'm interested in ...
What would you like to know?
What day is it on?
What time does it start/finish?
Where do they meet?

WRITING

Starting and finishing an email

Hi there / Hi ... / Dear ...
I want to tell you about ...
Write soon.
Bye for now / Best wishes

Prepositions of time

at 9.30, **at** 11.00
in the morning, **in** the afternoon, **in** the evening
on Friday, **on** Saturday
BUT: **at** night, **at** the weekend

LANGUAGE SUMMARY
UNIT 3

GRAMMAR

Present simple and adverbs of frequency

0% —————————————— 100%

never	sometimes	often	usually	always

They **are never** late for school. She **is always** friendly.
We **never play** football. He **always gets up** early.
We **sometimes go** swimming in the sea.
I **often play** volleyball in the summer.
Lucy **usually goes** mountain biking at the weekend.

Rules

We use adverbs of frequency to talk about how often we do things.
Adverbs of frequency go after the verb *be*, but before other verbs.

like / don't like + -ing

love	I **love** play**ing** table tennis.
like	I **like** chatt**ing** with my friends.
don't/doesn't mind	I **don't mind** gett**ing** up early. It's OK.
don't/doesn't like	Rosie **doesn't like** tidy**ing** her room.
hate	My mum **hates** cook**ing**.

Rules

We use *like*, *love*, *hate* and *don't mind* + *-ing* to talk about likes/dislikes.

can and *can't*

Affirmative

I/You/He/She/It **can** swim.
We/You/They **can** use Jack's car.

Negative

I/You/He/She/It **can't** play volleyball.
We/You/They **can't** chat in the library.

Questions	Short answers
Can you speak French?	Yes, I **can**. / No, I **can't**.
Can she ride a horse?	Yes, she **can**. / No, she **can't**.

Rules

We use *can* and *can't* (*cannot*) to talk about ability and permission.
After *can*, we don't use *to* before the verb.

must and *mustn't*

✓	All students **must** wear the correct uniform.
✗	Students **mustn't** talk during the exam.

Rules

We use *must* to talk about obligations and rules.
We use *mustn't* to talk about things that are not permitted.

VOCABULARY

Sport

athletics
ballet
gymnastics
ice hockey
mountain biking
rugby
skateboarding
surfing
swimming
table tennis
taekwondo
volleyball

Action verbs

catch
climb
jump
kick
ride
run
skate
ski
swim
throw

SPEAKING

Asking for suggestions

What shall we do?

Making suggestions

Let's do something.
Why don't we play table tennis?
How about going mountain biking?
What about taking a picnic?

Responding to suggestions

That doesn't sound very exciting.
That sounds like fun.
Great idea!

WRITING

Expressions of frequency

Every Saturday/Sunday/weekend, I ...
Once a month / Twice a week, I ...
I always/usually/often/sometimes/never ...

Punctuation

We use:

- a full stop (.) at the end of a sentence.
- a question mark (?) at the end of a question.
- a comma (,) to separate parts of a sentence, and between words in a list.
- an exclamation mark (!) to show emotion.

LANGUAGE SUMMARY UNIT 4

GRAMMAR

Present continuous: affirmative, negative and questions

Affirmative	Negative
I'**m cooking** dinner.	I'**m not doing** my homework.
He/She/It'**s having** lunch.	He/She/It **isn't watching** TV.
We/You/They'**re playing** a video game.	We/You/They **aren't studying**.
Questions	**Short answers**
Are you **listening** to music?	Yes, I **am**. / No, I'**m not**.
Is Ben **reading** a book?	Yes, he **is**. / No, he **isn't**.
Is it **raining**?	Yes, it **is**. / No, it **isn't**.
Are they **wearing** trainers?	Yes, they **are**. / No, they **aren't**.

Rules

We use the present continuous to talk about things that are happening now.

We form the present continuous with the verb *be* + the *-ing* form of the main verb.

We put the verb *be* before the subject to form questions.

Present continuous and present simple

Present continuous	Present simple
I'**m drinking** a cup of tea right now.	I sometimes **drink** coffee.
It **isn't raining** at the moment.	It often **rains** in London.
Tom'**s doing** his homework now.	Sam always **does** his homework after dinner.
What **are** you **doing** today?	What **do** you usually **do** on Saturday?

Rules

We use the present continuous to talk about things that are happening now. We often use time expressions like (*right*) *now* and *at the moment* with the present continuous.

We use the present simple to talk about regular routines, habits and facts.

VOCABULARY

Places in a city

castle
department store
hotel
library
market
monument
museum
restaurant
shopping centre
square
theatre
train station

The weather

It's cloudy.
It's cold.
It's foggy.
It's hot.
It's icy.
It's raining.
It's snowing.
It's stormy.
It's sunny.
It's warm.
It's windy.

SPEAKING

Asking for and giving directions

Excuse me, I'm looking for ...
Is it far?
It's a five-minute walk.
Go straight on.
Turn right/left.
Go past the bank.
It's on the left/right.

WRITING

Writing a message

I'm spending the weekend in ...
I'm staying with my ...
At the moment / Now, we're ...-ing ...
I'm having a really good time!
See you at/on ...! / See you soon!

Adverbs of degree

It's **quite** hot.
It's **very** hot.
It's **really** hot.

LANGUAGE SUMMARY UNIT 5

GRAMMAR

Countable and uncountable nouns + *some* and *any*

	Countable nouns		Uncountable nouns
	Singular	Plural	
+	There's **a** potato.	There are **some** vegetables.	There's **some** yoghurt.
-	There isn't **an** apple.	There aren't **any** sandwiches.	There isn't **any** juice.
?	Is there **an** egg?	Are there **any** tomatoes?	Is there **any** rice?

Rules

Countable nouns are things that we can count. Uncountable nouns are things that we can't count.

Countable nouns have a singular and a plural form. To make the plural form, we usually add *-s* or *-es*. Before a singular countable noun, we use *a* or *an*.

Uncountable nouns only have a singular form.

Before uncountable nouns and plural countable nouns, we use *some* in affirmative sentences and *any* in negative sentences and questions.

Quantifiers: *much*, *many*, *a lot of*

	Countable	Uncountable
+	She eats **a lot of** bananas.	He drinks **a lot of** juice.
-	I don't eat **many** eggs.	I don't drink **much** milk.
?	**How many** vegetables do you eat in a day?	**How much** fruit do you eat?
	A lot. / **Not many.**	**A lot.** / **Not much.**

Rules

We use *a lot of* before plural countable nouns and uncountable nouns to talk about quantities.

We use *not many* and *not much* in negative sentences to talk about small quantities. We use *not many* with plural countable nouns and *not much* with uncountable nouns.

We use *how many* and *how much* to ask about quantity. We use *how many* with plural countable nouns and *how much* with uncountable nouns.

VOCABULARY

Food and drink

apples
bananas
beans
bread
cereal
chicken
eggs
fish
fruit
hot chocolate
ice cream
jam
meat
milk
orange juice
pasta
potatoes
rice
salad
sandwich
sugar
toast
tomatoes
vegetables
water
yoghurt

Health

active
fit
healthy
hungry
lazy
thirsty
unfit
unhealthy

SPEAKING

Ordering food and drink

Can I help? / What can I get you?
Anything to drink? / Anything else?
Is that to eat in or take away?
That's ... pounds, please.
Your food is just coming.
I'd like ..., please.
Can I have ...?
I'll have ...
To take away. / To eat in.
Here you are.

WRITING

Instructions

Fry ...
Add ...
Cut ...
Cook ...
Serve ...

Sequence words

First, cook the beef.
Then, cut the garlic.
Next, add the tomato sauce.
Finally, cook the spaghetti.

LANGUAGE SUMMARY UNIT 6

GRAMMAR

Comparative and superlative adjectives

Short adjectives		
Adjective	**Comparative**	**Superlative**
small	small**er**	the small**est**
nice	nice**r**	the nice**st**
fit	fit**ter**	the fit**test**
healthy	health**ier**	the health**iest**
Long adjectives		
Adjective	**Comparative**	**Superlative**
modern	**more** modern	**the most** modern
difficult	**more** difficult	**the most** difficult
Irregular adjectives		
Adjective	**Comparative**	**Superlative**
good	**better**	**the best**
bad	**worse**	**the worst**
far	**further**	**the furthest**

Rules

We use a comparative adjective + *than* to compare two things/people.

When an adjective is one syllable, we usually add *-er*.

When a one-syllable adjective ends in *-e*, we add *-r*.

When a one-syllable adjective ends in consonant + vowel + consonant, we double the final consonant and add *-er*.

When an adjective ends in *-y*, we change the *y* to *i* and add *-er*.

When an adjective is two or more syllables, we usually use *more* + adjective.

We use a superlative adjective to say that something is more than all the others in a group. We use *the* before the adjective.

When an adjective is one syllable, we usually add *-est*.

When a one-syllable adjective ends in *-e*, we add *-st*.

When a one-syllable adjective ends in consonant + vowel + consonant, we double the final consonant and add *-est*.

When an adjective ends in *-y*, we change the *y* to *i* and add *-est*.

When an adjective is two or more syllables, we usually use *most* + adjective.

(*not*) *as ... as*

	(*not*) *as ... as*
+	It's **as** fast **as** a leopard. I'm **as** tall **as** my brother.
-	It **isn't as** big **as** an elephant. Sam **isn't as** fast **as** David.

Rules

We can use *as* + adjective + *as* to say that two things are the same.

We can use *not as* + adjective + *as* to say that two things are different.

VOCABULARY

The natural world

beach
desert
forest
island
lake
mountain
rainforest
river
sea
sky
volcano
waterfall

Wild animals

bat
bear
beetle
elephant
frog
leopard
lion
monkey
mosquito
parrot
penguin
shark
snake
spider
tortoise
whale

SPEAKING

Buying a ticket

Can I help you?
I'd like a ticket / two tickets, please.
Is there a discount for children / young people / students?
That's ... in total.
Here you are.
Here are your tickets.
Here's your change.

WRITING

Animal facts

... are one of the most dangerous animals on Earth.
They live in the forests/mountains/ocean in ...
They can grow to ... m long.
They can weigh ... kg.
They can live for ... years.
They usually eat ...
During the day, they ...
At night, they ...

too and *also*

Lions usually hunt at night. Leopards **also** hunt at night.
Lions usually hunt at night. Leopards hunt at night, **too**.

LANGUAGE SUMMARY
UNIT 7

GRAMMAR

be: past simple

Affirmative	Negative
I/He/She/It **was** in the park. We/You/They **were** at school.	I/He/She/It **wasn't** tired. We/You/They **weren't** hungry.
Questions	**Short answers**
Was the weather nice? **Were** the beds comfortable?	Yes, it **was**. / No, it **wasn't**. Yes, they **were**. / No, they **weren't**.

Rules

We use the past simple form of *be* (*was* and *were*) to talk about situations and states in the past. The past simple forms of *be* are *was* and *were*.

There was / There were

	Affirmative	Negative
Singular	**There was** a laptop.	**There wasn't** a TV.
Plural	**There were** two cars.	**There weren't** any dogs.
	Questions	**Short answers**
Singular	**Was there** an orange?	Yes, **there was**. / No, **there wasn't**.
Plural	**Were there** any eggs left?	Yes, **there were**. / No, **there weren't**.

Rules

We use *there was* (singular nouns) / *there were* (plural nouns) to say that something existed in the past.

Past simple affirmative: regular verbs

I **wanted** a new bike. They **travelled** to Paris.

Spelling Rules

Most verbs: want > want**ed**, enjoy > enjoy**ed**

Verbs that end *-e*: dance > dance**d**, love > love**d**

Verbs that end *-y*: study > stud**ied**, try > tr**ied**

Verbs that end consonant + vowel + consonant: travel > travel**led**, stop > stop**ped**

Object pronouns

Subject	Object	
I	me	**I** went to the party. Maria invited **me**.
you	you	**You**'ve got a heavy bag. I can carry it for **you**.
he	him	**He** doesn't understand. Can you help **him**?
she	her	**She**'s late. Can you drive **her** to the station?
it	it	**It**'s very cheap. Shall we buy **it**?
we	us	**We** were late. Sophie arrived before **us**.
they	them	**They** were at the park. Dan was with **them**.

Rules

After verbs or prepositions, we use object pronouns.

VOCABULARY

Clothes

boots, coat, dress, hat, jacket, jeans, jumper, shirt, shoes, shorts, skirt, socks, T-shirt, tie, trainers, trousers

Regular verbs

arrive, borrow, collect, enjoy, love, play, travel, try, use, want

SPEAKING

Shopping for clothes

Can I help you?
What size do you need?
The changing rooms are over there.
Any good?
You can pay over there.
Have you got this shirt / these shorts in (red/green)?
Small/Medium/Large
Can I try it/them on, please?
How much is it / are they?
I'll take it/them.

WRITING

Writing about past events

For me, ... was a fantastic / an interesting year.
There were some great films.
There was some great music.
We listened to ... / We watched ...
We loved/liked ...
It was exciting/funny/cool/great.

Giving examples

There were some great films, for example *Incredibles 2* and *Black Panther*.

LANGUAGE SUMMARY
UNIT 8

GRAMMAR

Past simple: affirmative, negative and questions

Affirmative	Negative
My grandma **enjoyed** the film. She **studied** Spanish at university.	They **didn't enjoy** the concert. They **didn't see** Jack at the party.
I **saw** *The X Factor* on TV last night.	My dad **didn't study** English at school.
They **gave** him a camera for his birthday.	My parents **didn't give** me any money today.
Questions	**Short answers**
Did you **like** the restaurant? **Did** Claire **grow up** in the USA? **Did** they **go** to the beach this morning?	Yes, I **did**. / No, I **didn't**. Yes, she **did**. / No, she **didn't**. Yes, they **did**. / No, they **didn't**.

Rules

We use the past simple to talk about completed actions in the past.

For regular verbs, we usually add *-ed* to the infinitive of the verb to form the affirmative.

When a verb ends in *-e*, we add *-d*.

When a verb ends in consonant + *y*, we change the *y* to *i* and then we add *-ed*.

When a verb ends in vowel + consonant, we usually double the consonant and add *-ed*.

We form the negative of regular and irregular verbs with *didn't* (*did not*) + infinitive.

We form questions with *did* + subject + infinitive.

Past simple: *Wh-* questions

Wh- questions
What did you **do** in Paris? **Where did** you **go** on Sunday? **Why did** you **leave** the party early? **When did** you **learn** to drive? **Who did** you **see** at the party? **Which jacket did** you **buy**? **How did** you **get** home last night? **What film did** you **watch** on TV? **What time did** his plane **arrive**?

Rules

We make questions with question words to ask for specific information about actions and situations in the past.

VOCABULARY

Life events

be born
buy a house
die
get a job
get married
go to university
grow up
have a baby
learn to drive
leave school
make friends
start school

Physical appearance

bald
beard
blond
blue
brown
curly
dark brown
glasses
green
grey
light brown
long
moustache
red
short
slim
straight
tall
thin
wavy
well-built

SPEAKING

Talking about your weekend

Did you have a good weekend?
What did you do?
How was it?
What was the food/music/weather like?
How about you?
It was great / amazing / really good / OK.
I went to ...
That sounds like fun! / That sounds good!

WRITING

Describing someone

He's/She's tall/slim/well-built.
He's/She's got blond/dark hair and blue/brown eyes.
He's/She's got a kind/friendly/serious face.
He/She was born in ... / He/She grew up in ...
After he/she (finished school), he/she ...
After that, ...
His/Her hobbies are ...

Using paragraphs

When you write an essay, organize your ideas into paragraphs.

Each paragraph contains a sentence about one topic.

When you change topic, start a new paragraph.

LANGUAGE SUMMARY
UNIT 9

GRAMMAR
will and *won't*

Affirmative	Negative
Trains **will be** faster. More people **will cycle** to work.	Planes **won't have** pilots. Our exams **won't be** easy.
Questions	**Short answers**
Will you **have** a big family?	Yes, I **will**. / No, I **won't**.
Will we **be** happier in the future?	Yes, we **will**. / No, we **won't**.
Will there **be** more cars on our roads?	Yes, there **will**. / No, there **won't**.

Rules

We use *will* and *won't* (*will not*) to make predictions about the future.

We form the affirmative with *will* + the infinitive of the main verb.

We usually use the short form *'ll* (*will*) after personal pronouns.

We form the negative with *won't* + the infinitive of the main verb.

We form questions with *will* + subject + the infinitive of the main verb.

be going to: future plans

Affirmative	Negative
I**'m going to stay** with my uncle in New York.	I**'m not going to stay** in a hotel.
He/She/It**'s going to travel** by train.	He/She/It **isn't going to rent** a car.
We/You/They**'re going to relax** on a beach.	We/You/They **aren't going to visit** the castle.
Questions	**Short answers**
Are you **going to go** sightseeing?	Yes, I **am**. / No, I**'m not**.
Is she **going to go** hiking?	Yes, she **is**. / No, she **isn't**.
Are they **going to stay** in a campsite?	Yes, they **are**. / No, they **aren't**.

Rules

We use *be going to* to talk about future plans.

We use *be going to* + the infinitive of the main verb.

When we use *be going to* in spoken English, we usually use the short forms *I'm*, *you're*, *he's*, etc.

VOCABULARY
Transport

bike
boat
coach
helicopter
on foot
lorry
motorbike
plane
scooter
ship
tram
underground

Holiday activities

explore the city
go hiking
go sightseeing
pack your bag
relax on a beach
rent a bike
stay in an apartment
take a bus tour
take pictures
unpack your bag
visit a castle

SPEAKING
Making arrangements

What are you doing on Saturday / at the weekend?
Are you doing anything in the afternoon/ evening?
Would you like to ...?
We're meeting at ...
Nothing special.
Sorry, I'm busy.
That sounds great.
Where are you meeting?
I'll see you then.

WRITING
Writing about holiday plans

In July/August, I'm going to go to ...
We're going to stay in a campsite/hotel.
I'm going to spend a week / a few days in ...
I can't wait.
I'm excited/nervous because ...
Write and tell me about your plans.

so and *because*

I want to improve my Spanish, **so** I'm going to do a language course.
I'm really excited **because** it's the last week of school!

IRREGULAR VERBS LIST

Infinitive		Past simple		Past participle	
be	/biː/	was/were	/wəz, wɒz, wə(r), wɜː(r)/	been	/bɪn, biːn/
become	/bɪˈkʌm/	became	/bɪˈkeɪm/	become	/bɪˈkʌm/
begin	/bɪˈɡɪn/	began	/bɪˈɡæn/	begun	/bɪˈɡʌn/
break	/breɪk/	broke	/brəʊk/	broken	/ˈbrəʊkən/
bring	/brɪŋ/	brought	/brɔːt/	brought	/brɔːt/
build	/bɪld/	built	/bɪlt/	built	/bɪlt/
buy	/baɪ/	bought	/bɔːt/	bought	/bɔːt/
can	/kən, kæn/	could	/kəd, kʊd/		
catch	/kætʃ/	caught	/kɔːt/	caught	/kɔːt/
choose	/tʃuːz/	chose	/tʃəʊz/	chosen	/ˈtʃəʊzn/
come	/kʌm/	came	/keɪm/	come	/kʌm/
cost	/kɒst/	cost	/kɒst/	cost	/kɒst/
do	/də, du/	did	/dɪd/	done	/dʌn/
draw	/drɔː/	drew	/druː/	drawn	/drɔːn/
drink	/drɪŋk/	drank	/dræŋk/	drunk	/drʌŋk/
drive	/draɪv/	drove	/drəʊv/	driven	/ˈdrɪvn/
eat	/iːt/	ate	/eɪt, et/	eaten	/ˈiːtn/
fall	/fɔːl/	fell	/fel/	fallen	/ˈfɔːlən/
feel	/fiːl/	felt	/felt/	felt	/felt/
find	/faɪnd/	found	/faʊnd/	found	/faʊnd/
fly	/flaɪ/	flew	/fluː/	flown	/fləʊn/
get	/get/	got	/gɒt/	got	/gɒt/
give	/gɪv/	gave	/geɪv/	given	/ˈgɪvn/
go	/gəʊ/	went	/went/	gone/been	/gɒn, biːn/
have	/həv, hæv/	had	/hæd/	had	/hæd/
hear	/hɪə(r)/	heard	/hɜːd/	heard	/hɜːd/
know	/nəʊ/	knew	/njuː/	known	/nəʊn/
learn	/lɜːn/	learnt/learned	/lɜːnt, lɜːnd/	learnt/learned	/lɜːnt, lɜːnd/
leave	/liːv/	left	/left/	left	/left/
lose	/luːz/	lost	/lɒst/	lost	/lɒst/
make	/meɪk/	made	/meɪd/	made	/meɪd/
meet	/miːt/	met	/met/	met	/met/
read	/riːd/	read	/red/	read	/red/
run	/rʌn/	ran	/ræn/	run	/rʌn/
say	/seɪ/	said	/sed/	said	/sed/
see	/siː/	saw	/sɔː/	seen	/siːn/
sell	/sel/	sold	/səʊld/	sold	/səʊld/
send	/send/	sent	/sent/	sent	/sent/
sing	/sɪŋ/	sang	/sæŋ/	sung	/sʌŋ/
sit	/sɪt/	sat	/sæt/	sat	/sæt/
sleep	/sliːp/	slept	/slept/	slept	/slept/
speak	/spiːk/	spoke	/spəʊk/	spoken	/ˈspəʊkən/
stand	/stænd/	stood	/stʊd/	stood	/stʊd/
swim	/swɪm/	swam	/swæm/	swum	/swʌm/
take	/teɪk/	took	/tʊk/	taken	/ˈteɪkən/
teach	/tiːtʃ/	taught	/tɔːt/	taught	/tɔːt/
tell	/tel/	told	/təʊld/	told	/təʊld/
think	/θɪŋk/	thought	/θɔːt/	thought	/θɔːt/
throw	/θrəʊ/	threw	/θruː/	thrown	/θrəʊn/
wear	/weə(r)/	wore	/wɔː(r)/	worn	/wɔːn/
write	/raɪt/	wrote	/rəʊt/	written	/ˈrɪtn/

AUDIO SCRIPTS

STARTER

S0.1 Page 4, Exercise 1

Monday Tuesday Wednesday Thursday Friday Saturday Sunday

S0.2 Page 4, Exercise 3

January February March April May June July August September October November December

S0.3 Page 4, Exercise 4

first second third fourth fifth twelfth twentieth twenty-ninth thirtieth thirty-first

S0.4 Page 4, Exercise 6

1	snack	7	folder
2	pencil	8	pencil case
3	pen	9	notebook
4	money	10	keys
5	water bottle	11	timetable
6	phone	12	earphones

S0.5 See SB Page 5, Exercise 6

S0.6 Page 6, Exercise 1

1	Egypt	7	Brazil
2	Mexico	8	Spain
3	the USA	9	Ireland
4	Japan	10	Argentina
5	France	11	the UK
6	Turkey	12	China

S0.7 Page 6, Exercise 2

Argentina – Argentinian
Brazil – Brazilian
China – Chinese
Egypt – Egyptian
France – French
Ireland – Irish
Japan – Japanese
Mexico – Mexican
Spain – Spanish
Turkey – Turkish
the UK – British
the USA – American

S0.8 Page 6, Exercise 3

1 **Where is this animal from?**
It's from China.
2 **Who is Daisy Ridley?**
She's a British actress.
3 **What is the capital of Brazil?**
It's Brasilia.
4 **How old are the pyramids in Egypt?**
They're 4,500 years old.
5 **Where are tacos from?**
They're from Mexico.
6 **What nationality is the footballer Marcos Asensio?**
He's Spanish.

S0.9 See SB Page 6, Exercise 4

S0.10 See SB Page 7, Exercise 7

S0.11 See SB Page 8, Exercise 1

S0.12 See SB Page 8, Exercise 3

S0.13 See SB Page 8, Exercise 4

S0.14 Page 8, Exercise 5

1 It's half past six.
2 It's quarter past one.
3 It's three o'clock.
4 It's quarter to ten.
5 It's quarter to twelve.
6 It's half past eight.

UNIT 1

1.1 Page 9, Exercise 1

Picture 1: bed, chair, desk, wardrobe, mirror
Picture 2: cooker, fridge
Picture 3: chair, sofa, table
Picture 4: bookcase, chair, desk, lamp, table
Picture 5: bath, mirror, shower, sink, toilet

1.2 See SB Page 10, Exercise 1

1.3 Page 12, Exercise 1

Male	Female
brother	sister
dad	mum
grandad	grandma
husband	wife
nephew	niece
son	daughter
uncle	aunt

Male and female

child cousin parent

1.4 See SB Page 12, Exercise 2

1.5 Page 12, Exercises 5 and 6

P = Presenter, E = Emma

P: Hello and welcome to *Famous Families*. Today's show is about the actor Chris Hemsworth and his family, and with me in the studio is our reporter, Emma. So, Emma, where is Chris from?
E: He's from Australia. His parents are both Australian – his dad, Craig, and his mum, Leonie.
P: I see. And is Chris married?
E: Yes, he is. His wife is Elsa Pataky. She's an actress from Spain.
P: An actress – that's interesting. So, have Chris and Elsa got any children?
E: Yes, they have. They've got three children: two sons and a daughter.
P: What are their children's names?
E: Their sons are called Sasha and Tristan.
P: Sasha and Tristan – unusual names.
E: Yes, and their daughter's name is India Rose.
P: India Rose, that's a lovely name. And has Chris got any brothers or sisters?
E: He hasn't got any sisters, but he's got two brothers, Liam and Luke. They're also actors.
P: Wow, acting is in the family.
E: Yes – so perhaps Sasha, Tristan and India Rose are stars of the future!
P: Yes, who knows?! Thanks Emma. And now it's time for some music. Don't go away!

1.6 Page 13, Exercise 5

P = Presenter, E = Emma

Famous Families: Stephen Curry

This week's Famous Families is about the famous basketball player, Stephen Curry.

P: Has Stephen got a sister?
E: Yes, he has. Her name's Sydel, and she's good at volleyball.

1
P: Has he got a brother?
E: Yes, he has. His brother, Seth, is also a basketball player.

2
P: Has he got a wife?
E: Yes, he has. His wife, Ayesha, is a TV presenter.

3
P: Have they got any children?
E: Yes, they have.

4
P: Have they got a cat?
E: No, they haven't, but they've got two dogs!

1.7 Page 14, Exercise 5

C = Carla, F = Felix

C: Hi, my name's Carla and I'm from Edinburgh in Scotland. I'm thirteen years old and I've got two sisters. I love animals – I've got lots of pictures of animals on my bedroom walls – and I've got a lot of pets. I've got two rabbits, a cat and three fish. I also like going to the cinema. My favourite film is *Harry Potter*.
F: Hi, my name's Felix. I'm English, and I'm from Manchester. I'm twelve years old. My birthday is next month. I've got a brother and a sister. They're really into music, but I prefer sport. I like football and basketball, and I'm in a basketball team at school. We're really good!

1.8 See SB Page 15, Exercise 1

1.9 See SB Page 15, Exercise 2

1.10 Page 15, Exercise 3

M = Megan, B = Ben, L = Lydia

M: Hi Ben. How are you?
B: Not bad, thanks. How are you?
M: I'm good. This is my cousin, Lydia.
B: Hi, Lydia. Nice to meet you.
L: Nice to meet you, too.
M: See you later, Ben.
B: Yes, see you.

1.11 See SB Page 16–17, Exercise 2

UNIT 2

2.1 Page 19, Exercise 1

1 get up
2 leave home
3 chat with my friends
4 have lunch
5 have a shower
6 tidy my room
7 watch TV
8 have dinner
9 go to bed
10 get dressed
11 have breakfast
12 do my homework

2.2 Page 19, Exercise 2

1 *[sound of shower running]*
2 *[sound of eating and crunching cereal]*
3 *[sound of jeans being pulled on and zip being pulled up, followed by sound of drawers opening and closing, then boy calling out 'Mum, where's my new T-shirt?']*
4 *[sound of phone alarm clock going off, and person yawning and getting out of bed]*
5 *[sound of boy calling out: 'Bye' and parents replying: 'Bye. Have a nice day.' Door closing.]*
6 *[sound of teenagers chatting and laughing]*
7 *[sound of girl saying goodnight to parents: 'Night mum, night dad.' 'Night Lucy, sleep well.']*
8 *[sound of bed being made, followed by sound of vacuum cleaner]*

2.3 See SB Page 20, Exercise 2

2.4 See SB Page 21, Exercise 3

2.5 Page 21, Exercise 4

1	talks	4	has
2	loves	5	finishes
3	teaches	6	chats

2.6 Page 22, Exercise 1

1 tablet
2 interactive whiteboard
3 Virtual Reality headset
4 3D printer
5 drone
6 computer
7 projector
8 wireless headphones
9 digital camera
10 laptop

2.7 Page 22, Exercises 3 and 4

C = Claire, A = Alfie

C: Today's podcast is all about a school with a difference. With me is thirteen-year-old Alfie. So, Alfie, where do you go to school?
A: I go to school in North London.
C: And what's different about your school?
A: It's a 'no technology' school. We don't use anything electronic or digital, like computers or laptops.
C: Really? What about your teacher? Does she use a computer or an interactive whiteboard?
A: No, she doesn't. The school doesn't use any technology and we don't have the internet.
C: So, how do you study?
A: Well, we have books of course! But we also have a lot of fun. We play games in our French classes, we paint and draw in our History classes and we go outside for Science lessons. In the afternoon, we do sport or we work in the vegetable garden.
C: What about at home? Do you watch TV? Do you play video games?
A: No, we don't. It's a school rule – no technology at school and no technology at home. We don't watch TV, we don't play video games, and we don't use mobile phones.
C: Wow, that's very different! So, do you like your school?
A: Yes, I do! I have more time to read books, to chat with friends and to do sport. I think my school is great!
C: Thank you Alfie.
So, what do you think?
Send me your comments and thank you for listening.

2.8 Page 24, Exercises 3 and 4

F = Flora, M = Megan

F: Do you want to join a club this year, Megan? I'm on the school website now.
M: Yes, I do. What clubs are there?
F: Well, there's a Sailing Club, a Basketball Club, …
M: They sound interesting.
F: … a Music Club, a Dance Club, …
M: Cool.
F: And there's also a Computer Club, and an Art Club.
M: Er, no thank you! I'm not interested in computers or art.
F: OK … What days are you free?
M: Well, I play football after school on Tuesday and Friday, so I'm busy on those days. I'm free on Monday, Wednesday and Thursday.
F: Do you want to go to a club at lunchtime, or after school?
M: Oh, after school! I don't want to go to a club at lunchtime because I do my homework and chat with my friends then.
F: Right, there's only one club for you then. It's the …

2.9 See SB Page 25, Exercise 1

2.10 See SB Page 25, Exercise 2

2.11 Page 25, Exercise 3

A: Hello. Can I help you?
B: Yes, I'm interested in the Drama Club.
A: When do they meet?
B: They meet on Monday.
A: What time does it start?
B: It starts at 3.30.
A: And what time does it finish?
B: It finishes at 4.30.
A: Cool. I'd like to join, please.
B: Of course. Have fun!

2.12 See SB Page 26–27, Exercise 2

2.13 Page 26–27, Exercise 4

1 Tonight I've got Science, Maths and English to do. Do we get a lot of homework? Yes, we do!
2 At my school, we wear black trousers and a white shirt. I don't like my uniform – it's boring!
3 We sometimes watch Spanish videos on the whiteboard or listen to Spanish songs. I like Spanish, but it's quite difficult.
4 My brother goes to school by bike, but I walk. It takes fifteen minutes. I meet my friends and we chat about sport or music.
5 I take sandwiches to school and I eat them with my friends. Today, I've got cheese and salad sandwiches, and an apple.

UNIT 3

3.1 Page 29, Exercise 1

1	rugby	8	ballet
2	taekwondo	9	gymnastics
3	volleyball	10	mountain biking
4	skateboarding	11	athletics
5	ice hockey	12	surfing
6	table tennis		
7	swimming		

3.2 See SB Page 30, Exercises 1 and 2

3.3 See SB Page 32, Exercise 2

3.4 Page 32, Exercises 4 and 5

Can you run, jump and climb? Then freerunning is for you! It's an amazing sport and it's easy to learn. There are lessons on Tuesday, 14 July. Are you interested? Then meet us at eleven o'clock at the park. That's eleven o'clock on Tuesday, 14 July, at the park. You must be thirteen or over.

Can you ride a bike? Do you like going fast? Then why not try BMX biking? It's very fast and a lot of fun, and you can also do tricks! The BMX Day is on Thursday, 16 July, at ten o'clock, at the Skate Park. You can use one of our BMX bikes, but you can't ride them without a helmet, and you must follow our rules. See you at the Skate Park, on Thursday, 16 July, at ten o'clock.

Do you like playing basketball? Then why not try 3-on-3 basketball? The rules are similar to regular basketball, but there are only three players in each team and only one basket. You mustn't run with the ball, and your team must throw the ball at the basket after twelve seconds. Want to try? Then come to the Sports Centre on Saturday, 18 July, at half past nine. That's Saturday, 18 July, at half past nine, at the Sports Centre.

3.5 Page 32, Exercise 6

1 Can you run, jump and climb?
2 You must be thirteen or over.
3 You can use one of our BMX bikes, but you can't ride them without a helmet.
4 You mustn't run with the ball.

3.6 See SB Page 33, Exercise 3

3.7 See SB Page 33, Exercise 4

3.8 Page 33, Exercise 6

Red Dragon Kung Fu Club

Rules: Under 18s

1 You must speak to your teacher with respect.
2 You mustn't use mobile phones in class.
3 All students must wear the correct uniform.
4 Your uniform must be clean.
5 You mustn't chat or play in class.
6 Parents must pay for all classes on time.

3.9 Page 34, Exercises 4 and 5

1

R = Receptionist, B = Boy

R: Hello, can I help you?
B: Can I have two tickets for *The Avengers*, please?
R: Yes, of course. That's £14.
B: Here you are. What time does the film start?
R: It starts at quarter past three.
B: Great, thanks.

2

B = Boy, G = Girl

B: Can we buy an ice cream? I'm really hot.
G: OK, but let's go swimming first.
B: Good idea. Then after lunch, let's go surfing.
G: Cool. What a great day!

3

R = Receptionist, G = Girl

R: Good morning.
G: Hello. We'd like to use the gym, please.
R: OK. How old are you?
G: I'm fourteen and my sister is twelve.
R: I'm sorry, but you must be thirteen to use the gym.
G: Oh, that's a pity. Can we play tennis?
R: Yes, you can. It's £6 to play.
G: Cool. Here you are – £6.

3.10 See SB Page 35, Exercise 1

3.11 See SB Page 35, Exercise 2

3.12 Page 35, Exercise 3

B = Boy, G = Girl

B: I'm bored. Let's do something.
G: OK. What shall we do?
B: Why don't we go shopping?
G: Mmm, that doesn't sound very interesting. How about playing basketball?
B: That sounds like fun. Let's call Dan and Lottie, too.
G: Great idea!

3.13, Page 36–37, Exercise 3

Sport in the UK

Gaelic football

Gaelic football is popular in Northern Ireland. It's a mixture of football and rugby. There are two teams of fifteen players. Players can kick the ball or run with it in their hands.

Golf

Scotland is the home of golf. There are over 550 golf courses in Scotland. The Old Course in St Andrews is the oldest golf course in the world. It's 600 years old.

Cricket

Cricket is popular in summer. At Edgbaston Stadium in Birmingham, some matches start at 11 a.m. and finish at 8 p.m. But players don't play for nine hours. They stop for lunch, and also for sandwiches in the afternoon!

Tennis

Wimbledon is a famous tennis competition in London. Fans come from all over the world to watch the matches and to eat the traditional snack: strawberries. During the competition, fans eat more than 1.6 million strawberries!

Running

The London Marathon is a famous running race. It's 42 kilometres long. 40,000 runners take part, and there's also a wheelchair race. Some people run in crazy costumes!

Surfing

Can you surf? The town of Newquay has got eleven beaches and is a great place to learn. Surfing competitions often take place here.

Rugby

Rugby is popular in Wales. Welsh rugby fans love singing. When the Principality Stadium in Cardiff is full of 74,500 fans, it's very noisy!

Football

There are two famous football teams in Manchester. Manchester United play in red shirts, and Manchester City play in blue shirts. Are you a fan of the 'reds' or the 'blues'?

3.14 Page 36–37, Exercise 5

1 **How often is the FIFA World Cup competition?**
It's every four years.
2 **What nationality is tennis player Naomi Osaka?**
She's Japanese.
3 **Where is this cricket fan from?**
He's from Australia.
4 **Which race includes swimming, cycling and running?**
The triathlon.
5 **In which Brazilian city is this Olympic stadium?**
It's in Rio de Janeiro.
6 **Which basketball team has got a bull as its mascot?**
The Chicago Bulls.

UNIT 4

4.1 Page 39, Exercise 1

1 Explore a museum
2 Stay in a hotel
3 Watch a play at the theatre
4 Walk round a market
5 Eat in a restaurant
6 Spend a day at a castle
7 Go shopping at a shopping centre
8 Visit a famous monument

4.2 Page 39, Exercise 2

1

W = Waiter, B = Boy

W: Are you ready to order?
B: Yes, please. I'd like a Margarita pizza, please.
W: And I'd like Spaghetti Carbonara.
B: And to drink? ...

2

F = female tannoy voice

F: The next train to leave platform 1 is the eleven o'clock train to Liverpool. Platform 1 for the eleven o'clock service to Liverpool.

3

G = Greg, A = Anna, L = Librarian

G: Hi, Anna.

A: Hi, Greg. How are ...

L: Shh, quiet please! People are studying.

4

M = Market stall owner

M: Melons, lovely melons, two for the price of one! Bananas, get your bananas, five for a pound.

5

A= Audience

A: Bravo!

6

M = Male voice in lift

M: First floor. Men's fashion. Children's shoes.
Going up. Doors closing.
Second floor. TVs and Computers.
Bedroom furniture.

7

R = Receptionist, M = Man

R: Good afternoon, can I help you?

M: Yes, have you got any rooms for tonight?

R: Just one moment ... yes, we do.

M: Great.

R: A single or double room?

M: A double room, please.

8

B = Boy, G = Girl

B: Hello? Where are you?

G: I'm in Trafalgar Square, where are you?

B: Trafalgar Square ... really, you're in Trafalgar Square? Me too, I'm near the fountain in the middle.

G: I don't see you ... ah, there you are! Hey!

4.3 See SB Page 40, Exercise 2

4.4 See SB Page 41, Exercise 2

4.5 See SB Page 41, Exercise 3

4.6 Page 41, Exercise 4

1 She's walking to work. Picture c
2 They're playing a game. Picture e
3 He's running. Picture d
4 She's going to a party. Picture f
5 She's riding a bike. Picture h
6 We're having fun on the river. Picture g
7 He's playing the trumpet. Picture b
8 I'm reading a book. Picture a

4.7 Page 42, Exercise 1

1 It's sunny.
2 It's cloudy.
3 It's windy.
4 It's raining.
5 It's snowing.
6 It's foggy.
7 It's icy.
8 It's stormy.
9 It's hot.
10 It's warm.
11 It's cold.

4.8 Page 42, Exercises 4, 5 and 6

L = Liv, J = Josh

L: Hi, Josh, Happy Christmas!

J: Hi, Liv! Happy Christmas to you, too! Are you having a nice day?

L: Well yes, but it's only eight o'clock in the morning here in Glasgow. What time is it in Perth?

J: It's eight o'clock in the afternoon.

L: Really? What's the weather like?

J: It's beautiful. It's hot and sunny. What's it like in Glasgow? Is it snowing at the moment?

L: Yes, it is. It's snowing and it's really cold.

J: You're so lucky! I love snow, but it never snows in Perth!

L: So, what are you doing today, Josh?

J: I'm at the beach with Mum and Dad. I'm surfing and swimming.

L: Wow! Do you always go to the beach on Christmas Day?

J: Yes, we do. We usually have a picnic or a barbecue on the beach, and then we stay here until the evening.

L: Are your mum and dad surfing, too?

J: Yes, they are, but they aren't very good! So, what about you? What are you doing right now, Liv?

L: I'm helping Dad in the kitchen.

J: Is your dad cooking lunch?

L: Yes, and there's a lot to do, so I'm going now.

J: OK, thanks for phoning. Say hello to your family.

L: Yes, and happy Christmas to all of your family.

J: Thanks. Have a great day.

L: You too. Enjoy your evening. Bye!

4.9 Page 44, Exercises 3 and 4

Hello, and welcome to Oxford. We're standing next to the Tourist Information, in the centre of this beautiful city. If everyone is ready, let's start our tour – follow me please ...

... So, at the moment we're walking along Broad Street. This beautiful theatre on the right is more than 350 years old. It's called the Sheldonian Theatre, and you can come here to see a music concert, or to listen to a talk. The sound inside the theatre is very good, but I must tell you, the seats are very hard and uncomfortable!

... Opposite the theatre there is a very famous bookshop. It's got more than 200,000 books: children's books, travel books, music books, every type of book you can think of! It's a great place to spend an hour or two, and it's also got a great café. You can have a coffee and a cake, and look at a book – all at the same time!

We're now turning into Parks Road, and this big building here is the Natural History Museum. If you're interested in insects, they've got lots of colourful and unusual insects here. There are also lots of birds and other animals. But, when I come here, I like looking at the dinosaurs, especially the Tyrannosaurus rex. It's really scary!

... There's a fantastic park next to the museum, but we haven't got time to go there now, so let's walk back to Broad Street and continue our tour from there ...

4.10 See SB Page 45, Exercise 1

4.11 See SB Page 45, Exercise 2

4.12 Page 45, Exercise 4

1

A: Excuse me, is there an [...] near here?

B: Yes, there is. It's called the Ashmolean. Go straight on and turn left into Saint Giles Street.

A: Sorry. Can you say that again, please?

B: Sure. Go straight on and turn left into Saint Giles Street. Turn left again into Beaumont Street, and it's on the right opposite the hotel.

A: Thank you.

B: No problem.

2

A: Excuse me. I'm looking for the [...].

B: OK, let me think. Go straight on and cross the road into Broad Street. Go past the bookshop and turn left. Then go straight on. It's on the right after the museum.

A: OK, so go straight on, cross the road, turn left after the bookshop and it's on the right after the museum.

B: Yes, that's it.

A: Thanks very much.

B: You're welcome.

3

A: Excuse me, I'm looking for the [...]. Is it near here?

B: It's not far. Go straight on and turn right. Go past the shopping centre and the bank and turn left. It's on your left, before the University Library. It's a five-minute walk.

A: OK, thanks for your help.

B: You're welcome.

4.13 See SB Page 46–47,

Exercise 2

4.14 Page 46-47, Exercises 5 and 6

I = Interviewer, M = Man, W = Woman, E = Elderly woman

I: Excuse me, can I ask you some questions, please?
M: Sure.
I: OK, what is your favourite season?
M: My favourite season is um ... winter.
I: Why?
M: Well, I play soccer in the summer and in the fall, and hockey in winter. I think you call it ice hockey in Britain, but here we just say hockey. I love hockey! That's why winter is my favourite season.
I: Thank you.
M: You're welcome.

I: Hello, can I stop you for a minute?
W: OK.
I: Today I'm asking people 'What's your favourite season?'
W: My favourite season? I think it's fall.
I: Why's that?
W: Because it's a good time to go running. I can put on my sneakers and go running in the park. The weather is perfect – like today. Then in November, it's the New York Marathon.
I: So you like running?
W: I love it! Bye now.
I: Bye.

I: Excuse me, what's your favourite season?
E: Well, it's not summer.
I: Really? Why's that?
E: New York in summer is hot. I always take my vacation in summer because I can't stay in the city – it's so hot. No, my favourite season is spring. The weather is usually good. You can go to the park to have a picnic. You can sit outside at restaurants. Yeah, spring.
I: Thanks very much. Have a nice day.
E: You, too.

UNIT 5

5.1 Page 49, Exercise 1

Breakfast: cereal, milk, yoghurt, orange juice
Second Breakfast: eggs, beans, toast, jam
Lunch: fish, pasta, salad, fruit
Snack: sandwich, hot chocolate
Dinner: chicken, rice, potatoes, vegetables

5.2 Page 49, Exercise 3

I get up every morning at half past six, and have breakfast at seven. For breakfast, I usually have cereal and fruit. At eight o'clock, I go to the gym, and I train until lunchtime. For lunch, I have chicken and vegetables, and I usually have a glass of orange juice.
After lunch, I have a rest, and then I do more training in the afternoon. I go home at about half past four, and I see my family before dinner. For dinner, I usually have fish with pasta and salad.

5.3 See SB Page 50, Exercise 2

5.4 Page 52, Exercise 2

active— lazy
fit— unfit
healthy— unhealthy
Pairs that aren't opposite: hungry, thirsty

5.5 Page 52, Exercises 4 and 5

I = Interviewer, B = Boy

I: Excuse me. I'm doing a questionnaire about health. It's very short. Can I ask you some questions, please?
B: Yes, no problem.
I: Great. Question one: How much fruit, and how many vegetables, do you eat in a day?
B: Oh, I probably eat five or more different types. I eat a lot of fruit – I love apples – but I don't eat many vegetables.
I: Thanks. Question two: How much exercise do you do in a day?
B: Er, I don't do much exercise. I sometimes play football after school, but not every day. I'm not very active.
I: OK. Question three: How many hours do you sleep at night?
B: Quite a lot! I sleep for about nine hours. I go to bed at about ten o'clock and I get up at seven o'clock.
I: Cool. Question four: How much time do you spend watching TV, playing video games or using your phone?
B: Mmm, probably about three hours a day. I don't watch much TV, but I spend a lot of time on my phone – I play a lot of games. Three hours, that's not very healthy, is it!
I: OK, Question five: How much water do you drink in a day?
B: That's a difficult question. Probably about a litre and a half a day. And I always have a glass of orange juice at breakfast.
I: Thanks. Last question. It's two hours before dinner and you're hungry. What do you do?
B: If I'm hungry, I have some toast with jam or honey.
I: OK, that's great. That's the end of the questionnaire. Thanks very much for your time!

5.6 See SB Page 53, Exercise 3

5.7 See SB Page 53, Exercise 4

5.8 Page 53, Exercise 5

1 How much sugar is there in a can of cola?
e A lot – about nine teaspoons.
2 How much fruit does a monkey eat in a day?
c A lot – about fifty different types.
3 How many burgers do people in the USA eat in a year?
a A lot – nearly fifty billion!
4 How much honey does a bee make in its life?
b Not much – only 1/12 (one twelfth) of a teaspoon.
5 How many eggs does a chicken produce in a week?
d Not many – about five.

5.9 Page 54, Exercises 4 and 5

G = Girl, B = Boy

G: Wow, these salads look amazing. I love mango! I want the Taste of Thailand salad.
B: Yes, but you're vegetarian and it's got seafood in it!
G: Ah yes, you're right. Hmm. Plant Power then, that's only got vegetables and nuts. What about you?
B: Not sure. I love Mexican food, but I don't really like chicken, so I'm not sure about the Mexican meatballs.
G: Why don't you have the Super Salmon? You like fish, don't you?
B: Ah yes, good idea. With some bread, too – I'm really hungry.
G: I'm not that very hungry, but I'm really thirsty. I want a nice big bottle of mineral water!
B: So, we know what we want? Shall we order?
G: Yes!

5.10 Page 55, Exercise 2

S = Server, A = Alina

S: Can I help?
A: Hi, I'd like the Plant Power salad, please.
S: Anything to drink?
A: Can I have an orange juice?
S: OK. Anything else? Any dessert?
A: Yes please, I'll have a chocolate cookie.
S: Is that to eat in or take away?
A: To take away.
S: OK, that's £8, please.
A: Here you are.
S: Thank you. Your food is just coming.

5.11 See SB Page 55, Exercise 3

5.12 Page 55, Exercise 4

W = Waitress, B = Boy

W: Hello, what can I get you?
B: I'd like the Korean Curry, please.
W: One Korean Curry. Anything else?

B: Yes, can I have a fruit salad?
W: Sure. Is that to eat in or take away?
B: To eat in.
W: OK, that's £7.75, please.
B: Here you are.
W: Thank you.

5.13 See SB Page 56–57, Exercise 2

5.14 Page 56–57, Exercises 5 and 6

S = Aunt Sheila, A = Alex

1

S: Hi Alex. How are you?
A: Hi Aunt Sheila. I'm fine, thanks. I'm decorating the house with flags. Everywhere is red, white and blue!
S: Wow, I can't wait to see it. What's your dad doing?
A: He's in the kitchen. He's making the food for the barbecue.
S: And what's the weather like there?
A: It's beautiful – hot and sunny.
S: Great. See you later.

2

A = Anita, Gm = Grandma, Gp = Grandpa

A: Hi Grandma. Are you wearing your new dress? It's beautiful.
Gm: Yes, I am. Thank you, Anita.
Gp: I'm also wearing new clothes, you know.
A: Sorry, Grandpa. You look nice, too!
Gp: Thank you! Now where's the rest of the family?

3

G = Girl, B = Boy

G: Oooh! I love watching fireworks.
B: Yes, they're really beautiful. Wow!
G: And I can't wait for tomorrow. My friend Cheng is in the parade. He's one of the lion dancers.
B: Cool! Can I be in the parade, too?
G: Sorry, it's all organized for this year. But maybe you can be in it next year.

5.15 Page 56–57, Exercise 7

Independence day in numbers

Every year, on 4 July, millions of Americans celebrate Independence Day. It's a celebration of America's independence from Great Britain in 1776. Offices and schools close for the day, and friends and families get together. 43% of Americans have a barbecue or picnic. Altogether, people spend more than $7 billion on food.

Americans love fireworks on Independence Day! There are more than 16,000 firework displays in the country, and 65% of people go to one.

UNIT 6

6.1 Page 59, Exercise 1

1	sky	7	lake
2	volcano	8	river
3	mountain	9	waterfall
4	desert	10	island
5	forest	11	sea
6	rainforest	12	beach

6.2 Page 59, Exercise 2

1 K2 is a very high mountain between China and Pakistan.
2 The Amazon is a river in South America. It's home to piranhas and caimans.
3 Half of the Earth's animal species live in rainforests.
4 Vesuvius is a volcano in Italy near the old city of Pompeii.
5 Angel Falls is a waterfall in Venezuela. It's 979 metres high.
6 Bali is a beautiful island in Indonesia. It's very popular with tourists.

6.3 See SB Page 60, Exercise 1

6.4 Page 61, Exercise 3

The Secrets of a Longer Life

Okinawa is a beautiful island in Japan, with mountains, forests and beaches. The people there enjoy a longer life than people in other parts of the world. A lot of them are older than 100! What's their secret?

- The weather in Okinawa is sunnier than in other parts of Japan.
- People eat healthier food, with lots of vegetables.
- People are more active in their free time. For example, they walk, work in their gardens or do tai chi.
- The air is cleaner than in a big modern city.
- People are happier because they spend a lot of time with family and friends.

6.5 Page 62, Exercise 1

A	elephant	I	mosquito
B	bear	J	shark
C	frog	K	whale
D	lion	L	bat
E	beetle	M	tortoise
F	parrot	N	snake
G	monkey	O	spider
H	penguin	P	leopard

6.6 Page 62, Exercises 4 and 5

G = Girl, B = Boy

G: Do you want to do a quiz about animals, Matt? There's one on this website.
B: Sure. I love quizzes.
G: OK, ready? Question 1: What is the strongest animal in the world?
B: Mmm, is it a bear? They're very strong.
G: Let's see. No, it's a beetle.
B: A beetle? But they're really small!
G: Yes, it says that some beetles can carry an object that is 1,000 times heavier than they are. So that's why they're the world's strongest animal.
B: I see. What's Question 2?
G: What is the oldest animal alive today?
B: Oh, I think I know this one. Is it a tortoise?
G: Let's see. Yes, that's right. The tortoise's name is Jonathan and it's about 200 years old! Question 3: What's the hungriest animal – the animal that eats the most food?
B: Mmm, is it an elephant?
G: Sorry, Matt. It's a whale. Blue whales eat about 4,000 kilograms of food a day.
B: Woah – that's about ... 12,000 pizzas! Amazing!
G: Not everything is about pizzas, Matt! So, Question 4: What's the most dangerous animal to humans?
B: Mmm, a shark?
G: I'm afraid not, Matt. It's a mosquito. Sharks kill six or seven people a year, but mosquitos kill more than 800,000 people, through malaria and other diseases. Last question. What animal can jump the furthest?
B: Mmm, is it a frog? They're good at jumping.
G: Wrong again Matt! It's a leopard. It says that some leopards can jump 15 metres.
B: Wow, 15 metres, that's incredible!
G: So Matt, your score is 1 out of 5. The animal world is more surprising than you think, isn't it?
B: Yes, it is. It's amazing!

6.7 See SB Page 63, Exercise 2

6.8 See SB Page 63, Exercise 3

6.9 Page 64, Exercises 3 and 4

A = Anneka, L = Lisa

A: Hi, Lisa!
L: Hi, Anneka. Listen, would you like to go to Walton Forest at the weekend?
A: Ooh, yes, I really want to go there! It sounds amazing!
L: Cool. Are you free on Saturday?
A: Mmm, Saturday's a bit difficult. My grandparents are here for the day. Sunday is better for me than Saturday.
L: OK, let's go on Sunday then.
A: Great. How do we get there?
L: We can go by bus or train.
A: Which is cheaper?

L: Just a minute. I'm looking at the website now. So, the bus is cheaper than the train.
A: OK.
L: But the train is faster than the bus.
A: Hmmm.
L: But wait a minute. It says here that the bus station is nearer to the forest than the train station.
A: OK, let's go by bus then. What time shall we meet?
L: The Treetop Challenge opens at ten o'clock, so shall we get the 9.30 bus. We can meet at my house at 9.15?
A: 9.15 in the morning? That's so early!
L: Yes, but it's good to go early because the forest isn't as busy in the morning.
A: OK. Sunday, 9.15 at your house. See you then!
L: Great. See you then.

6.10 See SB Page 65, Exercise 1

6.11 See SB Page 65, Exercise 2

6.12 Page 65, Exercise 3

A = Assistant, B = Boy

A: Hello, can I help you?
B: Yes, we'd like to visit the museum. Is there a discount for students?
A: Yes, it's half price if you have a student card.
B: Great! We'd like four tickets, please.
A: OK, that's £16 in total.
B: Here you are.
A: Here are your tickets, and your change.
B: Thanks.
A: Enjoy your visit!

6.13 Page 66–67, Exercise 5

G = Tour guide, Gr: Group, B = Boy, G = Girl

1
B: It's dark in here, and there's an echo.

2
T: These are also some of the world's oldest trees. Some are more than 2,000 years old.
Gr: Wow ... Amazing! ... 2,000 years.

3
B: Phew, it's hot. Pass the water, please. I'm really thirsty.
G: Oh no, the bottle's empty.
B: What?
G: I'm only joking! Here you are.

4
B: I can't look down! We're so high.
G: It's OK. Don't be afraid. The bridge is safe.

5
T: Good morning and welcome to our tour. Now, this is very important: you mustn't feed the animals and you mustn't put your hands near the water. These reptiles are very dangerous.

6
G: Wow, the water is so loud!
B: Look at my clothes! I'm really wet!
G: Yes, it's lucky we've got some dry clothes in our bags!

UNIT 7

7.1 Page 69, Exercise 1

1	jeans	9	shorts
2	coat	10	skirt
3	boots	11	T-shirt
4	shirt	12	jumper
5	shoes	13	tie
6	hat	14	trousers
7	dress	15	jacket
8	trainers	16	socks

7.2 See SB Page 70, Exercise 1

7.3 Page 71, Exercise 6

The 1950s

There was often a phone in people's homes, but there weren't any mobile phones.

Fridges were very popular in the 1950s. There was often a fridge in the kitchen, but there wasn't always a washing machine because they were expensive.

For children, there were books and toys, but there weren't any computers or games consoles.

Clothes for adults were a bit boring. There were dresses and skirts for women and suits for men.

But for teenagers, there were colourful skirts, jeans and leather jackets. And there was rock 'n' roll music!

7.4 Page 72, Exercise 3

want, wanted	use, used
love, loved	borrow, borrowed
arrive, arrived	travel, travelled
collect, collected	enjoy, enjoyed
play, played	try, tried

7.5 Page 72, Exercises 4 and 5

P = Presenter, A = Amy, Z = Zac

P: Hello. Today's show is all about crazes. What crazes were popular when you were younger, and why were they popular? Let's speak to Amy. So Amy, tell us about a popular craze.
A: When I was about 9, Pokémon Go was really popular. It was a really fun game! People played it on their mobile phones. They walked around town and they tried to collect virtual Pokémon monsters on their phones. The monsters were in lots of different places – in parks and restaurants, in museums and cinemas, and in front of famous buildings. I loved it, and all my friends loved it, too!
P: And why was it popular?
A: It started in summer, so it was hot, and people wanted to be outside. Also, it was easy to play, and it was new and exciting.
P: Great, thanks Amy. Now, let's speak to Zac. Zac, have you got a crazy craze for us?
Z: Yes, I have. A few years ago, there was a dance that was really popular. It was called the Floss or Swish Swish. We all danced it at school, and then some of our teachers learned it, too! Famous people danced it on TV, footballers danced it in stadiums ... everybody wanted to do it!
P: Why was it so popular?
Z: Well, it was a difficult dance, but it was a lot of fun. And we all wanted to learn it because we wanted to be better and faster than our friends.
P: Cool. Thanks Zac. If you know any more crazy crazes, then call us on 0787654 ...

7.6 Page 73, Exercise 2

The Story of the Floss

A few years ago, a fifteen-year-old schoolboy, Russell Horning, invented a funny new dance called 'the Floss'. He uploaded a video of the dance to YouTube. The singer Katy Perry watched the video and she liked it. She invited Russell to dance with her on a TV show. Russell travelled to New York to be on the show. He danced the Floss on national TV! Children and adults tried to copy him. Later, Epic Games used the dance in their video game, *Fortnite*. Suddenly the Floss was a global craze!

7.7 See SB Page 73, Exercise 3

7.8 Page 73, Exercise 4

/t/	/d/	/id/
finished	arrived	collected
liked	tried	started

7.9 Page 74, Exercises 4 and 5

E = Eva, F = Frank

E: Hey, Frank, can you help me?
F: Sure, Eva. What is it?
E: I'm looking for a present for my brother. It's his birthday and I don't know what to get him. There are some nice things on this website.
F: Oh yes, coolpresents.com ... well, what does your brother like? Is he sporty?
E: Yes, he is.
F: OK. What about this bag for his sports things?
E: Mmm, he's already got a new sports bag.
F: Right, what about this watch then? It's really nice.

E: Frank, it's £39.99! It's really expensive! I love my brother, but ... not that much!
F: Yeah, OK! So, this cap's really cool and it's only £5. Does your brother like caps?
E: Yes, he does. Great idea! I can get him these sunglasses, too – they're really funny!
F: Yes, that sounds good – a cap and some sunglasses. When's your brother's birthday?
E: Err ... it was yesterday. I'm a bit late with the present.
F: Oh, Eva!

7.10 See SB Page 75, Exercise 1

7.11 See SB Page 75, Exercise 2

7.12 Page 75, Exercise 3

A = Assistant, G = Girl

A: Hello. Can I help you?
G: Have you got this sweatshirt in red?
A: Yes, we have.
G: Can I try it on, please?
A: Of course. What size do you need?
G: Small.
A: Here's a small in red. The changing rooms are over there.
A: **Later ...** Any good?
G: Yes, thanks. I'll take it.
A: OK. You can pay over there.

7.13, Page 75, Exercise 4

1 Five pounds
2 Eight pounds ninety-nine or Eight ninety-nine
3 Ten pounds seventy-five or Ten seventy-five
4 Seventeen pounds fifty or Seventeen fifty
5 Four pounds twenty-five or Four twenty-five
6 Thirty-nine pounds ninety-nine or Thirty-nine ninety-nine
7 Two pounds seventy-five or Two seventy-five
8 Three pounds sixty or Three sixty

7.14 Page 75, Exercise 5

1	£24.99	4	65p
2	£12.35	5	£3.49
3	£17.70	6	80p

7.15 See SB Page 76–77, Exercise 2

7.16 Page 76–77, Exercise 5

1 **She played Hermione Granger in the *Harry Potter* films. Who is she?**
b Emma Watson.
2 **He directed the first two *Jurassic Park* films. Who is he?**
a Steven Spielberg.
3 **How old was Macauley Culkin when he acted in the film *Home Alone*?**
b nine years old.
4 **In the *Toy Story* films, Woody and Buzz Lightyear lived with a boy called ... ?**
a Andy
5 **In the movie *E.T.*, the alien wanted to phone ... .**
c home
6 **At the end of *Titanic*, Rose dropped something into the sea. What was it?**
c a necklace.

UNIT 8

8.1 Page 79, Exercise 1

1 leave school
2 learn to drive
3 start school
4 get a job
5 get married
6 be born
7 buy a house
8 have a baby
9 die
10 make friends
11 grow up
12 go to university

8.2 Page 79, Exercise 3

1 The footballer, Lionel Messi, left Argentina to play for Barcelona when he was thirteen.
2 The actor Daniel Radcliffe bought his first house when he was eighteen.
3 The singer Ariana Grande was born in 1993.
4 The singer Bruno Mars went to school in Hawaii.
5 The actress Penélope Cruz grew up in Spain.
6 Before he was famous, the actor Hugh Jackman got a job as a clown!
7 Kimani Maruge from Kenya started primary school when he was 84 – the oldest person ever!

8.3 See SB Page 80, Exercises 2 and 3

8.4 Page 82, Exercise 2

Height and build: short, thin, tall, well-built
Hair colour: grey, dark brown, red
Hair type: curly, bald, wavy, long, straight
Eyes: blue, brown
Other: beard, moustache, glasses

8.5 Page 82, Exercises 5 and 6

I = Isabel, L = Lewis

I: Hello and welcome to *Film Magic*. I'm Isabel.
L: And I'm Lewis.
I: This week, we're looking at make-up and special effects in films.
L: And we're talking about the films of Zoe Saldana.
I: Let's start with *Avatar*. As Neytiri, Zoe had blue skin, big yellow eyes and long straight hair. She looked completely different.
L: So how did they create the character? Did they use make-up?
I: No, they didn't. They used a special camera to film Zoe's face. The small camera was on a helmet on Zoe's head. It filmed all of the movements in her face.
L: So, they used a small camera to film her face. Then what did they do?
I: Then they used a computer to change the colour of her skin, to make her eyes bigger and to add other things, for example her ears and hair.
L: Wow, so there wasn't any make-up? They just used a special camera and a computer?
I: Yes, that's right. Neytiri was completely digital.
L: Then, in *Guardians of the Galaxy*, Zoe played Gamora. She had green skin and red hair. Did they use computers for that, too?
I: No, they didn't. To create Gamora, they just used make-up – lots of green make-up! There weren't any computers.
L: Amazing! How long did the make-up take?
I: It took five hours in the first film and four hours in the later films!
L: Wow, five hours. That's a long time!
I: Yes, it isn't easy to be green!
L: You're right! Well, that's all we've got time for this week. Join us again next week for more *Film magic*.

8.6 See SB Page 83, Exercise 3

8.7 See SB Page 83, Exercise 4

8.8 Page 84, Exercises 4 and 5

1
Last Saturday, I went to a concert at Rock City Stadium with my family. First, we went to the shop in the stadium, and I bought a Cool Penguins T-shirt. Then we watched the concert. It was one of the best evenings ever! The band was fantastic, and we all sang along with their songs.
2
Last Sunday, I went to a basketball match with my dad. It was Redland Rockets against Glasgow Giants in the final of the All-Stars Cup. We arrived early and had lunch next to the arena, before the match. Did I have a good time? Yes and no! It was a great day and an exciting game, but our team didn't win. It was 111–110 to Glasgow Giants.
3
Last weekend, I was in a dance show with my dance club. My friends and I danced to two songs by Bruno Mars. It was really good fun, and the audience loved it,

too! But I was really tired at school on Monday, because after the show we had a party with all of the other dancers!

8.9 See SB Page 85, Exercise 1

8.10 See SB Page 85, Exercise 2

8.11 Page 85, Exercise 3

B = Boy, G = Girl

B: Did you have a nice weekend?
G: Yes, it was really good, thanks.
B: What did you do?
G: I went to the cinema with Harry. We saw the new *Star Wars* film.
B: What was it like?
G: It was fantastic. The special effects were amazing!
B: That sounds good!

8.12 See SB Page 86–87, Exercise 3

8.13 Page 86–87, Exercise 5

1 Nelson's real name was Rolihlahla. He started using the name Nelson on his first day at school!
2 For eighteen years, Nelson was in prison on an island. His room was 2x2 metres. There was no bed – Nelson slept on the floor.
3 As a young man, Nelson loved sport, especially boxing. He exercised regularly in his room in prison.
4 In 1993, he won the Nobel Peace Prize.
5 Nelson always made his own bed, even when he was president.

UNIT 9

9.1 Page 89, Exercise 1

1 a ship in Australia
2 a scooter in Italy
3 a lorry in India
4 a motorbike in the USA
5 a coach in Switzerland
6 a bike in the Netherlands
7 an underground train in Japan
8 a helicopter in Canada
9 a tram in Portugal
10 a boat in France
11 on foot in the UK
12 a plane in Egypt

9.2 See SB Page 90, Exercise 1

9.3 Page 91, Exercise 2

Holidays in Space

For very rich people, a trip into space is already possible. But in the future, more people will travel into space. There will be space hotels, but they won't be very big, so there will only be about eight beds. It will be a different type of holiday. People will have amazing views of the Earth, but they won't leave the hotel at all. And without gravity, it won't be easy to have a shower, so people probably won't want to spend a long time in space!

9.4 See SB Page 92, Exercise 1

9.5 Page 92, Exercise 5

P = Presenter, C = Conor, L = Luke, J = Jaz

P: Hello, and welcome to *Here comes the summer!* Let's have our first caller, please.
C: Hello, it's Conor.
P: Hi, Conor. What are your plans for the summer?
C: I'm going to go to Wales with my family.
P: Nice! How are you going to travel?
C: Well, we usually travel by car, but this year we're going to travel by train.
P: And where are you going to stay?
C: We're going to stay with my cousins – they live near the beach.
P: That's great. What are you going to do there?
C: I'm going to go surfing. We all love surfing in my family.
P: Thanks Conor! Who's our next caller?
J: It's Jaz here.
P: Hello, Jaz. So where are you going to go?
J: I'm going to go to France with my sister and my mum and dad.
P: How are you going to get there?
J: We're going to go by coach and by boat.
P: By coach and by boat – that's cool. Where are you going to stay?
J: We're going to stay in a campsite. I'm really excited. We're going to rent bikes and visit some castles.
P: Sounds good. Thanks, Jaz. Who's next?
L: It's Luke.
P: Hi, Luke. So where are you going to go this summer?
L: We aren't going to have a holiday this year. We're going to stay at home in London.
P: OK. So what are you going to do?
L: Well, a Spanish friend is going to stay with us. We're going to go sightseeing in London.
P: Sounds amazing. Have a great time, Luke. Now let's ...

9.6 See SB Page 93, Exercise 5

9.7 See SB Page 93, Exercise 6

9.8 Page 94, Exercises 5 and 6

D = Daisy, J = Jordan

D: Hi, Jordan. Where are you? Adam and I are already here. George's band is playing in ten minutes!
J: Sorry, I had some homework. My dad said I needed to do it before I went to the festival.
D: OK, so where are you now?
J: I'm on the bus. I'll be there really soon. Did you have your picnic?
D: Yes, we did. Sorry, we didn't save you any food.
J: Don't worry! I had lunch at home.
D: So, what are you doing later, after George's band finishes?
J: I haven't got any plans. Why's that?
D: Adam and I are staying to watch the fireworks. Do you want to watch them with us?
J: Yeah sure, that sounds cool.
D: My mum's meeting us at eight o'clock and driving us home. We can take you home, too.
J: Brilliant, thanks. I'll let my dad know. Right, the bus is at the park now. I'll see you in two minutes.
D: Just in time! See you!

9.9 See SB Page 95, Exercise 1

9.10 See SB Page 95, Exercise 2

9.11 Page 95, Exercise 3

J = Jess, G = Greg

J: Hi, Greg. Are you doing anything on Saturday afternoon?
G: Nothing special. Why's that?
J: I'm going to a football match. Would you like to come?
G: Sure! That sounds great. What time are you going?
J: We're leaving my house at two o'clock.
G: OK, I'll see you then.

9.12 See SB Page 96–97, Exercise 2

9.13 Page 96–97, Exercises 6 and 7

Five facts about the London Underground

Fact 1:
The London Underground was the world's first underground train system. It opened in 1863 and there were only seven stations. Today, there are more than 270 stations.

Fact 2:
Five million passengers use the Underground every day. But it's not only people that use the Underground. The tunnels are also home to half a million mice. If you visit London, look carefully – perhaps you'll see one!

Fact 3:
The shortest journey on the Underground is twenty seconds long. It's between Leicester Square station and Covent Garden station. It's only 260 metres. But it's one of the most popular journeys with tourists!

Fact 4:
In 1924, a baby was born on the London Underground. It was a little girl called Marie. She was born at a station called Elephant and Castle.
Fact 5:
Hundreds of musicians sing and play in the stations and tunnels every day. Before he was famous, the singer and guitarist Ed Sheeran often played in the London Underground!

REVIEWS

R1 Listening, Page 100, Exercises 3, 4 and 5:

C = Charlie, S = Sara, J = Jack

1
C: I love relaxing at the weekend after a busy week at school. I usually get up late on Saturdays and Sundays! I don't like getting up early at the weekend. I like watching TV, especially box sets. I've got a big TV. I also sometimes play computer games with my friends. I never tidy my room during the week or at the weekend. I'm very untidy. My mum isn't happy about that!

2
S: I usually get up early and tidy my room on a Saturday morning. I'm a tidy person, so it isn't a big job. I always have a big family lunch at the weekend. After lunch, I love chatting with friends on my phone. I don't like leaving home at the weekend! I like staying at home!

3
J: I do taekwondo on a Saturday morning. I don't get up early and I don't tidy my room. I hate tidying my room – it's boring! My taekwondo class starts at 11 a.m. and I train for an hour and a half. Taekwondo looks easy, but it isn't! I like learning new moves – and now I can jump and kick very high. I've also got a lot of friends at the Taekwondo class. I like chatting with them before the club starts, and we usually have lunch together, too. On Sundays, I do my homework.

R2 Listening, Page 102, Exercises 4, 5 and 6

R = Radio presenter, H = Hannah, P = Pierre, A = Alba

R: Good afternoon everyone. It's two o'clock on Saturday, 3 December. We are in the UK. It's raining and it's cold! Brr! What's the weather in your country today? Hannah is waiting on line 1. Hello, Hannah!
H: Hi! I'm in Perth, in Western Australia. Perth is the biggest city in Western Australia and it's also the sunniest city, in my opinion! The nearest Australian city is Adelaide, and it's more than 2,000 kilometres away! In fact, Perth is nearer Indonesia than another Australian city!
R: Wow! That's amazing, Hannah! ... and what are you doing right now?
H: Right now, I'm on the beach with my friends and I'm talking to you! Some of my friends are playing volleyball, two of my friends are cooking on a barbecue. They're cooking fish, chicken and vegetables. I'm very hungry. My favourite food is fish ... so I'm very happy!
R: And ... which season is it?
H: It's summer here. The weather is usually hot and dry at this time of year. February is the hottest month. December and January are the best months to visit my hometown. There are four rivers, nice beaches and a lot of museums near here.
R: Thanks, Hannah. Now it's over to Pierre on line 2. Where are you calling from?
P: Hi! I'm calling from Quebec City in Canada. It's early here – eight o'clock in the morning, but I'm outside and I'm playing ice hockey with my friends. We're all very fit and active and we love playing winter sports, especially at this time of year. In fact, I'm fitter in winter than I am in summer. It isn't snowing at the moment, but it's very cold and icy. We're playing on a frozen lake, but it isn't dangerous. You can go ice skating here, too! Quebec City is a great city, especially for winter sports. There's an ice hotel here – it's the only one in North America, and it's the coldest! There are also a lot of markets here in December. I love it here!
R: That's great Pierre! And finally on line 3 it's Alba.
A: Hi! I'm in Mexico City. It's earlier than it is in Quebec. It's seven o'clock in the morning here. It's warm and sunny. I'm walking to the market to buy some bread and cakes for breakfast. I'm standing in front of a beautiful building. It's called Bellas Artes and it's a theatre, museum and music venue. There aren't many people on the streets at this time in the morning. There are a lot of food stalls in this part of the city and the people are cooking food to sell. In my opinion, the best street food is a chicken torta: it's like a very big sandwich with bread, meat, chicken, cheese, salad and tomato sauce. Mmm ... my favourite! I'm very hungry!

R3 Listening, Page 104, Exercises 4, 5 and 6

D = Daz, I = Ines, N = Nick

1
D: I really like athleisure – clothes that combine sport and fashion. These are my new blue trousers. What do you think? I love them! They arrived this morning.

I also love sports T-shirts with writing on them. I've got a new red T-shirt with writing on it. But my favourite clothes are my black and white trainers. They're so cool! I bought these trainers last week with my pocket money. I'm going to wear them to my friend's party next weekend.

2
I: I have a lot of clothes and I love the skater style! It's my birthday next week. I'm going to buy some jeans with my birthday money, and my sister is going to buy me a white T-shirt. But one of my favourite clothes is my baseball cap ... it's red and very cool! I got it a few years ago at a baseball game when I was on holiday in New York City! I spent all of my holiday money on it – it was very expensive!

3
N: I'm excited because tomorrow is the first day of the summer holidays! I'm going to go to sightseeing in Paris with my family for ten days. We're going to do a lot of sightseeing! My weather app says it won't be cold, but it will rain. I'm going to pack my bag tonight. I'm taking all my summer clothes: my favourite red shorts, my green shoes, my black and white shirt ... and a raincoat for the rain. Paris here I come!

LITERATURE

L1 See SB Page 112, Exercise 3

L2 Page 112, Exercise 6

I know. I remember my first day at work. Jim looks at me. There is a question in his eyes. 'You want to know how I got the message. Right?'

'That's right,' says Jim.

'The message came out of the printer at seven o'clock this morning. Now I think I know why.' More answers come into my head. 'Last night, Jack began to type the message into his computer. Someone – maybe Strode or Fallon – went into the laboratory and saw him. Jack quickly sent the message. He typed 22.00 hours next to 'print', the time when you are usually here.

But Strode turned off the electricity to stop you working. The electricity came on again early this morning. And at seven o'clock this morning the message came out of the printer. It was nine hours late – because of the problem with the electricity.'

We are quiet for a moment. Jim looks very serious.

'Is anything wrong?' I ask.

'Yes,' Jim says. 'Where is Jack now?'

'I don't ...' I hear a noise and stop speaking. The noise is coming from outside. We go to the window.

The guard is not sleeping any more. He is standing in front of his office. A big, black car is driving through the main gate. It is Strode's car. Strode is driving. Fallon is sitting next to him. There is a gun in Fallon's hand.

L3 See SB Page 115, Exercise 3

L4 Page 115, Exercise 6

The Picture

By the time they got to the village shop, they were both wet and cold.

'Let's get the things we need, then go back to the cottage,' Pattie said.

'OK,' Will said. 'I want to get out of these wet clothes.'

They got some vegetables, a big bottle of Coca Cola, and some other things.

They were not in the shop for long. When they came out again, the road was like a river of rainwater and Pattie got water in her shoes.

They stopped in the doorway of another shop. There were a lot of old books, and old postcards and pictures of the village in the window. Pattie took off her shoes to get the water out of them.

Suddenly, Will said, 'Look, Pattie! Look at that picture!'

It was a small picture near the front of the window.

'It's a picture of Sea Bird House!' Pattie said.

There were some words under it: 'Sea Bird House, 1884. Some people call it 'the smuggler's house' because George Fenton, the smuggler, lived there.'

'Smugglers!' Will said. 'Do you think that smugglers lived in Sea Bird Cottage? Maybe they put the contraband there.'

'Yes!' Pattie said. 'Maybe they put it in the cellar.'

'But there isn't a cellar,' said Will. And then he remembered the strange noises. 'Or is there?'

L5 See SB Page 116-117, Exercise 4

L6 Page 116-117, Exercise 6

Partners

Maria heard someone behind her. She walked along near some big windows. In the windows she saw a man following her. She stopped. He stopped and looked at a newspaper. She went on. He followed her again. She felt afraid, but she wanted to laugh, too. She moved, he moved. She stopped, he stopped.

Maria looked at the man. She said, 'Are you following me? I'm going to class. Do you want to come too?'

He was very surprised and he laughed.

'Who are you?' Maria asked.

'Er ... I ...' He did not want to tell her.

Maria began to walk away. She was late for class. He ran in front of her.

'I'm Barry Lyle. Harriet Beecham is – was – my wife's sister.'

Maria went cold. What did he want from her? She looked at his face. 'I'm sorry about Harriet,' she said.

'Oh. Harriet ... Yes. Thank you,' he said. 'You didn't know Harriet?'

'No, I didn't know her,' Maria said.

'Ah ... What happened after you found her?' Barry asked.

'The police took her away. I didn't watch.'

'I see. Did they look for her ... er ... shoe there, where you found her?'

'I don't know. I didn't stay.'

'Are the police there now? Can we go and see?'

EXAM PRACTICE

E 1.1 See SB Page 118, Exercises 1 and 2

E 1.2 Page 118, Exercise 4

2 Where is Tom's phone?

T = Tom, M = Mum

T: Mum! I can't find my phone? Do you know where it is?
M: Is it in your bookcase?
T: No, and it isn't on my desk.
M: Is it in your schoolbag?
T: Oh yes, it is! Thanks, Mum!

3 Which photo are they looking at?

A = Anna, G = Gabby

A: Is this a photo of your family, Gabby?
G: Yes, it is. Look! You can see my parents and my brother. And me, of course!
A: And are these two people your grandparents?
G: Yes – my mother's parents. My father's parents live in Canada, so we don't see them often.

4 Which is Jake's house?

G = Grandma, J = Jake

G: So, Jake. Tell me about your new house. Do you like it?
J: It's great, Grandma. It's got a big garden at the back, and it's near the park.
G: Oh – so you can play football with your friends after school.
J: Yes. The only problem is the traffic. It's quite noisy at night.
G: Oh, that's a pity!

5 When is David's party?

D = David, Z = Zara

D: Hi, Zara. It's my birthday on 12 March. It's a school day, but Mum says I can have a party next weekend. Can you come?
Z: Next weekend? ... hmm ... the 16th and 17th of March? I'm busy on the 16th, but I'm free on the 17th.
D: That's lucky – my party is on the 17th.
Z: Great, see you then!

E 3.1 Page 120, Exercise 1

T = Teacher, M = Maria

T: So, are you ready to start?
M: Err ... OK ...
T: What's your name?
M: Maria.
T: And how old are you?
M: Thirteen.
T: Where do you live?
M: Madrid.
T: What's your favourite subject at school, Maria?
M: Um ... History.
T: And what do you usually do at the weekend?
M: I watch TV.
M: Sorry – can you repeat the question?
T: What do you usually do at the weekend?
M: I watch TV.
T: Please tell me something about your bedroom.
M: It's small.

E 3.2 Page 120, Exercise 3

E = Examiner, M = Maria

E: Good morning. What's your name?
M: Maria.
E: And how old are you?
M: I'm thirteen.
E: Where do you live?
M: I live in Madrid.
E: What's your favourite subject at school?
M: Well, I'm good at Maths, but I love History. It's my favourite subject.
E: And what do you usually do at the weekend, Maria?
M: Lots of things! I usually watch TV and play computer games. I also like riding my bike and I sometimes visit my grandma, too.
E: Please tell me something about your bedroom.
M: Well, I share it with my sister. It isn't very big, but we like it. We've got a bookcase for our books and a lot of pictures on the walls.
E: Thank you, Maria.

E 5.1 Page 122, Exercise 1

1 There's a music festival in the park on 17 October.
2 The tickets are £9.00 each.
3 The music begins at 1.30.
4 For more information, call 07386 446 281.
5 My name is Mrs Jones ... spelled J-o-n-e-s.

E 5.2 See SB Page 122, Exercise 3

E 5.3 Page 122, Exercise 5

T = Teacher

T: OK everyone. Listen please. I want to give you some information about the new school cooking club. Some of you have activities every Thursday and Friday, so this club is on Wednesday between 3.30 and 4.30 in the afternoon. It starts next week on 9 January, and finishes on 6 March.

The club is with a new teacher, called Mr Gastrell. That's spelled G-A-S-T-R-E double L. He's got lots of amazing meals for you to cook at the club. They are very healthy, too! The club costs £2 a week.

So ... what are you going to cook in the first lesson? You are going to cook chicken and rice with vegetables – very healthy! Remember to bring the chicken and vegetables with you.

E 7.1 See SB Page 124, Exercise 2

E 7.2 Page 124, Exercise 3

M = Mum, T = Toby

M: How was your shopping trip Toby? Was the new shopping centre nice?
T: Yes, I liked it, Mum. It's really big, and I found some amazing trainers ... and they were cheap, too! But there were a lot of people there. It was very busy!
M: Oh no! How did you travel to the shopping centre? Is it far?
T: It was very far – so I didn't go on foot. But there's a bus stop opposite the train station so I went by bus.
M: Were there many places to eat? And was there a cinema?
T: No, there wasn't a cinema, but there were some really nice restaurants and a sandwich shop.
M: That sounds great. What did you buy?
T: I bought jeans. What do you think? Last month they were £50, but today they are only £20! Do you like them?
M: Well, the size is fine. And they're cheap, too! But ... they're purple! I don't like the colour!
T: Well, I love purple, Mum. It's my favourite colour. I think they're perfect!

E 9.1 Page 126, Exercise 3

T = Teacher, To = Tomas

T: Hi Tomas! Can I have your topic form, please? OK, let's start. What are we going to talk about today?
To: Skiing.
T: OK. And ... can you ski?
To: Yes.
T: Great! When did you learn to ski?
To: Sorry? Can you repeat the question?
T: When did you learn to ski? How old were you when you started skiing?
To: Four years old.
T: ... and where did you learn to ski?
To: In Krahule. In Slovakia.
T: And ... why do you like skiing?
To: Can you repeat the question?
T: Yes, of course! Why do you love skiing?
To: Oh, I love snow! And going fast!
T: Can you snowboard as well?
To: No.
T: Have you tried snowboarding?
To: Yes. Once.
T: Is skiing better than snowboarding?
To: Yes.
T: Why? Why is it better?
To: Snowboarding is ... is ... I don't like it.
T: OK ... So, are you going skiing again soon?
To: Yes, in December. We are going to Jasna.
T: Thank you, Tomas. That was a good start! Now, let's think about how we can make this better for your exam ...

E 9.2 Page 126, Exercise 4

E = Examiner, To = Tomas

E: Hi Tomas! Can I have your topic form, please? OK let's start. What are we going to talk about today?
To: My favourite sport, skiing.
E: OK, great. Can you ski?
To: Yes. I go skiing with my family every year.
E: So, when did you learn to ski?
To: When I was four years old. My father was my teacher! He's very good at skiing.
E: Where did you learn?
To: In Krahule. It's a very small village. There aren't many ski lifts, but it was perfect for learning to ski.
E: Why do you love skiing so much?
To: I'm sorry, can you repeat the question?
E: Yes, why do you love skiing?
To: Oh, I love the mountains, the fresh air ... and I love going really fast. It's very exciting!
E: Can you snowboard as well?
To: No, I can't. I tried snowboarding, but I didn't like it. In my opinion, it's more difficult than skiing. Can you ski or snowboard?
E: No, I can't, unfortunately! So, are you going skiing again soon?
To: Yes, I'm going skiing next month with my family. We're going to Jasna. We will stay in our favourite hotel there and we will go skiing every day.
E: Thank you Tomas!

VLOG
UNIT 1

My new home

BACKGROUND

Ioan is from the UK. At the moment, he lives with his parents but now it's time for him to move out. In this vlog, Ioan talks about moving to his new home. He talks about the different rooms in his parents' house and describes the things he wants to take with him to his new place.

LANGUAGE

The following target language items are recycled from Unit 1: *bookcase, chair, cooker, desk, fridge, lamp, mirror, sink, table, wardrobe*. These are detailed in bold in the Unit 1 vlog script on TG page 304. You may wish to pre-teach the following words and phrases: *drawings, keep, memories, move out, outfits, stay, stuff, throw away*.

NOTE: Ioan uses some phrases which sts might find difficult to translate: ... *It's time to (move out/find)* ... (It is a good idea to do something now); *Why not (take all of them)?* (There's no reason why I can't take all of the outfits); ... *let things go* ... (throw away things you don't need). Ioan also uses some grammar that sts don't meet until later in the SB: present simple (*I have, I do, I spend*, etc.) to talk about possessions and routines; present continuous (*I am taking / I'm not taking, They're staying* ...) to talk about things happening at this moment in time; *can* (... *you can help* ..., ... *I can't take* ...).

The Richmond Learning Platform has a vlog activity to focus on the vocabulary of this lesson. Sts see the complete lexical set from SB page 9 and click the words they hear on the vlog. Alternatively, if focusing on the words in class, the timecodes are as follows: *desk* (0:36, 1:00); *table* (0:38); *chair* (0:46); *lamp* (0:48); *mirror* (0:49); *bookcase* (1:12); *wardrobe* (1:21); *cooker* (1:49); *sink* (1:34); *fridge* (1:50). These are detailed in bold in the Unit 1 vlog script on TG page 304.

PREPARE

21st Century skills

FIND OUT

In the past, young people in the UK left their family home in their late teens or early twenties. Now, over 25% of 20-34-year olds still live at home with their parents. Some of them leave home (for example, to go to university) and then return later. They're called 'boomerang kids'.

WATCH

Watch the vlog together. At the end, ask sts to write one sentence with a fact that they learned from Ioan's vlog. Then ask some of them to read their sentences aloud.

Ask sts the following true/false noticing questions from the video, playing it again for sts to check their answers:

- *There is a laptop computer on Ioan's desk.* (true: 0:28–0:43)
- *Ioan's bed is on the right side of the bedroom.* (false (it's on the left): 1:59–1:11)
- *The door to Ioan's house is blue.* (false (it's red): 1:59–2:10)

With stronger classes, you may also wish to focus on the following words and phrases which also relate to the home: *my parents' house* (0:09); *my new place* (0:17); *study* (0.30); *the things that live there* (0:42); *(my desk) is home to (sth)* (1:01); *workspace* (1:05); *bedroom* (1:10); *kitchen* (1:40).

REFLECT

21st Century skills

FIND OUT

Sts can use the activity below to find out more about their classmates and their homes. First, elicit the question sts need to ask. (*Do you live in a* ... / *Where do you live?*).
Encourage sts to mingle and talk to as many different classmates as possible, using the same questions. Ask one or two sts to report back to the class.

- *Find out how many of your classmates live in:*
  - » *a house*
  - » *an apartment*
  - » *somewhere different, for example a boat or a caravan*
- *Talk to your classmates about their favourite room at home. What is your favourite room? What are your classmates' favourite rooms?*
- *Think about the place where you do your homework and revision. Describe your workspace to your classmates. Is it similar to theirs?*

You could also ask sts to watch the vlog again for homework (either with or without subtitles).

VLOG
UNIT 2

Morning routine

BACKGROUND

Tati is a student from London who vlogs about her daily activities. In this vlog, Tati is at home. She talks about her typical morning routine, from the time she gets up in the morning to the time she leaves the house to study.

LANGUAGE

The following target language items are recycled from Unit 2: *get dressed, get up, have a shower, have breakfast, tidy my room*. These are detailed in bold in the Unit 2 vlog script on TG page 304. You may wish to pre-teach the following words and phrases: *go downstairs/upstairs, my alarm goes off, take a while, feel refreshed, make time to do something, wake up*.

NOTE: Tati uses two phrases which sts might find difficult to translate: *So, let's get right into it* (Let's start), and *I'm all ready for the day ...* (I'm ready for the day ...). She also uses some grammar that sts don't meet until later in the Student's Book: *can* (*... this can take a while*) to talk about possibility; present continuous (*... I'm having tea and toast*) to talk about something happening now.

The Richmond Learning Platform has a vlog activity to focus on the vocabulary of this lesson. Sts see the complete lexical set from SB page 19 and click the words they hear on the vlog. Alternatively, if focusing on these words in class, the timecodes are as follows: *get up* (0:19); *have a shower* (0:29, 0:34); *get dressed* (0:43); *have breakfast* (1:04, 1:15); *tidy my room* (1:23, 1:29). These are detailed in bold in the Unit 2 vlog script on TG page 304.

PREPARE

21st Century skills

FIND OUT

Tati describes her morning routine in the vlog, and talks about what she has for breakfast. Write this sentence on the board and ask sts to guess or research the correct answer a, b or c.

In Britain, people drink ... million cups of tea a day.

a 65 million   b 115 million   c 165 million

(correct answer: c)

WATCH

Watch the vlog together. At the end, ask sts to write one sentence with a fact about Tati's day. Then ask some of them to read their sentences aloud.

Ask sts the following noticing questions from the video, playing it again if necessary for sts to check their answers:

- *What day is it?* (Monday: 0:27)
- *Does Tati drink green tea or white tea for breakfast?* (green tea: 1.14)
- *What colour is Tati's bedroom door?* (white: 1:54)

With stronger classes, you may also wish to focus on the following words and phrases relating to daily routines: *my alarm goes off* (0:16); *get out of bed* (0:27); *wake up* (0.36); *coming home* (1:31); *leave the house* (1:48); *have a good day* (1:48).

REFLECT

21st Century skills

FIND OUT

Sts can use the *Find someone who* activity below to find out more about their classmates and their morning routines.

First, elicit the questions sts need to ask (*What time do you get up? What do you have for breakfast? Do you tidy your room every day/How often do you tidy your room?*)

Encourage sts to mingle and talk to as many different classmates as possible, using the same questions. Ask one or two sts to report back to the class.

- *Find someone who:*
  - » *gets up at seven o'clock*
  - » *has the same breakfast as Tati*
  - » *tidies their room every day*
- *Talk to your classmates and find out what they have for breakfast. Use the information to draw a bar chart showing the number of sts who have cereal, toast, coffee, etc.*

You could also ask sts to watch the vlog again for homework (either with or without subtitles).

Life as an athlete

BACKGROUND

Nina is a ballet dancer from the United States. Her ambition is to be a professional dancer, so she practises six days a week. In this vlog, Nina talks about life as an athlete. and the things that athletes have in common such as hard work, practising every day and having instructors or coaches to help them improve.

LANGUAGE

The following target language items are recycled from Unit 3: *ballet, gymnastics, surfing, swimming, volleyball*. These are detailed in bold in the Unit 3 vlog script on TG page 304. You may wish to pre-teach the following words and phrases: *be serious about something, get better, jump, movement, powerful, train, turn, twist*.

NOTE: Nina uses some phrases which sts might find difficult to translate: ... *the work it takes* ... (the work you must do to be successful),*'cos* (because), ... *get something just right* (do something correctly). She also uses some grammar that sts don't meet until later in the Student's Book: past simple (*started, tried, was, went swimming, liked, preferred*) to talk about things she did or liked in the past; present continuous (... *I'm training* ...) to talk about what she is doing now; *could* (*How could surfing ... be like ballet?*) for possibility; and zero conditional (*If you're thinking about joining a sport, go for it!*) to give advice.

The Richmond Learning Platform has a vlog activity to focus on the vocabulary of this lesson. Sts see the complete lexical set from SB page 29 and click the words they hear on the vlog. Alternatively, if focusing on the words in class, the timecodes are as follows: *ballet* (0:14, 0:44, 1:07); *swimming* (0:49); *gymnastics* (1:00); *surfing* (1:34); *volleyball* (2.04). These are detailed in bold in the Unit 3 vlog script on TG page 304.

PREPARE

21st Century skills

FIND OUT

The colours of the five circles on the Olympic flag represent the five continents of the world that take part in the Games: Africa (black), The Americas (red), Asia (yellow), Australia (green) and Europe (blue). If you have time and internet access, put sts into pairs and ask the to find out what the circles represent.

WATCH

Watch the vlog together. Ask sts to write one sentence with a fact from the vlog. Then ask some of them to read their sentences aloud.

Ask sts the following noticing questions from the video, playing it again for sts to check their answers:

- *How many football players are there?* (four: 0:23–0:25)
- *Is the athlete in the park a man or a woman?* (a woman: 0.41)
- *What colour are the children's surfboards?* (red and blue: 2:02–2:05)

With stronger classes, you may also wish to focus on the following words and phrases which also relate to sport: *athlete* (0:21, 0:33, 0:40); *the sport they practise* (0:39); *dancing* (0:55); *training to be/become a professional* (1:22); *skills* (1:41); *dance teachers* (2:01); *surf instructors* (2.02); *coaches for sports* ... (2.03–2.04).

REFLECT

21st Century skills

FIND OUT

Sts can use the *Find someone who* activity below to find out more about their classmates and the sports they do. First, elicit the questions sts need to ask. (*Do you do ballet? Are you in a sports team? Do you want to be a professional athlete?*). Encourage them to mingle and talk to as many different classmates as possible, using the same questions. Ask one or two sts to report back to the class.

- *Find someone who:*
  - » *does ballet*
  - » *is in a sports team*
  - » *wants to be a professional athlete*
- *Talk to your classmates and make a list of all the different sports that they do.*
- *Find out how many hours a week your classmates spend doing sports.*

You could also ask sts to watch the vlog again for homework (either with or without subtitles).

VLOG UNIT 4

My top five things in Paris

BACKGROUND

Natalie Hall is a British vlogger from London who specializes in travel vlogging. She's also interested in cooking and fashion. In this vlog, she takes us on her recent trip with her friends to Paris, France. She show us the landmarks she visits and the top five sights she sees. Her journey includes shopping, visiting museums and famous landmarks.

LANGUAGE

The following target language items are recycled from Unit 4: *library*, *market*, *monument*, *museum*, *restaurant*, *shopping centre*. These are detailed in bold in the Unit 4 vlog script on TG page 304. You may wish to pre-teach the following words: *full*, *busy*, *painting*, *luxury*, *view*.

NOTE: Natalie uses some phrases which sts might find difficult to translate: ... *iconic* (a famous thing or person), ... *we've just had an explore in* ... (we've visited a place and explored it), *panoramic view* (a wide view of an area) *filled with* (a place that is full of something) ... *the most recognisable place* (a place that a lot of people know about). She also uses some grammar that sts don't meet until later in the Student's Book: past simple (*had*, *visited*, *was/wasn't*).

The Richmond Learning Platform has a vlog activity to focus on the vocabulary of this lesson. Sts see the complete lexical set from SB page 39 and click the words they hear on the vlog. Alternatively, if focusing on the words in class, the timecodes are as follows: *museum* (0:22, 0:29, 0:33); *market* (1:02); *shopping centre* (1:15); *restaurant* (1:17); *library* (1:28), *monument* (2:08). These are detailed in bold in the Unit 4 vlog script on TG page 304.

PREPARE

21st Century skills

FIND OUT

If you have time and internet access, you could ask sts to guess how many visitors the Louvre has each year and then find out the answer online (more than 10 million). Whose guess was the closest?

WATCH

Watch the vlog together. Ask sts to write one sentence with a fact they didn't know before they watched the vlog. Then ask some of them to read their sentences aloud.

Ask sts the following noticing questions from the video, playing it again for sts to check their answers:

- *How many museums does Natalie talk about?* (two; the Louvre: 0:21, the Musée de l'Orangerie: 0:40. Also the Pompidou Centre (exhibitions and modern art: 1:34)
- *Name one thing Natalie says the market sells.* (books/ antiques: 1:05)
- *What does Natalie eat for lunch?* (a sandwich: 2:24)

With stronger classes, you may also wish to focus on the following words related to places in a city which are also heard on the vlog: *art gallery* (0:43); *river* (0:58); *book store* (1:25); *tower* (2:05); *hill* (1:59); *building* (1:59); *park* (2:25).

REFLECT

21st Century skills

FIND OUT

Sts can use the *Find someone who* activity, and questions below, to find out more about their classmates and the places they visit.
First, elicit the questions sts need to ask. (*Do you go to a restaurant every weekend?/How often do you go to a restaurant? Do you visit/go to a library? Do you usually stay in hotels on holiday?/Where do you usually stay?*).
Encourage sts to mingle and talk to as many different classmates as possible, using the same questions.
Ask one or two sts to report back to the class.

- *Find someone who:*
  - » *goes to a restaurant every weekend*
  - » *sometimes visits a library*
  - » *usually stays in a hotel on holiday*
- *What are the top five places to visit in your town or city?*
- *Talk to your classmates about museums. Who knows the most unusual museum? What is it about?*

You could also ask sts to watch the vlog again for homework (either with or without subtitles).

VLOG UNIT 5

Farmers' market

BACKGROUND

Bokang is from South Africa. She has a vlog called *The B Word* and she blogs about her life. In this vlog, she describes a visit to a local farmers' market. There's a lot of different food at the market. Bokang buys a drink, a sandwich and a snack.

LANGUAGE

The following target language items are recycled from Unit 5: *chicken, fruit, orange juice, potatoes, sandwich, vegetables*. These are detailed in bold in the Unit 5 vlog script on TG page 304. You may wish to pre-teach the following words and phrases: *farmers' market, freshly squeezed, juice stand, local, selection, snack, stall.*

NOTE: Bokang uses some phrases which sts might find difficult to translate: *... being out and about ...* (going to interesting places outside your home); *once the main meal was done* (after the main meal); *there you go* (it's ready). She also uses the word *fruits* – in British English *fruit* is an uncountable noun. However, in some English-speaking countries, such as the USA and South Africa, *fruit* is countable and has a singular and plural form (*one fruit, two fruits*). Bokang uses some grammar that sts don't meet until later in the Student's Book: *going to* (*I'm going to the market ...*) to talk about a plan; and past simple (*was, decided, thought*) to talk about things that happened at the market.

The Richmond Learning Platform has a vlog activity to focus on the vocabulary of this lesson. Sts see the complete lexical set from SB page 49 and click the words they hear on the vlog. Alternatively, if focusing on these words in class, the timecodes are as follows: *chicken* (0:40, 1:28); *fruit* (0:41, 1:04); *vegetables* (0:41, 1:04); *sandwiches* (0:42, 1:23); *juice* (0:45); *potatoes* (1:44-1.46). These are detailed in bold in the Unit 5 vlog script on TG page 304.

PREPARE

21st Century skills

FIND OUT

If you have time and access to the internet, arrange sts in pairs and ask them to find photos of a farmers' market in their town/country. Have them list ten food and drink items people can buy there. Pairs could then compare their lists.

WATCH

Watch the vlog together. Ask sts to write one sentence with a fact that they learned from the vlog. Then ask some of them to read their sentences aloud.

Ask sts the following noticing questions from the video, playing it again for sts to check their answers:

- *What are Bokang and her friend eating in the car?* (ice cream: 0:20)
- *What fruit do you see at the juice bar?* (oranges, lemons, apples: 1:01–1:05)
- *What colour dress is Bokang's friend wearing?* (black and white: 1:25–1:27 & 1:55 & 2:14)

With stronger classes, you may also wish to focus on the following words and phrases which also relate to food and drink: *freshly squeezed ... juice* (0:44); *dishes* (0:48); *juice stand* (0:57); *ginger* (1:13); *main meal* (1:34); *snack* (1:39); *potato stand* (1:44); *cut up* (1:45); *fry* (1:46); *flavour* (1:48).

REFLECT

21st Century skills

FIND OUT

Sts can use the *Find someone who* activity below to find out more about their classmates and the food they eat.
First, elicit the questions sts need to ask.
(*Do you go to markets? Do you want to try South African food? Can you cook?/What can you cook?*).
Encourage sts to mingle and talk to as many different classmates as possible, using the same questions. Ask one or two sts to report back to the class.

- *Find someone who:*
  - » *goes to markets*
  - » *wants to try South African food*
  - » *can cook something interesting*
- *Do a class survey to find the best places to eat in your town/city.*
- *Talk to your classmates about their favourite food. Do they know how to cook it?*

You could also ask sts to watch the vlog again for homework (either with or without subtitles).

Exploring the island of East Java

BACKGROUND

Steve is from the United States. He is a travel vlogger and he makes videos about the different places that he visits. In this vlog, Steve describes a trip to Indonesia and talks about the amazing places he went to while he was on the island of East Java.

LANGUAGE

The following target language items are recycled from Unit 6: *desert*, *forest*, *island*, *lake*, *mountain*, *river*, *volcano*, *waterfall*. These are detailed in bold in the Unit 6 vlog script on TG page 305. You may wish to pre-teach the following words and phrases: *bottom*, *explore*, *hike*, *in the dark*, *mile*, *raft*, *top*, *travel around*, *view*.

NOTE: Steve uses some phrases which sts might find difficult to translate: ... *It makes sense* ... (It is easy to understand); *all the way* (from the beginning to the end); *there you go* (it's ready). Steve also uses some grammar that sts don't meet until later in the Student's Book: *going to* (*We're going to explore* ...) to talk about a plan; *can* (*You can see* ..., *you can ride* ...) to talk about things that are possible; and past simple (*hiked*, *made*, *saw*, *spent*, *visited*, *went*, *woke*) to talk about things that happened on his trip.

The Richmond Learning Platform has a vlog activity to focus on the vocabulary of this lesson. Sts see the complete lexical set from SB page 59 and click the words they hear on the vlog. Alternatively, if focusing on these words in class, the timecodes are as follows: *island* (0:13); *waterfall* (0:37, 0:45, 2:29. 2:40); *river* (1:02); *volcano* (1:14, 1:36, 1:40, 1:49); *mountain* (1:20, 1:31); *desert* (1:42); *lake* (2:08); *forest* (2:36). These are detailed in bold in the Unit 6 vlog script on TG page 305.

PREPARE

21st Century skills

FIND OUT

Indonesia is an archipelago – a country made up of islands. Write this sentence on the board. *Indonesia has ... islands*, then ask sts in pairs to guess how many islands make up the country of Indonesia. (answer: over 16,000).

WATCH

Watch the vlog together. Ask sts to write one sentence with a fact that they learned from the vlog. Then ask some of them to read their sentences aloud.

Ask sts the following true/false noticing questions from the video, playing it again for sts to check their answers:

- *There are four plants in Steve's room.* (false (there are two): 0:05–0:18)
- *Steve rides an orange raft down the river.* (true: 1:05–1:12)
- *There are a lot of people at the top of Mount Ijen.* (false (there is one person): 2:13–2:21)

With stronger classes, you may also wish to focus on the following words and phrases which also relate to the natural world: *view* (0:58, 1:24); *active volcano* (1:14); *Mount* (1:52); *sunrise* (2:03); *crater* (2:09); *wall of water* (2:35).

REFLECT

21st Century skills

FIND OUT

Sts can use the *Find someone who* activity, and questions below, to find out more about their classmates.
First, elicit the questions sts need to ask. (Do you like adventure holidays? Do you want to visit Indonesia?) Encourage sts to mingle and talk to as many different classmates as possible, using the same questions. Ask one or two sts to report back to the class.

- *Find someone who:*
  - » *likes adventure holidays*
  - » *doesn't like adventure holidays*
  - » *wants to visit Indonesia after watching the video*
  - » *doesn't want to visit Indonesia after watching the video*
- *Think about the natural world. What places do you like to visit in your country? Do your classmates like to visit the same places?*
- *Talk to your classmates about the natural world. What natural wonder would you like to see? What natural wonder is the most popular?*

You could also ask sts to watch the vlog again for homework (either with or without subtitles).

VLOG
UNIT 7

I know nothing about fashion

BACKGROUND

Ben is from Canada but he lives in London. He makes videos about his life. In this vlog he talks about the clothes he likes to wear and why he feels good wearing them.

LANGUAGE

The following target language items are recycled from Unit 7: *coat, hat, jeans, jumper, shirt, shoes, skirt, socks, tie, trainers*. These are **highlighted** in the Unit 7 vlog script on page 305. You may wish to pre-teach the following words and phrases: *charity shop, fall apart, feel good, hoody, long/short sleeves, pound (currency), tie* (v).

NOTE: Ben uses one or two phrases which sts might find difficult to translate: *it keeps me warm* (I feel warm when I wear it); *wear something out* (wear something outside the house); *brand new* (completely new); *... with my hair down* (used to describe long hair that is free and not tied). Ben also uses some grammar that sts don't meet until later in their course: *will* (*... it will be fun / inspire me ...*) to predict the future.

The Richmond Learning Platform has a vlog activity to focus on the vocabulary of this lesson. Sts see the complete lexical set from SB page 69 and click the words they hear on the vlog. Alternatively, if focusing on the words in class, the timecodes are as follows: *skirt* (0:33, 0:35); *jumper* (0:44); *shirt* (0:53); *tie* (1:10); socks (1:16, 1:24) *trainers* (1:34); *shoes* (1:36); *jeans* (1:43, 1:46); *coat* (2:01); *hat* (2:06). These are detailed in bold in the Unit 7 vlog script on TG page 305.

PREPARE

21st Century skills

FIND OUT

There are a few clothing words that are not the same in American and British English. Write the following British words on one side of the board: *jumper, trousers, trainers, jacket, dressing gown* and check that sts know them. Then write the following American words on the other side of the board: *bathrobe, sneakers, sweater, blazer, pants* and ask sts to match pairs of words. (answers: jumper/sweater, trousers/pants, trainers/sneakers, jacket/blazer, dressing gown/bathrobe)

WATCH

Watch the vlog together. At the end, ask sts to write one sentence with a fact that they learned from the vlog. Then ask some of them to read their sentences aloud.

Ask sts the following true/false noticing questions from the video, playing it again for sts to check their answers:

- *Ben's skirt is red.* (false (it's black): 0:30–0:42)
- *Ben has got four pairs of jeans.* (false (he has got three pairs): 1:43–1:59)
- *Ben buys some trainers at the charity shop.* (false (he buys a jumper): 2:31–2:44)

With stronger classes, you may also wish to focus on the following words and phrases which also relate to clothes: *fashion* (0:19); *made for men* (0:35); *hoodies* (0:45); *long-sleeve shirt* (0:53); *long sleeves* (0:54); *short sleeves* (0:57); *blazer* (1:07); *patterns* (1:20); *pair of sneakers/shoes* (1:33, 1:37); *tight-fitting* (1:46); *comfy* (1:51, 2:30); *brand new* (2:01).

REFLECT

21st Century skills

FIND OUT

Sts can use the *Find someone who* activity below to find out more about their classmates and their clothes. First, elicit the questions sts need to ask. (*Do you like Ben's clothes? Why do you/don't you like them?*) Encourage sts to mingle and talk to as many different classmates as possible, using the same questions. Ask one or two sts to report back to the class.

- *Find someone who:*
  - » *likes Ben's clothes – why?*
  - » *doesn't like Ben's clothes – why not?*
- *Talk to your classmates about your favourite item of clothing. What colour is it? Where did you buy it? Why do you like it? When do you wear it?*
- *Think about the shops in your town/city where young people like to buy clothes. Talk to your classmates and find out what are the most popular shops. Why are they popular?*

You could also ask sts to watch the vlog again for homework (either with or without subtitles).

VLOG
UNIT 8

My grandpa and his life story

BACKGROUND

Rebecca is a student from the United States. At the moment, she is living and studying in the United Kingdom. In this vlog, Rebecca talks about her family history. She tells us about how her grandparents met, she describes their life in East Africa, and she explains why her dad decided to move to the USA.

LANGUAGE

The following target language items are recycled from Unit 8: *be born, get a job, go to university, grow up, have (children), get married*. These are detailed in bold in the Unit 8 vlog script on TG page 305. You may wish to pre-teach the following words and phrases: *fix, grandpa, make memories, multicultural family, Navy, proud, road trip*.

NOTE: Rebecca uses some phrases which sts might find difficult to translate: *... you guys ...* (an informal way to talk to everyone watching the vlog); *His family didn't have a lot of money growing up* (a shortened way of saying 'His family didn't have a lot of money when he was growing up'). Rebecca uses some grammar that sts don't meet at this level: *have to do something* (*... he had to get a job*) to talk about past obligation; *should* (*... you should be proud ...*) to give advice; and *will* (*I'll see you ...*) to refer to a future time.

The Richmond Learning Platform has a vlog activity to focus on the vocabulary of this lesson. Sts see the complete lexical set from SB page 79 and click the words they hear on the vlog. Alternatively, if focusing on these words in class, the timecodes are as follows: *was born* (0:20, 0:30); *growing up* (0:32); *get a job* (0:36, 1:09); *got married* (1:00; 1:09); *drive* (1.16), *go to university* (1.56). These are detailed in bold in the Unit 8 vlog script on TG page 305.

PREPARE

21st Century skills

FUN FACT

The USA is one of the most multicultural countries in the world. New York is an example of a multicultural American city. It has a population of eight and a half million people and over three million of them were not born in the USA. Half of all New Yorkers speak a language that isn't English, at home.

WATCH

Watch the vlog together. Ask sts to write one sentence with a fact from the vlog. Then ask some sts to read their sentences aloud.

Ask sts the following true/false noticing questions from the video, playing it again for sts to check their answers:

- *There are four colours on the Italian flag?* (false (there are three): 0:29–0:33)
- *Rebecca's aunt is standing with a lion?* (false (her uncle is standing with a lion): 1:04–1:07)
- *VEXEDBECCA is the name of Rebecca's Twitter account?* (True: 2:13–2:18)

With stronger classes, you may also wish to focus on the following words and phrases which also relate to life events: *life story* (0:18); *be in (the Navy) for ... years* (0:48–0:51); *meet someone* (0:54–0:57); *make memories* (1:26–1:27); *move (to another place)* (1:46, 1:52); *live (in a place)* (1:58); family history (2:05).

REFLECT

21st Century skills

FIND OUT

Sts can use the *Find someone who* activity, and the questions below, to find out more about their classmates and their families. First, elicit the questions sts need to ask. (*Do you anything about ...? / What do you know about ...?*).
Encourage sts to mingle and talk to as many different classmates as possible, using the same questions. Ask one or two sts to report back to the class.

- *Find someone who knows an interesting fact about:*
  - » *Italy*
  - » *Ethiopia*
  - » *the USA*
- *Find out how many of your classmates would like to study in another country. Which country?*
- *Talk about your parents and grandparents. Is your family multicultural? Have you got any relatives living in other countries?*

You could also ask sts to watch the vlog again for homework (either with or without subtitles).

VLOG
UNIT 9

Transport in Europe

BACKGROUND

Natalie lives in London. Last year she bought a train pass and travelled around Europe. She visited Paris, Berlin, Prague and Budapest. In this vlog, Natalie talks about the cities that she visited and all the different types of transport she used in each city.

LANGUAGE

The following target language items are recycled from Unit 9: *bike, plane, scooter, tram, underground*. These are detailed in bold in the Unit 9 vlog script on TG page 305. You may wish to pre-teach the following words and phrases: *environmentally friendly*, *get around*, *hire*, *international*, *pass (n)*, *regional*, *system*, *ticket*.

NOTE: In this vlog, Natalie uses one or two phrases which sts might find difficult to translate: *... pretty far away from each other* (a long way from each other / not close to each other), *a little bit* (not much), *... via an app* (by using an app).

The Richmond Learning Platform has a vlog activity to focus on the vocabulary of this lesson. Sts see the complete lexical set from SB page 89 and click the words they hear on the vlog. Alternatively, if focusing on the words in class, the timecodes are as follows: *bike* (0:17); *underground* (0:24, 1:27, 1:32, 2:04); *scooter* (1:38, 1:43); *tram* (1:55, 1:58); *plane* (2:19). These are detailed in bold in the Unit 9 vlog script on TG page 305.

PREPARE

21st Century skills

FIND OUT

If you have time and access to the internet, you could ask sts to find out which four cities have the longest underground systems in the world. (1 Shanghai, 2 Beijing, 3 London, 4 New York). Alternatively, prepare them for the video by writing *London, Paris, Berlin, Budapest* and *Prague* on the board and setting a time limit for them to find three different ways to get around each city.

WATCH

Watch the vlog together. Ask sts to write one sentence with a fact that they learned from the vlog. Then ask some of them to read their sentences aloud.

Ask sts the following noticing questions from the video, playing it again for sts to check their answers:

- *What colour is Natalie's bike?* (*red:* 0:15)
- *What day of the week did Natalie and her friends hire electric scooters?* (*Wednesday:* 1:46–1:47)
- *What is the number on the side of the tram in Prague?* (*24:* 1:58)

With stronger classes, you may also wish to focus on the following words and phrases which also relate to transport: *bus* (0:21, 2:05); *flight* (0:43); *rail* (0:45); *regional and international trains* (0:49); *train* (0:55, 1:04, 1:09); *metro system* (1:19); *metro ticket* (1:23); *metro* (1:31); *tram pass* (1:54); *walking* (2:14); *flying* (2:22); *methods of transport* (2:30).

REFLECT

21st Century skills

FIND OUT

Sts can use the activity below to find out more about their classmates and the transport they use.
First, elicit the question sts need to ask. (*How do you come to school?*)
Encourage sts to mingle and talk to as many different classmates as possible, using the same questions. Ask one or two sts to report back to the class.

- *Find out how your classmates come to school, and make a bar chart to show the most popular ways of travelling to school.*
- *Look at the transport words on page 89 of the Student Book. Put them in order from the best to the worst, then compare your ideas with your classmates. What is the most popular way to travel?*
- *Describe an interesting journey you made. Where did you go? How did you travel there? Why was the journey interesting?*

You could also ask sts to watch the vlog again for homework (either with or without subtitles).

Homes on wheels

BACKGROUND

The Tiny House Festival is taking place in Colorado, USA. Visitors come to these festivals to see the unusual homes that people create in very small spaces. British travel vloggers and mobile homeowners Bee and Theo are at the festival and they show us some of their favourite tiny houses. These include a motorhome made from wood, a complete house on wheels, and a tiny, very colourful mobile home. Each home is different, and there are a lot of ideas for Bee and Theo's own mobile home.

LANGUAGE

The following target language items are recycled from Unit 1: *there is / there are + a, an, some, any*; prepositions of place; *have got*; *bed, bedroom, big, bookcase, comfortable, small, sofa*.

You may wish to pre-teach the following words: *air conditioner, mobile home, roof, staircase, stove, tiles, wheels*. Point out that a *cooker* is called a *stove* in some English-speaking countries, including the USA.

PREPARE

21st Century skills

FIND OUT

Tell sts they will watch a video about an unusual type of home. If you have time and internet access, you could ask sts to find out about the Tiny House Movement and look at the inside of some tiny houses. They could work individually and find a tiny house they like, then compare their ideas in pairs or groups.

WATCH

Watch the video together. See TG page 306 for Unit 1 culture video script. Ask sts to write one sentence about the tiny house they liked best. Then, ask some of them to read their sentences aloud.

Ask sts the following noticing questions from the video, playing it again for sts to check their answers:

- *What colour is the first mobile home?* (grey/silver: 0:06)
- *What piece of furniture has a FOR SALE sign on it?* (a table: 1:06)
- *What are Theo and Bee holding at the end of the video?* (American flags: 2.37)

REFLECT

21st Century skills

COMPARE CULTURES

Ask questions to encourage sts to think about similarities or differences with homes in their own country, e.g.:

- *What is a typical home like where you live?*
- *Are houses on wheels popular in your country? Why/ Why not?*
- *Is it easy to live in a house on wheels in your country? Why/Why not?*

After watching the video, put sts into pairs or small groups to discuss one or more of the following questions:

- *Think about the advantages and disadvantages of living in a mobile home. Would you like to live in a mobile home? Why/ Why not?*
- *Why do you think Bee and Theo visit the Tiny House Festival? What can they learn there?*
- *'Visiting very tiny houses can help us organize our own bigger space.' Is this true? Why/Why not?*

Monitor while sts work, then collect some ideas from the class.

You could also ask sts to watch the video again for homework (either with or without subtitles). There are comprehension questions for them to answer about the video on the Richmond Learning Platform.

School in 1927

BACKGROUND

In this video, three real families leave their twenty-first century lives behind and spend a month in a Welsh coal mining town. TV cameras film them as they try to live the same way as families in 1927.

In the video, we see the children at school as if it is 1927. There are no computers or tablets in the classroom. The teacher writes everything on a blackboard for the children to see. He is very strict. His job is to prepare children for the school exam. In 1927, Children usually go to school until they are fourteen, but they can leave school six months early if they have a job. Steffan is thirteen and a half, and today is his first day of work at the local coal mine.

LANGUAGE

The following target language items are recycled from Unit 2: Present simple; *computer*, *leave home*, *lesson*, *tablet*, *technology*.

You may wish to pre-teach the following words and phrases: *blackboard*, *coal mine*, *schoolchildren*, *standard*, *strict*, *'the day we've been waiting for'*.

PREPARE

21st Century skills

FIND OUT

Tell sts they will watch a video about school life in a Welsh coal mining town in 1927. If you have time and internet access, you could ask sts to find photos of schools in the 1920s. Ask them to describe the buildings as well as the classrooms, and the teachers and children.

WATCH

Watch the video together. See TG page 306 for Unit 2 culture video script. Ask sts to write one interesting fact about school life in 1927. Then, ask some of them to read their sentences aloud.

Ask sts the following noticing questions from the video, playing it again for sts to check their answers:

- *What musical instrument is in the classroom?* (a piano: 0:28)
- *How many children take the exam?* (six: 1:23)
- *What colour is Steffan's house?* (white with red doors and windows: 1:44)

REFLECT

21st Century skills

COMPARE CULTURES

You could ask questions to encourage sts to think about similarities or differences between Wales and their own country, e.g.:

- *Think about the children in the video. Do you think life for children was similar in your country in the 1920s? Why/Why not?*
- *How is the 1927 classroom similar or different to your classroom today?*
- *Today, children in Wales leave school when they are sixteen or eighteen. What is the school-leaving age in your country?*

After watching the video, put sts into pairs or small groups to discuss one or both of the following questions:

- *School in the 1920s is not the same as school today. Do you think it's better now? Why/Why not?*
- *In the programme, Steffan leaves school and starts work in the coal mines because he is thirteen and a half. Today, there are countries where children and young teenagers leave school in order to work. What jobs do they do? Why do they do them?*

Monitor while sts work, then collect some ideas from the class.

You could also ask sts to watch the video again for homework (either with or without subtitles). There are comprehension questions for them to answer about the video on the Richmond Learning Platform.

CULTURE VIDEO
UNIT 3

Soccer in Soweto

BACKGROUND

Soccer City near Soweto is the largest football stadium in Africa and was home to the 2010 World Cup. In this video we take a look at the Soweto Derby: the Kaizer Chiefs against the Orlando Pirates. Football may be an international sport, but in Soweto the distinct combination of freestyle, music and dance gives football a very South African feeling and style. From the loud music of the vuvuzelas to the 'African warm-ups', where typical exercises are combined with song and dance, we see how Soweto has taken football and made it its own.

LANGUAGE

The following target language items are recycled from Unit 3: Adverbs of frequency; *like* + *-ing*; *can*; *fan*, *match*, *stadium*, *team*.

You may wish to pre-teach the following words: *fan, show, skills, trumpet, vuvuzelas*. Point out that *football* is called *soccer* in some English-speaking countries, including the USA, New Zealand and Australia.

PREPARE

21st Century skills

FIND OUT

Tell sts they will watch a video about an unusual kind of football. If you have time and internet access, you could ask sts to find out how many different countries have hosted the FIFA World Cup (seventeen up to and including Russia 2018) and which is the only African country to host it (South Africa).

WATCH

Watch the video together. See TG page 306 for Unit 3 culture video script. Ask sts to write one sentence with a fact they didn't know before they watched the video, then, ask some of them to read their sentences aloud.

Ask sts the following noticing questions from the video, playing it again for sts to check their answers:

- *What colour are the chairs in Soccer City?* (orange: 0:16)
- *What is the name of the country on Dan's T-shirt?* (South Africa: 1:30)
- *What colour is the children's school uniform?* (blue, black and white: 2:25)

REFLECT

21st Century skills

COMPARE CULTURES

Ask questions to encourage sts to think about similarities or differences with their own country, e.g.:

- *How are football matches in South Africa similar to football matches in your country? How are they different?*
- *Which sports are popular in your country? Why are they popular?*

After watching the video, put sts into pairs or small groups to discuss one or both of the following questions:

- *Are there any musical instruments played at sports games in your country?*
- *Can you think of any other types of sports from around the world that have music and dancing? What are they?*

Monitor while sts work, then collect some ideas from the class.

You could also ask sts to watch the video again for homework (either with or without subtitles). There are comprehension questions for them to answer about the video on the Richmond Learning Platform.

CULTURE VIDEO
UNIT 4

Holidays at home

BACKGROUND

Ellie lives and studies in Brighton, UK. It's a popular seaside town and a lot of of people visit it each year. Brighton is Ellie's hometown, so she doesn't often do the same things as tourists who visit her town. This video follows Ellie when she decides to be a tourist for the day. She visits the popular tourist sights, buys postcards, visits the fairground and eats traditional fish and chips on the beach.

LANGUAGE

The following target language items are recycled from Unit 4: Present continuous; present continuous and present simple; *market, sunny, theatre, warm.*

You may wish to pre-teach the following words and phrases: *fairground ride, fairy-tale* (adj), *go sightseeing, palace, pier, postcard, sea life, sun cream.*

PREPARE

21st Century skills

FIND OUT

Tell sts they will watch a video about a student doing tourist activities in Brighton, a famous British seaside town. If you have time and internet access, you could ask sts to find out where Brighton is in the UK, and what tourists can see and do there.

If not, put sts into pairs or small groups and ask them to think about a well-known seaside town in their own country. Ask them to make a list of things to see and do there, then elicit ideas from the class.

WATCH

Watch the video together. See TG page 306 for Unit 4 culture video script. Ask sts to write a sentence about one thing they would like to see or do in Brighton. Then, ask some of them to read their sentences aloud.

Ask sts the following noticing questions from the video, playing it again for sts to check their answers:

- *What colour are Ellie's sunglasses?* (brown: 0:57)
- *How much is the dress that Ellie wants to buy?* (£10: 1:30)
- *How does Ellie travel home?* (by bike: 3:16)

REFLECT

21st Century skills

COMPARE CULTURES

You could ask questions to encourage sts to think about similarities or differences between their town and Brighton, e.g.:

- *Brighton is on the south coast of England. How close to the sea is your town/city?*
- *A lot of British tourists and tourists from other countries visit Brighton. Does your town/city have a lot of tourists? Why do they want to come to your town/city?*
- *Would you prefer to live in Brighton or your own town/city? Why?*

After watching the video, put sts into pairs or small groups to discuss one or both of the following questions:

- *Do you think Ellie's idea to be a tourist for a day is a good idea? Do you think you can learn anything about your own town by doing this?*
- *How can tourists find out more about the places they visit? What are the best places for tourists to visit in your town? Why?*

Monitor while sts work, then collect some ideas from the class.

You could also ask sts to watch the video again for homework (either with or without subtitles). There are comprehension questions for them to answer about the video on the Richmond Learning Platform.

Diwali in New York

BACKGROUND

People living in New York come from many different cultures. The city has five boroughs (districts), including Queens. Jackson Heights is part of Queens and it is sometimes called 'Little India' because a lot of Indian Americans live here. Every year, in October or November, they celebrate *Diwali*, the Festival of Light.

In this video, we meet a dancer called Mickela Malozzi. She is visiting Queens for *Diwali*. She tries some of the food and dances to a *Bhangra* song. Bhangra is a type of traditional music and dance from the northern part of India. Mickela has a great time enjoying *Diwali* without leaving New York!

LANGUAGE

The following target language items are recycled from Unit 5: Countable and uncountable nouns + *some* and *any*; Quantifiers: *much*, *many*, *a lot of*; *chicken*, *rice*, *festival*, *traditional*, *celebration*.

You may wish to pre-teach the following words: *culture*, *energy*, *goat*, *performance*, *street food*, *sweet*.

PREPARE

21st Century skills

FIND OUT

Tell sts they will watch a video about how Indian Americans celebrate *Diwali* in New York (it is can be pronounced both /diwa:li:/ and /diva:li:/). If you have time and internet access, you could ask sts to look at a map of New York and find out where Queens is. They could also look at photos of the *Diwali* celebrations in India and New York City, and find videos of *Bhangra* music and dancing.

WATCH

Watch the video together. See TG pages 306–307 for Unit 5 culture video script. Ask sts to write one new thing they learned from the video. Then, ask some of them to read their sentences aloud.

Ask sts the following noticing questions from the video, playing it again for sts to check their answers:

- *What is the Jackson Diner?* (a restaurant: 1:11–1:12)
- *How many different Indian sweets does Mickela buy?* (one (burfi): 1.35)
- *What colour is the costume Mickela wears for the dance performance?* (green: 2.35)

REFLECT

21st Century skills

COMPARE CULTURES

Encourage sts to think about similarities or differences in their own culture and celebrations:

- *Does your town/city have a mixture of people from different cultures?*
- *What festivals do people in your country celebrate?*
- *Bhangra is a traditional type of Indian music and dance. What are the traditional types of music and dance in your country?*

After watching the video, put sts into pairs or small groups to discuss one or both of the following questions:

- *Why do people like to eat food from different places? Is it better to eat traditional food? Why/Why not?*
- *When people move to a new country, they often celebrate days and festivals that are important in the country they come from. Why do you think they do that? Are there any examples where you live? Do local people join in the celebrations?*

Monitor while sts work, then collect some ideas from the classroom.

You could also ask sts to watch the video again for homework (either with or without subtitles). There are comprehension questions for them to answer about the video on the Richmond Learning Platform.

CULTURE VIDEO
UNIT 6

Marvellous mountain biking

BACKGROUND

Richard Parks is an extreme athlete. He is cycling in the *Yak Attack* mountain bike race in the Himalayas. It's the most difficult bike race in the world. The race is ten days long and Richard and the other riders have problems from Day 1. At the start, they find it difficult to ride in the heat. Higher up in the mountains, it is freezing cold which is as bad as the heat. The way down is easier, but near the end of the race a truck hits one of the cyclists. Thankfully, it is nothing serious. Richard and the other competitors finish the race together. They are all winners in this race.

LANGUAGE

The following target language items are recycled from Unit 6: Comparative adjectives; *(not) as ... as ...*; Superlative adjectives; *highest, hundred, mountain, thousand.*

You may wish to pre-teach the following words and phrases: *cramp, cyclist, degrees, exhausted, extreme athlete, freezing, minus* (for temperature), *rider, truck.* Point out that a *lorry* is called a *truck* in some English-speaking countries.

PREPARE

21st Century skills

FIND OUT

Tell sts they will watch a video about Richard Parks, who is taking part in an extreme cycle race called *Yak Attack*. If you have time and internet access, you could ask sts to find out one or two facts about *Yak Attack* online.

WATCH

Watch the video together. TG page 307 for Unit 6 culture video script. Ask sts to write one interesting fact about the *Yak Attack* cycle race. Then, ask some of them to read their sentences aloud.

Ask sts the following noticing questions from the video, playing it again for sts to check their answers:

- *What is on top of Richard's cycle helmet?* (a camera: 0:23)
- *What number is on the front of Richard's bike?* (nineteen: 0:42)
- *What is the height on the sign at Thorong-La Pass?* (5,416 metres: 2:28)

REFLECT

21st Century skills

COMPARE CULTURES

You could use questions to encourage sts to think about similarities or differences between sports that people do around the world, e.g.:

- *What extreme sports can people do in your region/ country?*
- *Britain's national sport is football. What is your country's national sport? What national sports have other countries got?*
- *Does your country have any national sports teams? What international competitions do they compete in?*

After watching the video, put sts into pairs or small groups to discuss the following questions:

- *Do you do any extreme sports? Why do you think people enjoy extreme sports?*
- *Would you like to enter a competition like Yak Attack? Why/Why not?*
- *Is it a good or bad idea to have competitions? Why?*

Monitor while sts work, then collect some ideas from the class.

You could also ask sts to watch the video again for homework (either with or without subtitles). There are comprehension questions for them to answer about the video on the Richmond Learning Platform.

TV time travellers

BACKGROUND

This video comes from a TV programme called *Back in Time for Brixton*. The Irwin family are from London. They leave their modern lives and spend one summer finding out what life was like for a Caribbean family living in London, in different decades of the twentieth century. In this video, we watch the family travel back to the 1970s and 1980s.

The 1970s are very colourful. People wear colourful clothes and use bright colours in their homes. For entertainment, the children play games and listen to cassettes, but the 1980s bring new forms of entertainment, including a colour TV. In the 1980s, the Irwin's get their first car and try American takeaway food.

LANGUAGE

The following target language items are recycled from Unit 7: *be*: past simple; past simple: regular verbs; object pronouns; *clothes, coat, in 1970, in the 1970s, shirt, shorts, used, week*.

You may wish to pre-teach the following words and phrases: *bright, DIY (do-it-yourself), hi-fi system, radio cassette player, remind someone of something, time traveller, travel back,* VCR (video cassette recorder).

PREPARE

21st Century skills

FIND OUT

Tell sts they will watch a video about life in Brixton in London in the 1970s and 1980s. If you have time and internet access, you could ask sts to find Brixton on a map of London and find photos of Brixton in the 1970s and 1980s.

WATCH

Watch the video together. See TG page 307 for Unit 7 culture video script. Ask sts to write one interesting fact that they learned from the video. Then, ask some of them to read their sentences aloud.

Ask sts the following noticing questions from the video, playing it again for sts to check their answers:

- *How many people are there in the Irwin family?* (six: 0:18)
- *The Irwins put some paper on the walls. What is the picture on the paper?* (palm trees: 0:57)
- *What American takeaway food do they buy?* (Kentucky Fried Chicken: 1:46)
- *What colour is Mr Irwin's football shirt?* (red and white: 2:19)

REFLECT

21st Century skills

COMPARE CULTURES

Ask questions to encourage sts to think about similarities or differences between life in Britain and within their own country in the 1970s/1980s. You could set this task as homework. Give sts a list of questions and get them to interview older relatives about life in the 1970s/1980s. Example questions include:

- *What sort of clothes did your parents and grandparents wear in the 1970s and 1980s?*
- *What did your parents and grandparents do for entertainment in the 1970s/1980s?*
- *What sort of technology did they have?*
- *Where there any American takeaway restaurants in your city or country at that time?*

After watching the video, put sts into pairs or small groups to discuss one or both of the following questions:

- *Which decade would you like to travel to? Why?*
- *Some people collect old technology. Can you think of any examples of things people collect? Why do you think people like to collect old technology?*

Monitor while sts work, then collect some ideas from the class.

You could also ask sts to watch the video again for homework (either with or without subtitles). There are comprehension questions for them to answer about the video on the Richmond Learning Platform.

CULTURE VIDEO
UNIT 8

A family history

BACKGROUND

Danny Dyer is a popular British actor. He wants to find out more about his family history. In this video, Danny discovers that a hundred years ago his ancestors were poor. Then he visits a family history expert. She shows him a family tree and tells him that many years ago, his family were rich. He visits the stately home that they lived in. Later, Danny finds out that one of his relatives was a king of England.

LANGUAGE

The following target language items are recycled from Unit 8: Past simple; *be born*, *have (children)*.

You may wish to pre-teach the following words and phrases: *ancestors, expert, family history, family tree, lord, Royal family, stately home.*

PREPARE

21st Century skills

FIND OUT

Tell sts they will watch a video about a popular British actor named Danny Dyer. If you have time and internet access, you could ask sts to find out one or two facts about Danny Dyer, for example, his age, where he's from, his family, his films.

WATCH

Watch the video together. See TG page 307 for Unit 8 culture video script. Ask sts to write one interesting fact about Danny Dyer. Then ask some of them to read their sentences aloud.

Ask the following noticing questions from the video, playing it again for sts to check their answers:

- *How many of Danny's children are in the garden with him?* (one: 0:23)
- *What colour is Danny's car?* (grey: 1:39)
- *What time is it when Danny visits the Royal family expert?* (10.35 a.m.: 2:10)

REFLECT

21st Century skills

COMPARE CULTURES

You could ask questions to encourage sts to think about similarities or differences between families in Britain and their own country, e.g.:

- *Families in Britain are getting smaller. Today, most families in Britain have only two children. Is this the same in your country?*
- *The TV programme with Danny is about famous people who find out about their family history. Do you have programmes like this in your country? Do you watch them? Why/Why not?*
- *Are people in your country interested in their family history? How do they find out about their family?*

After watching the video, put sts into pairs or small groups to discuss one or both of the following questions:

- *Who would you be happy to have as your ancestor? A king? An actor, like Danny? Or maybe a scientist or a great athlete?*
- *Is it important to know about family history? Can this information help in your life today?*

Monitor while sts work, then collect some ideas from the class.

You could also ask sts to watch the video again for homework (either with or without subtitles). There are comprehension questions for them to answer about the video on the Richmond Learning Platform.

Tasty travels

BACKGROUND

Celebrity chef Nadiya Hussain lives in the UK. She's British, but her parents are from Bangladesh. She became famous after winning *The Great British Bake Off* – a TV baking (cooking) competition. In this video, she travels to Bangladesh to visit her relatives and explore the country. She starts in Dhaka, the capital of the country, then travels south on the river. While she is travelling, she cooks for some of the people that she meets.

LANGUAGE

The following target language items are recycled from Unit 9: *will* and *be going to*; *boat*, *car*, *explore*, *motorbike*, *take (a boat)*, *train*, *visit*.

You may wish to pre-teach the following words and phrases: *captain and crew, celebrity chef, ferry, grilled chicken, overnight, rickshaw.*

PREPARE

21st Century skills

FIND OUT

Tell sts they are going to watch a video about a celebrity chef who is travelling around Bangladesh. If you have time and internet access, you could ask sts to find out some information about the country. For example, where it is, what countries it is next to, the capital city, and the popular foods.

If not, arrange sts into small teams and write some facts, words and numbers about Bangladesh on the board. Teams compete to guess what they refer to. For example: *Asia* (the continent), *India and Myanmar* (its neighbours) *Dhaka* (the capital), *Taka* (the money), *1947* (when it became a country), *the tiger* (the national animal), *cricket* (the national sport), *20,000,000* (the population), *Bangla/ Bengali* (the language).

WATCH

Watch the video together. See TG page 307 for Unit 9 culture video script. Ask sts to write a sentence about something they liked in the video (e.g. the rickshaws, the food, the clothes). Then, ask some of them to read their sentences aloud.

Ask the following noticing questions from the video, playing it again for sts to check their answers:

- *What is Nadiya making at the beginning of the video?* (a cake: 0:10–0:13)
- *What colour is Nadiya's backpack?* (grey: 1:08)
- *What type of fruit does Nadiya use to make her special grilled chicken?* (lemons: 1:52)

REFLECT

21st Century skills

COMPARE CULTURES

You could ask questions to encourage sts to think about similarities or differences between Bangladesh and their own country, e.g.:

- *How is your capital city similar to Dhaka? How is it different?*
- *Nadiya cooks outdoors in the village. How often do people in your country cook outdoors?*
- *Would you like to visit Bangladesh? Why/Why not?*

After watching the video, put sts into pairs or small groups to discuss one or both of the following questions:

- *What forms of transport are popular in your country? Why are they popular?*
- *What do you like to see and do when you travel to a new place?*

Monitor while sts work, then collect some ideas from the class.

You could also ask sts to watch the video again for homework (either with or without subtitles). There are comprehension questions for them to answer about the video on the Richmond Learning Platform.

VLOG SCRIPTS

UNIT 1

My new home

I = Ioan

I: Hello, my name's Ioan, and it's time for me to move out of my parents' house.

I have a lot of stuff. I need to decide what to take to my new place, so maybe you can help me. Let's take a look.

The study. This is where I do most of my work and spend most of my day. First, my **desk**. It's just an old **table**, and I'm not taking it with me. But, I am taking some of the things that live there. This is my sister's old **chair**, my mum's old **lamp**, and a **mirror** I got from my art class. I am taking all of them with me. But most of all, my **desk** is home to drawings that I don't want to throw away, but don't know where to keep. I liked my workspace, but it's time to find a new one.

The bedroom. My **bookcase** is very full. I buy a lot of books and I am slowly reading them, but I haven't finished them all yet. My **wardrobe** has a lot of clothes in it. How do I decide which outfits I need? Why not take all of them?

The kitchen. Obviously, there are some things I can't take with me. My happiest memories are in the kitchen, but they're staying here with the **cooker**, the **sink**, and the **fridge**. But that's OK. It's good to let things go.

Thank you for helping me pack. Bye!

UNIT 2

Morning routine

T = Tati

T: Hi everyone, my name is Tati and today I'm going to show you my typical morning routine as a student. So let's get right into it!

First, my alarm goes off at 7 a.m. and it's time to **get up**. Usually, I am very tired so this can take a while. After I get out of bed, it's time to **have a shower**. I prefer to shower in the mornings, as it definitely helps me wake up and feel refreshed for the day. After I have a shower, next it is time to **get dressed**. These are my clothes for today.

At eight o'clock, I go downstairs and **have breakfast**. Breakfast is the most important meal of the day, so I always make time to have breakfast. Today, I'm having tea and toast.

After breakfast, I go back upstairs to **tidy my room**. I like to tidy my room in the mornings, because I like coming home to a clean room.

At 8.30, I'm all ready for the day ahead of me and it's time to leave the house and have a good day.

So that's it! I hope you enjoyed watching my morning routine as a student. Bye!

UNIT 3

Life as an athlete

N = Nina

N: Hello everybody, and welcome to this video. My name is Nina. I am from the United States and I am a **ballet** dancer.

Today, I want to talk about life as an athlete and the work it takes. But what does it mean to be an athlete? Well, let's take a look. Anyone who is serious about the sport they practise is an athlete.

I started doing **ballet** at three years old. But as a young girl, I tried other sports, too. When I was eight years old, I went **swimming** twice a week. I liked it a lot, but dancing was already hard work, so two sports was difficult. I also tried **gymnastics** 'cause my friends at school did it. But I always preferred **ballet**. It is difficult, but powerful and beautiful. And now, I'm training to become a professional, so I dance six days a week.

Each sport is different, but they all have a few things in common. How could **surfing**, for example, possibly be like **ballet**? Well, each person works hard to improve their skills for their sport. We spend hour after hour practising. We want to get that movement, that jump, that twist, that turn just right.

For me, the other very important thing that we all have in common is that we don't do it alone. Dance teachers, surf instructors, and coaches for sports like football and **volleyball**, they are the ones who teach us and help us get better at our sport. If you are thinking about joining a sport, go for it! It's so much fun. And having fun is a really important part of being an athlete.

Thank you for joining me, and I'll see you next time!

UNIT 4

My top five things in Paris

N = Natalie

N: Hello, and welcome to this video. My name is Natalie and I recently visited Paris. Here are the top five things I did with my friends.

Number one: we visited the Louvre **Museum**. Well, we didn't actually go inside. It's a really popular **museum**, so it was full. The **museum** has the world-famous *Mona Lisa* painting, so I wasn't really surprised by how busy it was.

Number two: I visited Musée de l'Orangerie, which is an art gallery filled with twentieth-century paintings. It's a lot more peaceful and quiet than the Louvre.

Number three: the River Seine. There is a big **market** along the river. They sell books and antiques here. It's very different to the Champs-Élysées, which is an avenue filled with luxury **shopping centres** and **restaurants**.

We've just had an explore in Shakespeare and Company.

This is a famous bookstore. It was like the **library** from *Harry Potter*.

Number four is Le Centre Pompidou.

So we've come to the Centre Pompidou. It's a lot of exhibitions, modern art. There's also an amazing panoramic view of all around Paris. It's amazing to see the city from a height where you can see all the hills and buildings. It's amazing.

Number five: the Eiffel Tower, which is a very famous **monument**.

So I've come to visit the iconic Eiffel Tower, which is probably the most recognizable place in Paris.

My friends and I ate our lunch in the park and admired the views of the famous **monument**.

I had a wonderful time in Paris. It's such a beautiful city and I want to go back one day.

UNIT 5

Farmers' market

B = Bokang

B: Hi everyone, my name is Bokang and I am a vlogger from South Africa. My channel is called *The B Word* and I share parts of my life and vlog being out and about, just like I am doing today.

Today, I'm going to the Fourways Farmers' Market in Santon, South Africa. The market has a big selection of food ranging from **chicken**, **fruit**, **vegetables**, **sandwiches**, freshly squeezed orange and apple **juice** and so many more delicious dishes.

I was thirsty, so my first stop was a **juice stand** called 'Impressed'. Here they use **fruits** and **vegetables** to make their **delicious juices**. My favourite is the orange, apple and ginger mix.

After that, I decided to find something to eat. There's a stall that sells delicious **sandwiches**. I decided to go for the **chicken** option, and mmm, it was good. Then, once the main meal was done, I thought it was time for a little snack. At this **potato** stand, they cut up potatoes, fry them, add some flavour and there you go! This one is definitely one of my favourites.

I really like the Fourways Farmers' Market. It's a great place to try some fantastic food. And now it's your turn to go to your local market and try some.

UNIT 6

Exploring the island of East Java

S = Steve

S: Hello! My name is Steve and I'm a travel vlogger from the United States. In this video, we are going to explore the **island** of East Java, in the country of Indonesia.

I spent some time travelling around this beautiful place, and I want to share with you some amazing places that I visited. The first place that I visited was this **waterfall** called Tumpak Sewu. Translated into English, this means 'one thousand **waterfalls**'. It makes sense, doesn't it? You can see it from the top, but you can also hike all the way down to the bottom for a very close view. The **river** from this waterfall is very strong, and a few miles away you can ride a raft for a crazy adventure.

Very near, there is an active **volcano** called Bromo. As a visitor, you can ride up the **mountain** next to it, to get a beautiful view of Bromo from the top. I went all the way up to the top of this **mountain**. From the top, I saw Bromo and three more **volcanoes**. At the bottom of the **volcanoes**, there is a large **desert**.

A few days later, I went to visit another **volcano** called Mount Ijen. I woke up very early and hiked in the dark. It was hard, but I saw a beautiful sunrise from the top! There's a bright blue **lake** in the middle of the crater, and you can walk all around it. It made me feel really small.

Last of all, I went to another **waterfall** called Madakaripura. This a huge wall of water in the **forest**. You can walk right under the **waterfall**.

Ahhhhh it's cold!

I had such an amazing time visiting these places. I love to travel!

UNIT 7

I know nothing about fashion

B = Ben

B: Hello, my name is Ben. I live in London, and I make videos all about life. I am from Canada, as you can see here.

I have something to tell you. I know nothing about clothes and fashion. I think it will be fun to show you some of my clothes. Maybe it will inspire me to buy better clothes.

OK, so here are some of my clothes. I own a **skirt**. This is a **skirt** made for men. I really like it. I love **jumpers** and hoodies, this is my favourite. I wear a lot of long-sleeve **shirts**, long sleeves. I like how they feel more than short sleeves. It keeps me warm when it's cold. It's cold a lot in the UK.

This is the only blazer that I own. I like it very much. I do know how to tie a **tie**, but I only have one.

Look at these cool **socks**! I like them so much. I really like when they have funny patterns. This one is chicken. I really love having funny **socks** – they're my favourite Christmas present.

This is my only pair of sneakers. People in the UK call them **trainers**. I only buy one pair of **shoes** at a time, until they fall apart.

Here are all of my **jeans**. I like tight-fitting **jeans**. These big grey ones are comfy, but I don't like wearing them out very much. When I have a day at home, I usually put these on.

Here is my brand new **coat**, which I love very much. It was a Christmas present. This is the only **hat** I own. I like to wear it with my hair down like this, because I have very long hair.

So, this is all the clothes that I have that I like. I really want to find some more clothes. Let's go to the charity shop and find some.

So, I'm back from the charity shop, and I found this! It's so comfy! I love it! This was only £3!

What you wear says something about you. I feel good when I wear clothes like this. My clothes aren't really pretty, but I feel good when I wear them. Wear clothes that make you feel good, no matter what. That's my advice.

Bye!

UNIT 8

My grandpa and his life story

R = Rebecca

R: Hey guys, welcome back to *Beccavision*. My name is Rebecca. And today, I want to tell you guys a little bit about my grandpa, and his life story.

I **was born** in the United States to a multicultural family. This is my grandpa. He was born in Italy. His family didn't have a lot of money **growing up**, so at the young age of eighteen, he had to **get a job** in the Italian Navy. He travelled to East Africa and he was in the Navy for many, many years. But, when he was in East Africa, he actually met my grandma.

They **got married** and they **had three children**: my aunt, my uncle and my dad. After my grandpa **got married**, he **got a job** fixing cars in Ethiopia. His favourite thing to do was to **drive his white car** and take his family on road trips. My dad, my aunt, my uncle, my grandpa and my grandma made amazing memories in this time.

My dad loved travelling so much, he decided to move to the United States. This is where **I was born**. And then, I moved to the United Kingdom. This is where I **go to university**, and this is where I live now.

So, thank you guys for watching. I hope you guys liked learning a little bit about me. Everybody has a family history and you should be proud of it. But for now, thanks for watching, and I'll see you later. Bye!

UNIT 9

Transport in Europe

N = Natalie

N: Hello, and welcome to this video which is all about transport.

My name is Natalie, and I live in London in the United Kingdom. Usually, I ride a **bike** around the city. Sometimes, I take a bus. Or sometimes, I use the famous London **Underground**. Recently, I went to Paris, Berlin, Prague and Budapest. I tried different ways of getting around in each city.

So these cities are all pretty far away from each other. But instead of taking flights between each one, I got an Interrail Pass – a type of ticket for regional and international trains across Europe. Why take a train? Reason number one: it's a little bit cheaper. And reason number two: it's much healthier for the environment to take trains. The views from the train are incredible. You can see more of the country by travelling on the train.

When I arrived in Paris, I used their Metro system to get around the city.

Just bought my first Metro ticket.

Their system was very similar to the London **Underground**. Berlin has a similar system to the Metro and **Underground**. But my favourite transport in Berlin was an electric **scooter**. My friends and I hired electric **scooters** via an app, and it was so much fun.

On to the third city, which was Prague. I bought a 24-hour **tram** pass. We have **trams** in London, too, but I never use them. I only use the **Underground** or buses.

In Budapest, I chose to walk everywhere. Walking is my favourite way to see more of a city.

On the way back to London, I took a **plane**. Flying takes two hours, but the **train** takes 24 hours.

And those were all of the methods of transport I took during my trip to Europe. I hope you enjoyed this video and you learned a little bit about how to travel in Europe. Bye.

CULTURE VIDEO SCRIPTS

UNIT 1

Homes on wheels

T = Theo, B = Bee

When we think of a mobile home, it looks something like this ... Or does it?
This is the Tiny House Festival in Colorado, in the USA. There are lots of homes here in many different shapes and sizes. But, they are all the same in one way: they've all got wheels, so they can visit different places.
T: *What's going on guys? So, we have just arrived at the Colorado Tiny House Festival and this place is massive.*
Travel vloggers Bee and Theo are at the Tiny House Festival. They show us around. This motorhome is an interesting shape, and it's made of beautiful wood. Inside, it's got a sofa and a bed. There's a bookcase for your books and all your things. There's also a window, so you've got a view of the places you visit.
This one actually looks like a real house. It's got an air conditioner and lots of windows. It's also got tiles on the roof. Inside, there's even a staircase that takes you up to a comfortable bedroom with a big bed.
B: *So, we've just stopped for lunch.*
Now, it's time for some food.
Small can also be beautiful. An unusual look outside and a really special inside. Great colours! And look at the bed by that big window. There's even a small stove.
Bee and Theo have now got a lot of cool ideas for their own home on wheels.
B: *So, thanks for watching guys and we'll see you on the next video.*

UNIT 2

School in 1927

T = Teacher

These students go on a trip to the past ... to 1927!
The children leave home at 6 a.m. This is their school. All the children aged five to thirteen are in the same class.
T: *Now, mind your fingers. I'll chop them off.*
The teacher isn't very nice.
T: *For really bad things, I've got this.*
He's very strict.
T: *It works.*
He uses a blackboard.
There isn't any technology in the classroom. There aren't any computers and there aren't any tablets. The schoolchildren enjoy the art lessons – they're fun.
T: *This is the day we've been waiting for, the day of the standard exam. Your big day.*
At the end of term, the students take an exam.
But Steffan doesn't go to school now. He is thirteen and a half now, so he goes to work. He works in the coal mine. This is his first day. He goes to work at 5 a.m. It takes an hour and a half.
It's hard work in the coal mine. It's also very dangerous.
School in 1927 is hard, but life for children in the coal mines is horrible.

UNIT 3

Soccer in Soweto

D = Dan

Welcome to Soccer City near Soweto in South Africa. It's the largest football stadium in Africa. Spain were the World Cup winners here in 2010. Today, 90,000 people are here for a big match called the Soweto Derby. The match is between two local teams: the Kaizer Chiefs and the Orlando Pirates.
South Africa has a very special football culture and South African fans always make a lot of noise. The noise is very loud because of the vuvuzelas. You find these trumpets at all South African football matches. Today, there are thousands of them. With the sound of the vuvuzelas it is like a big party. People love dancing and singing at the match.
At half-time the fans get an extra show. Dan Magness, a famous British football freestyler, can do fantastic tricks with a football. Freestyle is very popular with young people in Soweto.
D: *I've just performed a perfect show in front of nearly 90,000 people. What a feeling!*
Dan goes into Soweto. He sees that even young children like doing freestyle. Freestyle is everywhere in Soweto. Chris is a South African champion freestyler. There is something different about freestyle in Soweto. It is almost like a dance. Lots of people say that this is because dancing is very popular in South Africa. These freestylers mix dancing and singing with football skills.
At this Soweto school the children do an 'African warm-up': singing and dancing before the match. You can see how football and dancing come together.
Football and freestyle are international sports. People like playing them all over the world. But here in Soweto, football and freestyle are also a big part of South African life.

UNIT 4

Holidays at home

E = Ellie

Ellie's a student and she lives in Brighton. Brighton is a famous British seaside town.
E: *I'm Ellie and I'm an art student in Brighton.*
Ellie has a busy student life, so she doesn't have much time for tourist activities, like sightseeing. Today she's trying something new. She wants to be a tourist in Brighton for one day.
E: *I've made a list of all the tourist activities I can do, and I'm gonna tick them off one by one, in one day.*
First, she prepares the things she's taking with her: a map, sun cream and sunglasses, as it's warm and sunny today. Now she's ready to go to the first place on her map.
The Brighton Pavilion is a fairy-tale palace built by a royal prince. It's over 200 years old. The Pavilion gardens are looking beautiful in the bright sunshine.
Next, she spends some time looking around Brighton's markets and interesting shops. And of course, all tourists buy postcards! It's time for a quick break. Ellie's enjoying a nice cup of tea.
Now for something a bit different. She's going to the aquarium!
E: *I'm so excited! I love sea life.*
She gets really close to the sea life.
Next, she's going to Brighton Pier, for some fun! Piers are popular in British seaside towns. Especially the fairground rides. After all the excitement, Ellie goes to the seafront. She's really happy. She's seeing her hometown in a new way. To end the day, she's having a traditional dinner of fish and chips on the beach.
But she isn't a real tourist, so she doesn't have far to go home!

UNIT 5

Diwali in New York

M = Mickela, S = Subrato

Queens is an area of New York City. Some people call parts of Queens 'Little India', because there are a lot of Indian Americans living there. Mickela Mallozzi has a lot of friends! Today, she's visiting some of them in Queens. They're celebrating Diwali together.
M: *Happy Diwali!*
Diwali is the Hindu Festival of Light. Hindus celebrate it every year, in India and all over the world. An important part of any festival is the food. Mickela meets

her friend Subrato for a special Diwali meal. They have some tandoori chicken, goat curry and rice.
M: *Mmmm, oh, it's delicious.*
For dessert, they go to an Indian sweet shop. There's a lot of choice. Mickela gets some *burfi*, a traditional Indian sweet.
S: *Very sweet.*
M: *Very sweet.*
Every year, there's a big Diwali street festival in New York. It's a chance for Indian Americans to share their culture with the whole city. Of course, food is a very important part of that celebration as well. Everyone gets to try Indian street food.
M: *I've got chickpeas, chicken and rice.*
M: *Ding da ding da ding. Almost, almost ... close!*
There isn't much time left before the dance performance.
M: *We're about to go on stage to perform our Bhangra song!*
Mickela loves Indian dancing ... and all that delicious Diwali food gives her plenty of energy.
M: *Happy Diwali ... Happy Diwali!*

UNIT 6

Marvellous mountain biking

O = Race official, R = Richard, C1 = Cyclist 1, C2 = Cyclist 2

Richard Parks is an extreme athlete. He travels all over the world for sports competitions.
Richard is ready for the most difficult bike race in the world. He flies to Kathmandu: the capital city of Nepal. This race is in the Himalayas – the highest mountains in the world. The race is more than four hundred kilometres long and takes ten days.
O: *Be safe and best of luck for everybody ... so, three, two, one ... go!*
The race starts. There are many dangers for the cyclists.
The temperature is 35 degrees. It's very hot. Richard is exhausted.
R: *I'm cramping.*
C1: *Awesome work.*
C2: *Well done, dude.*
R: *Alright guys! Awesome!*
C2: *Well done.*
Now, they're higher than before and there are new dangers. There's lots of snow at 4,500 metres and the temperature is freezing at minus ten degrees.
R: *Today was a tough day.*
This is the highest point in the race. It's five and a half thousand metres high.
R: *I can say that's a first for me, climbing five and a half thousand metres.*
Going down looks easier ... but sometimes it's more dangerous than going up. The race is almost over when a truck hits another rider. But, it isn't as bad as it looks. After the accident, the riders want to finish the race together. They're all winners.

UNIT 7

TV time travellers

MsI = Mrs Irwin, MrI = Mr Irwin, S = Sister, B = Brothers

This is the Irwin family from London. They are time travellers for a week, trying life from 1940 to 1980. Today, they're travelling back to 1970. Their clothes are very colourful. Mrs Irwin is wearing an amazing yellow coat.
MsI: *Oh wow!*
This is their house in 1970.
MsI: *Nice dining area.*
In the 1970s, the colours were also very bright in homes. In the 1970s, people liked doing DIY in their free time, putting paint or paper on the walls. The Irwins decide to add more colour to their house.
MsI: *How's it going boys?*
MrI: *Nearly there.*
MsI: *It's looking good. It reminds me of the West Indies.*
There was no internet in the 1970s, so the children play games. But what's this? They have a new radio cassette player. People used them to record music.
Now, it's 1980. The Irwins have lots of new things: a hi-fi system and a colour TV. They also have a car. They go to buy American takeaway food.
S: *Hi guys!*
B: *Hey.*
S: *Dinner! Look what we got ... boys wake up!*
This was new, and very popular in the 1980s. There were lots of new things in the 1980s. This is a VCR, a video cassette recorder. People recorded television programmes on them. Now it's time for some exercise, in 1980s football shirts and shorts. In the 1980s, things were different. Football wasn't a popular sport for women. The Irwins say goodbye to the past with a small party. They enjoyed living in the past and learned a lot, but they were all happy to go back to their normal lives.
MrI: *Number 1, ya know. Yeah, yeah, yeah, yeah, yeah ...*

UNIT 8

A family history

D = Danny Dyer, LT = Lord Tollemache, P = Peter

Danny Dyer is a British actor. He was born in London and still lives there today. He's very famous.
Danny has children, but he doesn't know anything about his ancestors. He wants to tell his children about their family history. So, he decides to find out more.
First, he goes to a library in London. He finds lots of information. He learns about his great-great-grandmother. She was poor and she had a hard life. A hundred years ago, all of Danny's family were poor. This makes Danny feel sad.
But what about further back in history? Danny sees a family history expert. She shows Danny his family tree. It's a map of all of his relatives. She tells Danny that four hundred years ago some of his relatives were rich and powerful.
Danny's family lived in this stately home. Lord Tollemache lives here now.
LT: *Hello, Danny.*
D: *Hello, young man!*
LT: *Very nice to meet you.*
D: *Absolute pleasure, yeah, pleasure.*
LT: *Welcome to Hellmingham.*
He's Danny's distant cousin. Danny learns more about his ancestors and their lives. He has one more visit to make in London. He meets an expert on the history of the Royal family.
P: *Hi, Danny.*
D: *Hi, Peter. Alright?*
P: *Nice to meet you.*
There's some exciting news. Danny's twenty-two times great-grandfather was King Edward III! Danny is amazed! His relative was the King of England! But will this change his life? For now, Danny says no.

UNIT 9

Tasty travels

SP = Sue Perkins

Nadiya is a famous British cook. She won *The Great British Bake Off*, a TV competition.
SP: *The winner is Nadiya.*
She became a celebrity chef in the UK. Now she's in Bangladesh. She's visiting some of her family there, and then she's going to travel around the country.
Dhaka is the capital city of Bangladesh. It is a huge city, with a population of 20 million. People travel around the city on trains, on motorbikes and bikes and in cars. Rickshaws are also popular.
Bangladesh has a lot of rivers, so boats are a great way of getting around. Nadiya's going to explore Bangladesh. She's going to leave Dhaka by boat. This type of boat is called a ferry. The ferry will travel overnight. Nadiya cooks dinner for the captain and crew.
The ferry arrives early in the morning. Now Nadiya's going to take a much smaller boat. They travel up the river slowly, enjoying the countryside. She arrives at a little village by the river. Nadiya cooks lunch for some of the people there. Her special grilled chicken. They'll love it! Everyone will enjoy Nadiya's cooking. And everyone has just one question: Will she cook dinner, too?
Subtitles: 'Is it tasty?' 'Very good'.

GRAMMAR ANIMATION SCRIPTS

UNIT 1

There's a cake on this chair!

B = Ben, J = Jake, V = Vicky

B, J: Hi, Vicky!
V: Oh, hi, Ben! Hi, Jake! Thanks for coming, guys! Ready to play?
J: Well, yes, but there aren't any empty chairs!
B: What a mess! There's a cake on this chair!
J: And there are books in front of the TV.
B: There are some clothes on the desk, and there's an apple on the carpet.
J: And there are some cups under the table.
V: Sorry, guys!
J: Come on Ben, let's help Vicky.
V: Thank you very much for helping me!
J: You're welcome! The room is tidy now.
B: The books are in the bookcase!
J: And there aren't any cups under the table!
V: And the clothes are next to the desk.
J: But, where's the cake?
V: Ben, watch out! The cake is behind you!
B: Oh! The cake is … here!
V, J: Oh, Ben!

I've got funny hair!

B = Ben, V = Vicky, J = Jake

B: Your games room is amazing, Vicky. You've got lots of cool things!
V: I know! I'm very lucky! I've got a computer and a video games console, and I've got lots of books.
B: I've got some e-books on my tablet, but I haven't got a games console. Have you got any video games, Jake?
J: Yes, I have. And I've got a guitar!
V: Wow! I haven't. Are you good at the guitar?
J: Well … not yet!
B: Look at this photo! Who are all these people?
V: This is my family. This is my mum and this is my Uncle David. He's got a dog, Bella. This is my Aunt Liz. She's got two children – my cousins, Isaac and Isabel. And this is my grandma, Jill. She's got a pet snake!
J: Wow! Who's this?
V: That's me! I'm a baby there!
B: Ah, you're very cute!
V: I know! But, I've got funny hair!

UNIT 2

He cleans the robots!

AR = Aunt Rose, M = Mr Jones, J = Jake, B = Ben, V = Vicky

AR: Welcome to the Science Fiction Museum! This is my friend, Mr Jones. Mr Jones works here. He's a museum guide.
J, B, V: Hello, Mr Jones. Nice to meet you!
M: Nice to meet you, too!
B: I love science fiction films! I want to be a film director one day!
M: That's great!
V: Tell us about your day, Mr Jones.
M: Well, I get up at seven in the morning. I get dressed and have breakfast. Then, I ride my bike to work. I don't take the bus. I get to my office and I check my emails. Then the visitors arrive. I show them all the amazing things in the museum.
V: Ah, it sounds interesting!
M: Yes! The café opens at one o'clock. I have lunch with my friend, Steve. Steve doesn't work in the mornings. He starts work at two o'clock. He cleans the robots!
B: Ah, I love this place! I watch lots of science fiction films. My favourite is *Planet of the Robots*!
M: We've got lots of robots from that film here!
B: Really? Have you got Robodog? Have you got CA-12? Come on, let's go and see them!
M: OK!

What does it do?

M = Mr Jones, B = Ben, J = Jake, AR = Aunt Rose, V = Vicky

M: Do you like CA-12, Ben? It's the star of *Planet of the Robots*.
B: Yes, I do! It helps the astronauts come back to Earth!
M: Correct. And this is Robodog.
B: I know! It's CA-12's pet!
M: That's right! Do you know everything about robot films, Ben?
B: No, I don't! I don't know everything. But I know a lot, because I watch a lot of films!
M: Good for you! Where do you watch them? At home or at the cinema?
B: Both!
J: Oh, no! Drew, come back!
M: What's this?
AR: It's our robot friend. Jake! What does Drew want?
J: I don't know. Drew! Switch off!
M: That's an amazing robot, Rose. Where do they sell them?
R: They don't. Drew's my creation. I'm an electrical engineer.
M: Wow! What does it do?
AR: It likes learning new things. But I think Drew needs a software update right now!
M: Good idea! Well, what do you want to see now, guys? More cool things?
B, J, V: Yes, please!
M: OK, let's go!

UNIT 3

I love eating popcorn!

J = Jake, B = Ben, V = Vicky

J: Hi, Ben!
B: Oh, hey, Jake!
J: How are things?
B: Great! I'm on my bike today. I love cycling! I always go cycling on Saturdays.
J: That's nice. I've got my guitar lesson now.
B: Wow! Do you take guitar lessons? That's amazing!
J: Yes, I like learning the guitar! I sometimes practise for three hours or more.
B: Three hours? That's a lot! Do you want to be a musician?
J: Well, no, but I love making music! I don't mind practising at all. It's easy! My teacher is very kind. She always helps me, and she sometimes organizes concerts, too.
V: Hi, guys!
J, B: Hi, Vicky!
V: What's the plan for today?
J: I've got my guitar lesson this afternoon, and Ben … well, Ben's

on his bike this morning! What about you?
V: It's my video game club today. We learn how to make video games and apps, too!
B: Wow! That sounds difficult!
V: Yes, but I usually enjoy it. And I love making video games! I never get bored when I'm there.
J: Good for you, Vicky!
V: What about this evening? Let's watch a film!
B: Great idea! I like going to the cinema! And I love eating popcorn!
J: Me too! See you later!
B, V: See you later, Jake.

You mustn't give up!

M = Mark, V = Vicky, G = Girl, B1 = Boy 1; B2 = Boy 2

V: Club rules. You must turn off your mobile phone. You must bring your own laptop. You can't use headphones. You can't eat or drink near the computers. You must complete the challenge.' Mmm. I hope the challenge isn't boring!
M: Hello, everybody. Welcome to our club for computer game programmers. As you know, to be a computer game programmer, you must be good at Maths. You can use your imagination, too, but you must always concentrate. Computer game programming is sometimes difficult, but you mustn't give up!
B1: Uh, I can't do this challenge! It's really difficult!
B2, G: Yes, it is!
M: OK. You've got one more minute! Do you need any help?
V: Yes! I've got it!
M: Congratulations, Vicky! Well done!

UNIT 4

Drew is playing the guitar!

J = Jake, B = Ben, V = Vicky

J: This is a great game, Ben! We need to guess what Vicky is doing now.
B: Mmm ... I think she's running.
J: No, she isn't running. She's riding a bike!
V: Correct!
J: My turn!
V: Mmm ... He's climbing!
B: No, he isn't! He's playing basketball.
V: Mmm ... He isn't playing basketball! He's cooking!
J: Good guess!
B: OK, now it's my turn.
J: Mmm ... I think Ben is running ...
V: And he's jumping!
J: And he's kicking ...
V: He's playing football!
B: Well done, guys!
V: Look! Drew is playing, too!
J: You're right! Drew is playing the guitar, I think!
B: Yes! Just like you, Jake!

Is it snowing now?

J = Jake, B = Ben, V = Vicky, AR = Aunt Rose

J: Look, guys. This website gives information about the weather in different cities.
B: Uh, that's useful for our homework. What's the weather like in Rome?
J: It's raining now in Rome!
V: Let's check out some more cities. How about ... New York? It sometimes snows in New York. Is it snowing at the moment?
J: Uh, yes it is! Look, people are wearing warm clothes.
V: What about Sydney? Is it snowing there right now?
J: Mmm ... No, it isn't. It's summer there! The sun is shining today. Look, people are wearing T-shirts.
B: It isn't always sunny in Sydney. It sometimes rains.
J: I know. But it isn't raining there now.
AR: Hello, everyone. What are you doing?
J: We're looking at the weather all over the world!
AR: Great! Are you working on a school project?
J: Yes, we are!
AR: Drew can help. Drew always knows about the weather!
V: Wow! That's amazing.
V, B, J: Thank you, Drew!

UNIT 5

Is there any cheese?

V = Vicky, J = Jake, B = Ben

V: What are you doing, Jake?
J: Well, it's a special day today. It's National Pizza Day!
V: So, you're making a pizza!
J: Yes! Hey ... you can help me!
V: Sure! OK, so there's some flour ... some salt ... some oil ... and there's some tomato sauce.
J: Perfect! Now for my favourite part, the toppings! First, the cheese. Is there any cheese?
V: Mmm ... no, there isn't any cheese.
J: Oh. Are there any vegetables?
V: No, there aren't any vegetables, but there's some fruit! There's an orange, there are some grapes, and there's a banana. Great! Let's make a fruit pizza!
J: A fruit pizza? Yuk! No, thanks. Let's have a takeaway!
B: Wait! We can make our own pizza! I've got some mushrooms ... I've got some olives ... and, of course, I've got some cheese!
V, B, J: Mmm!
J: This is a great pizza! Happy National Pizza Day, everyone!
V, B: Happy National Pizza Day!
B: Yummy!

How many questions are there?

V = Vicky, J = Jake, B = Ben

V: Hey, look at this. It's got a lot of information about food.
J: Mmm ... Interesting!
V: Oh, there's a quiz here! Let's do it.
B: Sure! How many questions are there?
V: There are only four. OK. Question one. How much sugar is there in a chocolate bar?
B: Mmm ... not much. About one teaspoon?
V: Wrong! There's a lot of sugar in a chocolate bar! About eight teaspoons!
J, B: Eight teaspoons?!
V: Yes! Question two. How much fruit do you need in a day?
J: Mmm ... a lot! Maybe three or four pieces?
V: Correct! You need a lot of fruit and vegetables! Question three. How much salt is there in a packet of crisps?
B: Oh, I like crisps. But I know there's a lot of salt in them!
V: That's right! You mustn't eat many crisps.
V: Last question. How much water do you need every day?
J: You need a lot of water! At least seven glasses a day!
V: Correct!
B: Let's have some water now!
J, V: Good idea! I'm thirsty!

UNIT 6

Which place is more interesting?

B = Ben , J = Jake

B: Hey, Jake, I like this map. But what are those things on it?
J: Those pins? They're all the places I want to visit one day!
Drew! Show us!
This is New York, in the USA. It's bigger than our town. Millions of people live there. It's more exciting, too. There are lots of jazz clubs! I love jazz!
This is Barcelona, in Spain. It isn't as big as New York, but I think it's more beautiful. There are lots of things to see. It's also warmer than New York, so I can spend lots of time outside!
Ah, this is Vesuvius, in Italy. Vesuvius is a volcano, so it can be more dangerous than other places!
B: Vesuvius looks really cool! I'd like to take pictures there! From a safe place ...
J: And this is the Sahara Desert, in Africa! It's great ... and it's hotter than most places in the world!
B: New York and Barcelona are good, but I think Vesuvius is better! It's more interesting!
J: Mmm. And finally ... the North Pole! It's further than Spain and Italy, but it's really cool! Ha! Ha! Ha! You can do more fun things there, Drew. For example, you can see a polar bear!
B: Ha! Ha! Ha! Wow, Jake! These are amazing places. Can I go with you?
J: Sure! What about you, Drew? Do you want to go with us?

The most intelligent animal!

J = Jake, V = Vicky

J: Hey, Vicky! How is the game project going?
V: Hi, Jake! Really well, thanks. Almost ready! Look. It's a quiz game about animals. There are eight different animals here and you compare them.
J: Mmm ... I think the frog is stronger than the mosquito. And the penguin is bigger and stronger than the frog. But the bear is the strongest!
V: Well done!
J: Mmm ... the spider is faster than the tortoise.
V: Good.
J: And the monkey is faster than the spider. But the lion is the fastest!
V: You're good at this!
J: Oh! What's this? Challenge round?
V: Ah, it gets more difficult now! So ... different animals, but this time, you choose one animal.
J: Mmm ... Well, I know the polar bear lives at the North Pole ... and the elephant lives in Africa and Asia ... so that means the right answer is the kangaroo! It lives the furthest away from Europe, in Australia!
V: That's brilliant, Jake!
J: 'Final question'!
V: Yes. This is the most difficult question in the quiz!
J: Mmm... 'Which is the most intelligent animal?' Oh, I'm not sure! Maybe it's the parrot ... or the elephant ... but what about a dolphin?
V: Oh, what? No Drew, you aren't an animal!
J: Do you think it's the dolphin, Drew? Let's see!
V: Correct!
J: Thank you, Drew! That's a great quiz, Vicky! I hope you get an 'A' for this project! It's the best!
V: Thanks, Jake!

UNIT 7

There weren't any laptops

J = Jake, AR = Aunt Rose, V = Vicky

J: What's this, Aunt Rose?
AR: It's a computer from the 1980s! It was my first computer.
V: Wow! It's very big!
AR: Yes, computers were big back then! There weren't any laptops.
J: Were there any tablets?
AR: No, there weren't.
V: Is this ... a mobile phone?
AR: Yes!
J: Mobile phones were very big, too!
AR: Yes, they were. And they were also very expensive.
V: Does the computer work?
AR: Mmm. Let's see ...
V: What's this? Where's the touch screen?
R: Oh, there wasn't a touch screen in the 1980s! Wait ... there was a book with the computer ...
J: A book?
AR: Yes. Here it is! It's got instructions!
V: But, why was there a book? Why can't you find all this information on the internet?
AR: Well, there was internet back then, but not usually in people's houses. It wasn't very common.
V: What are you doing, Drew?
AR: I think Drew is writing a little program!
J: That's really cool, Drew!

Ben needed some new clothes!

B = Ben, V = Vicky, J = Jake

B: Hi, guys! Oh! I'm really tired!
V: Here ... have some lemonade! Why are you tired? Tell us about your day!
B: Well, it's Saturday and I wanted to go shopping for some clothes. I walked to the department store. There were lots of people there! I was there for two hours!
J: Two hours? Why?
B: Well, I arrived at the store, and I tried on some jeans ... I looked at a shirt, too. I really liked it! Then I tried on some shorts, a jacket and some trainers.
V: Wow, that's a lot of clothes!
B: I know! The shops opened at ten, and I only finished shopping one hour ago!
J: That's OK. You've got lots of new clothes now!
B: No, I haven't.
J: What do you mean?
B: I tried on lots of clothes, but then ... I walked to the bookshop. There were some great books about photography there. Look! This one is about African jungles! Do you like it? This one is about South America! This one is about penguins! And this one is about the world's biggest cities!
J: Oh ...
V: So ... you haven't got any new clothes?
B: No, but I've got four fantastic books! I love them!

UNIT 8

He became famous!

B = Ben, J = Jake

B: Hey, Jake. What are you doing?
J: Oh, hey, Ben! I'm working on my school project. It's a presentation about my favourite singer and guitarist.
B: Sounds interesting!

J: Can I show you? You can tell me what you think.
B: Sure!
J: OK, here it goes. This is Ed Sheeran. He was born in England in 1991 and grew up in a small town. Ed learned to play the guitar before he left school, and he also wrote songs. He didn't like school, but his school friends thought he was very talented! He started recording his own music when he was a teenager. He played the guitar and sang his own songs on YouTube. People loved them! After that, he didn't stay in his hometown. He left home and moved to London. He won lots of prizes and worked on songs with other artists. Now he's famous all over the world!
B: Ah ... So, you do want to be a musician!
J: Well ... not really, but ... well, maybe! But don't tell anybody!
B: Ha! Ha! Ha! It's OK, you can tell me! Well done, Jake. That was a great presentation!
J: Thank you!

Did they like your photo?

J1 = Judge 1, B = Ben, J2 = Judge 2, V = Vicky, J = Jake

J1: Thank you for entering the competition, Ben. We really liked your photograph.
B: Thank you.
J1: We've got some questions for you. Where did you learn to take photographs? Did you go on a photography course?
B: No, I didn't. My dad showed me.
J2: When did you start taking photographs, Ben?
B: Oh, I was very young. I think I was seven years old!
J2: Wow! Did you get your first camera when you were seven?
B: No, I didn't. I used my mum's camera. But she gave me my own camera for my twelfth birthday.
J1: Did you take photographs of things and people in your house?
B: Yes, I did. I also photographed things outside, in the garden and all over our town.
J1: Great. Well Ben, thank you very much for coming in. We received lots of photographs, so we've got a big decision to make!
B: That's OK. I can wait! Thank you very much. Bye!
B: Hi, guys!
V, J: Hey, Ben!
V: How did the interview go?
B: They asked me to wait for an email.
V: I see. Well, can we see the competition photograph now?
B: Oh ... OK, here it is.
V: Oh, Ben! That's beautiful!

UNIT 9

When will it be ready?

AR = Aunt Rose, J = Jake

J: Hi, Aunt Rose.
AR: Oh, hi, Jake.
J: What's this?
AR: I'm designing a new machine. It's a flying bike!
J: A flying bike? Wow! That's amazing! Will it have wings?
AR: No, it won't. It will look like a normal bike!
J: Well, how will it fly?
AR: It will have four engines. They will use power from the sun!
J: That's amazing! Will it go fast?
AR: Yes, it will! It will fly at 70 kph! To go faster, you will need to cycle a little quicker. To go slower, you will need to use the brakes.
J: Just like a normal bike!
AR: Yes, but you will be in the air! To land, you will press a special button. The bike will stop and slowly go back down.
J: Ah ... Aunt Rose, that's incredible! When will it be ready?
AR: Oh, I really don't know.
J: Well, my birthday is in three months!
AR: Oh, it won't be ready on your birthday, Jake! Maybe next year!

We're going to go on holiday!

AR = Aunt Rose, J = Jake, V = Vicky, B = Ben

AR: Lemonade for everyone!
J: Thanks, Aunt Rose!
AR: You're welcome! So, Vicky, what are you going to do this summer?
V: I'm going to go to Spain with my family. We're going to stay in a hotel and we're going to go sightseeing!
AR: Sounds exciting! What about you, Jake?
J: Well, I'm going to visit Scotland with my mum! We're going to stay in Edinburgh. The Edinburgh Festival will be on.
AR: Great! And what about you, Ben? Are you going to go on holiday?
B: Well, no, I'm not. My mum and dad are busy this summer, so we're going to stay here. Are you going to be here, Rose?
AR: Yes, I am!
V: Hey, what's Drew doing with Ben's tablet?
AR: I don't know. Drew! Come back!
B: What's this, Drew? An email for me?
B: Huh? Photography competition ... What? Wow!
V: What?
B: Dear Ben, Congratulations! You won first prize in the competition! The prize is a weekend for three on a summer surfing school. You're going to go to the best beach in the country and you can take two friends! Enjoy the sun, the sea and the surf!
Ha! Brilliant! We're going to learn to surf!
R: Wow! I'm really pleased for you!

WORKBOOK ANSWER KEY

STARTER

1 November, Saturday, May, Monday, Friday, July, December, Tuesday

2 1 Italian lesson 2 English test 3 party 4 my birthday

3 1 third of March 2 twenty-fourth of February 3 sixteenth of June 4 first of April

4 1 timetable 2 earphones 3 pencils 4 phone 5 keys
Mystery word: *money*.

5 1 Joanna 2 Marta 3 Ali

6
1 I love your sister's dress.
2 These are my friend's/friends' bikes.
3 Where is Mr Smith's house?
4 My cousins' names are Lou and Anna.

7 1 My parents' 2 The teachers' 3 My brother's 4 Tom's 5 Julia's

8 1 Her 2 my 3 She 4 His 5 He 6 We

9 1 These 2 That 3 This 4 Those

10 1 Spanish 2 Turkish 3 Brazilian 4 Argentinian 5 Egyptian 6 French 7 Chinese 8 American

11 1 **w**hite 2 **y**ellow 3 **b**rown 4 **o**range 5 **p**ink 6 **g**reen 7 **b**lack 8 **p**urple 9 **g**rey 10 **b**lue

12 1 aren't 2 Is 3 'm 4 isn't 5 Are 6 's 7 aren't 8 isn't 9 aren't 10 is

13
1 Where are you from?
2 Who is the president of your country?
3 How old is your sister?
4 What colour is your bag?
5 Where is your school?

UNIT 1

Vocabulary

1 1 lamp 2 cooker 3 toilet 4 bookcase 5 sink 6 table 7 bed 8 desk

2 1 – 2 ✓ 3 – 4 ✓ 5 ✓ 6 – 7 ✓ 8 ✓ 9 –

3 1 e 2 f 3 a 4 b 5 d 6 c

4
1 wardrobe, bookcase
2 sofa, mirror, lamp
3 fridge, table, cooker
4 toilet, bath, sink

Reading

1 b

2 1 F 2 T 3 F 4 T 5 T

3 1 dirty 2 uncomfortable 3 untidy 4 empty

Grammar

1 1 There are 2 isn't 3 are 4 aren't 5 There's 6 isn't

2
1 There are some clothes in the wardrobe.
2 There aren't any tomatoes in the fridge.
3 There are some apples in the kitchen.
4 There are some bananas on the table.
5 Are there any books in the bookcase?

3 1 Is there 2 there isn't 3 there's 4 Are there 5 there are

4 1 T 2 F 3 F 4 F 5 T

5 1 in 2 on 3 next to 4 under

6 1 under 2 on 3 next to 4 behind 5 in

Vocabulary and Listening

1 1 husband 2 grandad 3 child 4 daughter 5 parent

2 1 uncle 2 sister 3 nephew 4 daughter 5 husband

3 1 cousin 2 nephew 3 daughter 4 grandad 5 brother 6 uncle 7 husband 8 aunt

4 1 – 2 ✓ 3 ✓ 4 – 5 ✓ 6 ✓ 7 ✓ 8 ✓

5 1 c 2 b 3 b 4 a

Grammar

1
1 Sophia has got six cousins.
2 I have got two dogs.
3 They haven't got a big family.
4 Has David got a nice bedroom?
5 How many brothers has Meghan got?

2 1 e 2 f 3 d 4 a 5 b 6 c

3 1 haven't 2 He's 3 hasn't 4 has 5 Have 6 has

4 1 She's got 2 Has she got 3 hasn't 4 have you got 5 I've got 6 Have you got 7 haven't 8 I've got

5
1 Lara's got a new phone
2 Have you got a pen?
3 Freddie hasn't got a bike.
4 They haven't got any bananas.
5 Has she got a dog?
6 We've got five cousins.

Speaking

1 1 How 2 This 3 Nice 4 meet 5 later 6 Bye

2 a 3 b 5 c 7 d 1 e 6 f 2 g 4

3
1 Fine, thanks
2 This is my friend
3 Nice to meet you
4 Nice to meet you, too
5 Bye

4 1 c 2 e 3 a 4 b 5 d

Writing

1 1 two 2 No 3 three 4 No 5 No

2 1 and 2 but 3 but 4 and 5 and 6 but

3 1 e 2 f 3 d 4 c 5 a 6 b

4 Students' own answers.

Review Unit 1

1 1 cooker 2 fridge 3 lamp 4 mirror 5 sink 6 sofa 7 table 8 toilet

2 1 in 2 under 3 behind 4 in front of 5 next to

3 1 are 2 any 3 aren't 4 there's 5 Is 6 isn't 7 there are

4 1 uncle 2 parents 3 husband 4 grandma 5 sister

5 1 have 2 has got 3 has it got 4 's got 5 has got 6 have they got 7 have 8 haven't got

UNIT 2

Vocabulary

1
1 We have lunch at 1.00.
2 On Sunday I tidy my room
3 After breakfast we get dressed.
4 I have a shower at 7.00.
5 We leave home at 8.00.
6 After dinner I do my homework.
7 In the evening we watch TV.

2 1 leave 2 tidy 3 watch 4 have 5 do 6 get

3 1 f 2 c 3 a 4 b 5 e 6 d

4 1 have 2 get 3 have 4 leave 5 have 6 tidy 7 do 8 have 9 watch 10 go

Reading

1 1 ✓ 2 – 3 ✓ 4 – 5 ✓

2 1 T 2 F 3 F 4 F 5 T 6 F 7 T 8 T

3 1 Geography 2 Maths 3 Music 4 Science 5 English

Grammar

1 1 gets up 2 doesn't go 3 eat 4 walks 5 don't sleep

2
1 Mr Ellis teaches Maths at my school.
2 Max sleeps in a very big bed.
3 My brothers don't have breakfast with me.
4 Charlie tidies his room on Saturday.
5 Jana and Lena don't like their cousins.
6 Yoko doesn't speak English.

3
1 Freddie and Max don't play football after school.
2 I don't live in France.
3 Mum doesn't leave home at seven o'clock.
4 My sister doesn't go to school in the village.
5 Lucas doesn't study History.

4 1 does 2 don't 3 has 4 do 5 doesn't

5
1 My English lesson starts at ten o'clock.
2 Mustafa comes from Turkey.
3 Paul and Dom don't go to bed at 8.00 p.m.
4 Susie doesn't play the guitar.
5 My mum speaks French.

Vocabulary and Listening

1 1 d 2 e 3 a 4 b 5 c

2 1 computer 2 camera 3 whiteboard 4 laptop 5 drone 6 projector

3
1 interactive whiteboards
2 projectors
3 Virtual Reality headsets
4 digital cameras
5 computers
6 wireless headphones

4 1 Layla 2 Seb 3 Seb

5 1 a 2 b 3 c 4 c

Grammar

1 1 Do, don't 2 Does, does 3 Do, do 4 Does, doesn't 5 Does, does

2 1 don't 2 Does 3 does 4 Does 5 doesn't 6 Do 7 do

3
1 No, they don't.
2 Yes, it does.
3 Yes, they do.
4 No, she doesn't.
5 No, I don't.

4
1 How do you make this cake?
2 When does the lesson start?
3 What do you eat for lunch?
4 How many apples do you have?
5 Where do you play tennis?
6 What time does Paul have lunch?

5 1 How many, do 2 Where do 3 When do 4 When does 5 How does 6 What time does

Speaking

1 1 in 2 know 3 on 4 start 5 when 6 meet

2 1 Sunday 2 10.15 3 12.30 4 school

3 1 ✓ 2 – 3 ✓ 4 ✓ 5 – 6 ✓

4
1 I'm interested in
2 What would you like to know?
3 Where do they meet?
4 What day is it on?
5 What time does it start?
6 What time does it finish?

5 1 c 2 e 3 a 4 b 5 d

Writing

1 1 at 2 at 3 In 4 In 5 On 6 In 7 on 8 at

2 1 10.00 2 3D printer 3 No 4 Tuesday 5 11.00

3 1 tell you about 2 at 7.30 3 My favourite 4 On Friday 5 Write soon 6 Best wishes

4
1 We meet at 5.30 on Tuesday.
2 My dad works at night.
3 What do you do at the weekend?
4 I get up early in the morning.
5 My music lesson finishes at 4.30.

5 Students' own answers.

Review Unit 2

1 1 have 2 get 3 have 4 leave 5 watch 6 have 7 do 8 go

2 1 plays 2 gets up 3 don't live 4 studies 5 wants 6 don't watch

3
b tablet
c wireless headphones
d digital camera
e projector
f drone

4 1 do 2 Do 3 don't 4 Does 5 doesn't 6 does 7 Do 8 don't

5
1 What time does Katie get up?
2 When do you do your homework?
3 How many brothers does she have?
4 What time does the lesson start?
5 Do your parents like pizza?
6 Do your teachers use interactive whiteboards?

UNIT 3

Vocabulary

1 ballet, gymnastics, volleyball, taekwondo, athletics, rugby, surfing, swimming

2 1 rugby 2 surfing 3 ice hockey 4 skateboarding 5 table tennis

3
1 ice hockey
2 ballet
3 mountain biking
4 surfing
5 taekwondo
6 rugby

4 1 play 2 do 3 play 4 does 5 go

5 1 does gymnastics
2 goes skateboarding
3 plays ice hockey
4 play volleyball
5 goes mountain biking

Reading

1 1 – 2 ✓ 3 ✓ 4 – 5 ✓

2 1 F 2 T 3 F 4 F 5 T 6 F 7 F

3 1 champion 2 success 3 helmet 4 ambition

Grammar

1 1 always, d
2 sometimes, c
3 often, e
4 never, b
5 usually, a

2 1 wearing 2 visiting 3 practising 4 walking 5 meeting 6 reading

3 1 Oscar never phones his friends.
2 I sometimes go to school by train.
3 Leah's bedroom is always tidy.
4 I often go running with my sister.
5 The bus usually arrives at 7.30.

4 1 I don't mind getting up early.
2 Do you like playing table tennis?
3 Emma doesn't like reading.
4 My dad hates doing exercise.
5 Umberto loves going to the gym.

5 1 usually visits
2 sometimes plays
3 is often
4 always go
5 is often

6 1 loves playing
2 hate going
3 doesn't mind tidying
4 like visiting
5 doesn't like watching

Vocabulary and Listening

1 1 e 2 b 3 a 4 f 5 c 6 d

2 1 skates 2 climbs 3 throws 4 rides 5 ski

3 Across
4 skate
5 climbs
7 swimming

Down
1 ride
2 throwing
3 catches
4 ski
6 kick

4 1 ✓ 2 – 3 – 4 ✓ 5 ✓ 6 ✓

5 1 No 2 Yes 3 Yes 4 Yes 5 No 6 Yes

Grammar

1 1 can 2 can't 3 can 4 can 5 can't

2 1 can 2 can't 3 can 4 can't 5 can

3 1 Lee can stay at my house.
2 I can't play the guitar.
3 My friends can't climb that tree.
4 You can take photos here.
5 David can ride a horse.

4 1 You must take a bottle of water.
2 Students mustn't chat in class.
3 Your dog mustn't sleep on the sofa.
4 Students must wear their school uniforms.
5 You mustn't jump on the bed.

5 1 must 2 mustn't 3 must 4 must 5 mustn't

6 1 Your shoes must be clean.
2 You mustn't talk to your friends in class.
3 Dad mustn't be late for work.
4 Parents must wait for their children outside the school.
5 They mustn't use their phones.

Speaking

1 1 shall 2 about 3 sound 4 fun 5 Why 6 idea

2 1 ✓ 2 ✓ 3 – 4 – 5 ✓ 6 ✓ 7 ✓

3 1 What shall we do
2 What about
3 That doesn't sound very exciting
4 Why don't we
5 Where shall we meet
6 Great idea

4 1 a 2 f 3 b 4 e 5 c

5 1 go 2 listening 3 meeting 4 ask 5 play 6 making

Writing

1 1 Saturday 2 Saturday 3 Sunday 4 Sunday 5 Saturday 6 Sunday 7 Saturday

2 1 On Monday, I go to Art Club.
2 This pizza is great!
3 Once a month, my mum goes to the theatre.
4 Can you ski?
5 Do you like going mountain biking?
6 My dad has got eight brothers and sisters!

3 1 every weekend
2 every Wednesday
3 sometimes
4 never

4 Students' own answers.

Review Unit 3

1 1 mountain biking
2 swimming
3 gymnastics
4 athletics
5 ice hockey

2 1 plays 2 do 3 does 4 go 5 plays

3 1 I sometimes play tennis on Thursday.
2 Pam never goes shopping with her mum.
3 He usually does his homework after dinner.
4 Jessie is often late for school.
5 I sometimes meet my friend Lulu after school.

4 1 like playing
2 doesn't mind helping
3 love watching
4 hates being
5 Does, like wearing

5 1 throw 2 swim 3 rides 4 kick 5 runs

6 1 must wear
2 mustn't swim
3 mustn't run
4 must bring
5 must pay
6 mustn't use

PROGRESS CHECK

Starter and Units 1–3

1 1 Mexico 2 British 3 Turkey 4 French 5 Japan 6 American

2 1 My parents' car is red.
2 This is my sister's bedroom.
3 Is that your grandparents' house?
4 These are Julia's pens.
5 Are you Emily's mother?
6 Alejandro's friends are French.

3 1 I 2 Our 3 her 4 He 5 It 6 Their 7 They 8 your

4 1 any 2 a 3 an 4 any 5 some 6 a

5 1 There are, next to
2 There aren't, on
3 There's, behind
4 There are, in front of
5 There isn't, under

6 1 tidies 2 don't use 3 get 4 watches 5 doesn't like 6 goes

7 1 Are his keys
2 Does Maria live
3 Do Clara and Alex go to school
4 Are Adam and Chris
5 Have Laura and Joe got
6 Is Susan
7 Do Alan and Tom play football
8 Has Paul got

8 1 she isn't
2 he does
3 she does
4 they don't
5 they don't
6 they aren't
7 they are
8 I don't

9 1 daughter 2 skateboarding 3 folder 4 athletics 5 interactive whiteboard 6 snack 7 games console 8 grandma

10 1 Grandma is often tired in the evening.
2 My sister always goes to bed at nine o'clock.
3 Ollie never tidies his room.
4 Mia's house is usually tidy.
5 I sometimes go mountain biking with my friends.
6 Lily often does her homework in the living room.

11 1 Can 2 can't 3 must 4 can't 5 mustn't 6 must

12 1 use 2 be 3 playing 4 have 5 taking 6 going

UNIT 4

Vocabulary

1 a 1 b 4 c 5 d 3 e 6 f 2

2 castle, hotel, train station, monument, shopping centre, square, theatre, market

3 1 e 2 d 3 a 4 b 5 f 6 c

4 1 library 2 market 3 restaurant 4 hotel 5 department store

5 1 monument 2 castle 3 market 4 restaurant 5 theatre

Reading

1 1 – 2 ✓ 3 ✓ 4 ✓ 5 – 6 – 7 ✓

2 1 a member of her family 2 good 3 the streets 4 market 5 park

3 1 Pol**ish** 2 Brazil**ian** 3 Chin**ese** 4 Russ**ian** 5 Span**ish** 6 Japan**ese**

Grammar

1 1 ✓ 2 ✓ 3 – 4 ✓ 5 – 6 ✓

2 1 am 2 is 3 are 4 having 5 are 6 climbing

3 1 're having 2 is looking 3 are talking 4 'm cleaning 5 is watching 6 are playing

4 1 He's looking at the paintings.
2 She's reading a book.
3 We're buying some food.
4 We aren't going to school.
5 I'm not having lunch.

5 1 is eating 2 isn't skating 3 's climbing 4 isn't swimming 5 's riding 6 aren't skiing

Vocabulary and Listening

1 stormy, cloudy, sunny, foggy, cold, windy, icy

2 1 b 2 c 3 b 4 a 5 c 6 b 7 c

3 1 foggy 2 stormy 3 snowing 4 raining 5 windy

4 1 Dad 2 Lucy 3 Lucy 4 Dad

5 1 F 2 T 3 F 4 F

6 1 b 2 c 3 b 4 b

Grammar

1 1 am 2 Is 3 isn't 4 doing 5 is 6 is 7 swimming 8 aren't

2 1 c 2 a 3 d 4 e 5 f 6 b

3 1 Are there people in the sea? Yes, there are.
2 Is the woman listening to music? Yes, she is.
3 Is the woman riding a horse? Yes, she is.
4 Is the man running fast? No, he isn't.
5 Are the women playing volleyball? Yes, they are.

4 1 Do they go 2 leaves 3 we're having 4 It never rains 5 He's chatting 6 are you doing

5 1 's snowing 2 eat 3 's having 4 goes 5 's climbing 6 's getting

6 1 George goes swimming every Saturday.
2 I'm tidying my bedroom at the moment.
3 Abbie usually gets up at seven o'clock.
4 Grace runs 15 kilometres three times a week.
5 Mum's having a shower right now.

Speaking

1 1 far 2 walk 3 straight 4 past 5 turn 6 on

2 1 ✓ 2 – 3 ✓ 4 ✓ 5 ✓ 6 –

3 C

4 a 4 b 7 c 2 d 1 e 3 f 6 g 8 h 5

Writing

1 1 Uncle Jack 2 a painting 3 a pizza 4 hot and sunny

2 1 c 2 e 3 a 4 b 5 d

3 a 2 b 3 c 1

4 Students' own answers.

Review Unit 4

1 1 castle 2 train station 3 monument 4 restaurant 5 market 6 hotel 7 library 8 theatre

2 1 'm not watching 2 isn't snowing 3 's listening 4 's raining 5 isn't having

3 1 e, g 2 b, c 3 f, h 4 a, d

4 1 Is, isn't 2 Are, are 3 Are, am 4 Are, aren't 5 Are, 'm not

5 1 'm visiting 2 're looking 3 love 4 have 5 studying

UNIT 5

Vocabulary

1 1 **s**andwich 2 **p**otatoes 3 **s**alad 4 **o**range **j**uice 5 **e**ggs 6 **p**asta 7 **b**eans 8 **f**ish

2 1 eggs 2 fish 3 fruit 4 milk 5 potatoes

3 1 b 2 e 3 a 4 f 5 c 6 d

4 1 sandwich 2 fruit 3 yoghurt 4 pasta 5 rice

5 1 toast, cereal, milk, egg, orange juice, yoghurt
2 chicken, rice, salad
3 fish, potatoes, beans

Reading

1 1 pizza 2 chips 3 cheese 4 burgers

2 b

3 1 T 2 F 3 F 4 F 5 T

Grammar

1 1 ✓ 2 – 3 ✓ 4 – 5 ✓ 6 ✓

2 1 any 2 some 3 any 4 some 5 some 6 some

3 1 c 2 e 3 a 4 f 5 b 6 d

4
1 There's some pasta in the cupboard.
2 Let's have some ice cream!
3 I don't want any milk, thanks. I don't drink milk.
4 Do you want a drink? We've got some apple juice.
5 I've got an apple in my bag.
6 There are some lemons in the kitchen.
7 There isn't any milk in the fridge.
8 Is there any bread in the cupboard?

5 1 any 2 some 3 any 4 some 5 any 6 some 7 any 8 any

Vocabulary and Listening

Positive adjectives (+)	Negative adjectives (-)
active fit healthy	lazy unfit unhealthy

2 1 unhealthy 2 hungry 3 fit 4 lazy 5 healthy 6 active

3 1 thirsty 2 hungry 3 unhealthy 4 lazy 5 unfit

4 1 lazy 2 unfit 3 healthy 4 active 5 unhealthy

5 1 Oscar 2 Oscar 3 Beth

6 1 T 2 T 3 F 4 F 5 F 6 T 7 F 8 F

Grammar

1 1 UC 2 C 3 C 4 UC 5 UC 6 C 7 UC 8 C 9 C 10 UC

2
1 My dad doesn't drink much coffee.
2 Tom plays a lot of basketball.
3 How many apples do you eat in a day?
4 I don't eat a lot of potatoes.
5 How much orange juice do you drink?

3 1 a lot of 2 many 3 many 4 much 5 many 6 much 7 a lot 8 a lot

4 1 How much 2 How many 3 How many 4 How much 5 How many 6 How many

5 1 c 2 f 3 e 4 a 5 b 6 d

6 1 How many 2 a lot of 3 How much 4 a lot of 5 a lot of 6 How many

Speaking

1 1 like 2 Anything 3 have 4 else 5 have 6 take away 7 Here 8 coming

2 a 5 b 2 c 4 d 7 e 3 f 1 g 6

3 1 d 2 c 3 a 4 b

4 1 c 2 a 3 e 4 b 5 d

5
1 Anything to drink
2 Can I have
3 Anything else
4 Any dessert
5 I'll have
6 Is that to eat in or take away
7 That'll be
8 Here you are
9 Your food is just coming

Writing

1
1 four people
2 onion and garlic
3 red pepper
4 about ten minutes
5 rice and a green salad

2 1 b 2 e 3 a 4 d 5 c

3 1 First 2 Then 3 Next 4 Finally

4 Students' own answers.

Review Unit 5

1 Across: 4 cereal 5 eggs 7 toast 8 rice
Down: 1 fruit 2 sandwich 3 pasta 6 salad

2 1 some 2 any 3 any 4 a, an 5 any, some

3 1 e 2 a 3 f 4 c 5 b 6 d

4
1 eggs, pasta, rice
2 potatoes, cookies
3 jam, bread

5
1 My dad drinks a lot of coffee.
2 There's a lot of butter in this cake.
3 There aren't many chairs in this room.
4 How many people can you see?
5 You've got a lot of video games!

UNIT 6

Vocabulary

1 1 island 2 mountain 3 waterfall 4 beach 5 desert 6 rainforest 7 forest

2 1 beach 2 forest 3 rainforest 4 mountain 5 waterfall

3 1 sky 2 beach 3 forest 4 desert 5 river

4 1 island 2 sky 3 sea 4 volcano 5 lake

5 1 F 2 T 3 F 4 T 5 T

Reading

1 b

2 a 6 b 2 c 5 d 4 e 1 f 3

3 1 two 2 see 3 volcano 4 year

4 1 a thousand 2 a hundred thousand 3 a million 4 a billion 5 a trillion

Grammar

1 1 F 2 T 3 T 4 T 5 T

2 1 than 2 younger 3 more difficult 4 as 5 easier

3 1 as 2 than 3 than 4 as 5 than

4 1 more exciting 2 better 3 easier 4 cheaper 5 funnier 6 more expensive 7 worse 8 further

5 1 fitter 2 hotter 3 longer 4 windier 5 bigger 6 hungrier

6 1 older 2 faster 3 cloudier 4 happier 5 more interesting 6 more beautiful

Vocabulary and Listening

1 1 **l**eopard 2 **m**osquito 3 **p**enguin 4 **s**nake 5 **w**hale 6 **s**hark 7 **l**ion 8 **d**onkey

2 1 tortoise 2 whale 3 penguin 4 snake 5 leopard

3 Across: 2 shark 3 bear 5 bat 6 monkey 7 lion 8 snake
Down: 1 parrot 4 frog 5 beetle

4 1 – 2 ✓ 3 ✓ 4 ✓ 5 – 6 ✓ 7 –

5 1 cold, icy 2 fast 3 60 4 intelligent

6 1 a 2 b 3 a 4 c

Grammar

1 1 Gavin 2 Lucy 3 Helen

2 1 best 2 most colourful 3 hottest 4 funniest 5 worst

3 1 biggest 2 most difficult 3 strangest 4 most interesting 5 hungriest 6 strongest 7 easiest

4 1 Antarctica is the coldest place on Earth.
2 The most famous river on Earth is probably the Nile.
3 This is the worst restaurant in town!
4 Christchurch, New Zealand, is the furthest capital city from London.
5 The best museum for children is the Natural History Museum.

5 1 the most exciting 2 the best 3 the furthest 4 the longest 5 the most expensive

6 1 most dangerous 2 longest 3 hottest 4 heaviest 5 smallest

Speaking

1 1 there 2 like 3 total 4 are 5 Here 6 change

2 a 2 b 7 c 1 d 5 e 6 f 3 g 4

3 1 d 2 c 3 a 4 b

4 a 3 b 1 c 4 d 5 e 7 f 2 g 6 h 8

5 1 We'd like to go to 2 Is there a discount 3 it's 4 students 5 're all students 6 'd like 7 tickets, please 8 that's £75 9 Here you are 10 Here are your 11 Thank you 12 here's your 13 Thank you

Writing

1 1 intelligent 2 grow 3 weigh 4 eat 5 sharks 6 day 7 also

2 1 Yes 2 eight 3 sleep 4 Yes 5 Yes

3 1 My tortoise moves very slowly. He eats slowly, too.
2 These spiders are huge. They are also very dangerous.
3 Black bears live in forests. They live in mountains, too.
4 They are very fast. They are also very intelligent.
5 Leopards live in Africa. They also live in Asia.

4 1 d 2 a 3 e 4 f 5 c 6 b

5 Students' own answers.

Review Unit 6

1 1 sky 2 mountain 3 desert 4 forest 5 island

2 1 The Pacific Ocean is larger than the Atlantic Ocean.
2 K2 isn't as high as Mount Everest.
3 Barcelona isn't as wet as Manchester.
4 The lake is colder than the river.
5 The food in Italy is better than the food in the UK.
6 The Palace of Versailles isn't as beautiful as the Taj Mahal.

3 1 leopard 2 lion 3 mosquito 4 parrot 5 penguin 6 shark 7 snake 8 whale

4 1 The cheetah is the best runner in the world.
2 The ostrich is the heaviest bird in the world.
3 Whales are the loudest animals in the sea.
4 These are the most colourful parrots in the world.
5 The Gobi bear is the rarest bear on Earth.

PROGRESS CHECK

Units 4–6

1 1 beach 2 museum 3 jam 4 department store 5 elephants 6 rainforest

2 1 are having 2 is studying 3 'm watching 4 's raining 5 are travelling 6 'm not wearing

3 1 d 2 h 3 f 4 g 5 a 6 b 7 c 8 e

4 1 monkey 2 hotel 3 penguin 4 island 5 potato 6 market 7 fruit 8 snake
Mystery word: *mountain*.

5 1 'm going 2 lives 3 works 4 isn't working 5 's visiting 6 'm learning 7 don't speak 8 understand

6 1 many 2 any 3 any 4 much 5 some 6 any

7 1 mountain 2 lake 3 fit 4 warm 5 castles 6 markets 7 vegetables 8 chicken

8 1 shorter than 2 as old as 3 more comfortable than 4 bigger than 5 more excited than 6 happier than

9 1 the best 2 warmer 3 older than 4 the highest 5 the most beautiful 6 more dangerous than

10 1 raining 2 icy 3 foggy 4 snowing 5 windy 6 cloudy 7 sunny

UNIT 7

Vocabulary

1 1 Isabel 2 Beth 3 Amanda

2 1 shorts 2 trousers 3 coat 4 socks

3 1 tie 2 trousers 3 hat 4 dress 5 shoes 6 T-shirt 7 shorts 8 trainers

4 a 1 shirt 2 trainers
b 3 skirt 4 jumper 5 boots
c 6 trousers 7 T-shirt 8 shoes

Reading

1 1 – 2 – 3 ✓ 4 ✓ 5 – 6 ✓ 7 ✓

2 1 F 2 F 3 T 4 F 5 F 6 T

3 1 hour 2 week 3 year 4 decade 5 century

Grammar

1 1 weren't 2 was 3 Were 4 was 5 Was

2 1 Was he at the train station?
2 They weren't in the kitchen.
3 It wasn't very hot on the beach.
4 Was the hotel comfortable?
5 The water was warm in the swimming pool.

3 1 was 2 Was 3 was 4 were 5 Were 6 weren't 7 were 8 was

4 1 c 2 a 3 f 4 b 5 d 6 e

5 1 Were there 2 There were 3 There wasn't 4 Was there 5 There was 6 There weren't

6 1 were 2 Was 3 was 4 was 5 Were 6 were 7 wasn't 8 weren't 9 were

Vocabulary and Listening

1 a 3 b 1 c 4 d 2

2
1 We enjoyed riding our bikes in the park.
2 My brother and I collected Pokémon cards.
3 We loved our little dog.
4 My brother wanted a new bike.
5 I borrowed my friend's skateboard.

3 1 wanted 2 tried 3 used 4 enjoyed 5 travelled

4 1 Uncle David 2 Uncle David 3 Lucy 4 Uncle David

5 1 F 2 T 3 T 4 F

6 1 c 2 a 3 b 4 c

Grammar

1 1 played 2 loved 3 painted 4 watched 5 enjoyed 6 rained

2
1 She stopped running because she was tired.
2 I tidied my bedroom at the weekend.
3 At the party I danced with my friend Sarah.
4 Two years ago, we travelled to China.
5 She studied Maths and Science this morning.
6 George loves playing the guitar. He practised all weekend.

3 1 invited 2 used 3 listened 4 talked 5 visited 6 opened

4 1 them 2 us 3 her 4 it 5 me 6 him 7 them 8 him

5 1 him 2 it 3 them 4 her 5 us 6 it 7 her 8 him

Speaking

1 1 got 2 try 3 size 4 rooms 5 good 6 much 7 them 8 pay

2 1 – 2 ✓ 3 ✓ 4 – 5 – 6 ✓

3 2

4 1 c 2 f 3 a 4 e 5 b 6 d

Writing

1 1 really 2 it 3 loved 4 popular 5 events 6 scored

2 1 three 2 amazing 3 Rime 4 the Netherlands

3 1 c 2 f 3 a 4 e 5 b 6 d

4
1 pencils and folders
2 beds and bookcases
3 monkeys and lions
4 jumpers and a coat
5 Students' own answers.

Review Unit 7

1 1 jacket 2 trainers 3 hat 4 T-shirt 5 shorts 6 boots 7 jeans 8 socks

2 1 weren't 2 was 3 were 4 was 5 wasn't

3 1 there weren't 2 there were 3 There was 4 Were there 5 Was there 6 there wasn't

4 1 f 2 e 3 a 4 c 5 b 6 d

5
1 I watched television on Saturday evening.
2 We studied in the evenings.
3 The train sometimes stopped at that station.
4 I loved the clothes in that shop.
5 My children collected World Cup cards.

6 1 b 2 b 3 b 4 a 5 a

UNIT 8

Vocabulary

1 1 have 2 learn 3 buy 4 go 5 leave 6 make 7 get

2 1 b 2 f 3 e 4 a 5 c 6 d

3 1 bought 2 was 3 had 4 learned 5 went 6 grew

4 a 5 b 3 c 1 d 8 e 2 f 7 g 4 h 6

5
1 started school
2 had, baby
3 got married
4 went, university
5 bought, house

Reading

1 a 5 b 2 c 7 d 8 e 1 f 4 g 6 h 3

2 1 c 2 a 3 c 4 b

3 1 audience 2 group 3 concert 4 album 5 village 6 singer 7 competition

Grammar

1 1 c 2 f 3 b 4 a 5 d 6 e

2 1 left 2 want 3 went 4 travelled 5 loved 6 got 7 have 8 had

3

Infinitive	**Past simple affirmative**	**Past simple negative**
meet	met	*didn't meet*
know	**knew**	**didn't know**
live	lived	**didn't live**
have	**had**	didn't have
join	**joined**	**didn't join**
make	made	**didn't make**
write	**wrote**	didn't write

4
1 I didn't see Marc this morning.
2 He didn't grow up in America.
3 She didn't win the competition.
4 I didn't tidy my room.
5 We didn't leave at ten o'clock.

5
1 She didn't want the book.
2 I met Karl in Venezuela.
3 He didn't know my name.
4 They didn't travel with us.
5 He wrote his phone number on the paper.
6 Andrew spoke Spanish very well.
7 Freddie didn't study Latin at school.
8 Emma left school when she was sixteen.

6
1 I spoke to Jamie yesterday.
2 My brother went to university.
3 Pia didn't listen to the song.
4 I didn't learn French at school.
5 We saw the movie last night.
6 Jack didn't walk to school this morning.
7 I didn't travel to Edinburgh by train.
8 She met her mum at the station.

Vocabulary and Listening

1 1 glasses 2 green 3 bald 4 slim 5 straight 6 thin

2 1 e 2 a 3 f 4 b 5 c 6 d

3 1 brown 2 dark 3 curly 4 moustache 5 tall 6 blond 7 long 8 glasses

4 1 ✓ 3 – 5 ✓ 7 ✓
2 ✓ 4 ✓ 6 –

5 1 F 3 F 5 T
2 T 4 F 6 T

Grammar

1 1 c 3 a 5 b
2 e 4 f 6 d

2 1 Did, come
No, she didn't.
2 Did, wear
No, he didn't.
3 Did, enjoy
Yes, they did.
4 Did, tidy
No, she didn't.
5 Did, buy
Yes, she did.

3 1 Did you finish
2 did you invite
3 did Martha spend
4 Did Matt tell
5 did Leah join
6 did you eat

4 1 Why did you go
2 Where did you see
3 How much did, cost
4 What time did, arrive
5 Who did you meet
6 What did you wear

Speaking

1 1 weekend 4 went
2 amazing 5 like
3 do 6 sounds

2 a 2 c 1 e 3
b 4 d 6 f 5

3 1 have 5 went to
2 it was 6 fun
3 you do 7 was
4 about you 8 like

4 1 e 3 f 5 h 7 g
2 a 4 b 6 c 8 d

Writing

1 1 straight 5 grew up
2 brown 6 that
3 face 7 got married
4 born 8 hobbies

2 1 Yes 3 No 5 No
2 Yes 4 Yes

3 1 e 3 a 5 b
2 c 4 f 6 d

4 My art teacher, Mr Flood, is great. He's tall and slim and he has got a friendly face. He wears glasses because he can't see very well. / He was born in Canada and grew up there. He got married when he was 30. His wife is English, and they moved to London in 1995. After that, he got a job at my school. / His hobbies are walking and reading. He also likes listening to music in the evenings.

1 b 2 c 3 a

5 Students' own answers.

Review Unit 8

1 1 bought 4 went
2 learned 5 got
3 left 6 made

2 1 were 4 had
2 got 5 grew
3 started 6 made

3 1 I didn't see my friend Lola at the weekend.
2 Kris wrote to me every day.
3 I didn't want to get a job in London.
4 Jamie bought flowers for his mother every Sunday.
5 Helen didn't work in a hotel.

4 1 they didn't 4 she didn't
2 he didn't 5 they did
3 I did 6 he didn't

5 1 Did your dad start his new job last week?
2 When did you meet your wife?
3 How long did you stay at your cousin's house?
4 Did your parents enjoy the film?
5 How did you make this cake?
6 Did they go to the beach yesterday?

UNIT 9

Vocabulary

1 1 underground 4 helicopter
2 scooter 5 motorbike
3 coach

2 1 helicopter 5 motorbike
2 on foot 6 underground
3 coach 7 plane
4 bike

3 1 scooter 4 tram
2 ship 5 on foot
3 plane

4 1 lorry 4 plane
2 motorbike 5 helicopter
3 tram 6 bike

5 1 coach 4 scooter
2 boat 5 ship
3 bike 6 on foot

Reading

1 1 ✓ 3 – 5 ✓ 7 –
2 – 4 ✓ 6 ✓

2 1 F 3 T 5 F
2 T 4 F

3 1 traffic 4 expensive
2 transport 5 travel
3 healthier

4 1 motorway 4 traffic
2 path 5 driver
3 view

Grammar

1 1 won't 3 will 5 will
2 will 4 won't

2 1 I think it will be hot tomorrow.
2 I think John will become a teacher after university.
3 Maria won't pass her English exam in June.
4 Will the party be fun on Saturday?
5 Most people won't drive cars in 2050.

3 1 No, we won't.
2 Yes, it will.
3 Yes, we will.
4 No, they won't.
5 Yes, they will.
6 No, they won't.

4 1 Megan will live in New York one day.
2 Ryan will make friends at his new school.
3 Lucy won't have any children before she's 35.
4 People won't have flying cars in 2050.
5 Astronauts will travel to Mars before 2100.

Vocabulary and Listening

1 1 g 3 a 5 d 7 e
2 c 4 f 6 h 8 b

2 1 d 3 e 5 c
2 b 4 a

3 1 packed 4 stayed
2 relaxed 5 visited
3 took 6 took

4 1 Sara 3 Sara
2 Dylan 4 Dylan

5 1 F 2 F 3 T 4 T 5 T

Grammar

1 1 'm 3 is 5 's
2 Are 4 Are 6 'm

2 1 Are 4 going
2 to have 5 get
3 aren't 6 isn't

3 1 going 3 are 5 aren't
2 fly 4 to 6 stay

4 1 Are you going to go sightseeing?
2 I'm going to go to university.
3 Is Sophie going to learn to drive?
4 They're going to buy a house.
5 Dan isn't going to go skiing with us.
6 I'm not going to tell Maria.

5 1 's going to take
2 'm not going to go
3 're going to explore
4 're going to unpack
5 isn't going to visit
6 'm going to take

Speaking

1 1 going 5 going
2 anything 6 are
3 special 7 see
4 Would

2 1 ✓ 2 ✓ 3 – 4 ✓ 5 – 6 – 7 ✓ 8 –

3 1 c 2 a 3 d 4 b

4 a 2 b 8 c 3 d 1 e 4 f 6 g 7 h 5

Writing

1
1 Wales
2 bikes and walking boots
3 her aunt and uncle
4 surf

2 1 so 2 because 3 because 4 so

3 1 e 2 a 3 b 4 d 5 c

4 Students' own answers.

Review Unit 9

1

Across	Down
4 boat	1 ship
5 plane	2 underground
7 scooter	3 coach
	6 lorry
	8 tram

2 1 will 2 won't 3 will 4 will 5 won't 6 won't

3
go hiking
rent a bike
take a bus tour
unpack your bag
visit a castle

4 1 c 2 e 3 a 4 b 5 f 6 d

5
1 're going to buy
2 'm going to get
3 isn't going to have
4 're going to travel
5 aren't going to visit
6 'm not going to learn

PROGRESS CHECK

Units 7–9

1 1 Were 2 wasn't 3 weren't 4 was 5 Was 6 were/weren't

2 1 straight 2 tie 3 blond 4 trainers 5 socks 6 well-built 7 moustache 8 hat

3 1 decided 2 went 3 bought 4 made 5 took 6 win 7 had 8 were

4 1 coach 2 bike 3 scooter 4 boat 5 ship 6 plane 7 lorry

5
1 get married
2 start school
3 pack, bag
4 go sightseeing
5 relax, beach
6 get, job

6
1 Alex sang some songs.
2 I often spoke to Mrs Brown.
3 My parents didn't know Gary.
4 Did your dad finish work at six o'clock?
5 The train stopped at Cambridge Station.

7
1 People won't live on other planets.
2 Are you going to meet Suzie later?
3 I'm not going to visit Harry.
4 Laura isn't going to go to university.
5 I think Jana will get a job.

8 1 Were 2 were 3 Did 4 didn't 5 was 6 going to 7 Will 8 won't

9 1 d 2 f 3 a 4 b 5 c 6 e

10
1 it wasn't
2 I am/we are
3 we did
4 she won't
5 there were
6 I'm not/we aren't

11
1 When did you meet Chloe?
2 How old will Grace be in 2050?
3 Is Tom going to university next year?
4 Did your parents give you that phone?
5 Why did you go to bed late last night?
6 Will people go on holiday in space?